The Official Arts & Letters Handbook

Second Edition

The Official Arts & Letters Handbook

Second Edition

Michael Utvich

RANDOM HOUSE
ELECTRONIC PUBLISHING
New York

The Official Arts & Letters Handbook, Second Edition

Composed and produced by Parker-Fields Typesetters Ltd.

Published in the United States by Random House, Inc., New York, and simultaneously in Canada by Random House of Canada, Limited.

Manufactured in the United States of America

0 9 8 7 6 5 4 3 2 1

ISBN 0-679-79152-3

Trademarks

New York Toronto London Sydney Auckland

Contents

PART TWO

Design Tips and Techniques

Foreword

Computers have transformed our power to communicate. Scarcely a few years ago, electric typewriters were the universal means to create business documents. The speed with which the PC has taken over the desktop has been matched only by the growth and development of sophisticated software tools for text, data, graphics, and now multimedia.

In developing Arts & Letters Express, we at Computer Support Corporation sought to stay true to our original vision: that computers represent an opportunity to empower all people to create visual communications. To accomplish this, we expanded on our original concept of a database of art components to a fully realized set of composable color building blocks. With our new Clip-Art Manager we now provide streamlined access to thousands of art components, designed to be assembled and composed into finished, professional output. In redesigning the interface we reconceived our approach to the electronic art board, in order to provide fast access to sophisticated features, enhancements, and effects. We even reinvented the core concepts behind clip art itself, with our trademarked Flex-Art series, in which a single figure can be broken apart and recomposed into thousands of unique variations.

Over the past fifteen years our vision was the foundation of a series of revolutionary products: *Picture Perfect, Diagraph, Arts & Letters Composer, Arts & Letters Graphics Editor,* and now *Arts & Letters Express*, the subject of this book.

Michael Utvich captures the power of Arts & Letters Express. His focus is not only on the technical software operations but on the joy of creation and the sense of opportunity that we want you to experience. Using the techniques, instructions, and examples presented here, you can get a feeling for what you can create if you take the time to work with Express. The issue is not to plug together a group of prefab art elements. The focus must be to develop your confidence to use the full power of the software to express your creative vision, and your visual intelligence to create works you can be proud of.

Our goal from the outset has been to give you the power to present your unique ideas in both words and pictures without being limited by the mechanics of drawing. We live in a visual culture. Arts & Letters Express provides the tools for you to discover new ways to give life to your insights. May you experience the joy and excitement of finding and developing new ways to truly express yourself.

Fred Schoeller
President
Computer Support Corporation

Preface: How to Use This Book

Arts & Letters is one of the revolutionary applications for Microsoft Windows. Using a unique graphic database approach to creating artwork on the computer screen, Express provides a tool for creating many exciting applications. This book has been written and designed to capture the unique power of the product and to provide direct, hands-on support to help you master the features and understand the many ways you can develop practical applications.

Book Structure

The book is structured in three parts. Part One is a tutorial for using the key design functions in Express; composing artwork from the graphic database, using text, designing charts, and creating and editing in free-form mode. Part Two focuses on design features and techniques, with techniques and graphic concepts to use advanced styles and effects features. Part Three focuses on using Express within your Windows computing system; it demonstrates how to use Express output in many popular Windows programs, as well as providing advanced operational tips and techniques for printing in color.

Coverage includes captioned figures and images and step-throughs, which are designed to help you implement techniques instantly. Open the book to any point that interests you and you will find the information you need to solve a graphic problem or learn the operations of a particular feature. The following is a chapter by chapter summary of the content and special features of the book.

Part One: Arts & Letters Features and Operations

Arts & Letters represents a unique solution for using computer graphics in Windows. Using a graphic database of thousands of images, it allows you to compose and edit professional artwork by combining and editing pre-created components. This section of the book presents the unique design assumptions built into Express, and focuses coverage on each of the major art subsystems (symbols, images, text, charts, freeform) built into the product. This part is also designed to function as a tutorial for new users. Chapters 3-6 contain instructions and step-through operations that will quickly familiarize you with all the basics.

Chapter 1 Introduction to Arts & Letters Express

This overview chapter discusses the unique art composition and editing system within Arts & Letters, the operation of the graphic database, and highlights key concepts used throughout the book.

Chapter 2 Getting Started

Setting up Express involves having a computer system with sufficient processing power to generate your work. This chapter discusses technical setup information—both what you need and why you need it. It also contains a tour of the dramatically redesigned Arts & Letters Express interface with illustrations and explanations of the new screen features, including menu flyouts, and pushpin dialog boxes.

Chapter 3 Composing with Symbols and Images

Express provides two ways for you to compose finished artwork with ready-made components: traditional wireframe symbols; and complete colored images, available through the redesigned Clip-Art Manager. This chapter presents techniques and operations you will need to place components into the working screen, and editing operations you use to shape them as you wish them to appear within a complete composition.

Chapter 4 Working with Text

The text system in Express contains 91 typefaces of its own, and allows you to create and edit text using type from your printer, including PostScript and TrueType. This chapter presents features and techniques that are used to place text and make typographic adjustments on screen. In addition, it covers special text-effect features that allow you to flow text around shapes and create dramatic, stylish text presentations.

Chapter 5 Creating and Editing Charts

Express charting features let you make standard bar, pie, line, point, and area charts, just like many other programs do. But other programs don't have over 10,000 building-block components that you can assemble into charts as backgrounds, illustration components, even as actual charting elements. This chapter covers charting features and operations, and presents techniques you can use to create stylish picture charts similar to those used in national magazines and newspapers using Express Charting.

Chapter 6 Freeform Mode: Drawing, Symbol, and Text Editing Freeform drawing and editing features allow you to create your own artwork from scratch or perform detailed edits to any of the 10,000 components that are included with the program. This chapter covers freeform drawing and editing operations, and detailed coverage of technical drawing and precision features for technical illustrations, schematics, or any other task you need to complete.

Part Two: Design Tips and Techniques

The graphic database of symbols and images in Arts & Letters allows you to create artwork by assembling ready-made pieces. In this section, the focus is on the high-powered design features, which let you customize these ready-made elements exactly as you wish them to appear. Screen captures show many effective ways you can transform basic art objects by adjusting the color, line, fill, and type characteristics or by applying special design effects.

Chapter 7 Designing with Styles The completely redesigned Styles menu allows you to create thousands of unique variations from each of the 10,000 symbols and images included in Express. This chapter focuses on the key style features and functions: Color, Line, Fill, Type, and Style bundles. Techniques and features are fully illustrated so that you can see how changes to various style elements can change the look and feel of any art element.

Chapter 8 Design Effects Professional graphic artists know how to create dramatic graphic presentations using 3-D projections, and textures, and by distorting shapes. Express does these things, too. This chapter covers feature operations and design techniques for the powerful family of Express graphic effects: Merge, Blend, Extrude, Warp, Transform, and more. Coverage focuses on designs you can create through individual features and by combining effects.

Chapter 9 Idea Gallery You can make many practical graphic designs within Arts & Letters, such as diagrams, signs, slides, presentations, posters, and more. This chapter focuses on a series of practical art applications you can use in business. They are supplemented with illustrations and examples of professional output, and samples of artwork created by the Express graphic team.

Part Three: Advanced Operations and Techniques

This section covers advanced operations and techniques within Express and Windows. Advances in Windows technology have made available new ways to export and place artwork from Express into any of your favorite Windows programs. This section also contains practical coverage of frequently asked technical points in feature operations and printing.

Chapter 10 Express & Windows Express can act as an art foundation system for all your Windows programs. The graphic database of 10,000 composable and editable graphic components makes it easy for you to create unique, customized artwork for all your Windows output. This chapter includes techniques and instructions to place Express artwork in over 20 popular Windows software programs, and demonstrates how Express can increase the graphic power of any Windows program.

Chapter 11 Printing Operations and Color This chapter covers printing and color-separation features in Express. In addition, coverage includes service bureaus and techniques to prepare your work to be printed externally.

Special Features To help you get information quickly, this book has been written using a number of structural elements that summarize important points. It presents operations in an easily understandable way, and help you link directly to important information elsewhere in the book.

Key Concepts Each of the main chapters has a section on key concepts and techniques presented in the chapter. Skimming these points before working with specific operations can help you become more proficient and increase your speed.

Tools Each of the main content chapters has a section on software tools immediately following the key concepts list. The tools section points out key software features on various menus that are important for operations in the chapter at hand.

Steps To help you be work on-screen successfully, features are explained and supported with step-through sections. Each of these Step sections presents the information for applying the technique(s) in step-by-step fashion.

Captioned Figures System Features, techniques, and tips are highlighted throughout the book with over 250 screen illustrations and many finished examples of Arts & Letters output. Figures are fully captioned so you can easily see and get the point without having to wade through and find the accompanying text. You can get a solid overview of many key points of coverage by skimming the captions and figures and keying to the related heading in the text.

What's New in Version 5.0?

New Features

Extrude
Color and brightness/contrast filters
Clip art database with Find feature
Thumbnail images
Greater typographic controls
Eyedropper
Easier stacking order adjustment
Browser
Selection within a grouped object
Virtually limitless number of objects
Intuitive object selection
Proportional sizing from the center of an object
Accel-O-Draw to speed screen redraws
OLE (Object Linking and Embedding)
Drag and Drop

New Interface

Content menu button functions
Icon identifiers of Express objects
Flyout toolbars and rollup menus
Pushpin dialog boxes
Windows-conforming accelerator keys

PART ONE

Arts & Letters Features and Operations

C H A P T E R 1

Introduction to Arts & Letters Express

Graphic Challenges

Computer graphic software has evolved to the point where there are so many packages on the market that choosing *one* is truly confusing. In the early days of computerized publishing and graphics, if you got a crude screen image onto a printed page you were happy. No longer. Windows and other environments now boast a staggering array of graphics tools that allow you to draw pictures from scratch, load clip art into documents, scan and edit color photographs, and include a variety of other applications.

Arts & Letters Express offers a unique graphic system that is dramatically different from all other Windows packages in its core design and in its programming assumptions. You can use it as an independent tool to develop a wide range of graphic enhancements, effects, business art, and illustrations; and you also can use it as a global graphic resource and place images, on demand, into virtually all Windows programs. As a result, the features that are available translate into a powerful tool for anyone, even those with rudimentary artistic skills, to create finished, professional graphics for a wide range of applications. This chapter provides an overview of the unique software design and graphic capabilities of Arts & Letters Express. It also will serve as a creative guide to any design or illustration you create using it. (See Figure 1.1.)

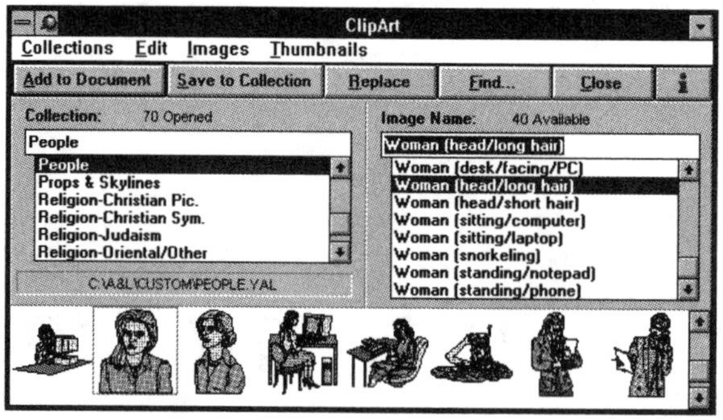

Figure 1.1
The Clip-Art Manager is part of the Arts & Letters integrated graphic database, which lets you interactively search, find, and compose images into finished artworks.

Ideas into Images

To understand the unique power of Arts & Letters Express, it is necessary to understand a number of key concepts and terms; some are commonly used in computer graphics, others are less common. The basis of this understanding was first conceived in the actual evolution of the Arts & Letters program, and grew out of the problems it wanted to solve.

Arts & Letters Express: A Little History

Arts & Letters Express evolved from a DOS-based graphic program that began its development over ten years ago. This program was designed to solve a problem common to aerospace engineers who are required to develop many schematic drawings that communicate complex technological designs. Their designs required them to develop special schematic skills and to use a variety of manual graphics tools that often proved to be laborious and time-consuming to execute. To make a long story short, the Diagraph program was designed to allow engineers, even those with a lesser degree of graphic skill, to assemble complex schematics by simply selecting predetermined shapes from a screen and then snapping them together to create finished output. The program stored an image alphabet of commonly used shapes, and provided an electronic page in which those shapes could easily be composed into graphically consistent, professional grade, schematic diagrams.

Arts & Letters Express evolved from this source into far-reaching graphics solutions, using a large-scale databank of ready-made shapes, fonts, and charting elements that can be assembled or composed into larger, more graphically complex works of art. In addition, Arts & Letters Express evolved an entire vocabulary for manipulating and editing these shapes, including color enhancements, graphic effects like blends, extrusions, and object warping, as well as automation features for storing sophisticated type, line, and fill effects. (See Figure 1.2.)

Bitmap vs. Vector Art

Many of the original computer drawing programs were raster or bitmap programs that created a pictorial image from a pattern of thousands of tiny dots. Such bitmapped or "paint" programs made it easy to draw simple shapes and to create highly textured backgrounds on the computer. The problem with such programs was that the dots along the edge of curved forms or lines often had a jagged or "stair-stepped" appearance that detracted from the overall quality of the art.

To compensate, Arts & Letters Express creates vector-based forms and figures instead of bitmaps. So, instead of creating a form as a pattern of dots, individual graphic "objects" were defined mathematically as a set of coordinates that could be interpreted by the computer. Vector-based drawing also makes it possible to draw clean, curved lines and complex, fluid, Bezier curves that don't have the "jaggies" associated with bitmapped programs.

Arts & Letters Express vector-drawing features allow you to instantly place geometric shapes, lines, fluid Bezier curves, and thousands of

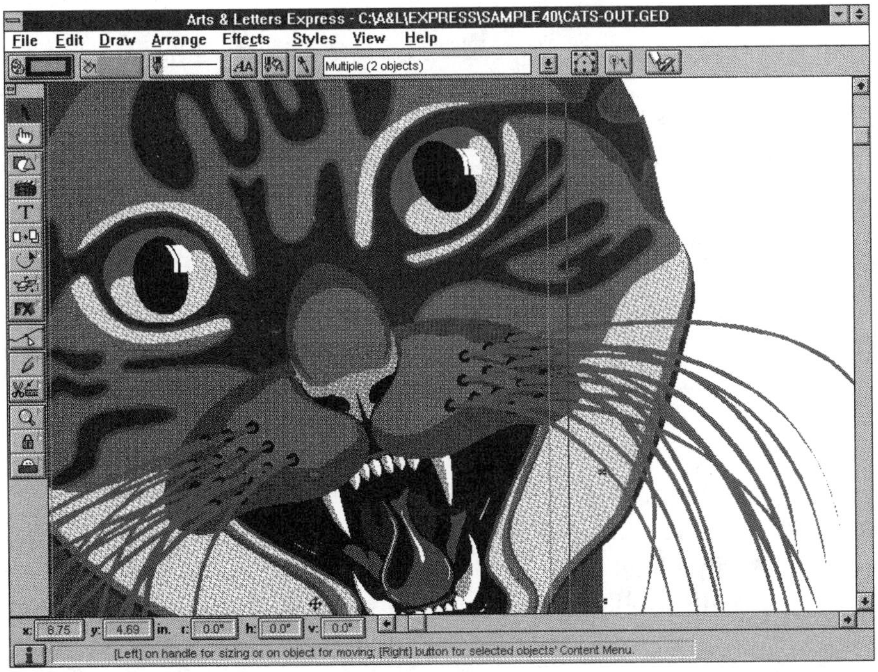

Figure 1.2
The image of the cat is a vector drawing formed of many individual, selectable art objects. You may select these components of the drawing, add textures, change colors or shading, and more.

ready-made symbols into drawings. Once in its workspace, you can fine-tune the shape, size, and position of individual elements and combine them with others to create instant, professional compositions in minutes. Constraint features, such as snapping to a line, an electronic grid, or a point on another object or line, give you more control during drawing and reduce the amount of time spent fine-tuning individual elements. You can manipulate objects on the computer screen, place objects in the front or back of a stack, and rotate, slant, and distort their shapes. Finally, each selectable graphic object can be enhanced with custom line attributes, size changes, textured form-fillers, and color. You also can apply automated special effects, including object warping, which distorts the shape of drawings and text but in a controlled way, and blends or extrusion effects, which change a flat drawing into a three-dimensional artwork.

Many bitmap "paint" and vector "draw" programs give you simple geometric shapes and collections of sample files to draw and play with. Simple core drawing tools, however, won't help you unless you have significant artistic skills already. Complex shapes must still be drawn freehand, or carefully assembled by stacking a number of individual geographic forms. Those who are not artists are often limited when using these products to create things as simple as flowcharts or diagrams, or confined to using the sample libraries of clip art that are provided with the software.

Professional artists using traditional paint and drawing programs can work very effectively with bitmap programs. However, even artists must manually draw complex compositions element by element—a process that often takes a great deal of time, even allowing for the speed and flexibility of the computer drawing tools provided.

Drawing vs. Composition

The early computer drawing tools were designed as electronic sketchpads. Typically, the screen consisted of an open drawing area surrounded by a number of electronic tools that permitted you to draw straight lines, curved lines, and simple geometric forms, such as rectangles and circles. Additional tools allowed you to add shading and other types of enhancements to drawn forms. Still others allowed you to edit the work you had done on the screen.

The Problem: Artistic Skill

The problem with traditional drawing programs is that they don't address the central problem of creating art, which requires some artistic skill. Some people have it, and some people don't. An experienced graphic artist could easily use simple tools to sketch and draw just as they would on paper. However, nonartists using these products couldn't do much more than draw simple forms on the screen. They couldn't draw people, objects, or other image elements on a screen any better than they could on paper.

Most conventional drawing programs try to get around this by including a family of sample art or "clip art." Generally, clip art consists of a few sample art files that can be used in a variety of different applications. These sample files tend to look canned and are often uninspiring. Nonartists have a choice: use the clip art or don't. As a result, the greatest value many nonartists get out of conventional draw programs is the ability to create fantastic boxes for flowcharts and little else.

Composition Power

Arts & Letters Express revolutionizes the concept of computer drawing by providing you with a whole built-in system of graphic symbols and art forms that you can easily plug into the screen. Unlike conventional computer artwork, which must be loaded from individual files, Arts & Letters Express images are accessed by number and may be placed directly into the screen at the click of a mouse. You may load as many art forms as you like and then edit, size, shape, and position, and then color them as independent graphic elements to form a complete composition. In effect, Arts & Letters Express uses the computer's schematic capabilities to remove the crucial requirement of drawing skill as a basis to create finished professional artwork.

Finished Art, Limited Flexibility

The key point to note about conventional, or paper, clip art is that it was designed as *finished, ready-made art.* It was not designed to be edited. The electronic versions of clip art, which were provided with conventional drawing programs or sold in separate libraries, were largely based on the same concept. The art was packaged by themes, in sets that could be used in business, advertising, sales, and other applications. Families of clip-art files presented a variety of visual concepts, neatly and concisely.

The problem with a more fully realized clip-art image is that it tends to express the individual character and style of the artist who created it. While an experienced graphic artist might not have problems reediting finished clip art, nonartists have a more difficult time. Because they lack the complete drawing skills necessary to edit finished clip art, their work often looks messy, distorted, and unprofessional.

A System of Flexible, Editable Drawings

Arts & Letters Express began with the assumption that something like conventional clip art was necessary to help graphic artists and nonartists create finished art. But rather than offer a set of completely finished files, Arts & Letters Express pioneered the use of electronic art forms. (See Figure 1.3.) Each Arts & Letters Express symbol has been designed as a highly flexible electronic sketch, which is open in design and can be easily combined with other electronic sketches to form a complete composition. For example, instead of presenting a set of fully realized clip-art drawings of the human face, Arts & Letters Express offers a portrait gallery consisting of different head shapes, different facial structures, different heads of hair, and other elements that may be combined by anyone—artist or nonartist—into an infinite number of finished artworks.

The Graphic Database

Arts & Letters Express is unique in large part because it combines two concepts that aren't often associated: *graphics* and *databases*. Also, since its inception, the handful of schematic diagrams in the original soft-

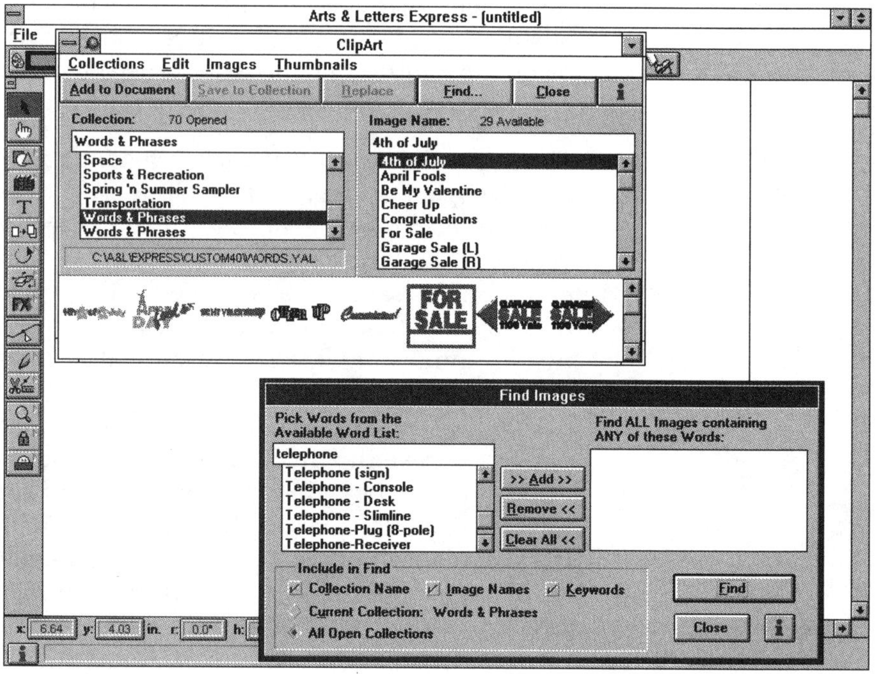

Figure 1.3
Using the Find option in the new Clip-Art Manager, you can type in words to search for or select from the list of all illustrations available in the system. Once found, you may load the image to the A & L screen or any other Windows program.

ware has grown to a network of over 10,000 ready-made images that you can access in a variety of ways through the Arts & Letters Express software.

Instant Access: The Clip-Art Manager

The portal to the Arts & Letters database is the new Clip-Art Manager (Figure 1.4). Type a word into the Clip-Art Manager and it will instantly present a variety of graphic images that you can instantly paste into the Arts & Letters Express screen or into any Windows program. The Clip-Art Manager screen also allows you to select the different libraries from a graphics database and preview individual images right on screen.

Unlike the vast majority of clip-art collections that are sold by themselves or included with mainstream graphics packages, Arts & Letters Express symbols and clip art were designed to work within this graphic database approach. Each symbol, icon, or component in a finished picture carries a unique database identification number. Each symbol was drawn on the screen and hand-digitized into a CAD art form and then stored in the specially compressed Arts & Letters Express graphic libraries that make up the database.

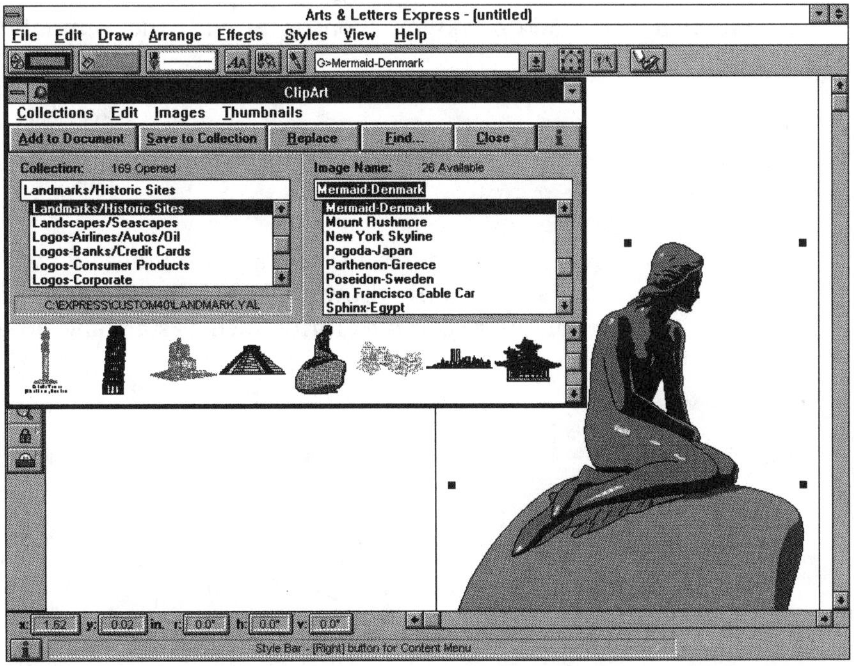

Figure 1.4
Instant Access
The Clip-Art Manager allows you to access fully developed images and simple line drawings from the classic Arts & Letters icon and pictorial libraries. Using thumbnail representations, you can select the image you want and drag it into the screen.

The Image Alphabet

The graphic database used by Arts & Letters Express allows you to fluidly access a library of images and designs. If you need to show a car, Arts & Letters Express gives you 20 or more simple generic car drawings, and a variety of ready-made, full-color images of *specific* automobiles, clearly indexed and named in the graphic database. Should you need to dress up a diagram with pictures of computers, peripherals, and network maps, Arts & Letters Express gives you generic diagrams, symbols, and realistic full-color images of *specific* computers and peripherals. If you want to create a pastoral scene, Arts & Letters Express has an array of mountain elements, clouds, trees, animals, and the sun. All are ready to assemble and plug into your composition.

Using the Arts & Letters Express "Image Alphabet"

At the core of Arts & Letters Express unique approach to creating and developing art is the *electronic image alphabet*. Rather than provide a simple set of essentially arbitrary clip-art files, Arts & Letters Express has been designed around an entire system of commonly used graphic images. These images have been conceived as an interchangeable lexicon of components.

Working with Simple Symbols

Conventional drawing programs give you simple line and basic geometric drawing icons to provide the foundation of your drawings, like this:

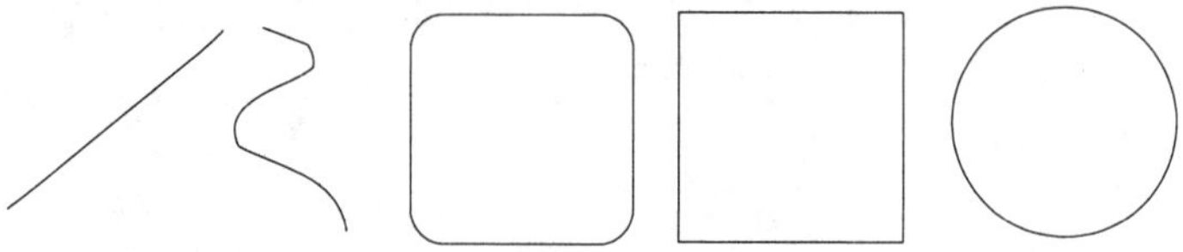

Arts & Letters Express also provides you with an expanded set of line and geometric drawing forms that include not only simple geometrics but more complex forms such as stars and others:

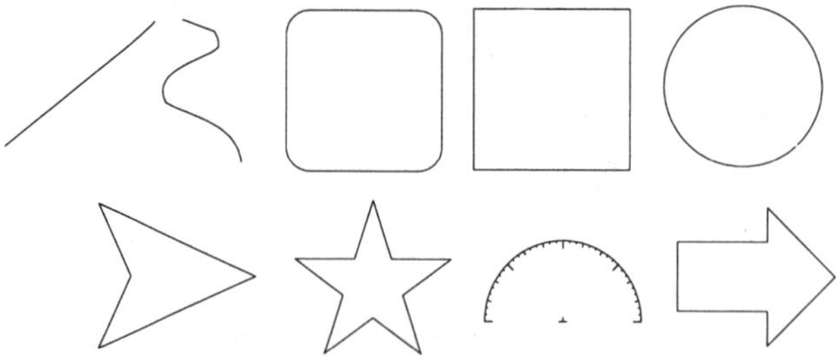

In addition to the basic forms, every one of Arts & Letters Express 10,000 custom art forms can be loaded and used exactly like a drawing icon in conventional drawing programs. Included are drawing icons for such everyday visuals as animals, trees, mountains, and clouds:

There are also complete sets of visuals for general business applications, including flowcharts and diagrams:

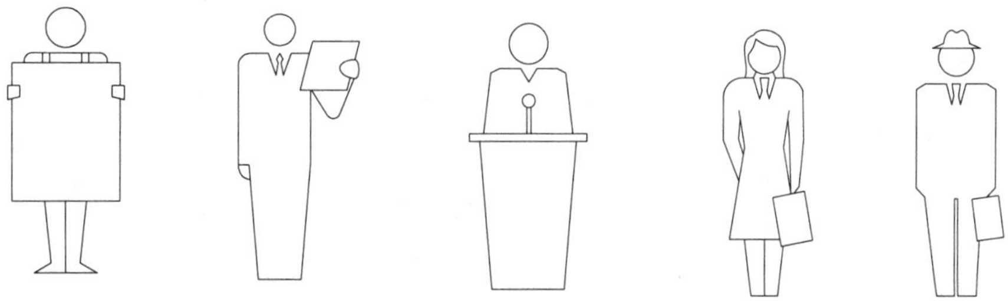

You can also draw a number of accents, 3-D geometric forms, and a variety of other supporting visual elements directly on the screen:

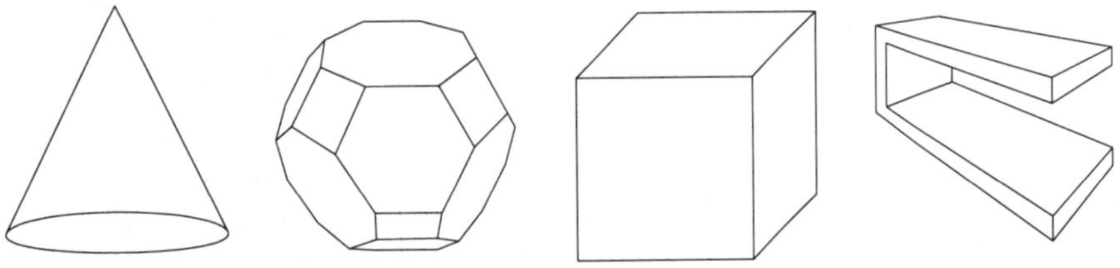

Arts & Letters Express provides a core set of 10,000 art forms with the software that allow you to build an enormous variety of graphic compositions. Each of the symbols and art forms may be used exactly like a drawing icon in conventional draw programs, and directly manipulated at the time you place it in the screen.

For example, take a standard symbol for a tree:

You may place the tree in the composition exactly as it appears in the book, or you may size and scale it into trees of many different sizes and shapes:

You may rotate symbols to any desired angle, either directly from the screen or by entering specific angles of rotation in a dialog box:

To achieve different effects of perspective or angle, you may stretch or flatten the symbol directly from the screen:

If you wish, you may copy the symbol directly on the screen and make a few quick changes to the interior fill characteristics to create a drop-shadow version of the symbol:

You can even create a shadow of the symbol in just a few minutes by copying it and making a few positioning edits and transformations, and then changing the interior color:

Unlike most computer clip art, which is generally presented in individual computer files, you may place an unlimited number of symbols into one Arts & Letters Express document. So, you can easily create a complete nature scene that includes a variety of trees, a mountain background, some clouds, and the sun:

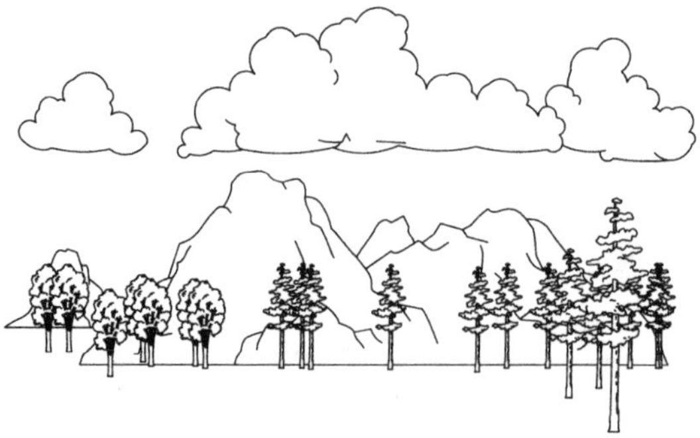

Each element in the composition may be individually sized and shaped without affecting the shape or position of others:

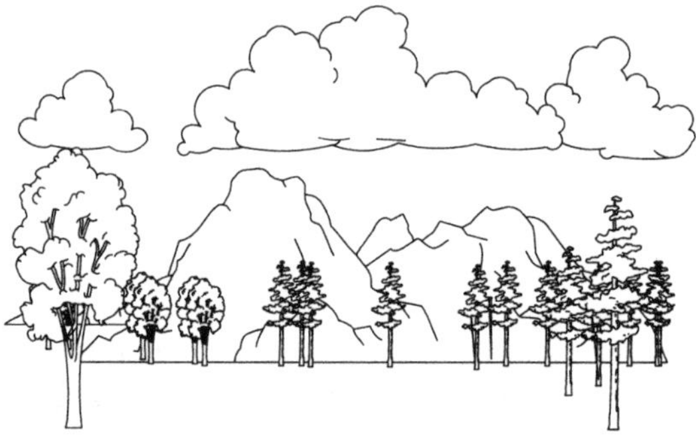

Editing Symbols in Freeform If desired, you may "explode" individual symbols into a collection of freeform objects that may be reshaped individually. After you have performed individual edits to the symbol using freeform drawing features, you may save it as an image that may be brought up in the screen at any time in the future.

You may select individual elements in the composition, make custom edits to line values, and add color or shading. Once you have completed all edits to individual elements and have finalized the composition, you may group it as a single graphic element and save the complete file.

Creative Text Arts & Letters Express also allows you to enter text into the screen and instantly apply a variety of different font effects to it:

Text Text

text Text

You may also "explode" the text into individual characters that can be manipulated and edited using freeform drawing features. Once edited, the text may be regrouped into a complete decorative headline effect, which, by the way, may be saved as an image that you can use, in this form, at any time in the future:

Text

Charting with Symbols

You can also use Arts & Letters Express to develop graphic charts, including pie and bar charts. These charts may be combined with any Arts & Letters Express symbol to create symbol charts and graphs:

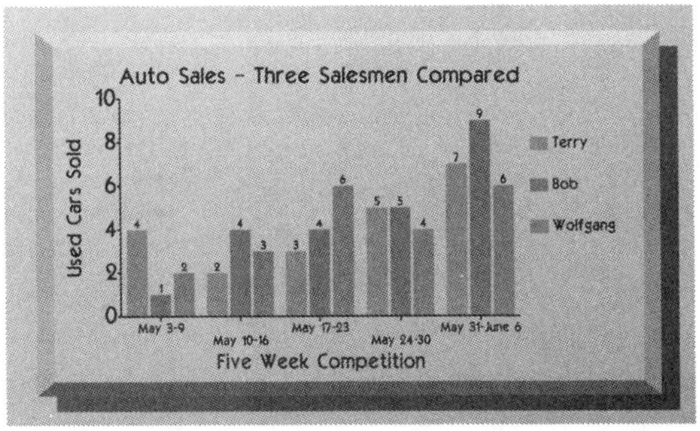

Enhancements and Effects

To automate symbol enhancement, you may store lists of attributes, including color, line attributes, fill patterns, and type styles into style overlays that can be applied to a selected art form or group. Different styles can instantly transform art forms or text to conform to your style standards:

You may create expanded dimensions of a single symbol by multiplying it through the blend feature:

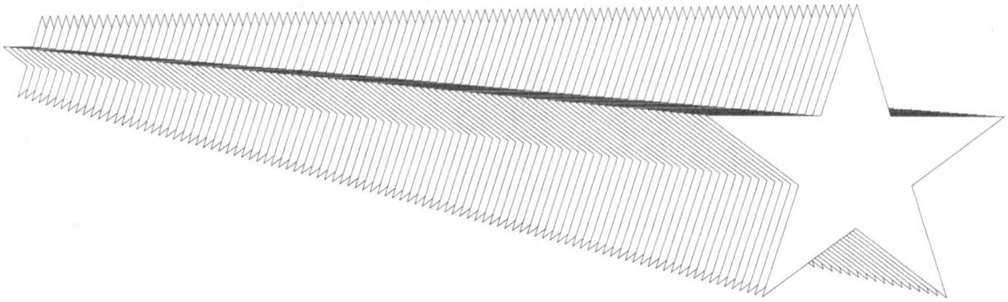

Selected text may be wrapped around a simple line form or a symbol shape:

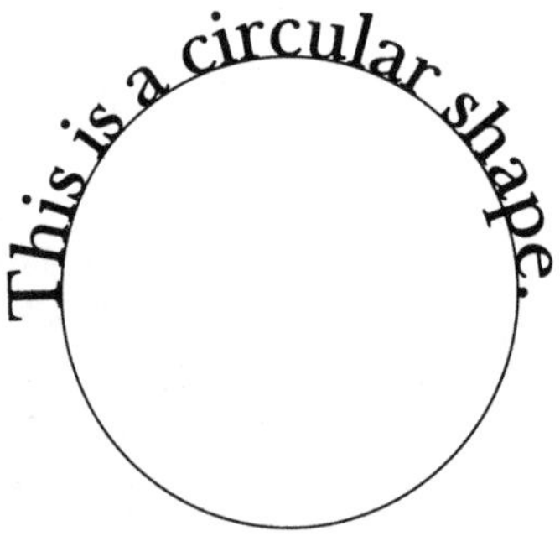

Using Extrude features, you can make a simple symbol into a three-dimensional form.

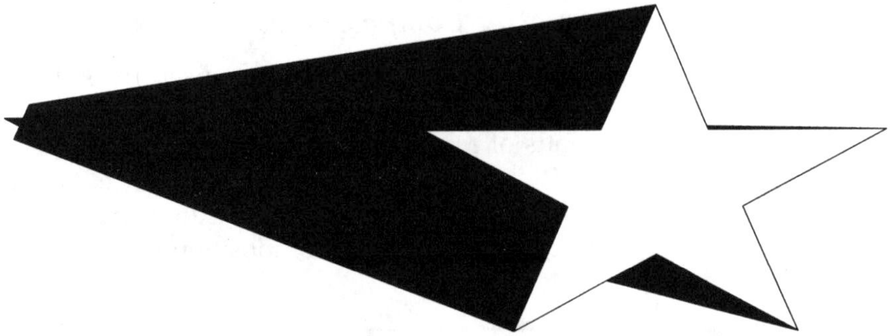

Using Warp/Perspective features, you can alter the shape of symbols or text and create large scale distortions or delicate adjustments in shape.

This sentence ripples across the page.

Merge and Cutout features allow you to assemble dramatic effects using shapes and backgrounds:

Creative Composition and Drawing

The image alphabet concept used by Arts & Letters Express enables you to compose complete drawings in seconds using libraries of thousands of ready-made graphic building blocks. You don't have to be an artist or have any drawing experience, and yet you can still compose artwork with highly sophisticated drawing effects, tricks of perspective, and a variety of composition forms.

Arts & Letters Express Features and Capabilities

The distinctive way that Arts & Letters Express creates and manipulates art enables it to be one of the most efficient drawing and composition systems available today.

Object-Oriented Drawing

Arts & Letters Express is a vector-based drawing program that creates art by combining a number of selectable *graphic objects*. A graphic object may be a simple line, a geometric form, or a freehand drawing.

Graphic objects may be drawn, shaped, resized, repositioned, and enhanced individually, or they may be combined into groups and two or more objects may be manipulated as a single entity. However, in freeform mode, only one object may be edited at a time.

The Arts & Letters Express screen gives you the largest possible area for viewing, drawing, and editing your work. And, at all times, you directly select the graphic object itself, not a simple representation of it. You always work directly on the actual object, and when you select it, the name or symbol number of the object is clearly labeled in the screen's title bar for ease of identification. Some drawing programs force you to work with the object outline only, allowing you to see the complete object along with its enhancements, color, and other attributes, only through an overlay preview screen (which, by the way, cuts your available drawing room in half).

With Arts & Letters Express, not only can you draw objects easily, you can perform a variety of sophisticated edits directly on the screen without having to go to a dialog box. You can copy, rotate, and slant individual objects, symbols, or groupings of objects by selecting the desired screen icon. Its object-oriented design makes it easy for you to assemble a complete composition while maintaining ready access to each portion of the drawing for editing and enhancement.

Integrated Composition and Drawing System

Arts & Letters Express integrates several powerful sets of features and capabilities into one program and command structure.

Drawing Features

Drawing features allow you to directly sketch on the screen using both standard shapes and complex Bezier curves. Handles on the curve lines allow you to pull the lines into shape, rather than redrawing them. (See Figure 1.5.) At any time, you may add a handle where desired to exactly control the shape and size of your design. A comprehensive system of drawing controls enables you to electronically control your freehand drawing, assuring easy joins between different lines, precise angles, and lines that snap onto defined areas in the screen.

Manipulation controls allow you to position and reshape symbols and freeform objects you have placed in the screen. You may group individual freeform drawings together, break complex groups apart, position objects to the front or back of the composition, and transform the drawing in a variety of ways.

The Symbol-Based Composition System

A second element of the Arts & Letters Express composition and drawing system are the 10,000 ready-made symbols and art forms available with the software (Figure 1.6). The software price includes 10,000 symbols,

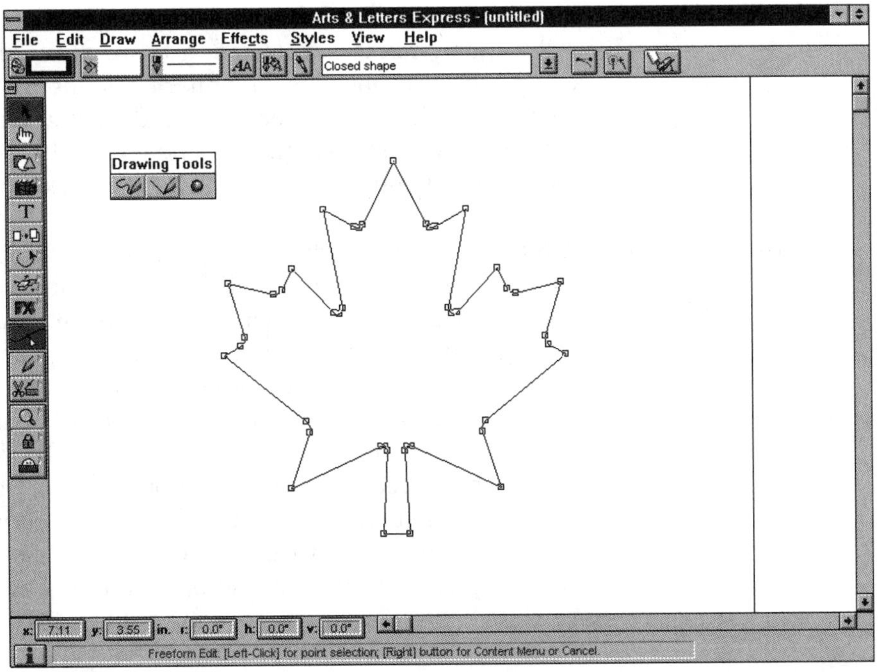

Figure 1.5
Drawing Features
The flyout drawing menu can stay on the screen, allowing you to select line and curve drawing tools to build your own artwork from scratch.

Figure 1.6
Symbol Composition
You can use either the quick flyout shape selector or the Symbol graphic database dialog box to select wireframes by number. Once in the screen you can manipulate and enhance them any way you want.

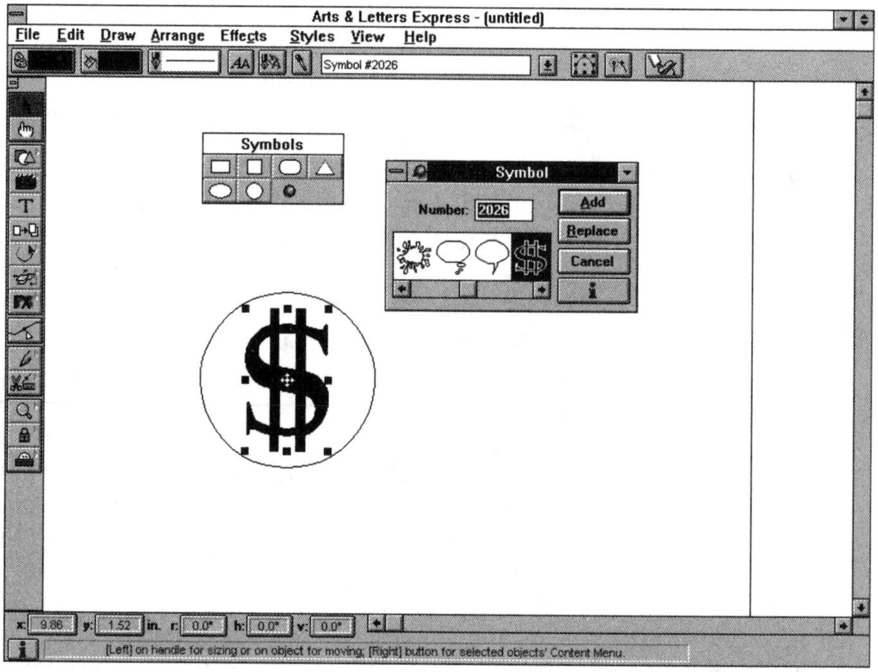

and additional optional libraries of specific technical, design, and business art also are available. (See Figure 1.7.)

All the symbols are designed to be assembled and edited into finished compositions. For the nonartist, symbols are an easy way to overcome their limited or nonexistent drawing skills. For artists, symbols are a way to compose quickly and avoid the tedium of sketching each individual element from scratch as ideas take shape.

Clip-Art Manager

A third element to Arts & Letters Express composition and drawing system are image libraries provided with the product. You can use them, or, using the Clip-Art Manager, you can create your own image libraries of groups and drawings that you create. Image libraries also allow you to create custom variations on the standard symbols provided.

The Clip-Art Manager is one of the most dramatically enhanced feature groups under Version 5.0. It has greatly expanded the automated approach to electronic composition used in previous versions. Thousands of full-color images have been preassembled into image collections and are ready to use when you install Express. Where it was necessary to individually load each drawing symbol and component in Version 3 software, the new features allow you to begin with complete complex images in color and break them apart for editing.

Figure 1.7
Clip-Art Manager
Collapsed to show only thumbnails, the Clip-Art Manager lets you load full images into the screen and build complex artworks by simply selecting, moving, and sizing individual elements.

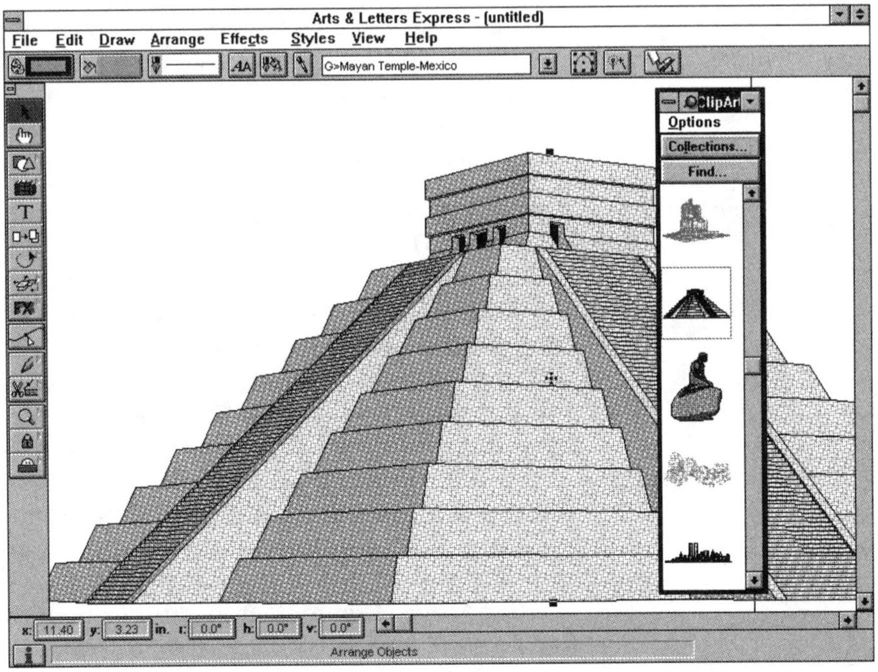

Arts & Letters Express contains many additional enhancements and new art libraries that were developed for a series of popularly priced Arts & Letters products, including Apprentice, Picture Wizard, Jurassic Art, and, for the multimedia Expo Series, Space Age, Air Power, and Planet Earth. You can select from specially created background settings; elaborately drawn figures, such as people, cartoons, and animals; image components, including cars, architectural renderings; and much more. The overriding goal in creating these new features is that you can create professional art by simply assembling and, if you wish, editing precreated components from a central database.

The Clip-Art Manager also permits you to assemble, save, and place your own custom drawing components which may include groups of art elements, freeform drawings, and standard symbols. This is a very powerful feature that many people don't use to the fullest. As you build larger drawings and business art, you can save useful components in an image library and insert them on demand, or simply drag and drop them directly into any Windows program via the Clip-Art Manager. This capability eliminates much of the need to simultaneously display multiple artworks, because you can save large and small components in a central place and load them where you need them right out of the database.

Image libraries allow you to expand the network of available symbols in Arts & Letters Express by creating your own or importing outside clip art through scanning or the direct importation of PostScript files. As you work with Arts & Letters Express, you can continually add to your image libraries for greater proficiency and flexibility.

Text Handling and Editing

Arts & Letters Express also contains a complete system for creating and editing text (Figure 1.8). You may enter text in the screen and maintain it in a form where the content can be edited and reedited as many times as you like. For decorative effects, you may convert the text into free-form graphic objects to be manipulated individually and used in combination with graphic symbols. Under Version 5, you can style and enhance text elements directly on screen, even change the typeface or styles of individual characters within a word.

Arts & Letters Express includes 91 of its own typefaces, which are equivalent to the most popular text and decorative styles in use today. It also permits you to import third-party typefaces from other vendors and either use them in their standard form or edit the character outlines into decorative variations. In addition, you have the option to select the fonts installed with your current printer, such as HP Laserjet fonts or Adobe PostScript typefaces, and use them within your Arts & Letters compositions.

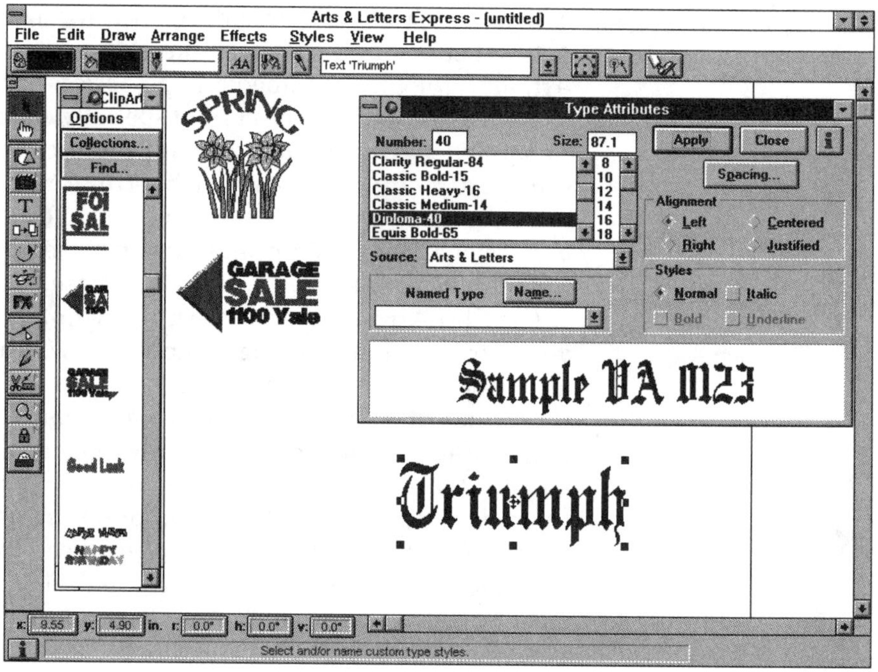

Figure 1.8
Text Handling and Editing
You can create logos using and shaping Arts & Letters text and combining them with graphics. Arts & Letters contains its own fonts and allows you to edit using the TrueType, PostScript, or other fonts in your selected printer. The Clip-Art Manager also contains special collections of stylized text effects.

The system for handling text is as flexible as it is for graphics. You may shape text into specialized forms, use it within graphic objects or as a background, shape it to a fluid form, and perform a variety of other visual tricks.

Charting Features

Arts & Letters Express provides you with the most comprehensive set of presentation tools available, including a charting feature based on its system of ready-made symbols (Figure 1.9). You may enter data directly into a spreadsheet grid, or cut and paste data grids into Arts & Letters Express from Windows-based applications, such as Microsoft Excel.

Once data is in the grid, you can build pie, line, point, and bar charts. The charting elements for displaying data are tied into the symbol system, allowing you many more choices for visual presentation than with dedicated charting products. For example, instead of a bar element in a bar graph, you can use graphic symbols, such as the icon of a man, a woman, a doctor, and so forth. In addition, you can use symbols as framing elements and backgrounds for Arts & Letters Express charts. This allows you to create interesting "picture graphs" similar to those frequently seen in such national publications as *Time*, *Business Week*, and *USA Today*.

The charting features in Arts & Letters Express, however, are not intended to rival the processing power found in a dedicated spreadsheet

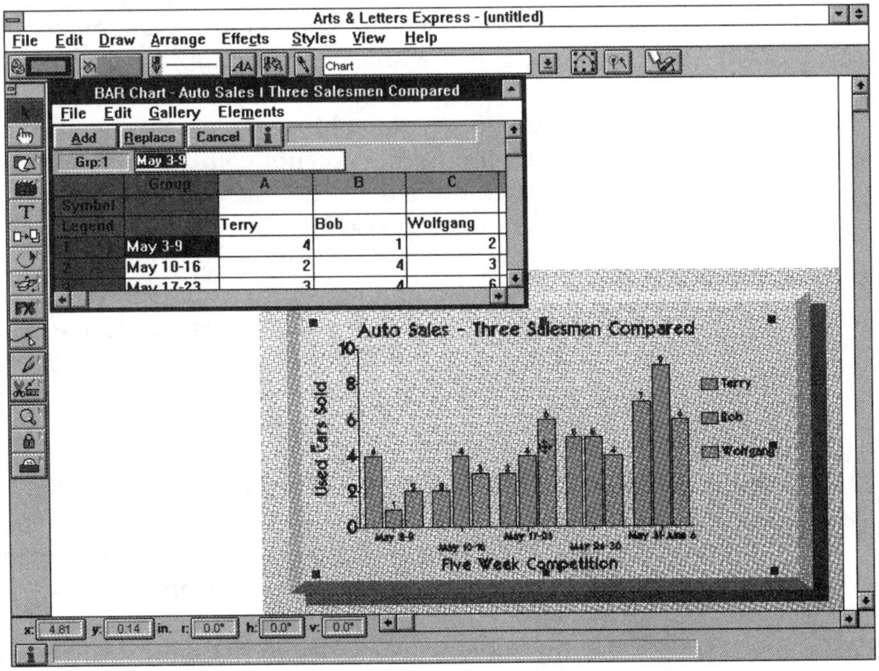

Figure 1.9
Charting
Charting features allow you to use standard bar, line, and pie graph components, or use symbols to dress up your charts with backgrounds and graphic enhancements.

application like Lotus 1-2-3, or Microsoft Excel. They are intended to support and enhance such applications by allowing you to use the Arts & Letters Express image alphabet and composition system with them to create unique and eye-catching graphics and visuals.

A Tour of the Graphics Database

The graphics database is the cornerstone of Arts & Letters Express, both in creating artworks entirely within the program or as an art resource to support your Windows programs. In Arts & Letters Express, each component, each accent, each background is part of the central database system and is designed to work with all the other parts of that system. This gives you extraordinary capabilities for creating a unified style without having to draw or create elements yourself.

Three Ways to Use the Database

Under Version 5, Arts & Letters Express gives you three ways to use the graphic database structure to compose and create original artworks.

1. Composing with Basic Symbols

Using the system of number-indexed symbols, called "wireframes," you can assemble a variety of ready-made drawings, designs, background elements, and other graphic components into a single composition, and then individually apply enhancements, custom sizing, and positioning. Using the database access numbers in the *Clip Art Handbook,* you can assemble complete images with all the accents provided, or select only the accents you desire. Since all numbered symbols are indexed in the database, each file you create in Arts & Letters Express becomes a database file. The unique advantage its Replace feature provides is the capability to replace any selected symbol with another by simply entering the database number for the new symbol desired. You can work with symbol composition to create diagram templates and other drawings that can be instantly customized by just saving the file under a new name and replacing any of the symbols shown with new ones instantly.

2. Composing with Ready-Made Images

The Arts & Letters Express Clip-Art Manager contains vastly enhanced groups of clip art, which are fully colored and assembled images that you can place in the screen. Unlike the standard symbol libraries, you can create your own image groups in the Clip-Art Manager and save them for insertion into any artwork you like. Once placed in the screen, you are free to break apart (ungroup) the image, select any of the component elements, and make edits or enhancements. You can even break it down to a freeform graphic and edit the actual line configurations in the drawing.

3. Placing Images with the Clip-Art Server

The entirely new Clip-Art Server, which is a minimized form of the Clip-Art Manager, is a window that can float independently of the Arts & Letters Express screen. The Clip-Art Server allows you to display and select from thousands of ready-made images, and either copy them into another program screen or embed them as OLE objects. The Clip-Art Server can place both standard Arts & Letters Express images and any custom symbols or images you have created and saved. This allows you extraordinary flexibility to create art, text, and charts based on uniform graphic style standards and deliver them in seconds to any Windows document.

Arts & Letters Express symbols are individual drawing elements. Within its large family of symbols, which is composed of many sublibraries (or groups) of symbols, there is great variety for accommodating different drawing tasks.

Groups of symbols also are made more powerful through a *unity of design*. That is, symbols in the same group are based on the same design approach, allowing them to be functionally interchangeable. If one symbol doesn't meet your need, you can use another, similar one, that will.

General Image and Master Drawing Collections

Arts & Letters Express includes a number of complete, ready-made, multielement images. These images are composite drawings that may be used as is or combined with other images, backgrounds, and accents. It is important to draw a key distinction between Arts & Letters system of images and the off-the-shelf "clip art" included in most competing packages. Just because a package gives you thousands of images doesn't mean they are easy to combine into images that fulfill your specific needs. Drawing styles used in off-the-shelf packages often look weird or out of place when assembled into a complete drawing. The Arts & Letters graphic database is built on the idea that each component, background, symbol, or image should work with all the others, providing you with the maximum degree of flexibility.

Most of the images available in the Clip-Art Manager are combined versions of existing Arts & Letters master drawings from the clip-art handbook. These images are composed of groups of separate Arts & Letters symbols that you may break apart and enhance with color, backgrounds, or reshaping, or delete them, if you wish. images are presented in a default color configuration, but you can easily edit the color or any other configuration you like. Once you've edited the individual components, you can assemble the image by selecting all the components and using the **Assemble Logically** selection in the Align option on the Arrange menu.

Flex Art Images

Certain image collections contain elements designed in accordance with Arts & Letters "Flex Art" system, which was developed to launch the Arts & Letters Jurassic Art package (Figure 1.10). For example, the *Nature-Dinosaurs Collection* contains the artwork developed for Jurassic Art. Individual figures of dinosaurs were drawn and digitized so they could be broken apart and posed in different configurations. Thus, each of the dinosaur drawings contains multiple joints that you can move, generally at the legs, neck, and tail. Using the Flex Art system, you can rotate or move these components to make hundreds of different dinosaur poses out of a single image!

The Flex Art approach can also be seen in the family of landscape backgrounds and select image elements. Here, the artwork was designed as a series of overlays so that you can insert animal and human figures into the foreground, middle ground, or background of a jungle scene, cityscape, or desert horizon. The master image is made up of

Figure 1.10
Flex Art
The unique Flex Art concept developed by Arts & Letters features figures that are made up of "moveable components," such as arms, body, and jawline. You may pose a single character in virutally unlimited positions, thus creating hundreds of custom variations from the same drawing.

layers that you select by using the new Stacking Order selector on the Arrange menu, you can put a human figure right into the driver's seat of a car easily and quickly by selecting art components on the screen.

Given the growing popularity of multimedia and animation programs, the Flex Art system in Arts & Letters provides a powerful tool to create animated figures and to make overlays for multimedia presentations and animated shows.

Expo Series Images

Arts & Letters image collections come with families of artworks specially developed for the Arts & Letters multimedia Expo Series, including *Space Age*, *Air Power*, and *Planet Earth* (Figure 1.11). These art families were designed as component elements that you can experiment with to create fanciful or practical images instantly. Using the Space Age collection, you can choose from a variety of space station components, which work very much like Lego blocks, to design your own space station right on the computer screen—much like NASA developers do.

ExpressArt

Unlike traditional Arts & Letters master drawings, which are composed of a series of digitized symbols and accents, the latest release of Arts & Letters Express includes a new group of high-quality freeform images (Figure 1.12). These images include the dramatic color graphics developed

Figure 1.11
Expo Series
This Series uses a highly modular system of objects which can be stacked and clustered in limitless ways to create your own unique space station or starship. High-quality backgrounds are included, so you can assemble professional, highly sophisticated images in minutes.

Fiugre 1.12
Express Art Cartoons
Another new development in the Arts & Letters graphic database are families of cartoon artworks developed entirely in freeform. These images have the fluid design of professional cartoons and a much more freehand design than many of the standard symbols or images.

for special projects by Arts & Letters and featured in its calendars and other applications. Since these images are drawn by hand, they are composed of a number of individual, freeform elements, each of which has been colored and textured. The results are figures and images with a wider range of subtle textures and three-dimensional effects than was possible in the standard system of composable master drawings.

You can still break apart any of the ExpressArt images and individually select and edit any of their components. You may also use the new Color Correction features in Version 5.0 to alter the master color and shadings in the drawings. From a composition standpoint, ExpressArt images may be selected from the Clip-Art Manager and used alone or combined with any symbol or image available in the Arts & Letters graphics database.

Logos and Text

Arts & Letters Express gives you a variety of creative ways to work with logos and text (Figure 1.13). The Words and Phrases collection in the Clip-Art Manager gives you a number of ready-made word designs suitable for posters, flyers, signs, and other applications. In addition, complete symbol libraries have been created containing many corporate logos and designs. Add to that the complete text system, which allows you to create your own logos using Arts & Letters' typeface library, symbols, and illustrations.

Just as with graphic forms, you can flatten or squeeze Arts & Letters typefaces directly on the screen. You may also "explode" a text string into a series of individual characters, which may be edited using all the freeform drawing features. You can enhance or distort individual characters

Figure 1.13
Logos and Text
Families of ready-made logos included in Arts & Letters showcase creative approaches to combining text and art objects. You may use these as models for your own logos. You may also access the entire business library of real corporate and product logos from the Clip-Art Manager. This collection includes such familiar logo designs as IBM, McDonalds, Coke, Visa, Mastercard, and American Express.

to create sophisticated display or decorative type effects. You may combine letter forms with drawings to create highly stylized graphic letters for a logo design.

To get the most out of the text system, you also can save any text string, enhanced or not, into a custom image collection. This allows you to create your own banks of text elements, in any typeface or type size, for use in signs, overhead transparencies, and flowcharts. They can be brought into the screen just like ready-made symbols and graphics. If you have a great number of compositions involving text, this capability alone can save you hours of time.

Charting Elements

In addition to the collection of 3-D geometric forms, arrows, and frames, Arts & Letters Express includes a family of symbols for use in charts and graphs (Figure 1.14). These include bar, pie, and line elements; grid backgrounds; and a variety of enhancements.

The charting feature automatically generates bar and pie graphs using data that has been entered. It also allows you to select different symbols to express the bar and pie design. The charting feature operates in sync with the symbol database, so you can enter the number code of any symbol you like for use as a chart element. In this way, you can use a house, a car, or a tree instead of a bar in a chart configuration.

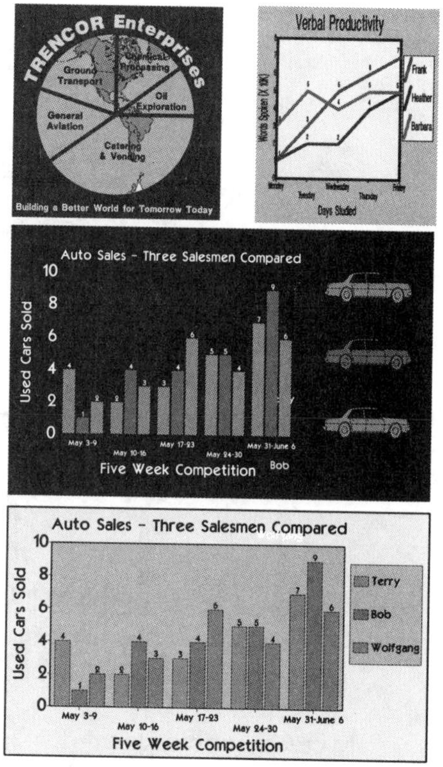

Figure 1.14
Charting Elements
Arts & Letters includes a set of standard charting elements for bar, line, pie, point, and area graphs. The real fun in Arts & Letters charting is using the whole range of symbols, particularly in bar graphs. This allows you to replace standard charting elements with graphics that auto-size to the correct charting height. A set of Chart Templates, including those shown, may be found in the Activity Manager.

The charting feature will distort the symbol to reflect the appropriate data relationship, just as it would expand the bar or other standard chart element. Using simple editing procedures, you can generate highly creative picture charts.

Cartoons and Fantasy

Arts & Letters Express includes the familiar cartoon series included in Version 3 with a dramatic new series of color cartoons (Figure 1.15). Cartoons may be used as standalone graphics or combined with backgrounds, dialog balloons, and other enhancements to create cartoon panels, even entire comic books. Full-color collections are available in the Clip-Art Manager for Cartoons and Fantasy drawings; add-in accents and enhancements may be found in the *Clip Art Handbook* and accessed through the graphic database by symbol number.

Conventional clip art often includes standardized "head shots"; that is, generic men, women, and children, for use in graphic compositions. Arts & Letters Express improved its clip art by creating a highly flexible portrait gallery. Instead of standard head shots, Arts & Letters Express gives you separate facial elements, facial shapes, hairlines, and other elements necessary to build a complete face.

Figure 1.15
Cartoons and Fantasy
Arts & Letters includes a complete set of ready-made cartoon components in the symbol libraries, such as the Money Talks and Angry Boss (shown). New "Toon Art" collections are freeform drawings often with softer edges and a more stylized art composition, such as the Skateboarder and Slugger (shown).

You may combine these separate elements into a virtually infinite variety of faces. You can make freeform edits to any of the elements to create your own portrait pieces. A simple freeform edit to a face allows you to change the expression from joy to shock. One design element may easily turn the hair color or shading pattern into 20 different ones. By adding pictorial elements available from other groups in the basic symbol library, such as hats, items of clothing, and others, you can draw people to order.

Pictorial Symbols

Pictorials are drawings of individual composition elements. The collection of pictorials in Arts & Letters Express includes individual elements of office furnishings and equipment (Figure 1.16). Other pictorials represent common images in nature, architecture, industry, sports, and domestic life.

Note that pictorials are *individual* components. They are not fully articulated images with textures and layers of accents. The simplicity of pictorial elements make them ideal for simple diagrams, sketches, and a variety of pictorial uses. Some pictorials come with several ready-made "accents," which are designed to provide highlights, enhancements, and add-ons to the basic drawing. For example, you can find a number of simple drawings that offer a contrasting color detail or shading effect

Figure 1.16
Pictorial Elements
The earliest Arts & Letters symbols were simple line drawings of common objects and icons of people in various walks of life. These simple pictorials can be customized with Styles or used as backgrounds and as standard pictorial elements. They are much less complex than the master image or freeform Express Art, and as such, are easy to adapt and use for diagrams and simple art compositions.

in an accent symbol. You can automatically assemble a complete drawing made up of the original pictorial symbol with accents using Align/Logical features.

As individual elements, pictorials are designed with enough details to fully represent an object; but they also are simple enough to edit and adapt to your own needs. As you work with pictorials, you may find that you want to create variations of the basic symbols. You can easily do this using freeform drawing features. In this way, pictorials provide both a standard system of ready-made art elements and the foundation of your own system of custom drawing symbols.

Icon Symbols

Unlike images or pictorials that represent real objects or people, icons are stylized symbols that represent various abstractions and relationships. Arts & Letters Express includes a large system of ready-made icons that can be used as simple visual enhancements to such documents as training materials, business presentations, and more (Figure 1.17).

The icon groupings in Arts & Letters Express standard library include a complete system of "stick-figure" people shown in a variety of actions and representing different professions. Additional icon symbols represent sports, family life, medicine, science, and technology.

The virtue of icons is their simplicity. The uniform design of Arts & Letters Express icons allows you to easily use them as is within larger

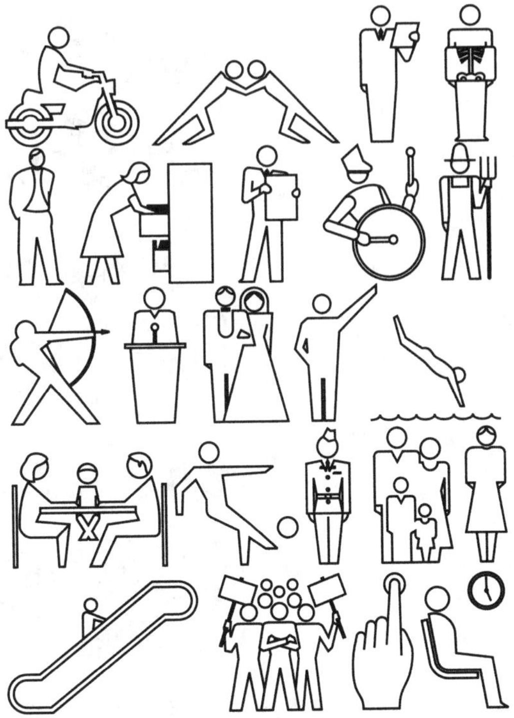

Figure 1.17
Icons
The icon system in Express incudes hundreds of images of people in various activities and representing a broad range of professions and sports. Adding your own custom backgrounds allows you to create entire systems of professional-looking icons in minutes.

compositions or to export them as independent files for use in desktop publishing or presentation graphics. Their simplicity of design makes them easy to enhance in a variety of ways.

One way to enhance icon forms is to place individual icons in a geometric or freeform background. By making even this simple enhancement, you can create framed icons that can be used as visual keys in books, published technical materials, and signs.

Another easy enhancement is to add 3-D quality drop shadows. By copying the icon and setting the copy in the back to solid black, gray, or a shade of color, you can create drop-shadow icons that have a professional look.

However you use icons, they are designed as a complete image alphabet that can be used as is, and edited, combined, and enhanced to create a virtually infinite number of art elements.

Abstracts and Devices

Accents are geometric patterns that can be used to garnish or embellish any composition. The standard symbol set includes a variety of accents such as flourishes and ornamental floral patterns (Figure 1.18). Other accents include op-art effects like stars, and starbursts. Still other accent groups include abstract designs similar to classical Japanese family crests.

Figure 1.18 Abstracts and Devices
Express includes hundreds of delicately drawn graphic abstracts and printer ornaments. These can be used in a variety of ways, from simple graphic ornamentation, as graphic backgrounds for text and/or figures, or as enhancements to charts, presentations, and diagrams.

Accents can be used in combination with line objects to create special framing effects. They also may be expanded to provide a series of interesting backgrounds for pictorials, images, or icons.

Because accents are abstract designs, they are highly flexible and can be manipulated to create an infinite number of effects through rotation, slanting, and stacking. You also can give them depth by creating a drop-shadow effect.

Keep in mind that accents, like all Arts & Letters Express art forms, can be "exploded" into a set of freeform objects that can be individually edited and manipulated. Working in freeform, you can use accents to create an astonishing variety of sophisticated and eye-catching art forms.

Arrows, 3-D Geometrics, and Frames

To easily enhance your flowcharts, Arts & Letters Express includes a set of ready-made arrow graphics, flowchart box frames, and 3-D geometric forms (Figure 1.19). Using these simple elements, you can assemble highly sophisticated flowcharts and diagrams in minutes.

Begin a flowchart with the desired frame symbols and place the frames in the position desired. Now add any of the ready-made arrow graphics. You have created a basic flowchart.

Given the wide selection of arrows, geometric forms, and framing elements in Arts & Letters Express, you don't have to be tied down to conventional flowcharts or presentation graphics. Size and shape 3-D

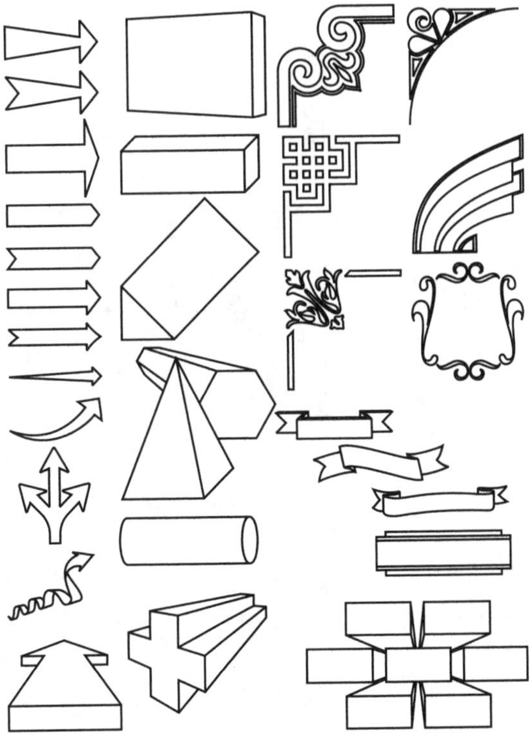

Figure 1.19
Arrows, 3-D Geometrics, and Frames
These graphic building blocks allow you to create elaborate diagrams and presentations, add callouts and pointers to graphic illustrations, even create your own stationery. This set of images includes series graphics that are designed to work together. For example, each of the arrow types shown at the left of the eillustration is part of a series of other arrows of different lenghts, but are all designed exactly the same.

geometric forms to give your flowchart boxes additional depth. Complement these forms with the matching 3-D arrows. You can also create flowcharts using two-dimensional frames and arrows and enhance them with drop-shadow elements.

By sizing, stretching, and flattening these design elements, you can create not only flowchart elements, but designs for presentation graphics. Use 3-D geometric graphics as backgrounds for icons, pictorials, and charts. Use arrows to enhance overhead transparencies or signs. Whatever your application, this group of design elements is highly flexible.

Maps and Flags

Many business and graphic applications require maps. Arts & Letters Express basic symbol library includes U.S. and world maps and national flags (Figure 1.20). Highly detailed maps, consisting of geographic forms, with separate line and text overlays for country, state, county, and city features, are included in the standard symbol set. These files allow you to configure the map layout exactly as you want and assemble the separate files instantly using Align features.

Using standard editing features, you can manipulate the map grid, add labels, and add 3-D effects for greater visual impact. With the sets of ready-made symbols, you can create a variety of "art maps," including

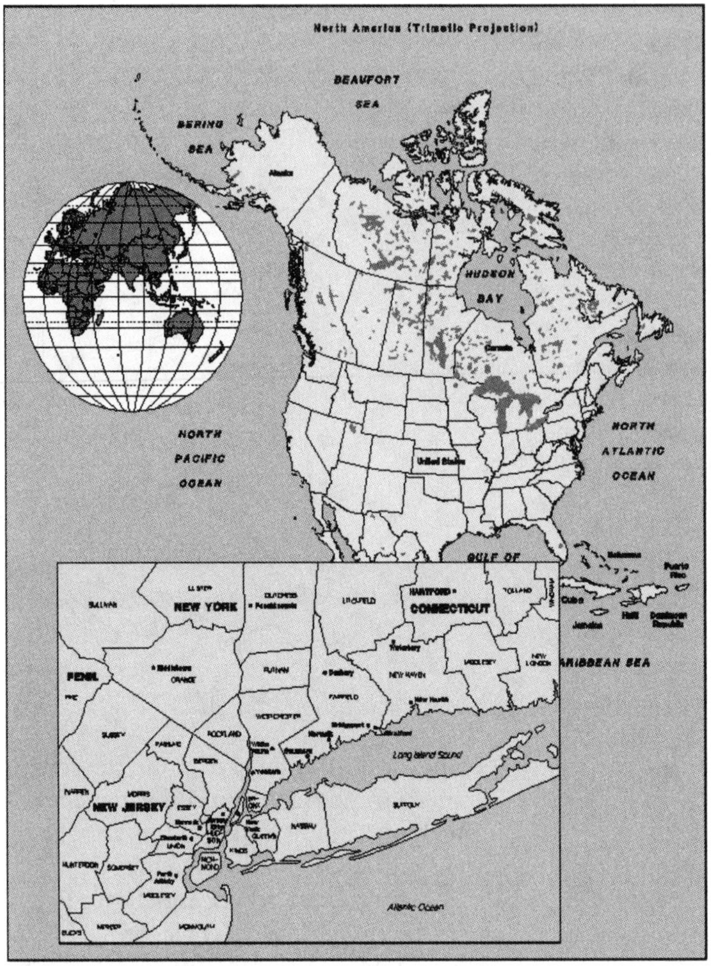

Figure 1.20
Maps and Flags
The Maps and Flags collections include a variety of map projections and closeup map configurations. Many Maps utilize a series of overlays: in the close up of New York City shown, the land mass is one symbol, the county lines another, and the key city points are yet another. This allows you to configure the individual map graphic in many variations by adjusting the fill color and texture of the land mass, as well as the characteristics of the marking lines.

stylized topological maps and a variety of maps for presentation graphics. Ready-made symbols can be used to illustrate the key business and industries in the mapped area.

Maps also can be used as backgrounds. Use a map to enhance text overheads, or as a background for a bar chart. Using clipping and mask features in Arts & Letters Express you can even create integrated chart maps in which the bar graph elements neatly fit into the mapped area.

Technical Illustrations

There are special symbol libraries in Arts & Letters Express for specific technical applications. Each of these image libraries comprises ready-made drawings that can be used as is, or integrated with backgrounds and other elements, or "exploded" into freeform graphics that can be edited (Figure 1.21).

Figure 1.21
Tecnical Illustrations
The labeled drawing of the human muscle system (shown) is representative of the families of technical images and schematics. Like other Express master drawings, this image is a composite of overlay components. The labels and titles can be easily removed and the image can be broken apart into selective elements. This single image can be used in literally hundreds of different ways depending on the technical point you wish to make.

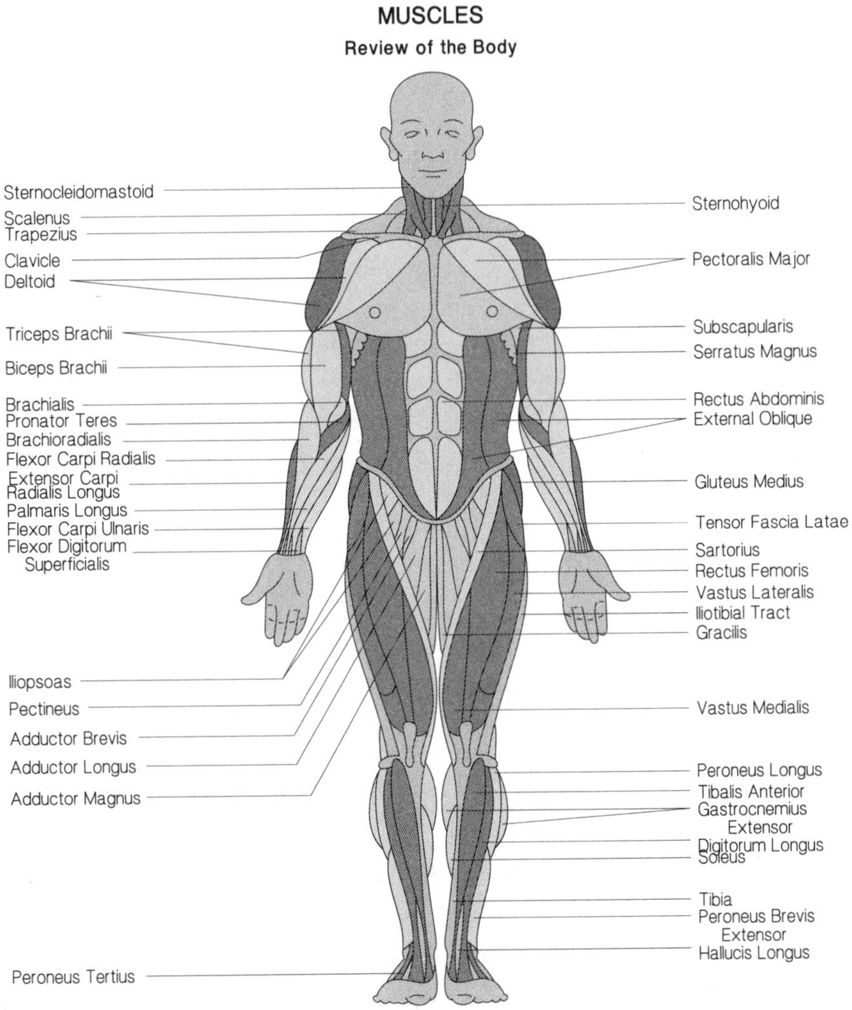

Anatomy Collection A variety of ready-made views of the human anatomy, including skeletal structure, nervous system, circulatory system, and major internal organs, can be used to create medical diagrams that can be labeled with text applied in Arts & Letters Express. In addition, portions of the drawings can be selected and adapted for closeup illustrations.

Aerospace Collections Aircraft and Space collections include many realistic drawings of airplanes and spacecraft, which can be used individually in presentation art or can be combined to create more complex compositions.

Computers The computer collection includes a group of highly accurate representations of a number of name-brand computer hardware and software products. These images can be used to create computer images, including system diagrams, presentation graphics, and advertisements. When combined with other Arts & Letters Express symbols, the computer elements can be used to create a representation of graphic software or text inside the computer image's screen.

Nature Arts & Letters Express includes entirely new collections of Nature images, such as families of animals, birds, insects, dinosaurs, natural backgrounds, and landscape components. In addition, the simple symbol drawings of animals and nature have been retained and are available through the symbol database as well.

Telecommunications The symbol database includes a set of drawings representing equipment and technical schematics of telephone technology. These drawings can be used for technical illustrations and schematic diagrams of telephone systems. The Clip-Art Manager also includes a complete *Communications* collection of various telephones and telecommunications hardware.

Technical Schematics In addition to technical images, Arts & Letters Express libraries include specialized collections of technical symbols, which can be assembled into "graphic sentences" that form complete schematic drawings. The principal libraries of technical schematics are the following:

- Chemical process flow
- Electronics and logic
- Pipe valves and fittings
- Pulp and paper process
- Telecommunications

Each of these libraries is a comprehensive symbol set; however, if additional symbols are needed, you can use any of them as the basis of an illustration, which you can save and use on demand.

Composition and Style Tools

The Arts & Letters graphic database provides instant access to thousands of images; the composition and style features give you highly automated means of combining these images into finished results. Arts & Letters Express contains three newly reconfigured composition menus and a newly redesigned object management system that offer you fast and easy access to enhanced tools that help you get results.

The major enhancement is the new Style Bar, which is a toolbar "strip"at the top of the screen that lets you access all the key enhancement and management features without opening a single dialog box. As images are loaded into the working area, you can control color, typeface, type size, and check all the image components using simple, easily viewed fly-out displays. (See Figure 1.22.) The convenient cascade menus allow you to pinpoint the exact change you wish to make without having to navigate through a complex master dialog box full of buttons and options. The composition system is designed to maximize working from the screen as efficiently as possible, and to resort to dialogs only when you absolutely have to.

Styles Menu

Arts & Letters was the first graphic software in the industry to offer a comprehensive system for saving and naming drawing attributes. Under the new Styles menu you may apply enhancements including color settings, line thickness, fill patterns, and typeface selections. For each of these styles, you may save the completed configuration under a custom-named style which can be summoned at any time with a mouse

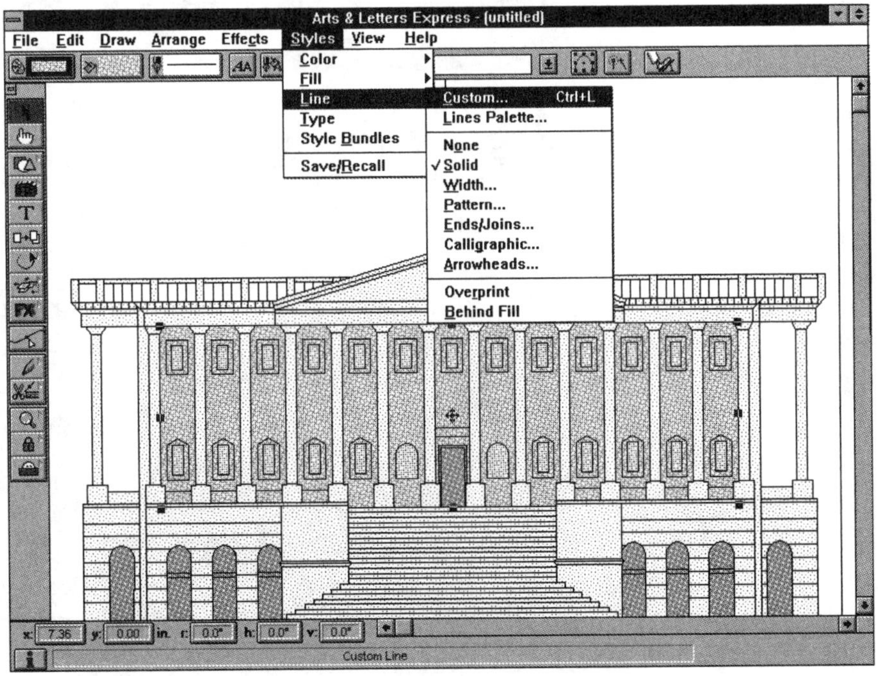

Figure 1.22
Styles Menu
Each option on the Styles menu operates off cascade submenus that let you select the simple or advanced attributes you wish to apply to symbols, image components, text, or charts.

click. This powerful naming system is the composition equivalent to the custom image collections mentioned earlier in this chapter. No matter what you want to do, either creating custom images or saving specialized enhancements, Arts & Letters Express is designed to help you work in the most efficient way possible.

Object Management

The new Object Browser is accessed either from the Style Bar, or from the Object Management option in the Edit menu. (See Figure 1.23.) In older versions of Arts & Letters, it was called the **Lock/Hide/Name** dialog box. This unique feature lets you see inside the graphic database to literally view the list of symbols and graphic components that make up each image. When you bring in an image or drawing and break it apart, you can instantly see its individual components. Selecting the name or symbol number of the component in the Object Browser automatically selects that component on screen. No more aimless clicking trying to select the right element!

Using the Object Browser, you can assign a custom name for any component in your drawing. In a drawing of a face, for example, you can name the eye, eyelid, mouth, nose, and so forth. You can also pinpoint

Figure 1.23 Managing Components
The Object Browser lists every graphic object and element in your drawing and lets you select them individually or in groups directly from the element list shown.

which elements are symbols and which are groups (which also could be ungrouped for further editing). To lock a component (to prevent editing) or hide it (to remove its display from the screen), just select the desired component and the feature you want.

Arrange Menu

The new Arrange menu (called Manipulate in former versions of the package) gives you the ability to stack individual art elements in a composition and align them in relation to the page or to each other. The Align features (Figure 1.24) are still some of the most powerful in the graphics software world. Using the unique Logical Alignment option, you can select all the pieces that make up an image and instantly reassemble it into a complete picture without any dragging, cropping, or minute mouse adjustments. The Arrange menu also contains the powerful Transform feature group that allows you to numerically activate the key positioning features in the Main Screen. You can set the exact position of the art element, set its degree of rotation or slant, and enter the exact size that you wish it to be without using drawing rulers or fussy guesswork.

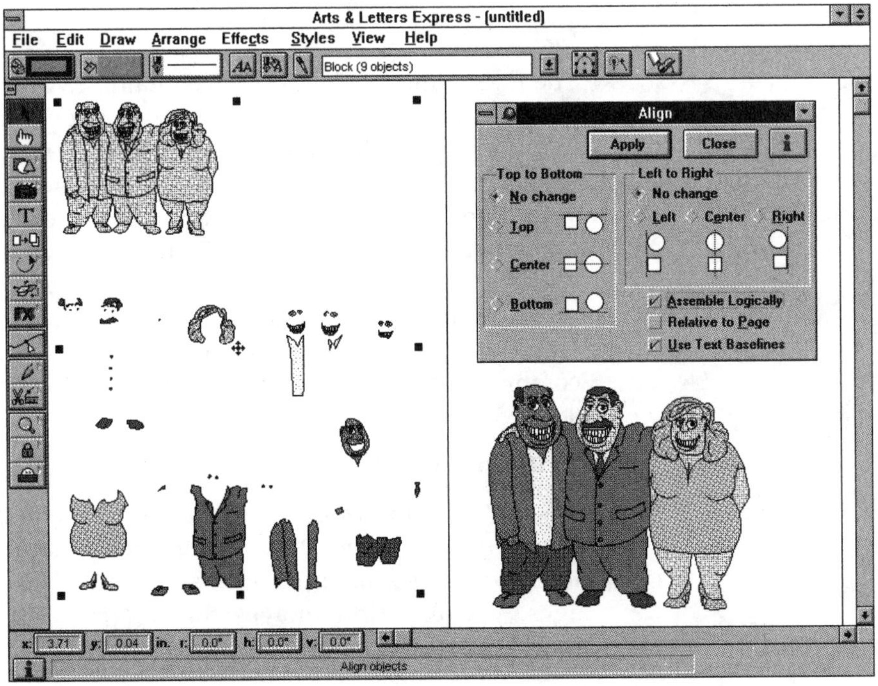

Figure 1.24
Logical Assembly
Images can be ungrouped and each of the component parts edited individually. Then, just select them all and reassemble them using the magical Logical Alignment option.

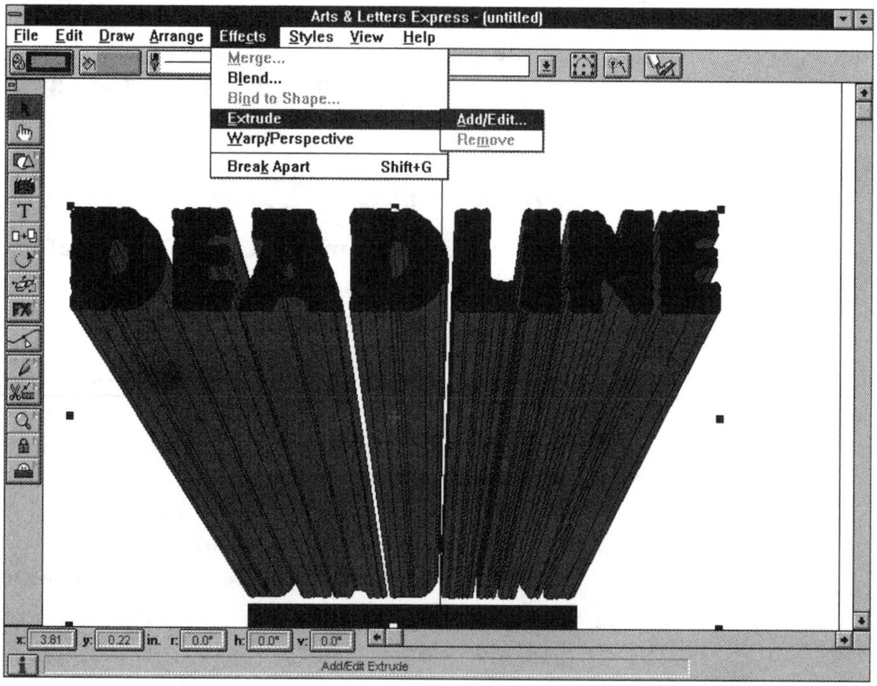

Figure 1.25
Dramatic Effects
The Effects menu allows you to develop professional graphic designs using symbols and text forms. The new Extrude feature, shown here, can turn a word or drawing into a three-dimensional element.

Effects

The Effects menu (Figure 1.25) contains a variety of high-impact design effects that you can activate from a dialog box without any hand drawing. You can multiply and evolve a single art form into many layers using the Blend feature. You can create unique cropping and fill effects with Merge. Using the new Extrude feature and the Warp/Perspective group, you can shape, distort, and explode a flat drawing into three dimensions.

Effects applied to an art element can be edited and removed afterward. Also, the entire effect can be edited, rotated, duplicated, and combined with other elements in the graphic database on demand.

Graphic Power

The Arts & Letters graphic database, in combination with the many powerful enhancement and composition features, gives you the ability to create professional art results instantly. Drawing from a bank of images, you can find images that match your ideas and experiment quickly and easily to find the best way to present your ideas graphically.

What's in It for You

The genius of Arts & Letters Express lies in a fundamental but subtle reality about the way we create: It is *always* much easier to be creative when we have something to work with—a model, an example, a template, etc. A blank page and an empty computer screen are voids we must fill with our creativity, and sometimes the hardest part is to connect a concept with an image. We can spend hours aimlessly shaping sketches on a computer screen without really getting an idea where we want to go.

The standard and optional drawing symbols that are the foundation of the Arts & Letters Express composition system are designed to help you *connect* the idea you wish to express with a visual image. You can select and integrate any number of drawing elements in Arts & Letters Express, delete them, replace them, move them, size them, enhance them, and as you do so, your creativity comes into play. Conventional drawing programs bring you to this level only after you have manually drawn all of the elements, or have found an individual clip-art file that looks vaguely like you can adapt it. Arts & Letters Express not only helps you to create art, it helps you to get your creative engines in gear and spend your time more effectively than you would if you had to draw everything by hand.

Benefits for Graphic Artists

The benefit of the standard symbol set comes in the early stages of conceptualization and composition. They give graphic artists the ability to compose a work of art. The standard symbols may not be the ultimate work, but they are invaluable. By eliminating the time and effort to draw individual elements, graphic artists can spend time composing and experimenting with different types of elements, backgrounds, and attributes. Because Arts & Letters Express symbols are so easy to manipulate, artists will find it easy to experiment with their perspective, shaping, and positioning. At any time, graphic artists also can access freeform drawing tools and, drawing on the intelligence in their fingers, sketch directly on the screen.

Benefits for Nonartists

The first question every Arts & Letters Express user must ask is whether you see yourself as an artist or not. If you do, great. If not, then you may have to change your thinking when using Arts & Letters

Express. The qualities that make up an artist are more than the technical skills associated with drawing, painting, or performing any manual processes we associate with creating art. Every good artist has more than just technical skill: they have an "eye," a sense of perception, an ability to see the world in an interesting way. Even if you don't have the technical skill to draw what you see, Arts & Letters Express can provide you with a powerful set of tools to transcend these limitations.

Use Your Creative Eye

If you don't think of yourself as an artist in the accepted sense, you can use Arts & Letters Express to create professional looking artworks simply by loading and integrating elements already drawn. You don't have to be limited by your lack of technical skill. You can experiment on the screen by sizing the elements, assigning different attributes to them, and manipulating them. The software gives you the tools to bring your vision into reality.

Another very real benefit for nonartists is that Arts & Letters Express allows you to create a wide variety of simple, practical artworks for everyday use in your business or profession. Even if you aren't interested in creating elaborate illustrations or works of art, Arts & Letters Express allows you to enhance your current business applications with effective visuals that enhance your ability to communicate. Use the ready-made symbols and the production power in Arts & Letters Express to develop your own system for creating professional presentation graphics, icons for proposals, reports and manuals, flowcharts, and technical illustrations. These compositions don't have to be fancy or elaborate, they can be simple sketches that help you involve an audience in your business communications.

Graphic Database Power

The power of a graphic package lies not so much in the results that are delivered, but how it provides you the tools to get those results easily. Arts & Letters is one of the pioneering software graphics systems. The unique graphic database concept goes beyond globs of random clip art favored by other programs in the market to provide you with an integrated visual alphabet you can access in seconds. The power of that concept lies at the very heart of what Arts & Letters can do for you and provides a reason why Arts & Letters has consistently garnered awards from editors and end users as the best computer art system in the industry.

CHAPTER 2

Getting Started

Understanding Your Tools

Most computer software is designed like a child's garden of secrets. There are the obvious features and options that you see from the main screen, but lurking behind every one is a hidden piece of magic. You can certainly use Arts & Letters Express very efficiently from the screen. At the same time, you can use it so much more efficiently if you take a few minutes to look at some of its hidden wonders.

This chapter focuses on technical requirements and performance tips to run Express, and includes a guided tour of the major screen features and a bit of technical background about the package itself.

System Requirements and Choices

The basic operating issues for Arts & Letters begin with your computer hardware. If you have a computer that can run Windows 3.1 efficiently, you can run Arts & Letters.

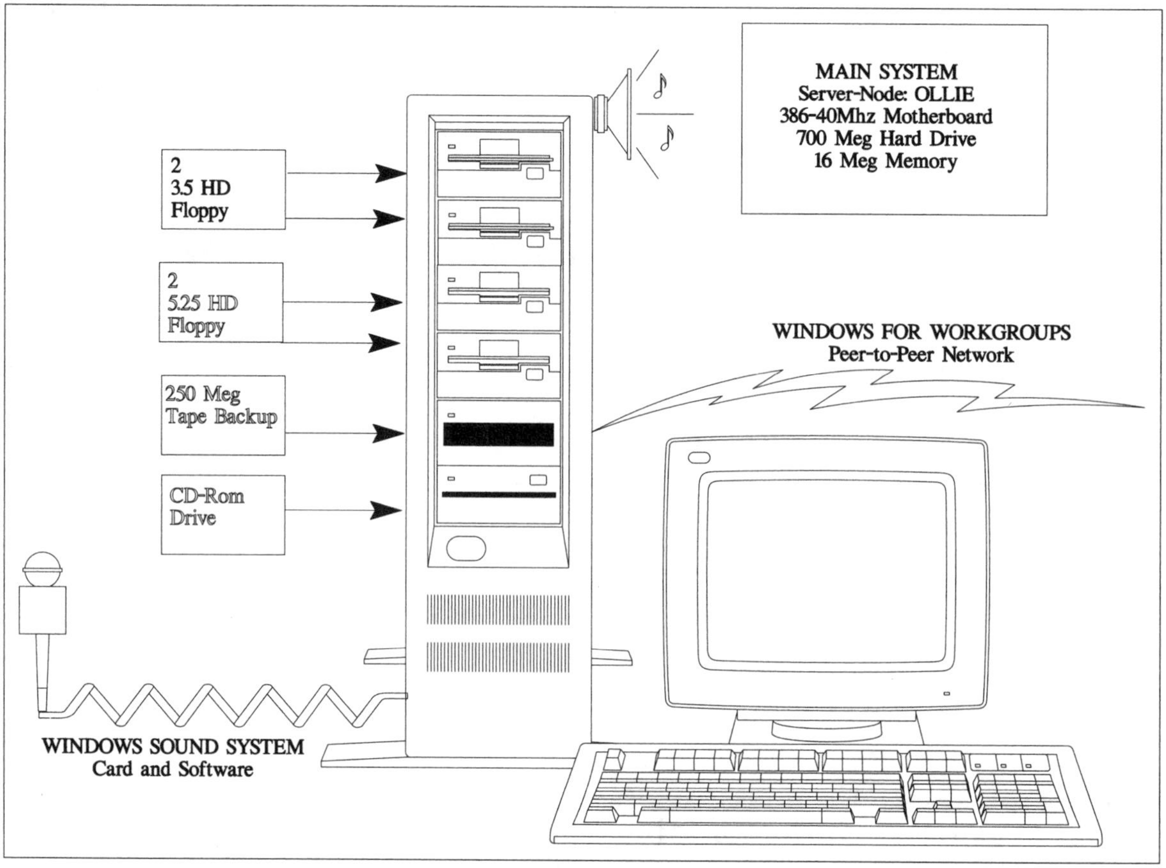

The main system used to create text and pictures in the writing of this book was a 486 system running at 66 Mhz with 16 megabytes of memory and 700 megabytes of hard disk space. Express and all of the third-party programs profiled later in the book were installed with banks of art files and adequate room for custom art that the author has created over the past four years.

Minimum System Requirements

The basic system required to run Arts & Letters Graphics Editor is a standard PC-386 machine with a minimum of two megabytes of memory. This matches neatly with the system operating requirements for Windows itself. Note that this is a minimum: the software will not run to its optimal speed or efficiency with this configuration, but it will run. Fully installed, Arts & Letters Express takes up about 16 megabytes of hard disk space. You should have an absolute minimum 40 megabyte hard drive in your system. By the time you put Windows, a few fonts,

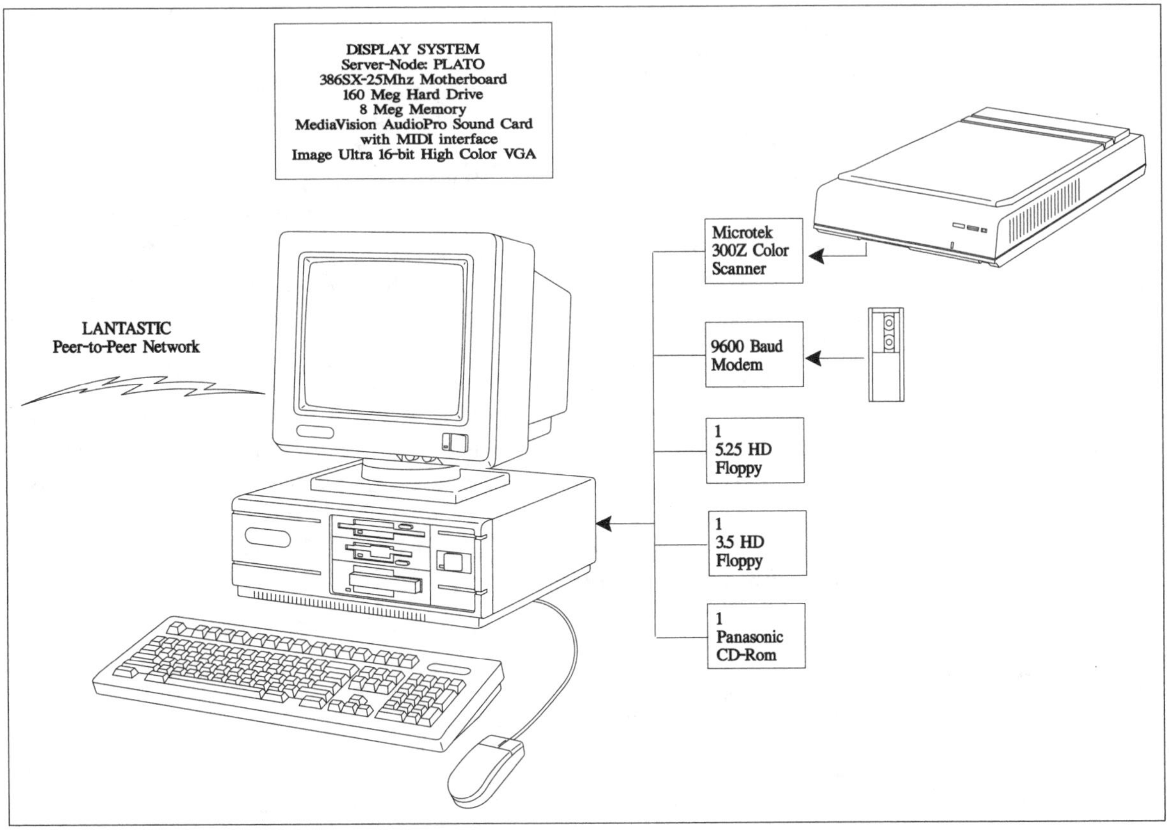

The production system used to create this book is where the word processor was installed. Chapters were written here while the main system was used to display Express and other packages for trial and verification of step-through techniques and other content. The network connection withe the main system was invaluable, allowing the two systems to function literally as a single computer.

and a golf game in there, you should be able to install Arts & Letters Express with room to spare.

Optimum System Requirements

To get the most out of Arts & Letters, install it on a fast 386 system (25 MHz or higher), a 486 or Pentium-based configuration with at least four megabytes of total system memory available. Eight or sixteen megabytes of memory are recommended if you want to run multiple Windows programs at the same time without serious degradation to software efficiency. Your hard disk should be minimum 80 megabytes for optimal use. This gives you plenty of room to maintain files on your hard drive and maintain a few extra software packages.

Since many Windows packages are lighting up like Christmas trees with added ornaments and lights, the size of all the related software you need is expanding. Add to that the flood of inexpensive fonts bundled with many programs—then add to that the fact that you need to have room to store the work you're actually doing. For optimal performance, you should be aiming at installing a 200 megabyte or larger hard drive to accommodate bigger, richer software packages, including Arts & Letters Express.

Finally, Arts & Letters is a vector-based graphic system, which is just a fancy way of saying that it creates artworks as a long and involved series of mathematical calculations. Math co-processor chips are included in the 486 and Pentium processors; if you are running a 386-based machine, you would be advised to look into installing a math co-processor. This can significantly speed up the display and editing of images in the Arts & Letters screen.

Microsoft Windows Tips

Arts & Letters Express is designed to run under Windows 3.1. If you're reading this book, you probably already know the basic Windows features and tools like the File Manager and the Program Manager. Once installed, Arts & Letters loads from the icon like any Windows program. Beyond the basics, there are a few tips and tricks in Windows you should be aware of.

OLE

Regardless of whether you pronounce "OLE" as a Swedish name or a Spanish cheer, it is an exciting, albeit often confusing, fact of life under Windows 3.1. OLE stands for *Object Linking and Embedding*, a nifty technical turn of phrase that describes a new way to translate information that is several technical tiers above, but related to, the ubiquitous Cut/Copy/Paste features in most Windows programs. OLE technology defines and manages computer objects—chunks of computer information that can "phone home" and automatically boot the program that created them (Figure 2.1).

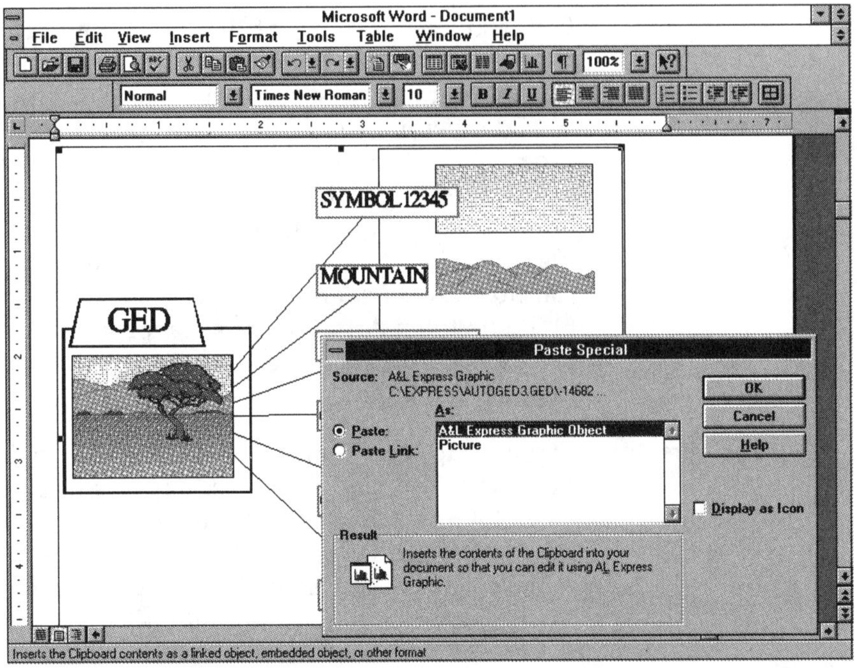

Figure 2.1
OLE Power
OLE takes Clipboard clumps of data and provides a means to cut and paste them in any compatible Windows program as "live" computer objects. Each object can phone home and summon its creation program for on-demand editing.

Objects vs. Files

The tricky concept at the heart of OLE is the concept of OLE *objects* vs. traditional computer *files*. Files, of course, are named chunks of data which you save, open, edit, and save again. Files are managed in all Windows programs through the File menu. Objects under OLE are managed in most Windows programs through the Edit (or equivalent) menu. Simply stated, OLE technology provides the means to retain the integrity of the chunks of data that you cut or copy in any Windows program, and gives you a series of options to Paste them into other programs using totally alien file formats. In this sense, OLE is like electronic collage, allowing data, graphics, text, even sound and video, to coexist in a single computer file. It signals a great step forward in computing capabilities.

Art Server for Windows

Arts & Letters Express is programmed to serve as an *OLE server* application in your Windows system. This means that Express can create objects that you can then place in any *OLE client* program. Most big-name word processors and spreadsheets are OLE clients, which means you can embed or link your Arts & Letters artwork directly into your word processor documents. When you activate the Express object in the page of the external program, the Arts & Letters program will boot and display automatically, allowing you to edit the art right at the source.

OLE features make use of the Cut/Copy features on the Edit menu of Express and other programs. To place an Arts & Letters object in an external program, the simple way is to select the desired art, copy it from the Edit menu, and use the Paste Special option in the receiving/client program. Paste Special gives you the options to paste the art, embed it, or link it through OLE.

If you embed the Arts & Letters composition in the external program file, the artwork is saved inside the external program file, so you can call up Arts & Letters and edit it whenever you want. If you create an OLE link to an Arts & Letters composition, that file is not saved inside the external program file, but remains independent and can be linked to other files in other programs.

OLE Versions Express supports Version 1.0 of OLE, the original format developed by Microsoft. Version 2.0 of OLE appears in some packages, but not all. Since OLE is a Microsoft technology for all intents and purposes, all Microsoft products tend to have the latest version. Other vendors support Version 1.0 or Version 2.0 in a somewhat scattergun fashion. Don't worry, Express's OLE configuration will work with any of the others.

Printer Fonts

Another Windows caution centers around printer fonts. Arts & Letters allows you to create artworks using the fonts available in your source printer or the included Arts & Letters custom typefaces. If you are using source printer fonts, bear in mind that what prints well on one device might not work as well on another. The Windows printer driver for your source printer will specify which fonts are available in that configuration. (See Figure 2.2.) If you decide to print on another device using the Setup Printer option, you may find that your type will change to match the supported fonts of the new printer. Since printing features and font management are controlled entirely by Windows, it is important to keep this in mind when using any printer fonts in your work.

Fancy Mice

The standard Windows mouse configuration features are located in the control panel. Essentially, they allow you to reassign the button configuration for right-handed or left-handed people. But major leaps in mouse technology hold forth a shimmering future: Microsoft's new serial mouse (Figure 2.3) includes dramatically enhanced mouse drivers that allow you to select fancy tricks like "wraparound" mouse movement, so that when the mouse disappears off the left edge of the screen

Figure 2.2
Fonts Maze
If fonts selected in the Type Attributes screen are your printer fonts, you may experience technical problems if you change to a different printer. Arts & Letters allows you to edit onscreen with your PostScript or HP format fonts.

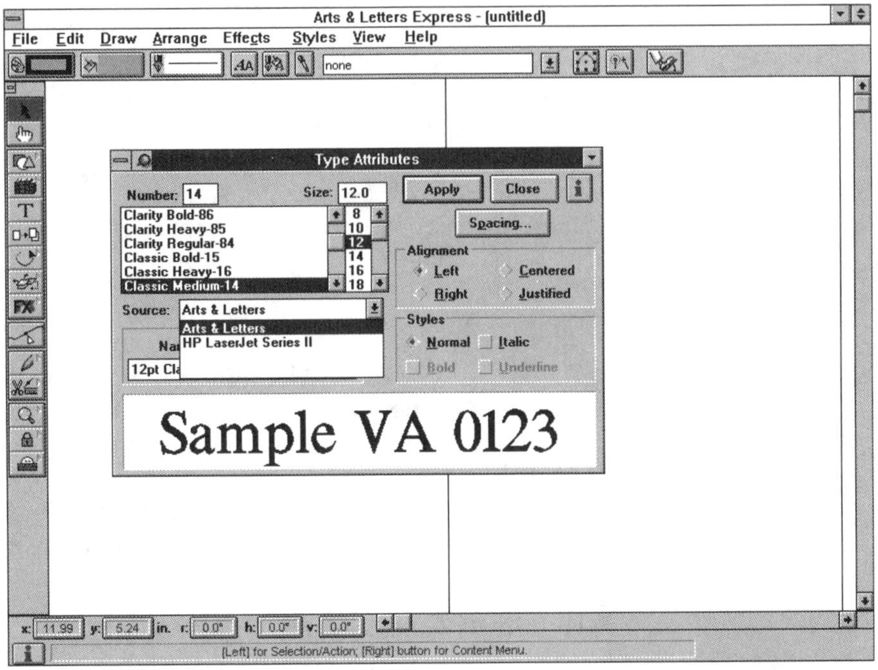

Figure 2.3
Fancy Mice
Using this hot new Microsoft serial mouse driver, you can make your mouse into a high-powered tool that navigates easier, even auto-magnifies the area around the cursor when you click the left button and a specified control key.

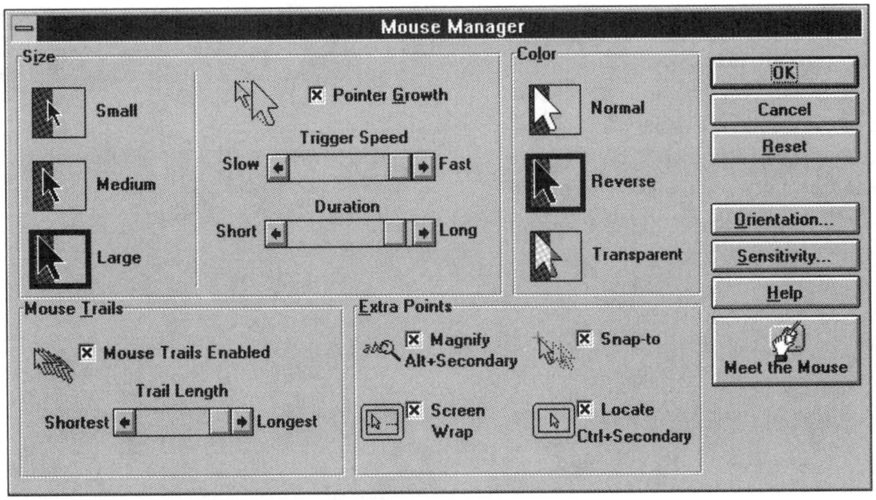

it "wraps-around" to the same place on the opposite right-hand side! Other enhancements allow you to combine a mouse click with one of the control keys (Alt, Ctrl, or Shift) to instantly magnify the area around the mouse pointer, and automatically center the mouse pointer in the page at any time. Since many manufacturer's make their mice compatible with Microsoft's standard (surprise!) these advanced drivers will enable you to be much more effective in using Express, no matter what mouse is in your house.

System Menu

The Windows System Menu may be accessed through the button at the upper-left corner of the Arts & Letters screen (Figure 2.4). This menu allows you to perform window management functions, including Minimize, Maximize, Move, Size, Restore, and Close windows. You may also use Switch To and the active window. Finally, this is where you activate the Decipher image processing and screen capture utility.

Windows Care and Feeding

Arts & Letters Express is a large-scale graphics package. It makes use of complex computations to stage and display your artworks on the

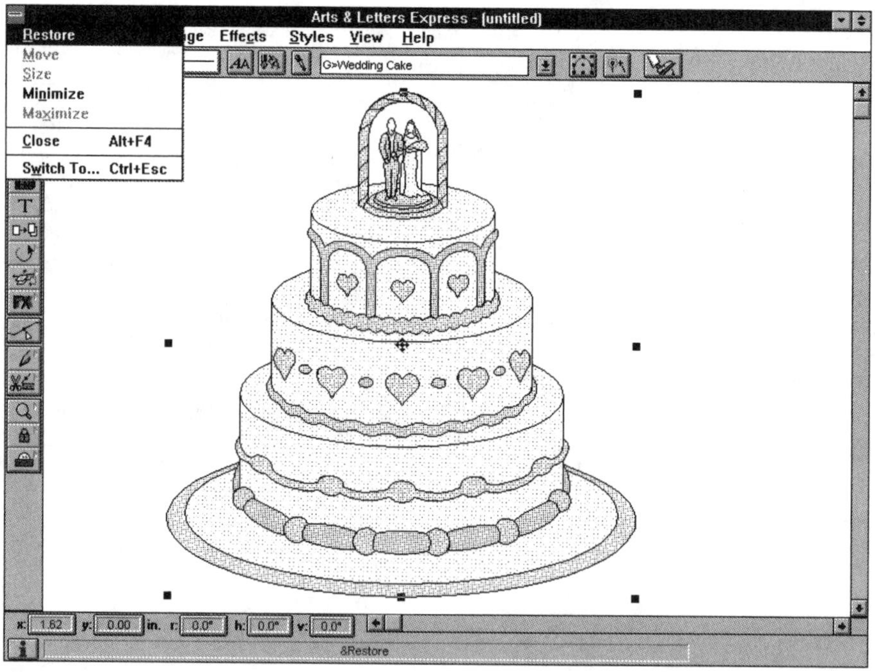

Figure 2.4
System Button
The System menu button that appears on the upper-left corner of the Windows screen is duplicated in the upper-left corner of many A&L dialog boxes. You use this drop down to close, control display, and position the window or dialog box.

screen. Remember that more memory makes Windows much speedier, so lacking sufficient memory or having too many other programs open takes up a lot of memory, and your Windows system resources may leave it and Express just plugging along. Use your common sense, save often, and you will get the best possible results from Express.

The Arts & Letters Screen Interface

Arts & Letters Express uses a Windows 3.1 style screen framework to display the tools available in the software. The screen design and operation have been dramatically reworked from previous versions, so even if you are an experienced Arts & Letters user, you'd be well advised to check through and see what's new and how the new screen can make you more efficient. The following is a summary of each of these screen tools and how they work within the Arts & Letters screen.

The Mouse

The Arts & Letters screen is operated primarily by the mouse pointer. The mouse is used to select screen features from icons located in the Toolbox in the Main Screen and from pull-down menus that may be accessed from the menu bar at the top of the screen. The mouse is the tool used in the working area of the screen to select graphic objects, edit them, draw freeform shapes, and build compositions from multiple objects. The key operating logic of the two key mouse buttons are:

- The left mouse button is the default or primary button used for almost all mouse operations. In this book, the terms *select* or *click on* mean to press the *left mouse button* unless otherwise specified.
- The right mouse button displays on-screen "pop-up" or "content" menus that allow you to select a variety of editing features right at the point of work (Figure 2.5). Contents of the pop-up menu depend on the feature you are currently using and the element you are editing. When editing text, the pop-up menu displays text-enhancement options; when editing a symbol, the pop-up displays object-editing options. Note that the right button is also used to disable any of the special drawing or manipulation features, such as Duplicate, Rotate, or Slant, you may have selected.
- When using the built-in Express Help system, the left mouse button is called the *primary mouse button*, and the right mouse button is called the *content menu mouse button*. An easy way to maintain the

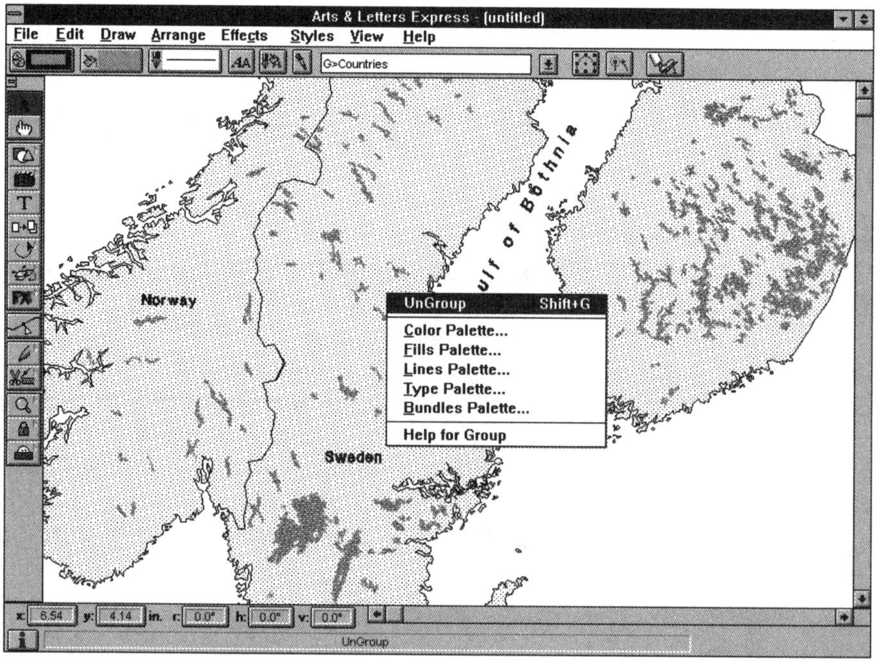

Figure 2.5
Mouse Pop-Ups
Depressing the right mouse button will display pop-up menus that allow you to execute the current selected feature more easily, and directly from the working area. The menu that appears depends on the feature you currently are using.

distinction is that the left/primary mouse button executes menu options on demand; the right/content mouse button displays a menu of editing or enhancement features for the objects directly beneath the current mouse position.

The Keyboard

While Arts & Letters is primarily a mouse-driven program, you can perform a wide variety of operations directly from the keyboard. Obviously, these include entering and editing text, but in addition, a great number of key editing, drawing, manipulation, and attribute features may be displayed by selecting a Control key and letter combination or using function keys.

Experienced users should note that the shortcut pairs and function key assignments for Express have been completely revised from those used in Arts & Letters Version 3 products. The design assumption of the shortcuts has been to focus on feature pairs and match commands to them. For example, the shortcut for Group is now Control-G; the shortcut for Ungroup is Shift-G. Other shortcuts, particularly for the editing features, have been brought into line with commands used in most other Windows programs; the shortcut for Copy is Control-C; for Paste is Control-V; and for Cut is Control-X.

Express makes full use of the menu hot-key features. Pressing the Alt key plus the hot key letter in a menu name displays the menu; typing the hot key of the desired feature on the menu activates it. You may also navigate the menus using the up and down arrow keys; the right arrow key will open a marked cascade submenu. Within dialog boxes, you may navigate through the feature options by pressing the Tab key to move forward; press the Shift-Tab to go back.

Pull-Down Menus and Cascades

The Menu Bar contains the names of all Arts & Letters screen menus beginning at the left of the screen, with the Help menu at the far right. You display menus by touching the menu name with the mouse cursor and clicking the mouse. To activate a feature, highlight it on the menu and click the mouse to select it.

Note that the standard Windows menu shows the keyboard command to activate all features at the right side of the menu. All features followed by a dialog box display are followed by an ellipsis (. . .), and any features not currently available to you are displayed in grayed-out text.

Arts & Letters Express makes extensive use of cascade submenus (Figure 2.6). These menu lists are marked by a small right-arrow at the

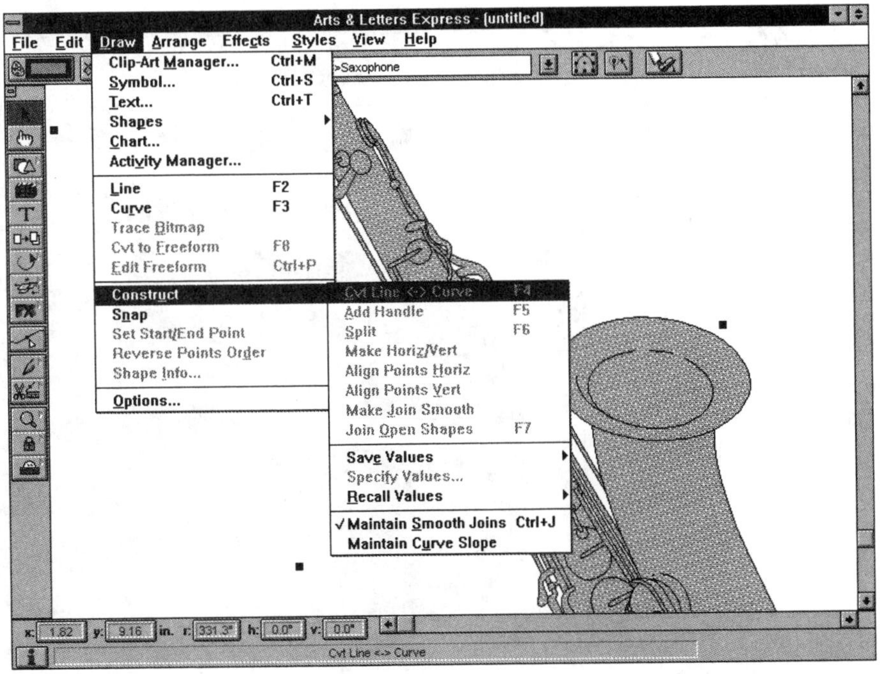

Figure 2.6
Cascade Array
Cascade submenus slide out from pull-down menus and allow you to avoid clicking through a chain of complex dialog boxes. Arts & Letters makes extensive use of cascade menus to help you select specific editing features directly from the main screen and menu bar.

far right-hand side of the menu opposite the feature name. When selected, the cascade menu shows a set of options for the selected feature. If you focus on your mouse skills, these features can be very rewarding; they are used in Express to allow you to select feature options, formerly buried in dialog boxes, directly from the screen.

Toolbox, Toolbars, Flyout Toolkits, and Pushpins

Once upon a time, graphic screens were mainly menu driven. Under the expanded design options of Windows 3.1, the hot new design approach is based on Toolkits, hot buttons, and button bars. Rather than forcing you to accept a locked screen design, this new approach lets you set up the screen with as many or as few instant access features as you like, and place them more or less where you want. (See Figure 2.7.)

Toolbars and Flyouts

The locked-in-place dual column Toolbox of Version 3 vintage Arts & Letters products has given way to a single column button-based Toolkit which is both movable and magical. Each button on the Toolkit either activates a major feature or acts as the handle to a small group of feature options which "fly out" when the button is selected. Express has added an additional wrinkle: each of these Toolbox flyouts has a graphic pushpin included. If you select it, the entire flyout becomes a

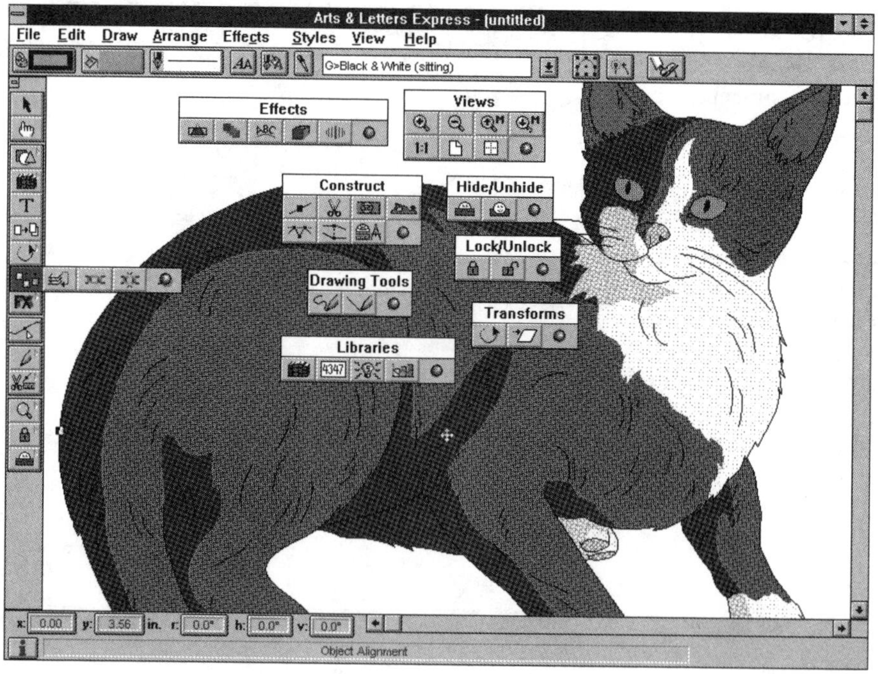

Figure 2.7
Flyouts and Mini-Toolboxes
Click on a construction icon and a flyout strip appears with selectable icons (check the Hint line at the bottom to see what they are). Click on the Pushpin and the flyout becomes a minitoolkit you can maintain on the screen as long as you need it.

separate, movable minitoolbox containing icons that activate a group of features. Select the Symbol icon on the Toolbox and you get six basic graphic shapes in the flyout. Pushpin it down, and a special minitoolbox appears which you can drag anywhere and select geometric shapes to your heart's content.

Style Bar At the top of the screen, you have the option to display a complete Style Bar that accesses most of the hot features from the Styles menu and a few others without opening a dialog box. Particularly ingenious are the color and other enhancement selectors (Figure 2.8). Select an object, point to the color button on the Style Bar, and a complete spectrum drops down in a flyout menu for you to select the desired color mix from the current palette.

Number Bar The Numeric Bar shows up at the bottom of the screen. It might appear to be just another of those earnest but boring displays that show the dimensions of the currently selected object. But look closer. Each of the listed dimensions, including the angle of rotation, is a hot button of the Transform dialog box. When you click on the desired statistic, you are fast-ported to a screen where you can numerically enter a desired value. No menu dancing required.

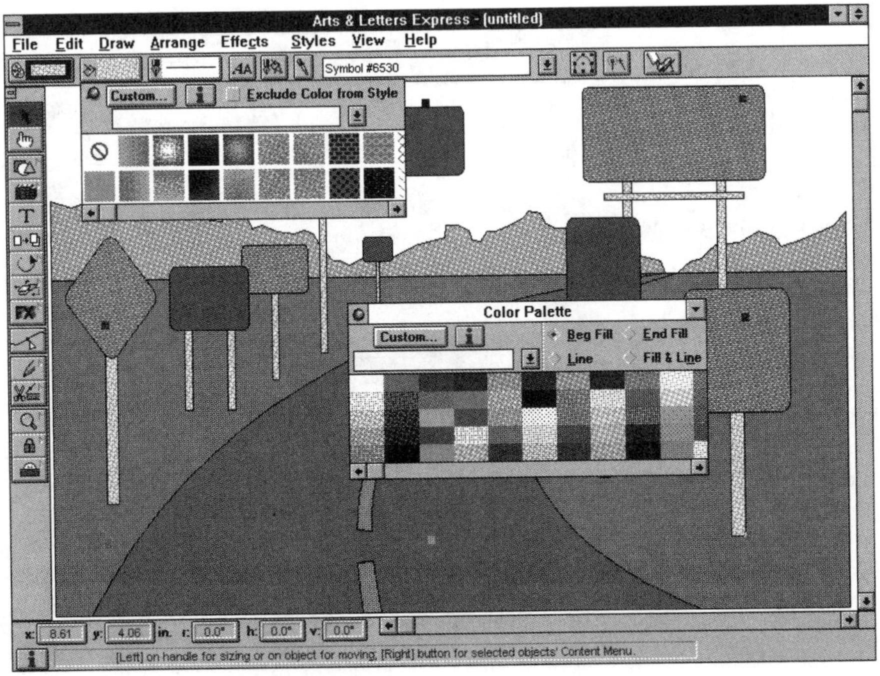

Figure 2.8
Style Bar Flyouts
The Style Bar also contains flyouts for the Styles menu that you can pushpin down to the screen, or slide right to the color or attribute you want. You may select various objects in the image and continuously apply colors or enhancements from the pushpinned flyout palette.

Hint Line The Hint line, also at the bottom, is a kind of minitutorial that tells you what the screen icons refer to as you slide your mouse over the Toolbox. All of these screen strips can be turned on or off in the Work Areas option of the View menu. By eliminating them, you gain a significant amount of working area.

Dialog Boxes

For features that require entry of numeric or text data, or selection from a list of feature options, Arts & Letters displays a dialog box as an overlay on the drawing screen (Figure 2.9). All features that carry dialog boxes are shown on the menus followed by an ellipsis (. . .). After operations are completed in a dialog box, you select **OK** or press the **Return** key and the dialog box disappears from view. The bar at the top of each dialog box can be selected and used to drag the dialog box display to any point within the screen.

Manager Screens

The graphic database in Arts & Letters operates through three dialog boxes that are uniquely designed as *manager screens*. They are:

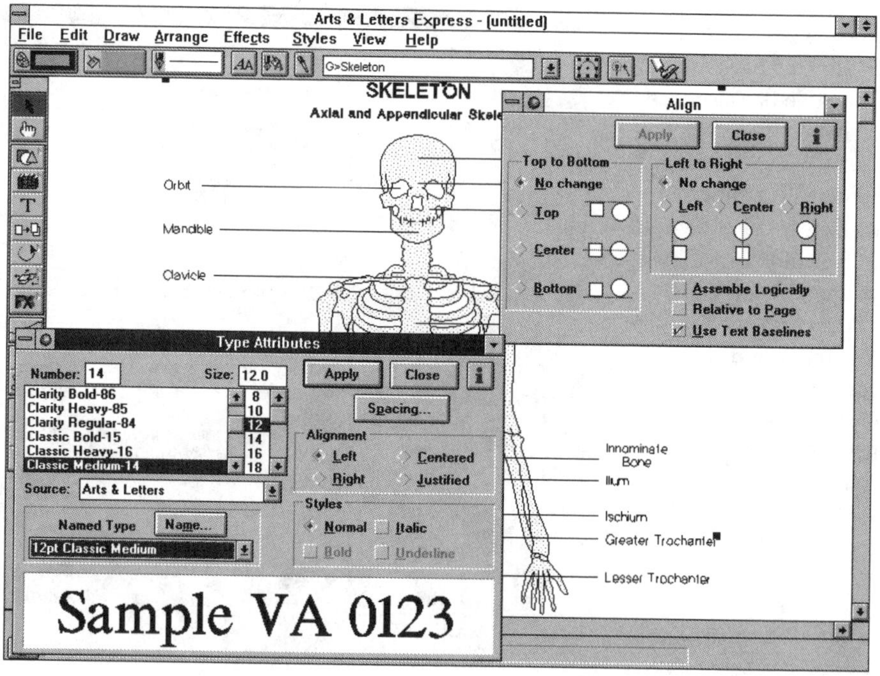

Figure 2.9
Dialog Boxes
Many dialog boxes in Arts & Letters give you a pushpin option which allows you to hold the dialog box right on the screen and operate other features of the software as you use it. This is a very high-production design feature that can save you a great deal of time and menu-dancing.

- Symbol dialog box
- Clip-Art Manager dialog box
- Activity Manager dialog box

The Symbol dialog box allows you to access the numbered symbol libraries. The Clip-Art Manager and Activity Manager (Figure 2.10) are identical screens, displaying (*.YAL) files. The Clip-Art Manager stores ready-made illustrations to plug into your document. The Activity Manager contains a group of automated templates and graphic tools, including automated forms for greeting cards and business forms, music paper and musical notation components, galleries of sophisticated formats for object warping, and charts. Use of the Activity Manager tools will be covered throughout the book where the context warrants.

Help Screens

Help screens are available from the **Help** menu situated to the far right of the menu bar. You may access help directly through the Help Index or by selecting **Help By Item**, which allows you to select any of the icons or selections on pull-down menus.

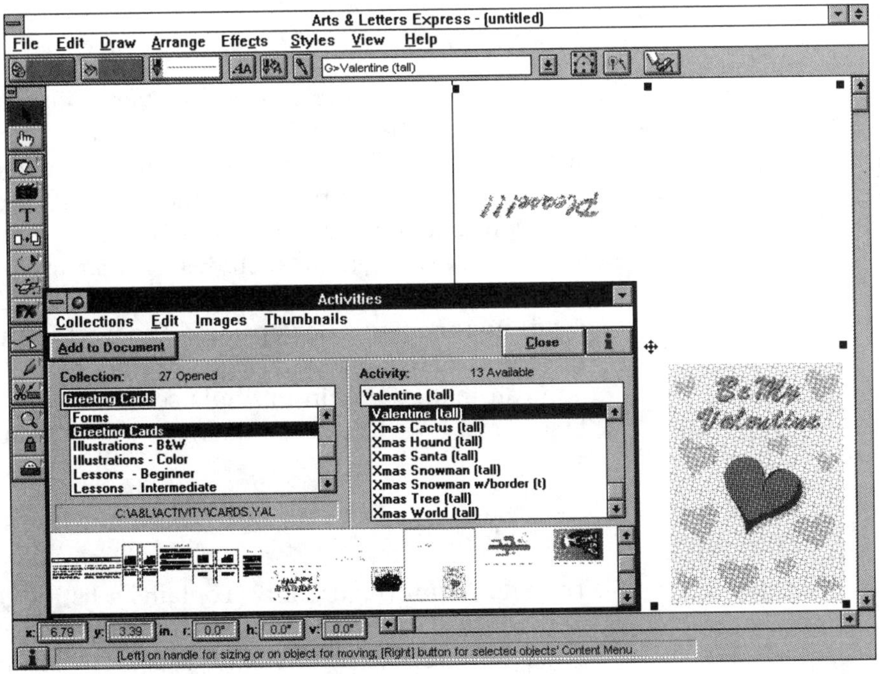

Figure 2.10
Activity Manager
The Activity Manager is a twin of the Clip-Art Manager and contains ready-made templates for a variety of art output, including greeting cards, forms, stationery, and a system of screen tutorial exercises, complete with on-screen step-by-step instructions.

Screen Rulers and Grid

You may display screen rulers at the left and upper edges of the drawing screen by activating them in the **Work areas** dialog box in the **View** menu. Tracking lines built into the rulers show your current horizontal and vertical position. Rulers take up some drawing screen space, so they should only be activated when you really need to measure or control the size of a graphic object.

Menu Gallery

The Arts & Letters Express screen has been redesigned so that you can do most simple art operations without using any dialog boxes, or a minimum number at best. The menu structure is still the basic framework in the package. Experienced users should note that serious shuffling has been going on there. The menu configuration under Express can be easily grasped if you imagine it as a series of operational groups. File controls the basic file operations; Edit, Draw, and Arrange provide features to place, move, and manage art elements; Effects and Styles provide art object enhancements and expanded effects; and View regulates how you see all this on the screen.

File Menu

The File Menu (Figure 2.11) is the operational command center for Arts & Letters. Features included allow you to open Arts & Letters document files (*.GED), save files, set up parameters for document pages, and print files. Additional selections allow you to directly import and export files in a variety of supported PC graphics file formats.

The Import selection includes a transparent link to Arts & Letters Decipher conversion program, and offers a dramatically expanded set of importation filter options. The new Defaults option allows you to save the current operating defaults of the software as a setup file. You can then maintain multiple setups for different projects and load them as you need them to minimize "macro" time spent making "micro" settings.

Edit Menu

The Edit Menu (Figure 2.12) contains a list of general editing capabilities, which allow you to Undelete operations, and select and deselect groups of graphic objects. Cut, copy, and paste features allow you to

Figure 2.11
File Menu
In addition to managing files and printing, this is where you can save your current screen configuration and style defaults into a loadable Defaults file. To bring back those defaults, just load the file any time.

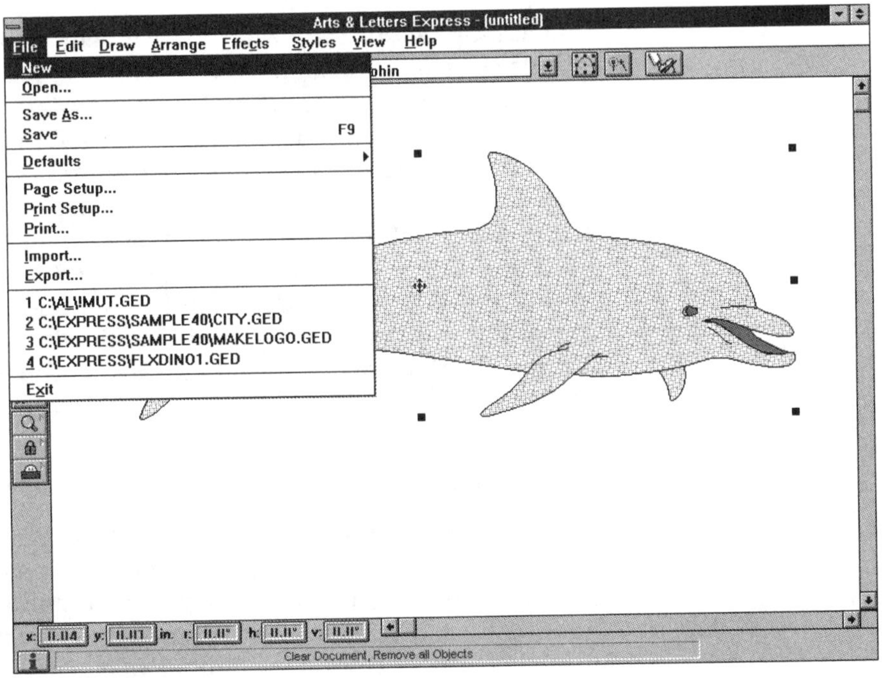

Figure 2.12
Edit Menu
The Object Management group makes it easy to find individual components of your artworks and select them for easy editing. The Object Viewer also appears in the Style Bar (at right, directly over the word "Correction") and displays a description of the object currently selected on the screen.

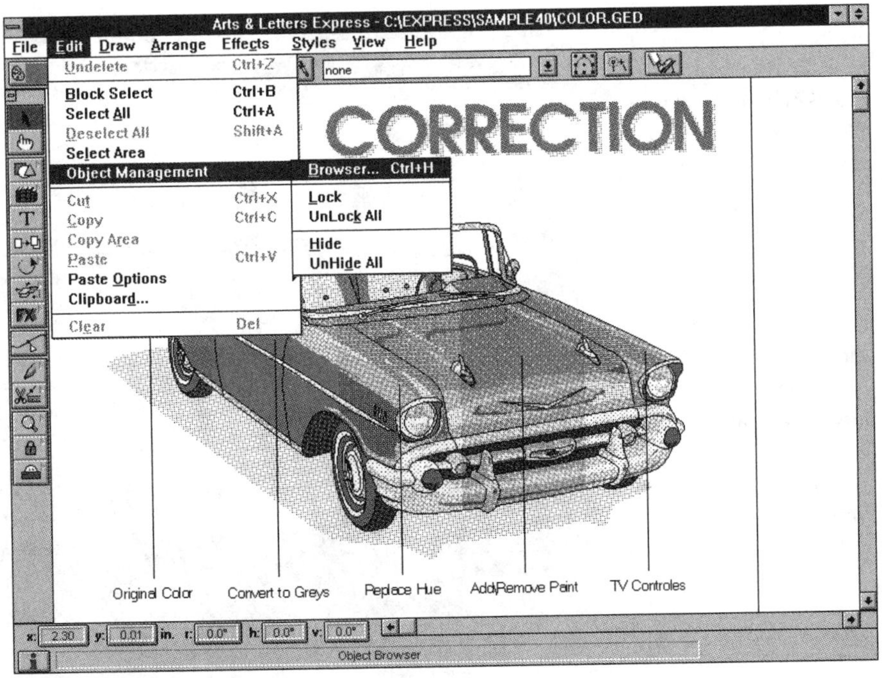

move graphic objects within a document or between different documents. This menu also gives you access to the Windows Clipboard, so you can directly move artwork and data between Arts & Letters and other Windows-supported applications, such as Microsoft Excel.

The new Object Management feature group includes an old friend (Lock/Hide/Name) under a new moniker (Object Browser), and provides quick features to lock and hide large groups of art objects. Note that this feature has nothing to do with OLE objects; its name derives from "art objects." The new Select Area option allows you to "rubber-rectangle" any area in the screen and select it. You may then copy, paste, export, or print that selected area, even if it slices through individual graphic symbols or illustrations—a fast output feature.

Draw Menu

The Draw Menu (Figure 2.13) contains the principal group of symbol-based and freeform drawing tools. From this menu, you can access the Symbol selector, Clip-Art Manager, Text, and Charts. You may select many of the key freeform drawing features, including Line and Curve drawing, Edit Freeform, and other freeform editing features. Options allows you to set the desired precision for drawing operations (general

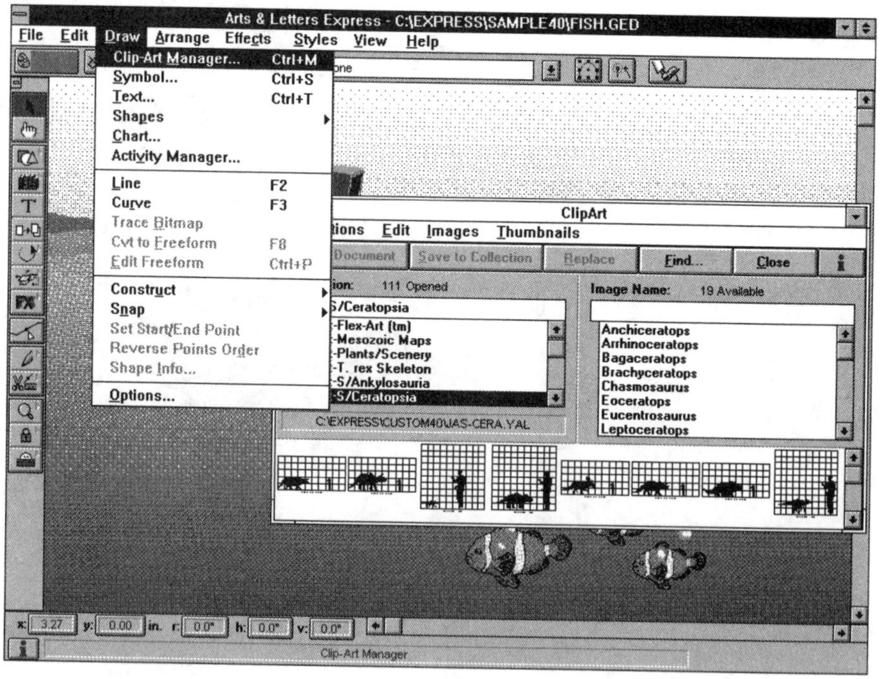

Figure 2.13
The Draw Menu
This is where you can select all the major art functions of Arts & Letters: Symbols, the Clip-Art Manager, Charts, Text, and Freeform drawing features. The Options selection here sets drawing parameters only; screen and display are controlled by the Options feature on the View menu.

operating preferences, including units of measure, snap-to grid, and others are set in the **Preferences** option on the **View** menu).

The two key selectors on this menu are the Symbol option, which lets you select individual symbols by number from the graphic database, and the Clip-Art Manager, which accesses the collections of images.

Experienced Arts & Letters users will note that the old Construct menu, containing high-end settings for freeform drawing, has disappeared and resurfaced as a Cascade group at the bottom of this menu. So all the line editing features are still here, but in an out of the way place. Note that these features can also be accessed through a series of flyouts right off the Toolbox.

Arrange Menu

This new menu (Figure 2.14) was born from the break up of the old Manipulate menu under Version 3. Features here are focused on moving images or groups of images around in the screen. Grouping, stacking, flipping, and alignment are all easy here. This is also the new home of what is arguably the most powerful single dialog box in the entire program: Transform, which allows you to control object sizing, positioning, rotation, and slant through numeric entries.

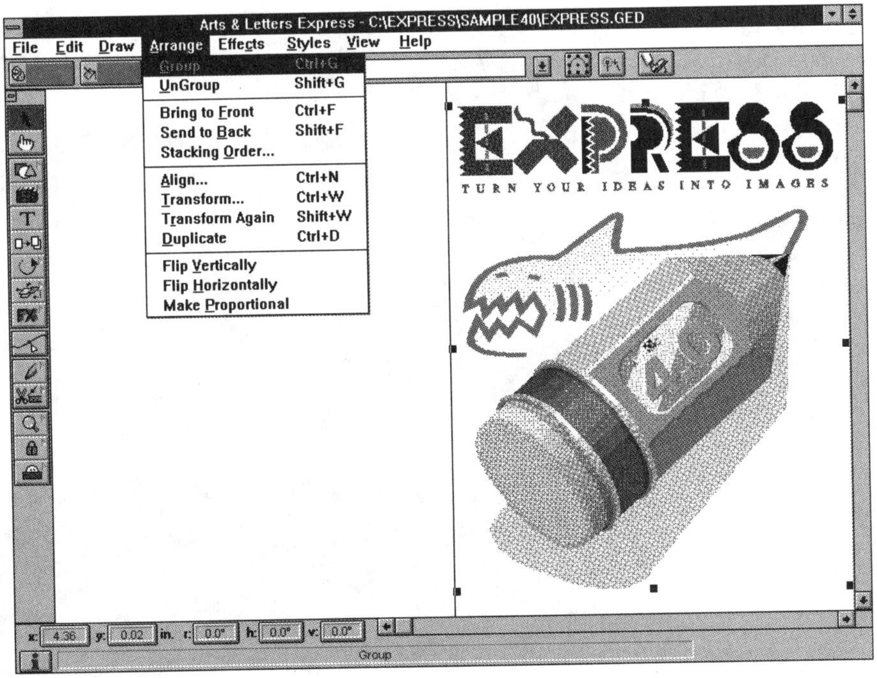

Figure 2.14
Arrange Menu
This contains all the features you use to manipulate individual elements and groups on the screen. The Transform feature allows you to set sophisticated manipulations numerically.

Effects Menu

The Effects menu (Figure 2.15) is the other half of the Manipulate menu breakup. Features here allow you to expand symbols and groups of elements into larger more complex composition elements. Using Blend, you can multiply and evolve an object in size and color. Merge allows you to create stylish cuts and cutouts. Bind to Shape maps text along a freeform line or an object shape. The new Extrude feature makes flat images into three-dimensional forms. Warp/Perspective provides multiple tools to shape text and art objects like Silly Putty.

Styles Menu

This menu (Figure 2.16) contains object-enhancement features, including color, line, fill, and type. Most of these features are best accessed from the new Style Bar for maximum efficiency. The menu design has exploded many of the old complicated dialog boxes into cascade menus that let you go directly to the enhancement effect you want without having to open a tunnel of dialogs. Under the Color option is the spectacular new Color Correction feature, which can phase a complete drawing consistently through the color spectrum. If you want a drawing in

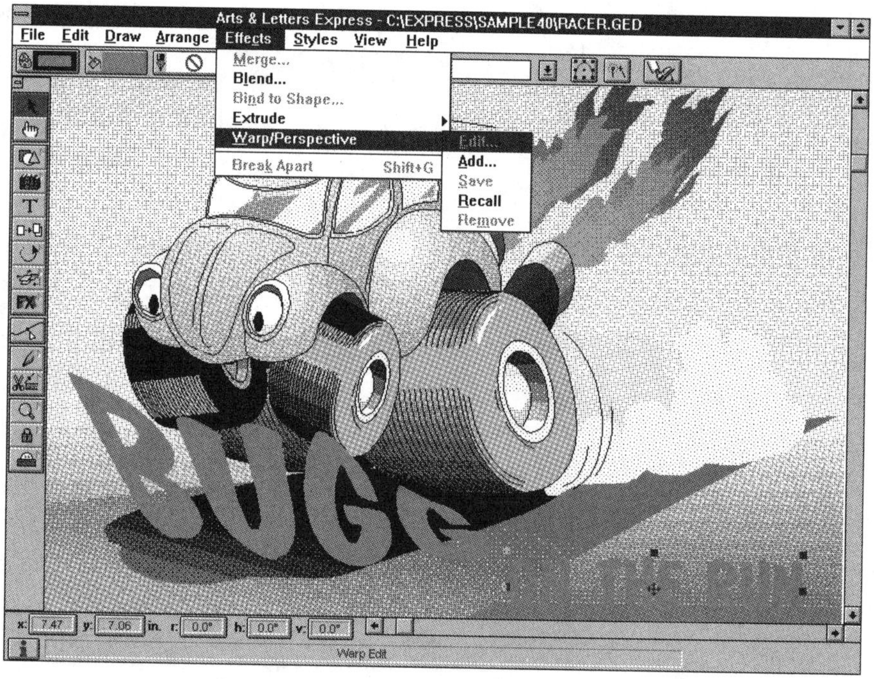

Figure 2.15
Effects Menu
This contains a group of dramatic composition features that let you create three-dimensional effects, layering, cutouts, shape distortions, and to even progressively evolve one shape into another. In the example shown, the word "BUGG" was created using the Warp/Perspective option, highlighted.

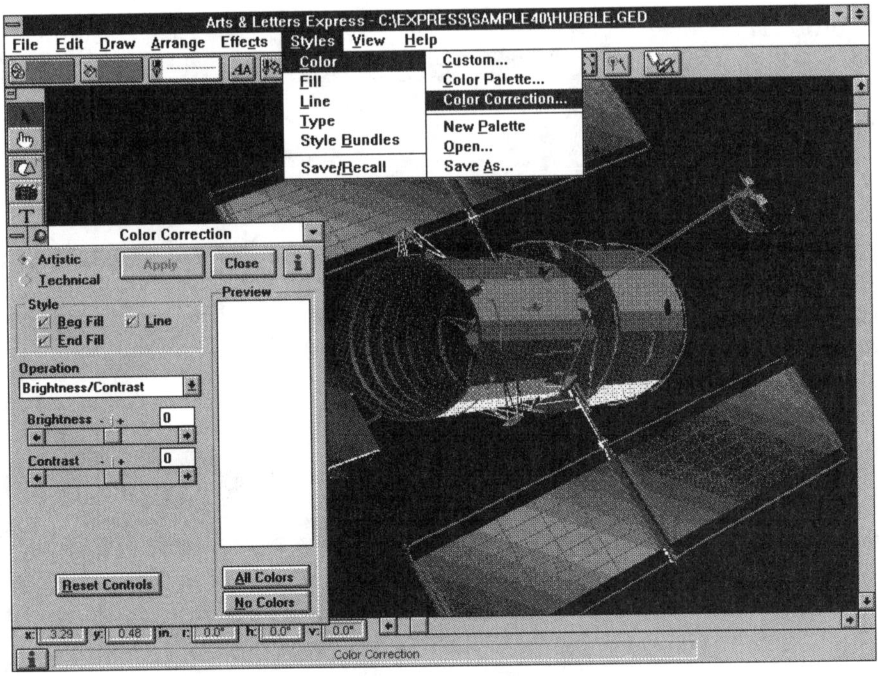

Figure 2.16
Styles Menu
Here is home to all the graphic and text enhancements—color, line, fill, and type. You also may save attribute configurations under a custom name and activate them on any object at the click of a button.

blue and shades of blue to change to red and shades of red, it's a click away using this feature. Style Bundles is a new name for the old Styles feature. It allows you to combine individual named styles—a named fill style, a named type style, a named line style—into one big megastyle that automatically applies a list of values at a single stroke.

View Menu

The View menu (Figure 2.17) allows you to control how you see your work displayed in the working area, both in terms of the actual area of the page displayed, and the freeform editing and control points shown. In addition, the **Preferences** option allows you to turn various features of the screen display on and off, including the Toolbox, Status line, Rulers, and Grid. This is also the place where you set the units of measure for the drawing grid (controls over drawing precision are set in the **Preferences** dialog box on the **Draw** menu).

Accel-O-Draw Depending on your hardware and memory configuration, display issues can significantly slow up screen redisplay and redrawing. Arts & Letters Express is designed with instant access programming, so you don't have to wait for the screen to redraw completely to begin editing.

Figure 2.17
View Menu
Beyond zoom, this menu gives you control over the screen display, grids, rulers, symbol and freeform editing points, and the ability to accelerate editing by suppressing a full display of all art elements on screen. The new Accel-O-Draw feature focuses all resources to draw the current illustration as fast as possible and automatically shuts off when finished.

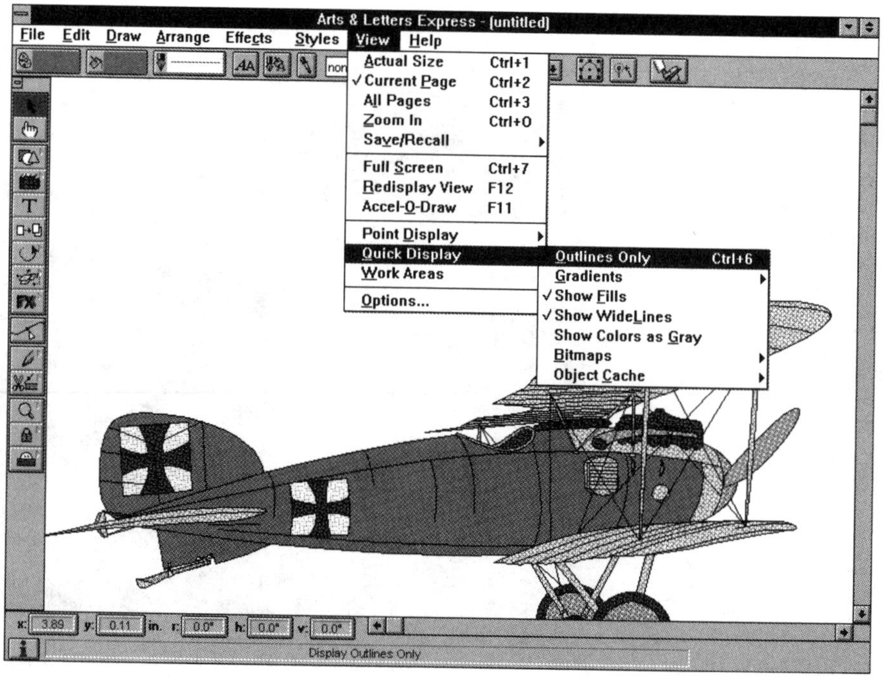

Just the same, you can use the display options here to turn off a variety of display enhancements and get a much more rapid, "quick and dirty," visualization of your edits in progress. The ultimate form of hyperspeed display is the new Accel-O-Draw feature. When activated, this feature automatically devotes all system resources in the software to redrawing the image on screen. As soon as the image is complete, it shuts off automatically.

Help Menu

The Help menu (Figure 2.18) lets you access Help directly on screen either from a general Help Index, or through context-sensitive Help. By selecting Help for Items (also available by pressing F1), you can click the mouse on any menu selection or icon on the screen and see the help display for that item without having to search the Index.

The user's guide and tutorials for the package have been made electronic, and are now integrated into the expanded Help system. Never forget, you can print Help topics on demand—that's what the Help Print features are there for.

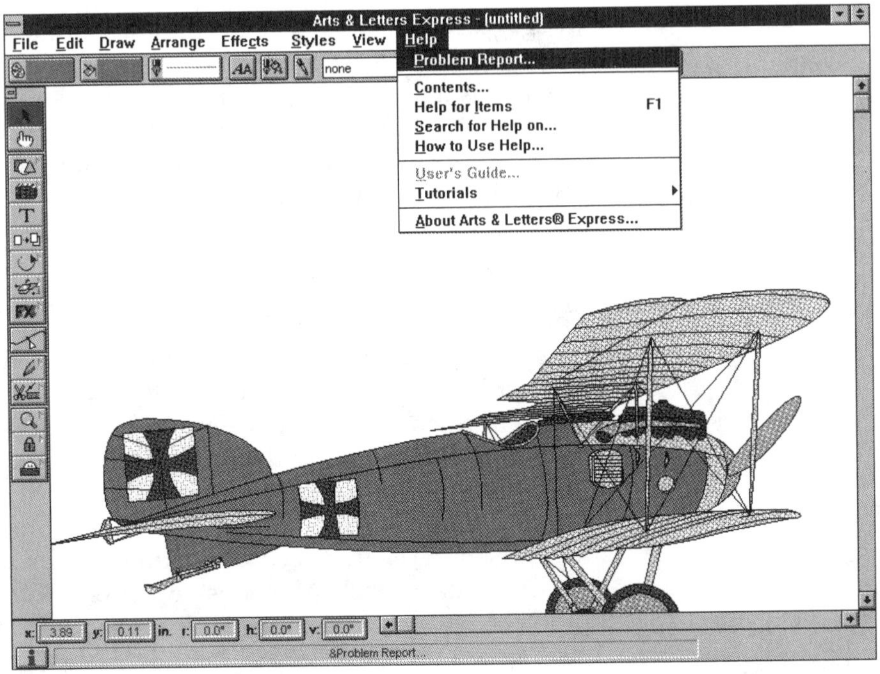

Figure 2.18
Help Menu
This contains full electronic documentation for all features of Arts & Letters. Available on demand, full user tutorials provide graphic, hands on exercises to teach you basic operations of sophisticated features.

Page Dynamics

To store and retrieve graphic information, Arts & Letters uses a unique system of programming. While it is not necessary for you to understand all the technical details, it is important that you understand the general concepts that are applied here, so that you can effectively create, save, and print your work.

The Graphic Document

Arts & Letters stores graphic information and symbol references that make up your drawing in what is called a *document*. A document is saved in a computer file called a GED file, short for *Graphic Environment Document*. A document may consist of a number of individual pages, in which you create drawings. This file structure permits you to save and store more than one drawing within a single computer file and to have each of those drawings available for printing individually or in a page-by-page series.

The number of pages in a document is a function of the size, margin settings, and final print resolution that you define for the page. Using the **Page Setup** dialog box (Figure 2.19) in the **File** menu, you can configure all the desired attributes of the page before you begin to work. If you are using larger pages, with small margins (so that the active drawing area in the page is larger) and high print resolution, you will have fewer pages in the document than if your pages are smaller and at a lower document precision.

Precision Output Tools

The critical point to note is that the graphic document format used by Arts & Letters is a tool for controlling precision in your output. At the highest levels of print resolution, Arts & Letters delivers output that can be printed on very high-resolution output devices and deliver extremely high clarity and detail. For most applications, you may not require such a high level of precision.

Arts & Letters achieves high levels of output precision by means of an invisible grid that records graphic information under a system of logical units per inch. Most desktop laser printers have an output resolution of 300 x 300 dpi (dots per inch). At its highest level of resolution, Arts & Letters delivers 2880 logical units per inch, which is exponentially more clear and better detailed than the desktop printing standard.

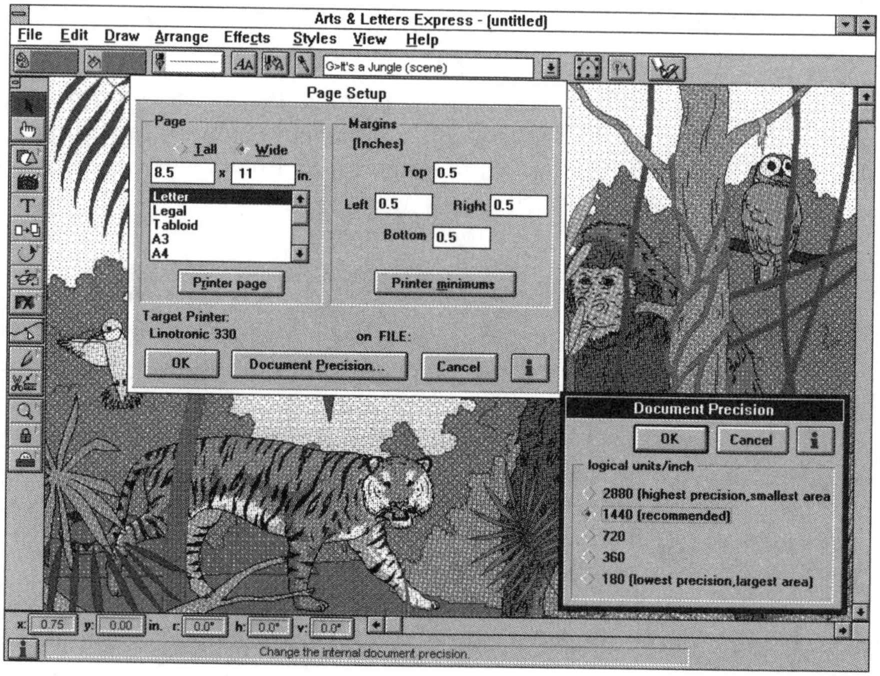

Figure 2.19 Precision Output Tools
Arts & Letters uses a system of logical units to control the precision and density of its output. The higher the number of logical units specified, the fewer pages in the Graphic Environment Document (GED). These features are primarily of interest to those developing color work for output at high resolution.

The higher the level of precision in the document, the fewer pages that are available. Also, the available active drawing area is smaller. To deliver extremely high resolution, more memory and graphic information is required. As you select lower levels of resolution, you have more pages available in the document and a larger output area to work with. For most presentation graphics and desktop publishing applications, the recommended resolution setting is 1440 logical units per inch, although you could go to one of the lower settings and still get excellent results.

The Page

A page is an area within a graphics document in which you draw individual artworks. The printing and file export features of Arts & Letters have been designed around the page as the basic screen area in which you can work. You may export the contents of a page to a filename, or you may print individual pages within a graphics document. Keep in mind that if you create a drawing that covers two or more pages in a document, Arts & Letters still treats them as individual pages, and when you print the document, you will get a series of pages that contain part of your drawing and not all of it.

You may configure the page using the **Page Setup** selection on the **File** menu. Your options include setting the size of the page, its orientation (*portrait* or standing up, and *landscape* or lying down), and the page margins.

For most works of art, it is best to create your work on a single page in the document and save that one page in its own GED file. For special applications, such as a two-page ad layout or a series of related graphics, you may find it convenient and useful to use multiple pages within the same document. After all, by using multiple pages, all graphic elements in the layout or graphic series are present in the same file and can be easily moved around the screen and interchanged with one another. This is a feature which you can't do easily if you're dealing with a series of separate computer files.

File Formats

One of the truly distinctive aspects of Arts & Letters is the way it handles graphic information. Many computer graphics programs store graphic information in individually loadable computer files. Because of its unique symbol-based composition system, Arts & Letters has a multilevel file structure in which different file types are used to retain your work for specific purposes in the software.

Library File Format: DLIB.ALL

Numbered symbol forms are stored in high-compression group files using the format DLIB###.ALL. These files contain the graphic information that defines the base "wireframe" of the symbol form, indexed by number. The *Clip Art Handbook* included with Express shows each of the wireframes with its index number. Enhanced symbols and master drawings that have related accent symbols are shown in parentheses beneath the main symbol number.

DLIB format files have two functions: first, they compress an immense amount of artwork so that it can be available on your system in a fraction of the space that separate individual computer files would require. Second, they provide a built-in linking system so that as you use symbols in your artworks, a representation of that symbol is displayed on the screen. When the work is saved in a GED file, a network link to the database number is stored, not the real graphic information. For this reason, GED files can contain huge complex artworks and remain relatively small.

You cannot create or save any symbols or edited versions of symbols into DLIB format files. They are locked. The DLIB format can contain only the wireframe of the graphic image. It cannot store colors, enhancements, special line configurations, or any other special setting.

Symbol File Type: INDEX.ALL

This file is the heart of the symbol graphic database. Symbols are made available in the screen through a single control file called INDEX.ALL, which loads a *representation* of a symbol into the screen when its number is called up. Note that when a symbol is still in symbol form, *the graphic information is not placed in the screen.* The symbol is created through a networking process based on the number. Only when a symbol drawing is converted to freeform graphic objects does the graphic information come into play. When you install symbol collections, the INDEX.ALL file is updated and knows where to locate your symbols that are stored in the DLIB##.ALL format.

Collection File Format: YAL

Collections are stored in another type of group database file called a YAL. This is not a technical acronym, but a contraction of the trademark Southern expression "Y'all." It was a contribution of a whimsically minded programmer. YAL files save symbols, graphic data, text, and graphic groups under user-defined text names. The YAL is a user-defined library format that can store not only graphic shapes and forms but the enhancements that go with them. Unlike the library file, these collection files can store finished, ready-to-use pictures, complete with colors, shading, and special line configurations. A single item under a YAL file may also contain symbols, freeform drawings, and text in the same image.

YAL files are cluster files: they allow you to save a long list of separate, accessible images inside the same file. You can use a YAL file to create a cluster of separate art elements for a given project, and then copy that file for use by anyone using Arts & Letters Express. Since the files are indexed by your defined user name, not by number, the graphic database concept is driven by key words.

The Clip-Art Manager is designed to access and manage all the YAL files in your system. Express comes with many ready-made families of YAL files, each containing thousands of ready-made images broken into topics. The Find feature in the Clip-Art Manager allows you to search through the text names based on keywords and find exactly what you are looking for.

Picture File Format: GED

When you save a picture in Arts & Letters, you use the GED (Graphic Environment Document) file format. The GED file format is a unique graphic construction that contains graphic information and listings of any symbols, by symbol number, contained in the file. A GED is a type of graphics manager in that it can re-create your drawing in detail without becoming an enormous, unwieldy, and space-consuming monster.

When using GED files, keep in mind that only freeform graphic information is stored in the file and is referenced by number. When the file is loaded, the graphic information in the file is created on screen and the GED file goes directly to INDEX.ALL to find the symbols it needs to complete the composition. If you have sent a GED file to someone using Arts & Letters on another system and they do not have all the symbols in their system that you used to create the composition, Arts & Letters will not be able to display the complete composition on their screen. In cases such as this, boxes will appear on screen to indicate the placement of the missing symbols. If, however, symbols are converted to graphic objects during the composition and drawing phases, all necessary graphic information to create the symbol image will be recorded in the GED file.

This programming reality is only a problem if you are using any of the available optional symbol libraries not included with the base software. All Arts & Letters version 3.0 and higher have the base set of

10,000 symbols with the package. But optional symbols may not be loaded on the systems of other individuals who receive your files. A good rule of thumb to follow is, whenever you are creating files using optional libraries, convert the symbols to freeform before saving them in the GED file. That way, all graphic information will be recorded into the file and anyone who receives that file can open it in Arts & Letters and have the complete composition available.

Import/Export File Formats

Arts & Letters allows you to export graphic information to external file formats including PostScript and CGM. And even the exporting features have an interesting twist. You may export the contents of a current page *or* you may directly export a group of selected objects or a

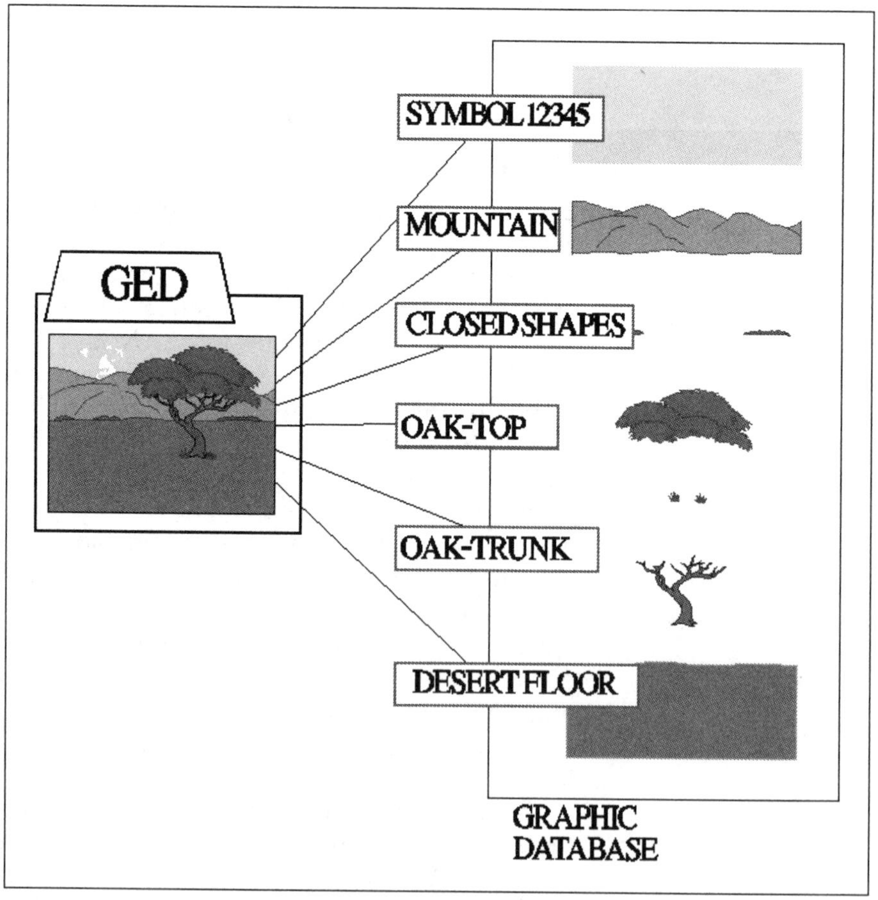

Figure 2.20
A & L Files Structure
The Arts & Letters system was designed on a foundation of locked high-symbol libraries that contain thousands of wireframe shapes and drawings in highly compressed form. These symbols provide the basis for the entire system of image collections The GED file accepts all forms of art generated in the software: freeform shapes, symbol shapes, graphic groups, and image components.

selected area on the screen. That means that you can draw a picture on the Arts & Letters screen and directly export that drawing into a file format compatible with your desktop publishing or other third-party software without even saving it as an Arts & Letters GED file. The unique power of this capability will be discussed and illustrated later in this book.

Arts & Letters comes with a companion program called Decipher that is used to perform Postscript file conversions, screen captures, and file conversions. The Import feature (Figure 2.21) provides a transparent portal to all of the import formats available through Decipher. Its set of filters has been significantly enhanced since the version 3 series of products.

Printing and Color Capabilities

Arts & Letters includes a highly sophisticated set of features that allow you to develop artwork in color and print your work in a variety of ways. The following is a general overview of these features. More detailed information on printing and color printing options can be found in Chapter 11. Using color in screen operations is covered in specific operations throughout the book.

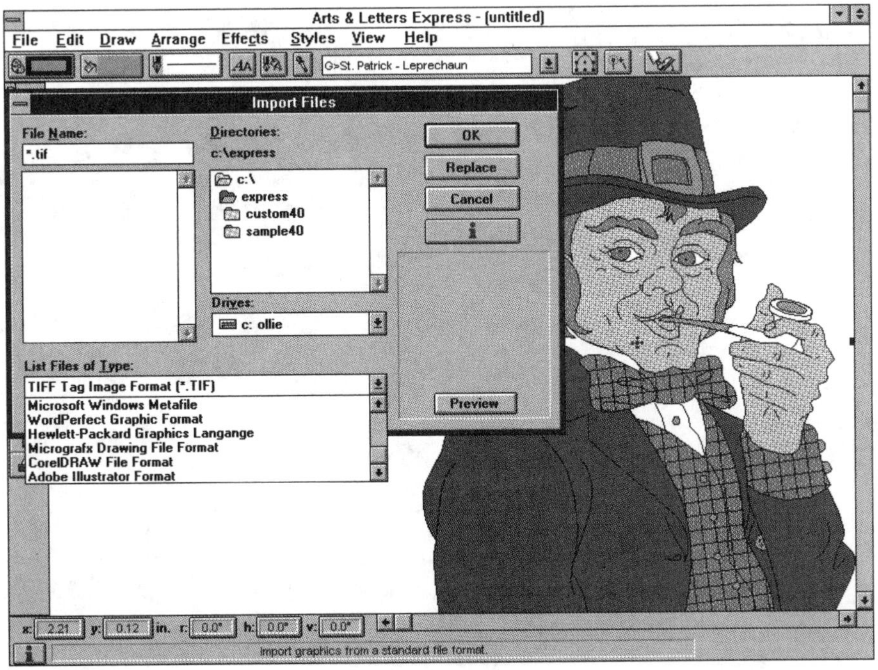

Figure 2.21
Enhanced File Import
The Import dialog box provides a transparent link to Arts & Letters built-in Decipher file management and conversion program. You may directly import vector-based artwork such as CorelDraw files into an editable GED format.

Printing Features

Arts & Letters gives you many different ways to print your work. File export features discussed in the previous section are, in effect, a way of "printing" your Arts & Letters files into different formats where they can be read and used by other software packages. The actual Print feature set includes options that allow you to print directly to your PostScript printer, create spot or process color separations, or print your document into a computer output file so that it can be printed by an external printing device, such as a Linotronic high-resolution imagesetter.

Printing features are based on your page setup. If print configurations for page size, margins, and other key elements differ from the setup of your page, you will be prompted to fix them before printing can proceed. Once in the printing screen (Figure 2.22), you can set your printing requirements: you have the option to print the entire document, selected pages in the document, or a group of selected objects which have not been saved into a GED file.

Color Features

When creating artwork in Arts & Letters, you have a sophisticated set of color control features that allow you to apply basic or mixed colors to

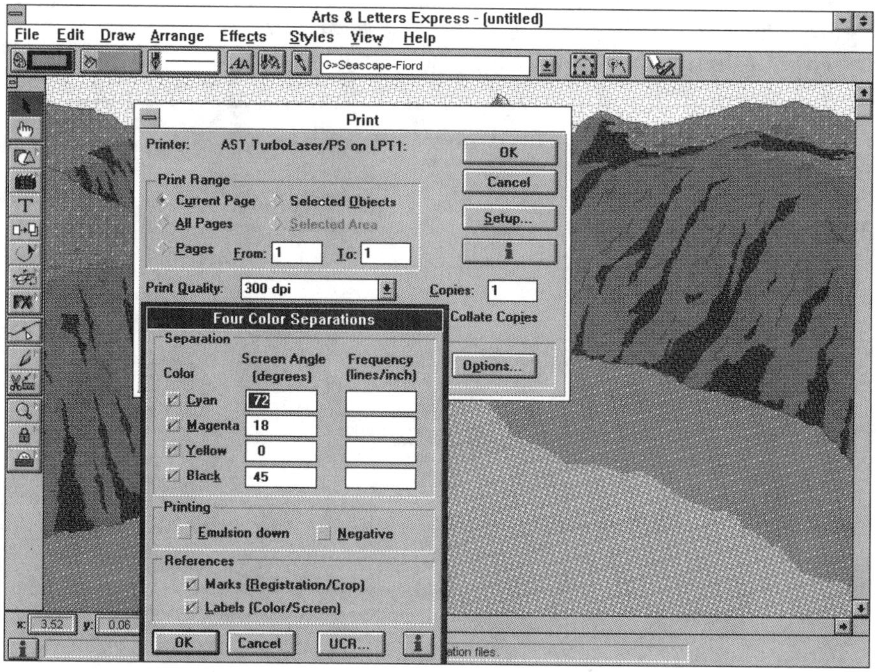

Figure 2.22
Printing and Color
The Print dialog box contains precision controls for printing color output to a variety of devices, using several key color models.

graphical line and fill values. The basic color dialog box functions as a separate standalone window with its own pull-down menus inside (Figure 2.22). These allow you to bring up additional windows so you can mix colors to precise numeric values based upon a number of available color models, including RGB and CYMK, or by selecting Hues from a color band.

Another powerful aspect of the color handling system are the ready-made color palettes. In Arts & Letters, you can create color mixes and give them logical, English-language names. These color mixes can then be saved into groups called palettes. This capability allows you to create highly specific color mixes for a project, and group all the color mixes for that project in a single file that can be displayed on the screen on demand. To apply a color mix, simply select the name of the palette desired.

Named color mixes may also be stored in Arts & Letters styles. A style can store specific line and fill attribute settings along with color mixes under a single name so that all of these attributes may be applied, in seconds, by selecting the style name.

Color editing features may be accessed from the option selection on the **Styles** menu or from icon selections in the stylebar which, for your convenience, display the currently selected color for line and fill values.

Integrated Feature Power

The screen interface and programming approach within Arts & Letters represents a solution used by a number of computer graphics problems. Specifically, they permit you to have powerful drawing capabilities, an instant composition system, text handling, and charting all within the same system of menus, features, and commands.

What is best about the Arts & Letters approach is that it consistently gives you more choices on how to use the software, and the tools to work the way you want to work. This integrated system of capabilities gives you much more flexibility and freedom than most conventional drawing software. However, it is somewhat unusual, and you should take a moment to experiment by setting up a page and familiarizing yourself with the operation of the graphics document concept.

CHAPTER 3

Composing with Symbols and Images

Using the Graphic Database

The graphics database of symbol wireframes and ready-made images in Express provides you with a powerful resource to summon and assemble individual artworks into complete professional compositions. The database exists on two levels. First is the database of number-indexed symbol wireframes, which is the foundation of the entire system. Each wireframe symbol may be sized, reshaped, rotated, slanted, colored, textured, and displayed in a virtually infinite range of line thicknesses, shades, and configurations. Second are the complete images available from the collections included with the Clip-Art Manager. These images are made up of multiple symbols, already assembled, enhanced, and displayed in full color. You may break apart or ungroup the images and edit the individual numbered symbols and freeform shapes that make them up. Whatever your communication need, Arts & Letters gives you a creative base to build from so that you don't have to start from scratch.

This chapter covers the basic operations for using symbols and the Clip-Art Manager in Arts & Letters Express. The focus is on electronic composition: how to place and edit Arts & Letters symbols and images in the screen, and how to shape, edit, and apply attributes to them. This chapter focuses on using the graphics database to assemble finished art rather than create it by hand. Features and operations for freeform drawing may be found in Chapter 6.

Fast Track Orientation

Information presented in this chapter is based on a number of key concepts and software features. These concepts are defined to help bring you quickly up to speed.

Key Concepts

Symbol Wireframes An Arts & Letters symbol is a number-indexed wireframe drawing. Each is basic line art, a rendered but not a finished work of art. Once the wireframe is placed into the working area, Express provides you with a wide range of tools to move, size, shape, color, and enhance it to make it look the way you want. Symbols may be selected using the Symbol option on the Draw menu. A full illustrated listing of symbols may be found in the *Clip Art Handbook* that is included in the Express package. When symbols are placed in the work area, they appear in the currently selected default color, but without any other enhancements.

Images/Pictures An Arts & Letters *image* or *picture* is a name-indexed full color picture. Images may be selected from the Clip-Art Manager option on the Draw menu. Symbol images may also be found in the *Clip Art Handbook*, as well as in the thumbnail representations that appear in the Clip-Art Manager screen. An image may be composed of groups of numbered symbols, freeform objects, or both.

Component/Element Any item of art or text—symbols, images, freehand drawings—in the working area is referred to here as a *component* or *element*. These terms are used to avoid tripping over the word *object*, which is the signal word used to identify groups of data under OLE.

Unique ID Each symbol or image carries a *unique ID* in the graphic database; symbols have a unique series number, and each image is identified by a text name. These elements are brought into the working area by selecting or entering the Unique ID.

Graphic Database

Arts & Letters was designed from the ground up, using an element linking concept that was founded on the use of a database of art objects. Symbols and/or images are selected using their unique ID from the database, and the Arts & Letters GED file accesses the unique ID reference to link the artwork into the saved composition. (See Figure 3.1.)

Database Links

Once an element is in place in the work area, the software retains its unique ID. This is unlike a blob of graphic data that is simply pasted somewhere by the Clipboard. The ID sets up a powerful linking capability that forms the foundation of the Replace command, which is found only in Arts & Letters. You can select a symbol form or an image in the working area and automatically replace it with another by simply selecting a new symbol number or image name. This powerful linking feature makes virtually any artwork you create in Arts & Letters Express into the template for another. The replaced element will automatically assume the size and position attributes that were set up for the original.

Electronic Templates

Each symbol and image in Arts & Letters Express is stored either in a mass library or in a collection format. As a result, you can never accidentally damage or change the foundation artwork. Each time you

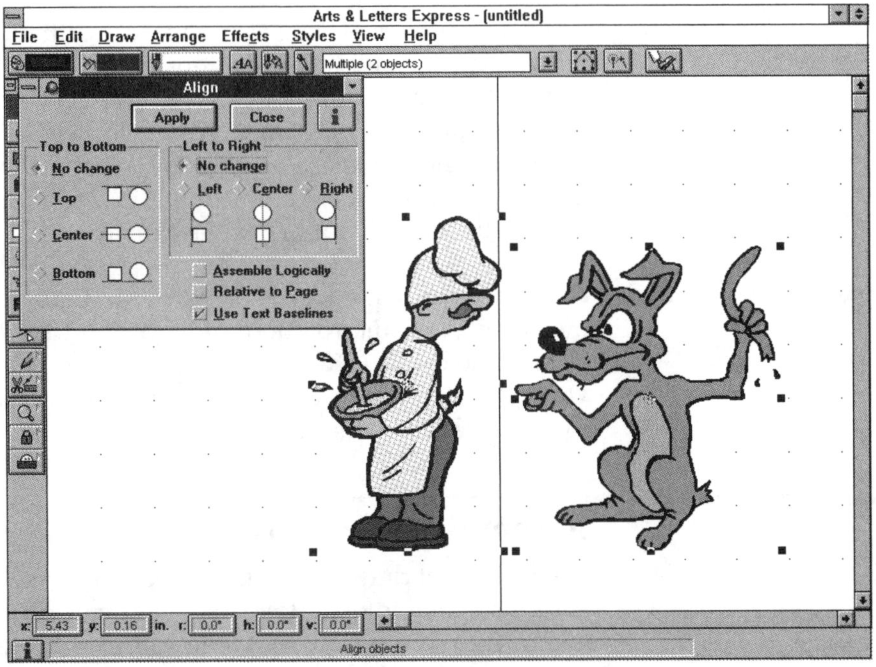

Figure 3.1
Align Dialog Box
The Align dialog box contains the Assemble Logically option that lets you assemble groups of numbered symbols into complete master drawings or images. You can take these drawings apart any time, color the different components, and snap them back together again.

place a symbol or image component into the screen, you work on a copy; therefore, the electronic template remains secure in the graphic database control files.

Tools

Draw Menu The Draw menu is home for all the key graphic database control screens (all of which can also be accessed through the Toolbar): Clip-Art Manager, Symbol dialog box, and Shape selector. Most of the other features on this menu are used in freeform drawing, covered in Chapter 6.

Edit Menu The Edit menu contains the master feature groups allowing you to select art components on the screen and Cut/Copy/Paste them within Arts & Letters or to other programs.

Arrange Menu The Arrange menu contains the key tools used to position, shape, and orient art elements in the working area: Group/Ungroup, Bring to Front/Back, Flip, and Align. This menu also includes the Transform dialog box, which allows you to set the size, position, rotation, and slant values numerically instead of approximating them by hand with the mouse.

Toolbar The Toolbar is the easiest way to access the major group of features used in symbol and image compositions. In addition to the Symbol and Clip-Art Manager icons, you may access element Duplicate, Rotate, and Slant features directly from the icon. Note the use of flyout submenus: a small triangle at the upper-right corner of a Toolbox icon means that it contains a flyout. For example, both Rotate and Slant options are available in the same flyout under the Rotate icon.

Hint Line At the bottom of the work area, the Hint Line contains the element's dimensions (x,y), the rotation angle (r), and the horizontal and vertical slant angle (h, v). Clicking on any of these dimensions in the Hint line will instantly display the Transform dialog box and allow you to specify these values numerically.

Assembling Artwork

The essence of drawing is a pencil point moving across a sheet of paper. An artist's moving hand creates lines, curves, and shapes. Drawing is one of the most ancient and simplest forms of expression, dating back to the dawn of human life. The obvious question is, of course, if drawing requires nothing more than pencil and paper, what's the point of bringing a computer into it?

Computers can automate processes performed by the mind and hand (Figure 3.2). Because the process of creating art is highly complex and time-consuming, the marriage of computers and drawing helps to save time. An artist may edit small sections of an electronic drawing instead of having to physically redraw the entire thing. A sketch, or segment of a sketch, may be instantly copied, stretched, rotated, and sized in an electronic file, where such operations would be very time-consuming if performed by hand.

Artists drawing electronically can play with different slant and rotation effects, sizes, line thicknesses, textured background patterns, and an infinite number of other effects that would take countless hours to create in traditional ways. To the greatest extent possible, the computer mimics the result of pencil, pen, or brush on paper. However, computer drawing is qualitatively different from traditional drawing. An artist accustomed to the feel and action of a pencil on paper or a brush on canvas must learn to use a new set of tools to be successful on the computer.

Figure 3.2
Assembling Artwork
The Wild West scene shown was not drawn as a single composition but assembled using various backgrounds, props, and figures from the Express graphic database. Many graphic programs give you lots of pictures, but none give you a system of components designed to be fluidly assembled into finished illustrations in minutes.

Graphic Elements in an Electronic Page

Graphic elements are, by definition, flexible in ways that hand-drawings are not. Because graphic elements are always separate from the "electronic paper" in which they appear, you have much more control over them, even after they have been drawn. For artists and nonartists alike, getting the most out of Arts & Letters Express depends on understanding this difference and all that it implies.

A graphic element may be used as a simple line form, as an electronic master that you copy and edit, or as the basis for a series of variations. In Arts & Letters a finished image always is "live" and electronically editable. In this way, a complete image can be copied and serve as the electronic parent for a stream of variations and refinements. Because the image is a composite of many graphic elements, it may be "broken down" into constituent parts. Parts of it can be copied into other works of art. Entire segments from a finished work may be "borrowed" as ready-made segments to be brought into a new work and edited to fit a new look.

File Operations

The Windows File/Open feature is more or less standard across the bandwidth of compatible Windows programs. Working with symbols and illustrations in Arts & Letters Express is the same. Your projects are saved into files using the Save command, and the Save As command is used when you first name the file when you create a copy of it under a different filename. To access and open your files, you use the Open command.

Working with GED Files

The Open command in Arts & Letters is your means of accessing saved work in Graphic Environment Document (GED) files. The GED format is unique in graphic arts software because it stores both *graphic information* and *database links*. When you work with symbols, which are loaded by number from the Symbol dialog box, you are, in effect, placing database links into the working area and a representation of the selected symbol is shown on screen. As you manipulate its size, rotation, and position, the new attributes are captured and saved in the GED file in relationship to the database file link. The graphic information for the symbol remains in the library files, and does not reside in the GED itself.

Symbol Display The same applies to images placed into the working area. Most of them are composites of symbol forms, so the GED works the same way. What is displayed on the screen is a representation of the symbols that make up the image along with the pre-created enhancements and colors assigned at the factory. You can break apart the representation and make changes to them, and the new attributes will be recorded in the GED file along with the database links to the correct symbols.

Freeform Graphics and Converting to Freeform

You can bring the graphic information that makes up a symbol wireframe into the GED file at any time. To do this, you execute the Convert to Freeform (F8) option on the Draw menu. When you do this, all the line and curve elements that make up the symbol are copied out of the foundation symbol libraries into your file. You can now make edits to the symbol form itself.

Accessing Symbol Graphic Information When you save the GED containing the exploded symbol, all the graphic information for that symbol will be saved in your file. Naturally, the more freeform graphic information you have in a file, the larger that file will be. File size is a problem with all graphics and publishing applications. Unless it is absolutely necessary for you to redraw the symbol art—for example, if you can't get the desired effect through flattening, stretching, or creating subtle distortions using the Warp feature—leave it in its base symbol form.

Freehand Graphics Any freehand drawings you create using the line and curve drawing tools are also saved entirely within the GED file. Once drawn, you may group or ungroup them, and assign attributes exactly as you do with standard symbols. Complete coverage of freeform drawing and editing may be found in Chapter 6 of this book.

File Open vs. Manager Screens

Most graphics programs allow you to open sample files and copy/edit material in them using the standard File/Open feature. (See Figure 3.3.) Arts & Letters provides a few such samples, but the vast majority of its sample art is saved and secured in databank files. So in a very real sense, the Symbol dialog box, the Clip-Art Manager, and its twin, the Activity Manager, all perform a second level of file opening functions in the software. When you "open" an image from these manager screens, you place a working copy into the screen. You cannot accidentally do anything to the graphic database images to alter or destroy them: they are standard features of the package.

Figure 3.3
File Opening Options
You may store complete compositions in the Graphic Environment Document (GED) through the standard File Open option. You may also use the Symbol, Clip-Art, and Activity Manager screens to open graphic database components directly into the work area. All such components are already saved in the graphic database.

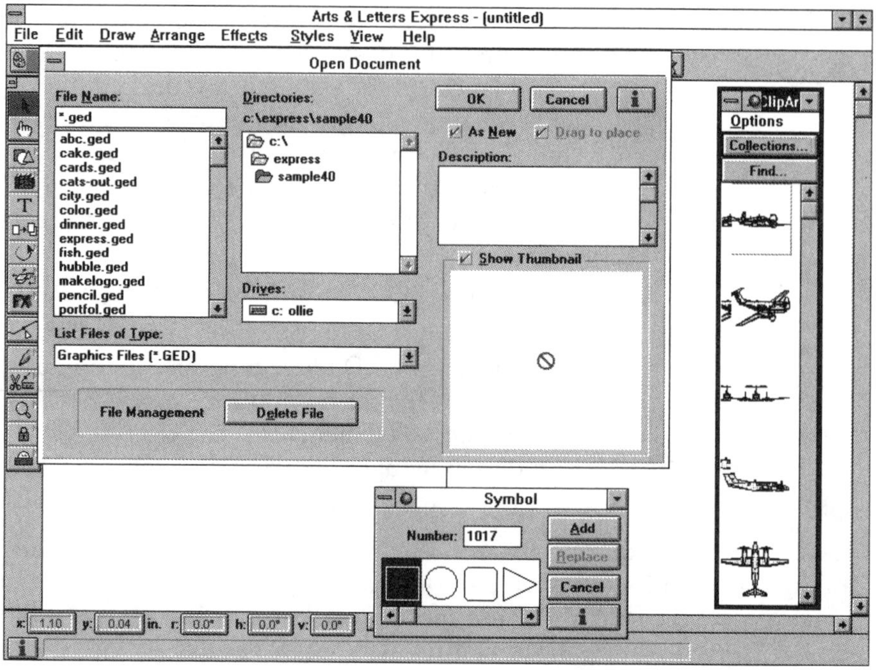

The Manager screens are a second level of the File/Open functions. You can use them to open up a long list of art components and drop them into the working area. From that point, you have a number of direct output options, only one of which is saving them into a standard GED file.

Output Options

GED files represent a dynamic means of saving a variety of graphic data, including symbols, images, freeform graphics, and links to bitmap files, such as TIFF and BMP formats. But you also can save output in Arts & Letters Express without saving a GED file. Essentially, you have three other options to secure output from Arts & Letters:

- Copy selected art to the Windows Clipboard and Paste as a BMP or metafile (WMF) into the page of another Windows program.
- Copy selected art to the Windows Clipboard and Paste as an OLE, which is embedded or linked into the page of another Windows program.
- Export the current page, selected objects, or selected screen area to an external file format, including Encapsulated PostScript, TIFF, CGM, BMP, or others.

Export to File You also have the option in Arts & Letters to simply load symbols, text, and illustrations into the work area and go directly to Export to write your work into another file format for use in other programs. This is a fast way to simply create art elements that will plug into other programs. This is particularly effective when you are simply using symbols, ready-made images, or when your custom artwork is saved in a YAL file elsewhere in Windows. The graphic database structure in Arts & Letters uses library files (DLIBxx.ALL) and collection files (*.YAL) as a context bank of saved artwork. It is simply not necessary to save a lot of GED's unless you will actually need to go back in and edit the compositions.

Placing Symbols

Symbols are the foundation of Arts & Letters composition system. Even if you are oriented more toward freehand drawing, understanding how to place, manipulate, and edit symbols is one of the basic operations of Arts & Letters that you must master. Freehand drawing features give you simple line and curve tools to draw with. For all other forms, including simple geometric shapes such as squares, circles, and triangles, you must use the symbols or freeform shapes provided. (See Figure 3.4.)

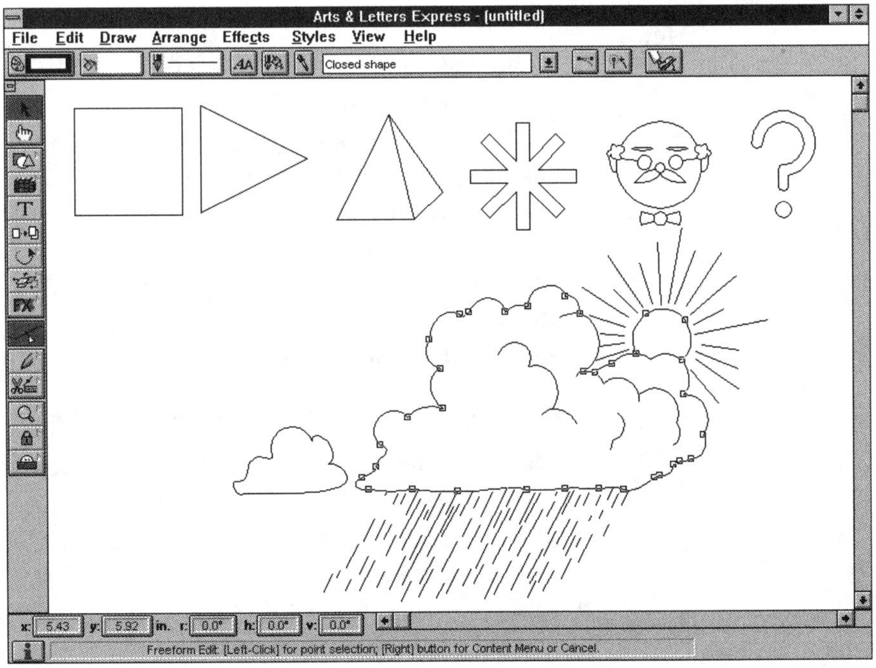

Figure 3.4
Placing Symbols
The Symbol dialog box allows you to select wireframe drawings by number. Each of these drawings may be shaped, colored, enhanced, and manipulated into literally infinite variations. Symbol wireframes represent an integrated bank of drawing templates for any artwork you produce.

Symbols are loaded into the document page using the **Symbol** dialog box in the **Draw** menu. Some of the basic form symbols are displayed in the dialog box and may be directly selected. All other symbols must be loaded using the identifying number appearing beneath the representation of the symbol in the *Clip Art Handbook*.

The **Symbol** dialog box may also be transformed into a freestanding window by selecting and "pushing in" the **Pushpin** in the **Symbol** menu Title bar. When used as a window, you can load a series of symbols directly into the page, then use the **Close** command on the **Symbol/Window** menu, or double-click the left mouse button on the pushpin to remove the window. This allows you to quickly assemble all the symbols you need for a composition, without resorting to a series of time-consuming pull-down menu operations.

Adding a Symbol

You use the mouse to load a selected symbol on the page. You may select one of the simple symbol forms displayed or enter the number displayed in the *Clip Art Handbook*. Note that for any of the symbols shown in the display bar inside the Symbol dialog box, you can simply double-click on the symbol you want, and click once in the working area to place it.

Steps: Adding a Symbol from the Menu

Use this operation to add a symbol from the Symbol dialog box.

1. Access **Draw | Symbol**.
2. Enter a symbol number or select a form from the display bar.
3. Select **Add** (or press Return).
4. The mouse cursor appears as the **Symbol Drawing** icon. Click the mouse in the working area to place the picture, or press and hold the left mouse button. (To distort the shape of the symbol as you draw it, depress and hold the **Control** key at the same time.)
5. Drag the mouse to create a framed area equal to the desired size of the symbol.
6. Release the mouse button and the symbol appears in the framed area.

Steps: Adding a Symbol from the Toolbar

Use this operation to display the Symbol dialog box using the Toolbar.

1. Place the mouse cursor over the Draw Elements icon (fourth from the top, bookshelf image).
2. Depress and hold the left mouse button and drag to the boxed number icon.
3. The symbol dialog box is displayed. Repeat the above steps to enter a number and place symbol.

Replacing a Symbol

If you load an incorrect symbol, or you wish to replace a symbol in the page with another, use the Replace feature. This will save you the effort of manually deleting the first symbol and creating a new framed area to place the new one in.

Steps: Replacing a Symbol

Use this operation to replace a symbol in the working area with another number indexed symbol (Figure 3.5).

1. Select the symbol to be replaced in the page.
2. Select the **Symbol** icon.
3. Enter the number of the replacement symbol.
4. Select **Replace**.

Placing Multiple Symbols

Most compositions will require two or more symbol elements. To speed up the process, you can use the **Symbol** dialog box as a separate window that remains on screen as you Add and Replace symbols. In this way you can simply and quickly place symbols in the page that you need and size and move them into place after all are in the page.

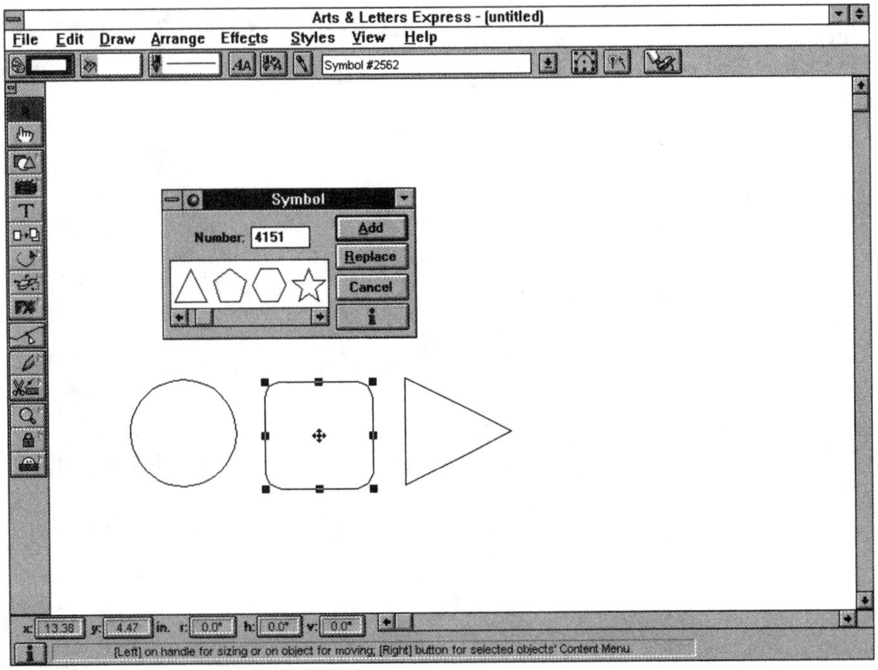

Figure 3.5
Replacing a Symbol
In the example shown, the square is selected on the screen and the number of a replacement symbol has been entered in the Symbol dialog box. When the Replace command in the dialog box is selected, the new symbol will replace the old and take on all of the enhancements assigned to it.

Steps: Placing Multiple Symbols

Use this operation to lock the Symbol dialog box to the screen to load multiple symbols.

1. Display **Symbol** dialog box, from the Toolbar or the Menu.
2. Select **Pushpin**.
3. Add the desired symbol.
4. Repeat this operation until all symbols have been placed.
5. To remove window from the screen, reselect **Pushpin.**

Working with Images and the Clip-Art Manager

Image Collections are a truly unique facet of Arts & Letters, as unique as its system of ready-made graphic symbols itself.

Image Databank

For the first time, Version 5 of Arts & Letters Express includes thousands of images and master drawings already assembled for you to use and available through the Clip-Art Manager, formerly known as the Custom Symbol dialog box (Figure 3.6). This databank of ready-made images is radically different than the file-based clip art included with

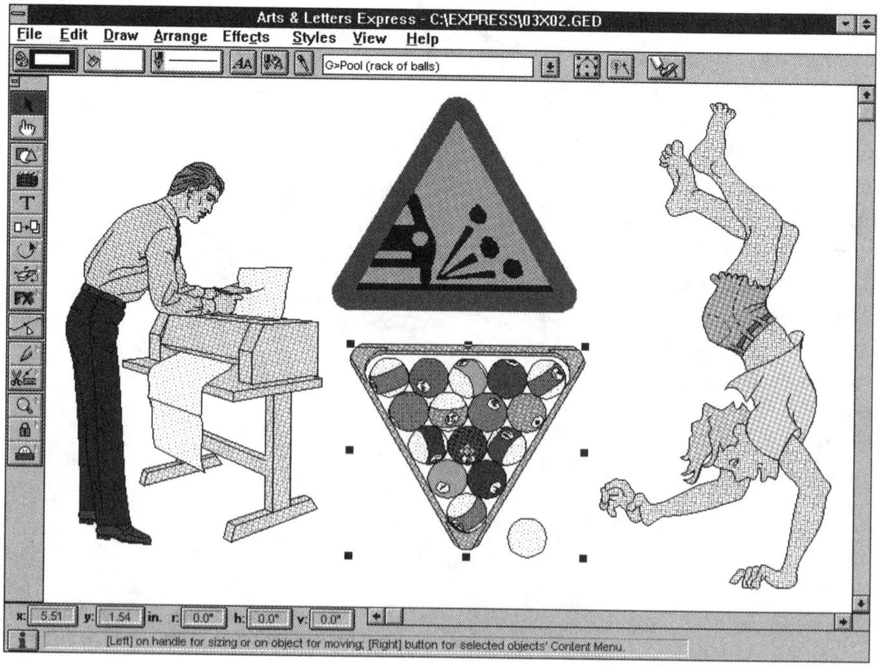

Figure 3.6
Placing Images
Images loaded from the Clip-Art Manager come into the screen as fully colored pictures, ready for use. Most images are based on groups of standard symbols and may be ungrouped to change the colors of various components, including backgrounds, details, clothing on figures, and more.

most graphic software. You select images from the collections and place them in the screen. In a matter of minutes you can select ten or more components and lay out a complete flyer, presentation slide, brochure cover, or anything you want, simply by navigating through the index.

Adding an Image

To load a selected image and place it on the page, use the Clip-Art Manager. It is designed to display images that are grouped by name in various collections. Unlike numbered symbols, you access images through written descriptions, visual thumbnails, and key words (such as "Computer," "Telephone," "Nature," "Automobiles") that reflect areas of topical interest. The Clip-Art Manager includes essentially the same features as the Symbol dialog box with several important exceptions.

Flexible Collections Collection files (all of which carry a .YAL extension) are *transportable* group files. You can copy them onto a floppy disk and send them to anyone else using Arts & Letters, and they can load the YAL files through the Clip-Art Manager in their screen without any installation procedure required. Image collections are also much more flexible than symbol libraries. You can remove images from them, add new images to them, and open as many as you like for use.

Since collections are linked into the graphic database through key words, the Clip-Art Manager includes an automated search feature very much like the Find option on your word processor. When you activate the Find option, you can specify a keyword or select from the alphabetized list of clip-art images for all the open libraries displayed in the selector.

Images vs. Symbols Like the Symbol dialog box, you may also Replace images onscreen. Unlike the Symbol Replace feature, which will apply any custom shaping, sizing, and enhancements to the replaced element, the Clip-Art Manager will place the artwork where the original was positioned, but retain none of these special characteristics. Interestingly enough though, the Clip-Art Manager's Replace command will allow you to replace any selected group or element with a component from any collection. This is a powerful feature that allows you to use any layout you have created in Express as the basis for a new design and simply plug new art into it in seconds. No other package on the market has this capability because no other graphics software is built around a powerful graphics database.

Steps: Adding an Image from the Menu

Use this operation to add a symbol from the Symbol dialog box.

1. Access **Draw | Clip-Art Manager**.
2. Select the desired collection in the **Collection** list.
3. Select the desired image in the **Image Name** list.
4. Double-click on the image name or select **Add to Document** or press **Return**.
5. The mouse cursor appears as the **Symbol Drawing** icon. Click the mouse in the working area to place the picture, or press and hold the left mouse button. (To distort the shape of the symbol as you draw it, depress and hold the **Control** key at the same time.)
6. Drag the mouse to create a framed area equal to the desired size of the symbol.
7. Release the mouse button and the symbol appears in the framed area.

Steps: Adding an Image from the Toolbar

Use this operation to display the **Clip-Art Manager** dialog box using the Toolbar.

1. Place the mouse cursor over the **Draw Elements** icon (fourth from the top, bookshelf image).
2. Depress and hold the left mouse button and drag to the electric light icon.
3. The **Clip-Art Manager** displays. Repeat the above steps to enter a number and place symbol.

Replacing an Image

If you loaded the incorrect image, or wish to replace a symbol in the page with another, use the Replace feature. This will save you the effort of manually deleting the first symbol and creating a new framed area to place the new one.

Steps: Replacing an Image

Use this operation to replace a selected image in the working area with another. (See Figure 3.7.)

1. Select the image or other element to be replaced in the page.
2. Display the **Clip-Art Manager** from the **Draw** menu or from the Toolbar.
3. Select the image name of the desired replacement symbol.
4. Select **Replace**.

Figure 3.7
Replacing Images
In the example shown, the apple in the working area has been selected and its replacement, the Apricots, are selected in the Clip-Art Manager. Just click on the Replace button at the top of the Clip-Art Manager, and the new one instantly replaces the old one.

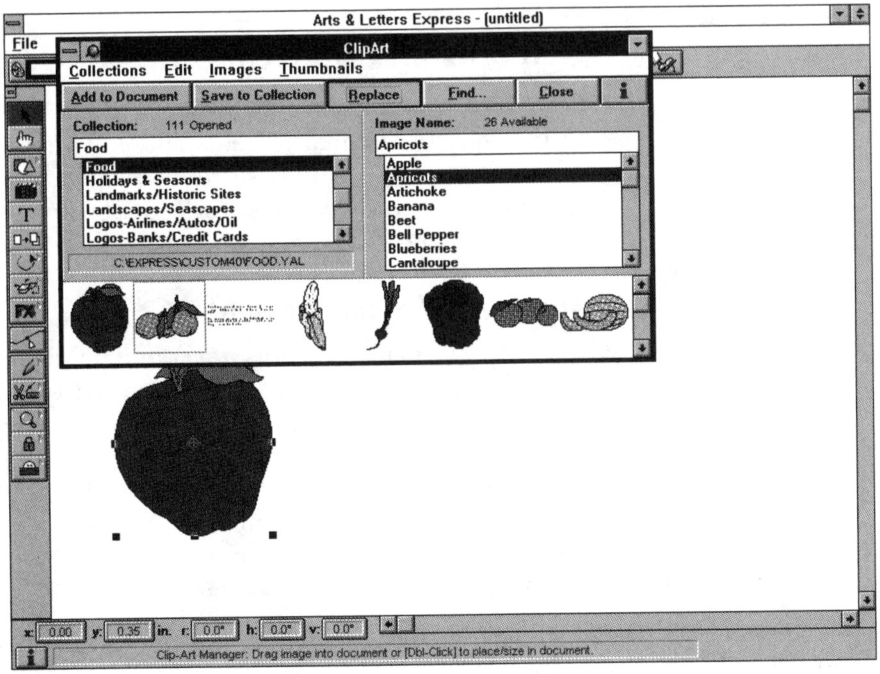

Placing Multiple Images

You may wish to use images as standalone artworks or as part of a larger composition, for example, placing multiple figures against a colored landscape background. To speed up the process, you can hold the **Clip-Art Manager** on screen as you Add and Replace picture elements. In this way you can simply and quickly place images in the page that you need, and size and move them into place after all are in the page.

Steps: Placing Multiple Images

Use this operation to secure the Clip-Art Manager to place multiple images into the working area.

1. Display the **Clip-Art Manager** dialog box from the Toolbar or the Menu.
2. Select **Pushpin**.
3. Select and add the image name of the desired image.
4. Repeat the operation until all symbols have been placed.
5. To remove window from the screen, reselect **Pushpin**.

Symbols and Images in the Working Area

Once placed in the working area, you can move, size, reshape, and perform a variety of enhancements and edits to fit each element into your overall composition. This section covers basic movement, sizing, and shaping procedures which work identically with symbol wireframes, images, text, and charting components in the Arts & Letters screen.

Moving and Sizing Symbols

Even though many symbols are complete drawings, made up of multiple graphic elements, a symbol drawn in the screen behaves as a single graphic element. Once you have drawn the symbol in the screen, you may move and size it in any way you wish.

To move and size a symbol (Figure 3.8), it must be selected, that is, surrounded by a set of small black sizing boxes. These sizing boxes are *handles* that you use with the mouse cursor to control the shape of the symbol form.

Steps: Moving Symbols and Images

Use this operation to move selected elements in the working area.

1. Place the mouse cursor anywhere over the symbol, but not touching any of the sizing boxes.
2. Depress and hold the left mouse button.
3. Drag the mouse to move the element, then release the mouse button.

Steps: Sizing Symbols and Images

1. Place the mouse cursor on any one of the four *corner* sizing boxes.
2. Depress and hold the mouse button.
3. Drag the rubber rectangle to the desired size and release the mouse button.

Shaping Symbols and Images

The representations of symbols that appear in the *Clip Art Handbook* illustrate the basic shape and detail of the symbol form. All Arts & Letters symbols are not frozen, like inflexible clip art, but highly flexible shapes that may be molded as you either draw them or use the mouse. Simply stated, the four corner sizing boxes allow you to size an element proportionally, the four center sizing boxes allow you to alter the size of one dimension (vertical or horizontal) at a time.

Standard Size and Variations

What you see in the *Clip Art Handbook* are the symbols in their standard *aspect ratio*. The aspect ratio can be defined as the relationship between the width and the height of the drawing. Without any advanced

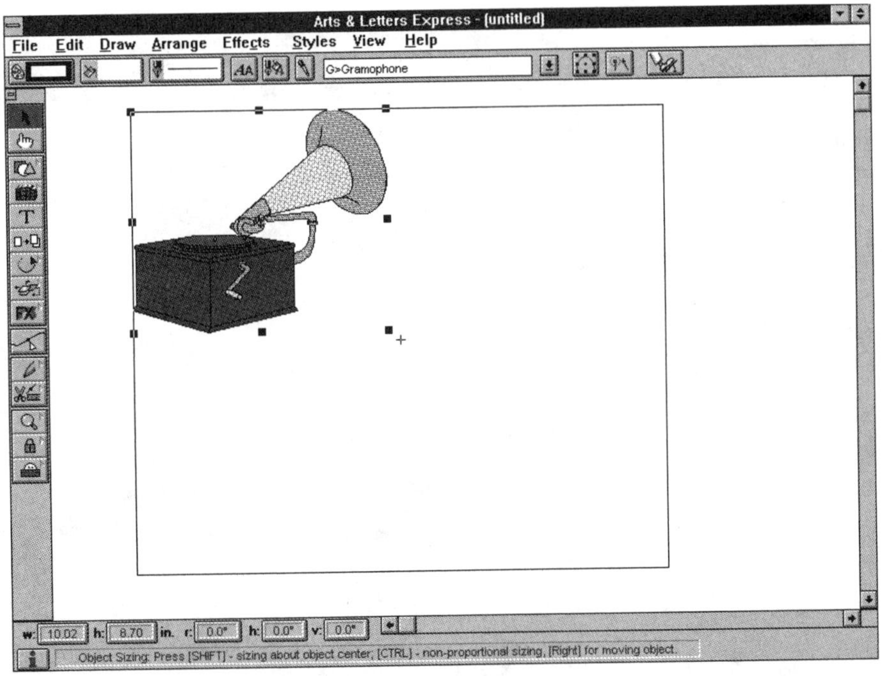

Figure 3.8
Sizing Elements
The large box in the example shown represents the new size of the selected element. To maintain the same height-to-width ratio, drag only from the corner sizing boxes to resize.

operations or freeform editing, you can instantly reshape any of the symbols using any of the four *middle* sizing boxes. These sizing boxes allow you to expand a single dimension of the symbol without affecting the others. If you wish to return the symbol to its original aspect ratio, all you have to do is select **Make Proportional** on the **Arrange** menu.

With this capability, you can reshape each of the standard symbols into a virtually infinite number of different shapes. By extending the height of a sun symbol without increasing the width, you create a tall, flat sun. By expanding the width of the sun without changing the height, you create a short, wide sun—all from the same symbol element.

This is one of the most powerful composition features in Arts & Letters, because it allows you to transform any of the basic graphic elements into infinite variations of itself.

Steps: Shaping Symbols and Images

Use this operation to change the vertical or horizontal dimension of any element from the working area (Figure 3.9).

1. Select the element to shape.
2. Place the mouse cursor on any of the *middle* sizing boxes.
3. Depress and hold the mouse button.
4. Drag the framed area to the desired position and release the mouse button.

Figure 3.9
Shaping Symbols and Images
Using middle handles on the top, bottom, and sides of the element allows you to distort the horizontal or vertical dimension, either for subtle configuration effects or for large-scale distortions.

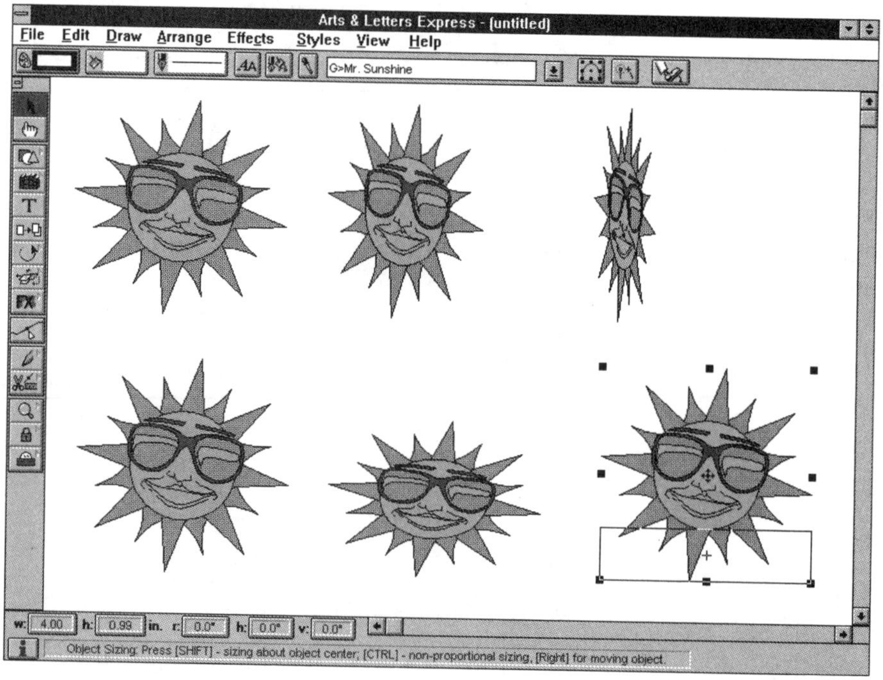

Manipulating Symbols and Illustrations

Arts & Letters allows you to compose and draw with three different sets of features and tools. You may compose an artwork from one or more of the standard symbol art forms provided, or draw your own forms freehand, or enter images of your own design. The beauty of the system is that you may use only one of these approaches or all three in the same drawing. As you enter art forms into the screen, you may manipulate them using a variety of tools in the standard operating mode to change the position, appearance, and character of the art form.

Manipulation Tools

Graphic element manipulation tools include Group, Rotate, Slant, and Duplicate, all of which are available as icons in the Toolbox. In addition, on the **Arrange** menu, there are tools to group and break apart graphic clusters and to move elements to the front and back of a graphic stack; additional tools are contained in the **Transform** dialog box that allow you to easily implement complex and sophisticated manipulations.

You may use these tools to manipulate *any selected element* in standard operating mode. This includes a standard symbol art form, a freeform drawing, an image, or any graphic group, or even more complex variations such as a graphic group that includes one or more standard symbol forms. Arts & Letters unique programming design allows you to use all of these drawing elements in concert to create finished art. For simplicity of communication, all selectable elements, including standard symbols, individual graphic elements, and grouped graphic elements, such as images, are referred to here as "elements."

Grouping Elements

Symbols or pictures can be grouped into graphic clusters that can then be manipulated as a single element (Figure 3.10). This is a basic tool in element-oriented drawing because it eliminates the need for you to constantly deal with masses of individual graphic elements. As the drawing evolves, completed elements of the drawing can be grouped and locked together so that they can be easily moved, sized, manipulated, and edited.

Block Groups

To group elements, you must select each element to be included in the group. When dealing with larger, more complex drawings consisting of many individual elements, this could be a tedious job. Enter the **Block**

Figure 3.10
Grouping Elements
The Group command on the Arrange menu will assemble selected objects into a single graphic group that can be uniformly sized and enhanced. Note that the Group command may be quickly executed using the shortcut Control-G, and the Ungroup feature using Shift-G.

Select feature (Figure 3.11). This tool allows you to draw a rubber rectangle on the screen (which appears with a dotted line border) around any group of graphic elements. When the rubber rectangle has been placed, every element inside it is automatically selected, and the number of elements selected is shown in the detail bar appearing immediately beneath the **File** menu name at the top of the screen.

Steps: Grouping Elements with Block Select

Use this operation to block-select a group of elements.

1. Select the **Block Select** icon in the Toolbox.
2. Draw the rubber rectangle around the graphic elements to be grouped.
3. Note the number of elements selected shown in the Status Bar at the top of the screen.
4. Select **Arrange | Group**. Note that **Group** appears in the Status Bar.

Grouping with Shift-Select

You may have situations in which **Block Select** is cumbersome and difficult because you only wish to select some of the elements from a group. In this case you use the Shift-Select operation. By holding down the **Shift** key as you click on the desired elements, only those elements you want to include are selected.

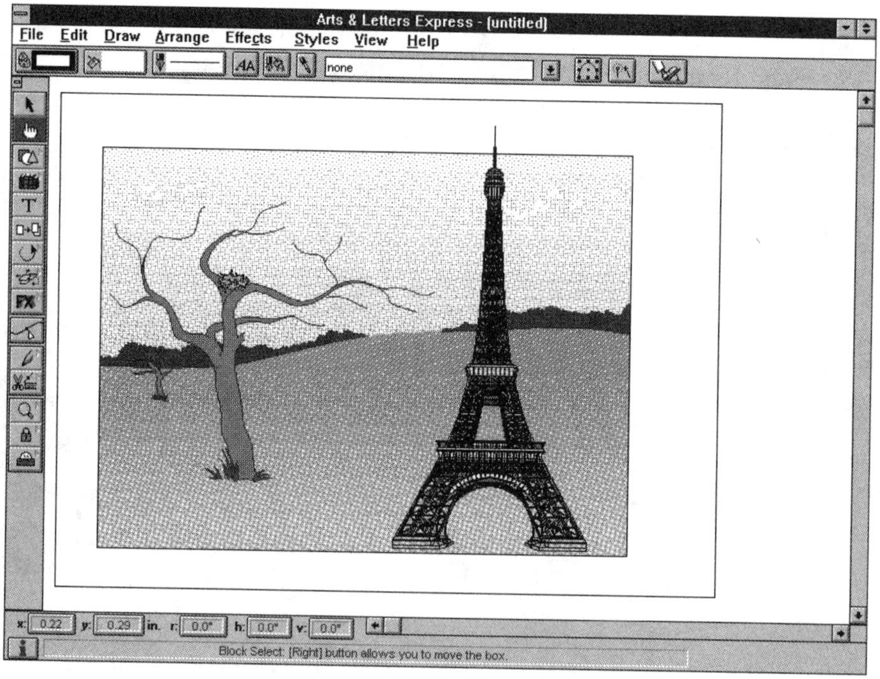

Figure 3.11
Block Select
In the example shown, the Eiffel Tower and the background are bounded by the rubber rectangle of the Block Select feature. Everything within this rectangle is automatically selected.

Once all desired elements are selected on screen, all you have to do is select the **Group** option on the **Arrange** menu, and the element grouping is complete. Once complete, you can move, size, rotate, slant, and duplicate the entire group as one.

Steps: Grouping Elements with Shift-Select

Use this operation to select a group of individual elements using Shift-Select.

1. Select the first element in the group.
2. Depress and hold the **Shift** key.
3. Click the mouse on the next element to be included.
4. Click the mouse on all additional elements to be included.
5. Select **Arrange | Group**. Note that **Group** appears in the Status Bar.

Ungrouping Clusters

Images and pictures are almost always groups, although individual symbols may be named in an image collection if you wish. When you display an image or any group of elements and symbols, you may wish to access the components inside the group. The **Ungroup** command on the **Arrange** menu and the **Break Apart** command on the **Effects** menu are identical commands that will explode the selected group into its constituent elements. A group may include other groups as well, so it may be necessary for you to ungroup several times in succession to get to the element you want.

Steps: Ungroup a Group

Use this operation to break apart a group of elements in the working area.

1. Select the desired group.
2. Verify that the selected item is a group in the display in the Status Bar at the top of the screen.
3. Select **Arrange | Ungroup** or **Effects | Break Apart**.

Breaking Apart Individual Symbols

Individual symbols cannot be ungrouped, but they can be broken down to their constituent freeform line elements. The feature that performs this task is called **Cvt to Freeform** and is located in the **Draw** menu. When a symbol is used as is, it retains its database link and the system recognizes it in the working area with its unique ID number. The minute you break it apart, you can access all the freeform elements that make it up, select them on the screen, and use all the moving, manipulating, and enhancement effects discussed in this chapter. You can also directly add or edit the freeform lines that make it up. You cannot reassemble it as the original symbol. Once broken apart, a symbol is just a bunch of graphic "stuff" in your screen. Note: When you convert a symbol to freeform, all the graphic information that makes it up is written into the GED file, so the size of your file will increase.

Steps: Convert Symbol to Freeform

Use this operation to break apart an individual symbol into its basic freeform elements.

1. Select the desired symbol on screen.
2. Select **Draw | Cvt to Freeform** or press **F8**.

Duplicating Elements

One of the most essential editing operations is the ability to duplicate a graphic element. Arts & Letters allows you to instantly duplicate any graphic element you wish using the **Duplicate** feature (Figure 3.12) available on the **Arrange** menu or from the **Duplicate** icon in the Toolbox. This feature is a screen-based feature that can be completed with the mouse cursor alone. When the **Duplicate** feature is enabled, the mouse cursor changes to the **Duplicate** cursor. To make a duplicate, just point on and drag the desired element and the duplicate is created instantly.

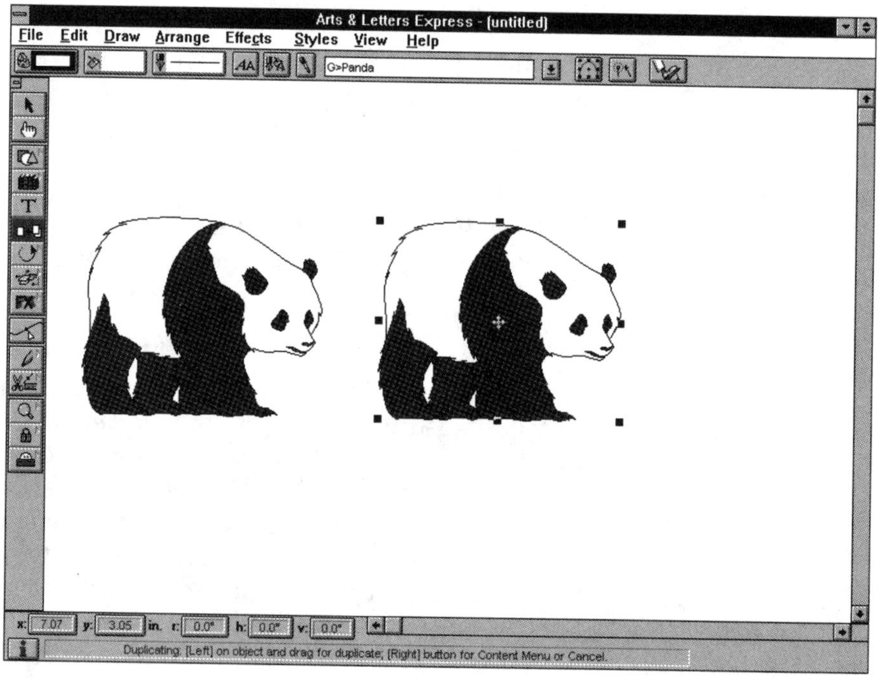

Figure 3.12
Duplicate
The Duplicate feature is an instant, onscreen means of making multiple copies of any element. Select the element and drag as many copies to any position in the working area. Use the Edit/Copy option only if you need to place art on the Windows Clipboard.

Duplicate vs. Copy

It is important to distinguish the **Duplicate** feature from the **Copy** feature on the **Edit** menu. The **Duplicate** feature works instantly on the screen; just drag the duplicate anywhere you like. The function of the **Copy** feature is to place an element into the Windows Clipboard. The only time you would use the **Copy** command within Express is to copy a selected element or group of elements from one Express file to another. In all other instances, within the same file, you should use **Duplicate**.

Steps: Duplicate Elements

Use this operation to duplicate a selected element.

1. Select the element to be duplicated.
2. Select the **Duplicate** icon in the Toolbox (or access **Arrange | Duplicate**). The **Duplicate** cursor appears.
3. Drag the duplicate to the desired position.
4. Click on the right mouse button or click on the Arrow icon to terminate **Duplicate** operations.

Accidental Duplication

One caution when using **Duplicate**: as long as the **Duplicate** cursor is displayed, every time you drag an element to a new position in the screen, you will be making more duplicates! Remember to click the *right* mouse button to turn off the **Duplicate** function when you have made the necessary duplicates to avoid having to delete unneeded or unwanted copies from the screen.

Rotating Elements

Another vital manipulation feature is Rotate (Figure 3.13). This allows you to spin a graphic element to any position around a set axis point. This feature allows you to take a standard graphic, such as a simple Arrow symbol, and change its direction so that it can be shown pointing up, down, left, right, or to any angle you desire.

Composing with Rotate

Using **Rotate** in combination with **Duplicate** allows you to instantly create complex composition effects in seconds. An excellent example of this can be found in the picture frame corner symbols found in the basic symbol set. Place the symbol for the frame corner, make three more duplicates of it, and rotate the three additional copies to the correct position to make up the four corners of the frame. Align them, group them, and you have created an ornate picture-frame effect in seconds.

Rotate Procedures

The **Rotate** feature operates interactively from the screen, using the **Transform Objects** icon, or it can be controlled by numeric values in

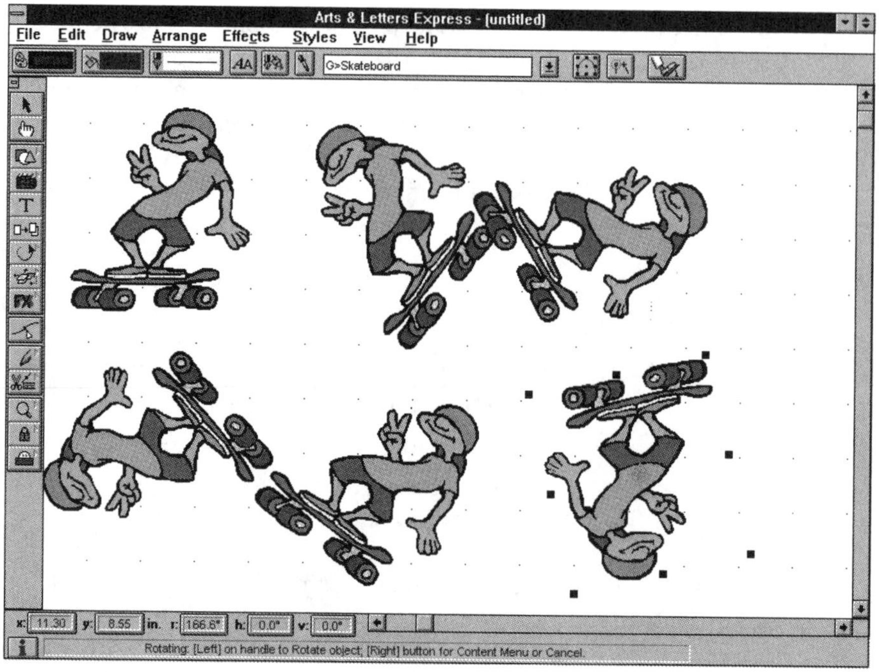

Figure 3.13
Rotating Elements
Select the Rotate icon and a rotation axis marker appears over the selected graphic. This image was created using Duplicate and Rotate in combination to quick copy the selected image and individually rotate three of the copies to different angles.

the **Transform** dialog box of the **Arrange** menu. When **Rotate** is first enabled, the pivot axis is placed in the exact center of the graphic element. You may move the pivot point to any place on or outside the element, to any corner of the element, or to any place along the outer edge of the element. In other words, you may spin the element around any point you wish to achieve the desired effect. Rotation is continuous, without any defined angles or constraints—unless you wish to enable the snap constraints that are available in the **Construct** menu. Just pull on the selector handles and the element spins around its axis until it has been rotated to the desired position.

Steps: Rotating Elements

Use this operation to rotate one element or a series of elements.

1. Select the **Transform Objects** icon in the Toolbox. Click on the first icon in the flyout.
2. Select the element to be rotated.
3. Verify that the pivot axis is in the desired place, or specify the point of rotation using **Arrange | Transform**.
4. To move the axis, place the cursor on the axis, depress and hold the left mouse button, and drag the axis to the desired position.

5. Place the mouse cursor on any of the selector handles, depress and hold the left mouse button, and drag the handle to rotate the element around the pivot axis.
6. Release the mouse button when the element has been rotated to the desired position.
7. Click on the right mouse button or click on the Arrow icon to terminate **Rotate** operations.

Slanting Elements

The **Slant** feature (Figure 3.14) is, in some ways, a variation on the **Rotate** feature. Like **Rotate**, it involves moving graphics around a pivot axis, which can be placed anywhere in the element you wish. Using **Slant** you can force graphic elements to tilt in subtle or exaggerated angles. The visual effect of slanting elements is to place them on different planes outside the two-dimensional confines of your screen. A simple picture of a house can be slanted in such a way that the house appears to be lying on a flat plane directly inside your screen.

Creative Slant

Slanting elements allow for an infinite variety of distortion effects. Elements can be tilted, flattened, angled, crunched, and stretched. When

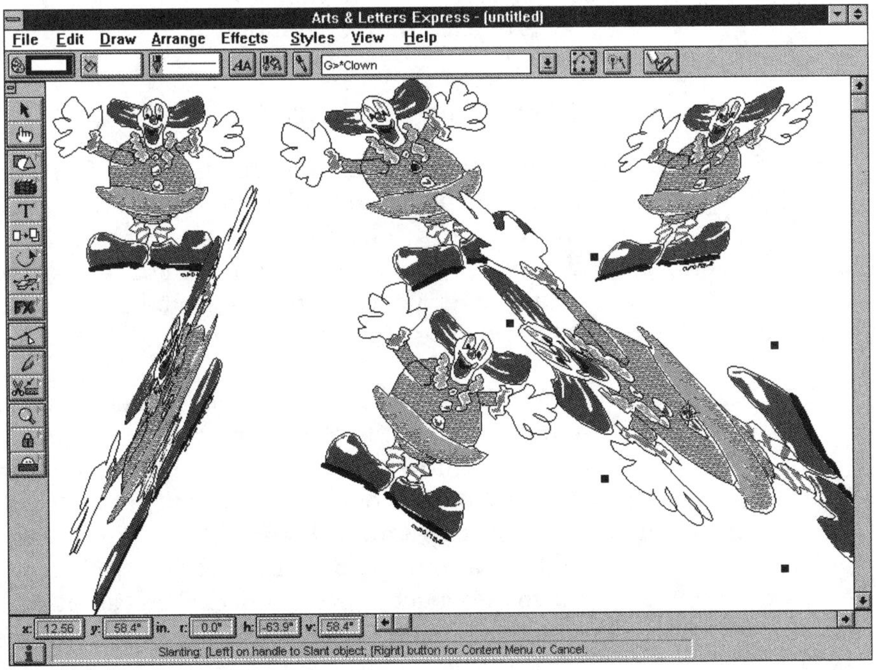

Figure 3.14 Slanting
Using the same pivot point as Rotate, Slant lets you tilt, flatten, and expand an object into virtual space. This feature is particularly effective when creating shadow effects in combination with Duplicate.

used in combination with the **Duplicate** feature, you can create dramatic drop shadow effects in which a nonslanted element is matched with a distorted, slanted shadow, or both elements are slanted to heighten the three-dimensional impact. Slant is generally a great way to create shadow components for real-world elements like trees, clouds, and figures.

Steps: Slanting Elements

Use this operation to slant a selected element, or series of elements.

1. Select the **Transform Objects** icon from the Toolbox. Select the second icon on the flyout.
2. Select the element to be slanted.
3. Verify that the pivot axis is in the desired place or specify the point of rotation in **Arrange | Transform**.
4. To move the pivot axis, place the mouse cursor on the axis, depress and hold the left mouse button, and drag the axis to the desired position.
5. Place the mouse cursor on selector handles and pull on the handles to slant the element.
6. Release the mouse button when the desired slant effect has been achieved.
7. Click on the right mouse button or click on the Arrow icon to terminate **Slant** operations.

Controlling Stacking Order

Images in Arts & Letters are made up of clusters of individually selectable elements often stacked on top of one another. To compose art effectively in Arts & Letters, you need to be able to control the position of individual elements and groups in the stack. That is, you need fingertip control over which element is to be at the front (top) of the stack and which is to be at the back (bottom) of the stack.

Stack Logic

Arts & Letters lets you position elements in a stack using the **Bring To Front** and **Send To Back** features in the **Arrange** menu. These features not only allow you to make simple positioning moves, sending elements to the bottom or bringing them to the top. The new Version 5 feature **Stacking Order** (Figure 3.15) makes it easy to display the stacking order in a complex drawing, select any element, and click the mouse to move the object to front or back. You can pushpin this dialog box to the screen and make continuous stacking commands and observe the result

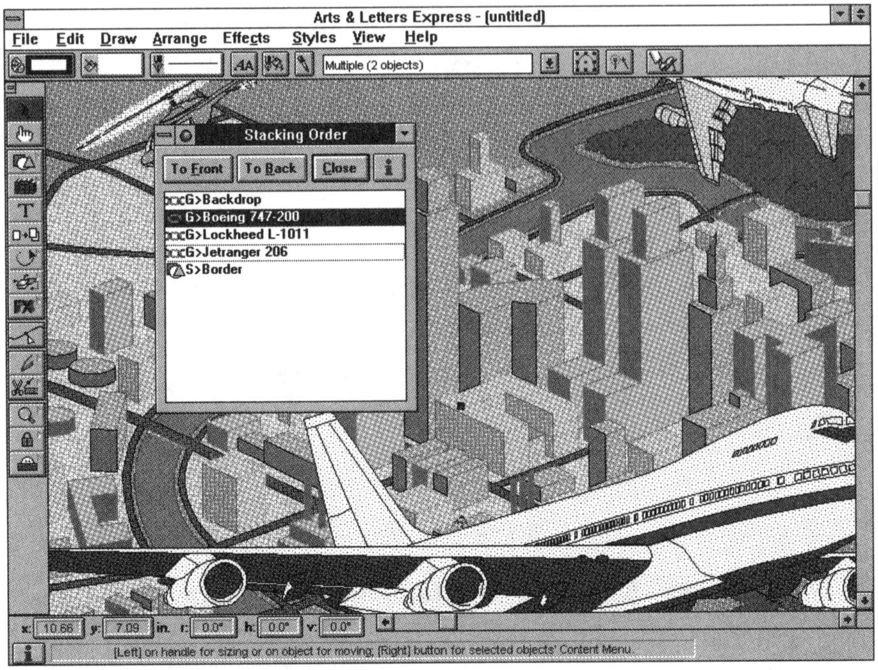

Figure 3.15
Stacking Order
In the screen shown, a scenic image with named components makes it easy to select the right jet plane and move it to foreground or background. Using the Stacking Order dialog box.

as you work. The display used in the **Stacking Order** dialog box is the same as the one inside the **Object Browser**, which is also displayed in the **Status Bar** at the top of the screen. Keep in mind that these features, like many others in Arts & Letters, can also be operated from the keyboard using the control commands featured at the right of the pull-down menu.

Steps: Positioning Elements to Front or Back

Use this operation to send a selected element to the top (front) or bottom (back) of a stack.

1. Select the element to be positioned.
2. Access **Arrange | Bring to Front** or **Send to Back**, as desired.
3. Select another element and repeat operation until desired effect is achieved.

Steps: Adjusting Internal Stacking Positions

Use this operation to make adjustments to the positions of symbols within a large stack.

1. Access **Arrange | Stacking Order**.
2. Select the **Pushpin** to secure the dialog box to the screen.

3. Position the **Stacking Order** dialog box so that you can clearly see the objects you are working on.
4. Select the desired element in the list. Note that the object is selected on screen at the same time.
5. Click on the Front or Back options as desired.
6. Select additional elements and stack moves until the desired effect is achieved.
7. Select the **Pushpin** to close the dialog box.

Transforming Elements

There are a number of applications where it is essential to have exacting control over positioning and element editing. The **Transform** dialog box on the **Arrange** menu is Arts & Letters' headquarters for specific, numeric-based positioning, and manipulation operations.

Transform by Number

The **Transform** dialog box (Figure 3.16) contains a set of features that allow you to specifically control element size, position in the screen, rotation, and slant factors. Rather than simply drag your mouse to perform element editing, here you enter specific control factors that permit

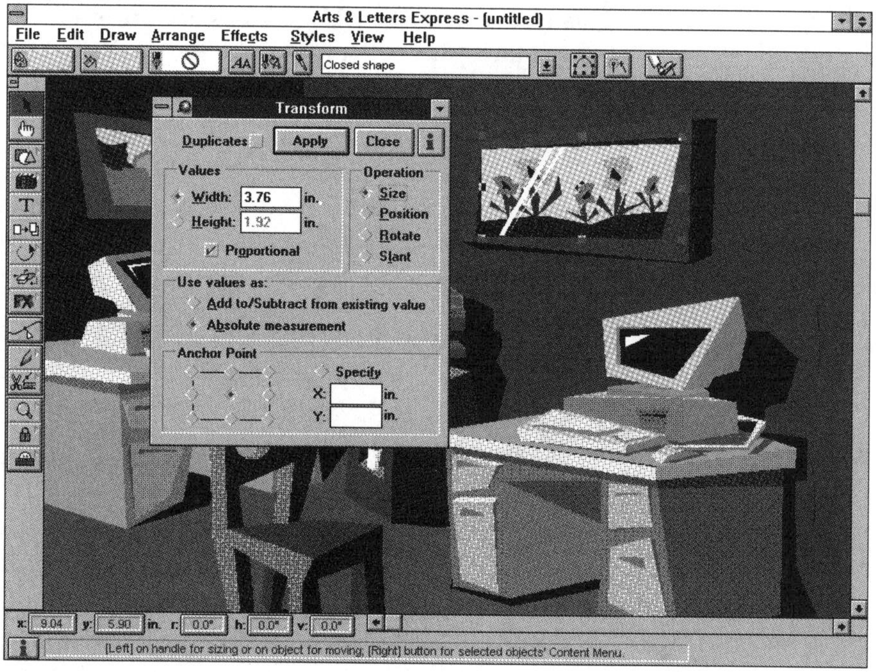

Figure 3.16 Transform
Size, Position, Rotate, and Slant may all be set as absolute dimensions or angles. Using the Add/Subtract option in the middle, you can perform relative sizing operations; for example, increasing the size of an element by 50%.

precise positioning of individual elements and allow you to more effectively control a large number of different elements.

Absolute Transform The Transform feature defaults to *absolute* measures; for example, the exact dimensions of the element displayed on the screen. The absolute transform feature operates in set dimensions by inches; it sets rotations by exact angles; and sets the position of an element to an exactly measured place on the screen.

Relative Transform You may also use **Transform** to enter *relative* values; for example, making a duplicate of an element which is 50% of the size of the original.

Transform gives you a professional edge when you need technical accuracy in your drawings, or when you want to make precise measurement of space and angles in complex clusters of elements. This dialog box has many different uses; it is a powerful design tool when used correctly. These uses will be covered in more detail later in this book.

Assigning Styles

The **Styles** menu is home to all of the enhancement attributes in Arts & Letters Express, including color, line styles, fill styles, and typographic control features. All of these enhancements may be accessed easily and directly from the Status Bar at the top of the screen. Applying styles to symbols or images is a standard procedure: select the object, and select the desired enhancement. For most simple enhancements, the new screen design of Version 5 makes it more or less unnecessary to go to the dialog boxes. You can apply colors from a flyout palette that drops down from the Status Bar, and select line and fill patterns the same way.

Custom Styles

The Styles menu has been redesigned to break out and improve access to the many custom attributes available under Arts & Letters. Each of the menu selections carries a cascade submenu that allows you to pinpoint the custom effects you wish to work with. Rather than go to a large master dialog box, you can cut right to the Calligraphic Pen effects option off the submenu. You may also select a variety of fill and typographic effects directly from the submenu, without a lot of dialog dancing. There are many eye catching effects you can generate using custom styles. You can create your own custom line, fill, color, and type styles—even group them into automated style bundles. The many creative applications of styles are covered in Chapters 7 and 8.

Enhancing Individual Elements

When applying styles to elements in your screen, there is one cardinal rule to keep in mind: It is best to enhance individual objects and not groups. For example, if you thoughtlessly select a group and apply a color to it and all elements in the group change to that color, all contrast is suddenly gone. The same applies to line and fill attributes as well. When enhancing an image, break apart the image and select individual components to enhance. When working with symbols, select one symbol at a time. There is one significant exception to this rule. When you are making a series of elements you wish to look absolutely identical in line, color, or whatever (for example, when developing a flowchart or diagram), you can block-select the group and apply a single attribute to all.

Enhancement Power through Styles

The Style Bar provides you with direct access to the most complex and dramatic feature of the software. You can apply color and line effects from the Style Bar by simply clicking your mouse. Each of the flyout dialogs on the Style bar give you a display to show you the available enhancements and the option of going to a custom dialog box to use more elaborate effects.

This new Style Bar feature underscores and emphasizes the power of Arts & Letters' style naming features. Arts & Letters was the first graphic arts package to provide a fully integrated style naming feature group that permits you to save your own custom color, line, fill, gradient, typographic, and other configurations under a name you specify. These flyout dialog boxes contain ready-made defined styles for you to use—and don't forget you can create your own versions and make them available in these convenient dialogs any time you like. (Specific steps and instructions to create custom named styles appear in Chapter 7.)

Steps: Applying a Color to an Element

Use this operation to apply fill or line color to a selected element.

1. Select the element to be colored in the working area.
2. Click on the **Color** flyout (first icon on the left of the Status Bar).
3. Select desired option (line, fill, line and fill, or the Beg/End options for color gradients).
4. Drag the mouse to the desired color and click the left mouse button.

Steps: Applying a Line Style to an Element

Use this operation to apply fill or line color to a selected element (Figure 3.17).

1. Select the element to be colored in the working area.
2. Click on the **Line** flyout (third icon from the left of the Status Bar).
3. Drag the mouse to the desired line style and click the left mouse button.

Steps: Applying a Fill Style to an Element

Use this operation to apply fill or line color to a selected element.

1. Select the element to be colored in the working area.
2. Click on the **Fill** flyout (third icon from the left of the Status Bar).
3. Drag the mouse to the desired fill style and click the left mouse button.

Managing Components and Elements

Arts & Letters includes a unique capability that allows you to assign English-language names to each element in a composition. The names

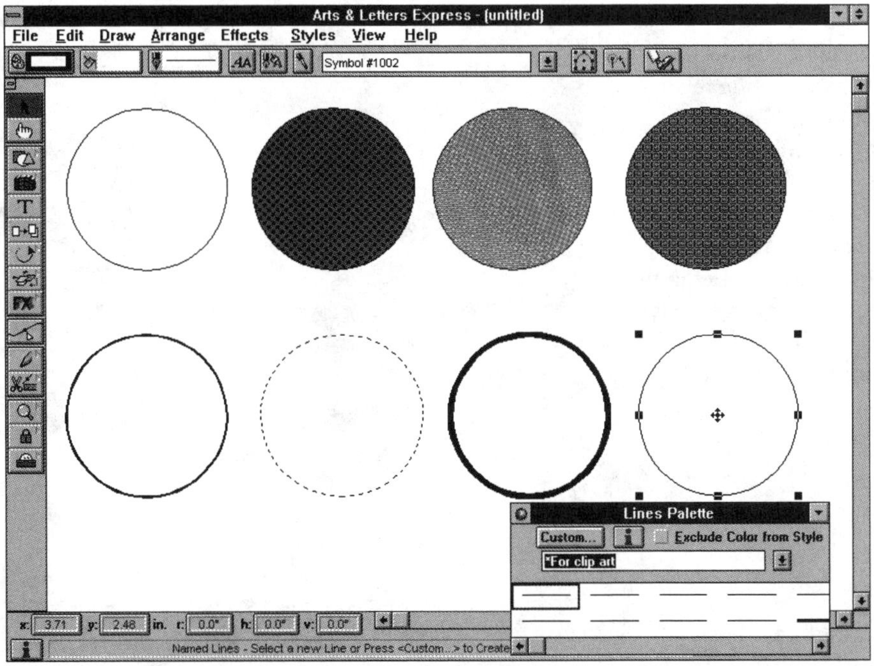

Figure 3.17 Line and Fill Enhancement
The circles shown were enhanced using the ready-made fill and line patterns available on the Style Bar flyout menus. At the bottom, the Line flyout has been pushpinned to the screen to permit interactive element selection and enhancement from the screen.

provide you, or any other individual using your files, with an instant indicator to whether the correct element has been selected for editing purposes, and a highly efficient way of working with complex compositions.

Using the Object Browser

Naming features are controlled through the **Object Browser** dialog box (Figure 3.18) available from the **Object Management** cascade menu on the **Edit** menu. This dialog box is a special configuration that remains on the screen through multiple operations and does not leave the screen until **Done** is selected. This allows you to name a series of elements in a single, straightforward operation, without a lot of going back-and-forth between menu and dialog box.

The **Object Browser** dialog box selects elements on the screen. That is, it works in the opposite way from most dialog boxes, which require that an element be selected on screen before they can function. In **Object Browser** you simply select one of the element descriptions from the list on the screen and the graphic element it relates to will be shown selected. At that point, you have the option of entering a name for the element. Note also that symbols in the composition are listed by number, and the type of element is specified by a letter code. Graphic

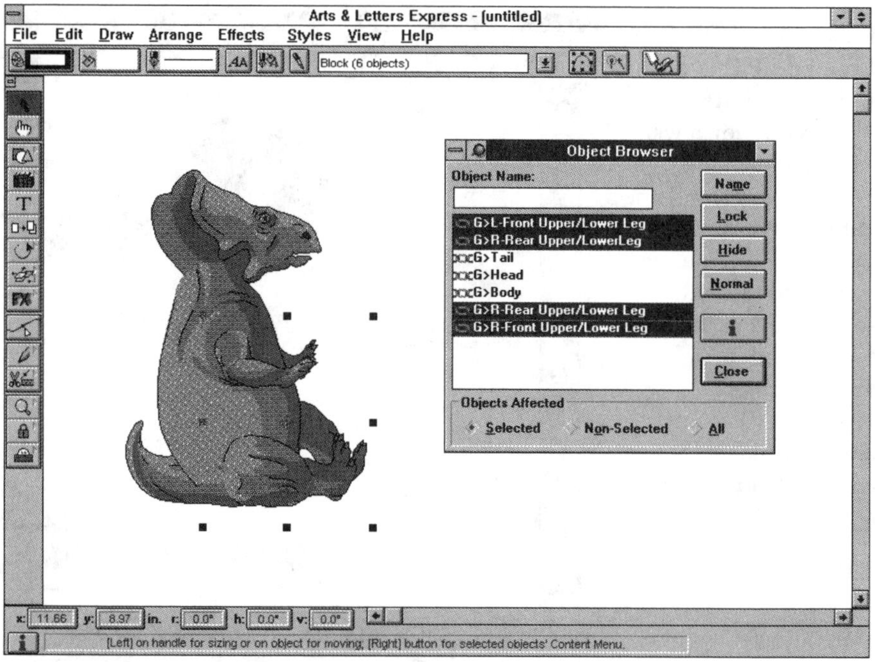

Figure 3.18
Named Elements
Looking inside this dinosaur through the Object Browser, you can select one or more named elements of the drawing. You may type in element names in the naming box in the Style Bar at the top of the screen as you work. It makes editing so much easier!

groups, for example, are coded **G**. Note also that you may select multiple elements from the list using **Shift-Select**.

Object Browser on the Status Bar

The **Object Browser** list appears as a drop-down menu near the center of the Status Bar at the top of the screen. There, it displays a description of the currently selected object. If none is selected, the display will say None. Otherwise, it will display the symbol number, image name, or a generic label for freeform elements (such as Closed Shape or Open Shape). Remember, you may assign a text label to any of these elements to make it easier for you (or anyone) to select inside the **Object Browser**.

Steps: Naming Graphic Elements

Use this operation to assign a name to a selected element.

1. Create a composition on screen.
2. Access **Edit | Object Management | Browser**.
3. Select an element description from the element list.
4. Enter the desired name in the **Object Name** box.
5. Select **Name**.

Locking Elements

You may also lock elements into the composition, which prevents you or anyone else from moving or altering the element as long as the lock remains in effect. You may, of course, reenter this dialog box at any time and unlock the element, which allows you to edit it as you wish.

Steps: Locking Graphic Elements

Use this operation to lock a selected element to suppress editing.

1. Select the description of an element to be locked in the **Browser** element list.
2. Select **Lock**.
3. The **Status** of the element will display a code **L**.

Steps: Unlocking Graphic Elements

1. Select a locked element in the element list.
2. Select **Normal**.
3. The **Status** of the element will display a code **N**.

Hiding Elements

The **Object Browser** dialog box also allows you to hide one or more elements from view. This is helpful if you wish to perform detailed editing on one or more elements in a composition and you don't want to be distracted by others. The procedure for hiding and redisplaying elements is identical to the process shown above for locking elements.

Global Operations

You may perform a variety of multiple operations automatically in the **Object Browser** dialog box using the **Elements Affected** selectors at the bottom of the dialog display. The default is for operations to affect only the element selected. However, if you wish to make a global change to all elements, say you want to unlock every element in a drawing, select **All**, and you only have to click once on the **Normal** selector to unlock all elements. Similarly, if you want to perform operations on every graphic element *except* the one currently selected, use the **Non-Selected** option, and the operations will be performed globally to all but the selected element.

This set of features is one of the most unusual and powerful in Arts & Letters. For it not only gives you a greater degree of control over your compositions by naming elements, it also enables you to control your artwork and prevent unintentional editing and damage.

Creating Your Own Collections

Where many programs are content to let you save your work in an external file format of their own, or export them to common PC graphics formats like .PCX and .TIF, Arts & Letters goes them one better. In Arts & Letters Express, any group of graphic elements may be saved in an image collection, which is defined by you. Once saved in the collection file, you may select the group by name and place it in the electronic page just like you would a standard symbol drawing. (See Figure 3.19.)

Create Your Own Graphic Database

Each image collection contains a list of symbol elements, defined and created by you and stored in a special computer file with a .YAL extension. Each element is identified in the list by naming a string that is long enough for you to specify an accurate description of the image element. You may create small symbol libraries that contain clusters of similar elements, such as Trees, Automobiles, or People.

You may create image collections that contain sets of graphic icons to use in training materials or in presentation graphics. You can even use

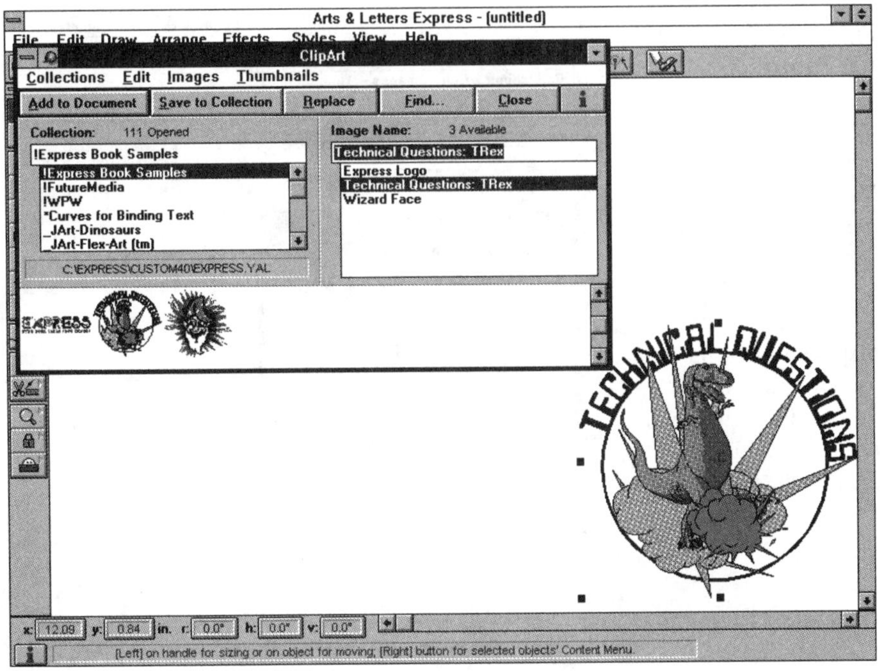

Figure 3.19
Custom Collections
The collection shown is a custom group of artwork the author created for this book. The components were created or broken out from other components in other collections or from sample GED files. Custom collections can be loaded into the Clip-Art Manager/Server and placed anywhere in Windows on demand.

image collections that contain groups of your favorite standard symbol forms. Just load the symbol form, convert it to freeform, group the free-form elements, and it's ready to be saved into a collection.

Saving Your Unique Combinations

You can customize any of the standard forms provided and *use them just like standard symbols.* This feature allows you to create and define a system of visual elements that many people in your organization can easily use. Since the .YAL files that contain image collections include all the necessary graphic information, they can be copied and sent to other Arts & Letters users that you are working with.

The system value of image collections is at the heart of what makes Arts & Letters unique. Where conventional draw programs allow you to save your work in discrete computer files, Arts & Letters gives you an added dimension by allowing you to save *drawing elements* that can be brought up and integrated on the screen in seconds.

Creating Collections

To store images, you must create one or more collection files (Figure 3.20). This operation involves specifying a computer filename (up to eight digits with a .YAL extension), the full name of the image library

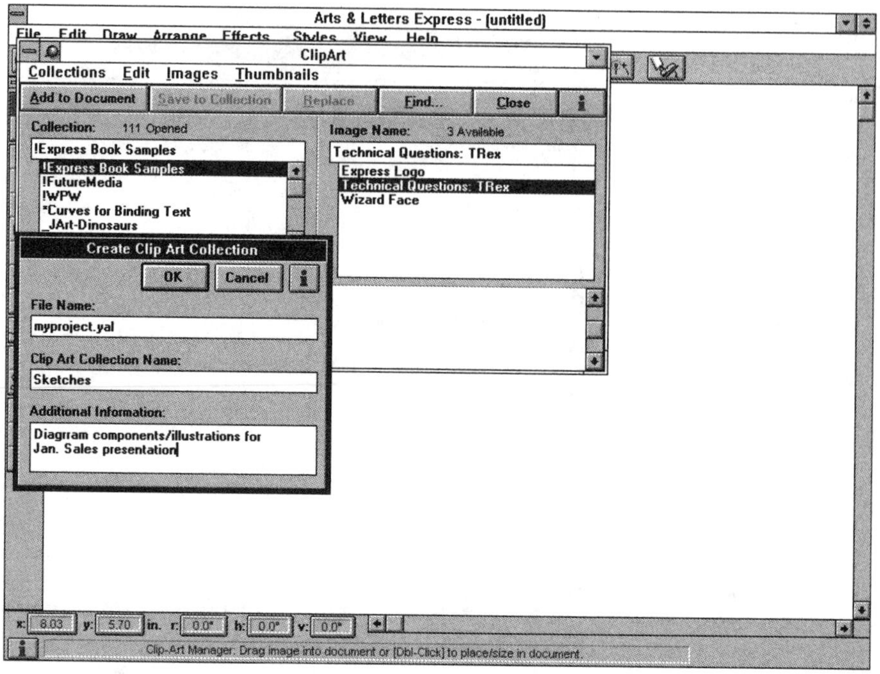

Figure 3.20
Creating Collection File
Selecting the New option in the Clip-Art Manager Collections menu brings up the Create screen. There, you specify a filename, a longer name to display in the Clip-Art Manager, and a description. After that, just select and Save components into this custom group file.

that appears in the library selector, and any descriptive information about the library contents that will help you or others identify its contents.

One final note. You may create an image collection file even if you have no symbols ready to place in it. The operation only involves creating the necessary computer file and saving it. Once created, the image collection file is like an electronic file drawer where you can enter and store images at any time you wish.

Steps: Creating a Illustration Collection

Use this operation to create a new collection in the Clip-Art Manager.

1. Access the **Draw** menu and select **Clip-Art Manager**.
2. Access the **Collection | New**.
3. Enter the desired **File Name**.
4. Enter the **Clip Art Collection Name** (which is displayed in the **Collection List**) in the box provided.
5. Enter any descriptive information about the library in the **Additional Information** box provided.
6. Select **Done**.

Storing and Naming Custom Symbols

Once you have created one or more collection files, you can enter and store symbols into them at any time. Unlike standard symbols, which are stored in a special, clustered electronic form, custom symbols are stored and recognized as a *group* of graphic elements, created with the **Group** option on the **Arrange** menu.

Any graphic element—freeform drawing, symbol, group, text, or chart—may be saved as an image. You simply select the desired element and access the Clip-Art Manager, enter a name, and save it into the selected library. For veteran Arts & Letters users, this is a much simpler process than in previous versions, and all elements in the screen are fully supported.

Steps: Storing and Naming Your Custom Image

Use this operation to store and name any graphic element or group into a collection.

1. Select the element to be stored in the working area.
2. Access the **Draw** menu and select **Clip-Art Manager**.
3. Select the collection to contain the new image.
4. Enter the desired name into the **Image Name** box.
5. Select **Save to Library**.

Object Editing Power

Arts & Letters is more than just a drawing program; it is a *composition system*, based on thousands of ready-made symbols, and it allows you the capability of designing your own system of interchangeable drawing elements. Viewed in that light, these tools are extremely powerful because they let you instantly take simple, prepared graphics and transform them into an infinite number of unique variations *without your having to draw a line.* The more you understand the integrated drawing and composition resources available to you in Arts & Letters, the more you will be able to create the kind of art you need efficiently and quickly.

CHAPTER 4

Working with Text

Creating and Editing Text

People do not communicate with images alone. Graphically enhanced text increases the power of words. All graphic programs have some form of onscreen text features. In Arts & Letters Express, there is a sophisticated text placement and editing system with over 90 custom typefaces in addition to the fonts installed with your printer. These typefaces allow you to communicate on multiple levels, with custom-styled characters that add visual power to text through shape, line, and angle. Arts & Letters Express is where images and words meet.

This chapter focuses on the core operations for handling standard text in Arts & Letters. *Standard text* means any non-freeform text element. Text characters, like symbols and images, are keyed into the Arts & Letters graphic database, and as long as they remain in standard form, they can be reedited even after the text has been manipulated or wrapped around another shape. Text editing and manipulation operations are identical to those described in Chapter 3 for drawing and editing. The operations described here will highlight Arts & Letters' more unusual features (see Figure 4.1), and show how to get the best value out of standard text elements.

Figure 4.1
Graphic Text
A dramatic effect like this can be created using simple Bind to Shape options in Express. Even in this dramatic configuration, the text content can be edited on demand, anytime you want.

Full coverage of freeform text editing operations can be found in Chapter 6; and coverage of sophisticated text effects can be found in Chapter 7.

Key Concepts

To work effectively with text in Arts & Letters, you must understand several key concepts that are slightly different from those used in working with graphics.

Typefaces Arts & Letters includes a set of 91 custom typefaces, which are loaded into your computer at the same time as the standard symbol sets. Arts & Letters' typefaces are designed to correspond with many popular commercial faces, including Times, Helvetica, Palatino, and more. These special Arts & Letters typefaces have been designed specifically to integrate with its unique graphical system of electronic composition. Third-party faces, such as those available through Adobe, Bitstream, or special font packages like ZSoft's SoftType, can be integrated into your Arts & Letters compositions, but you won't have the same level of individual character editing and flexibility with those faces.

Type Format When you type a text string in the **Enter/Edit Text** dialog box and place the string in the screen, the text exists in **Type** form. This is analogous to a standard symbol that is first placed in the screen. Text in **Type** form may be selected, and the text string can be edited and reedited in the **Enter/Edit Text** dialog box; different typefaces may be applied to the whole text string from the **Type Styles** menu.

Standard Text Editing You may use the **Convert to Freeform** option on the **Draw** menu to explode standard type into freeform graphic objects. Like a symbol, once broken apart, all the king's horses and all the king's men can't put your text string together again. New features in Version 5 allow you to make spot edits to individual characters within a text string and save entire standard text strings into an image collection without converting them to freeform objects.

Multiple Meaning of "Styles" "Style" is a popular word with computer interface designers. In Express, the word is used in several related senses and it is important to keep them straight. First and foremost, the **Styles** menu (Figure 4.2) is home to all style-related (formatting) features. Each of these features (color, line, fill, type) contains a number of individual attributes (color selection, line thickness, fill pattern, typeface, type size, and so forth) that

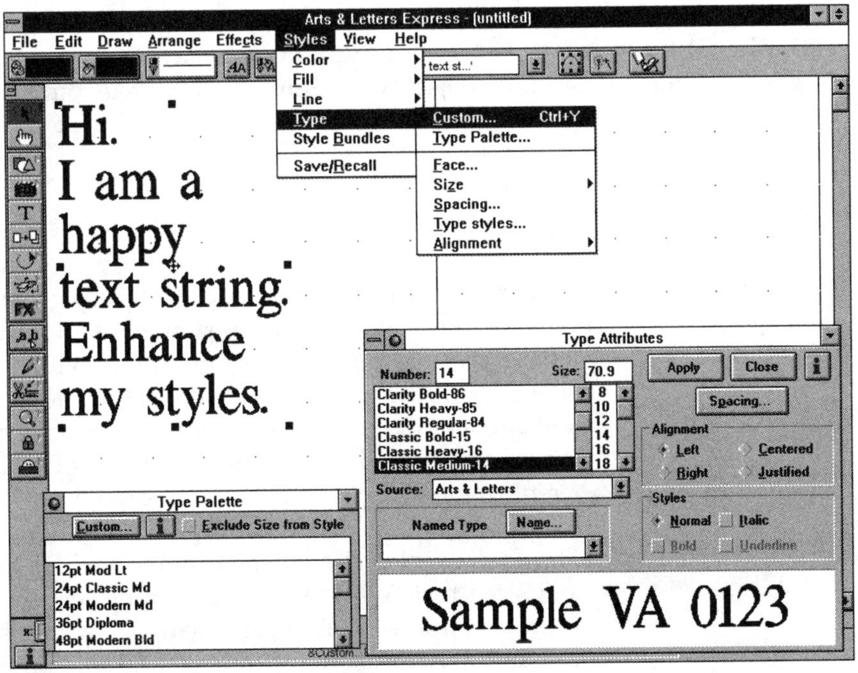

Figure 4.2 Styles, Style, and Named Styles The Type Attributes dialog box, a.k.a. "Custom," is the master control for Arts & Letters typography. Choose features from the menu Cascade, or named styles from the list in the Style Bar flyout (lower left).

you may select. When individual attribute selections or groups of them are saved under a custom name, using the **Name** feature in any of the **Styles** options, you have **Named Styles**. Express is designed to encourage you to use these named styles to automate your work. Flyout menus on the Style Bar display only named styles—either those defined at the factory or those you define yourself, for selection.

Type Styles When text is in **Type** form and has not been converted to freeform, you may apply and edit the Styles of the text string, including the desired typeface and style, text alignment, and spacing. Spacing controls consist of a family of adjustments that allow you to set the letter spacing, word spacing, line spacing (leading), and kerning. In addition, you may condense or extend the type string using a control provided. These features make it easy for you to develop custom display text effects based on exacting typographic standards.

Text in Graphic Groups Just like standard symbols and graphic objects, one or more letter characters may be selected and grouped. This allows you to break a text string out of its Type configuration, make individual character edits, then regroup all the letters in the text string into a single graphic object. Once grouped, you can easily move and manipulate the edited text string, and you have the option to save it in a custom symbol library.

Binding Text to a Shape A text string in **Type** format may be conformed to the outline of any graphic object, including a symbol, custom symbol, or graphic group. This allows you to develop integrated graphic and text effects easily on screen.

Tools

Tools for creating, editing, and configuring text are fundamentally the same as those used to place symbols and edit in freeform. However, text exists in two editable forms: Type, which retains the logical, editable flow of the text string; and freeform text, in which the text string and the letters that make it up function as graphic objects. Therefore, the way you use the available tools to work with text are somewhat different from symbol composition or drawing.

Toolbox The Toolbox displays the **Text** tool as well as tools to duplicate, rotate, and slant text. When local text editing features are selected, the **Freeform** icon in the Toolbox will change to a special **Text Editing** icon that displays a flyout menu of character editing options.

Draw Menu This menu contains the selectors for both **Text** and **Clip-Art Manager**. Also, this menu contains the features that enable you to convert a text string to freeform and edit individual characters.

Styles Menu Features in this menu display typographic Styles that can be applied to selected text. In addition, text line and fill characteristics can be controlled using line and interior attribute settings.

Effects Menu Many of the special graphic features in this menu are perfect for creating dazzling text effects, including using text as a "cookie cutter" over a pictorial background; extrude-and-warp features that let you shape and expand a word or text string into three dimensions; and Bind to Shape, which allows you to flow text around a graphic object or a freeform line.

Symbols of Expression

The alphabet began as a collection of symbols that permitted us to translate speech into a visual form. Speech combines sounds and inflections. The printed word, like the spoken word, involves degrees of subtlety that use visual inflections to express an overall impression. Printing evolved into symbols and characters using a variety of shapes, stroke thicknesses, and details for every typeface.

An Integrated System for Text and Graphics

Arts & Letters Express offers a creative interface between text and graphics. It provides a rational system for creating graphics through a ready-made graphic alphabet that allows you to easily create your own graphically enhanced alphabets. It helps you to develop text with the same freedom and individuality it makes available for graphics. Very simply, Arts & Letters treats both text and graphics as symbols. For example, a symbol for a tree, a house, an airplane, and a human face may be manipulated and edited in the same way as letter characters such as L, E, T, or R. (See Figure 4.3.)

This unified approach to developing and editing text and graphics gives you extraordinary design flexibility. Where conventional drawing programs often offer only limited text handling capabilities, or control text through a separate set of controls and functions, Arts & Letters integrates text handling into the same system it uses to compose graphics. In Arts & Letters, you can move and size text the same as graphics;

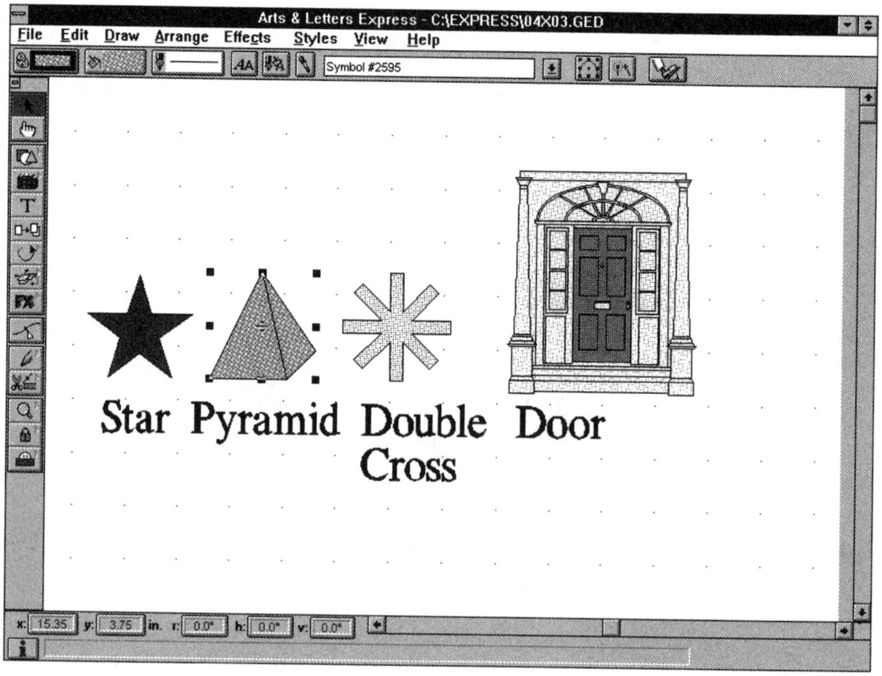

Figure 4.3
Forms, Pictures, Text
Text can be added as another level in the graphic database to label art elements, but you can use text as an art element in combination with graphic components to assemble "word art," logos, and presentation text.

you can rotate, slant, duplicate, and manipulate text the same as graphics; and you can develop custom variations on text just as you would for graphics. You can create everything from simple text labels for graphics in a flowchart to highly decorative logo effects that blend letter characters and graphic symbols into a seamless, unified composition.

Standard Text

Arts & Letters allows you to edit text as a rational string of letter characters in the graphic database. Once you have entered text into the screen, you may reselect that text and make corrections, additions, or deletions to its content. You may control the display of text by specifying point sizes, typefaces, and type styles. You may also define specific values for leading, letter spacing, kerning, and word spacing. Treated as graphic elements, individual letters may be resized, customized, and additional elements added. Custom fill values may be selected, line weights altered, and character shapes enhanced. You may create graphics from text characters, and vice versa, using the same system of tools you use for graphics. In addition, you have the option to explode text into a collection of freeform shapes and edit the character shapes in detail (see Chapter 6).

Creating Text Elements

Creating a finished text element in an Arts & Letters document involves two distinct operations. First, you must type the text string into the **Enter/Edit Text** dialog box (Figure 4.4), which appears when either the **Text** icon or **Text** on the **Draw** menu is selected. This dialog box is solely devoted to text entry and does not contain any attribute options or typographic controls. Once text has been entered into the text area, you may add it to the document just like a standard or custom symbol.

Text Format and Styles

When text is first placed in the screen, it is in **Type** format and the string retains its logical internal structure. You may select the entire string as a special graphic group, but you may not select individual letters in the text *from the screen*. You may, however, select the entire text string and reaccess the **Text** icon. The **Enter/Edit Text** dialog box will then appear with the text of the paragraph intact and fully editable.

Once the desired text appears on the screen, the second thing you do is apply *typographic styles* to it. This feature set may be found under the **Type** selection in the **Styles** menu. Using the **Type Styles** dialog box,

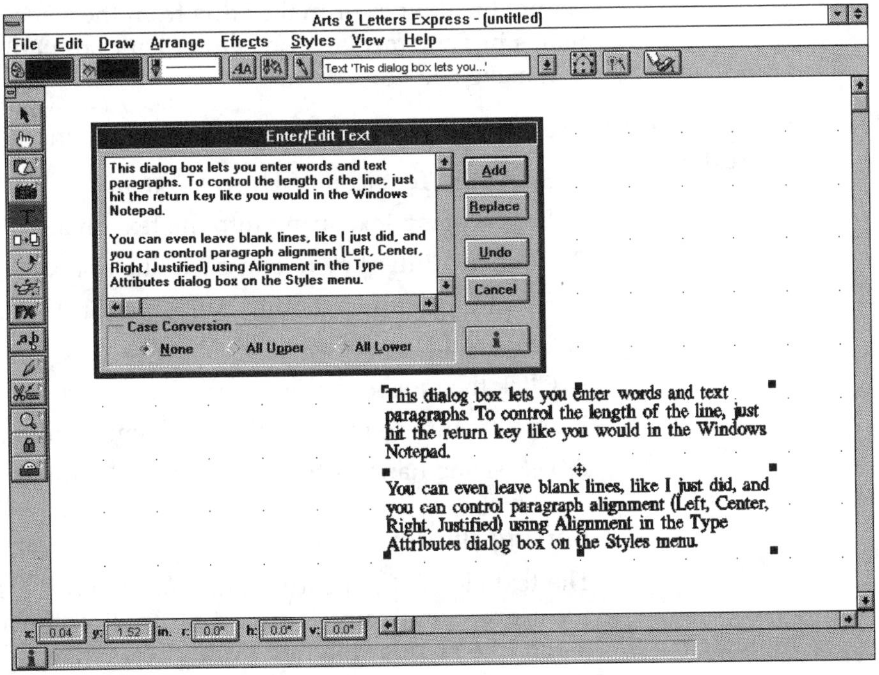

Figure 4.4
Enter/Edit Text
This dialog box controls the words and phrases you want to place in the Arts & Letters screen. You can either Add new text blocks or select existing blocks, edit them, and Replace your changes.

you may select the desired typeface, size, style, alignment, and spacing for the selected text. Keep in mind that these Styles may only be applied to text when it is in **Type** format. Once text has been converted into freeform, individual characters become graphic objects and can be edited the same as any other graphic element. In freeform, text loses its internal structure, so that you may no longer edit it from the **Enter/Edit Text** dialog box.

Typing the Text String

To enter any text string from a single letter to a complete paragraph in the Arts & Letters screen, you must use the **Text** icon or the **Text** selection on the **Draw** menu, both of which bring up the **Enter/Edit Text** dialog box.

You may type a line or a paragraph of text into the dialog box. You must press the **Enter** key to end a line because the dialog box does not automatically force text to wrap within the visible area. If you type a line longer than the width of the dialog box, the text entry area automatically scrolls to the right as you type.

When entering text, as you are typing it, try to visualize how you wish the finished text to appear on the screen. Remember that the resulting text element will be a single complete graphic element and you cannot break lines or make edits from the screen. As long as the text remains in **Type** format, you can return to the **Enter/Edit Text** dialog box and make text edits there.

Steps: Typing the Text String

Use this operation to place a string of text in the working area.

1. Select the **Text** icon or **Draw | Text**.
2. Begin typing text string into the text area.
3. Press the **Enter** key to end each line of text.
4. Select Case Conversion to All Upper or All Lower as desired.
5. Select **Add**.
6. Click the mouse in the page.
7. Use the mouse to move the text element into place.
8. Use sizing handles to adjust the size of the text element.

Editing the Text String

The text element appearing on your screen is a single graphic element, *not* a graphic group (Figure 4.5). In **Type** format, text behaves very much like standard symbol drawings when they are first placed into

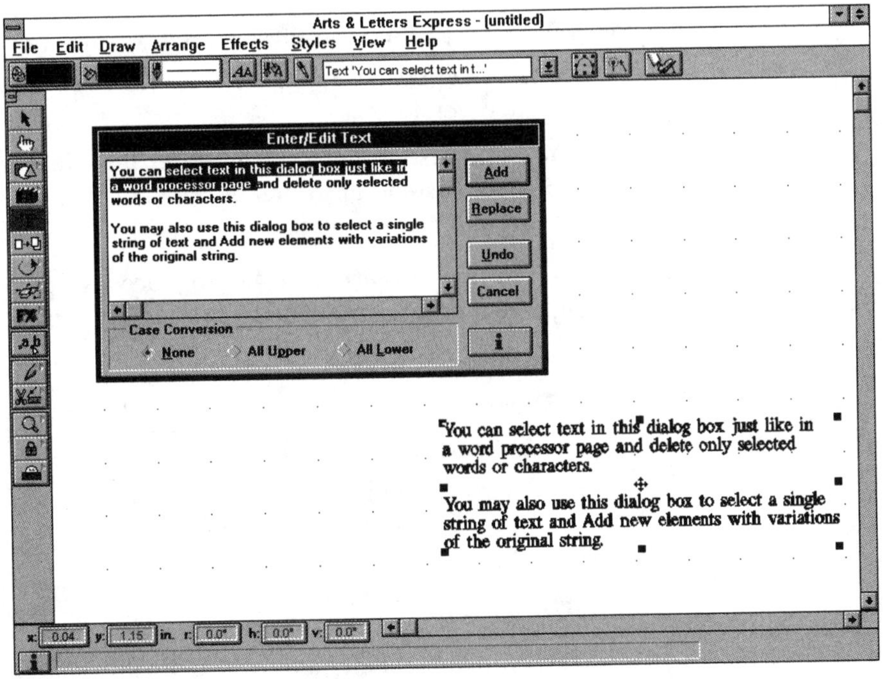

Figure 4.5
Editing Content
The dialog box acts like a minipage to let you select and enter new text to an existing block. Using the Replace command, the edits will appear right in the original block on the screen. Capitalization controls appear at the bottom of this dialog box. Paragraph alignment controls—Left, Right, Center, Justified—are available in the Custom Type features on the Styles menu.

the screen. As long as the text remains in **Type** format, it may be selected and edited using the **Text** icon.

The simplest form of text editing is to make changes to the text in the **Enter/Edit Text** dialog box and replace the original with the edited version.

Steps: Editing the Text String

Use this operation to change the content of a text string already in the working area.

1. Select the text element to be edited in the screen.
2. Select the **Type** icon or access **Draw | Type**.
3. The **Enter/Edit Text** dialog box appears with all text highlighted. You may press the **Del** key to delete all the highlighted text or you can drag the text cursor to select a portion of the text to delete.
4. Click the mouse once to deselect the entire text block.
5. Position the cursor over the text to be edited and click the mouse to place the text cursor.
6. Use the keyboard to enter or delete text.
7. To select portions of a text string, press and hold the mouse button as you drag the mouse over the desired text.

8. Use the **Undo** option to restore text to its original form.
9. Select **Replace** to replace the original version on the screen with the edited version.

You may use the text in the **Enter/Edit Text** dialog box as a template and place edited variations of the base text in the screen while leaving the original version intact.

Steps: Adding a Variation of the Text String

Use this operation (Figure 4.6) to place a second text string in the working area based on the content of a selected original.

1. Select the text element on screen.
2. Select the **Text** icon or access **Draw | Text**.
3. Edit the text as desired.
4. Select **Add** to place the edited version of the text in the screen. (The original will still be in place.)

Arranging Text

The complete text element may be manipulated on the screen using the standard manipulation features available in the Toolbox, including

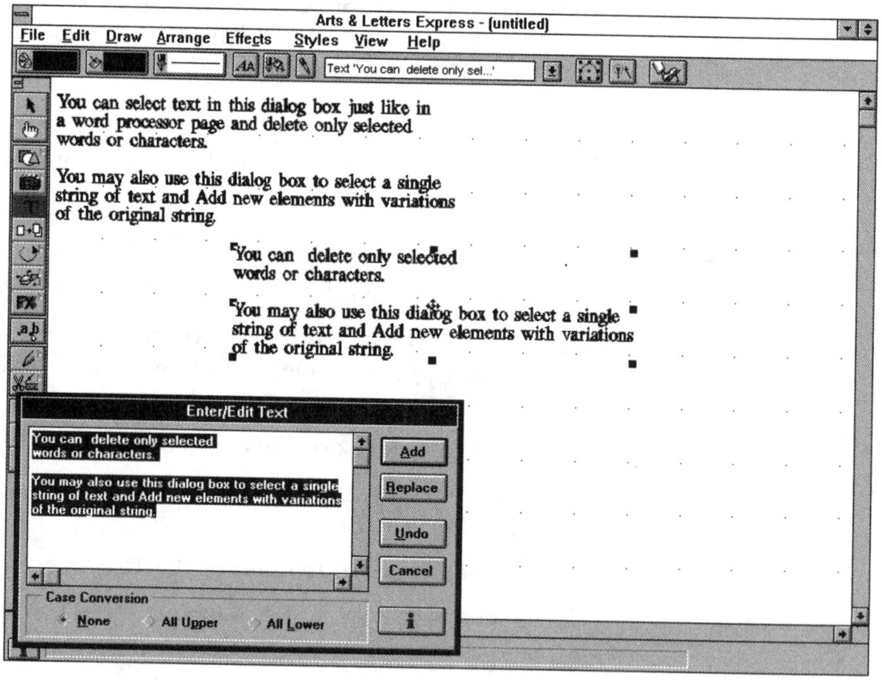

Figure 4.6
Variations
Using the Add feature will place a new copy of the text in the screen, even if the original block of text is still displayed in the working area.

Rotate, Slant, and Duplicate. These features work exactly as they do for symbol forms and freeform drawings with the exception of the **Slant** tool. When using the **Slant** tool with a text element in **Type** format, the text will slant slightly, but will not completely conform to the slant aspect shown by the rubber rectangle. One useful trick is to use Slant with a text object made up of multiple lines. The baselines of the text object will correspond to the slant, allowing you to create interesting, angled paragraphs of text. If the text is converted to freeform and the letters are regrouped into a single element, the **Slant** feature works exactly as it does with graphic forms.

Editing in Type Format Even in **Type** format, text may be worked as a graphic element. You may easily move it around the screen, size it, and reshape it by altering the aspect ratio, that is, the relation of height to width in the text string. This allows you to instantly shape your text elements into a variety of different display configurations without converting to freeform and losing the ability to edit the string using the **Text** icon.

Moving Text

You may move a text element, just like a symbol or a freeform graphic element, anywhere you wish on the screen. In **Type** format, all the letters in the text string are locked together as a single graphic element that moves as one.

Steps: Moving Text Use this operation to move a selected string of text within the working area.

1. Select the text element on screen.
2. Place the mouse cursor over the text element without touching any of the black sizing boxes. (You may move the object without sizing it, even if you are touching one of the handles, by pressing both mouse buttons at the same time.)
3. Depress and hold the left mouse button as you drag the text element to the desired position.

You may increase or decrease the size of text elements using the sizing boxes that appear when the text is selected. Note that when you increase or decrease the text size, the exact point size of the text in its current size is displayed in the **Size** indicator in the **Type** dialog box, which is accessible from the **Styles** menu.

Steps: Sizing Text

Use this operation (Figure 4.7) to change the size of text in the working area while maintaining the aspect ratio (the relationship between width and height of the text string).

1. Select the text element on screen.
2. Place the mouse cursor on one of the *corner sizing boxes.*
3. Depress and hold the mouse button and drag mouse to resize the text element.

Stretching or Flattening Text

You may also distort the appearance of the text string by stretching or squashing the entire word. Reshaping allows you to create a number of dramatic text effects while maintaining the text in fully editable **Type** format.

Steps: Reshaping Text

Use this operation (Figure 4.8) to flatten or stretch a selected string of text in the working area.

1. Select the text element on screen.

Figure 4.7
Sizing Text
Like graphic symbols and illustrations, the corner handles allow you to increase the size of the text without stretching or flattening it. You may set precise sizes numerically, using the Size (Absolute) option in the Transform dialog box on the Arrange menu.

Figure 4.8
Reshaping Text
The middle handles on the top and bottom allow you to flatten or stretch text directly from the screen. You may set distorted sizing numerically in the Transform dialog box. When the Proportional option for Size is turned off, you may set the height and the width exactly as you choose.

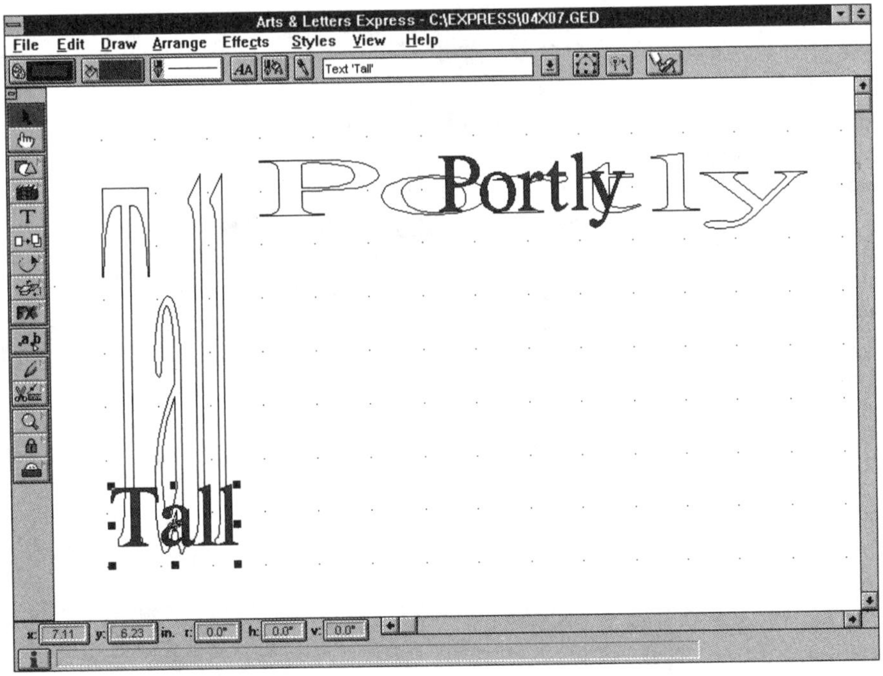

2. To increase or decrease the width of the text element, place the mouse cursor on the *middle* sizing box on either the left or right side of the text element.
3. To increase or decrease the height of the text element, place the mouse cursor on the *middle* sizing box on either the top or the bottom of the text element.
4. Press and hold the left mouse button and drag the mouse to reshape the text.
5. To return text to its original proportions, select **Arrange | Make Proportional**.

Duplicating Text

You may also make copies of entire text elements using the **Duplicate** icon in the Toolbox (Figure 4.9). This allows you to easily create drop shadow effects using a string of black or solid-color text in the background and a copy of the same text in a different shade or color in the foreground. If you use the **Group** command in the **Arrange** menu to lock the drop-shadow effect together, the two strings of text can then be manipulated as one.

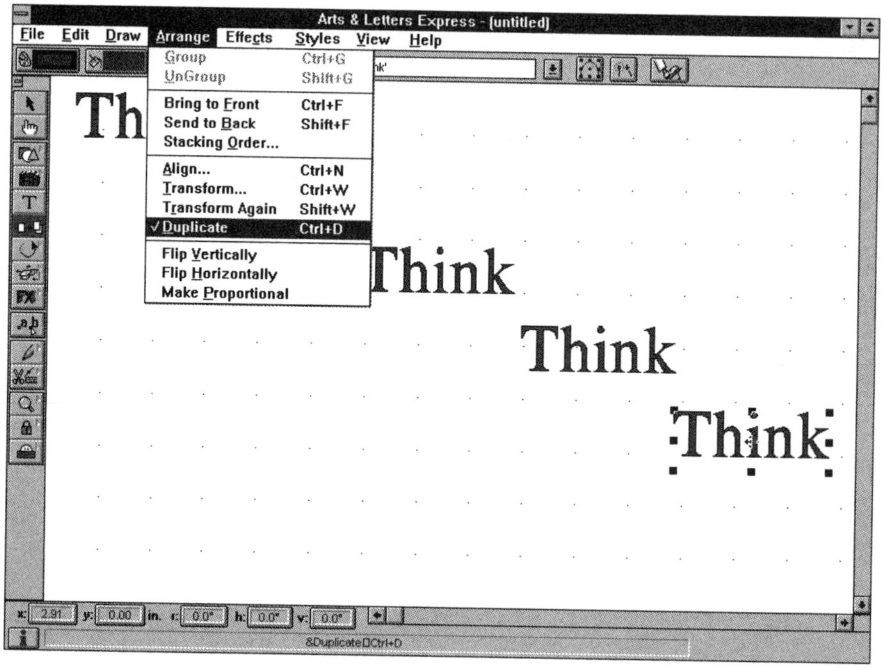

Figure 4.9
Duplicating Text
Access this feature from the icon or the Arrange menu. Duplicate is a quick way to create a group of words that all have the same size, font, and color. Duplicate one word, select each of the copies and edit the content to a new word.

Steps: Duplicating Text

Use this operation to create a duplicate of selected text in the working area.

1. Select **Duplicate** icon or access **Arrange | Duplicate**.
2. Select the text element to be duplicated.
3. Drag the duplicate copy to desired position.

Rotating Text

You may rotate a complete text element using the standard **Rotate** features (Figure 4.10). As with symbol graphics, you may drag and place the rotation pivot at any place within the text element or on its edges. Rotation allows you to tilt text slightly or to place it at vertical angles.

Steps: Rotating Text

Use this operation to rotate a selected string of text in the working area.

1. Select the text element to be rotated.
2. Select **Rotate** icon or access **Arrange | Transform**.
3. To move the rotation pivot, place the mouse cursor on the pivot, press and hold the left button as you drag the pivot to the desired point.

Figure 4.10
Rotating Text
For many reasons, turn, turn, turn. Duplicate plus Rotate lets you make a series of words that communicate the right angle.

4. Use any of the sizing boxes on the text element to pull it around the pivot point.

Applying Text Styles

Once the text appears in its desired form on screen, you may set the specific typographic Styles desired using the **Type** option on the **Styles** menu. This dialog box allows you to select one of the 91 typefaces provided by Arts & Letters as well as third-party typefaces available in your printer. You may set the size and style of the type, the alignment of paragraph text, and spacing values for the text (Figure 4.11).

Keep in mind that these features are only available as long as the text is in **Type** format and has *not* been converted to freeform graphic objects. When configuring your text, be sure to make all typographic attribute settings *before* you convert the text to freeform for individual character editing or other operations. Once converted to freeform, Arts & Letters no longer recognizes letter characters as text—they are graphic objects just like any symbol character.

Figure 4.11
Text Styles
The many designer typefaces in Arts & Letters allow you to graphically enhance text to correspond with the message you are communicating.

Type Style Features

There are several ways to access type formatting features by using the menu or the Style Bar. Because type formatting features offer so many options, a quick review of these screens will help you to use them effectively.

Type Attributes Dialog Box/Custom

The complete array of type formatting features may be accessed through the **Type Attributes** dialog box, which is available under the menu selection **Custom** in the **Styles** menu, or through the **Custom** button option in the Type flyout menu on the Style Bar. The **Type Attributes** screen allows you to select typeface, size, type style, alignment, spacing, and other options from a central dialog box.

Type Palette Flyout

The Style Bar at the top of the screen contains a flyout menu that displays the available type styles. Like all Style Bar options, you can select from these named style attributes, but not the typefaces and other options that appear in the full Type Attributes dialog box. Arts & Letters Express comes with a set of ready-made type styles. If you wish to apply a new typeface and other attributes from the flyout, select the **Custom** option and the full Type Attributes dialog box will be displayed.

Type Style Pop-Up Menu

When text is selected in the working area, pressing the right mouse button will display a pop-up menu (Figure 4.12) that provides the same options as the Style Bar. You can directly access all named styles for color, fills, line, and type characteristics by sliding the cursor to the desired selection. You must hold the right button down and release it over the desired selection. If you make no selection from the pop-up menu, the Text entry dialog box is displayed.

Style Menu Cascade

The **Type** option is operated like all Styles menu options from a master cascade menu. This menu contains an array of type formatting options, including typeface, size, spacing, type styles, and alignment. These allow you to go directly to the editing option you want and bypass the full **Type Attributes** dialog box. This will help you speed up individual detail edits. For any operation involving multiple format edits, go directly to the **Custom** option and display the master dialog box.

Point Edit Option

Version 5 includes a new feature that allows you to directly edit individual characters within a full text string. When you double-click on the text string in the working area, a set of graphic handles will appear, allowing you to select one or more characters in the text string. Once selected, you may use the standard formatting selections on the menu, or the flyout, to make changes to those individual characters alone.

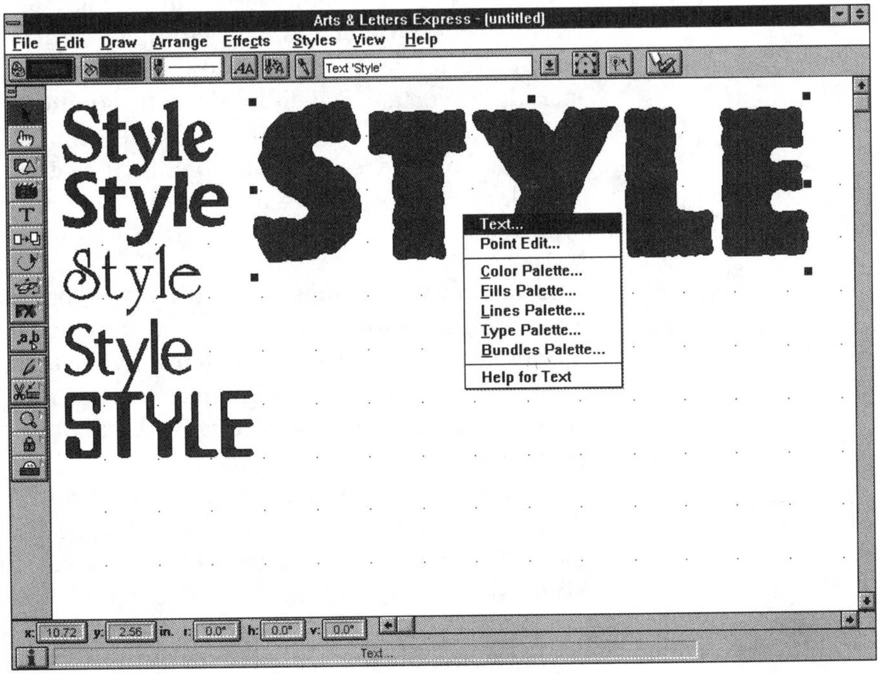

Figure 4.12
Text Style Pop-Up Menu
The right mouse button displays a pop-up menu that lists the features displayed as icons in the Toolbar and in the Style Bar across the top. You can select the edit tools directly as you work.

Note that when standard text is selected in the working area, Arts & Letters Express will change the Freeform Editing icon on the Toolbar to the **Point Edit** icon, which allows you to display the editing handles around the text.

Selecting Typefaces and Styles

Arts & Letters includes a complete family of custom typefaces. Most of these typefaces are equivalents of popular type styles available from other vendors. A chart showing the Arts & Letters typefaces and the names of the popular faces they resemble may be found in the *Clip Art Handbook*. In addition, representative character sets of all Arts & Letters typefaces are shown in the *Clip Art Handbook* to aid you in selecting the desired typeface for your project.

Typefaces and the Graphic Database Typefaces in Arts & Letters are identified both by name and by series number. Using the series number of the typeface in the *Clip Art Handbook*, you can simply enter it in the **Number** selector above the typeface list. This is a great convenience when you're in a hurry and don't have time to sort out the difference between complex typeface names like *Modern Light Extended* and *Modern Medium Condensed.*

Type Families Each typeface family may have many available typestyles. For example, Arts & Letters typefaces all include a Normal and Italic style. If PostScript Printer fonts are selected, a wider range of styles is available, including Normal, Italic, Boldface, Strikeout, and Underline, or combinations of those styles. The Italic selector is used to create slanted type—in some faces slanted type may be called italic, oblique, or slant. The slant control feature allows you to specify the slant angle for the typeface.

Type Size Arts & Letters provides you with two ways to select the size of type. The scroll selector, next to the list of typefaces, contains many commonly selected type sizes, which may be instantly click-selected with the mouse (Figure 4.13). For custom type sizes, you may enter the desired size directly in the **Size** entry box above the scroll selector in increments of one-tenth of a point.

Another interesting trick to keep in mind with both size selectors is that they can be used to set the default type size for new text entered in the screen. For example, if you select a type size of 18 points in the **Type Styles** dialog box, that becomes the default type size in Arts & Letters. When you add new text using the **Text** icon, that text will automatically appear in the default type size (in this case, 18 points) when you simply

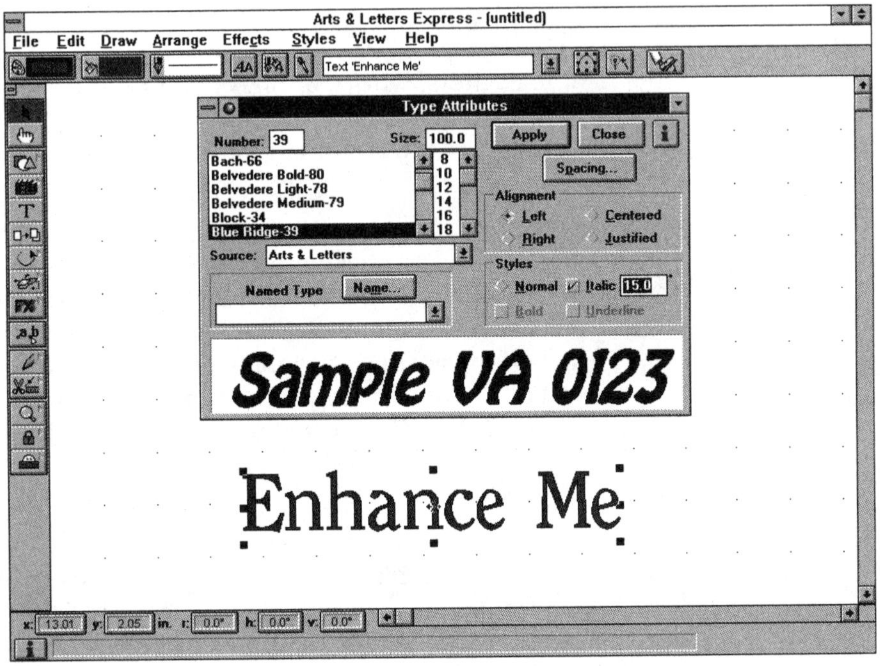

Figure 4.13
Type Attributes
The main Type Attributes dialog box allows you to select the typefaces, size, and type styles available for each typeface (middle-right of dialog box display). The Name feature lets you save the specs you enter under a name you define and apply them to any other text in seconds.

click the mouse in the screen and don't drag the mouse to draw the type. If you do drag to draw the text, the correct size of what you have drawn will be shown in the **Size** selector, and it will immediately become the default type size.

Steps: Selecting Typeface, Size, and Style

Use this operation to select a typeface, size, and type style for text in the working area.

1. Select the text element.
2. Access **Styles | Type | Custom**.
3. Enter the correct series number in the **Number** entry box, or select the desired typeface name from selector.
4. Enter the desired size in the **Size** selector, or select the desired type size from selector.
5. Select **Style**.
6. Click on the desired type style (the only available options are shown in black).

Setting Text Alignment

Single letters, words, or lines don't need to be aligned because they are all single-line text elements. Paragraph text, on the other hand, requires alignment controls for left, center, right, and justified presentations.

Paragraph Alignment

If you enter complete paragraph text into the screen or shorter elements, such as titles with two or more lines, you may need to control the alignment of the text within the element. For example, you can center a two-line title using the Alignment centering option without having to physically manipulate and center the text on screen. Similarly, you can create left-aligned, "ragged-right" paragraph text using the left Alignment option. To set up right-aligned side captions, use the Alignment option. It will align text to the right side of the element, creating a "ragged-left" effect.

Alignment Options

To create solid block paragraphs with clean right and left edges, use the justified alignment option (Figure 4.14). However, note that justified text in Arts & Letters, as in a word processor or desktop publishing program, may require special adjustments for kerning and line and word spacing. This is because the process of justifying text adds spaces in

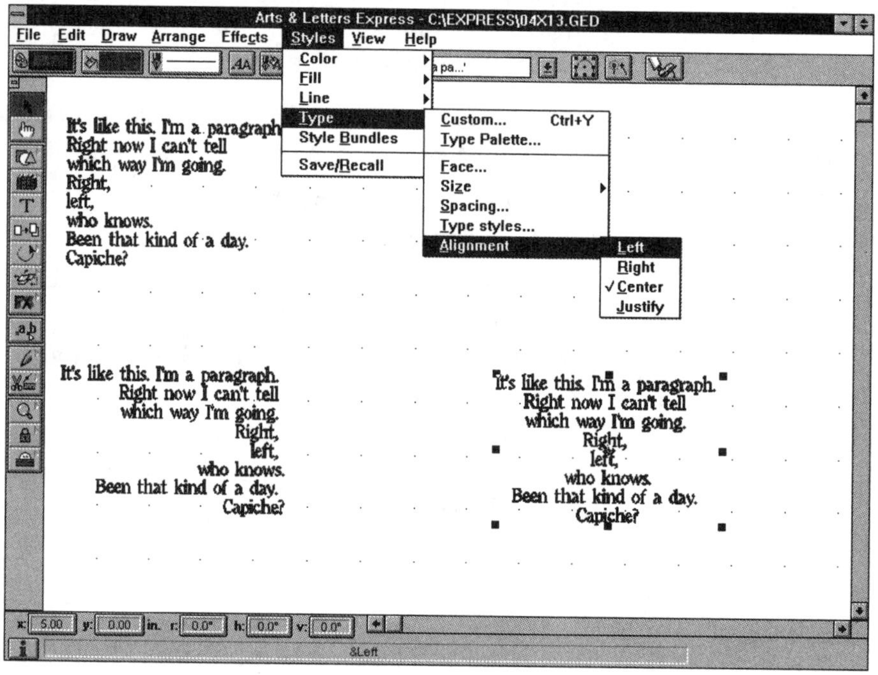

Figure 4.14 Alignment Options
Use text alignment to set text position *inside* a text element. Use the Alignment features to set the position of the entire text element in relationship to the page or other objects.

lines of text to force the left and right ends of each row of text to line up perfectly. Depending on the width of the paragraph and the length of the words, this process can cause an uneven, choppy display of text with large, gaping holes between words. Spacing controls (discussed later in this chapter) help you to spread out and equalize these extra spaces between words, reducing the choppy text presentation often associated with justified text.

Steps: Setting Text Alignment

Use this operation to select alignment for text blocks of two or more lines. Note that for single line text blocks, it is easier to position the text block with the mouse or using the standard element Align features on the Arrange menu.

1. Select the text to be aligned.
2. Access **Styles** | **Type** | **Alignment**.
3. Select the desired alignment.

Setting Spacing

Text spacing features allow you to control the space relationships between lines, words, and individual letter characters (Figure 4.15). This typographic feature is important because it gives you control over the

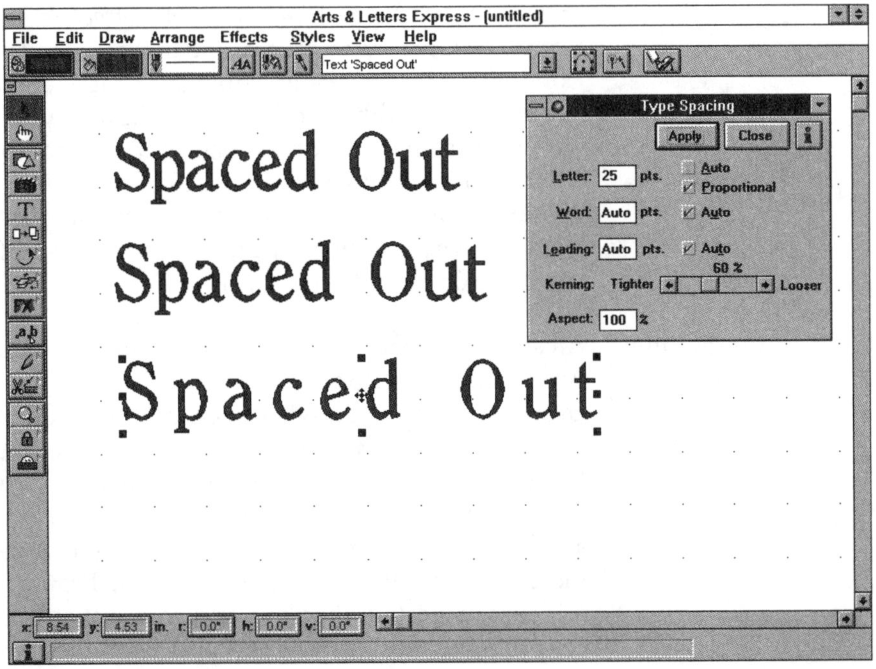

Figure 4.15
Setting Spacing
Spacing features let you control the distance between words or letters using standard typographic controls and measures. You may also adjust spacing between lines in paragraphs of two lines or more. Use Align and Transform to control spacing between text and other art or text elements.

relative spacing, character flow, and relative positioning of text characters in commonly used units of typographic measure. Without these controls, you would be forced to manipulate individual text characters from the screen and have to "eyeball" the results.

Spacing Options

Four spacing options in the **Type Spacing Adjustment** dialog box allow you to control text presentation in the following ways:

Letter Adjusts spaces between letters in a word. Best used to control large gaps in justified text.

Word Controls the minimum space allowed between words on a line. Used in conjunction with letter spacing, it can smooth out spacing in justified text paragraphs.

Leading Also known as *line spacing*, this allows you to set the amount of space between lines of text in a paragraph.

Kerning Allows you to uniformly adjust space between characters to make a line display looser or tighter.

Condensed or Extended Text Strings

In addition to standard text spacing capabilities of letter, word, line spacing (leading), and kerning, the **Type Spacing Adjustment** dialog box allows you to Condense or Extend the typeface display. The key distinction to note here is that kerning allows you to increase or decrease space *between standard letter characters*; the condense and extend features allow you to control the thickness of *letter characters themselves.* Condensing the text causes all letter characters in a string to have a narrower stroke width than in the standard form. That is, more text will fit within the same horizontal space in the page. Extending the text causes all characters to have thicker stroke width than in the standard form—giving the letters more power and emphasis. You may make these adjustments by entering percentage points reflecting the degree of condense or extend effects you wish.

Auto Settings

All standard spacing controls are set to auto-spacing by default. That is, Arts & Letters automatically enters a default spacing value when you create the text. If you wish to change this default value, you must turn auto-spacing off and enter the desired value in the entry box provided. In addition, letter spacing is set to a default value of **Proportional**. This means that letter spacing assumes that the amount of space on the line allotted to each character is *proportional* to the width of that character, so there is a smooth, even flow of text. If Proportional spacing is turned off, Arts & Letters displays text in a *monospace* format, in which each character, regardless of width, is allotted the same amount of space on a line. This is "typewriter" spacing, and is not visually attractive and tends to look less professional. Note also that when proportional spacing is off and monospacing is in effect, you lose the ability to kern, that is, adjust space between letters.

Steps: Setting Spacing

1. Select text for spacing operations.
2. Access **Styles | Type | Spacing**.
3. To enter custom letter spacing value, select **Auto** so that no **X** appears in the box and enter desired value.
4. To enter custom word spacing value, select **Auto** so that no **X** appears in the box and enter desired value.
5. To enter custom leading, select **Auto** so that no **X** appears in the box and enter desired value.
6. To enter custom kerning value, click mouse on the scroll arrow to kern tighter or looser, as desired.

Naming Text Styles

To save time in applying standard text styles, Arts & Letters includes an attribute naming selection in the **Type Styles** dialog box. These naming features allow you to assign a name of your own devising to a *collection* of type styles, including typeface, type size, type style, alignment, and spacing values.

Automation through Text Styles

Once you have set up and assigned a name to a collection of styles, you can instantly apply those styles to text from the name list in the **Type Styles** dialog box. The obvious benefit of this feature is to save time. You don't have to remember each individual attribute and apply it individually each time you need it. But there is another, somewhat more subtle benefit. By creating and naming a family of commonly used type styles, you make it possible for yourself and others working with you to *consistently* apply the *correct* styles. In other words, this feature helps you to develop and implement typographic style standards that can be applied in your overheads, technical drawings, diagrams, and even illustrations.

Quick Naming

The best time to name a style is when you create it in the **Custom | Type Attributes** dialog box (Figure 4.16). After all desired attributes have been entered, select the Name option and enter a name for the custom configuration you just entered. From that point, the named selection will be displayed in the Type Palette and in the flyout menus on the Style Bar.

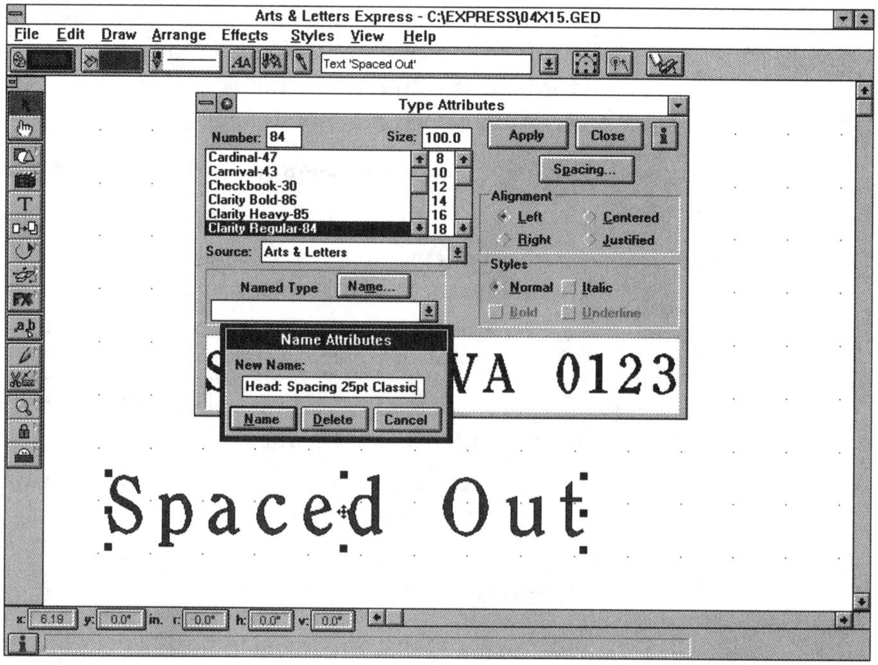

Figure 4.16
Naming Text Styles
Typographic attributes are a pain to remember when you're trying to re-create the same effect for different text. Take an extra second and save your attributes under a name. You can pop it onto any text from the flyout from that point on.

Pickup Naming

You also can save a text style name retroactively by simply selecting a string of text that has the attributes you want to capture and go to the Custom selection on the Styles menu or the Style Bar flyout. All the attributes of the selected text will be displayed; just activate the Name selection and type in the desired name.

Steps: Naming Text Styles

Use this operation to assign a name to a list of type attribute selections made in the Type Attributes dialog box.

1. Select text in the working area.
2. Access **Styles | Type | Custom**.
3. Make any changes to styles, including typeface, type size, type style, alignment, and spacing.
4. Select **Name**.
5. Enter the desired name for the attribute set (e.g., 24ptDiplomaCent for 24-point Diploma type, centered).
6. Verify that the named attribute set appears in the named attribute selector at the bottom of the dialog box.

Steps: Pickup Naming

Use this operation to save the attributes of a selected string of text in the working area.

1. Select text with the desired attributes.
2. Access **Styles | Type | Custom**.
3. Select **Name**.
4. Enter the desired name for the attribute set.
5. Verify that the named attribute set appears in the selector at the bottom of the dialog box.

Point Editing Text

When you type a word or string of text in the **Enter/Edit Text** dialog box, you create a single text element that is placed on the screen. In previous versions, it was not possible to edit individual words or letters within that element. Under Version 5, you may use an entirely new text editing capability called **Point Edit** to select individual characters and assign custom typeface, size, type style, and other attributes to them (Figure 4.17).

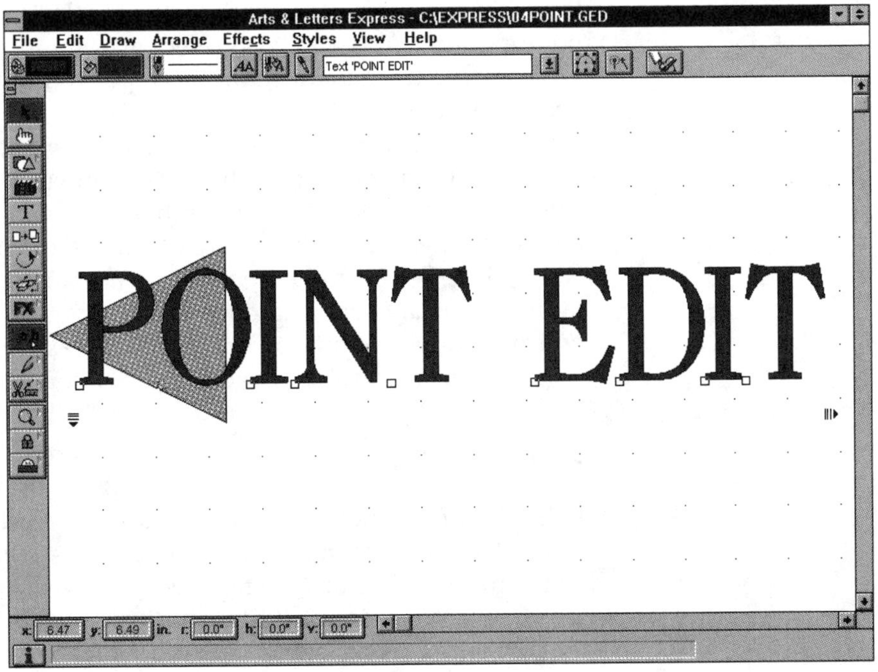

Figure 4.17
Point Editing Text
The arrow is pointing to the Point Edit icon, which appears any time standard text is selected. Note the handles under the left of each character. Select one or as many as you like and selectively enhance and format characters inside the element.

Individual Character Formatting

This capability allows you to create words with multiple formatting effects, including a big first character or drop caps, mixing typefaces in a single word, or altering the size of individual characters in a word. You may also use this feature to create paragraphs of text and assign different fonts and sizes to the title words in the paragraph.

Point Edit Benefits

Using **Point Edit** retains the text in standard form, so you may edit the content using the **Enter/Edit Text** dialog box any time you wish. Under the old feature array, creating specially formatted text blocks involved one of two workarounds. The first was to break the text into freeform and make changes to individual characters. In doing this you lose the ability to edit the content text or access any of the type style features, because freeform text takes the characters out of the graphic database system. All Arts & Letters sees is a bunch of freeform objects. The second option was to create a series of individual standard text blocks, even special text blocks for single letters, and then align and size them to create the desired effect.

Selectable Handles

Point Edit doesn't appear on the Styles menu, but is activated directly from the Toolbar or the text pop-up menu. Click on a text block and hit the right mouse button, and you can select **Point Edit** from the text pop-up menu. You may also select it from an icon on the Toolbar (the Freeform Editing icon instantly changes to **Point Edit** mode as soon as text is selected on screen).

Activating **Point Edit** mode places a square shaped graphic handle to the left of each character in the text element. Handles appear as white squares when open, and filled in black squares when selected for editing. You may use the full array of selection features, including Block-Select, Shift-Select, and individual mouse pointer selections to highlight individual characters or groups within the text element. Once selected, you may now use any of the standard text Styles options to change typeface, size, type style, spacing, and so forth.

Point Edit Operations

Point Edit operations will work with standard text only. Once text is converted to freeform, as far as Express is concerned, it is no longer text. Grouping freeform text characters will not restore editability. Note that you may use **Point Edit** operations on text which has been shaped and enhanced using sizing boxes and higher-end features such as Bind to Shape, Extrude, and Warp. This synergy allows you to use **Point Edit** to refine positioning of spacing in designer text layouts as well as change color and typeface. (See Figure 4.18.)

Steps: Activating Point Edit Mode

Use this operation to open **Point Edit** mode for a selected string of text in the working area.

1. Select the text in the working area.
2. Select the **Point Edit** icon, or click on the right mouse button and drag mouse to **Point Edit** option.
3. Verify that **Point Edit** handles appear under each character in the text element.

Steps: Selecting a Character

Use this operation to select a single character in **Point Edit** mode.

1. Verify that **Point Edit** mode is active.
2. Place the mouse cursor over the desired character and select the handle at the bottom left of that character
3. Verify that the handle shows as a solid black square.

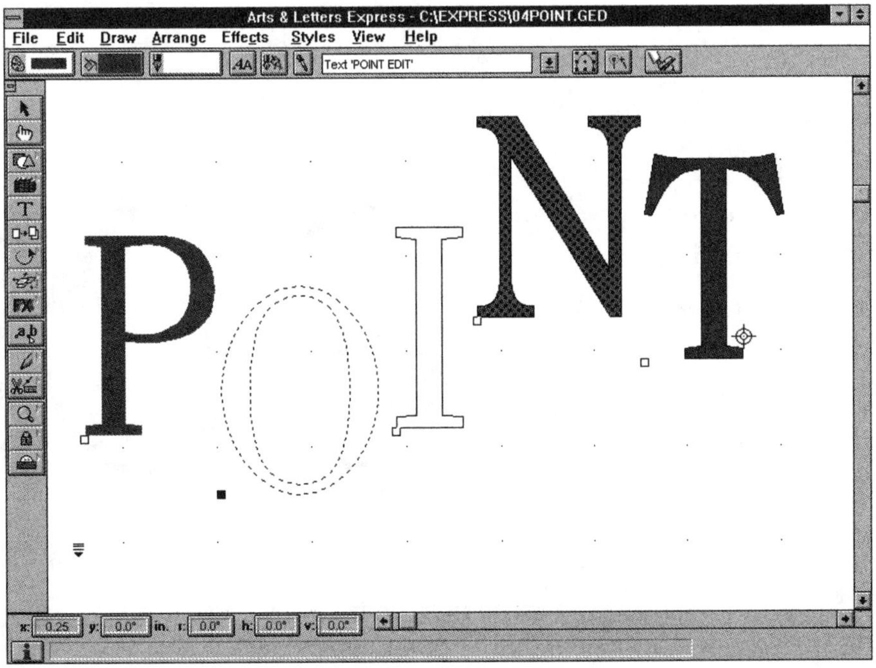

Figure 4.18
Point Edit Operations
The word is still standard text but every letter has different positioning, line, color, and fill attributes. You can still edit the content of this text, even with all of these changes.

Steps: Selecting Group of Multiple Characters with Block Select

Use this operation to select a continuous group of characters using Block Select in **Point Edit** mode.

1. Verify that **Point Edit** mode is active.
2. Select **Edit | Block Select**.
3. Depress the left mouse button and drag the Block Select lasso around the character group you wish to select.
4. Release the left mouse button.
5. Verify that all the desired character handles appear as solid black squares.

Steps: Selecting Random Multiple Characters with Shift-Select

Use this operation to select a continuous group or multiple random characters using Shift-Select in the **Point Edit** mode (Figure 4.19).

1. Verify **Point Edit** mode is active.
2. Place the cursor over the first character handle to select it, and click the left mouse button once.
3. Depress and hold the Shift key.

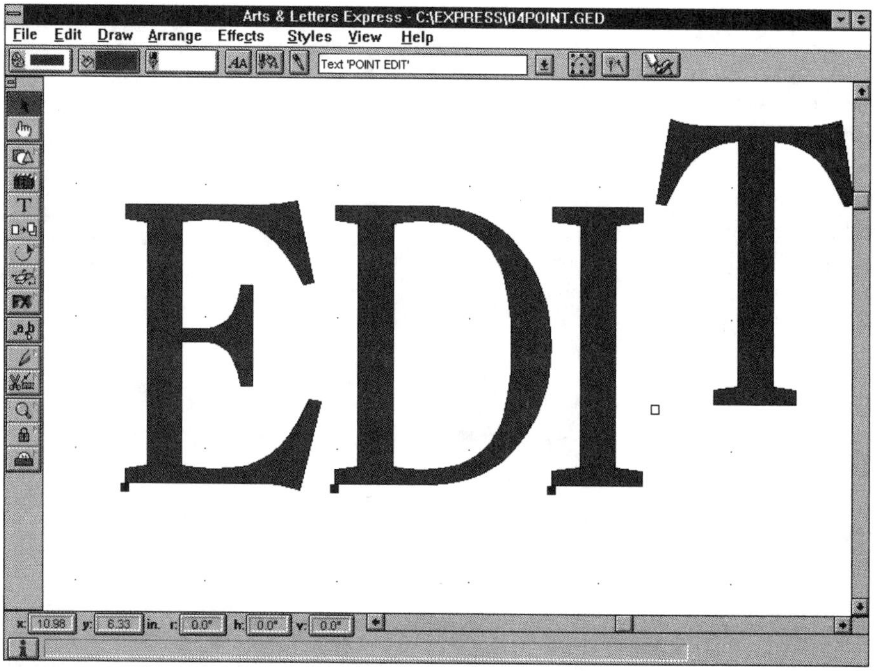

Figure 4.19
Multiple Point Edit
Selecting multiple points lets you make coordinated edits to groups of letters in the word or phrase. For example, selecting every other letter would allow you to make a zigzag pattern of the word by simply dragging the selected group down slightly.

4. Place the cursor over any additional handles anywhere in the text element and click the mouse to select.
5. Verify that handles for all desired characters display as solid black squares.

Formatting with Point Edit

Once you have selected handles in **Point Edit**, the procedure to apply formatting choices and selections are exactly the same as those used for selected text elements. You may use the flyout menus on the Style Bar to select line or fill colors, line patterns, fill patterns, and named text styles. For more detailed edits, you may access the Styles menu and select any of the options there to enhance the selected characters.

Typical Point Edit Enhancements

Typical **Point Edit** enhancements include:

- Creating large first characters.
- Applying different type styles (bold, italic, or bold-italic) to selected characters or words in a text element.
- Adjusting spacing of individual characters in a text element.
- Highlighting key words or title strings.
- Changing the color of individual letters or words in the text element.
- Assigning special graphic fill patterns or line attributes to selected characters in the text element.
- Assigning graphic gradient patterns to characters or words in the text element.

Alignment and Point Edit

The one enhancement you may rarely use with **Point Edit** is the Text | Alignment option. As noted earlier in this chapter, Alignment is an option that you use only when the text element contains two or more lines. It then allows you to align that block of text as Left, Center, Right, or Justified. Remember that if the effect you desire involves this kind of positioning, use the Alignment option first on the entire text element. You may then select groups of words or lines within the group and align them differently as you wish using Point Edit.

Binding Text to a Shape

Arts & Letters Express contains a group of highly sophisticated graphic effects you may apply to selected symbols, illustrations, and text elements. These effects include Merge, Warp, and Extrude. One of the high-end effects, called Bind to Shape, is unique to text. This section will focus on Bind to Shape operations; coverage of other high-end graphic effects for text and graphics can be found in Chapter 7.

Standard Text and Bind to Shape

Under Version 5, the Bind to Shape option (Figure 4.20) works directly with standard text. This allows you to wrap a word or text string along a curve, around a circle, or in many other forms, and retain the ability to edit the content. However, the shape you use as the basis for the text flow must be a freeform shape. The basic procedure to use this feature is a simple matching of text to form. The key stages are:

1. Type and place the text element.
2. Select shape and convert to freeform.
3. Select Start Point on the shape.
4. Select both the text and shape and make Bind to Shape selections.

Bind to Shape Options

Once the text and the shape have been selected together, the **Bind to Shape** on the **Effects** menu becomes available (Figure 4.21). The dialog box contains options, all graphically illustrated, that describe the

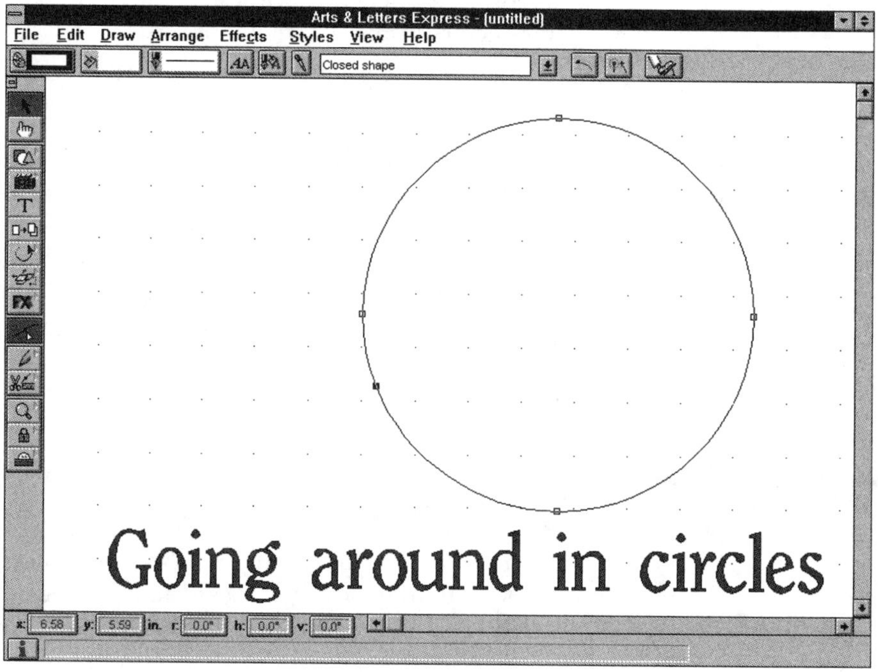

Figure 4.20 Binding Text to a Shape
After setting the starting point on the freeform circle shape, the text is ready to be snapped onto the form. The text may just appear in the shape of the form, or include the form as part of the finished effect.

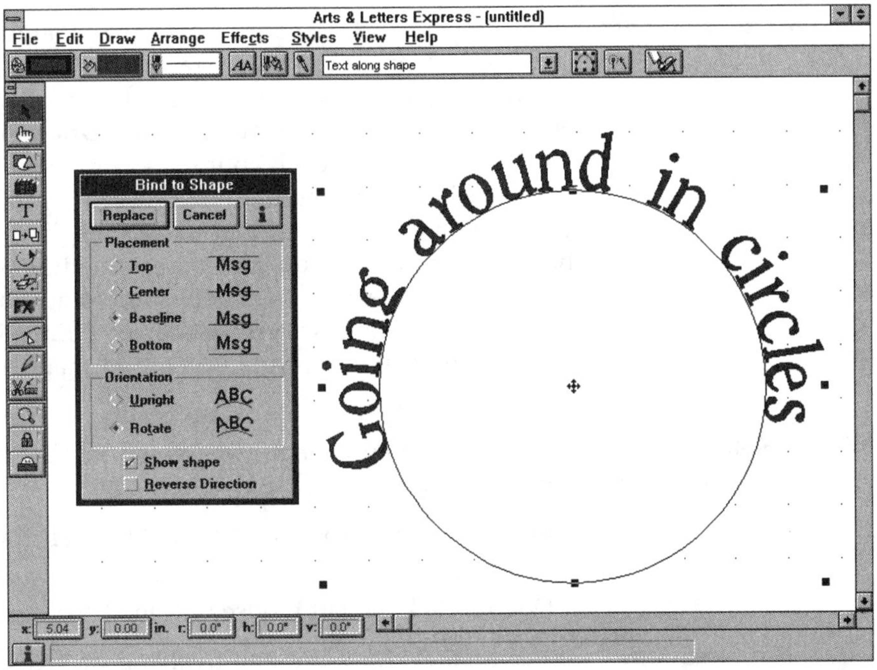

Figure 4.21
Bind to Shape Options
The option commands relate to the physical text and how it positions to the line of the shape. Note that the Show shape option allows you to hide the circle form in the final effect, but retain it hidden for later editing of the bind-to-shape group.

relationship between the text and the line of the shape element. Options include the **Center**, and most commonly used, the **Baseline** of the text, the "Top" option means binding the **Top** of the text line to the shape; and the **Bottom** means the very bottom of the text expression (touching the bottom of the descenders in letters like "g" and "q") to the shape line.

Orientation options let you specify whether the text characters Rotate to flow with the shape line or remain Upright even as the shape line moves up and down. Additional selections allow you to run the word backward (for mirror image effects), and to show or suppress the shape, so you can have the fluid text alone, displaying with or without the shape form or line.

Bind to Shape Operations

Bind to Shape involves using standard text in combination with a freeform line or graphic shape. Freeform lines or shapes *must* be used because, for this feature to work, you need to be able to specify exactly where on the line or in the form the text is to begin. This type of operation can only be done within the line or drawing itself.

Start/End Point

For the most exacting control over this operation, you have the additional option of specifying a starting or ending point on the graphic object. By selecting the graphic object that will serve as the text shape, the **Set Start/End Point** feature on the **Draw** menu becomes available. Select it, and double-click your cursor on the point on the shape where you wish the text to begin. Then proceed through the binding-to-shape operation, and you'll find that the text begins at the exact point on the shape you indicated. You can change the direction the text is drawn on the shape by selecting the shape, accessing **Shape Info** on the **Draw** menu, and enabling **Reverse Order of Points**. This will draw the text backward from the opposite end of the shape and is useful in creating mirror effects.

Steps: Setting Start Point for Text

1. Draw the freeform shape or convert symbol to freeform.
2. Select **Draw | Set Start/End Point**.
3. Move the cursor to a position on the freeform object where the text is to begin.
4. Double-click the left mouse button. A handle appears at the point.

Bind to Shape Process

You can either draw the line freehand or break apart any of the thousands of symbol components to create a shape form for your text. The standard key command to break apart any symbol drawing is **F8**, the shortcut key for the **Cvt to Freeform** option on the **Draw** menu. Once converted to freeform, the selected shape (yes, it must be selected) will make available the Set Start/End Point option on the Draw menu. This feature changes the cursor to a question mark and an arrow. Click the arrow on the place that you wish to define as the start or end point and your shape is ready to use.

Steps: Binding Text to a Shape

1. Select the **Text** icon.
2. Enter the desired text string.
3. Draw freeform shape or select symbol and select **Draw | Cvt to Freeform** (**F8**).
4. Verify that the shape is selected and select **Draw | Set Start/End Point**.
5. Click the arrow cursor over the point on the shape where text flow is to begin.
6. Verify that a black square handle appears on the shape.
7. Click the mouse on the shape to display the standard element sizing boxes.
8. Depress and hold the Shift key.

9. Select the text element on screen.
10. Verify that both the text and shape are selected in the working area.
11. Access **Effects | Bind to Shape**.
12. Select the desired positioning.
13. Select **OK**. The text is bound to the shape. Note that both the text and the shape remain editable after this operation.

Content Editing

What is really amazing about this feature is that the text remains editable after being bound to a shape, and you can return to the **Enter/Edit Text** dialog box (Figure 4.22) and change the wording if you wish. You may also experiment with different placements of the text in the **Bind to Shape** dialog box and use the **Replace** command to change the way the text flows along the shape.

Steps: Change Bind to Shape Text Content

Use this operation to change the content text in a bind-to-shape group. This capability is very powerful because it allows you to shorten or lengthen the text content to fit without having to break apart the group and start from scratch.

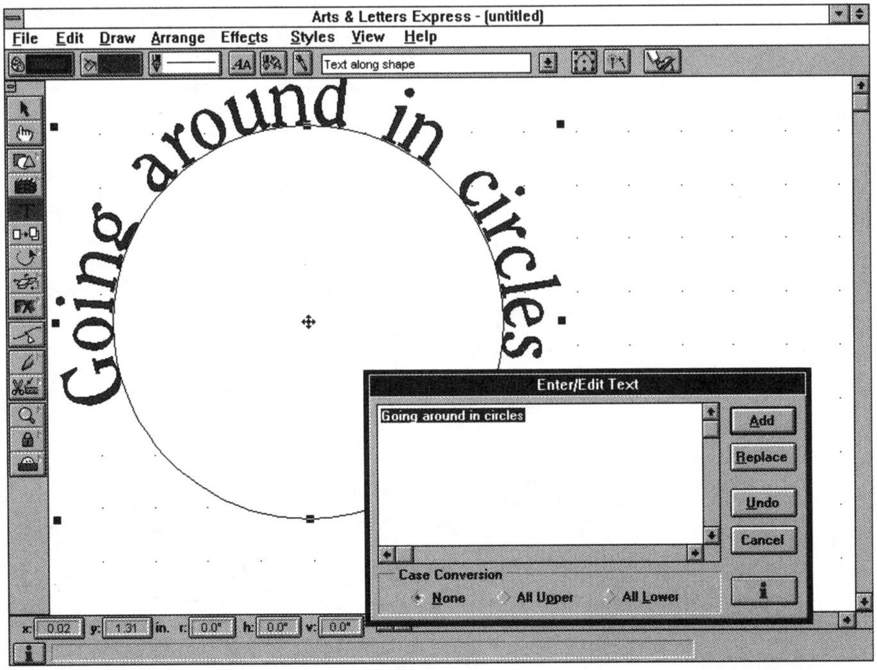

Figure 4.22 Content Editing Even in the bind-to-shape format, you can still edit this text directly from the Enter/Edit Text dialog box like any other standard text.

1. Select the finished Bind to Shape group in the working area.
2. Access **Draw | Text**, or select the **Text** icon.
3. Enter new text in the dialog box display.
4. Select **Replace**.

Text as Graphics

Because Arts & Letters uses the unique concept of a graphic database for symbols and illustrations, as long as your text is in standard form, you have the power to exchange typefaces, perform dramatic enhancements to the text format, and still retain the ability to make content edits at any time you want.

The ability to present, control, and design text is essential to effective communications. Arts & Letters gives you extraordinary freedom to work with text any way you wish. By combining the text system with the powerful database of graphic forms, symbols, and illustrations, you can create highly professional results by simply assembling and positioning ready-made components.

CHAPTER 5

Creating and Editing Charts

Creating Charts

Charts allow you to create pictures based on data. Using graphic images of text you can demonstrate and dramatize relationships between key points of data as part of an overall communication. Arts & Letters provides a built-in charting engine to work with the complete graphic database of texts, symbols, and images. The charting features in Express do not have all the bells and whistles found in many dedicated charting products, nor do they have the charting feature sets inside the leading Windows spreadsheet packages. But the charting capabilities that Arts & Letters gives you is focused and unique. Drawing upon the graphic database of thousands of images, you can create stylish and sophisticated picture charts. You can size either standard or 3-D charting symbols, and you can use any of the thousands of pictorial images and icons in your charts. Arts & Letters makes it easy for you to create charts that also tell your story in pictures.

This chapter covers basic techniques and operations used to create charts in Arts & Letters Graphics Editor. The focal point of the discussion here is to explain charting features and all the operations necessary to complete finished chart materials. Additional coverage of special effects, styles, and design techniques for charts can be found in Chapters 7, 8, and 9.

Fast Track Orientation

The charting features covered in this chapter are based on a number of key concepts. Your understanding of these key concepts in advance will help you more fully understand each operation presented later in the chapter.

Key Concepts

X-Axis and Y-Axis

Charts measure the relationship of one type of information against another. For example, you can show automobile sales over a period of time. The scale of sales figures can then be represented as a vertical line (Y-axis) and the time, say one year, can be represented as a horizontal line (X-axis). Data can then be plotted in a chart based on the intersection of the two axes. (See Figure 5.1.)

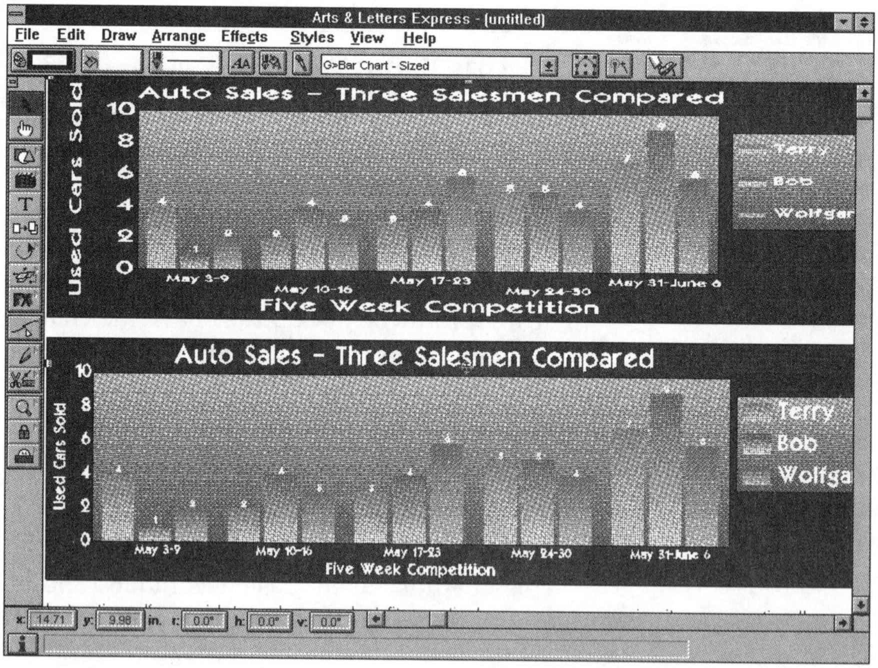

Figure 5.1
Chart Components
The two charts shown illustrate the key elements of auto-generated charts in Arts & Letters: the Y-axis (vertical), X-axis (horizontal), title (top), and X/Y axis labels (left and bottom). To the far right are the legends indicating the name of the salesman and the color used to represent him in the chart bars.

Chart Titles and Labels

Chart titles are text elements in the chart graphic that name the chart. Typical chart titles will show the main title and several subheadings, as well as the values represented by the X-axis and Y-axis. Chart labels also are the text elements that mark and identify the different data elements in the chart, such as the individual bars in a bar chart or the pie slices in a pie chart.

Legends

Labels describe in text form the data being interpreted. Legends are a way of describing or labeling the chart elements. For example, in a bar chart, legends would specify the data represented by each bar, using the differences in color or shading in the bar as references.

Background and Backdrop

The chart background is the area of the entire chart, including titles, legends, and all other elements. The chart backdrop is the space behind the live area of the chart, including the actual bar graphics and pie slices.

Values

The actual data included in the chart, that is, the numbers represented by the bar, pie, or line graphics, are referred to as the chart values (Figure 5.2).

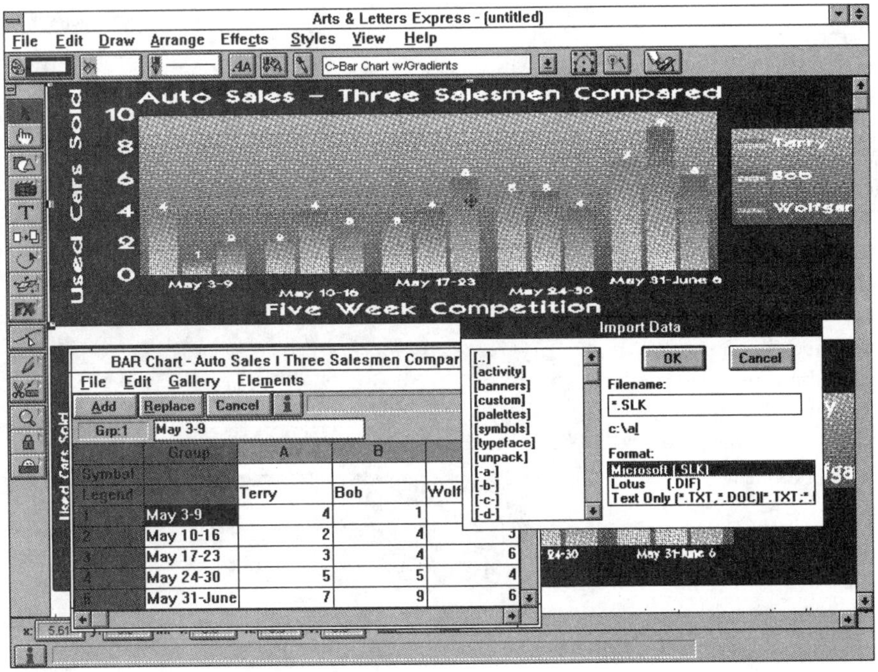

Figure 5.2
Chart Data
In the example shown, the upper chart is selected and the Chart dialog box (lower left) displays its numeric values in rows and columns. The Chart Titles entry screen below (lower right) displays the labels entered for the chart and the x/y axes.

Rows and Columns Data in the charting grid is entered in horizontal rows or vertical columns. Features in the charting screen allow you to edit the data in the grid by deleting and inserting rows or columns. Columns must be edited and adjusted in the appropriate width to accept a full data record.

Range The charting grid is a framework for data entry. At various times, you may need to make charts out of only part of the information within the charting grid. A range is the selected area within the charting grid. That is, you may only wish to chart the first four rows and the first two columns in a larger grid. That selected area is called the range.

Chart Data

Charts are pictures derived from a grid of data or from numeric values in the **Chart** dialog box. There are a variety of ways to place this data (Figure 5.3). You can, of course, enter the data directly in the Arts & Letters data grid in the **Chart** dialog box. With Version 3.1, you can directly import files containing data compiled in a number of popular spreadsheet applications, including Lotus 1-2-3, Microsoft Excel, or data created in any application that has been converted to straight ASCII (text) format. You may paste data using the Clipboard directly from any Windows application.

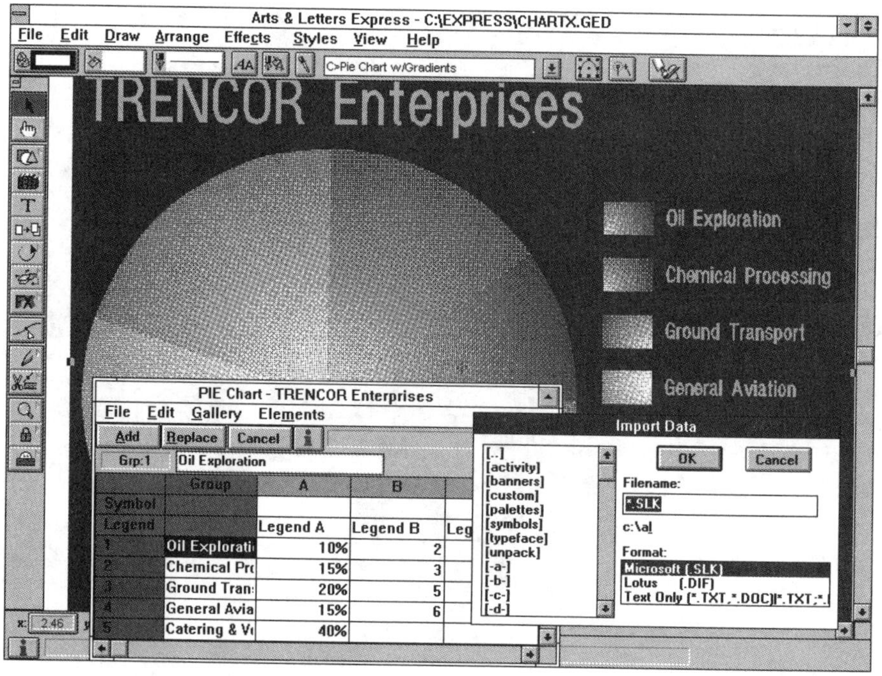

Figure 5.3
Chart Data
You can enter data directly into the chart grid in the chart dialog box. You may Copy and Paste data from data grids in other Windows spreadsheet programs, or you may use the provided file import to bring data from external programs directly into the Express Chart dialog box (lower left).

Chart Data File Format

Spreadsheets manage data in a variety of different file formats. These file formats are configured for a variety of uses in the software and contain different coding values that perform specific software operations. To import data into Arts & Letters for charting, you must use the specific file formats supported for Microsoft Excel (SYLK) or Lotus 1-2-3 (DIF) or a straight ASCII text file that contains no software control codes. If you attempt to import an unsupported file format, the operation will not work correctly.

Tools

To create charts in Arts & Letters, you will be using a number of key tools in the Arts & Letters screen. The following is a description of those tools and how they relate to the charting features.

Draw Menu This menu displays the **Chart** option, where you may bring up the Charting subscreen. It also contains the convert to freeform option, which allows you to break up and edit the finished chart as a collection of freeform graphic objects.

Charting Subscreen The charting subscreen is a full window within Arts & Letters that can be maximized to fill the entire screen to facilitate working with the grid and entering the data into the grid.

Windows Clipboard This Windows feature allows you to enter data from external Windows-based applications like Microsoft Excel. By copying a range from an Excel spreadsheet into the Clipboard, that information can be directly entered into the Arts & Letters chart data grid using the **Paste** feature on the **Edit** menu.

Presentation Power

The charting features included with Arts & Letters provide a built-in set of functions for recording, storing, and processing data, which can then be interpreted into visual form. This allows you to create an entire set of presentation materials including text overheads; complete bar, line, pie, and point charts; diagrams; images; and virtually any type of presentation media you wish directly within the Arts & Letters screen.

Build Charts from Data

You may enter data directly into the charting grid, or you may import it using the Windows Clipboard directly from parallel applications, such as Microsoft Excel, which are also running under Windows. Once data is in the grid, you may select Arts & Letters symbols by number for the bar, pie, or line graph, or by point charting elements you wish to be used to create the chart. The charting gallery allows you to select the type of chart and make adaptations to the look of the final chart. In Version 3.1, you can also import chart data in DIF, SYLK, and ASCII text formats.

Chart Editing But the power of Arts & Letters charting doesn't end by running data through the grid and simply turning it into a graphic. Once you have the completed chart, it may be edited using the full power of Arts & Letters Express. You may manipulate the chart using standard editing options, including Slant, Rotate, and Duplicate. You may break the chart into individual graphic objects and manipulate the look and presentation of the chart and make special adjustments to individual elements. With the symbol composition power of Arts & Letters, you may add backgrounds and artwork to the chart to give it a highly visual character that is simply not possible using standard charting software packages.

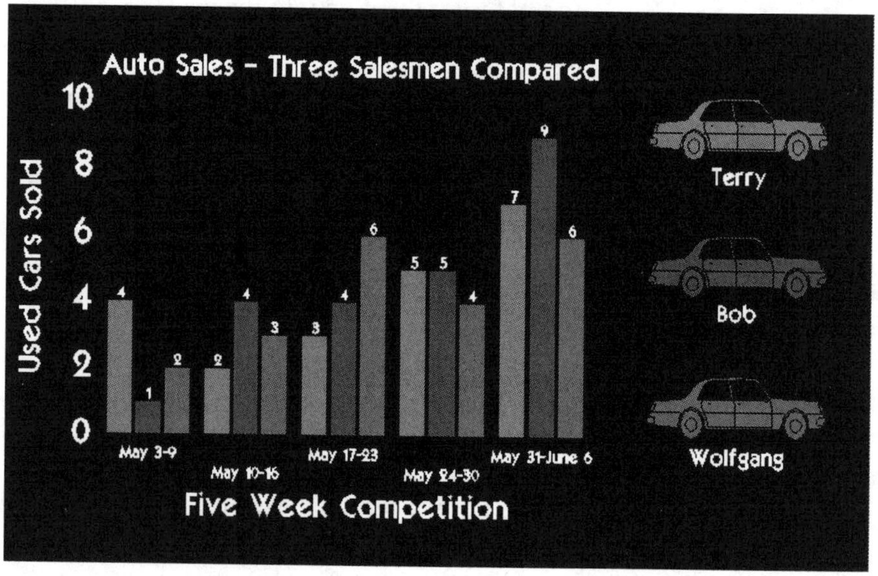

Pictorial Graphics

Pick up a national publication like *Time, Business Week,* or *USA Today.* Such publications often feature charts and graphics that include not only statistical relations shown in bar or pie graphs, but the chart itself has been reconfigured to resemble a picture, often with humorous cartoon-like elements, drawings, blended color backgrounds, and accents or icons for emphasis. The charts you create with Arts & Letters can be edited and enhanced to make precisely such highly professional designs.

Arts & Letters charting features were never intended to match the intensity of those available in a dedicated chart or graphics processor such as Lotus Freelance. They were designed to provide a means of processing data within the already powerful graphics composition system of Arts & Letters so that you get a presentation tool that allows you to do things quantitatively and qualitatively different from those done by any other graphics or illustration package on the market.

Symbol Charting

Where an artist may have the leisure time to draw and edit a high-quality illustration or other work, charts are intrinsically for business, and business art must be done quickly, to fit tight, seemingly impossible, deadlines. The marriage of a symbol-based composition system and grid-based charting allows you to select charting symbols, try out different variations, integrate charts with text, and even add pictorial elements and backgrounds in a fraction of the time required by dedicated charting packages.

What is most powerful about Arts & Letters charting is its level of interaction with the powerful and highly developed set of features already within Arts & Letters. This can give you presentation options you have never had before, and all within a program designed to make the most of your time and creativity.

Chart Types

The type of chart format you use is largely dependent on your application and the most effective way to communicate data to your audience. If you are attempting to show the comparative sales for a line of cars, an appropriate chart solution would be to build a bar chart with a bar representing the sales of each model. If, on the other hand, you want to demonstrate the change in sales volume for a single line of cars over the period of a year, you might choose a single line to represent the changes over the course of a year.

Charts represent both an artistic and conceptual challenge. The challenge is not just to demonstrate the relationships between individual chunks of information, but to find the most easy to understand and appealing way to present that relationship. Arts & Letters gives you the most complete and unique set of capabilities to carry your message.

There are five different types of charts supported within Arts & Letters Graphics Editor, each of which offers a different visual capability for specific visual communication problems.

Area Charts

Area charts are a variation of line charts that include two or more line graphs within the same chart. To demonstrate the difference between values on the individual line graphs, the areas between the lines are shaded.

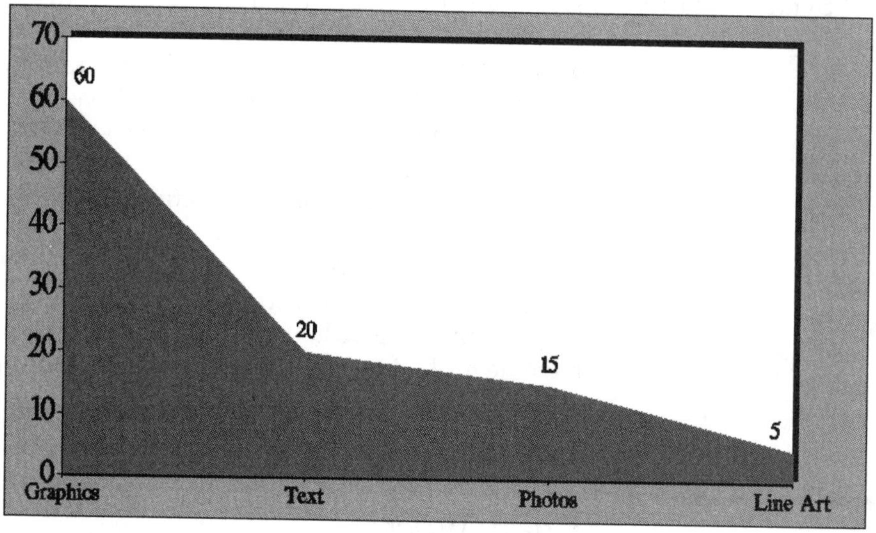

Bar Charts

Bar charts are made up of bar graphics whose size is based on the quantity of each column in the chart. They show relations in quantity over equal time intervals. For example, a good application would be to represent sales of different commodities over the same time period.

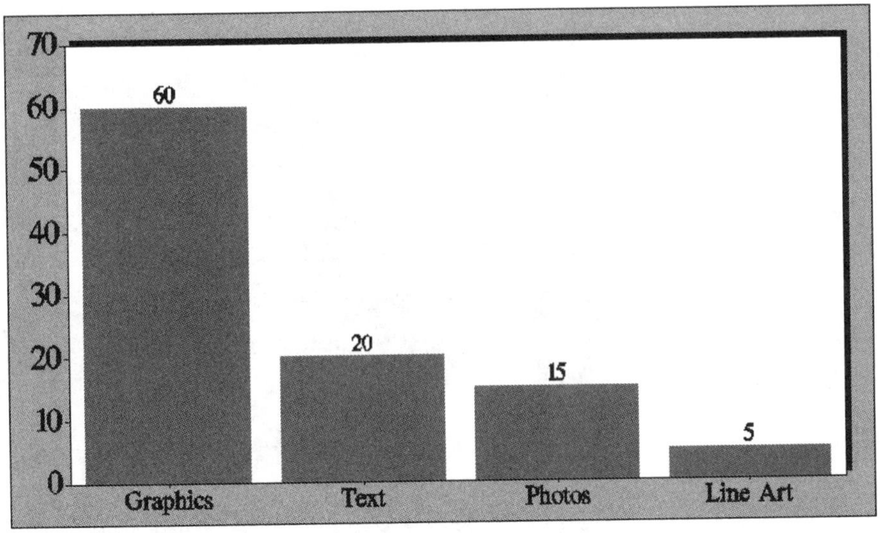

Clustered Bar Charts

Clustered bar charts allow you to compare multiple levels of information over equal time intervals so that you are aware of a larger progression of information.

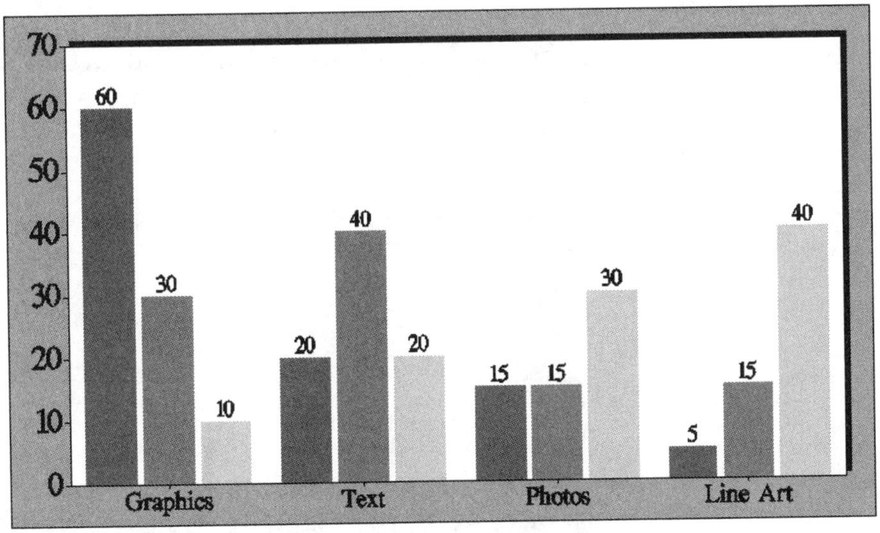

Pie Charts

Pie charts are used to show relative percentages of a defined whole, with each slice representing a part of the whole.

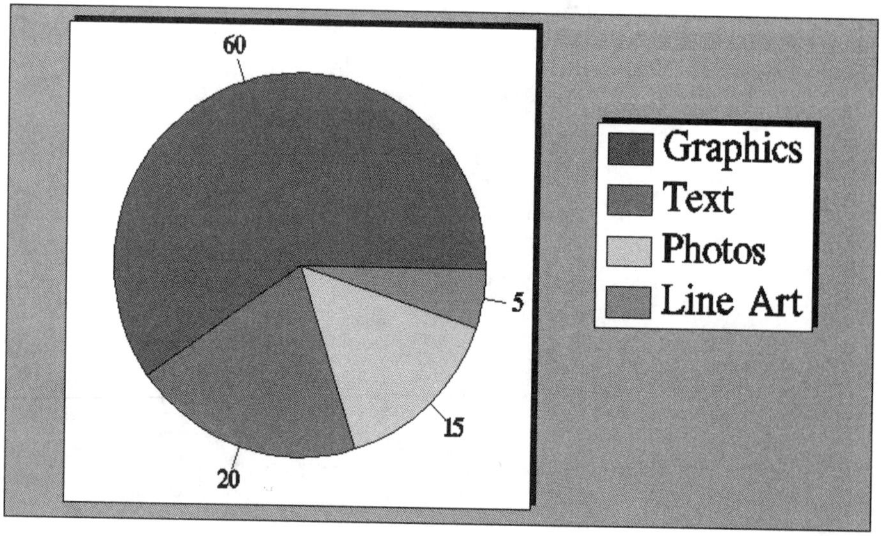

Line Charts

Line charts represent data in a continuous line that shows fluctuations in data, not unlike a wave.

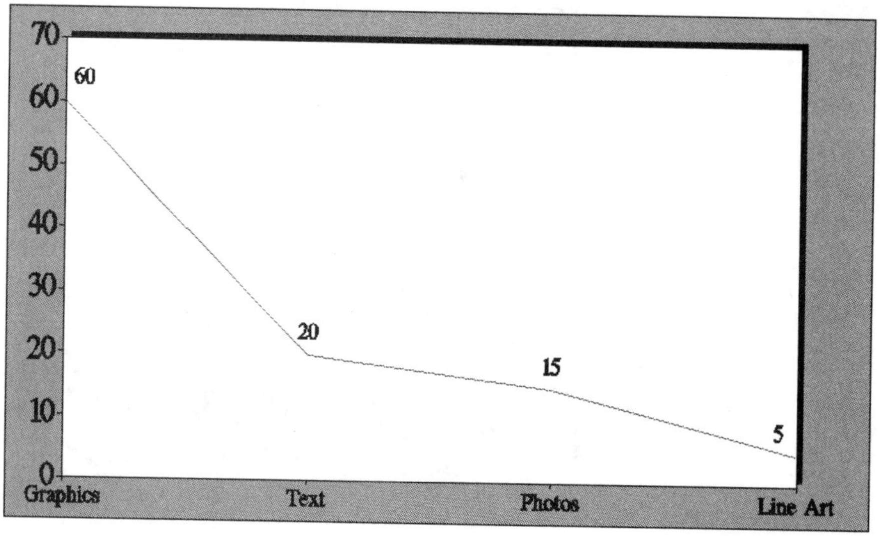

Point Charts

Point charts show values at specifically targeted points in time.

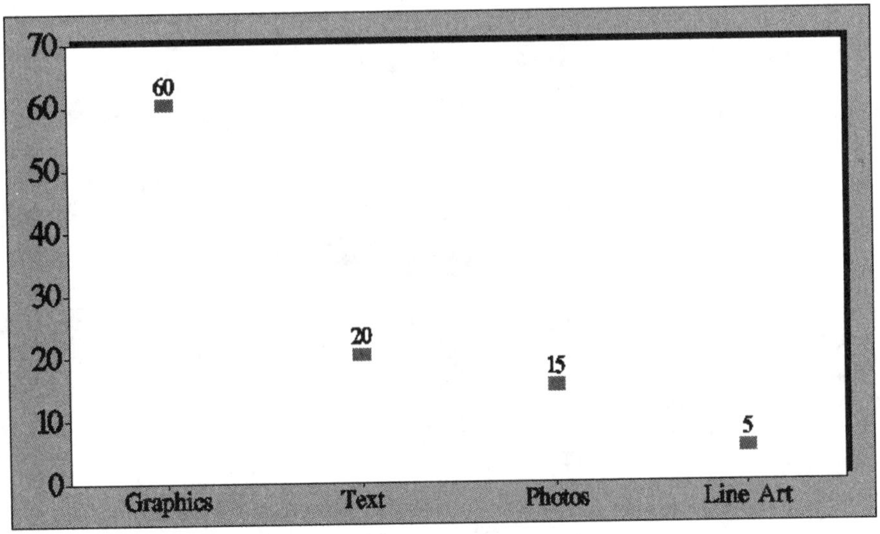

Selecting Elements

To begin with, the Chart dialog box (Figure 5.4) offers you a number of elements in the chart for you to use at your discretion, including:

- Chart Titles
- X- and Y-Axis Scales
- Legend
- Values
- Background
- Backdrop
- Backdrop Shadow

You don't have to have labels if you don't want them. You may wish to use an Arts & Letters symbol as a label. In that case you can turn off the option to produce labels. You also may wish to eliminate the background framing area or the backdrop behind the live area of the chart.

Steps: Selecting Elements

Use this operation to select the elements you wish to be included in your chart. When selected, the element will be displayed with a checkmark beside its name in the **Chart** dialog box **Elements** menu.

1. Access **Draw | Chart**.
2. Access **Chart | Elements** and select **Styles**.
3. Select the desired chart elements. Selected elements are displayed on the menu with a checkmark.

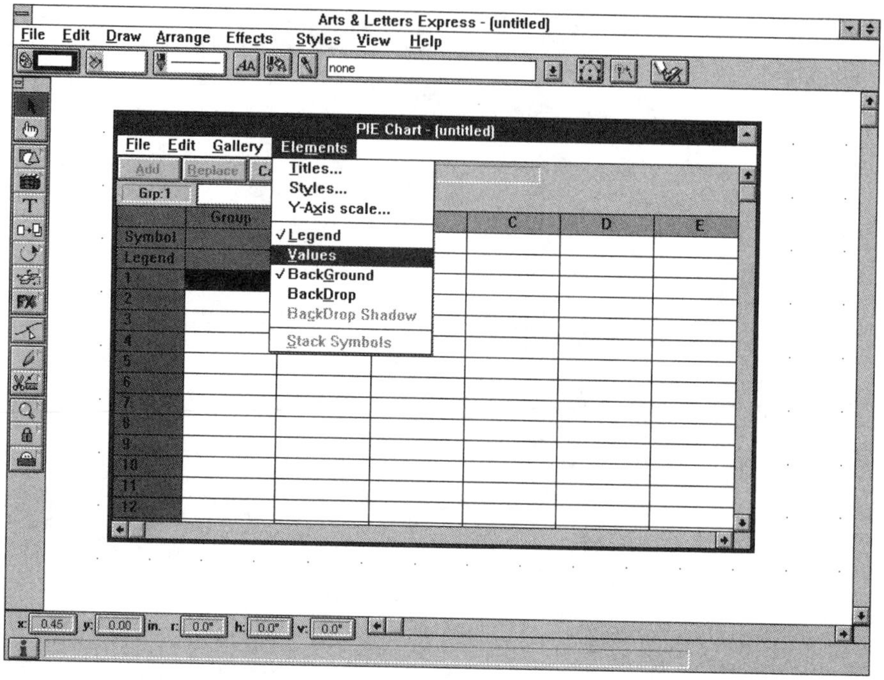

Figure 5.4
Selecting Elements
You may turn on various components of a chart by selecting or deselecting them in the Elements menu of the Chart dialog box. Note that the finished chart can be broken into elements using the Ungroup or Break Apart options, allowing you to customize the layout and add other art elements.

Defining Chart Titles and Labels

Once you have decided which elements you wish to have in the chart, you should enter the text elements that represent the title and the labels for the X-axis and the Y-axis (Figure 5.5). These values will be displayed for reference as you enter data in the chart dialog box.

Steps: Defining Chart Title and Labels

Use this operation to enter the text for the desired chart title and labels.

1. Access **Draw | Chart.**
2. Access **Chart | Elements** and select **Titles.**
3. Enter the chart title, X-Axis title, and Y-Axis title in the areas provided. You may leave one or more elements blank if you wish. (Note that pie charts do not have axis titles.)

Legends and Labels

The data in the chart is identified by labels on the rows and column legends. These labels are entered directly from the charting subscreen. Columns of information are identified by letter: A, B, C, and so forth. Rows of information are identified by number: 1, 2, 3, and so forth.

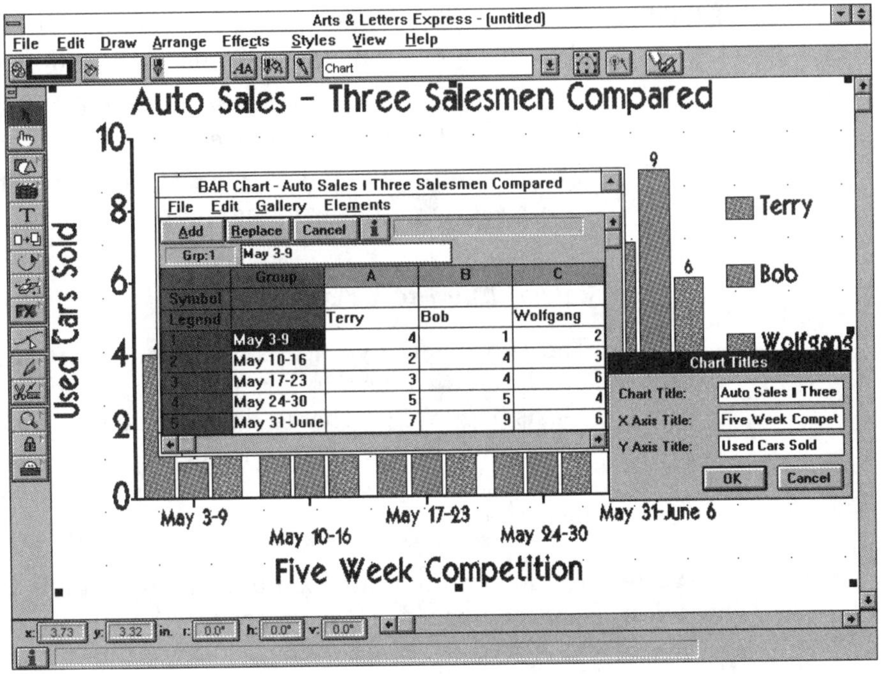

Figure 5.5
Chart Titles and Labels
The title at the top and the labels for the Y-axis (Used Cars Sold) and X-axis (Five Week Competition) are entered into the Chart Titles subdialog; the group labels on the X-axis (May 3–9) are entered into the Group column of the Chart grid; the Y-axis numbers are set using the Y-Axis Scale option on the Chart Elements menu.

Labels of columns will appear on the horizontal, or X-axis; labels of rows will appear stacked down the vertical, or Y-axis. You may arrange data in any way it makes sense to you. If you want to display sales of a set of items over a year, you may enter the months of the year either as row headings or column headings. Whatever your selection, enter the names of the items in the opposite axis.

Enter labels for columns in the white boxes opposite **Legend** and for rows in the white boxes beneath the word **Group**. Note that the colored boxes in the grid are not active and may not accept entry of text or data.

Steps: Specifying the Legend

Use this operation to identify the columns of data in the chart grid that will appear in the Chart Legend.

1. Access **Draw | Chart**.
2. To enter column labels, click the mouse in the white box at the **Legends** line in column **A**.
3. Enter the label.
4. Click the mouse in the white box in the same row beneath column **B** and enter the label. Repeat for each column.

Steps: Labeling Chart Columns

Use this operation to specify labels for groups of data in the chart grid that will appear on the X-axis in the final chart.

1. Click the mouse in the white box in the **Group** column opposite the number **1** and enter the label.
2. Press **Return** to move to the next box down in the **Group** column. Repeat for each row in the chart.

Specifying the Y-Axis Scale

The Y-axis is the vertical axis of your chart and is the one most commonly used to display a range of values for elements included in the X-axis (Figure 5.6). That is, a typical chart may show five different products on the horizontal X-axis such as automobiles, and the Y-axis will display a scale of dollar ranges against which sales of each product are displayed.

Automatic Y-Scale Generation

The minimum and maximum values on the Y-axis are generated automatically, based on the values entered into the data grid. The values are computed based on a numeric algorithm which automatically sets the axis scale value, but doesn't give you any control over it.

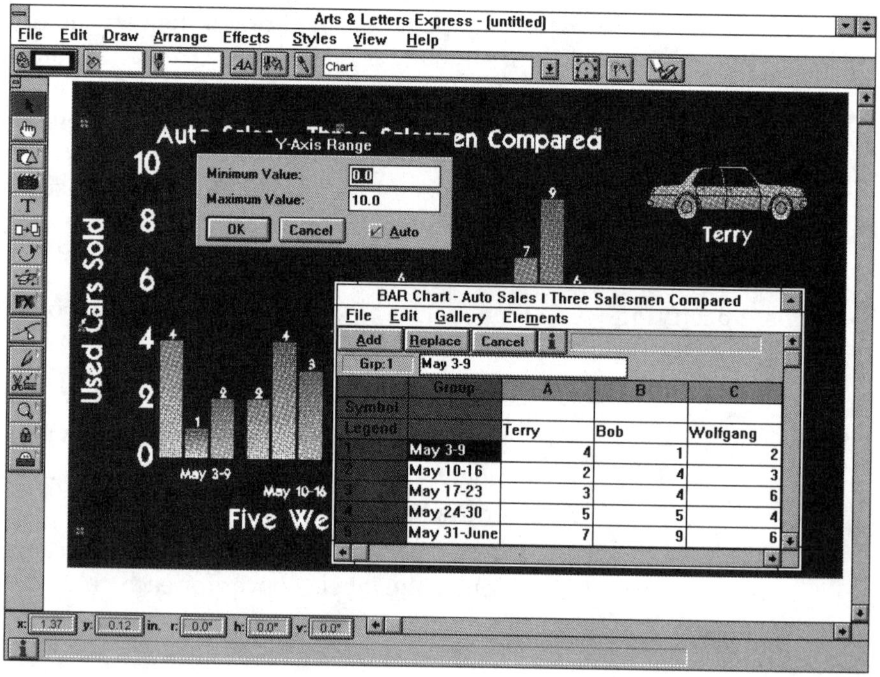

Figure 5.6
Specifying the Y-Axis Scale
The Y-axis (vertical) displays the range of data as an index to the graphic information displayed in the chart. The Y-axis values are generated automatically from the data, but you can override this using the Y-Axis Range dialog box in the Chart dialog box. This allows you to set custom values to display on the Y-axis.

Custom Y-Axis Settings

The **Y-Axis scale** option on the **Elements** menu lets you enter minimum and maximum values for the Y-axis, no matter what values are in the data grid. This allows you to set up the Y-axis as a clean scale in round numbers, for example **0–$1,000**. Data entered in the grid will be displayed in relation to the scale values you enter.

This feature also allows you to expand the scale of the Y-axis beyond the data values entered, for example, if you wish to alter the range of data against which the graphics are displayed. The data for the chart may have a maximum value of 10 (dollars, units, whatever). You can use the Y-Axis scale option to show a range of 25 (dollars, units, whatever) on the Y-axis. This will make the graphics representing the data look comparatively small against the scale value you have chosen. This feature is excellent if you wish to make variations on the same chart. You can duplicate the entire chart, and a copy of the data will go with the duplicate. You can then make alterations to the Y-axis scale to show how the same data stacks up against different frames of measurement.

Specifying the Y-Axis Scale

Use the operation below to enter a custom value for the Y-Axis scale. Note that Express will automatically set the Y-axis scale based on the highest values in your data. This is an optional feature you can use to customize the range against which your data is shown.

1. Access **Draw | Chart**.
2. In the **Chart** dialog box, access **Elements | Y-Axis scale**.
3. Enter the lowest value on the Y-axis in the **Minimum** line.
4. Enter the highest value on the Y-axis in the **Maximum** line.
5. Enter data and complete the chart. The Y-axis will reflect the minimum and maximum values you entered.

Selecting Chart Type

To produce a desired type of chart, you must select it from the **Gallery** menu in the **Chart** dialog box (Figure 5.7). The chart gallery lets you select Area, Bar, Line, Pie, or Point charts.

Once data is in the data grid, you may experiment with different looks for the chart by changing the type. So, if you initially select a pie chart and you would like to look at the same data in a bar chart, you have only to reaccess the gallery and select a bar chart and the data will be shown in a bar chart.

Figure 5.7
Chart Type
The **Gallery** menu lets you interpret the data entered into the grid in a variety of chart formats. Note that data entry may have to be adapted for different chart types. For example, a single pie chart cannot display the data on three separate salespeople over a time period as in the chart shown.

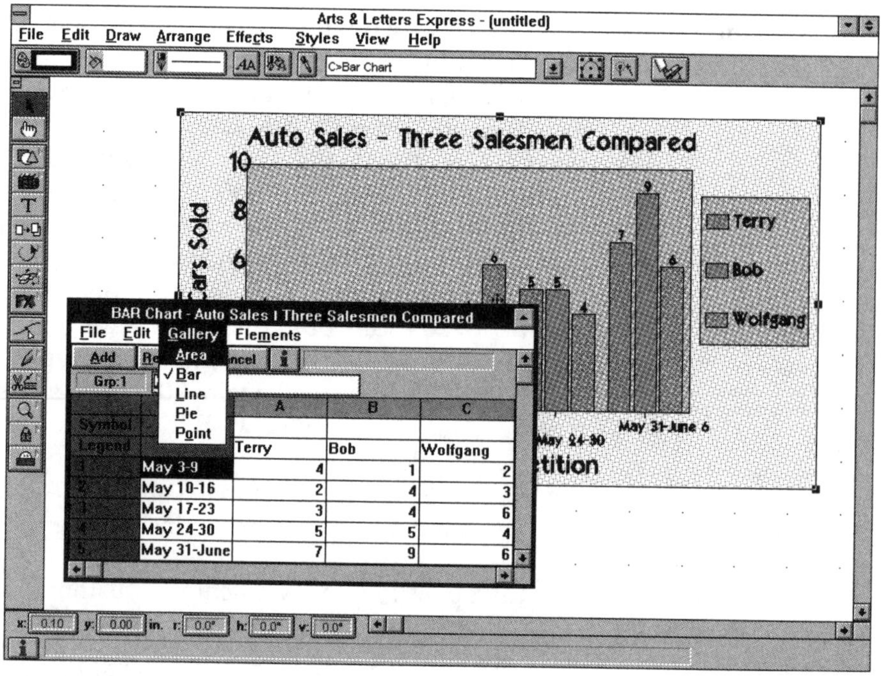

Steps: Selecting Chart Type

Use this operation to select the type of chart layout to display the data entered in the chart grid.

1. Access **Draw | Chart.**
2. Access **Chart | Gallery**.
3. Select the desired chart type. The currently enabled chart type is displayed with a checkmark.

Once you have properly set up the chart, the chart dialog box will be an effective matrix for entering and editing chart data.

Entering Data

The data grid provided in Arts & Letters is an open framework for the direct entry of data. You may place your mouse cursor in the box representing Column A, Row 1 and begin typing in data and statistics. When you press the **Return** key, you automatically advance down to the next cell in the column.

Once data has been entered in the grid, you may select ranges of data within the overall grid for editing, using the Cut, Copy, and Paste features. If you want a column or line to move to a new location, you select the range and manipulate it using the features of the **Edit** menu on the **Chart** dialog box.

Steps: Entering Data

Use this operation to type data into the chart grid.

1. Access **Draw | Chart**.
2. Click the mouse in the white box at the intersection of Column A and Row 1.
3. Type in the data entry and press **Return** to move down the column to the next cell in the chart.
4. You may enter data in any cell by using the mouse to select that cell.

Importing and Exporting Data

You may import ready-made data from such applications as Microsoft Excel into the Arts & Letters charting grid using the Windows Clipboard. To do this, you copy a range from a working Excel spreadsheet into the clipboard and paste it into the Arts & Letters charting grid. (See Figure 5.8.)

Importing and Exporting Data Using the Clipboard

Note that the Arts & Letters charting grid defaults to only 5 columns and 50 rows. You should bring in a limited range from Excel, and not a massive spreadsheet. Arts & Letters charting features were not designed to match the enormous charting and processing power of a dedicated spreadsheet application and are best used for simple charts.

Steps: Importing Data Using the Clipboard

Use this operation to import a block of data from any Windows spreadsheet grid or table configuration using the Clipboard.

1. Open the desired program containing the table or spreadsheet grid where the data is located.
2. Select a range of data to be used in an Arts & Letters chart.
3. Copy the data range into the Clipboard.
4. Access **Draw | Chart**.
5. Select a data cell. This cell marks the top-left cell for the data.
6. Select **Edit | Paste** in Arts & Letters to paste the data into the grid.

Importing Data from a File

You may also import data directly into the Arts & Letters chart screen from any spreadsheet or data management application that can write

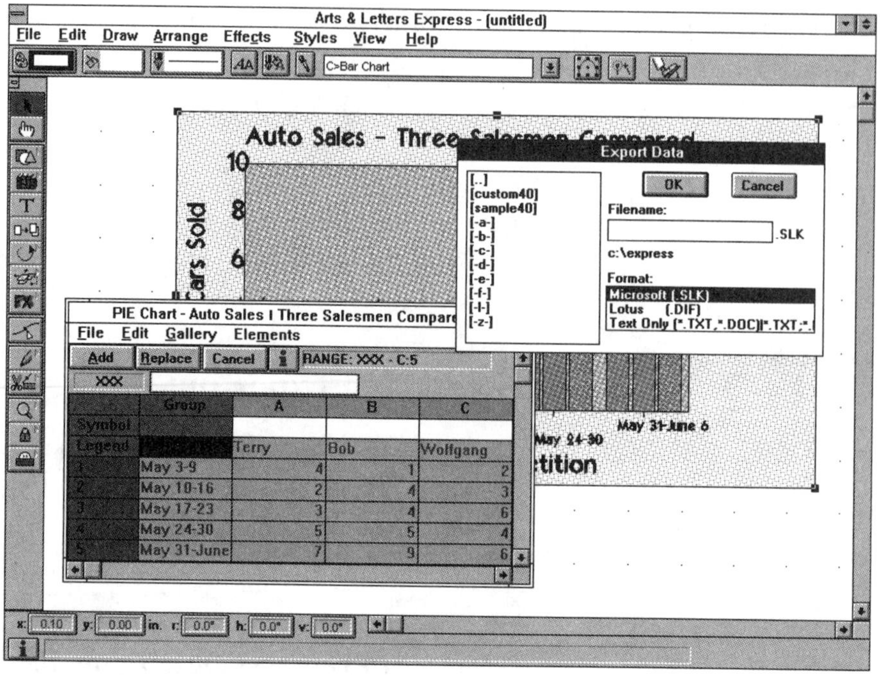

Figure 5.8
Importing and Exporting Data
The Import and Export screens allow you to bring in and send out data to major spreadsheet applications or as ASCII text. You may also select data in the Express Chart grid and copy it anywhere in Windows via the Clipboard.

the data to an ASCII (text) file. ASCII files are basic text and should contain the data only, without any software control codes. You don't necessarily need a spreadsheet application to create an ASCII file. Most of the popular word processors, including WordPerfect and WordStar, include an ASCII text entry feature.

Importing Chart Data from a File

Use this operation to import data into an Express chart in one of the supported file types.

1. Access **Draw | Chart**.
2. Select a data cell. This cell marks the top-left cell for the data.
3. In the **Chart** dialog box, access **File | Import**.
4. Select the desired file type.
5. Display the drive and/or subdirectory containing the data file. Select the file. Select **OK**.
6. The data appears in the Arts & Letters charting grid.

Exporting Data from a File

You may also export data from the Arts & Letters charting grid to a file which can be read by another spreadsheet application. This is especially useful if you have entered a complete data grid in Arts & Letters that you wish to edit in your spreadsheet for other purposes, or if you have made changes to an imported file while in Arts & Letters and want those changes to be available in the originating spreadsheet or database software.

Exporting Chart Data from a File

Use this operation to export selected data from the Express chart grid to an external file.

1. Access **Draw | Chart**.
2. Create the chart you desire in the grid.
3. Use the mouse to highlight a range within the charting grid, if desired.
4. In the **Chart** dialog box, access **File | Export**.
5. Select the desired file type.
6. Display the drive and/or subdirectory where you wish the exported file to be written.
7. Enter the filename for the data and select **OK**.
8. The data in the Arts & Letters charting grid (or specified range) is written to the filename.

Special Chart Effects

Arts & Letters creates standard graphic chart formats and custom variations via the graphic database. The Symbol entry line in the Chart grid allows you to enter the index number of any symbol from the symbol wireframe database (but not images from the Clip-Art Manager). These symbols can either be extended and stretched as a bar element, or stacked so that multiple images of the selected symbol make up the graphic bar.

Since the graphic database contains representations of a broad range of business images, you can make bar elements that look like factories, automobiles, clothing, machinery, and more. When combined with the full range of Arts & Letters editing features, you can break apart the chart group when generated and move around components, and adjust the width and scale of various chart elements to create artworks out of your data.

Chart Styles

Express will generate charts you create in default colors and backgrounds, allowing you exacting control of the appearance of all the elements, including the typography of the title and label elements through the Chart Attributes dialog box. This feature is unique because it allows you to assign styles to components within the chart group without breaking it apart for editing. You may directly access the Custom screens for all the Styles menu features including Color, Line, Fill, and Type. You may also apply any named styles you have created directly to chart elements (Figure 5.9).

The screen mimic in the Chart Styles screen allows you to see the selected colors for the various chart components and select them by name. Another nice touch is that this feature works retroactively. You can take an existing chart created by you or someone else and simply recolor and enhance it to match a new presentation you are making, or duplicate the source chart and make different color variations for printing the same graphic in black and white and also in color slides. For detailed coverage of the operation and application of Styles, see Chapter 7.

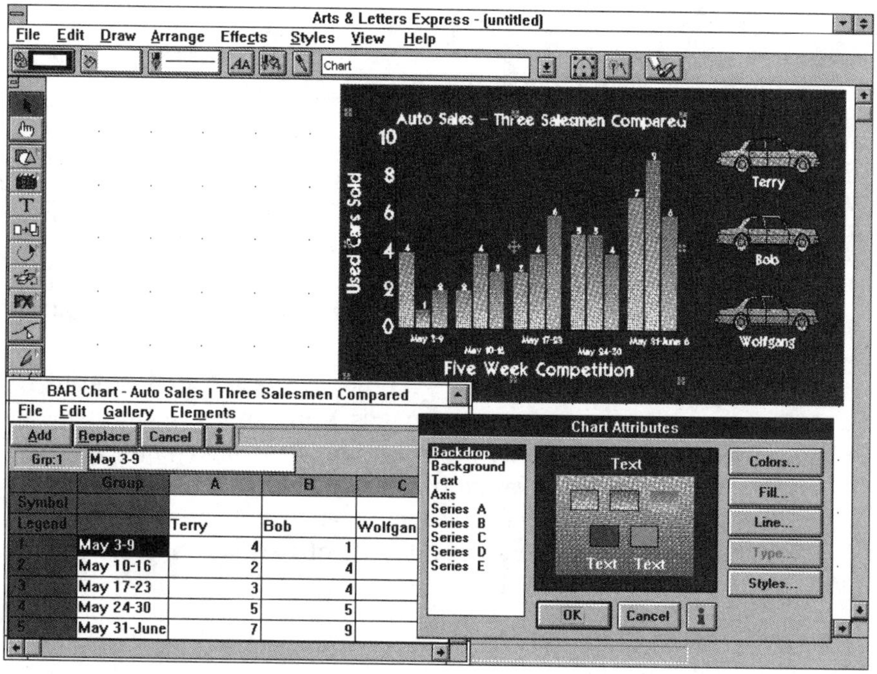

Figure 5.9
Chart Styles
The Styles menu on the Elements menu is a direct internal port to the entire styles menu that you can use when designing your chart, or retroactively editing it after the chart group has been created.

Steps: Applying Chart Styles

Use this operation to apply color, line, fill, and type styles to components in your chart. Note that these steps can be performed before you create the chart, or, as shown, retroactively, by selecting any standard chart (not exploded using Ungroup or Break Apart).

1. Select the chart group in the working area.
2. Access **Draw | Chart**.
3. Access **Chart | Elements | Styles**.
4. Select the desired component of the chart at the left of the **Chart Attributes** screen.
5. Select the desired Style to edit (at the right).
6. Make desired changes.
7. Continue selecting chart components, and make changes until complete.
8. Select **OK**.

Selecting Chart Symbols

Charts are created in Arts & Letters using standard symbol forms that are automatically expanded to reflect the relative amount of data entered into the column. The standard symbol set includes a complete family of ready-made charting elements, including 3-D bars, flat bars, pie slices, and more. When setting up your chart, you should enter the number of the symbol character you wish to express the information in the chart (Figure 5.10).

Charting with 15,000 Symbols

One of the most exciting things about the chart feature set is that you are *not* limited to the defined chart symbols to express charts. For bar and point charts, you can use any one of the up to 15,000 prepared symbols as chart elements, including icons, accents, pictorials, and others. Pie charts always use standard pie slices; and line charts are always drawn with lines, no matter what symbol you specify.

Obviously not all symbols are ideal for charting purposes. But, using this feature, you can create some highly interesting charting effects with the standard icon set. For example, instead of using a bar graphic, use a symbol for a man. The icon symbol will be shown in correct relationship to each column of information, growing and shrinking as the data does. In short, you have the option in Arts & Letters of making charts highly pictorial instead of just simple chart forms.

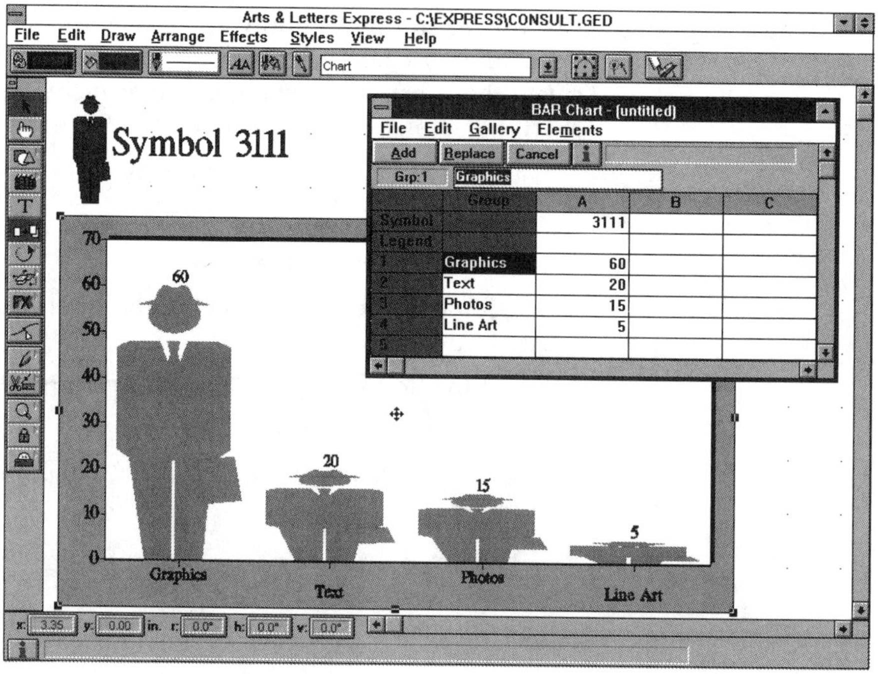

Figure 5.10
The Symbol entry line allows you to use any of the symbol wireframes as chart elements. This is most effective using bar chart configurations. The selected symbol will expand just like the bar, and distort to reach the correct numeric representation of the data.

Steps: Selecting Chart Symbols

Use this operation to enter custom symbols for use as graphic display elements in charts.

1. Access the *Clip Art Handbook.*
2. Select the desired chart symbols (bar, line, pie).
3. Enter the symbol number at the top of each column you wish to display.
4. You may use the same symbol in each column, or different symbols in each column.

Creating Stacked Symbol Charts

The charting features allow you to enter symbols for dedicated charting elements directly into the charting grid, such as bars, pie slices, lines, and so forth. For bar and point charts, you may replace these elements with any symbol, such as icons; each will grow and shrink to represent the amount of data.

You may also develop stacked symbol charts in which any symbol may be used without distortion. Instead of representing a data value as a tall bar, you may elect to represent it as a stack of car symbols the height of the bar.

Symbol Effects

Each symbol in the stack is shown in the correct aspect ratio so that you have a highly pictorial chart effect instantly. You may vary symbols for each column or row of data entry so that different symbols appear, visually describing the data they represent.

Stacked symbol charts are highly visual and effective, particularly when representing comparative data for different products or items. Using stacked symbols to represent the actual content of the data, such as sales of cars shown as a tall stack of cars, makes labeling less necessary and allows you to create presentation graphics that are almost entirely visual and pictorial.

Steps: Creating Stacked Symbol Charts

Use this operation to create bar displays of stacked symbol components based on the symbol number you enter into the Symbol line for each column. The stacked symbol format will multiply the number of symbols in a stack to reach the correct bar height indicated by the data.

1. Access **Draw | Chart**.
2. Access **Chart | Elements** and select **Stack Symbols**.
3. Enter chart data into as many columns as needed.
4. Enter the desired symbol into each column heading. You may use the same symbol for each column or different symbols, as you wish.

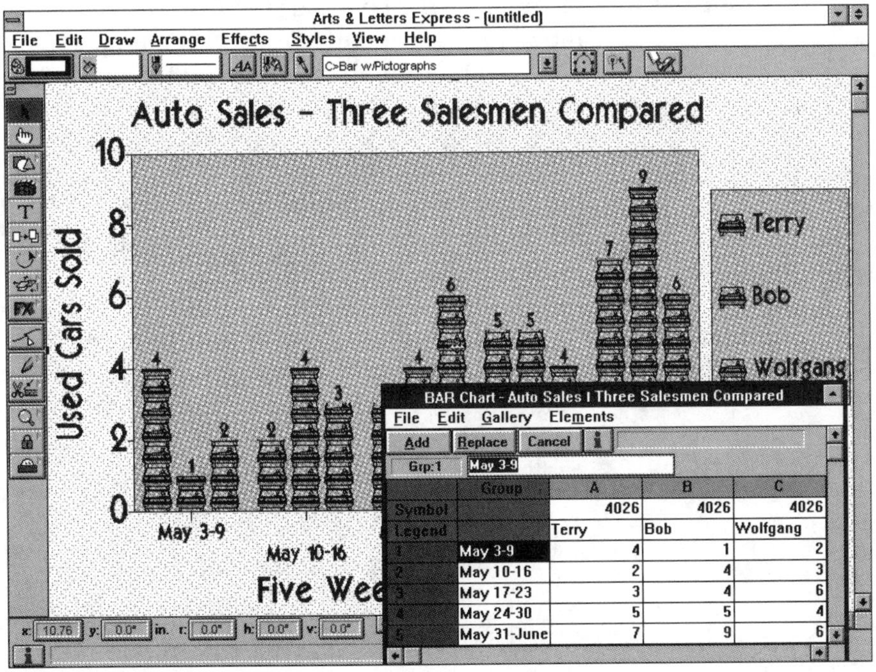

Figure 5.11
Stacked Symbol Charts
The symbol entry line in the chart grid allows you to enter any of the 15,000 symbol wireframes to use as graphics in your chart. In the example shown, the symbol numbers for the auto icon are placed in the Symbol line, and these symbols are shown in stacked formation.

5. Add the chart to the screen. Each data column will be represented by a series of stacked symbols.
6. Optional: For greater editing freedom, you may break apart the chart using **Arrange | Ungroup**.

Exploded Symbol Charts

Charts are generated by symbols that are automatically sized to reflect the relationship between different columns of data, backgrounds, backdrops, and text. You may edit individual elements in a chart by using the **Ungroup** command on the **Arrange** menu.

Adding Backgrounds and Accents

This permits you to create some highly interesting graphic effects by using the chart features to alter the size and relationship of individual symbols. Standard chart bars themselves are not visually distinctive, but they serve to demonstrate the relations between data. But, say you want to present the data more pictorially by using a drawing of a guitar instead of a bar to show data relationships. You can enter a custom symbol for each column in the data grid, and you will get a bar chart in which the bars are all guitars, or cars, or even buildings!

Arranging Chart Components

There's an even more interesting spin to this concept. Suppose you break apart the chart so that the sized guitars can be manipulated and moved independently. You can then create a cluster graphic in which you can stack the smaller bars on top of the larger ones, each in a different color. You can even select the larger guitars which have been stretched vertically, based on the data in the column, and extend their horizontal dimension so that they appear in proportion. By exploding the chart from its default form, you may find a wide variety of highly interesting ways to manipulate the bars and other elements. Take time to experiment. It's worth it.

Steps: Creating Exploded Symbol Charts

Use this operation to break apart and recompose elements in a chart group. Note that when you break apart the chart graphic itself, you cannot select and reedit the source data. To avoid this problem, duplicate the chart group before you break it apart, and drag the copy to another page in your GED file as a backup.

1. Access **Draw | Chart**.
2. Enter or import chart data as needed.
3. Enter numbers of desired pictorial symbols into the space provided in the charting grid. Add the chart.

4. Select the chart and select **Arrange | Ungroup**.
5. Move and position the individual bar/pictorial elements to the desired position.
6. Note: To reshape symbols stretched by the charting operations, do not use **Arrange | Make Proportional**. This will flatten the vertical dimension. To make the different bar elements appear in proportion, pull on the sizing handles in the middle on either the left- or right-hand side of the symbol.

Point Edit and Chart Labels

When a chart is broken apart using the Ungroup or Break Apart command, you may individually select the text elements that make up titles and labels. The selected text may then be sized uniformly with the mouse as a selected graphic, or you may edit it with any of the Type options on the flyout Type palette or the Type option on the Styles menu (Figure 5.12).

Point Edit If you want to create special effects with chart labels, you can select the title or label components and individually edit characters using the Point Edit mode. When any block of standard text in Express is selected,

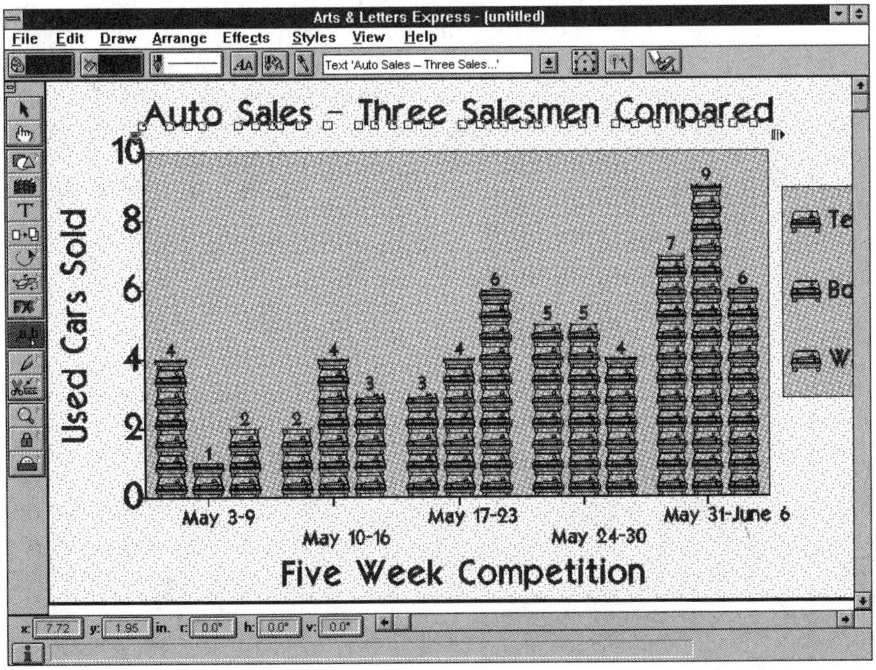

Figure 5.12
Point Edit and Chart Labels
When a Chart group is broken apart, the text labels may be selected and edited as a group with Type Styles, or individual characters may be enhanced and moved using the Point Edit feature group.

the Freeform icon changes to the Point Edit icon. Click on it, or select Point Edit from the right mouse button pop-up menu, and you can select individual characters in the Title or Label string.

Data Security with Duplicate

This capability is particularly useful if you are creating picture effects with charts and you want to shape text to flow in the composition or give emphasis to special characters or individual words in the title. Remember that once the chart has been broken apart, you can't reassemble it and reaccess the data. The best strategy is to duplicate the chart complete with data and retain the original. Break the duplicate apart and edit as you see fit: You'll have the original tucked away on another page in the GED file if you need to reaccess the data and regenerate the chart.

Enhancing Charts with Artwork

Charting is a master feature of Express that has links to the graphic database, the text system, and the whole family of editing and effects. You can interpret data in many ways simply by taking advantage of the range and diversity of the built in artwork in Arts & Letters.

Once a chart has been generated, you can easily disassemble it so that all the components—titles, bars, labels, and legends—become free-floating graphic components. This allows you to recompose the chart any way you want, adding images, backgrounds, and enhancing individual charting components. Using the full range of editing, styles, and special design effects, you can create arresting and powerful chart layouts by simply using your mouse.

CHAPTER 6

Freeform Mode: Drawing, Symbol, and Text Editing

The graphic database in Arts & Letters is a unique, automated system for using the computer as a graphic tool. Along with the symbol wireframes, images, text, and charts is the Freeform mode, which allows you to break any of the art components or text into collections of straight and curved line elements. (See Figure 6.1.)

This chapter presents operations and design techniques that will help you make best use of the freeform drawing tools available in Arts & Letters Express for drawing and editing symbols and text forms. It focuses on features of the drawing and editing system and ways to combine the Standard mode editing features with those available under Freeform mode.

Fast Track Orientation

The operations presented in this chapter are based on a number of key concepts. Understanding these concepts in advance will help you get the most out of the information presented here.

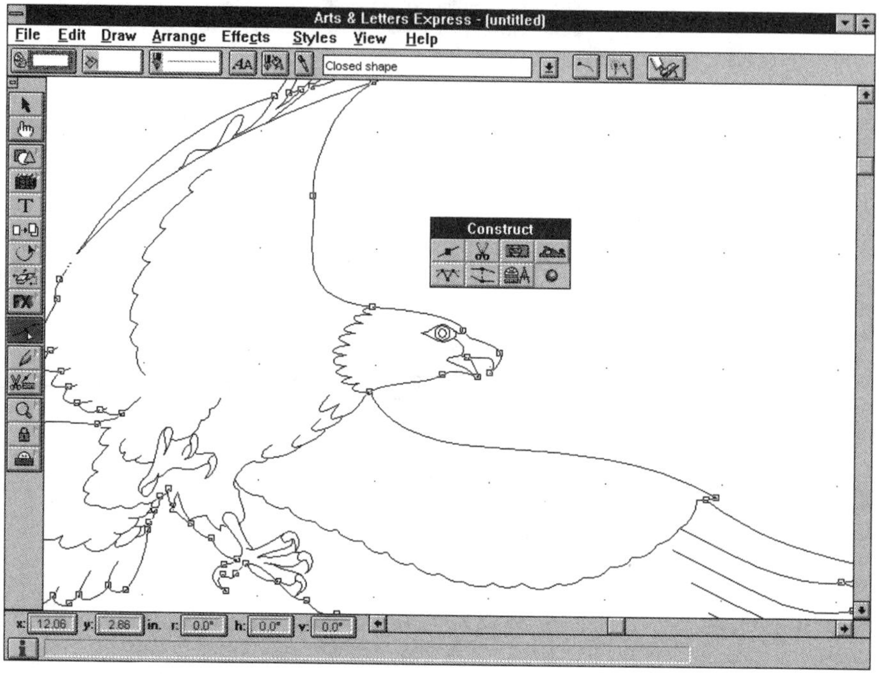

Figure 6.1
Construct Features
This group operates in Freeform mode and allows you to edit individual line elements. The drawing of the bird, shown, is a symbol exploded into freeform. The main outline of the figure is selected and displays editing handles on the line.

Key Concepts

Drawing Controls

The Construct option on the **Draw** menu contains features that allow you to set defined controls on Arts & Letters' two fundamental drawing elements: lines and curves. You do not have to use these if you do not wish to, but they are available at any time during drawing and editing to give you precise control over the character and position of lines and curves, as well as how they connect or join to one another, and the degree of accuracy and position of those lines.

Save and Recall

The Save and Recall capabilities allow you to define specific line lengths and to define precise angles between them. You may also define precise X and Y coordinates and recall those coordinates when you wish. This capability is very useful in technical drawings and similar applications.

Element Handle vs. Point Handle

Element handles are the small, black-filled sizing boxes that appear around graphic elements in standard editing mode. Point handles are the same size as element handles, but they are shown as an outline square with a white interior and solid black when selected. Point handles are used to physically drag line end points when you're in freeform editing mode. You can view both the element and point handles when a freeform element is selected by turning on **Point Display | Freeform Points** in the **View** menu or by toggling the **Freeform Points** icon in the Toolbox.

Control Points Control points (Figure 6.2) are special handles available with curved lines, but only in freeform editing mode. They allow you to reshape the curve, whereas point handles allow you to move, lengthen, and edit the curved line itself. To view control points, you must select **Point Display | Control Points** on the **View** menu. Once enabled, you click the left mouse button on any point handle on a curved line and the control point will appear.

Smooth Joins There are two controls that regulate the character of joins between line and curve segments. A standard join between line and curve segments allows the line to pivot freely at the join point into hard angles. A smooth join locks the line to the curve so that the line cannot pivot or angle at the join point. **Maintain Smooth Joins** is a toggle feature. When activated, it automatically makes all line/curve joins smooth. **Make Join Smooth** is a local editing feature that allows you to make an individual line/curve join smooth. Both features are available on the Construct flyout on the Draw menu.

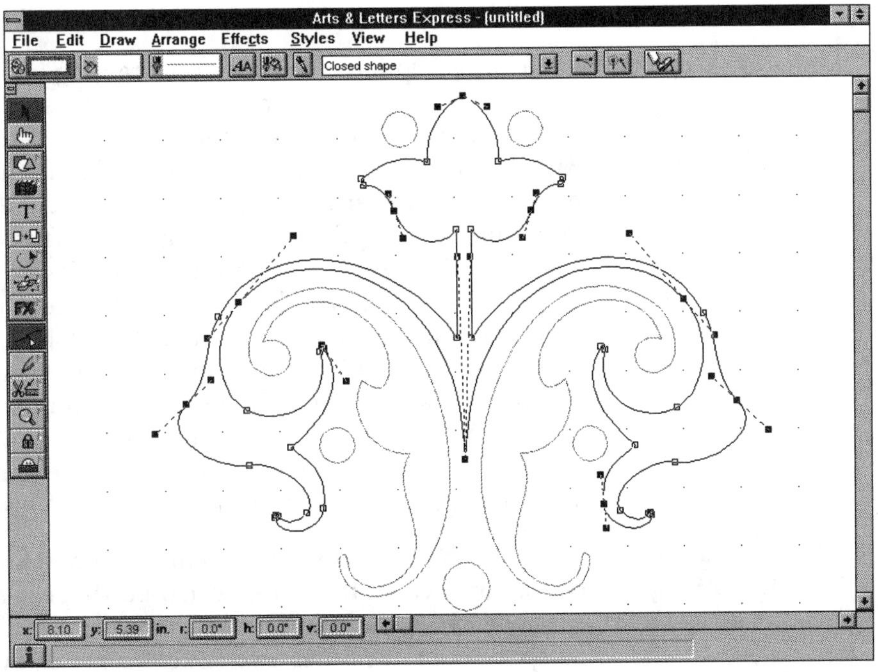

Figure 6.2
Control Points
Control points are special freeform editing handles for curved line segments. Only selected point handles will display control points. The boxes at the end of the dotted lines can be rotated to twist curves at the point handles, in the center of the dotted lines.

Maintain Curve Slope As you edit a curve, you may wish to maintain the slope of the curve. This control allows you to automatically maintain the slope of a curve as you edit in freeform.

Snap Lines and curves in Arts & Letters are a series of defined points on the page. You may use any of several snap features that allow you to automatically snap lines to points, to other lines, to curves, and to positions within a defined grid, without having to manually manipulate the line or engage in a lot of trial-and-error editing.

Snap Radius Snap features operate within a defined box around a point, line, curve, or coordinate in the snap grid. The radius of this circular area is called the *snap radius* and may be controlled and set using the **Snap Options** selection on the **Construct** cascade on the **Draw** menu.

Bezier Curve Accuracy Arts & Letters creates curved lines based on what you draw in the screen and automatically smoothes out imperfections into a fluid, seamless line. However, if you want to retain the exact character of the original line, with all its "imperfections" in place, you must increase the level of drawing accuracy using the **Preferences** selection on the **Draw** menu. By setting the accuracy of the curve sketching to a low value, such as within 2 or 3 pixels, Arts & Letters will not automatically smooth out your line and deliver a more accurate representation of the original. If you want more automatic smoothing, increase the accuracy setting accordingly.

Drawing Accuracy In Drawing Options, you may set drawing accuracy using a range defined by pixels. The lower the pixel range is set (e.g. accuracy within 1 pixel), the more accurately the curve will reflect your drawing. The Faster option speeds up the process by fitting the curve into the page, if possible with fewer bezier curve line segments. Better takes more time to calculate the optimum line segments. This option is required only when drawing very precise curves. When Detect Corners is activated, the desired Smooth Join Angle, which is set in the Draw Options dialog box, will automatically smooth joins between line/curve or curve/curve segments connected at less than this angle. Finally, Complex Curves is an option that regulates the number of curve segments in a sketched curve. When turned Off a single bezier curve segment will be used to translate your curve drawing; when On the curve may be broken into several Bezier curve components.

Open Shapes vs. Closed Shapes An open shape is any line or curved shape that does not completely enclose an area on the screen. A closed shape is any line construction or curve in which the start and end points meet. Only closed shapes may accept interior attributes, such as color, raster, or vector patterns.

Tools

Toolbox The Toolbox is the central source for all freeform drawing tools. Immediately beneath the main group of tools at the top appears the Freeform editing icon, followed by icons for line and curve drawing, adding handles, and more. Beneath that group of tools is another group that allows you to control sophisticated Draw and Construct features directly from the screen.

Shape Selector New in Version 5, the Shape selector contains a group of specially designed "smart shapes." These are not the same as standard symbol shapes, but, like symbols, must be converted to freeform if you wish to edit them in Freeform mode. These shapes are designed to place and edit more accurately than symbol shapes. The rounded rectangle form in the Shape Selector, for example, can be distorted in height and width without dragging or distorting the angle of the curves at the four corners. Use these shapes for simple geometrics in your drawings, or for any effect requiring simple geometric shapes.

Edit Menu The Edit menu contains the Cut, Copy, and Paste features, as well as tools allowing you to select all freeform handles or specific groups of handles. This is also where you access the Object Management features, including the Object Browser, which allows you to easily select elements within a group without breaking apart the group. The Edit menu is also home to the OLE features, Cut, Copy, and Paste, and the new Copy Area.

Draw | Construct Menu In addition to the main symbol, custom symbol, text, and chart features, this menu (Figure 6.3) contains the basic freeform drawing features, most of which can be selected directly from an icon in the Toolbox, by a keyboard control command, or by a function key. In Version 5, all tools used to control freehand drawing and editing are contained in a Construct cascade under the Draw menu, including controls on line and curve joins, snap features, and the family of set and recall features for angles, line length, X and Y positions, and perpendicular lines.

Using Freeform Features

Freeform features in Express allow you to make sophisticated revisions to art elements in the database, wireframe index numbers, image names, standard text, and chart components. (See Figure 6.4.) When converted to freeform, these elements lose their graphic database identity and become simple collections of freeform objects.

Figure 6.3
Draw | Construct Option
The entire Construct menu from Version 3 is now tucked away as an option in the Draw menu. This menu is home to most of the advanced freeform line editing features. These features may also be accessed from the Construction flyout on the Toolbar.

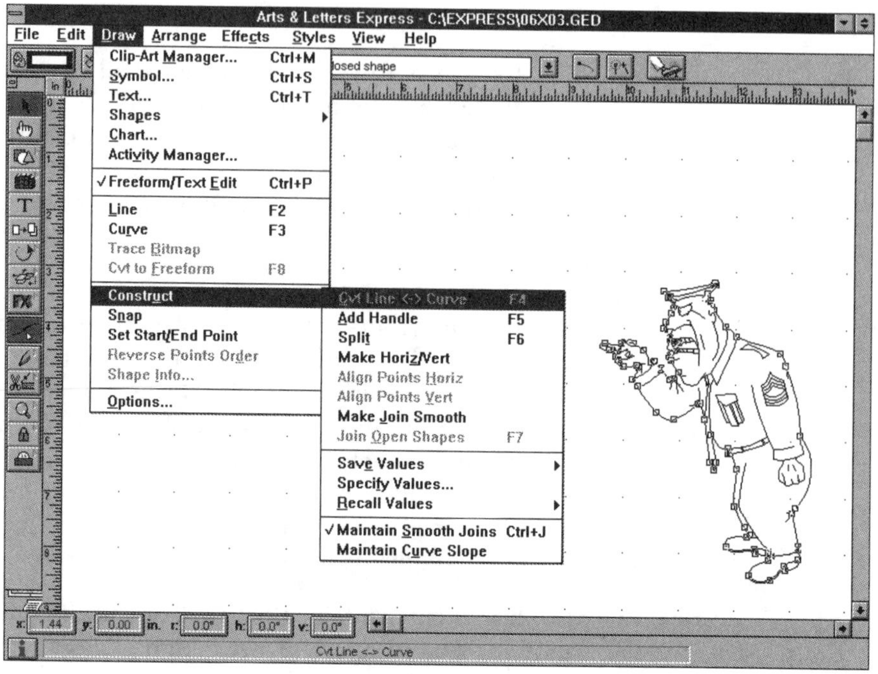

Figure 6.4
Freeform Features
Freeform features can be used to create variations on symbol art forms. In the example shown, freeform features can be used to add or revise details in symbol-based maps which are included in the graphic database.

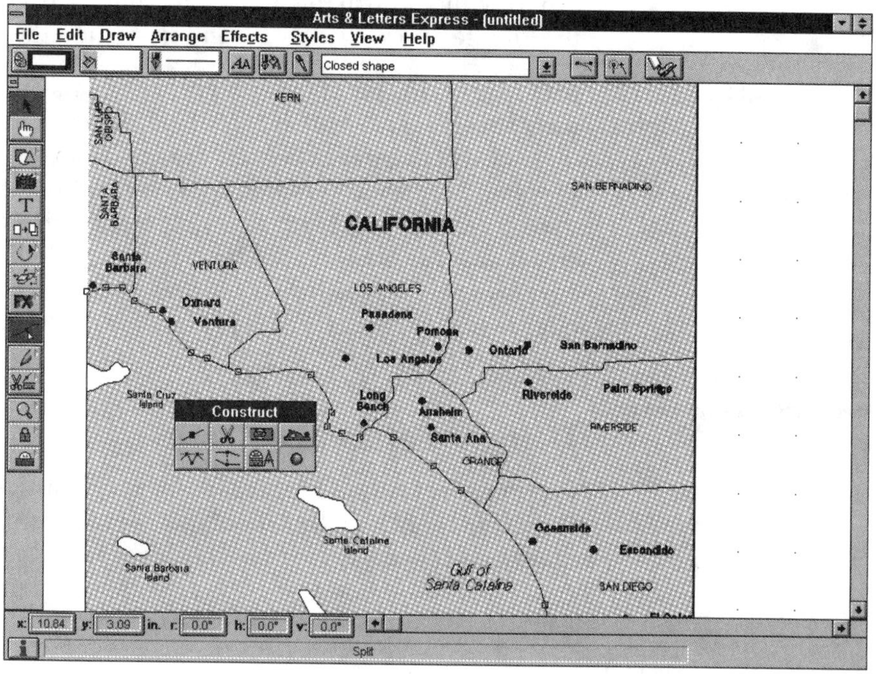

Standard Mode Editing

Using distortion and sizing features, you can make dramatic or subtle edits to art components; and the sophisticated Warp, Extrude, and other special effect options let you create controlled distortions of shapes and text that would take a trained professional hours to do by hand. New in Version 5 is the capability to load numbered symbols and text directly into YAL format image files without converting them to Freeform. (You can work quite comfortably in Express without ever accessing these features.)

Freeform Mode Editing

Freeform mode can be considered optional. Depending on your level of artistic skill, you may never need to use freeform. On the other hand, it allows you to make detailed and sophisticated edits to the actual shapes and components of a drawing. For example, if you explode a symbol wireframe of a human face into Freeform, and you will have access to the hundreds of individual line elements that make it up. You are then free to add, delete, edit, and reshape lines within the drawing to create your own custom variations.

Drawing from Scratch

You may, of course, draw your own compositions from scratch using the high grade professional editing tools provided. For technical illustrations and schematics, you also will find that Freeform mode contains an elaborate system of point and line editing controls that allow you to work easily with detailed and complex line and curve components.

Permanent Freeform Conversion

Above all else, note that once you have broken apart a symbol, a text string, or chart into freeform, you take it completely out of the graphic database. From that time on, the drawing is just a collection of elements that you can work with and group into simple graphic drawings.

Freehand Drawing on the Electronic Canvas

There is no way to exactly replicate on a computer screen the subtlety and precision of pencil on paper. Computers work in entirely different ways from old-fashioned hand drawing to create lines and shapes.

However, the computer can do many things that cannot be done in a hand drawing. For one thing, the computer screen is a highly sophisticated electronic grid, which allows you to create and edit artwork by recording the specific position of lines and shapes as points in the electronic grid. On the simplest level, this allows you to sketch any line in that grid, save it, and bring it up on the screen again for editing and revision.

Controlled Drawing and Editing

The space on the screen not only receives and records simple forms, it can control them as they are entered. For example, you can define drawing grids on the screen that force the lines to snap to specific points. You may also instruct the computer to automatically snap the lines you draw to match other line forms. That is, the screen can be set up to make lines automatically join the points in other drawing elements on the screen. Arts & Letters has fully implemented the concept of controlled drawing, far beyond a system of line and form snap features, that includes a detailed set of controls over line angle and length. If you wish to continue a line of an exact length and a precise angle from another line, you may specify that relationship and automatically implement it on the screen.

Automated Freehand Drawing

The capabilities of the freeform drawing features in Arts & Letters are just another example of this book's theme, which is to *automate the drawing process*. No matter how attached you may be to your pencil, Arts & Letters offers tools for precision and control over line forms and shapes that you never dreamed of before. By configuring screen grids (Figure 6.5), setting automatic line and point "snap" relationships, and using the specify and recall features to their utmost, you may create a "hot" workspace that automatically brings your drawings into precise relationships without a lot of aggravating trial and error.

Editing Electronic Sketches

Another dimension of the freeform features in Arts & Letters involves editing an electronic sketch. Traditionally, when you draw a rough, freehand sketch on the screen, such as to sketch out a general concept, you would have to discard the sketch and start from scratch to create a "comp," or a finished piece. In Arts & Letters, your rough drawing can form the basis of the finished piece. You can reform lines and shapes within constraints, and use control points and line handles to pull elements into the finished shape.

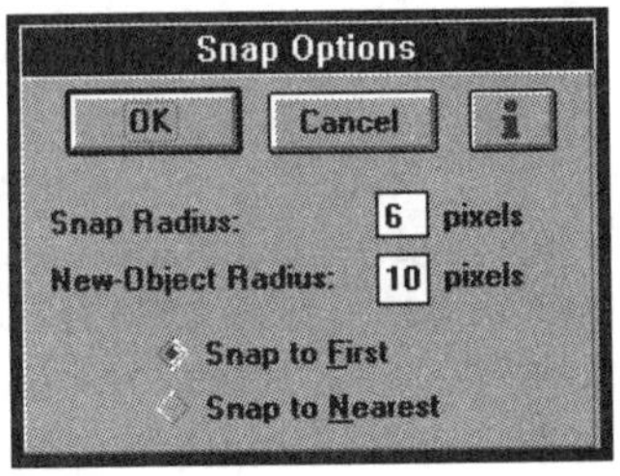

Figure 6.5
Electronic Canvas
Express includes rulers and a snap-to screen grid which are particularly effective in Freeform mode. The scale of the screen grid and the units of measure for the rulers are controlled through the Options selection on the View menu.

Freeform Drawing Constraints

The drawing controls in Arts & Letters are designed to be applied individually, as needed. Some, like **Maintain Smooth Joins**, **Maintain Curve Slope**, or the snap-to grid, may be defined as a consistent condition in the screen—meaning they are always active. Others, such as **Save Values | Angle**, or **Recall Values | Length** are defined and specifically activated on point handles and drawing elements only as needed. Even if you are accustomed to drawing by hand, you will find that the precision and control allowed by these tools during drawing or editing can significantly help you save time and effort.

Editing Freeform Art in Standard Mode

Standard mode contains powerful editing features for symbols, images, text, and charts. Once you leave Freeform mode, the lines and forms you have drawn are translated into graphic elements that may be rotated, slanted, enhanced, and reshaped. That is, you have not only the drawing tools at your disposal, but the general editing tools, which can completely reshape your freeform drawings at the stroke of a mouse.

However you choose to use the freeform tools in Arts & Letters, keep in mind that the key word is "free." You can simply draw and edit your drawing as you might in a conventional drawing package, or you can set up a control system to realize your vision more quickly and completely.

Preparing to Draw

Before drawing a line, it is a good idea to review all of the key drawing preferences and screen setup options. These features allow you to create an electronic canvas exactly suited to your purpose. Since drawing is a precision activity, you may find yourself needlessly wrestling with problems that could easily be addressed by using automatic preferences.

The key decision to make is whether you want to have an open, fluid, freehand environment, which lets you draw curved and straight lines as you wish, or to have a constrained system for controlling the position and placement of lines. The Express freehand drawing features can do either, including precise regulation over the character and display of Bezier curves and the sensitivity of line joins. The following section will take you through the key drawing and screen setup options so that you can create the most effective environment for your work.

Drawing Preferences

Setting up a freeform drawing system with constraints begins with the **Preferences** selection on the **Draw** menu (Figure 6.6). Note that there is another **Preferences** screen available from the **View** menu, but it deals with the general operating preferences of the program. The **Drawing Preferences** screen, which appears when you select **Preferences** from the **Draw** menu, allows you to control specific aspects of freehand drawing features, including settings for the operation of joins, curve sketching, and bitmap auto-tracing features.

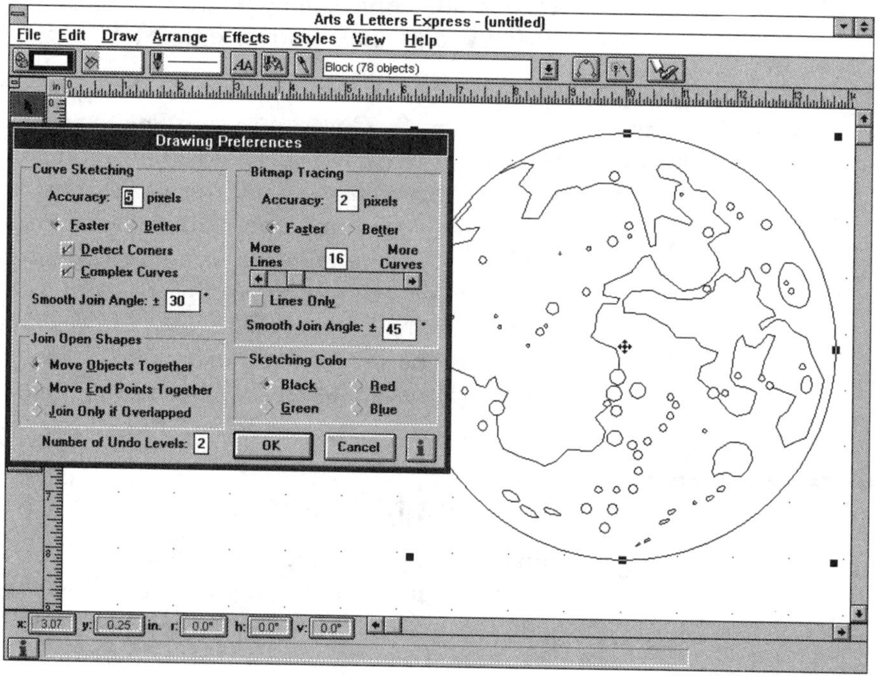

Figure 6.6
Drawing Preferences
This dialog box, opened from the Draw menu, sets the character of the electronic canvas for freeform drawing and editing. You can configure the screen to support rough, quick sketching to highly accurate and precise freehand drawing.

Curve Sketching Settings When setting curve controls, keep in mind that you have a choice between a system for precise freeform drawing or fast freehand drawing. The greater the level of precision required, the more work the software must perform, and the more time necessary for drawing operations. You may specify the accuracy of curve drawing in pixels, but remember, the tighter the accuracy, the more time the software will need to create the freeform curve and save it. You may also specify the level of drawing accuracy desired.

Corner Options The selection for **Detect Corners**, when activated, automatically recognizes and does not smooth out hard corners drawn with the curve-drawing cursor. A hard curve is any curved line at a sharper angle than that entered for **Smooth Join Angle**. For example, if **Smooth Join Angle** is set to 30 degrees, then a 35-degree angle drawn with the curve tool will be considered a corner, and not smoothed out.

Curve Quality and Display **Complex Curves** affects how curved lines are drawn on the screen. If it is turned on, Arts & Letters will draw the curved line in the appropriate Bezier segments that closely represent how it was originally drawn. If turned off, curves are drawn as a single Bezier segment no matter how complex the original sketch is. As with many features in Freeform mode, this feature involves an essential choice between speed and accuracy, and between rough sketching and precise, detailed drawing. This means that the software requires more time for complexity and precision than it does for simple, loose drawing. Only you know what your needs are for a particular project. But understand that you now have the power to set up the software specifically for your drawing needs.

Join Open Shapes The **Drawing Preferences** dialog box contains several settings that set values for **Join Open Shapes**. The **Join Open Shapes** command on the **Draw** menu is an editing function that controls how two, separate freeform elements can be joined together. To implement this feature, select the two open shapes at the same time using **Shift-Select**, and then select **Join Open Shapes**. This feature is a powerful and important one because, among other things, it allows you to turn open shapes into closed ones, which can accept Fill values. The default value for this is to **Move Elements Together** so that simple joins take place. But you also can set up joins so that you only **Move End Points Together**, or that lines **Join Only When Overlapped**.

End Points The best way to understand the value of these settings is through onscreen experimentation. The default value for joins works for most freeform drawing situations. However, if you are drawing a complex form that is, in effect, a continuous line, you may wish to create it by joining a series of lines and curves together at the end point. For this situation, **Move End Points Together** lets you do just that easily and automatically. If you are making a highly precise drawing and you don't want lines to join when they fall within the snap radius of one another, **Join Only If Overlapped** lets you limit joining to only those lines that overlap on the screen.

Setting Up Snap Features

Snap features allow you to automatically force elements into defined relationships or positions without a lot of trial and error or manual, micropositioning with your mouse. Three snap features in Arts & Letters allow you to define a "live" grid that (1) forces line and curve segments to snap to cross-points in the grid; (2) forces lines and curves to snap to particular points on other line and curve segments; and (3) forces lines to snap to an existing line or curve segment on the screen.

Snap Control Features

The operation of all Snap features are controlled through the **Snap Options** selection on the **Construct** cascade in the **Draw** menu (Figure 6.7). In this dialog box, you can set the snap radius, which is the live distance around a point or handle in which snap features operate. The larger the snap radius, the more loosely you can draw and make use of snap features. However, a large snap radius tends to mitigate the level of precision in your drawing. If you have many line and curve elements placed closely together, a large snap radius may cause lines and curves to snap to the wrong point, necessitating you to edit and rework your drawing.

New Element Radius

The **New Element Radius** is the snap radius around the end points of a line or curve element. If you want to continue a line or curve from the end point of the previous one, this sets the snap radius within which the connection will happen automatically. Again, the larger the snap radius, the more loosely you can draw, but you'll lose precision in tight situations.

Snap-To Controls

Snap to First or **Snap to Nearest** sets the default value for which point the line snaps to. **Snap to First** means that the line segment will snap to the *first point* in the document within the snap radius. **Snap to Nearest** means that it snaps to the *nearest point* within the snap radius.

The best way to understand the impact of technical settings such as these is through direct on-screen experimentation. Draw a few lines with the default settings enabled and watch what happens. Then make

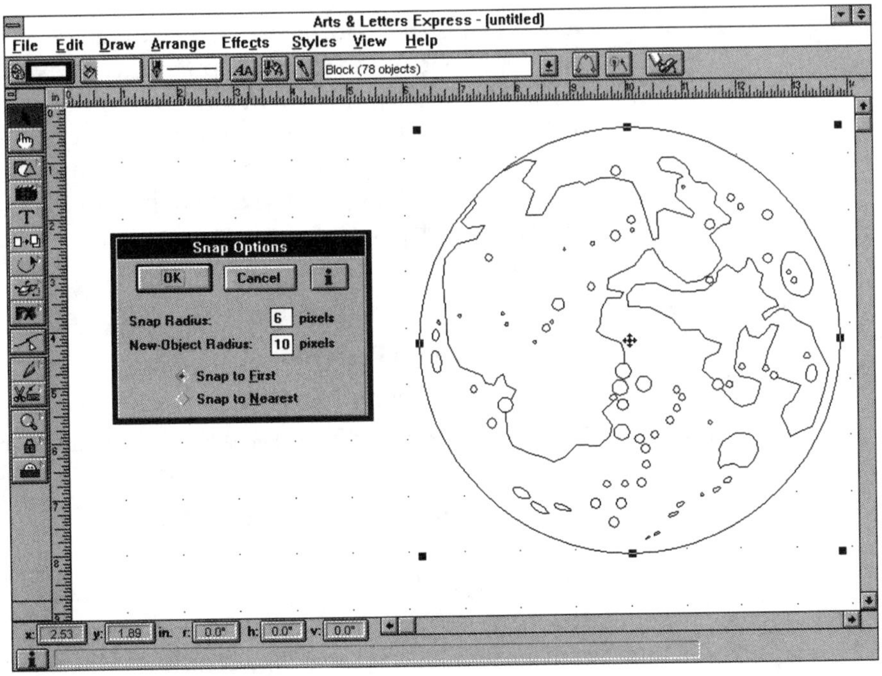

Figure 6.7
Snap Options
This option, available from the Snap cascade on the Draw menu, allows you to configure the operation of the snap features. Snap features make line forms automatically line up to the grid, or points in the page, or to line and curve segments.

a few dramatic changes to the snap and new element radius settings. The more dramatic the change you make, the easier it is to see and conceptualize the result. The bottom line is that you are setting a system of limits for snap features that, depending how these are set, can help you both in loose freehand sketches and in precise technical drawing applications.

Snap-To Grid

The snap-to grid is, in effect, an electronic grid that can be activated in the drawing screen as a matrix for all your drawing operations. Imagine drawing on a sheet of grid paper in which the line and curve elements were forced to snap to cross-points within that grid.

Like all snap-to features, the grid is fundamentally a tool for precision drawing, although it can have value in simple freehand sketching by providing automatic limits and anchor points for elements in your drawing. The grid is displayed using the main **Preferences** dialog box available on the **View** menu. Here you may define the grid increments—literally, the length of the sides of the boxes in the electronic grid. You may also elect to display the grid on the screen as a pattern of dots so that you can see where the live points are as you draw.

Single Active Snap Selection

When using the grid, keep in mind that Arts & Letters allows you to keep only one of the three snap features active at a time. The reason for this is, essentially, that, with all the programmed relationships for snap features operating at the same time, you run the risk that there will be an overlap and a conflict between snap imperatives and Arts & Letters. In effect, it's asking itself "Do I snap to the grid, or the closest point, or to the nearest line?" As you draw, you may need to change the snap feature currently in effect as your drawing needs changes.

Steps: Setting Up the Grid

Use this operation to set the desired density of the drawing grid.

1. Access **View | Preferences.**
2. Select units of measure.
3. Select the desired grid increment. The smaller the increment, the tighter and more precise the grid.
4. Verify that Show: Grid is selected.

Point Display

The final setup issue is to select the desired display of points on the screen. In Freeform mode, point handles on curves and lines are displayed for editing purposes. These handles represent the only place on a line segment that can be selected, moved, adjusted, or used as join locations with other line elements. You may drag directly at any point on a curve segment.

Freeform Points

Point display in Freeform mode is automatic. Using the Point Display option on the View menu and selecting the toggle for Freeform Points, Express will show all the editing points for a freeform graphic element *when it is selected* in Standard mode. (See Figure 6.8.) Note that points only display for the selected graphic element in both Freeform and Standard modes, but this can be somewhat frustrating if you're not used to freeform drawing features. Turning on Freeform Points and seeing them in Standard mode is an editing convenience, which is helpful when you are joining a number of line elements or doing detailed editing. For normal operations it can be distracting, and it is recommended that you leave this option off unless you really need it.

Control Points

Control points are used for curves only. When the Control Points are activated, also using the Point Display option on the View menu, control points will display on all selected handles on a curved line. Control points facilitate the turning and rotation of curved line segments by extending a dotted line bar out from the point on the line. By dragging either end of this bar, you can curve and turn the line segment in very detailed ways.

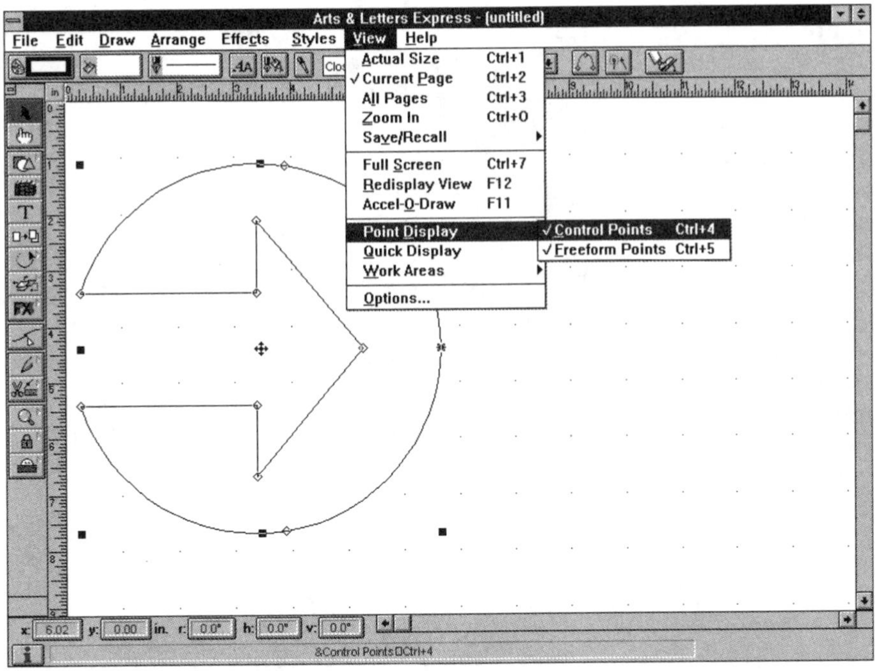

Figure 6.8
Point Display
When Freeform Points is activated using the option shown, freeform handles display in Standard mode. Note that the arrow graphic shown shows both standard selection handles around the perimeter and freeform handles within. Freeform handles can be selected only from within Freeform mode.

Freehand Drawing

Once you have set up the screen and the preferences for the level of drawing sensitivity and control you desire, operating the drawing features is simple. Express gives you two fundamental drawing tools: a line and a curve. This is a common approach in graphic software. Line elements cannot be accidentally curved in editing; they angle at defined points. So be careful about which element you select for your drawing. You do have the option to change a drawn element from a line to a curve or vice versa, if you later decide you want to change.

Drawing with Line and Curve

The Line and Curve drawing icons are the principal drawing tools. As soon as the Drawing icon (pencil, fifth from the bottom of the Toolbar) is selected, the flyout lets you select either **Curve** (the default) or straight **Line**. Each of these tools when selected instantly moves you to Freeform mode and changes the cursor to either a line or curve drawing configuration. (See Figure 6.9.)

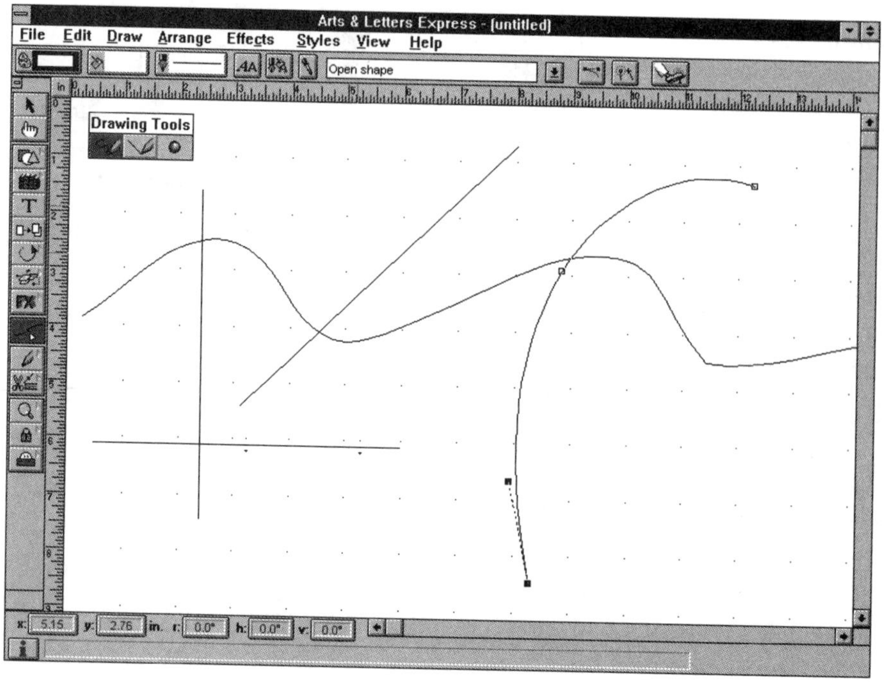

Figure 6.9 Drawing with Line and Curve
With the Drawing Tools flyout thumbtacked to the screen, you may select the tool you desire to create a variety of curve and line forms. The vertical and horizontal straight lines were easily aligned by holding down the Shift key as the line was drawn.

Moving between Modes

In Freeform mode, the Express screen will display the currently selected line/curve elements with graphic line handles displayed. Note that by selecting the right mouse button, the first item on the pop-up menu gives you the option to go back to Standard mode (e.g. cancel Freeform mode). In Standard mode, your drawing element is displayed just like a selected symbol or image, with eight sizing boxes around the full perimeter.

Steps: Draw a Straight Line

Use this operation to draw a single segment straight line. Note that holding down the Shift key as you draw will constrain the line to be exactly vertical or horizontal.

1. Select the **Line Drawing** feature from the Toolbox or the **Draw** menu, or press **F2**.
2. Depress and hold the left mouse button.
3. Drag the mouse to create the line segment.
4. Release the left mouse button.

Steps: Draw a Multi-Segment Straight Line

Use this operation to draw a multi-segment straight line with the Line Drawing tool.

1. Select the **Line Drawing** feature from the Toolbox or the **Draw** menu, or press **F2**.

2. Depress and hold the left mouse button.
3. Drag the mouse to create the line segment.
4. Release the left mouse button and do not move the mouse.
5. Depress the left mouse button.
6. Drag the mouse to create the next line segment.
7. Release the left mouse button.
8. Repeat drawing segments until the multi-segment line you wish is complete.

Steps: Draw a Curve

Use this operation to draw a curve using the Curve Drawing Tool.

1. Select the **Curve Drawing** feature from the Toolbox or the **Draw** menu, or press **F3**.
2. Depress and hold the left mouse button.
3. Drag the mouse to create the line segment.
4. Release the left mouse button.

Steps: Draw a Multi-Segment Curve

Use this operation to draw a multi-segment curve using the Curve drawing tool.

1. Select the **Curve Drawing** feature from the Toolbox or the **Draw** menu, or press **F3**.
2. Depress and hold the left mouse button.
3. Drag the mouse to create the curve segment.
4. Release the left mouse button and do not move the mouse.
5. Depress the left mouse button.
6. Drag the mouse to create the next curve segment.
7. Release the left mouse button.
8. Repeat drawing segments until the multi-segment line you wish is complete.

Steps: Change from Freeform to Standard Mode

Use this operation to display your freeform graphic in Standard mode.

1. Select line form in Freeform mode.
2. Press the right mouse button once.

Steps: Change from Standard to Freeform Mode

Use this operation to display your freeform graphic in Freeform mode.

1. Select line form in Standard mode.
2. Press the right mouse button once.

Drawing with Shapes

The shape selector contains a selection of basic geometric shapes. You can access these same shapes as symbols in the selector inside of the Symbols dialog box (Figure 6.10). Shapes are "smart art forms" that offer a higher degree of drawing precision than standard symbols. In standard mode, shapes size more accurately and precisely than symbols do. The easiest way to see the difference is the rounded rectangle form. When distorted in length or height, the symbol will distort the curved angles at the corners; the rounded rectangle shape will maintain the curve at the corner without distortion. Shapes must be converted to freeform, just like symbols, if you wish to edit them in Freeform mode.

Steps: Place Freeform Shapes

Use this operation to place freeform shapes in the working area.

1. Select the Shape icon on the Toolbar, or select **Draw | Shapes** and the desired shape.
2. Click the mouse in the working area, or depress and hold the left mouse button and drag the shape to the desired size.

Specifying Angle and Length

Precision drawing requires that you be able to define and replicate exact angular relationships between line elements. Arts & Letters supports this with a set of features that allow you to define the angular relationship between a pair of lines, to recall that relationship, and then apply it to any other pair of lines that you wish.

Saving Angles

You may store an angle in memory and then recall it in any other set of lines. Setting an angle from the screen simply involves using Block-Select or Shift-Select to select the two end points of a line segment or the dotted control point line segments. Once you activate the **Save Values | Angle** option on the **Construct** submenu (Figure 6.11), all you have to do is click on either end point, and the angle of the line segment will be saved into memory and available for recall.

Recall Angles

The recall process involves selecting two point handles of another line segment and recalling the stored angle. The line on which the point handle is selected will automatically move to the correct angular relationship.

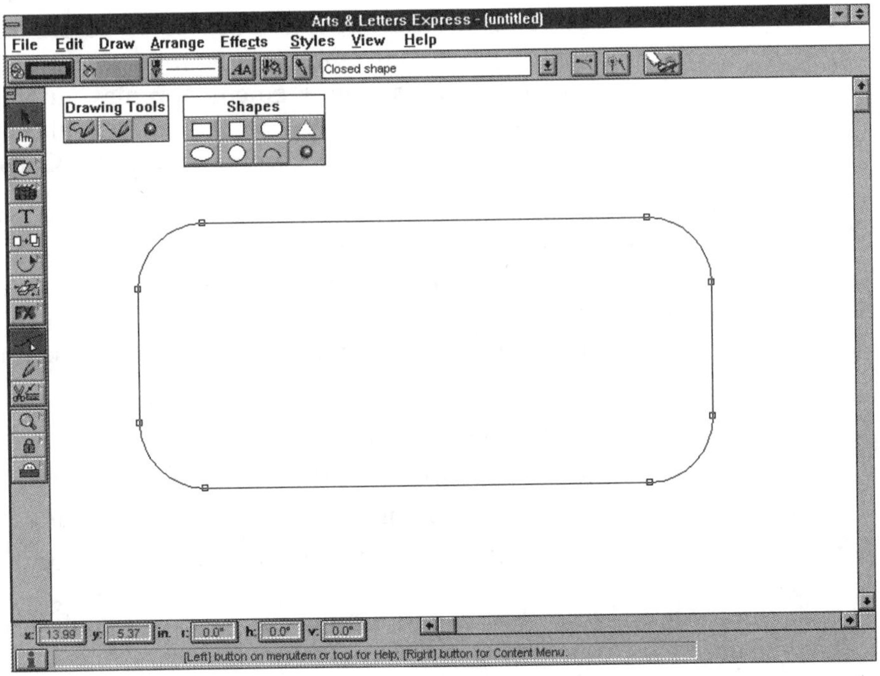

Figure 6.10 Drawing with Freeform Shapes The Shape flyout lets you place shapes into the working area. Shapes can be converted to freeform and edited in Freeform mode just like standard symbols.

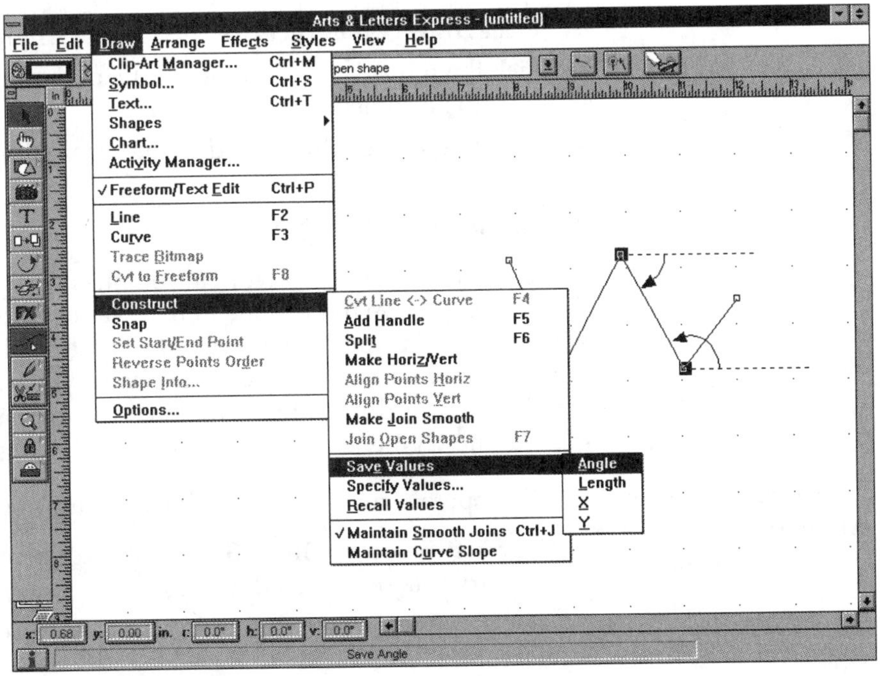

Figure 6.11 Specify Angle and Length Select two handles in the drawing and Express saves the exact angle of the line they define. That exact angle can be Recalled on any other selected line. These features support exacting line alignments and positioning for precision drawings.

Perpendicular Line A perpendicular line is at an exact, 90-degree angle to another line segment. Arts & Letters allows you to instantly control perpendicular lines in relation to any line segment. You may automatically adjust the position of all lines you wish to be perpendicular to that line by using the **Recall Perpendicular** command on the **Construct** submenu in the **Draw** menu.

Steps: Saving an Angle from a Line Segment Use this operation to save the angle of a desired line. Note that the angle is computed against a horizontal line (zero degrees) running to the right of the selected handle. You will get a different angle value, depending on which end of the segment you select to save.

1. Use **Shift-Select** or **Block Select** to select point handles at either end of a line segment in a drawing.
2. Select **Draw | Construct | Save Values | Angle**.
3. Click the mouse on the desired point handle.
4. The Angle will be set and stored in memory.

Steps: Recalling an Angle from a Line Segment Use this operation to recall the saved angle from one line segment to another.

1. Use **Shift-Select** or **Block Select** to select point handles at either end of the line you wish to carry the angle.
2. Select **Draw | Construct | Recall Values | Angle**.
3. Click the mouse on the point handle of the line where you wish the angle to be copied.
4. The angle will be duplicated in the second line.

Saving a Curved Angle

You can do the same thing for curved lines using the concept of curved-line slope. A curve has a slope (angle) value measured at each of its two end points. You may save this value and recall it to a corresponding point on another curved line. In this way, you can use Save/Recall Angle features to duplicate or match the curve slope on two or more curved line segments.

Steps: Saving an Angle from a Curve Segment Use this operation to save the angle of a curve segment.

1. Use **Shift-Select** or **Block Select** to select point handles at either end of a curve segment in a drawing.
2. Select **Draw | Construct | Save Values | Angle** or **Specify Values**.

3. Click the mouse on the point handle at the angle you wish to set.
4. The angle will be set and stored in memory.

Steps: Recalling Values | Angle from a Curve Segment

Use this operation to recall saved angle values from one curve segment to another.

1. Use **Shift-Select** or **Block Select** to select point handles at either end of the curve you wish to carry the angle.
2. Select **Draw | Construct | Recall Values | Angle**.
3. Click the mouse on the point handle of the curve where you wish the angle to be copied.
4. The angle is duplicated in the second curve.

Saving and Recalling Values for X and Y

Your drawings in Arts & Letters are stored using defined coordinates in the screen. Coordinates are created using the horizontal axis (X-value) and the vertical axis (Y-value). Any point in the screen will have both a horizontal position on the X-axis and a vertical position on the Y-axis. The two point positions, taken together, define the exact position of that point.

Saving Point Coordinates

Arts & Letters allows you to define a specific point on the screen and use that setting to force other points to that exact position. Let's say you have made a drawing of a house and you wish the vertical position of the roofline on the left to be exactly the same as the vertical position of the roofline on the right. You could engage in a great deal of measuring using screen rulers, or attempt to set up the drawing so these positions were at snap points in the grid. A much easier way to do this is to use the **Save** or **Recall Values | Y** feature which, in effect, copy the exact vertical position of the roofline on the right to the one on the left.

Point Coordinate Editing Examples

Once understood, this is one of the most powerful drawing and editing features you have available. It can eliminate a great deal of manual micropositioning and messing around with the mouse. Because all you have to do is click on the control point for the roofline on the right, and select the **Save Values | Y** option from the **Construct** option in the **Draw** menu (Figure 6.12). Now that exact vertical position has been stored in memory, so you can select the control point on the left of the house that you wish to move. Select **Recall Values | Y** and the point moves to the exact vertical position specified.

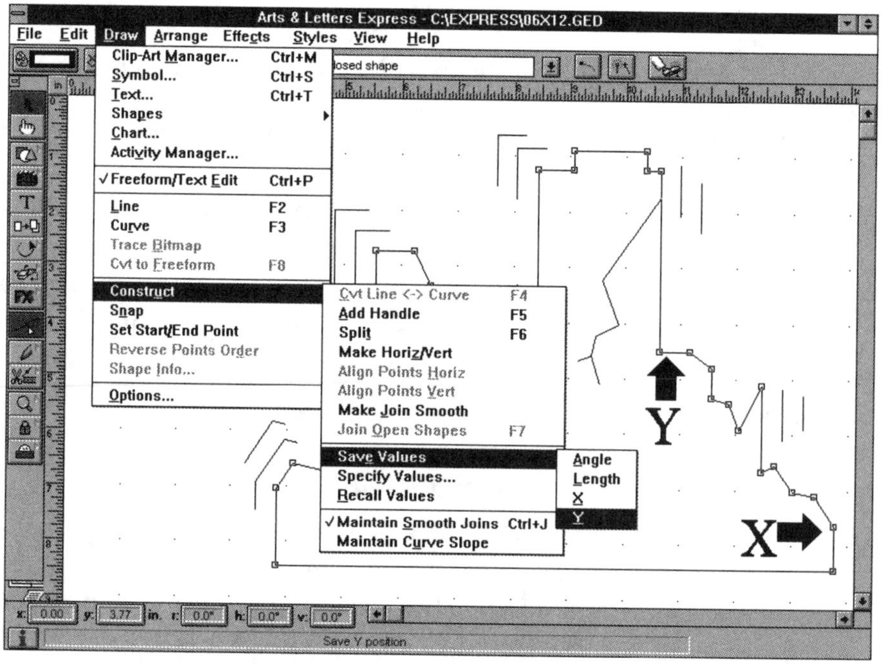

Figure 6.12
Save and Recall X/Y
Point alignment comes to the rescue of this quaking city. The Y (vertical) position indicated by the arrow can be saved and recalled on nearby points to raise the roof; the X (horizontal) position indicated by the arrow can be saved and recalled to fix the broken walls.

Using Point Coordinates

The Save or Recall Values | X and Y features are used to copy exact vertical and horizontal relationships. Used singly, they can instantly align individual parts of your freeform drawing to the desired position. Used together, they enable you to align two graphic elements at a specific point on the screen.

Steps: Saving Values | X or Y

Use this operation to save the X (horizontal) or Y (vertical) position values for a selected freeform point on the screen.

1. Access **Draw | Construct | Save Values | X** or **Save Values | Y**.
2. The **Save** cursor appears. Click the mouse on the point handle that represents the X (horizontal position) or Y (vertical position) value you wish to set.
3. The X or Y value is now set.

Steps: Recalling Values | X or Y

Use this operation to recall saved X or Y values from one point to another.

1. Access **Draw | Construct | Recall Values | X** or **Recall Values | Y**.
2. The Recall cursor appears. Click the mouse on the point handle you wish to reflect the Save Values | X value (horizontal position) or the Save Values | Y value (vertical position).

3. The point with any lines attached to it moves automatically to the defined Save Values | X or Save Values | Y value.

Saving and Recalling Length

The **Save Values | Length** feature in the **Construct** option in the **Draw** menu operates in exactly the same way the other Save | Recall functions do (Figure 6.13). You select end points of a line or curve segment and use **Save Values | Length** to store that length in memory. By selecting another line or curve segment and using **Recall Values | Length**, you can create a line of the same length as the original.

Steps: Saving Length

Use this operation to save the length of a line segment.

1. Use **Shift-Select** or **Block Select** to select the point handles at the end of a line segment.
2. Access **Draw | Construct | Save Values | Length**.
3. The length is stored and available.

Step: Recalling Length

Use this operation to recall the saved length of one line segment and applying it to another.

1. Use **Shift-Select** or **Block Select** to select the point handles at the ends of a line segment.
2. Select **Draw | Construct | Recall Values | Length**.
3. Click the mouse on the point handle at the end of the line you wish to adjust to reflect the selected length. The other point will remain stationary.

Using Specify Values Features

Save and Recall features may be operated directly from the screen, allowing you to capture angle values, line length, and the vertical and horizontal positions of line handles, and then copy those values to other line or curve segments in your drawing. The **Specify Values** features on the **Construct** option in the **Draw** menu allow you to precisely define those values numerically (Figure 6.14).

Configuring Line Elements with Specify Features

Specify features are used as editing functions to reconfigure angles, line length, and the X or Y position in something you have already drawn. The **Specify Values** dialog box has been designed to stay on the screen until you select **Done**. Other menus may be pulled down and software operations can continue while it is present. Using this dialog box, you

Figure 6.13
Saving Length
Express allows you to select any handle and save the exact line length between that and another connected handle. You can then select any other line segment and Recall that exact length.
Save | Recall features can save you hours of hand drawing.

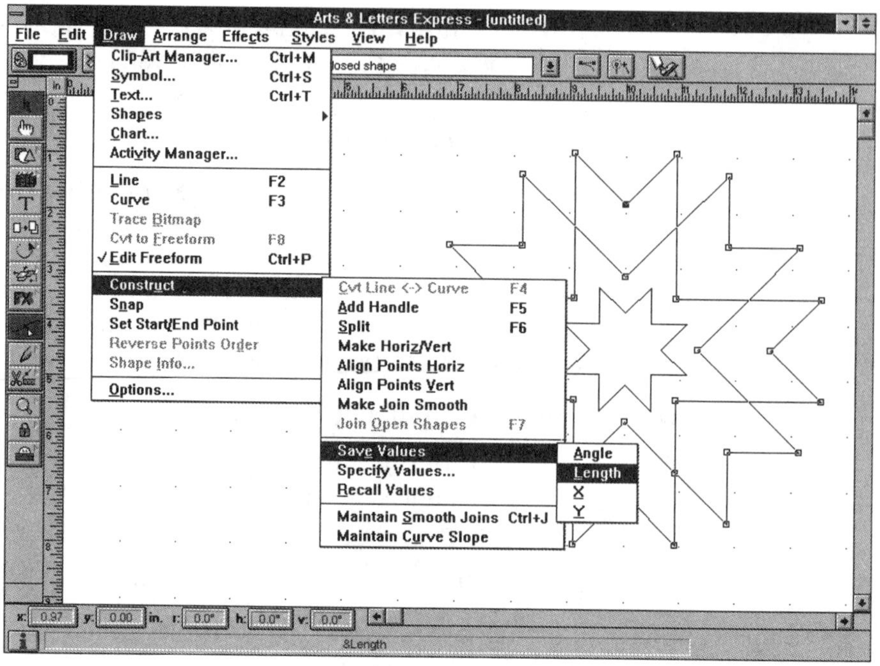

Figure 6.14
Specify Values
The Specify Values dialog box lets you select and define the specific horizontal position (X), vertical position (Y), line segment length, and line angle.

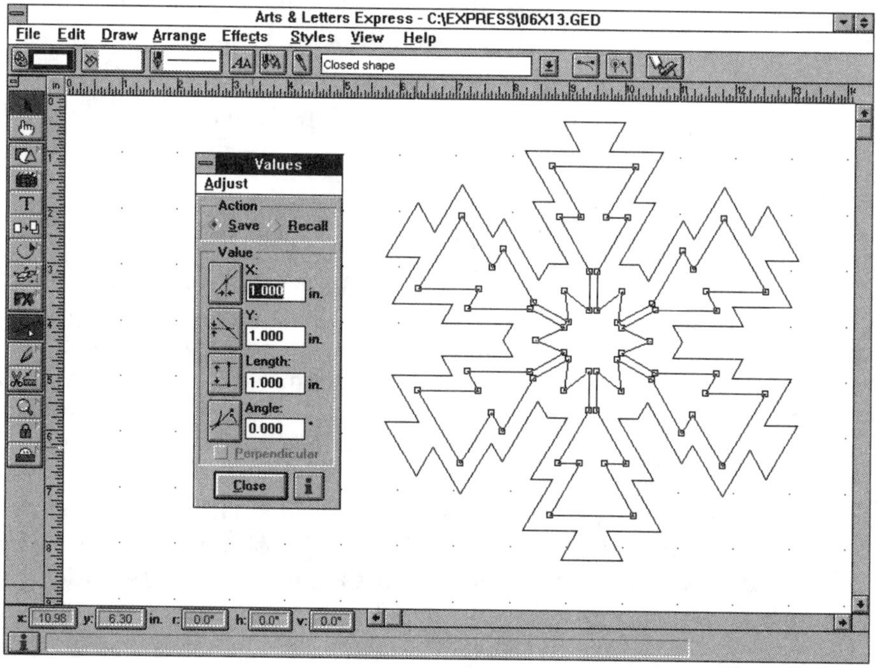

may select a series of line and curve elements in your drawing and apply specific values to them and see the results instantly reflected on your screen.

Steps: Using Specify for a Line Segment

Use this operation to save a defined value for a line segment. Once you have saved the desired value, you may select the end points of any line segment on the screen and use the standard Recall operation to translate those values to the segment.

1. Use **Shift-Select** or **Block Select** to select points at the end of a line segment.
2. Access **Draw | Construct | Specify Values**.
3 Verify **Save** is selected.
4. To Save the line length, enter the exact value in the **Length** box.
5. To Save the line angle, enter the exact value in the **Angle** box.

Steps: Using Specify for a Point

Use this operation to specify the X (horizontal) or Y (vertical) values for a selected point.

1. Select a point handle on a line you wish to edit.
2. Access **Draw | Construct | Specify Values**.
3. Enter the X value (horizontal position) or the Y value (vertical position).

Editing in Freeform Mode

Freeform mode provides you with a full range of detailed editing options. All of the angle and line controls described in the previous section can be used, and, in addition, you have the option to apply basic relationships that affect how your lines, joins, and other components are edited on the screen.

Selecting Freeform Elements

You may select freeform elements in Standard or Freeform modes. When selected in Standard mode (Figure 6.15), the freeform element will be displayed within a standard array of sizing boxes. Once selected in Standard mode, simply click the right mouse button to move to Freeform mode. This option is not available for any standard symbols, images, or text that have not been converted to freeform. To move from Freeform mode to Standard mode, click the right mouse button again.

Freeform mode is element driven, meaning that you may not select a series of freeform elements while remaining continuously in Freeform

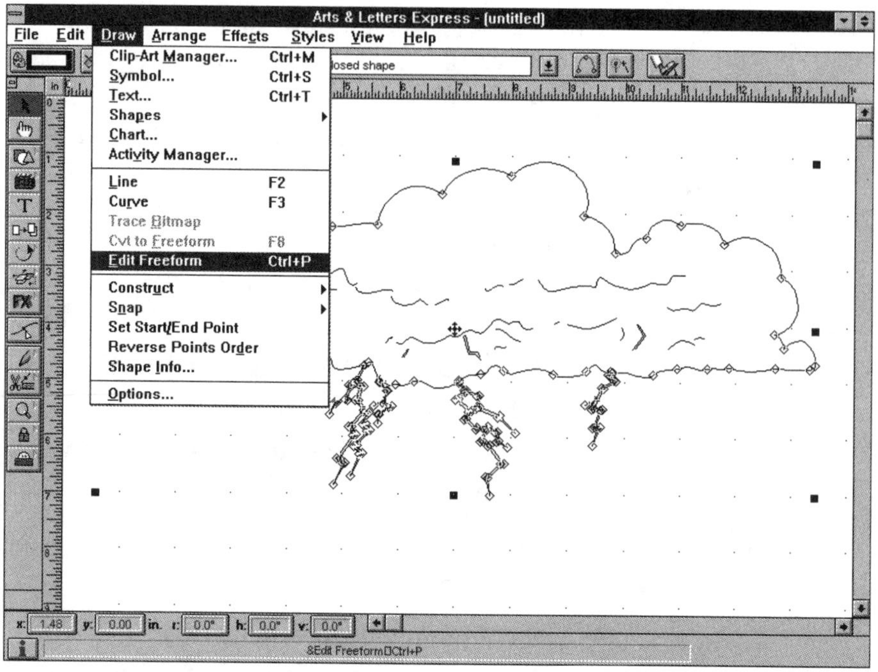

Figure 6.15
Selecting Freeform Elements
In the example shown, freeform points are active and the storm is selected in Standard mode. Note the sizing boxes around the edge. By activating the Freeform Text Edit option on the Draw menu, Freeform mode is enabled, and all the editing handles in the cloud will be selectable.

mode. Selection takes place from Standard mode. You then execute the Freeform mode option and its editing features are available.

Steps: Selecting a Freeform Element in Standard Mode

Use this operation to select a freeform graphic from Standard mode. Note that all Standard mode editing features, including moving, sizing, alignment, grouping, and Styles can be applied to the freeform element.

1. Verify you are in Standard mode.
2. Place the cursor over the element and click the left mouse button.

Steps: Enabling Freeform Mode for a Selected Element

Use this operation to activate Freeform mode for a freeform element selected in Standard mode.

1. Select the freeform element in Standard mode (follow the previous group of steps).
2. Click the right mouse button once.

Steps: Returning to Standard Mode

Use this operation to exit Freeform mode and change selection to Standard mode.

1. Verify that the element is selected in Freeform mode, and that editing handles are displayed.
2. Press the right mouse button once.

Editing an Individual Point

To reshape a drawing, the simplest technique is to pull on a single point handle, which forces the lines attached to that point to follow as you drag the point to a new location. This allows you to make small-scale and large-scale revisions in a freeform sketch or in a converted symbol.

Steps: Editing an Individual Point Use this operation to edit the position of an individual point in a freeform object, line, or curve segment.

1. Place the freeform cursor over a point handle to be moved.
2. Depress and hold the left mouse button as you drag the point to a new location on the screen.
3. All lines attached to the point will extend to the new location, reshaping all or a portion of the drawing.

Editing Multiple Points

To make a larger change in the drawing, you may edit more than one point at a time. You may individually click on point handles in the drawing, or use the **Block Select** icon to draw a rubber rectangle around a group of points you wish to move at the same time.

Steps: Editing Multiple Points Use this operation to edit the position of a group of selected points within a freeform object, line, or curve segment.

1. Use **Shift-Select** or **Block Select** to select a group of points to be moved. (See Figure 6.16.)
2. Depress and hold the left mouse button as you hold the cursor over one of the selected points and drag the mouse to the desired location.
3. All the selected points move in unison to the new position; lines attached to them will automatically reshape.

Maintaining Smooth Joins

In a drawing, you need to connect different line segments to complete the image. The common end points of lines and curves in a drawing are called *joins*, and joins may be of two different types. *Corner* joins define an angle, such as the corner of a square or rectangle, and are intended as sharp turning points in your drawing. *Smooth* joins are connections between different line segments intended to be fluid and elastic, so that two line or curve segments can function as one.

Join Options During editing, you may make edits that pull lines sharply out of their original configuration as the drawing is reshaped. You will need to be

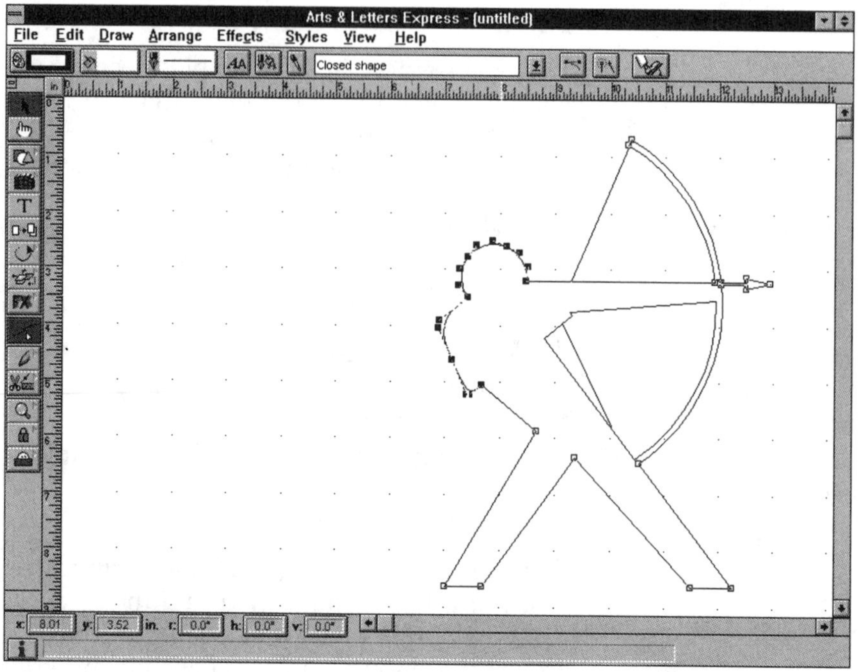

Figure 6.16
Selecting Multiple Points
The handles around the head of the archer, highlighted in black, are all selected and can be dragged or moved as a group. All other handles in the form are not selected and will not be affected when the selected points are moved.

able to control this action so that smooth joins are not pulled into many harsh, sharp angles. The **Maintain Smooth Joins** feature from the **Construct** option in the **Draw** menu has been designed to help you prevent joins from losing their integrity. **Make Joins Smooth** allows you to smooth individual joins.

Maintaining Curve Slope

Slope is the angle measurement for curve segments. There are two slope values for each curve, measured at the end points. When the **Maintain Curve Slope** option is activated, these angle/slope values are maintained as the curve is edited or resized. This feature allows you to make adjustments to the shape of the curve while maintaining the key angle relationships that define it.

Maintain Curve Slope is a toggle; when selected, it is displayed on the menu with a checkmark.

Closing Open Shapes for Symbols and Freeform Elements

An open shape is any graphic element where the end points do not meet (Figure 6.17). A box made up of a number of different line

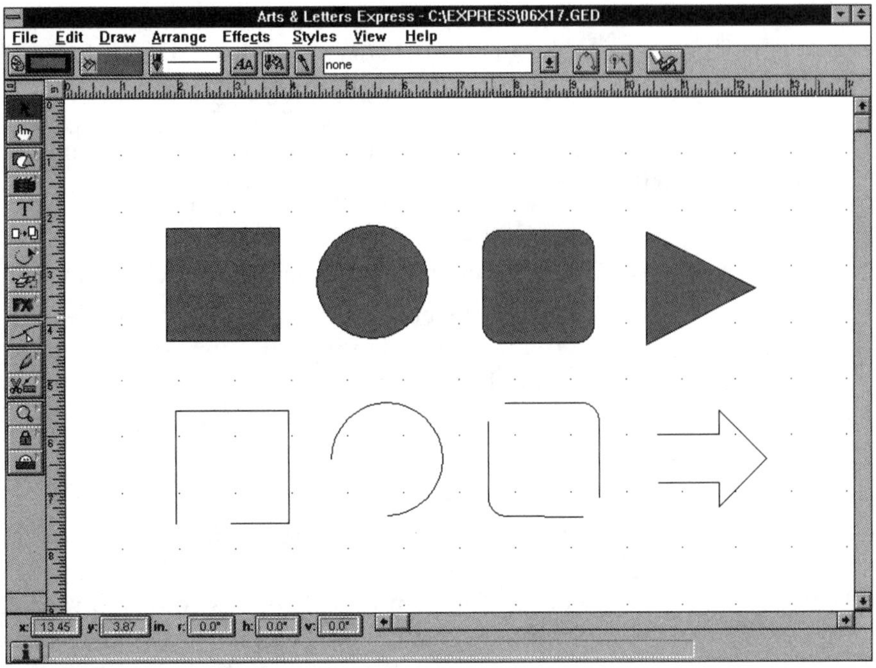

Figure 6.17
Open and Closed Shapes
The group of forms at the top are closed shapes, which can accept a fill color; those at the bottom are open shapes, which cannot accept a fill color. You can join open shapes into closed ones for more flexibility in applying styles and interior colors.

graphics can be a closed shape; a freeform curved line in which the end points meet is a closed shape. Straight lines and simple curved lines are open shapes. Only closed shapes can accept interior values, such as color, shading, and special patterns.

Working with Closed Shapes

During editing, you will need to close shapes to create fillable graphic elements, particularly when editing symbol forms that are converted to freeform. You also may wish to create a set of closed shapes for a customized version of the drawing.

Closing Shapes

It is critical for this type of editing that you know how to close open shapes or combine several open shapes into one closed shape. The open or closed shape status of a selected element is displayed at all times in the Style Bar. The easiest way to close a shape is to either extend the line segment or draw additional lines or curves so that the start and end points meet.

Steps: Closing Open Shapes with Line

Use this operation to connect the end points of an open shape using a line segment.

1. Select **Draw | Construct | Snap to | Points**.
2. In Freeform mode, click on the **Line** icon.

3. Draw one or more additional line segments to connect the end point of the line or curve with its start point.
4. Verify that the Style Bar displays Closed Shape.

Steps: Closing Open Shapes with Curve

Use this operation to connect the end points of an open shape using a curve segment.

1. Select **Draw | Construct | Snap to | Points**.
2. In Freeform mode, click on the **Curve** icon.
3. Place the cursor on the end point of the open shape you wish to close. Draw an additional curved segment to connect with the start point.
4. Verify that the Style Bar displays Closed Shape.

Joining Open Shapes

There is another way you can join open shapes that allows you to select multiple elements in standard editing mode and force them to lock together. The **Join Open Shapes** control on the **Construct** cascade of the **Draw** menu allows you to select two separate lines and automatically connect them at their nearest ending points. Rather than redrawing, this is an assembly feature that is particularly useful when working with converted symbols.

Steps: Using Join Open Shapes

Use this operation to connect two open line or curve segments.

1. Click on the **Freeform Editing** icon to leave Freeform mode.
2. Use **Shift-Select** or **Block Select** to select both line elements to be combined.
3. Verify that the number of elements selected in the Style Bar is 2.
4. Select **Draw | Join Open Shapes**.
5. The individual elements will be connected at their end points.

Controlling Vertical and Horizontal Position

Let's say you drew a freeform line that isn't quite horizontal or vertical and you need it to stand straight up or to lie flat. You could redraw the line, of course, or you could go into Freeform editing and pull on the point handles of the respective line with the Snap Grid enabled to bring it into position.

Instant Horizontal and Vertical Lines

Make Horiz/Vert (Figure 6.18) automatically makes lines horizontal or vertical with the click of a mouse. All you have to do is select a segment, activate the **Make Horiz/Vert** feature, and click on the point

Figure 6.18
Make Horiz/Vert
The selected line, shown with handles at either end, will be made vertical as soon as the Make Horiz/Vert feature is activated. This is a quick-alignment feature for freeform lines that helps you get straight verticals or horizontals in seconds.

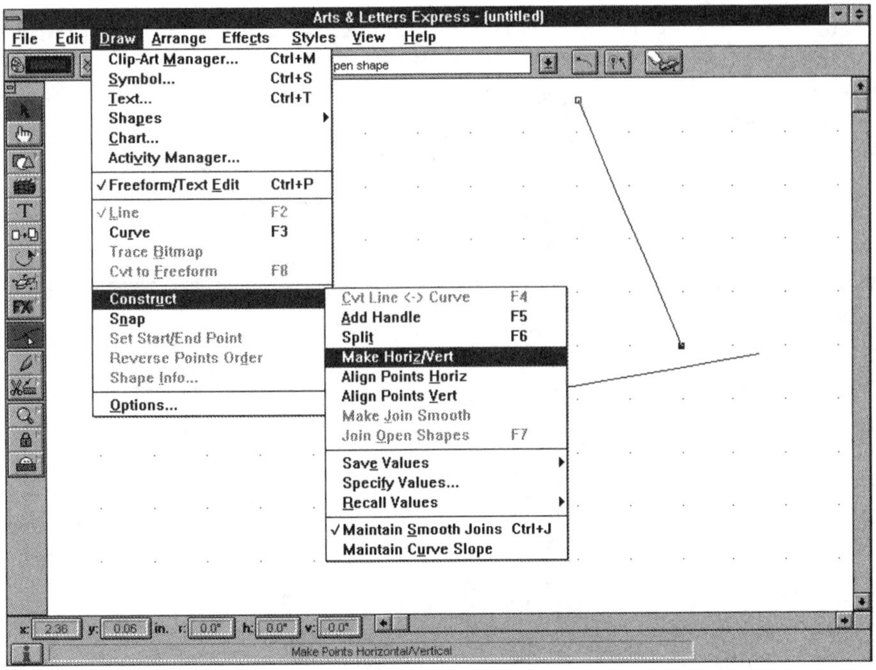

handle you wish to move to make the required adjustment. The other point will remain stable as the selected point snaps the line to a vertical position or horizontal position.

The orientation of the line after using the **Make Horiz/Vert** tool is determined by the original orientation of the line. If a line is more vertical, it will be made vertical. If it is more horizontal, it will be made horizontal.

Steps: Using Make Horiz/Vert

Use this operation to make a line or curve segment horizontal or vertical.

1. In Freeform Editing mode, select **Draw | Construct | Make Horiz/Vert**.
2. Select the point handle that must move to make the adjustment.
3. The line automatically adjusts to horizontal or vertical position.

Changing Lines to Curves and Vice Versa

During the course of editing, you may find the need to change a defined line so that it can be edited as a curve or vice versa. You can do this by selecting both end points of the line or curve segment and using **Cvt Line to/from Curve** from the **Construct** cascade on the **Draw** menu (Figure 6.19).

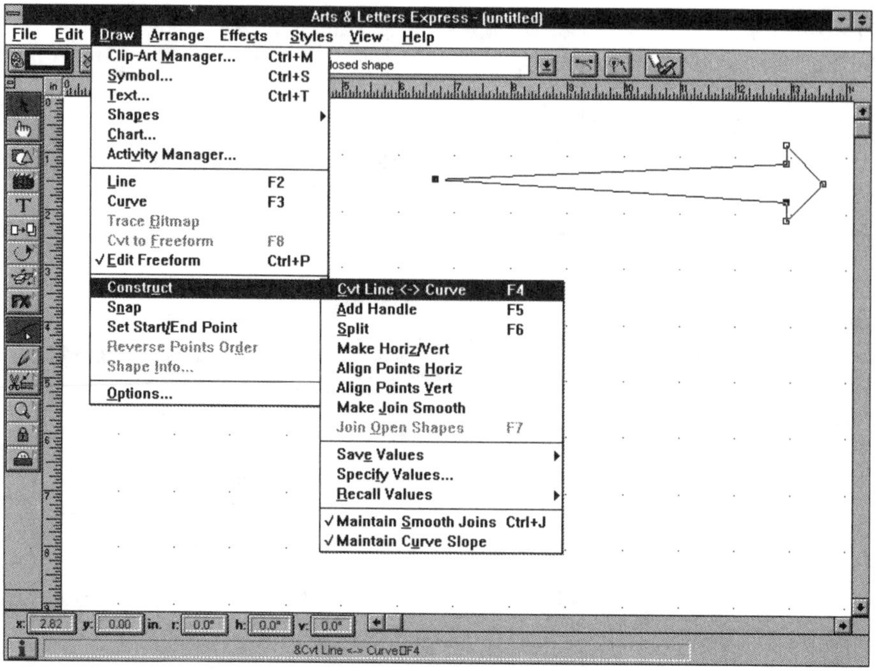

Figure 6.19
Changing Lines to Curves
In the example shown, the long angled line from the left-most point to the back of the arrowhead is selected. When converted to a curve using the option shown, it can be edited into a wavy line.

This is a deceptively simple feature, yet it has enormous implications when you are drawing. The ability to change lines to curves, so that they can be more fluidly edited, and to lock curves into solid straight lines, allows you a great deal of power to reshape a drawing, particularly a converted symbol, without drawing a line.

Steps: Changing Lines to Curves and Vice Versa

Use this operation to convert a curve to a line or a line to a curve segment.

1. Use **Shift-Select** or **Block Select** to select both end points of a line or curve segment.
2. Select **Draw | Cvt Line to/from Curve**.
3. The line has been transformed to a curve or vice versa.
4. Optional: In operations in which a line has been changed to a curve, use the **Add Handle** icon to add new handles within the curved line to reshape it more easily.

Adding Handles for Editing Flexibility

Handles are the points along lines and curves for controlling them. On the ends, they allow for connection and selection for feature operations. Within the line or curve, they serve as instant join points, or places you can pull on to reshape the line or curve instantly. Adding handles gives you the ability to add more detail or definition to a line or curve form.

Add Editing Points

The **Add Handle** feature allows you to create editing flexibility instantly by adding handles at any point you wish along the line segment. You may access the feature from the Toolbox, the Draw menu, or by hitting the **F5** key. Once enabled, the **Add Handle** cursor appears (the same graphic that appears in the Toolbox), and you can click on any point on the line to create a new handle (Figure 6.20).

Steps: Adding Handles

Use this operation to add editing handles to any line or curve segment.

1. Click on the **Construction** flyout; the **Add Handle** icon is the default.
2. Double-click the left mouse button at the position on the line where you wish the new handle to appear.
3. You may pull on the new handle to reshape the line or curve.
4. When handles are added to straight lines, they can automatically function as corner joins, if you wish. Just pull on the new handle and the straight line becomes a corner join instantly.

Splitting Lines and Curves

A companion feature to adding handles is the Split line feature, available from the **Construct** cascade on the **Draw** menu. You may split a line in two in the same way that you add a point, by clicking on a

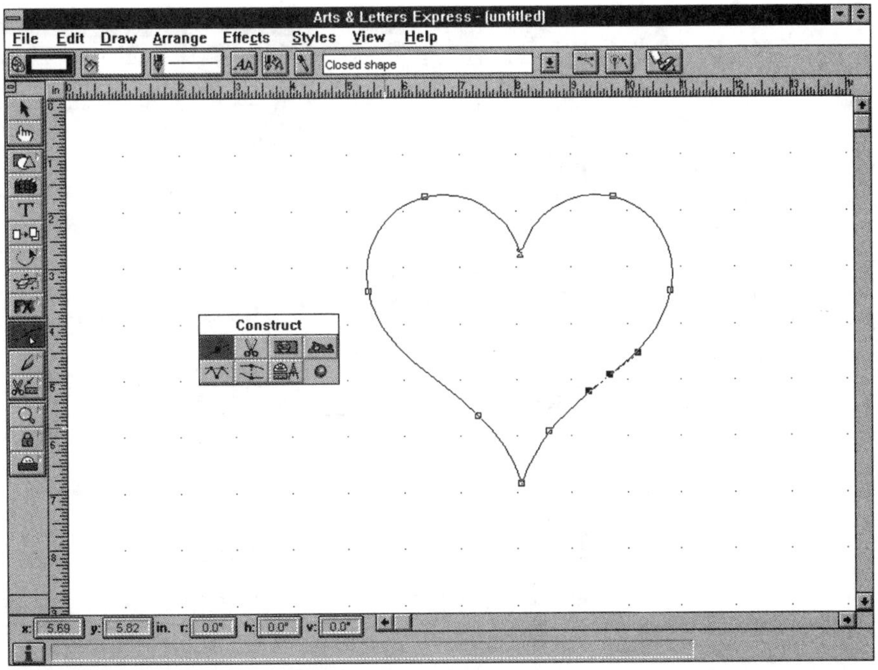

Figure 6.20 Adding Handles/Splitting Lines
These features allow you to either add a handle, for greater editing flexibility, or to cut the line in two. In both cases, select the appropriate icon (Add Handle is shown selected, Split is the Scissors next to it) and click where you want to add the handle or split the line.

position on the line. Once the line is split, you will have two new end points on either side of the split. You may now move either of the end points to the place desired.

Steps: Splitting a Line

Use this operation to break a straight or curved line segment into two sections.

1. Click on the **Construction** flyout; slide to **Split** icon (scissors).
2. Note the cursor changes to the Split icon.
3. Click the cursor at the point where you wish to split the line.
4. Select the desired segment of the split line.
5. Click right mouse button to edit the line in Freeform mode.

Point/Line Alignment

New in Version 5 is a feature that allows you to align selected points in freeform drawing to a set horizontal or vertical position (Figure 6.21). This is an automated group feature that, in certain cases, you can use instead of an individual Save or Recall X, Y position. The features operate on a simple syntax: You select all the points in the desired freeform shape you wish to align and then activate the feature. A vertical or horizontal bar appears on the screen and you drag the bar into place and

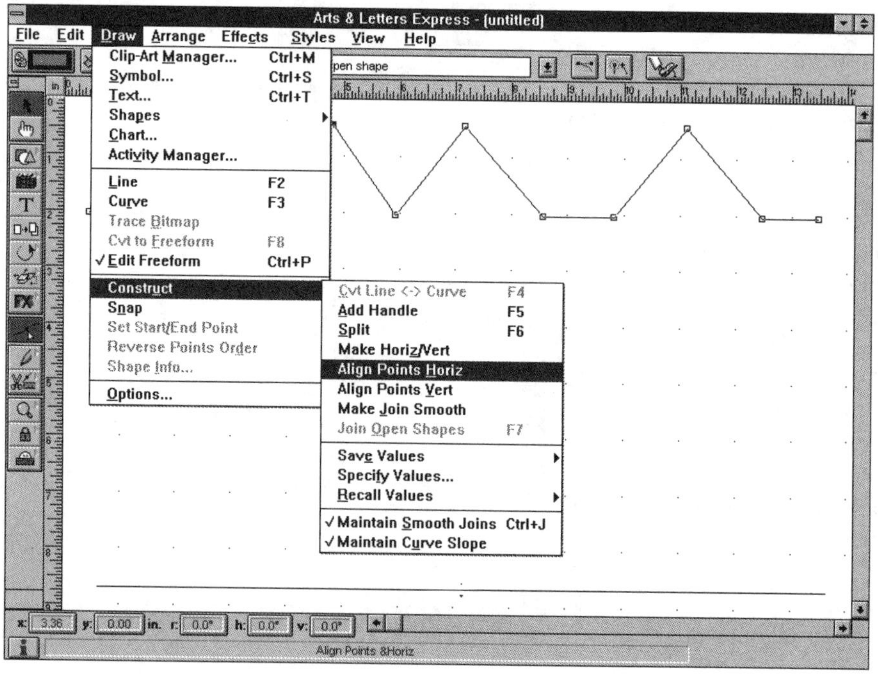

Figure 6.21
Point/Line Alignment
Selected points on a line can be auto-aligned to a vertical or horizontal position. When the feature is activated, a graphic bar allows you to drag a line to the desired horizontal or vertical position.

click the mouse to place it. All selected points and line segments attached to those points will instantly align.

Steps: Aligning Points to a Vertical or Horizontal Position

Use this operation to align selected points to a vertical or horizontal position.

1. Select individual handles to be aligned.
2. Select **Draw | Construct | Align Points Vert**, or **Draw | Construct | Align Points Horiz**.
3. Drag the alignment guide to the desired vertical or horizontal position.
4. Click the left mouse button.
5. Verify that points are aligned.

Freeform Editing Text, Symbols, and Images

Any number-indexed, wireframe symbol in Express can be exploded into Freeform by simply selecting it and pressing the **F8** key. Once this Convert to Freeform option is complete, you have complete access to all the line elements that make up the symbol. For simple symbol icons, this allows you to change its shape or to create variations of it. Since images in the Clip-Art Manager are largely collections of symbol wireframes and symbol accents, you will have to break them apart so you can get at the symbols that make them up. Conversion to freeform always takes place from the numbered symbol level.

Editing Shapes

Freeform editing allows you to directly edit the shapes of symbols by adjusting the position of one or more line handles (Figure 6.22). This allows you to create subtle or dramatic variations of the existing 10,000 forms in the symbol graphic database. Using graphic handles and line/curve editing displays, helps even an inexperienced artist to adjust graphic lines and point positions in the exploded symbol and create a highly professional result. Starting with a pre-existing drawing and making edits is much easier than attempting to draw something new yourself.

Shape editing is particularly effective for the simple icons, pictorials, and other line drawings that are part of the graphic database. You can create your own variations on any of the icons and once your shape revisions are made, you can then save them in a GED file; or you can group them as a single graphic element and save them individually to a YAL Image collection in the Clip-Art Manager. From the Clip-Art Manager, you can use your edited versions like any image. Just drop it in anywhere you need it.

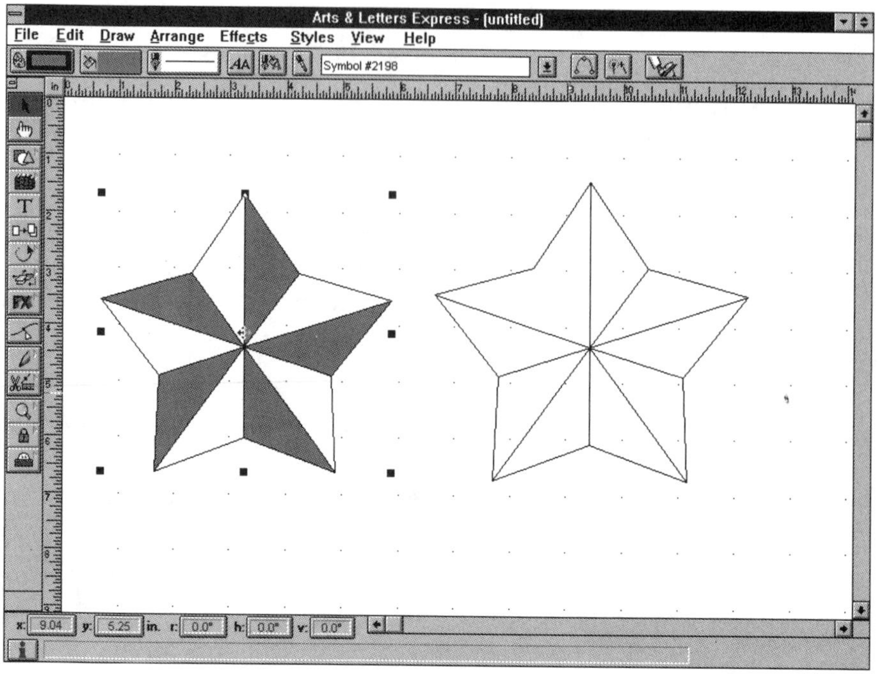

Figure 6.22
Symbol Editing
You can use Freeform mode features to make internal edits to standard symbols, such as the one on the left, and add or remove line elements, as in the example on the right.

Deleting Lines and Segments

Freeform features allow you to delete line segments or complete line components from exploded symbol forms. For simple symbols, this allows you to use one of the icons, printer ornaments, or other forms as a graphic background, and build what you want by starting from a whole and editing it down to what you want. You can also create phase effects by exploding a symbol and progressively saving versions with more line elements removed. This series of symbols can then be used to create an evolutionary effect: showing the symbol stripped and evolving to a greater degree of complexity in your final work.

Adding Lines and Segments

You may also add handles and line segments to symbol-based artwork. This is more touchy in that you have to know beforehand what you're trying to accomplish artistically. But if the edits are simple enhancements, anyone can do it. Remember that Freeform mode contains a full set of features that allow you to exactly specify the length and angle of line segments and to control curve angles as well, just like the Transform dialog box does for standard graphic elements. If you don't trust your hand, you can access the computer controls; they will increase your precision by letting you make simple feature selections.

Exchanging Lines and Curves

When editing exploded symbols, you can dramatically alter their shape by using the Convert Line to Curve feature. This is most commonly used to translate straight line elements into curved lines and then changing the shape or appearance of a symbol by altering the curve. You also can go the other way and flatten out curved elements in a symbol by forcing them into a straight line configuration. This is a simple editing technique, but a powerful one.

Combining Art Forms Once you're down to the basic line elements and joins, you can combine two symbols at the line level to create a unique variation based on two or more symbols. This can be used, for example, to incorporate a logo or other graphic text directly into the line construction of a symbol, such as placing your company label on one of the graphic images of a truck or building. You can save the edited freeform combination as a graphic group in a YAL format file which will then be available through the Clip-Art Manager.

Editing Text Freeform editing of text works the same way as symbol art forms. However, conversion is a one way street: once exploded, the graphics cannot be recognized by the Enter/Edit Text dialog box or by the Type Attributes features. What you will have is a bunch of graphic forms that can be edited any way you desire. Before converting text to Freeform mode, it is a good idea to duplicate a copy of it as a backup, so you retain a duplicate of the text in Standard mode. This gives you the ability to experiment freely in Freeform mode without losing the original text string and having to re-create it from scratch. When text is converted to freeform, Express breaks down all the components in the text string to freeform objects but maintains them in grouped format. So, right after the Convert to Freeform operation, you will have a graphic group for the entire word or text string. You can then ungroup that text string to access individual letters. Note that letters such as "O" and "B" that are composed of several graphic forms will be grouped individually. You have to ungroup the individual letters if you wish to get down to the editable freeform graphics underneath.

You can use the graphic composition of these characters to your advantage, however. By editing the position, size, or placement of the graphic components within the letter form; you also can create many variations on different letters by simply mouse dragging (Figure 6.23).

Security Duplicates Working with symbol and line elements in freeform is a detailed business. Depending on the effect you are trying to achieve, you may find yourself wasting time with a lot of trial and error. One effective technique is to progressively save iterations of your edited symbols as you make changes. The Duplicate function allows you to drag and drop a duplicate of any selected line form or group at any time. As you make

Figure 6.23 Editing Text Characters Exploding text characters into freeform opens the components that make up the characters. Express automatically groups these letters, so you have to break apart the letter groups to edit the base freeform graphics as shown.

changes, periodically group the edited symbol so that all line forms are included and drag a duplicate to one of the empty pages in the screen. This provides you with a master, so that if you mess up one, you'll have backup readily at hand.

Undo Levels

You may set up to nine Undo levels within freeform drawing only. The Undo levels relate to edits made within an individual freeform object. For example, if you are editing a symbol outline drawing that has been converted to freeform, you may make a variety of adjustments to positions of line handles, add and delete handles, and so forth. The Undo levels will work within that specific freeform object only. If you are moving between different objects, the multiple Undo levels will not work. To set the desired number of Undo levels, enter the desired value in the Number Of Undo Levels option at the bottom of the Drawing Options dialog box, available from the Options selection on the Draw menu.

Freehand Drawing and Symbol Editing

Features for symbol editing in Freeform mode are the same as those described earlier in this chapter for Freehand Drawing. Once exploded, you may use any and all of these features and operations to edit the symbol.

Working with Symbols in Freeform

Freeform conversion of symbols is a one way street. Once exploded into their line components, they may be grouped in Standard mode, but never restated as number-indexed symbols in the graphic database. This prevents you from using the Symbol Replace command with them.

The following is a quick toolkit of operations you should use when taking symbols into Freeform mode.

Steps: Quick Convert Symbol to Freeform

Use this operation to convert a selected symbol to freeform using the keyboard.

1. Select the symbol in the working area.
2. Press **F8**.

Steps: Convert Symbol to Freeform from the Menu

Use this operation to convert a symbol to freeform from the Draw menu (Figure 6.24).

1. Select the symbol in the working area.
2. Select **Draw | Cvt to Freeform**.

Steps: Save Edited Symbol in YAL File

Use this operation to save your edited symbol in a YAL file in the Clip-Art Manager. This is the fastest way to make your edited symbols available for use in any document, so that you can load them just like any of

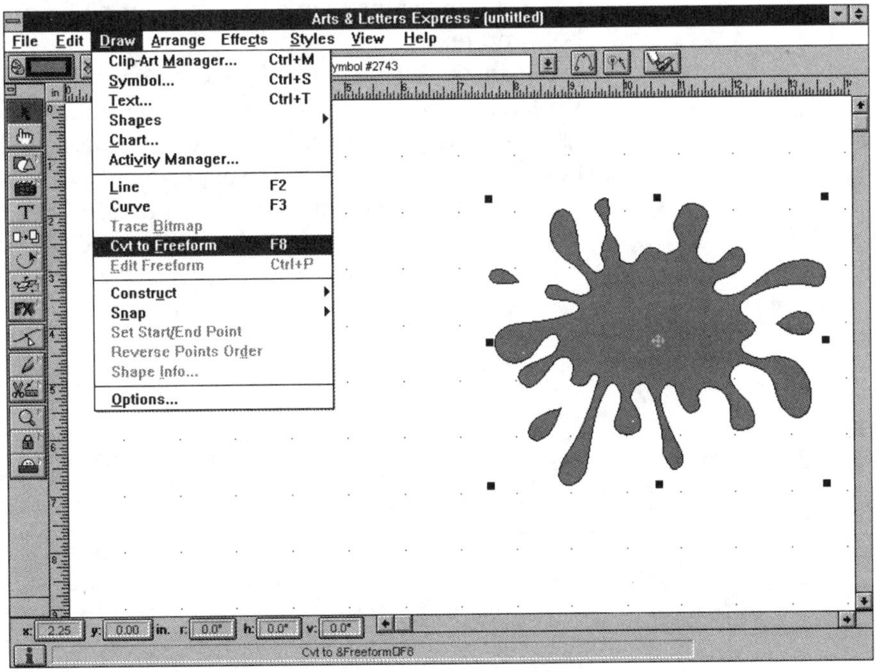

Figure 6.24
Convert to Freeform
Select the symbol and select the feature, and the symbol explodes into freeform shapes. You cannot, however, reverse the process.

the included illustrations. See Chapter 3 for instructions on creating your own custom YAL file collection.

1. From Freeform mode, press the right mouse button to return to Standard mode.
2. Select all line/curve components in the edited symbol drawing.
3. Select **Arrange | Group**.
4. Access **Draw | Clip-Art**.
5. Select your custom collection from the Collection list.
6. Type in the desired element name in the Image Name line.
7. Select **Save to Collection**.

Precision Drawing Features

The family of precision drawing features in the Freeform mode lets you develop many sophisticated effects by changing the actual composition of drawings, images, and text, or by creating your own freehand drawings. The level of precision and control in Freeform mode is one of the fundamental advantages of computerized drawing. Regardless of whether you are a professional or inexperienced artist, you can get spectacular results using Freeform mode features to edit the base symbols and text.

For those with technical tasks at hand, or who simply want the convenience of automatic controls in the screen, these features are easy to use and indispensable. You may find them a little intimidating at first, but if you take some time to experiment with them, you'll be amazed at how easy they make it to draw freehand with great precision, as well as to edit symbols, configure text, and create charts.

PART TWO

Design Tips and Techniques

C H A P T E R 7

Designing with Styles

Creating Design Effects

One of the most unique aspects of Arts & Letters Express's graphic database is its systematic approach. The thousands of puzzle pieces that are available as symbol wireframes and grouped into images allow you to make custom enhancements by simply breaking images apart and applying styles to the individual or multiple components.

The graphic database and the symbol, image, text, chart, and free-form operations allow you to put art forms into the working area, but styles add an entirely new level to your element's look, presentation, and the amount of detail you can include. In fact, styles are the foundation of design in Arts & Letters Express.

Styles are the next design layer above the graphic database. The integrated style system allows you to create and save custom sets of style attributes (Color, Fill, Line, Type) that can be applied to any art object from the Style Palettes in the Style Bar, are grouped and applied from the Style Bundles Palette.

This chapter is a guided tour of the options and capabilities of the Styles menu (Figure 7.1). It provides illustrated techniques for making practical use of all its features. Techniques here also will make use of the positioning features on the Arrange menu, as well as other features. Special graphics effects are covered in Chapter 8, and a gallery of ideas and projects is presented in Chapter 9.

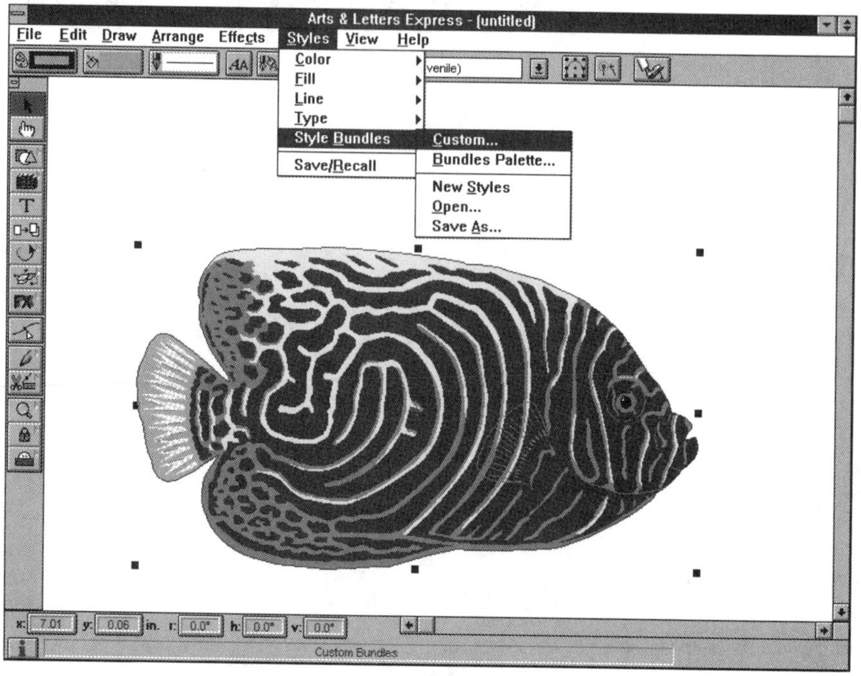

Figure 7.1
Styles
The completely redesigned Styles menu (formerly Attributes) in Express contains features that allow you to color and customize symbols and images. You may select features conveniently arrayed on the cascade submenus here, or access and apply named styles from the palettes, which are accessed directly from the Style Bar directly beneath the menu line.

Fast Track Orientation

This chapter is based on a number of key operating concepts. Understanding these concepts in advance will help you apply these operations more quickly and effectively.

Key Concepts

Symbol and Variations Each symbol in Arts & Letters may be configured into hundreds of variations without any freeform drawing or editing necessary. The basic form of the symbol is shown in the *Clip Art Handbook*. Using standard editing tools including Duplicate, Slant, and Rotate, allows you to alter the shape, position, and visual character of the symbol.

Images and Variations Images in the Clip-Art Manager are groups of symbols and, in some cases, freeform elements. When placed in the working area, the image can be broken apart and each of its components can be easily edited with styles. Using the Assemble option in the Align dialog box, you can reassemble the pieces by simply selecting and aligning them.

Symbols as Line Drawings When a symbol's fill color is set to White or None, each symbol appears as a line drawing. One easy way to vary the appearance of a symbol is to change its line weight and pattern. By experimenting with dashed line patterns for textured outlines, thicker line weights, and different corner joins, you can create an amazing number of visual effects from one basic symbol.

Symbols as Filled Shapes By eliminating the line that defines a symbol, a symbol may be expressed as a filled color or gray area. Without the line, the symbol generally looks softer, and does not exhibit the crispness associated with the line drawing. Reduced to a filled area, a symbol can have an entirely different character and can be used further to create interesting visual effects.

Selection within Groups Version 5 Group features allow you to select individual symbols and objects within a group and apply enhancements to them without ungrouping. (See Figure 7.2.)

Slant Slanting is a controlled distortion of the symbol form. As the symbol is slanted, it pivots around a visual axis. This has the effect of flattening and expanding the shape as you move the mouse. Slanting can be used in a variety of ways to suggest 3-D effects and create shadows, and, in combination with blends, to create sophisticated, progressive distortion effects.

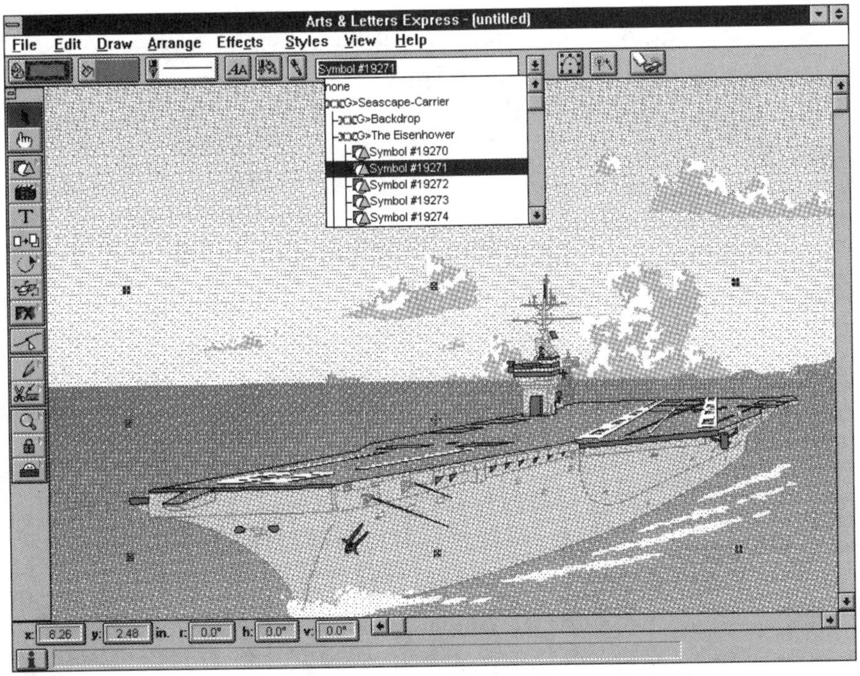

Figure 7.2 Selecting within Groups
Express allows you to select and enhance symbols without breaking up groups. The Object Viewer drop-down box displays the components in the group that you can select. Selection handles around the aircraft carrier are cross hatched—a new group-selection feature.

Rotation Rotation is a positioning device that allows you to tilt and turn symbols to a desired angle. Standard rotation takes place around a pivot axis in the center of the drawing. The pivot axis may be moved to any position in the document to create interesting rotation effects, particularly when there are multiple copies of the same symbol.

Stacked Symbols In their standard form, symbols are line drawings that may be manipulated, shaded, and enhanced. By stacking two or more copies of the same symbol, slightly offset in position, individual symbol forms can be given much greater depth and solidity. Stacked symbols can be used to create drop shadows, figure shadows, and background elements that make the symbol form seem much more finished.

Select and Multi-Select Styles are applied to selected objects only. Many graphics packages require you to select the object before accessing the style option (such as line, color, or fill). The new pushpin feature, present in all style dialog boxes and flyouts, allows you to lock the style features to the screen and interactively select the art form and immediately apply the style. If you wish to apply a style value to multiple objects, you may do this in a single operation. Use Block-Select or Shift-Select (see Chapter 3) to select a group, and the style values you choose will automatically be applied to all.

Define Named Styles You may select options within individual style dialog boxes (e.g., Line, Fill, Color) each time you apply styles (Figure 7.3). Express gives you the option to save the configuration of options under a Style Name. This helps you avoid having to repeat and re-create complex style settings. Note that Naming options are available through style flyouts as well as in the dialog boxes. Using these features is *strongly recommended* as a method of maintaining consistency in your work and reducing your edit and design time.

Retroactive Named Styles When a style-enhanced element is selected on screen, the style attributes it contains are immediately registered in the various style dialog boxes and flyouts. You can use this to capture style configurations from the example art or from any files created by it, including line treatments, fill patterns, gradients, and more. Select the element containing the attributes, go to the appropriate style screen, and name the attributes. From that point on, you may apply them to any other elements you wish by simply selecting the name.

Style Bundles To further automate style enhancements, you may create style bundles, which function as *master* styles in Express. A style bundle contains two or more named styles from any of the style dialog boxes. So in one operation you can combine a typographic style with a fill and a line style and apply all three of these named styles to a single selected element. The use of this feature is *strongly recommended* to maintain consistency and reduce your work time.

Tools

The tools you will use to implement operations in this chapter are summarized below.

Draw Menu The **Draw** menu is where you load symbol forms, images, text, and charts into the screen. You may access symbol and text dialog boxes from the Toolbox as well. In addition, this menu contains the features that allow you to convert symbols into freeform graphics.

Edit Menu The **Edit** menu contains features that allow you to easily select groups of symbols and graphic objects as well as to cut, copy, and paste symbols.

Arrange Menu The **Arrange** menu contains a number of powerful features for symbol composition including Group, Align, and Transform. In addition, Arrange menu features allow you to control stacking position, and to flip and position elements as you want them.

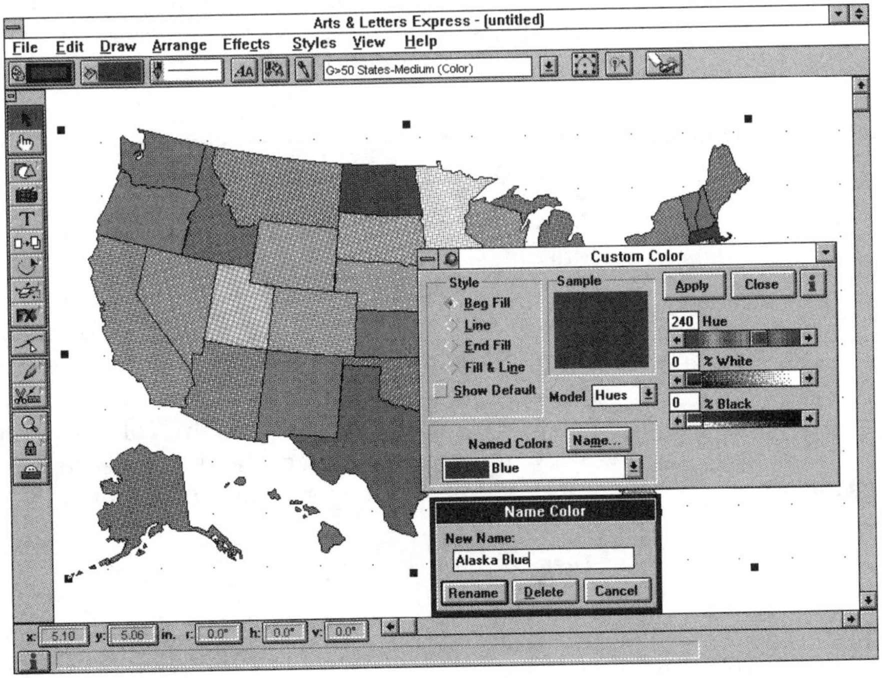

Figure 7.3
Named Styles
Named style features in all the Custom dialog boxes operate like design macros. You can save a list of style enhancements and apply them to any art form directly from the individual style palettes.

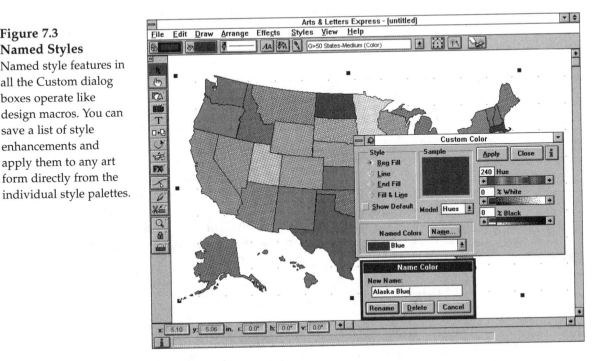

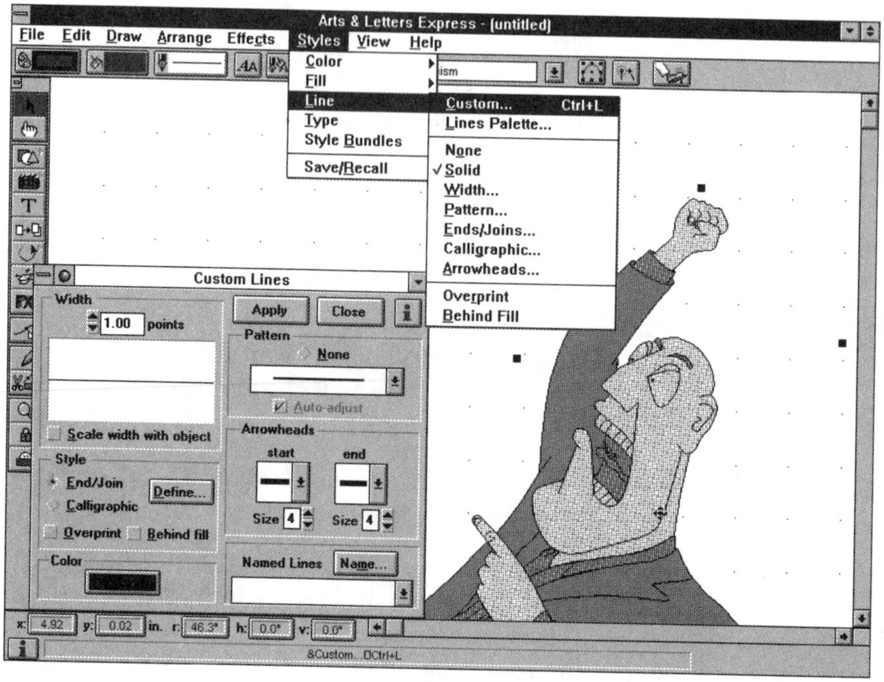

Figure 7.4
Styles Menu
Each option on the new Styles menu is structured identically, with cascades, allowing you direct access to features, and a system of uniform Custom and pushpin features for fast batch styles operations.

Styles Menu The **Styles** menu (Figure 7.4) allows you to set characteristics for line, interior, color, and type. Commonly used attribute settings in each dialog box may be saved under a name you define.

Symbol and Variations

Most symbols that appear in the *Clip Art Handbook* are simple line drawings, shaded in a uniform gray background. Looking at the representation, you might think that is all there is to each symbol, because Arts & Letters symbols function more like drawing icons than clip art. Using standard editing features from the main screen and menus, you can reconfigure each symbol into hundreds, even thousands, of variations by altering the line weight, color, shading, image rotation, and slant. You can also enhance and add depth to symbols through duplicate and transform operations performed with a click of the mouse.

Integrated Symbol Design

One of the great benefits of Arts & Letters symbol library is its *integrated system* design. Conventional clip art tends to be arbitrary and limited. A clip-art library may supply you with several similar elements, but it is essentially a take-it-as-is system. Arts & Letters not only gives you a much greater choice of art elements in more libraries, but the symbol library designs often include ready-made variations that you can easily select (Figure 7.5). The obvious benefit here is that you save time by not having to endlessly reconfigure the same basic drawing. Another, more subtle, benefit is that the designs of all the Arts & Letters libraries share a common visual approach. The symbol elements you select tend to blend more effectively than files picked from two or more packaged clip-art libraries. This will save you the time integrating the different elements on the screen.

Quick Layout Techniques for Heavy Deadlines

When you need to create art quickly, you can assemble and enhance the standard symbols included with the Arts & Letters software. The comprehensive system of graphics, images, icons, business graphics, and symbols is all you need.

Take time to experiment with the techniques presented here and throughout this chapter. Nothing here is difficult; you can create many

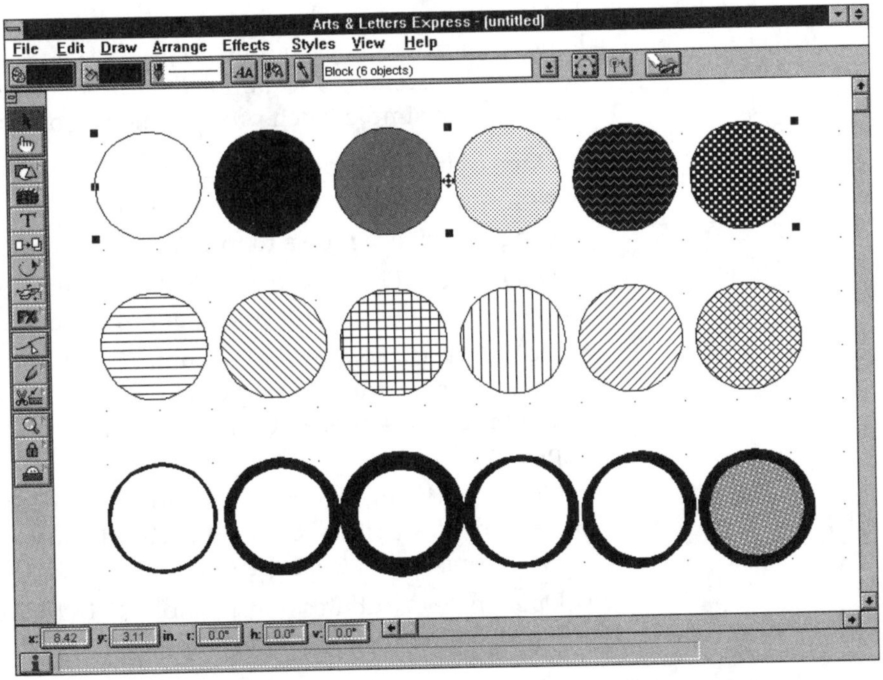

Figure 7.5 Variations on a Theme
Simple circles, many styles. Styles allow you to take basic symbol forms and change the look, color, interior attributes, even the shape and thickness of the line defining the form.

sophisticated effects by simply moving the mouse. Bring up some of your favorite symbols and experiment with different line weights, line patterns, or remove the line element entirely. Practice with different interior colors and textures. As you make simple changes, you will see the range of options available to you.

Pushpins and Batch Operations

All of the dialog boxes used to load symbols, image, and text, and to place styles, are equipped with a pushpin option in the dialog box or flyout Title Bar. This allows you to save significant time by avoiding "menu dancing." Traditional Windows dialog boxes required you to select the element and then select the feature to apply to it. Push-pinned dialog boxes can be maintained in the working area as long as you need them—this forms the basis of highly automated batch operations.

Automated Enhancement

As you become more accustomed to using the style flyout menus off the Toolbar and Style Bar or the dialog boxes off the menus, you can train yourself to think in batch terms. Load all the art elements you want, position them, then push-pin the color screen to the working area and make all desired color changes in one pass. Organizing your work along these lines will enable you to come up with draft art much faster.

Batch Logic

The more you apply batch concepts to your work, the more you can logically structure your output in Arts & Letters and more easily develop art elements to be used in other programs (Figure 7.6). An example of a simple batch process might look like this:

- Open Symbol dialog box and pushpin. Load all desired symbols into working area and release the pushpin.
- Drag and size symbols to form a rough sketch of the composition.
- Open Color Flyout and the pushpin. Select each symbol and apply the desired line and fill colors, and release the pushpin.
- Open Line dialog box and pushpin. Select each symbol and apply the desired line attributes to the first symbol. Name the attribute set for use on other symbols. Complete desired operations and release the pushpin.
- Open Fill dialog box and pushpin. Select each symbol and apply the desired fill attributes. Name each attribute group as you create it. When finished, release the pushpin.
- Open Type Attributes and pushpin. Select each text string and apply the desired attributes, and release the pushpin.

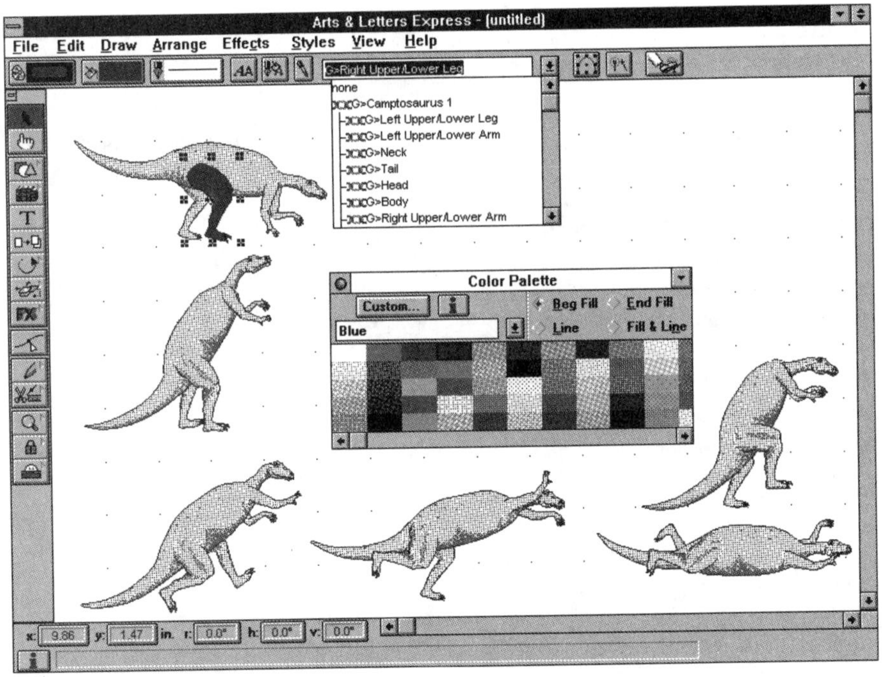

Figure 7.6
Batch Logic
With the palette push-pinned to the screen, you can select objects and directly enhance them using no menus or dialogs; using the internal group selection feature, you don't even have to break up graphic groups to enhance objects inside the group.

As you follow a style batch process like this, you will find a number of ways to automate your work through the use of named styles, selecting multiple symbols, and seeing the results of these structured enhancements displayed immediately.

Named Styles and Style Bundles

Named styles are groups of style attributes, just like graphic groups are a collection of freeform objects and symbols. Making style settings and doing them accurately is a time-consuming process. This is particularly true if you are seeking to achieve a specific design effect that works across a composition or is used in multiple compositions. Save your attribute sets under names as you create them. You can always delete unused name sets later. Having the named set available as you work is a major automation technique, and can save you significant time developing and editing your work.

Naming Symbols and Freeform Elements

The Express screen configuration contains a dramatic enhancement to one of the most powerful features in Arts & Letters: element naming. In the Style Bar is a text display and entry line that identifies the type of element that is currently selected (Figure 7.7). If a numbered symbol is selected, the symbol number is displayed, and groups and freeform

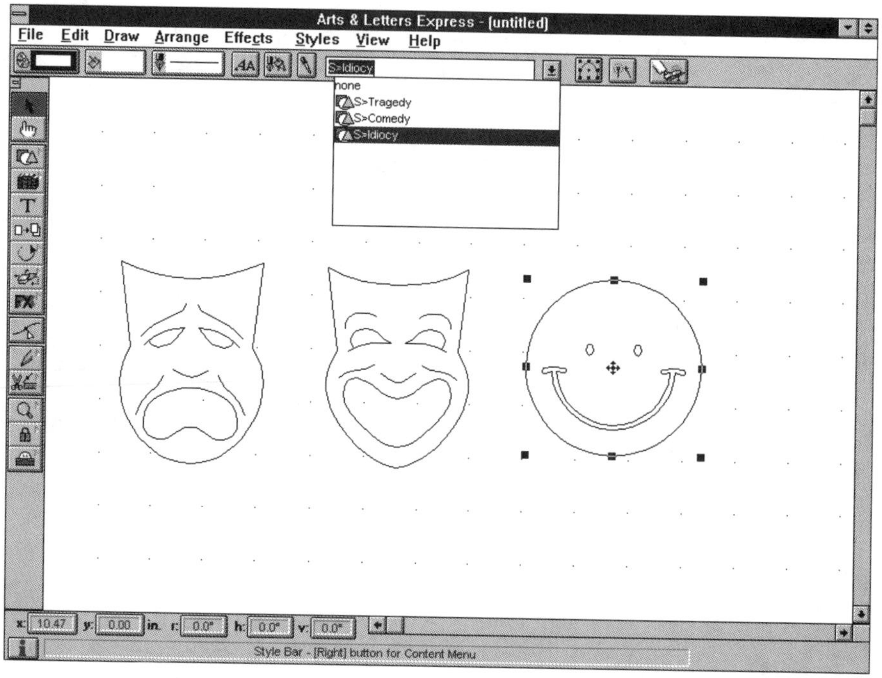

Figure 7.7 Naming Symbols and Freeform Elements The Object Viewer in the Style Bar allows you to fast-type a name for any selected object or group. Note that the names are preceded by the S symbol identifier. This feature allows you to define your own names for symbols and art elements.

shapes are noted. You have the option to name each element in your drawing as you create it on the screen. Just click on the text in the display and it is selected automatically. Now type in the desired name.

Since symbol numbers don't help you figure out the identity of each symbol in a given composition, when putting together a drawing, take a couple of seconds and type in a descriptive term for the selected symbol. Applying a symbol name does not affect the symbol's status in the graphic database. The display will show the name with an annotation that the element is a symbol. You may still select the named symbol and replace it with others at any time you wish.

Apply Styles within a Group

You can select individual elements from any group by double-clicking on the group then clicking on one of its elements. Once selected within the group, the element can be edited or enhanced with color, line, fill, or type styles. For example, without ungrouping you can select one part and rotate it alone. To select within a group, double-click on the group. The uppermost object in the group that is underneath the cursor is selected. A single click can choose another object in the group. The object handles surround the selection and its specific styles will appear in the Style Bar.

The Elements of Design

Designing art begins with the presentation of each element in the composition. Symbol wireframes, text, and freeform shapes may exist in a number of visual aspects in Arts & Letters. There also is a set of design elements that set the foundation for how styles are used and the effects created with them. Each symbol wireframe and master image in Express allows you to enhance individual components and to create hundreds, even thousands, of unique variations.

The same elements of design that apply to symbols apply to both text and freeform shapes. You may use them as plain outline forms, fill them, even make them hollow so that other art forms show through from behind. Using styles effectively begins with understanding the key configuration options that allow you to develop themes and variations in Express.

Art Forms as Line Drawings

The most basic configuration of any symbol is as a simple line drawing (Figure 7.8). Most symbols are shown in the *Clip Art Handbook* with a gray shading, which makes them seem more solid. However, as line drawings, those symbols can present a highly professional, uncluttered look to a variety of business communications. To display any symbol as a line drawing, simply change the interior color to white.

Arts & Letters allows you to control the interior attributes of symbols using the **Fill** dialog box on the **Styles** menu. Note that if interior values are set to **None**, the symbol will display as a line drawing and will be functionally transparent, so that any symbol, or a part of any symbol sitting beneath it will show through. If you don't wish this to happen, change the interior value of the symbol to **Solid** and set the interior color to **White** on the **Color** menu.

Steps: Symbols as Line Drawings

Use this operation to set a symbol, text, or closed freeform shape as a line drawing. Note: You may also use the None option in the Custom Fill dialog box. This option will make the element transparent to any other elements behind it.

1. Select the symbol on screen.
2. Access **Styles | Color**.
3. Verify that **Fill** is selected in the **Named Colors** dialog box.
4. Select **White**.

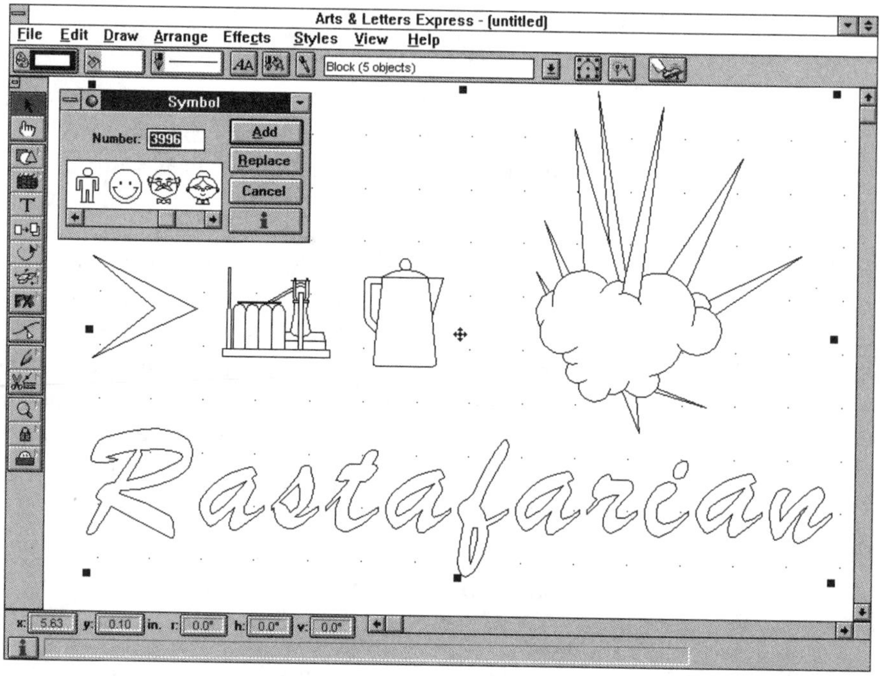

Figure 7.8
Art Forms as Line Drawings
Art or text forms can be presented as simple wireframe outlines. Each of the artworks in the symbol and image library and text elements can easily be configured to work as simple line drawing elements in the screen.

Art Forms as Solid Shapes

The opposite approach from line drawing is to present a symbol shape as a filled, or solid, form. Certain symbols, especially those that are simple outlines, such as many icons, accents, and some inset graphic pictorials, lend themselves to this because they don't have much internal detail (Figure 7.9).

You have the option when using symbols as a filled form to retain or eliminate the surrounding line sketch that defines the symbol. You can perform many interesting tricks with different configurations of line and fill patterns. For example, you can set a black line around a light fill pattern for standard fill effects.

If symbols are placed over a background, you can use a darker fill pattern with the line color of the symbol set to white, which makes the symbol form stand out from the background.

Experiment with different shades and textures. The number of possible shading textures available lets you create an incredible number of variations on a simple shape.

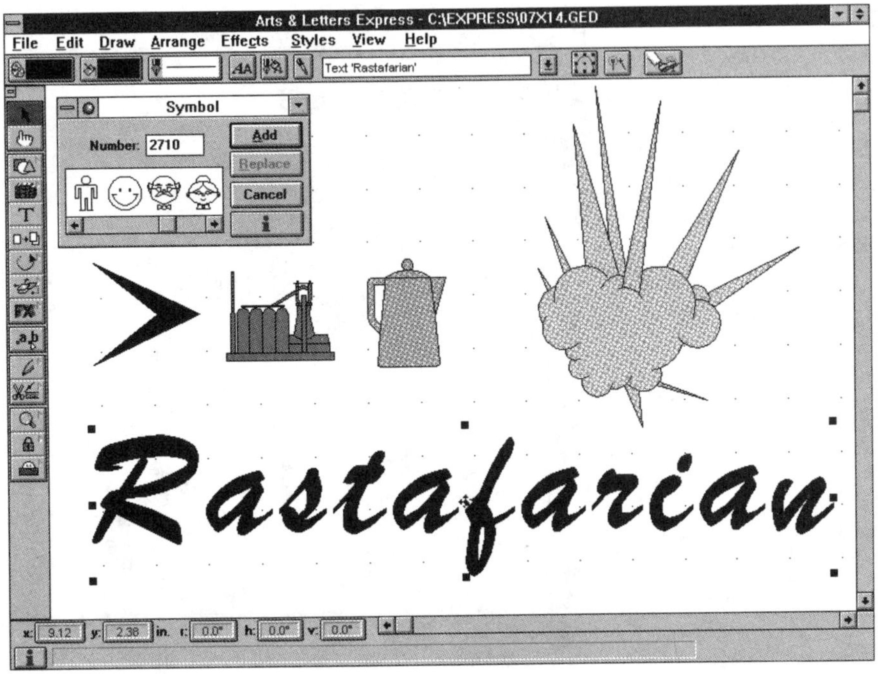

Figure 7.9
Art Forms as Solid Shapes
Applying colors to the wireframes and text outlines creates an entirely different look and impression using the same symbol. Each art form in Express works like a template that you can use to create hundreds of unique variations by simply selecting features with the mouse.

Steps: Symbols as Filled Forms

Use this operation to set the internal fill pattern to solid for any symbol, text, or closed freeform shape.

1. Select the symbol on screen.
2. Select **Styles | Fill | Solid**.

Art Forms as Textured Shapes

Symbols, text, or shapes may also be textured, as well as line drawings, and solid elements (Figure 7.10). Textures are added via the Fill Style option. There are two principal types of textures: standard fill patterns (vector or bitmap) and gradients. Textures in a symbol shape can be used to create a number of highly arresting effects. Textures can give the symbol a richer impact through a combination of pattern and shape. Fill patterns allow you to change the art form from solid to any variety of shade and texture.

Textured symbols can be shown with or without the wireframe line. Using gradients and fill patterns, this allows you to create textured backgrounds and to use symbols as textured accents in larger compositions.

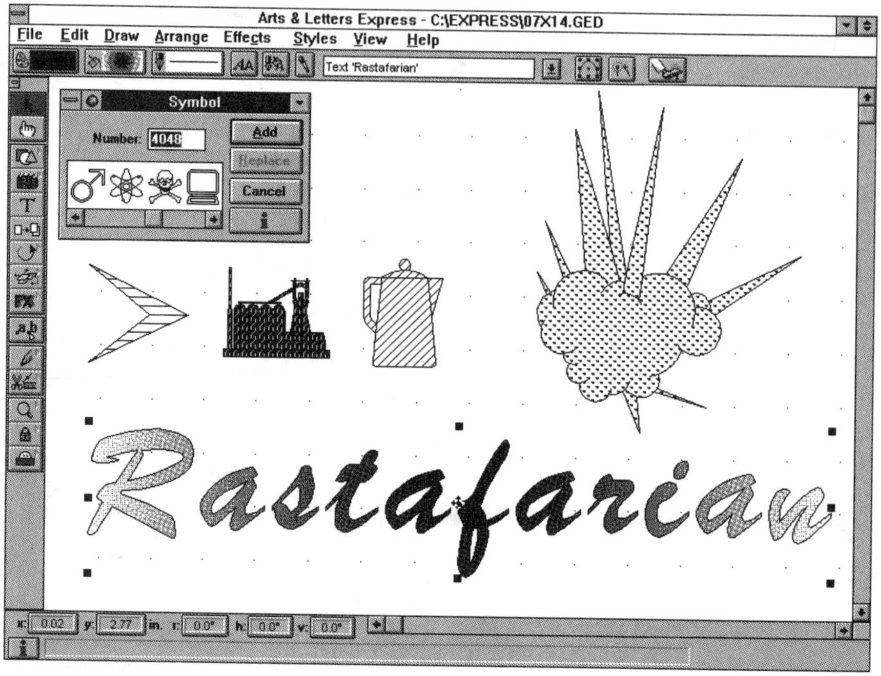

Figure 7.10
Art Forms as Textured Shapes
Changing solid fill to a variety of textured Vector, Raster, and Gradient patterns allows you to create additional variations using exactly the same art element.

Steps: Symbols as Textured Forms

Use this operation to set a textured pattern in any symbol, text, or closed freeform shape element.

1. Select the symbol on screen.
2. Access **Styles | Fill | Custom**.
3. Select Raster, Vector, or Gradient.
4. Select the desired texture.

Base Composition: Relative Size, Shape, Angle, and Position

In addition to the three symbol presentation options discussed above, the basis of your composition is established through the size, aspect ratio, and position of the symbol, text, and freeform components (Figure 7.11).

Size

Using the corner selection handles in Standard mode, you may drag any element in the Express screen to a desired size. The graphic database provides you with a wide range of choices and selections for art components, any of which may be used for different purposes in your compositions. Abstracts and pictorials may be used as small objects in a

Figure 7.11
Base Composition
The size, aspect ratio, angle of rotation, and position on the screen are basic aspects of a symbol's composition. Express lets you design complete compositions by manipulating and transforming these individual elements from the ground up.

diagram or flowchart, or as backgrounds in others. When you factor in the presentation values—wireframe, solid, or textured—you will see that even the simplest wireframes can function both as representative art objects, or provide a framework for subtle backgrounds and accent effects.

Shape Aspect ratio refers to the relationship between the height (Y) and the width (X) of the drawing. When you click a symbol, image, or text component into the screen, it is displayed in its normal aspect ratio. By using the middle selection handles on the top and sides of the element, you can change the width or the height of any element in the screen. Subtle or dramatic distortions of the aspect ratio may be necessary to make a given component fit with other elements in a composition. The correct aspect ratio may be restored at any time by selecting a distorted object and accessing the **Make Proportional** option on the **Arrange** menu.

Angle Rotation and slant options allow you to change the angle of the element as you wish. Rotation, in particular, allows you to directly control the angle at which a given symbol, image, text, or freeform component is shown. These positioning effects can be used not only to tilt the element but to invert it. When you look at pictorials and abstracts in the

Clip Art Handbook, note that they can be inverted, as well as flipped horizontally. The Rotate feature allows you to adjust an angle continuously; Flip Horizontal and Flip Vertical, on the Arrange menu, allow you to make simple presentation changes with a mouse.

Position and Stacking: Foreground and Background

The placement of elements establishes the composition. Placing elements is as simple as dragging them where you want them. With multiple elements, stacking all or part of a component is often required. The graphic database gives you many options for combining separate elements into a whole. Elements used as detail points on one composition can be used as a background in another.

If you are using a framing element, such as a geometric form, flowchart box, or one of the custom frame elements, it may be a good idea to remove the interior fill entirely by setting it to **None**. This way, all symbols contained in the frame will show through the frame and you won't have to worry about pushing the frame to the back of the composition.

For most background and foreground operations, the standard commands are **Stacking Order, Send to Back** on the **Arrange** menu (**Shift-F** from the keyboard), or **Stacking Order | Bring to Front** (**Ctrl-F** from the keyboard). Using keyboard commands is an effective way to quickly position foreground and background elements.

Composition by the Numbers: Transform

All of the positioning and sizing operations discussed here can be performed using the mouse or by using the **Transform** dialog box on the **Arrange** menu (Figure 7.12). Transform is arguably the single most powerful editing dialog box in the package; and you should be aware that fine editing points can be addressed directly here. By clicking on any of the dimension or angle measures shown in the Hint line at the bottom of the screen, Express will port you directly to the entry line for that dimension in the Transform dialog box. Detailed coverage of Transform techniques and advanced operations appears in Chapter 8.

Operating the Style Features

Unlike most software menus, in Express each Styles menu is structured and organized in the same way. Styles are also accessible directly from the redesigned Style Bar (Figure 7.13). Express gives you so many ways to access style features that you could easily get confused about the most efficient and effective ways to access these features for any given task. This section provides a practical overview and guide on using the Styles features and how to use the access options.

Figure 7.12
Transform
The Transform dialog box, a wizard of a feature, displays the precise angle of rotation of the sorcerer at upper right. This dialog box allows all base composition operations—sizing, positioning, rotation, and slant—to be set by number.

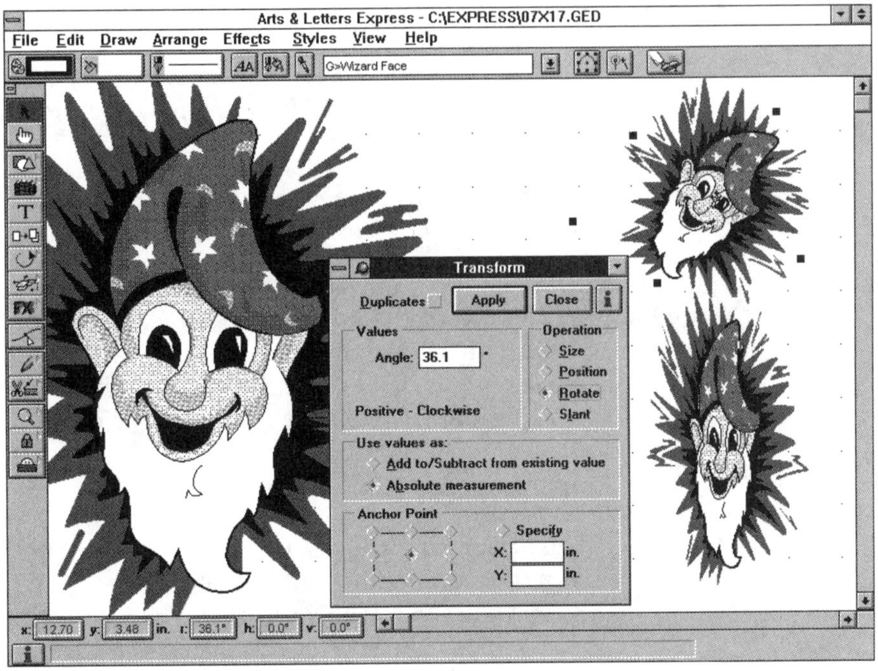

Figure 7.13
Custom Style Features
Each of the Styles options has a master or Custom screen that allows you to define custom style values for that feature and save it under a unique style name. Named styles are displayed in the Palette dialog boxes, which can be easily accessed from the Style Bar.

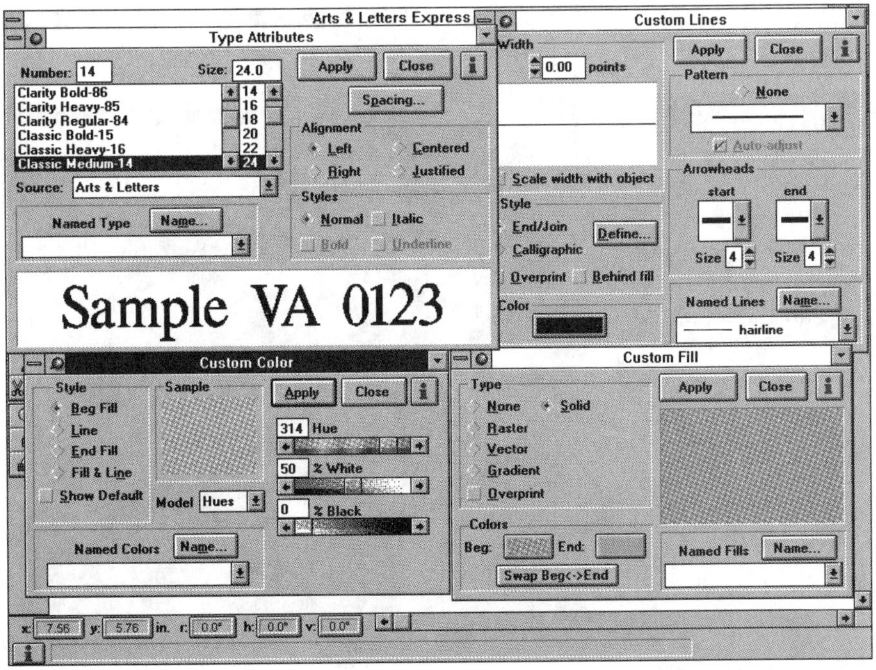

Styles Access

You may access styles features from two key places in the screen design: from the menu or from the newly designed Style Bar.

Styles Menu Cascades The styles menu is built around a series of cascade submenus that allow you to select from the array of style options without being forced to go to a main dialog box. Note that the cascades are shortcut commands to access key dialog boxes.

Style Bar At the top of the screen, the Style Bar contains icons to select flyout screens of the key Style palettes, as well as an entry box to enter object names (Figure 7.14). The Style Bar enables you to access style features with the mouse, which is the most efficient way.

Styles Screens

The design of the Styles features is based upon a set of dialog boxes and selection screens that are available for each of the four major Styles options: Color, Fill, Line, and Type. The location and function of these display screens is consistent and each is designed to help you accomplish specific tasks.

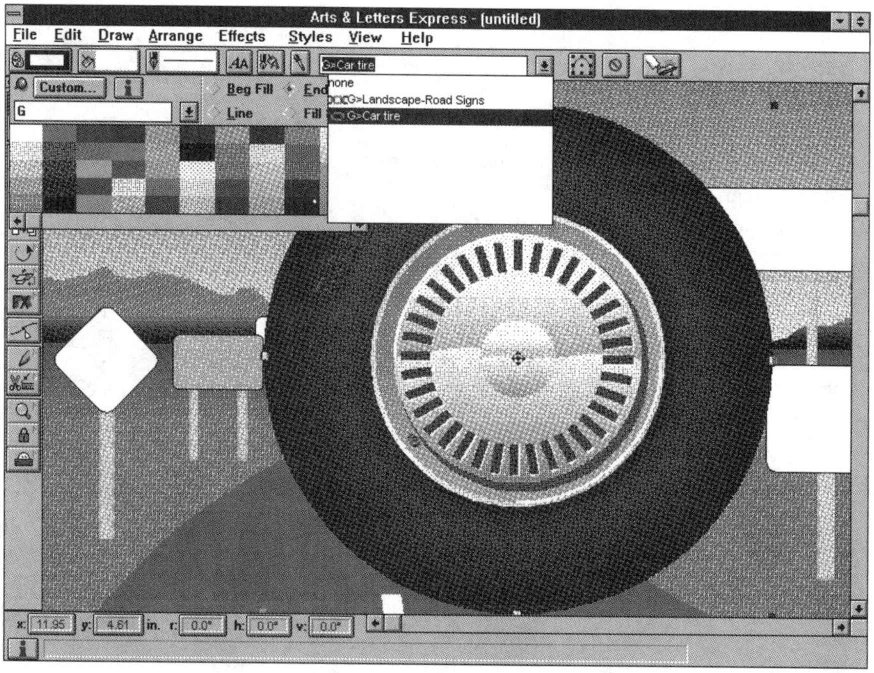

Figure 7.14
Style Bar
A toolbox for enhancements, the Style Bar at the top of the screen contains all the Style Palettes as drop-downs. Press the pushpin and the drop-down becomes a flyout. The Object Viewer is there to make it easy to select objects, groups, or objects within a group right from the list, or directly from the screen.

Custom Dialog Box

A Custom dialog box type is available for each of the four style types. This is the master dialog where you can make custom style settings for a selected object. The Custom dialog box also allows you to access all of the style options available from a single screen. Use this dialog box when you wish to create or enter a unique color mix, a special line thickness, a selected fill pattern, or a specialized typographic configuration. The Custom dialog box may be accessed from the Styles cascade menu for the desired style, or by selecting the Custom button in the style flyout. All Custom dialogs may be push-pinned to stay on screen for batch operations.

Custom Dialog: Style Naming Features

Each Custom Dialog Box contains a style naming line, so that you may assign a name to the custom style settings without leaving the dialog box or accessing another feature. Naming a set of style attributes will immediately display that named set of attributes on the Palette screen for that particular style (Figure 7.15).

Flyout/Palette

Each style has its own Palette screen, which displays an array of ready-to-use style enhancements included in both the default style set and named styles defined by you. You simply click the desired palette item to apply to the selected element. The Palette screen doubles as the Style Bar flyout toolkit for each of the styles. So the current Color Palette

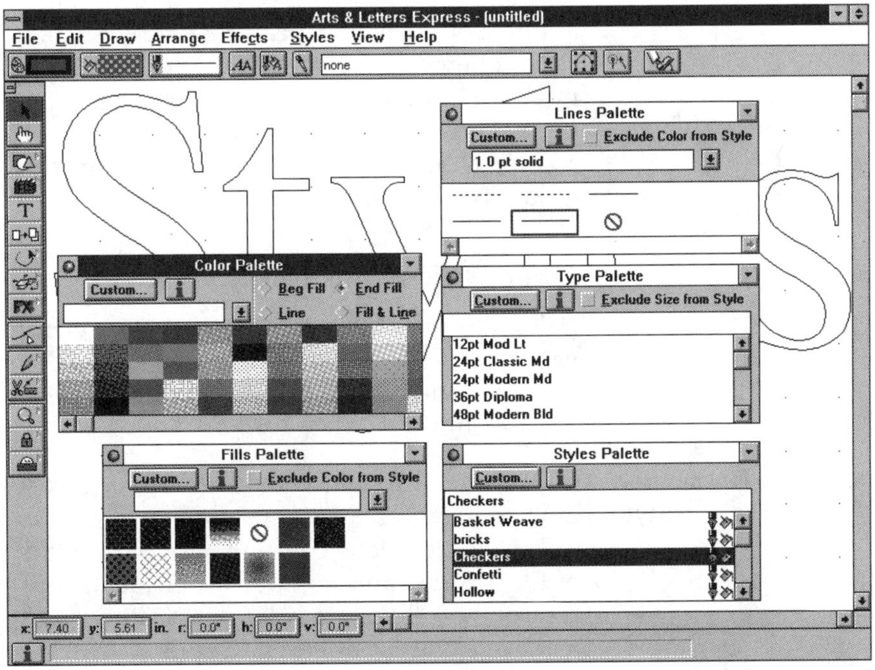

Figure 7.15
Style Palettes
Each of the Styles options has a Palettes screen that displays all named Styles for that feature. If you make a habit of naming your style configurations, they automatically show up in the Palette and may be easily accessed from the Style Bar. For frequently used styles, this feature can save a great deal of time and effort.

appears on the Color flyout, the Line Styles palette on the Line flyout, and so forth. Each of the Palette flyouts has a Custom button allowing you to directly access the Custom dialog box without having to go to the menu. All Palettes may be push-pinned to stay on screen for batch operations. All palettes display a Named Style entry line. You may select named styles from the palette or you may save the style attributes of the currently selected element by typing a name in the line provided in the Palette screen.

Style Options

Each style has a list of options that you may access. For color, you can load new premixed palettes. Fills allow you to select vector, bitmap, and gradient options. Line styles support special calligraphic pen and other options. Each of these options allows you to make detailed and unique style configurations to apply to one or more art forms. Most important: Option settings are stored and retained when you create a Named Style in the Custom dialog box. Options may be accessed from within the Custom dialog box for the style, or accessed directly from the cascade submenu for the given style off the Styles menu.

Designing with Color

Arts & Letters has been consistently a pioneer software package in the application, use, and printing of color. Color is the foundation of all styles offered in Express. The color you select for elements is the foremost application of styles in your compositions. Even if you are showing a simple symbol wireframe drawing as a black line, you are making a color choice. This section focuses on practical applications of the Color Styles features in Express.

Color Design Considerations

Color allows you to enhance individual elements in a composition in a variety of ways. The following are a number of key design and composition functions accomplished through the Color Styles features. (See Figure 7.16.)

Color as Foundation Style

Color Styles are unique in that they interact with all of the other styles in Express. You may set custom line attributes with Line Styles, but the Color features alone control Line Color. You may set or define a variety of fill patterns and textures for elements, but the Color features alone control the Fill texture color. Text features set typography, but the Color features alone control the text color.

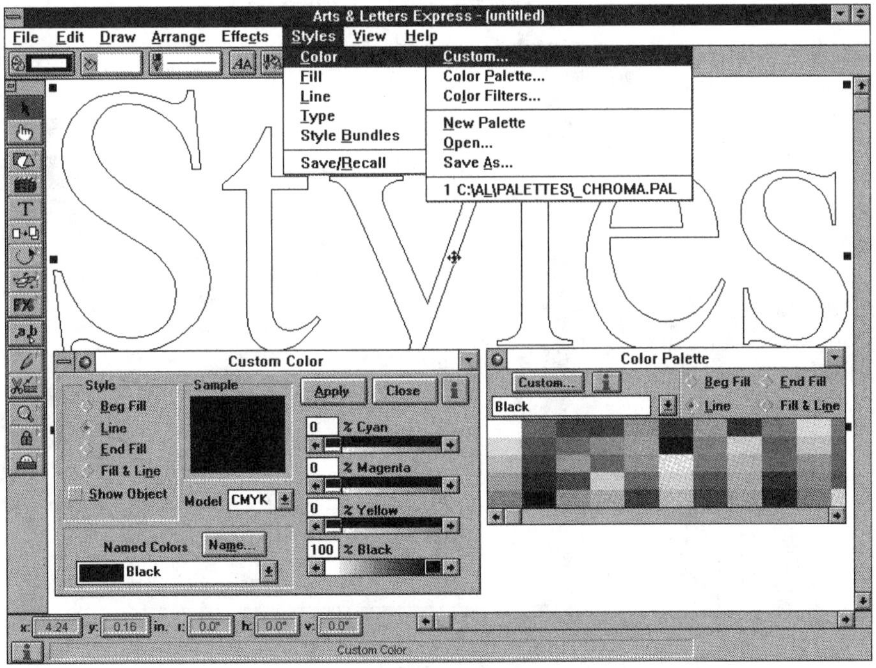

Figure 7.16
The Color Menu allows you to access the Custom Color and Color Palette screens, and to access the premixed palettes that can be opened and loaded into the Palette flyout.

Color , Grayscale, or Black and White

If you are printing the final work in black and white, or grayscale, you should be working in these colors on the screen. If you are working to output the final as color art, then you should be working in the final color.

Line, Fill, and Gradient

Color may be applied to a selected element in three principal ways: first, to define the color of the element's line; second, to define the fill color of the element, and third, to define a multicolor gradient range used as a fill pattern in the element. The Color flyout on the Style Bar allows you to select these options from the same display. (Note that there are not separate flyouts for line, fill, and gradient color.) The Beg Fill and End Fill options in the Color flyout define the color range that makes up a gradient; for single color applications, selecting Beg Fill gives you the one color you want.

Object Density: Solid and Shadings

Color is a key tool in defining the density of an object in the screen. The default palette provides you with the basic black, white, and primary colors, and a range of shadings and mixes to apply to selected elements. Using color or grayscale shadings allows you to vary and control the density and solidity of the selected element (Figure 7.17). Density and shading are key elements in a composition. They are also

Figure 7.17
Object Density
Color and shading alone can dramatically affect the graphic density and weight of an art form. The basic Express Color Palette provides a range of solid colors and shadings, so you can select the density and shading you want.

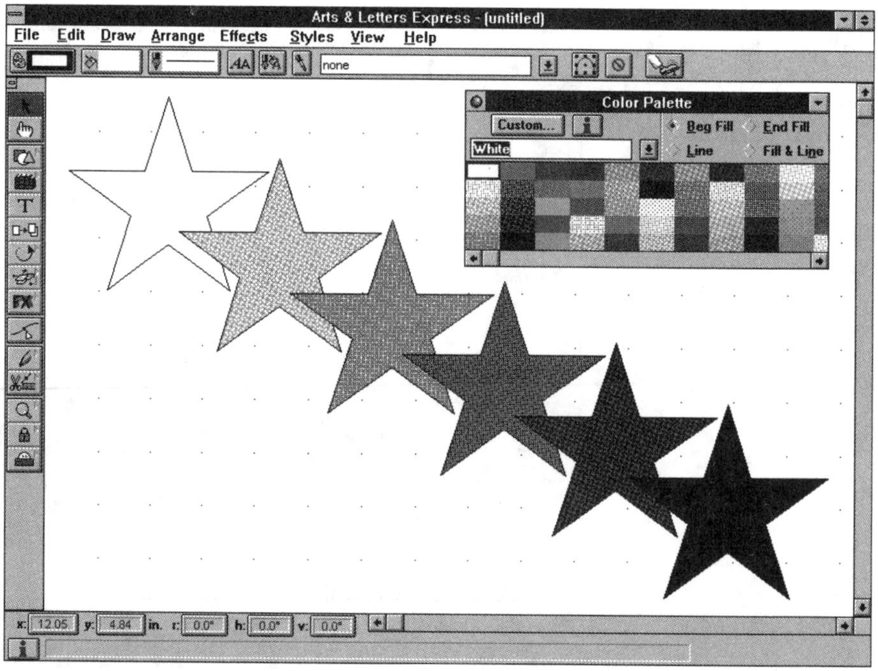

highly important when developing special effects such as drop shadows, blends, and shadow effects. (See Chapter 8.)

Color Menu

The array of features on the Color menu allow you to perform key style functions. The following is a brief review of all the color options that appear on the menu.

Custom Display **Custom Color** dialog box to create and name unique color mixes, using one of three selected color models:

- RGB
- CYMK
- Hues

Color Palette Display the currently active color palette on the screen. This is the same screen as the flyout from the Color icon on the Style Bar.

Color Correction The advanced color editing dialog box is covered in detail later in this chapter.

OVER 10,000
CLIP-ART
IMAGES
MasterCard
VISA

Drag-n-Drop All 10,000 Clip-Art Images

Now you can review the available images in a collection as thumbnails, select the image you want, drag it from the Clip-Art Manager, and drop it in your work space. In addition, you can search selected collections for images by keywords. Type "automobile," or "car," or "vehicle," for example, to build a temporary library of all automobile related images.

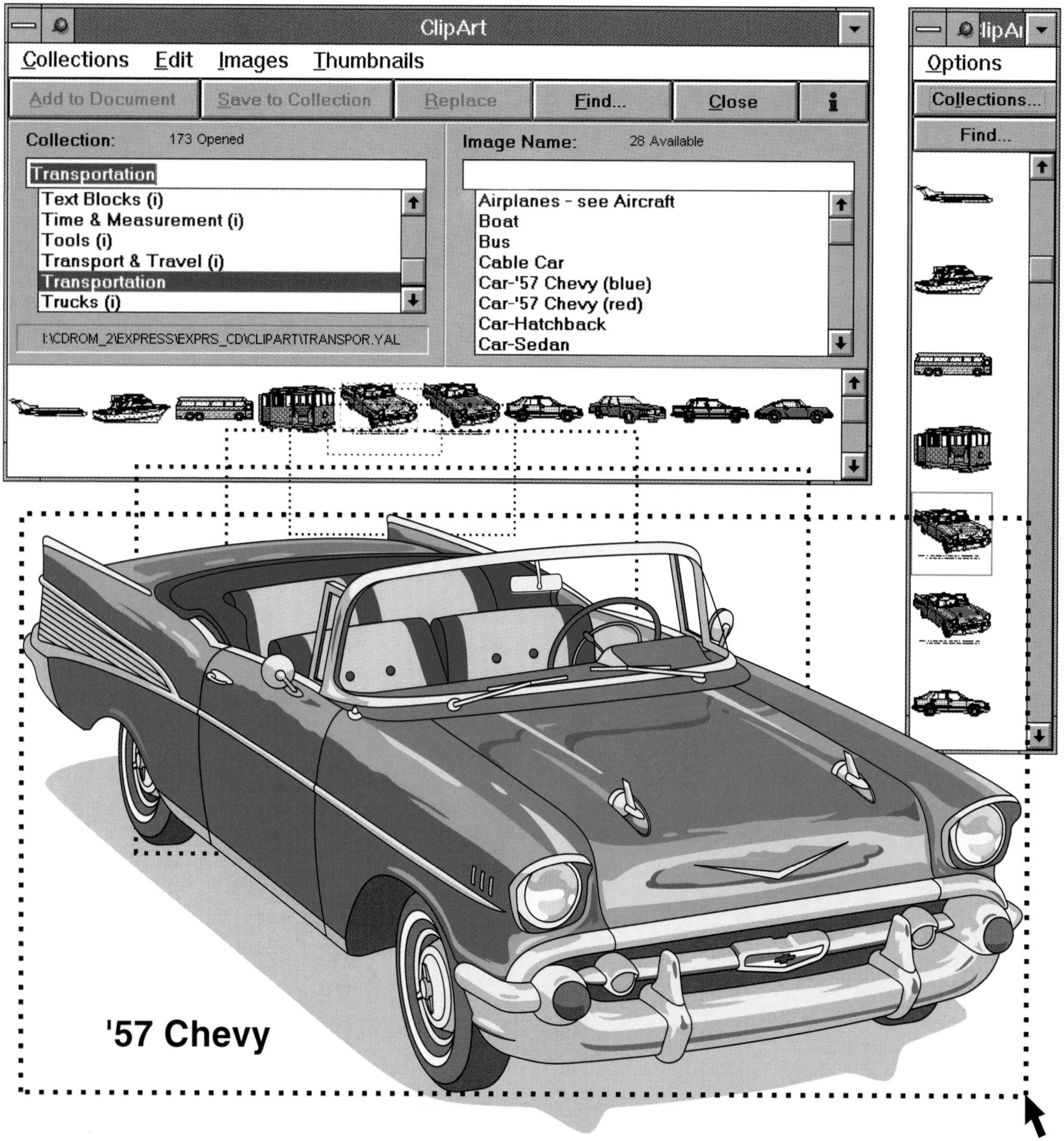

'57 Chevy

Color Filters

The Color Filters feature of *Express* allows you to apply a variety of color operations to entire documents, selected groups or individual objects. You can isolate specific colors within a group without breaking it apart or specify which attributes of the selected objects will be affected: beginning fill, end fill, and lines.

You can choose to make your adjustments in an artistic mode (shown) with a gallery of predefined adjustments or use a technical mode to create your own adjustments.

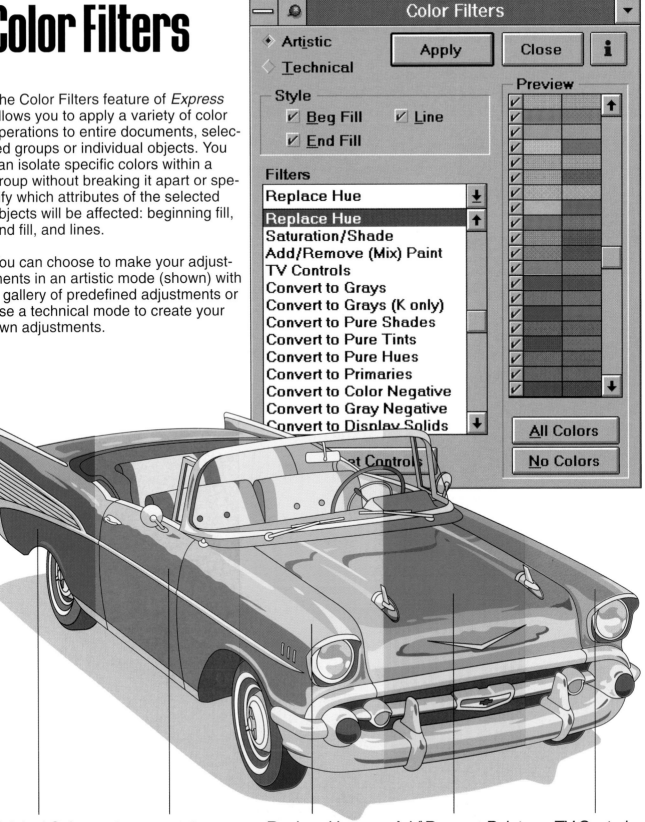

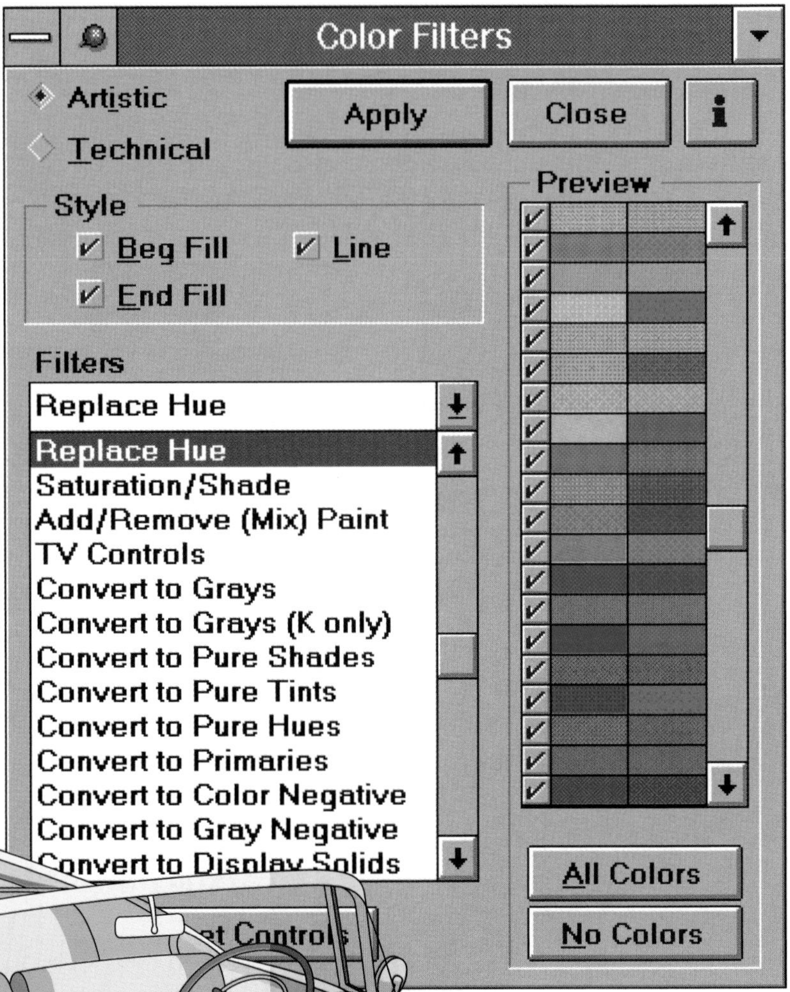

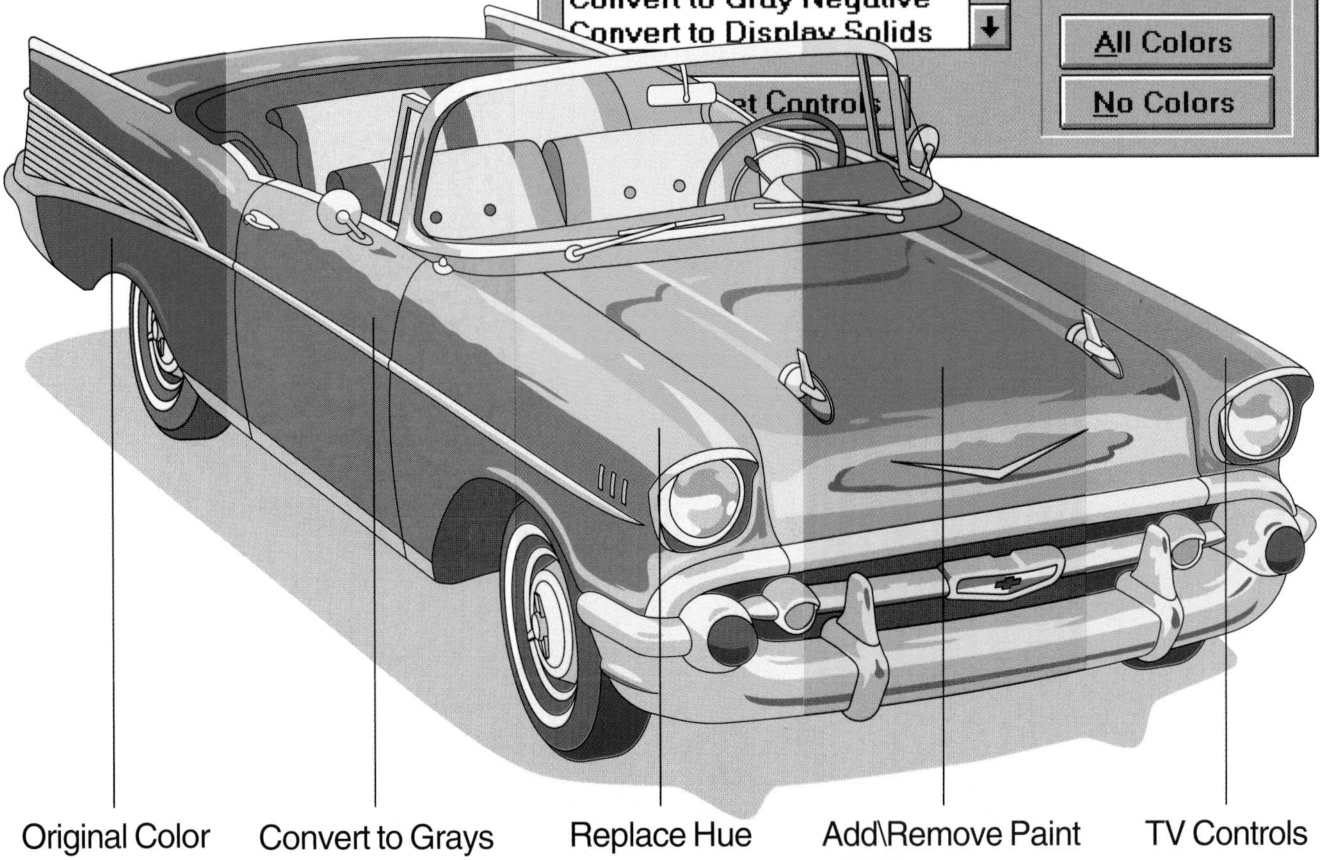

TEXT DESIGN FEATURES

You can create spectacular effects with text using a variety of features in *Express.* Bind text to a shape, extrude text, warp text. Cut holes, create clipping masks, and apply gradient fills.

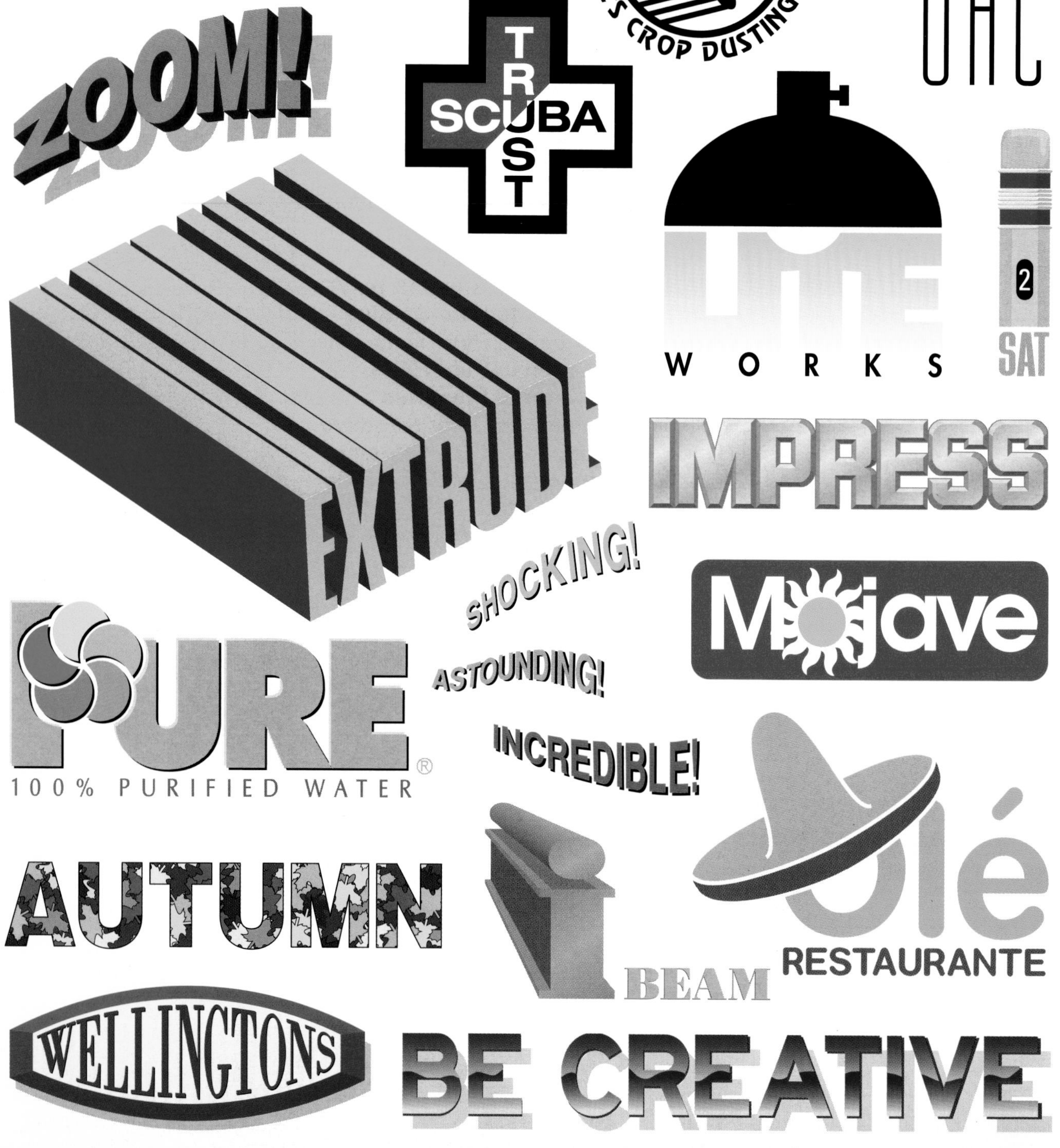

PROCESS–COLOR (CMYK) SEPARATIONS

Express automatically separates a color image into four separate images. Plates produced from the color separations are used on a printing press to recombine the four process colors (cyan, magenta, yellow, and black).

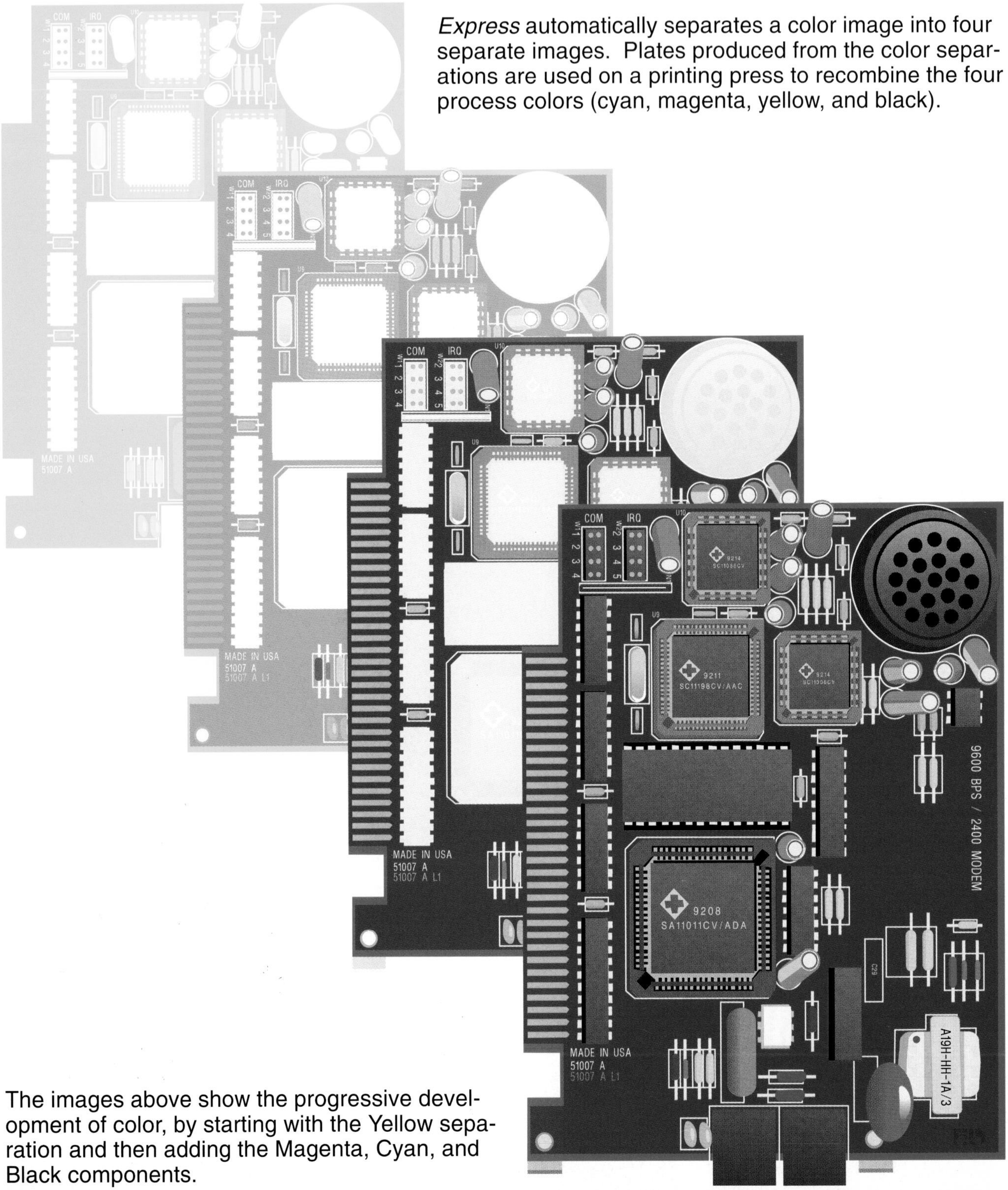

The images above show the progressive development of color, by starting with the Yellow separation and then adding the Magenta, Cyan, and Black components.

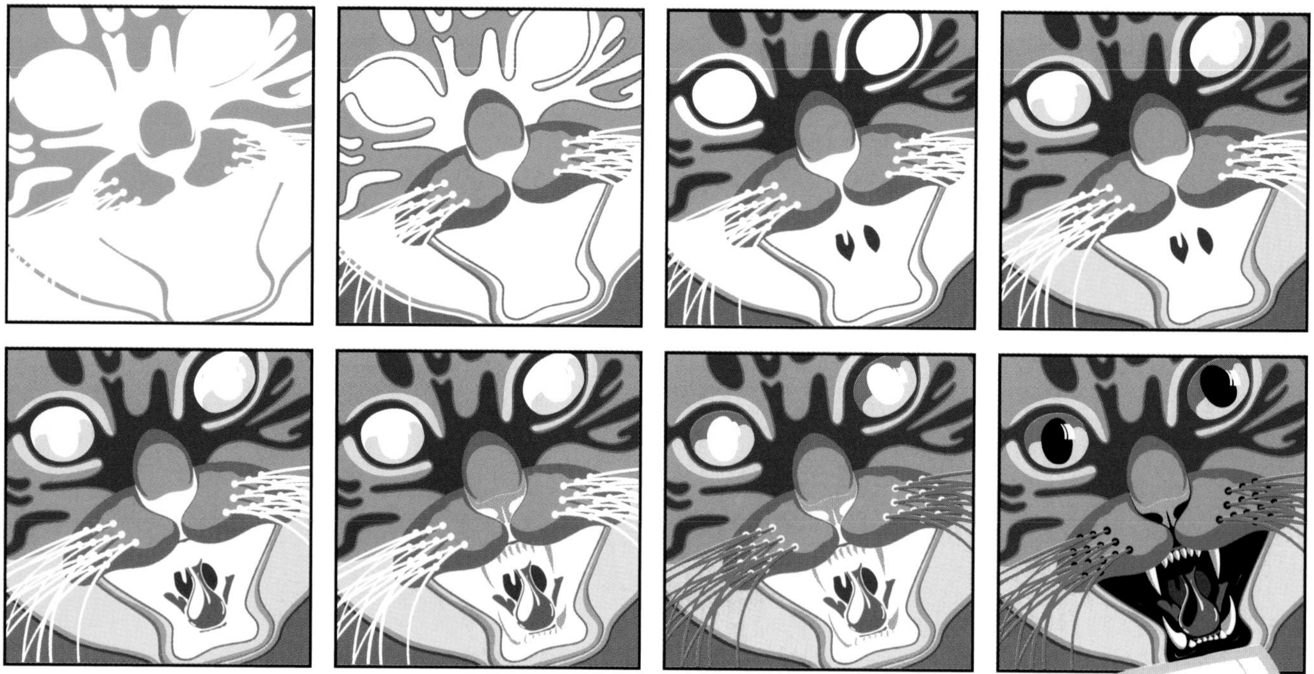

SPOT–COLOR SEPARATIONS

Express can create spot-color separations for silk screen or offset printing. The illustration above was created using eight colors. The final composition was silk screened onto T-shirts, printed on posters, and imaged directly to film for use in advertisements and other applications.

TEXTURES WITH GRADIENT FILLS

Individual freeform objects within these compositions were given color gradient fill patterns to add depth and texture to the compositions.

SCANNED PHOTOGRAPHS

You can import highly textured scanned photos and other images into *Express* and enhance them with clip art, text, and freeform drawing, to create integrated compositions.

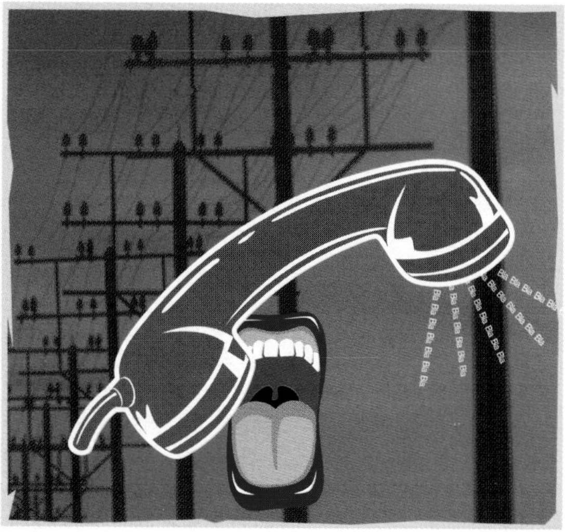

S
K
Y
"Excuze me, while I kiss the sky."
– Jimi Hendrix, in Purple Haze

CHARTING FEATURES

Arts & Letters *Express* automatically generates pie, line, and bar charts that can be combined with clip art, text and 24-bit scanned photographs.

New Palette Use New Palette to create your own palette of custom colors. This feature clears the current palette and removes all colors. As you name mixes in the Custom screen, they will be added to this new palette.

Open This option allows you to Open any custom palette file you create or any of the ready-made color palettes provided with Express. All palette files are stored in the \PALETTE subdirectory under the \A&L main directory and appear with a uniform *.PAL file extension. The default palette file that is shown when the software is installed is stored as _CHROMA.PAL.

Save As This option allows you to save a New Palette you create from scratch, or to save changes you make to any of the standard or custom palettes

Applying Colors

For standard color operations, use the color palette in the flyout menu. To save time, apply colors to all the elements in the screen in a single operation. Begin by push-pinning the color palette to the screen. Then select and color each element as desired.

Coloring Symbol Art Forms Colors are applied to selected symbols uniformly throughout the symbol. Arts & Letters treats a symbol drawing in its original form as a complete graphic object. So, when you first place the symbol, you cannot select individual components of it and apply different colors to them. To do that, the symbol must be converted to freeform graphic objects, which can be individually selected.

Warning: Check Type The color palette contains four selection options that control Line and Fill color selections. Always check to see what is selected before clicking on the desired color. The four options are:

- Beg(in) Fill [DEFAULT]
- End Fill
- Line
- Fill & Line

Standard color operations use a two-color format: one line color and a different fill color. Even when fill colors are used, the standard line color is black. If you want a uniform line and fill color, or you want to change the line color, check the type options and select what you want before choosing the desired color.

Line Colors

Line color defaults to black, which is the common color for maintaining a crisp line on a symbol wireframe, text, or freeform objects. You may wish to change the line to white, to display the art form against a dark background or to remove the outline from the art form.

Steps: Applying Line Colors

Use this operation to change the line color. When the palette is push-pinned to the working area, repeat this process until you are finished. Select the pushpin again to dismiss the palette. (See Figure 7.18.)

1. Select the object to be colored.
2. Select the Color icon in the Style Bar.
3. Select Line type.
4. Click once on the desired color mix.
5. Verify that the color is applied to the line.

Fill Colors

The palette display defaults to fill color, and the Fill palette defaults to Solid fill color. If a texture or pattern shows up with your selected color, access the Fill Palette and select the solid color option. Note that if no color appears in the selected symbol or element, the Fill may be set to None. Open the dialog box and change the None value to Solid and your fill color will be accepted.

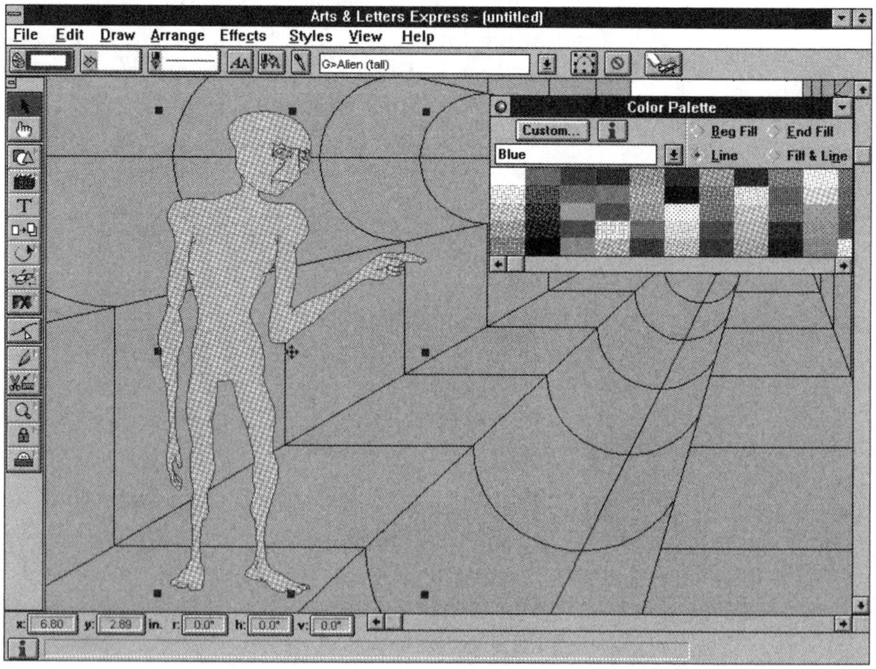

Figure 7.18 Applying Line Colors Take a moment for a close encounter with the color palette and check to make sure you have selected the Line type, as shown at the right, to set the color of the line. The Color Palette is used for line, fill, and gradient settings.

Steps: Applying Fill Colors

Use this operation to select a fill color for a selected element. When the palette is push-pinned to the working area, repeat this process until you are finished and select the thumbtack again to dismiss the palette.

1. Select the object to be colored.
2. Select the Color icon in the Style Bar.
3. Verify that Beg Line is selected.
4. Click once on the desired color mix.
5. Verify that the fill color is displayed.

Steps: Applying Line and Fill Color

Use this operation to apply the same color to both the line and interior of an art element (Figure 7.19). When the palette is push-pinned to the working area, repeat this process until you are finished and select the pushpin again to dismiss the palette.

1. Select the object to be colored.
2. Select the Color icon in the Style Bar.
3. Select Fill & Line type.
4. Click once on the desired color mix.
5. Verify that the desired color is displayed.

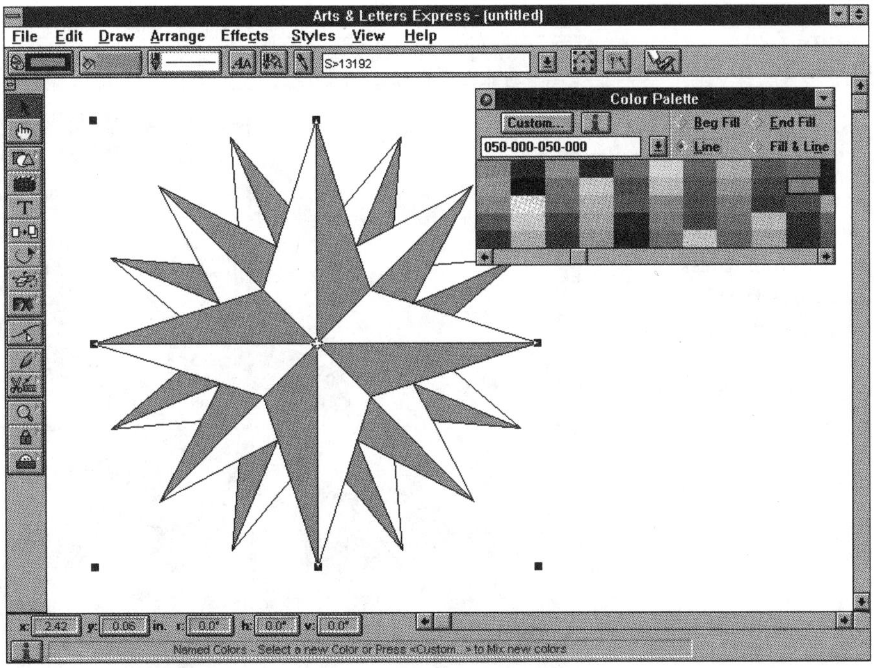

Figure 7.19 Applying Line and Fill Colors

If you want both the line and fill to be the same color, use the setting provided in the Palette. Take time to check these settings or you'll be back, somewhat sheepishly, making edits you shouldn't have to make.

Using Custom Color Palettes

Express includes a set of color palette files, which are stored in the \PALETTES subdirectory. These palettes include general colors, variations on common color groups (such as grays, browns, and blues), as well as specific named colors for the human body, buildings, forests, food, and many others.

Palette Options

When starting out in Arts & Letters, take a moment to familiarize yourself with the color palettes included in the software. It may save you hours of trial and error in color mixing. In addition, the colors are already mixed and named (in English), and are editable. That is, you can load one of the color palettes, select individual colors within the palette, make changes, and save your variation into the palette file or append additional color mixes into the palette.

Steps: Open Custom Palette

Use this operation to load a custom color palette (Figure 7.20).

1. Access **Styles | Color | Open**.
2. Select the **\PALETTES** subdirectory from the file list.
3. Select the desired color palette from the list displayed.

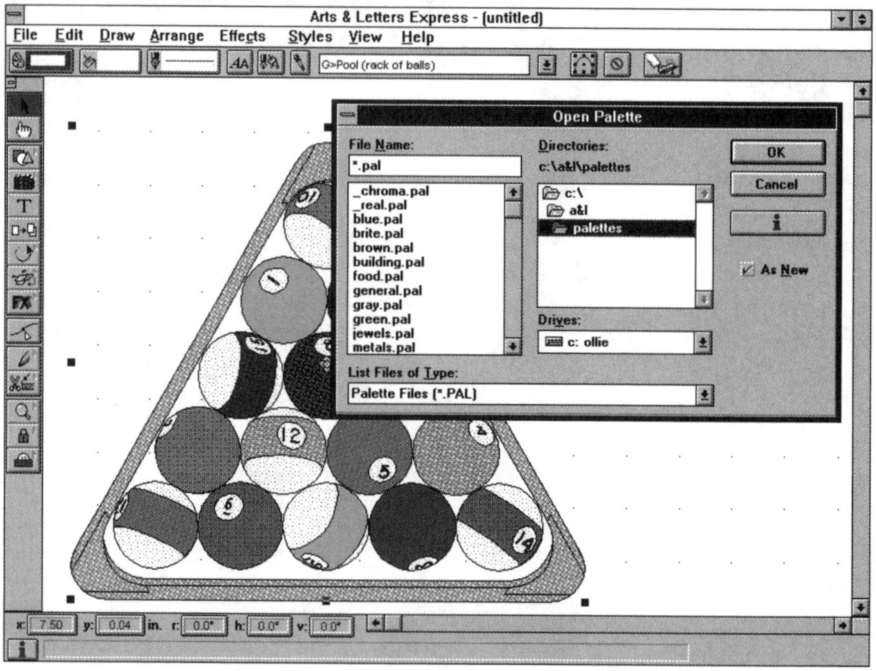

Figure 7.20
Open Custom Palette
Using the Open command on the Styles | Color cascade menu, you can display the list of prebuilt palettes in Express and load these files into the Color Palette. Note that the file at the top of the list shown is the default palette.

4. Select **OK**.
5. Select the Color icon from the Style Bar and verify that the new palette is displayed.

Steps: Restore Default Palette

Use this operation to restore the default color spectrum palette.

1. Access **Styles | Color | Open**.
2. Select the **\PALETTES** subdirectory from the file list.
3. Select the _CHROMA.PAL.
4. Select **OK**.
5. Select the Color icon from the Style Bar and verify that the default palette is displayed.

Coloring Images

Images from the Clip-Art Manager are complex art forms that are generally stored as graphic groups. Different components in the group may carry contrasting colors. Express gives you two ways to edit the color of images: Break Apart the groups to color individual symbols and freeform objects, or use the Color Correction options.

Image Groups

The images in the Clip-Art Manager are all groups of symbols and occasionally freeform objects. They come precolored. Major groups may consist of a number of smaller groups; so you may have to break apart a series of groups to be able to select and color the individual parts. Once the various components have been colored, you can select all of them and reassemble the image using the Assemble Logically option in the Align dialog box from the Arrange menu.

Master Symbol Groups

In the standard symbol set shown in the *Clip-Art Handbook*, note that a number of master symbols have ready-made "accents" or highlights shown as numbered symbols in parentheses beneath the main symbol index number (Figure 7.21). Many of these master symbols are preassembled illustrations available in the Clip-Art Manager. Symbol accents are often used to add shading or three-dimensionality to figures, images, arrows, and highlights, such as eye color and other points in larger images. You may individually load the accents and the master drawing, color them, and then assemble them using the Align Logically option in the Align dialog box on the Assemble menu.

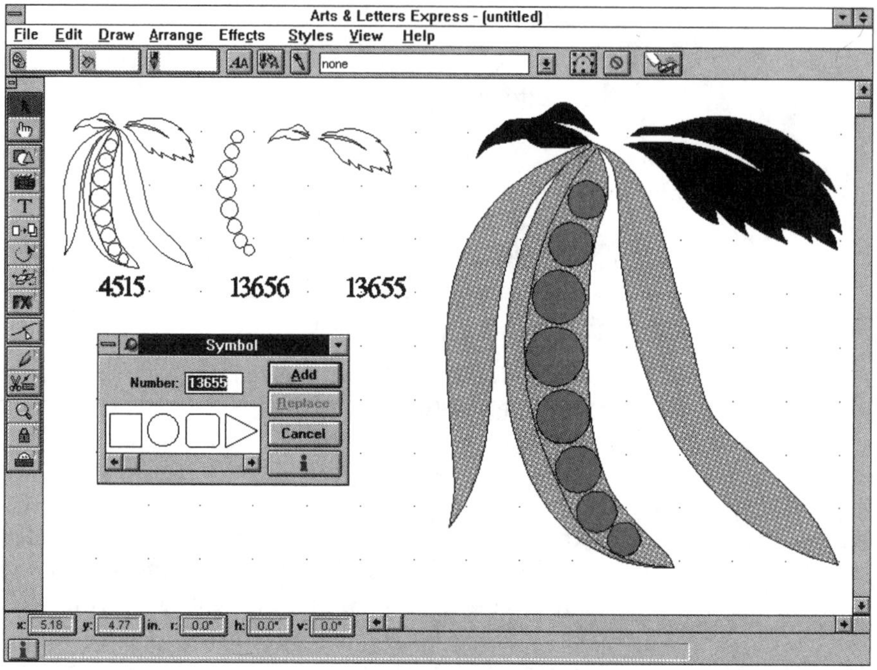

Figure 7.21 Master Symbol Groups
The main drawing of the peas (4515) has two indexed symbol overlays. These components may be separately colored and snap-assembled using the Logical option in the Align dialog box. The result is the shaded and colored artwork shown at right.

Breaking Apart Image Groups

Whether you are breaking apart a Clip-Art Manager image or assembling a master drawing from symbols and accents, Express allows you to easily work with components and to color the artwork. The graphic database design of these components makes it easy to create hundreds, even thousands of uniquely colored configurations of the same drawing.

You may also use Select Within Group, new in Version 5.0, to select individual components in a larger graphic group and compose them. If you select the object using Select Within Group and don't move it or drag it to another place on the screen, you may place the style enhancement quickly and easily. Select Within Group does permit you to drag the object out of position and, if you do this, it can be difficult to move the object back in place. For editing larger, more complex groups, it is recommended that you use the traditional Break Apart/Ungroup function, perform your editing tasks, then select all objects in the image, and reassemble using the Assemble Logically option in the Align menu as presented in this section.

Steps: Breaking Apart Illustrations

Use this operation to break apart a selected image from the Clip-Art Manager.

1. Access **Draw | Clip-Art Manager**.
2. Select the desired Collection from the list.
3. Select the desired Image Name from the list.
4. Select Add to Document.
5. Click the mouse in the working area to place the image.
6. Select **Arrange | Ungroup**.
7. Display the Object Browser list from the Style Bar, select any subgroups, and Ungroup them as well.
8. Select the desired symbol.
9. Select the Color icon.
10. Verify that the desired Color type is selected (Beg Fill, End Fill, Line, Fill & Line).
11. Select the desired color.
12. Repeat the color operation with each symbol in the image.

Steps: Reassembling the Image

Use this operation to reassemble the ungrouped, recolored image.

1. Use Block-Select or Shift-Select to select all element in the image.
2. Access **Arrange | Align**.
3. Select Assemble Logically.
4. Select **OK**.

Applying Styles within a Group

Express includes enhanced Group features that let you select and enhance components within a group without breaking it apart. This feature is perfect for editing ready-made images, but you will have to get used to the process of selecting the appropriate symbol in the stack. The Object Management features, which contain the Object Browser, are, in effect, the Group Manager. Note that the Object Viewer is included in the Style Bar; so, as you select a group and use internal group-select features, the symbol index number or element description of the currently selected object will be displayed in the Viewer screen.

Internal Selection Handles

When you use internal Group select, the display of the selection handles will change slightly. Instead of the solid black boxes for standard element selection, the selection handles will be boxes of the same size

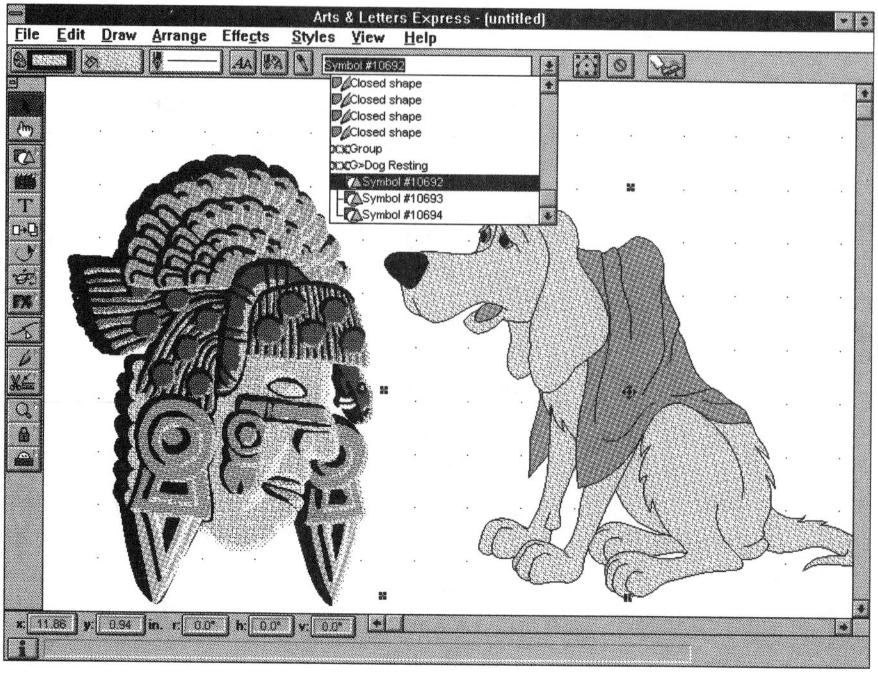

Figure 7.22
Styles within a Group
Note the crosshatch selection handles around the symbol component of the tired dog. You can apply color, line, or fill styles to this symbol without breaking apart the group. The Aztec, left, represents some newer art images, which are made up of freeform objects (Closed Shape in the list shown) that must be selected and enhanced individually.

broken by a white cross. If you experiment on the screen with selecting within a group, the display of the different handles will be very clear. (See Figure 7.22.)

Using Undo

When using internal Group select features, you will often select symbol numbers that represent one among several layers of a complex image. Since this number tells you nothing about which element you have selected, you may be unsure of what part of the picture you have selected. In this case, you can experiment by applying a color to the selected element and see what changes take place. If you have selected the wrong portion of the drawing, immediately access the Undo feature at the top of the Edit menu. You can return and continue selection operations until you get the part of the drawing you're looking for.

Pushpin Styles

When using internal group select, you should have the style palettes or Custom screens available and push-pinned to the screen. This allows you to select individual elements within the group and instantly click on the desired styles at each selection. You also may have all of the Palettes or Custom screens active at the same time, if you wish. This approach can significantly save time and effort when applying a series of enhancements to a number of art elements.

Steps: Apply Styles within a Group: Screen

Use this operation to select individual art elements within a grouped graphic or image and to apply a style.

1. Display the desired group on the screen.
2. Place the mouse cursor over the area of the grouped graphic you wish to select.
3. Double-click the mouse over the graphic.
4. Verify that the crosshatch selection handles appear around the selected element.
5. Verify that a symbol number, text, or freeform detail appears in the Object Viewer in the Status Bar.
6. Select the desired style to apply to the selected object.

Steps: Apply Styles within a Group: Viewer

Use this operation to select elements within a group using the drop-down Viewer list in the Style Bar (Figure 7.23).

1. Display the desired group on the screen.
2. Place the mouse cursor over the area of the grouped graphic you wish to select.
3. Double-click the mouse over the graphic.

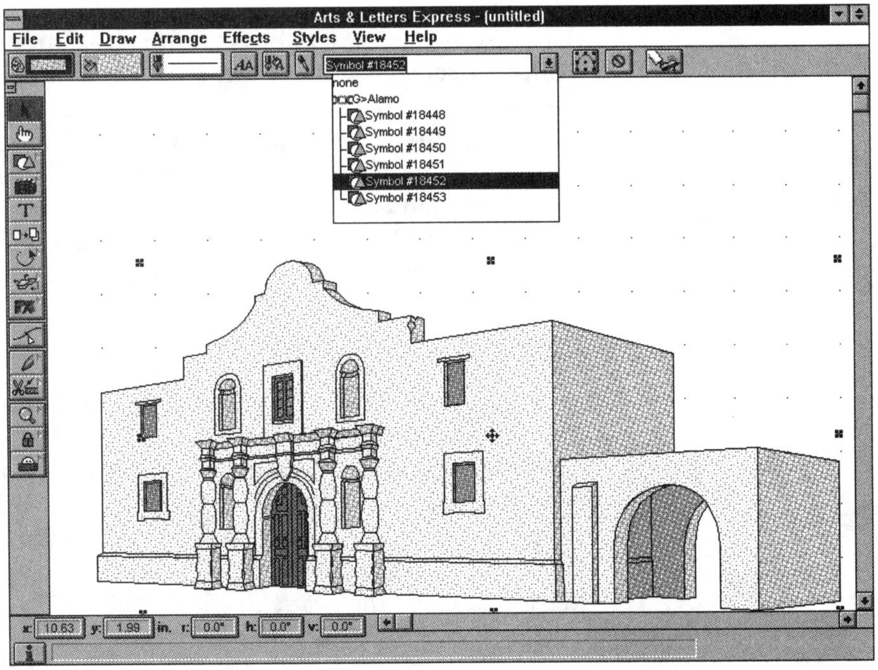

Figure 7.23
Viewer
You can select within a group by clicking on the image and checking the selection detail in the Viewer box, or you can select any of the elements in the Viewer drop-down list and the selection will be made in the screen.

4. Click on the menu arrow beside the Object Viewer and verify that a list of elements within the group is displayed.
5. Click on the desired element index number or description in the Viewer menu.
6. Verify that the object is selected with its handles, and that the object number or description is displayed in the Viewer box.
7. If necessary, repeat the process to select another element from the Viewer.
8. Select the desired style to apply to the selected object.

Color Mixing and Editing

Express provides you with fully defined color styles and a system of ready-mixed palettes that can enhance the features for most projects you undertake. At the same time, Arts & Letters is designed for professional color applications and includes features that allow you to customize mixes and edit color values using its sophisticated features. See the color pages for examples of Arts & Letters's color capabilities.

Color Models

An artist uses paint and brushes, but you can't stick a paintbrush into a computer screen. So just how is color created in a computer? There are two generally accepted color models in the computer industry that are used to create, display, and output color. These models essentially define a basic foundation of colors, and as the intensity of one or more of the foundation colors is changed, shades are mixed. Exact color mixes can be specified using numeric values that correspond to the percent of each basic color in the mix (See Figure 7.24).

Colors by Number

It is important to emphasize that the computer controls color mixes through numeric values. What the computer does is use percentage values of the foundation colors to control the color mixing. If you've ever mixed housepaint to create a specific shade, you've seen something close to this principle at work. You begin with a basic white and add a tad of bright red to create a pale pink. As you increase the percentage of the added color, the shade deepens.

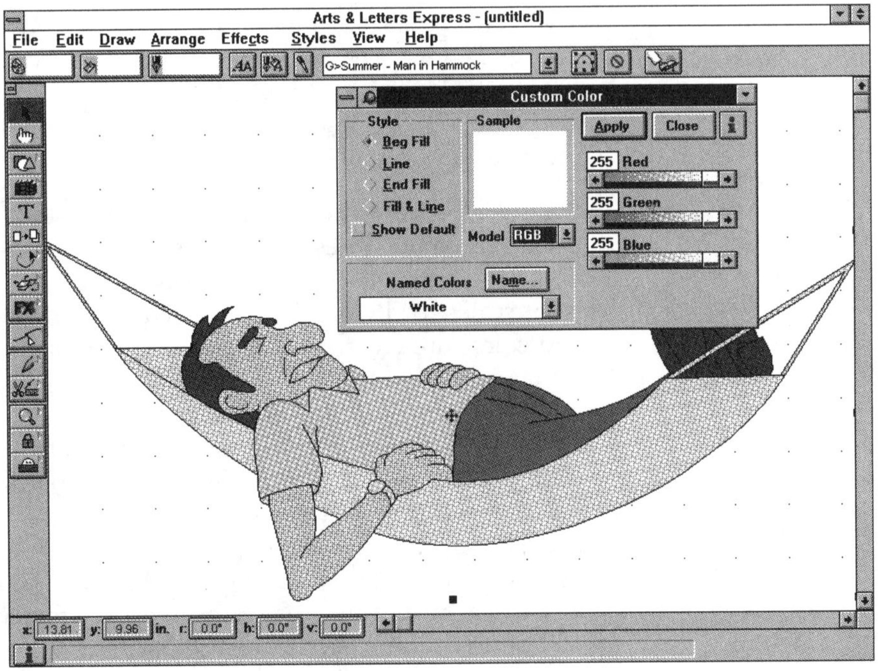

Figure 7.24
Color Models
In the Custom Color dialog box, you may select the desired color model for editing, and mix colors using the scale editors shown at the right of the dialog box.

Using Color Models In the **Custom Color** dialog box you have the option to select one of three available models to create color on the screen. Colors are controlled through a sliding scale for each basic color. You can exactly specify a color mix by recording the name of the color model and the values for each scale in the mix. It is, of course, much easier to save your color mixes under a name in a color palette, but it's more important that you understand that the numeric values for each color in the model are the means of defining and holding precise color mixes on the computer screen.

Model 1: CMYK CMYK (Cyan-Magenta-Yellow-Black) are the base colors that define all colors. White is the zero value on the scale for each of the foundation colors. As the percentage of color in each scale is increased, colors are created. On the screen, all three colors at 100% is pure black. However, *printing* at 100% of C, M, and Y creates mud. The only way to get a crisp black is to specify it separately. CMY is based on the assumption that white is, by definition, all colors (white light through a prism creates the color spectrum), and that different color shades are created by *subtracting* color values from pure white. This is called a *subtractive* process of color definition.

CMYK is the color model used to create process-color separations in Arts & Letters. The color file is broken down into its Cyan, Magenta, Yellow, and Black components. When the three colors (without black) are printed on the same sheet by a professional printer, the result is an image of continuous-tone color.

Model 2: RGB RGB (Red-Green-Blue) uses these three colors as its foundation set to define all colors. These colors are closer to the "primary" (red, yellow, blue) color set we were taught in school. The zero value in all three color scales for RGB is black (which is defined as the absence of color), and colors are created by *adding* colors to black. Rather than using percentage values as CMYK does, RGB color is expressed as 256 settings within a scale, or defined color values.

RGB is the color model used by most color monitors to define the color you see on the screen. Due to the variation of quality and technical considerations between screens, it is possible for a numerically defined RGB mix (or any other color model, for that matter) to look different on two different screens. Therefore, to a certain extent, there is a built-in uncertainty regarding whether the colors you see on screen will be accurate when printed on paper.

Model 3: Hues The color hues selector in the **Color Mixing** dialog box allows you to select color hues from an available spectrum and then vary the intensity of those hues using sliding scales of black and white. This screen is much easier to use because of the straight spectrum scale. It is also an effective way to mix shades of gray, which do not require a specific color model.

The **Hues** dialog box is useful because you can use it to quickly define the color you want. Once the color is mixed, you may select either of the two other models and you will see the numeric values in that model for the color you have just mixed.

Color Mixing

The **Custom Color** dialog box allows you to mix custom colors using one of the three defined color Models. Once you have configured a color mix to your liking, you may save it by naming it, and make it available for use with a click of your mouse.

Mixing Operations Mixing colors is a highly subjective and delicate art. As you adjust the various color elements to create a mix, the **Custom Color** dialog box displays percentage values for CYMK, or the color index numbers 1–255 for RGB, or index numbers for Hues. Each color in the mix is displayed directly above the scroll bar. Each mix then is a balance of colors in various percentage relationships. (You could record the percentage for each color to monitor the correct color mix, but that would be time-consuming and highly inaccurate.)

Steps: Color Mixing

Use this operation to mix and name a custom color.

1. Select the symbol on screen.
2. Access **Styles | Color | Custom**.
3. Select Models and select the desired color format.
4. Use color mixing scroll bars to adjust the desired color mix. The color mixed is shown in the middle bar at the bottom of the screen.
5. Select Name.
6. Enter the desired color name.
7. Select Name to exit the Name Color screen.
8. Select Apply.

Adding Color Mixes to the Current Palette

You may create and save your own color mixes using the Name option in the **Custom Color** dialog box. Any custom mix you create and name will be added to the currently selected palette. This means that you can enhance the master _CHROMA.PAL group with your own mixes, or you can define your own custom palette using the New Palette option on the Color cascade submenu and each named color will automatically be displayed in the palette.

Steps: Add a Color Mix to the Current Palette

Use this operation to add a named color mix to the currently selected default or custom palette.

1. Access **Styles | Color | Custom**.
2. Select the element to receive color mix.
3. Select the desired color Model.
4. Mix color as desired using the color bars.
5. Select Name.
6. Enter desired text or numeric value to serve as the color mix name.
7. Select Name to close the Name Color subdialog box.
8. Select Apply to close the Custom Color dialog box.
9. Select the Color icon in Style Bar and verify new color mix is displayed in Palette selector.

Color Correction

Breaking apart a multicolored image and individually coloring elements is an effective but time-consuming process, particularly if you do it often. Version 5 contains an entirely new feature that provides a sophisticated and flexible solution to this problem. The Color Corrections screen, accessed off the Styles | Color cascade menu, is a complete color control subsystem. You can instantly change the look and color relationships of any image element or a complete composition simply using the mouse.

Color Filters

The new Clip-Art Manager makes it easy to display and load thousands of colored images. Each of these images is precolored for your convenience. Color Filters is a new color management feature that works, in part, as a companion to the Clip-Art Manager, allowing you to transform the color array in an image or illustration in a variety of controlled ways. Breaking apart a multicolored image and individually coloring elements is an effective but time-consuming process, particularly if you do it often.

Color Mapping

The Color Correction dialog box operates off the principle of color mapping (Figure 7.25). When you select a color image and display the Color Correction dialog box, it automatically breaks down the image and identifies all the colors, shades, and mixes in the selected element, and then displays them to the left of the Preview mimic. As you select editing options in the dialog box, the edited resulting color is displayed to the right of the Preview screen.

Modes of Operation Color Filters has two modes of operation: Artistic and Technical. The Artistic mode provides a series of filter overlays. As each is selected from the Filter drop-down in the Color Filters dialog box, a set of control options or scroll bars appears below. The Artistic mode allows you to make color edits along more intuitive lines. Here, you can instantly convert a color image to a color negative, a grayscale, or a grayscale negative. You may also adjust brightness and contrast either for the entire artwork or for specific colors within it. The Technical mode gives you direct access to the color models, also featured in the Custom Color dialog box, and allows you to make specific mix edits to selected colors. You may edit a single color, all, or a selected group.

Figure 7.25
Color Filters
The Color Filters feature is designed to help you automatically edit the precolored images included in the Clip-Art Manager. The Artistic function (shown) allows you to make sophisticated edits from the menu; the Technical function lets you make edits using the core color models.

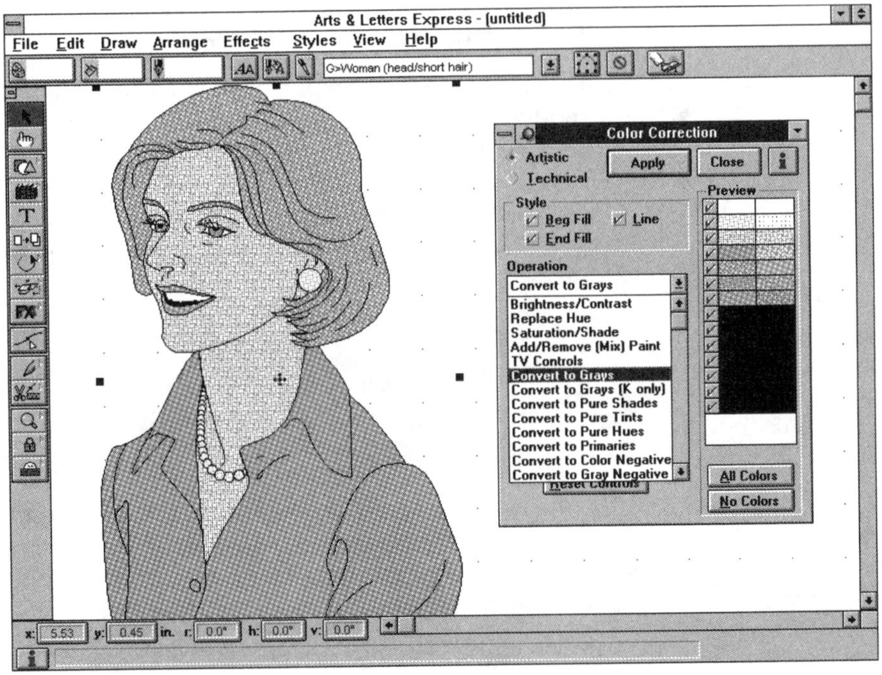

Color Selection

The display in the Color Filters dialog box contains a two column Preview display with a scroll bar. The colors in the left column are those in the currently selected object; the right colum will display a preview of the edits and adjustments you make to color. Note that this is just a Preview function: the color edits are made to the actual object only when the Apply button is selected.

At the far left of the Preview area are a series of checkboxes for each line in the Preview grid. When a check appears, that color is active for editing: Changes you make in either Artistic or Technical modes will be displayed; when the check does not appear, that color is not selected for editing. You may use the All Colors button at the bottom of the Preview to select all colors for editing; the No Colors button will clear the checks from all colors if you wish to select only one or a small number.

The Style selection area at the top of the dialog box allows you to specify the types of color objects that are displayed and subject to editing. With all three options and Line selected, Beg Fill, and End Fill, you display all colors in the selected image or object. You may constrain what is shown by selecting only one or two of these options.

Color Filters: Artistic Mode

Unless you are an expert in color publishing and output, the Artistic mode is the primary way you should use this feature (Figure 7.26). The Artistic mode provides a list of ready-made filters that automatically transform the colors in your selected object. Some filters include their own special adjustment features, which allow you to make adjustments to the effect. Some of the most notable effects you can create with these filters include:

- Convert object to color negative
- Convert object to grayscale
- Convert object to grayscale negative
- Adjust brightness/contrast for object

Keep in mind that Color Filters operate on selected colors only. When the dialog box is opened, all colors in the selected object are selected for editing, by default. You have the option to select only a few colors for editing by clicking on the checkbox opposite the color in the Preview area.

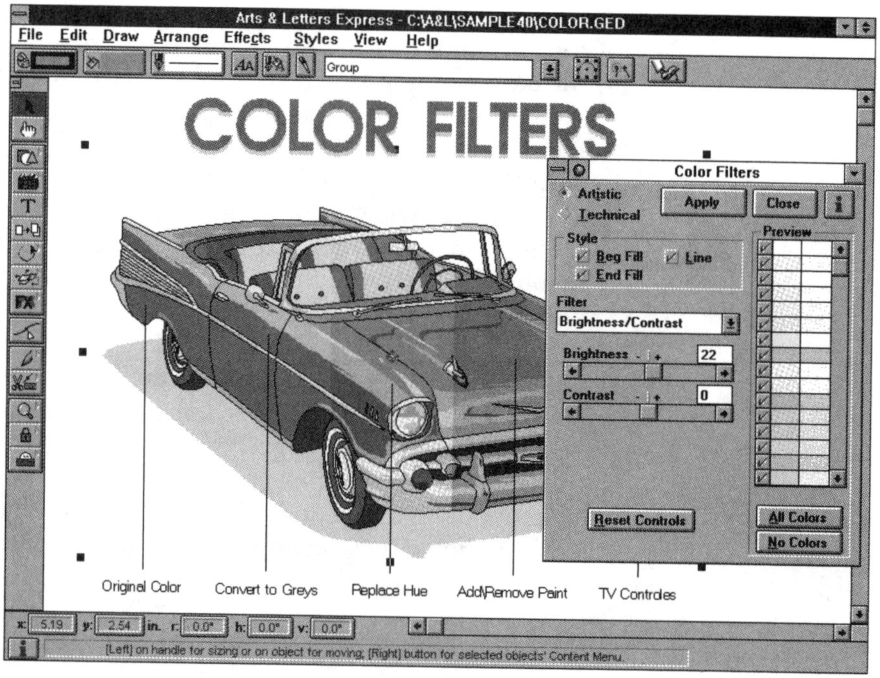

Figure 7.26
Artistic Mode
The Brightness/Contrast Filter (shown) displays scroll adjustment tools that, when selected, allow you to adjust the brightness and contrast of the selected colors in the Preview area. Changes are shown in the right hand column as you move the sliders; however, changes are not made to the selected object until you select Apply.

Steps: Apply Color Filters in Artistic Mode Use this operation to apply a selected color filter from the Artistic mode.

1. Select desired image or object to be edited.
2. Access **Styles | Color | Color Filters**.
3. Verify that Artistic Mode is selected.
4. Verify that all the colors you wish to edit are selected, and those you do not wish to edit are deselected in the Preview display.
5. Select the desired filter from the Filter drop-down.
6. Check the filter effect by comparing the original color in the left Preview column with the filter changes in the right Preview column.
7. Make any desired adjustments using filter-specifid controls (displayed directly below the Filter drop-down line). Check the filter changes in the right Preview display.
8. To apply the filter changes, select Apply.

Color Filters: Technical Mode

Technical mode uses the same color editing models and features as Color Mixing. Rather than applying preset filters like the Artistic mode, here you work directly with components of a particular color. The editing assumptions and key concepts are the same here as for Color Mixing (see Color Mixing earlier in this chapter), but this dialog box allows you to simultaneously edit a whole range of colors across an entire illustration or a multi-colored image.

The editing operation begins by selecting the colors you wish to edit in the Preview areas. All colors that are checked will be subject to the editing operations you make; and the preview will show in the right hand column. You can edit freely within the dialog box; your edits will show up in the finished object only when the Apply button is selected. Select the desired color model—RGB, CYMK, or the Hues selector. You may add to or subtract from a particular component using the Brightness option; map a full range of color component values to a larger or smaller range, using the Contrast option; or Replace a selected color component with another. These three operations work in parallel with each other, so that you may make settings for Brightness, Contrast, and Replace and execute all three in a single Apply operation.

Technical mode also allows you to experiment with a variety of adjustments to color hues and intensity. The scope of changes and adjustments here that are possible are so broad and far-reaching that it is a good idea for you to experiment here at the outset. Make several duplicates of a

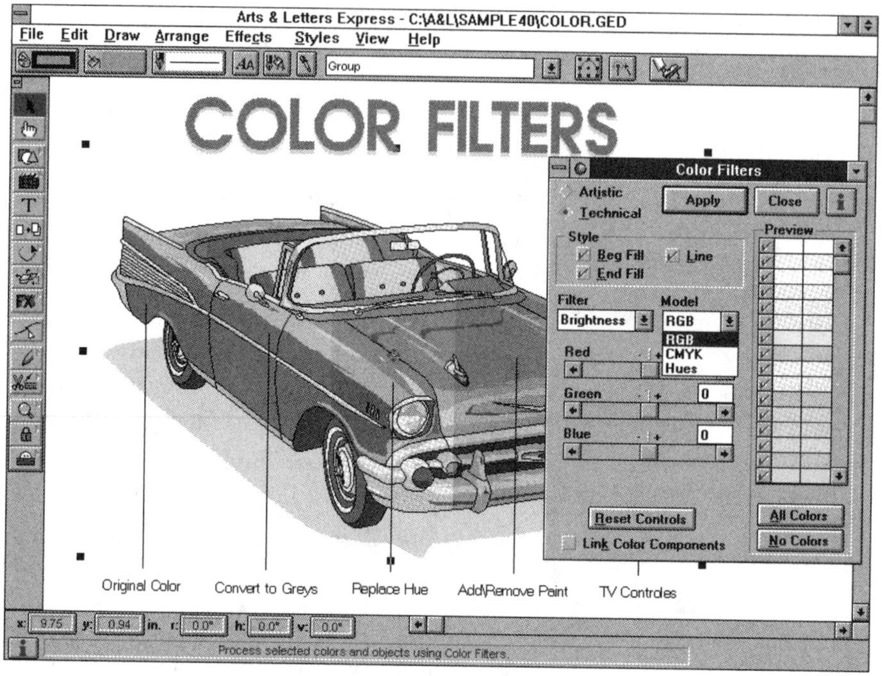

Figure 7.27
Technical Mode
Color Filters in Technical mode allow you to replace selected colors or edit Brightness and Contrast values working directly with the same color models used in mixing operations. You can literally edit the components of the selected colors and make detailed changes to improve the final printed appearance of your work.

single color image and edit it in a variety of ways and Apply the changes to the object.

Steps: Apply Color Filters in Technical Mode

Use this operation to apply a selected color filter from the Artistic mode.

1. Select desired image or object to be edited.
2. Access **Styles | Color | Color Filters**.
3. Verify that Technical mode is selected.
4. Verify that all the colors you wish to edit are selected, and those you do not wish to edit are deselected in the Preview display.
5. Select the desired filter from the Filter drop-down menu.
6. Select the desired color model from the Model drop-down menu.
7. Check the filter effect by comparing the original color in the left Preview column with the filter changes in the right Preview column.
8. Make any desired adjustments using filter-specifid controls (displayed directly below the Filter drop-down line). Check the filter changes in the right Preview display.
9. To apply the filter changes, select Apply.

Designing with Fill Attributes

Fill attributes control the texture of symbols, text, and freeform shapes. Fill patterns and textures may be applied to standard text, symbols, image components, and closed freeform shapes. Fill patterns may not be applied to line forms and open freeform shapes. By definition an element must have an interior to be filled.

Fill Menu

The array of features on the Color menu allow you to perform key style functions (Figure 7.28). The following is a brief review of all the color options on the menu as they appear.

Custom Displays the **Custom Fill** dialog box to create and name unique fill patterns using the available options.

Fills Palette Displays the currently active Fills Palette on the screen; this is the same screen as the flyout from the Fill icon on the Style Bar.

None Removes fill; makes object transparent.

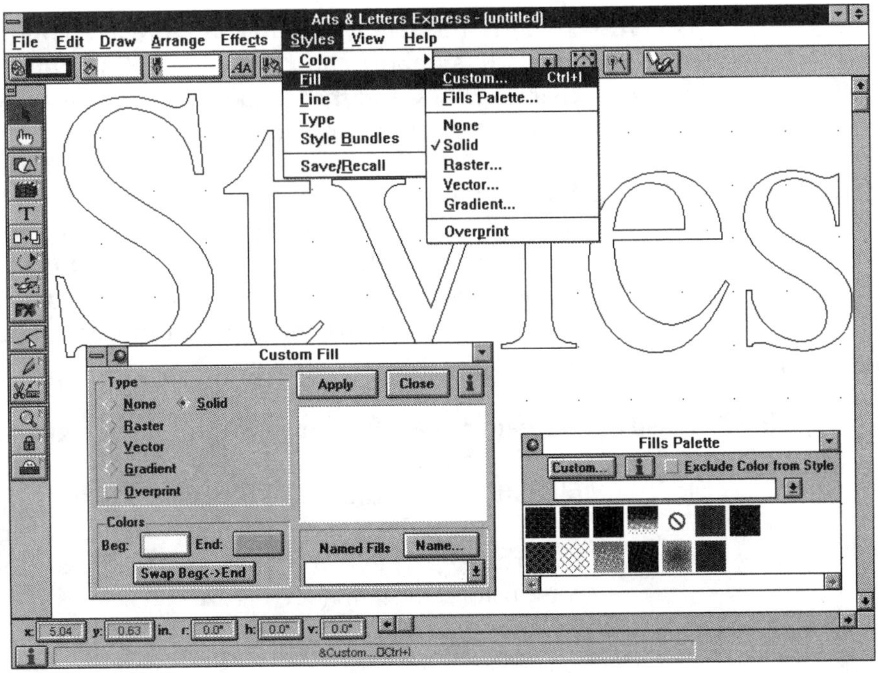

Figure 7.28
The Fill Menu lets you select a variety of fill switches (None, Solid) and specialized textures (Raster, Vector, Gradient). Fill features set the base for how colors are shown in the interior of art forms and text.

Solid	Makes the color selected for the fill solid; removes any fill patterns, textures, or gradients.
Raster	Allows you to select from a list of bit-mapped fill patterns and textures. You may separately define a color for the selected pattern.
Vector	Allows you to select from a list of vector fill patterns and textures. You may separately define a color for the selected pattern.
Gradient	Allows you to define a color gradient using a Beginning and End Color, as well as set the internal pattern, angle, and other characteristics of the gradient.

Fill Operations

Fill attributes are controlled through the **Fill** dialog box on the **Styles** menu. The four interior selections allow you to define the symbol or text as transparent (no interior characteristics), solid (solid-colored interior), and raster or vector fill patterns, which may be selected by number.

No Fill Fill attributes allow you to configure and control a number of enhancements to symbols and text. By selecting **None**, you remove all interior characteristics, and the symbol or text is transparent. Any form appearing behind the transparent, now windowlike symbols, will show through.

Selecting Textures Vector and raster texture patterns may be applied to selected symbols or graphics. These allow you to add textured fill patterns inside symbol forms as well as text characters. Note that the textured fills will appear in the selected interior color. So, each symbol can carry a wide variety of textured patterns that add additional depth and character to the image.

Object Density Fill patterns allow you to control the weight of symbols and text. Depending on whether you have applied a solid color or a heavy or light fill pattern, you can make a symbol instantly appear light and delicate or heavy and dramatic. Take a moment to experiment with different fill patterns to get a clear idea of the flexibility they add to your symbol composition system. (See Figure 7.29.)

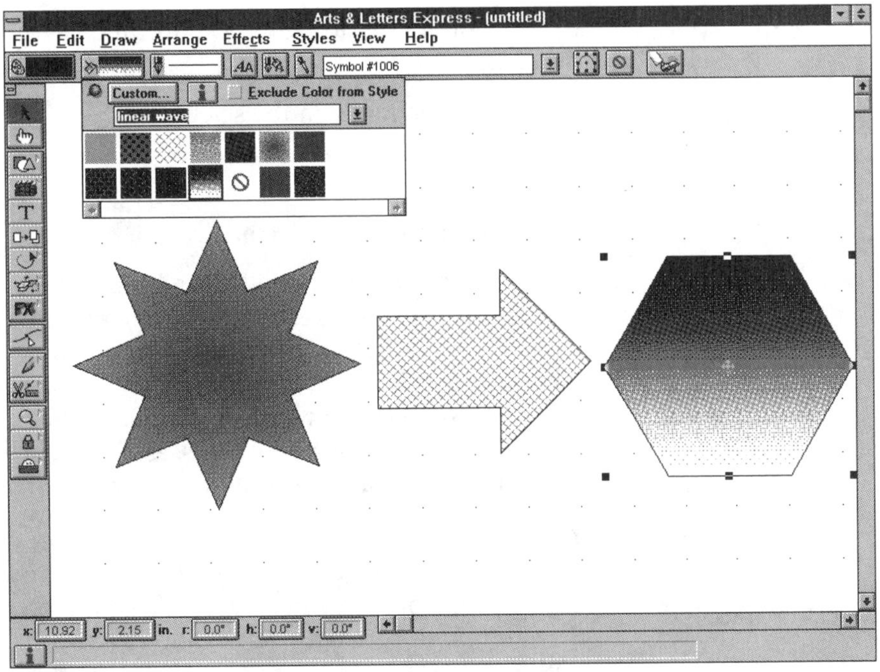

Figure 7.29 Applying Fill Patterns You can select numbered fill patterns from the Custom menu, or save your favorite configurations with color using the Name option, in the Custom dialog box, or the Palette flyout.

Steps: Applying Fill Patterns Use this operation to apply a fill pattern to a selected element on the screen.

1. Select the symbol on the screen.
2. Access **Styles | Fill | Custom**.
3. Select Desired Type.
4. Use up/down arrow-scrolling buttons to display numbered patterns, or enter a desired pattern by number. (Note: Patterns are shown in the *Symbol Handbook*.)
5. Optional: You may save the selected pattern under a defined user name using the **Name** option.

Solid Fill

For many if not most applications, solid is the default fill format for elements in the working area. When configured as solid, the element is nontransparent and stacks over other graphics in the background. An object cannot accept color if it is not assigned one of the fill patterns (Raster, Vector, Gradient) or is defined as solid.

Steps: Applying Solid Fill

Use this operation to apply a solid fill pattern to a selected element on the screen.

1. Select the symbol on the screen.
2. Access **Styles | Fill | Solid**.

Transparent Fill Patterns

The None option in the Fill style group allows you to remove any fill characteristics from the selected element and allow it to become transparent (Figure 7.30). The None setting can cause confusion if you are not used to it. If you find yourself clicking on a symbol or other element and it refuses to accept a color, it is likely that the Fill characteristics are set to None. This option expresses the element as a transparent line drawing, which can be useful for a number of stylistic effects.

Transparent Stacks

You can use this capability to create a nested set of "show through" symbols that fit together without the necessity of moving them to the front or back of the symbol stack. Another interesting use for removing the symbol fill is when you wish to reverse the image (white on black). With the interior attributes removed, only the line element defining the symbol or text remains.

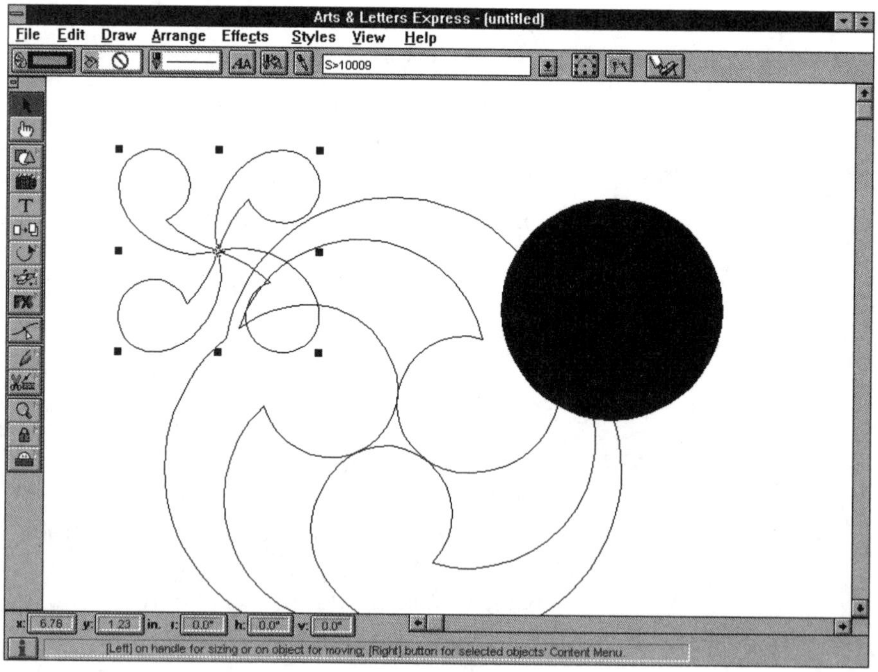

Figure 7.30 Transparent Fill When Fill is set to None, the object becomes transparent and shows other objects that are stacked behind it. If you wish to create objects that are empty white objects against a white background, use the Solid Fill option with the color set to White. In that form, the object will overprint graphics and backgrounds behind it.

Contrast Line on Background The None option can be used as a style device, particularly when you are placing line drawings over a darker background. The background will show through the transparent art form, and by setting line color to White or another light color mix, you can reverse the display of any symbol.

Solid White Option By setting the interior attributes to solid and the color to White, the symbol will appear to be a simple line drawing, but it will not be transparent. You can then stack the solid white line drawing over backgrounds and have it stand out as a complete, filled element.

Steps: Removing Fill Use this operation to make a selected element on the screen transparent.

1. Select the symbol on the screen.
2. Access **Styles | Fill | None**.

Raster Fill Patterns

Raster fill patterns are bitmaps, or patterns of dots. Express provides a scaled menu of bit-mapped fill patterns to select from that allow you to vary the density and texture of a selected art form. Because raster patterns are based on dots, they can provide a highly textured and subtle character to art forms, graphics, and text. The scale of patterns is progressive, so you will see very light and open patterns followed by others of progressive increasing density.

Maintaining Element Form When a Raster fill pattern is used, the internal texture varies in intensity. To maintain a clear visual sense of the shape or text characters, you may retain the line around the edge of the symbol, text, or freeform object as a frame to the pattern. Maintaining the form in this way makes the pattern a decorative texture to the form without losing its clear shape or identity (Figure 7.31).

Removing Element Form By changing the line's color or texture around a textured element, you can slowly fade the clean edge to create a softer, more ethereal presentation. This is particularly effective when using a raster pattern as a background or shadow for other elements. Removing the crisp line around the edge leaves just the pattern to fade into the background.

Steps: Applying Raster Fill Patterns Use this operation to apply a raster fill pattern to a selected element on the screen (Figure 7.32).

1. Select the symbol on the screen.
2. Access **Styles | Fill | Raster**.
3. Select the desired type.

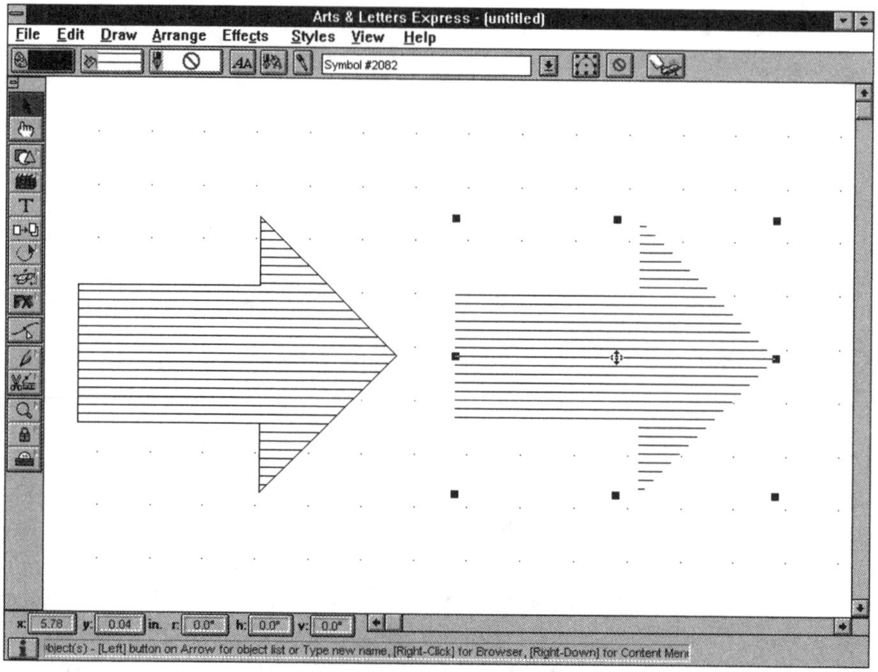

Figure 7.31
Element Form
The fill pattern can define an external shape with or without the framing line around the art form. Structured fill patterns work better for these effects. Note that the pattern of lines creates a crisp image either with the framing line or without it.

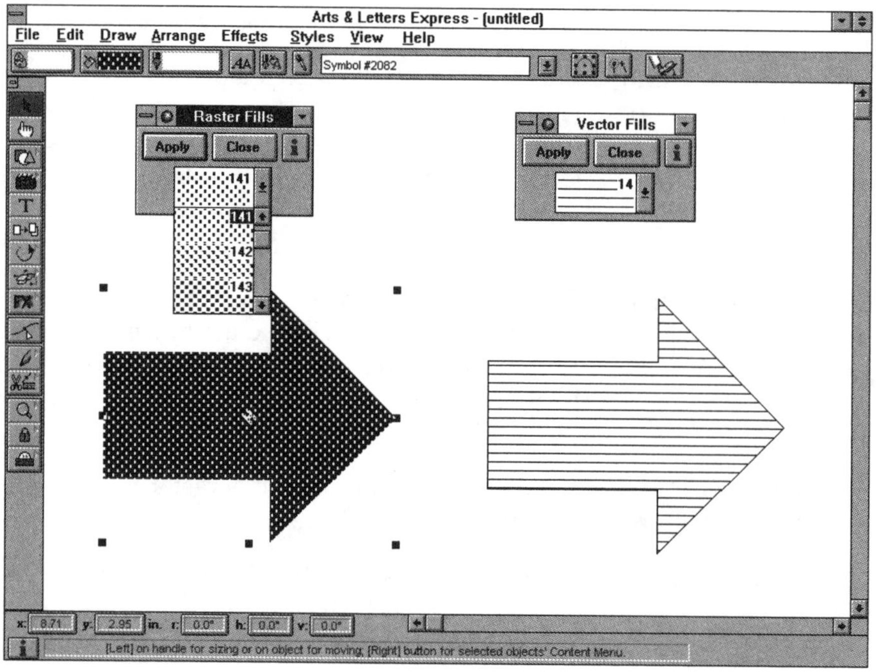

Figure 7.32
Raster and Vector
The Raster (BitMap) and Vector patterns can be selected from simple subdialogs accessed from the Fill cascade on the Styles menu. Using the full Fill | Custom menu, you can select color attributes as well.

Vector Fill Patterns

Vector fill patterns are composed mostly of structured lines and grids. As a vector-editing package, Arts & Letters creates forms using mathematical equations. Vector fill patterns are created the same way. Where raster patterns are textured with patterns of points, vector patterns tend to be crisp and structured.

Grids and Lines Vector fill patterns are an ideal way to create grids or line configurations to use as backgrounds for other objects or for text. The fill pattern group includes straight, vertical, diagonal, and cross-hatch effects that can be used in a variety of ways to create business diagrams and charts.

Text Enhancements Crisp line patterns make excellent highlights for text characters. A display typeface can acquire a whole new look with a pattern of colored lines filling the characters. In addition, you can play with drop shadow effects, and remove the exterior text framing line so that the line pattern alone defines the shape of the letters.

Steps: Applying Vector Fill Patterns Use this operation to apply a fill pattern to a selected element on the screen. (See Figure 7.32.)

1. Select the symbol on the screen.
2. Access **Styles | Fill | Vector**.
3. Select the desired type.

Designing with the Color Gradient

In addition to the standard fill patterns discussed above, Version 3.1 includes a new color gradient fill option (Figure 7.33). The gradient is, in effect, an automatic color blend that can be used as a fill value for text, freeform objects, and symbols. The Gradient option can be applied to symbols, freeform objects, and text. You can use this option to create linear and starburst backgrounds for your compositions, as well as to create a variety of interesting, graduated color patterns within individual composition elements instantly.

Beginning and End Colors A graduated pattern progresses between a selected **Beginning** and **End** color. Click on the color bars for first and last and the **Color** dialog box appears. You may go to the **Custom Color** dialog box and mix your own colors for **Beginning** and **End**, or use one of the premixed palettes available. The **Swap Beg End** button allows you to instantly reverse the color selections.

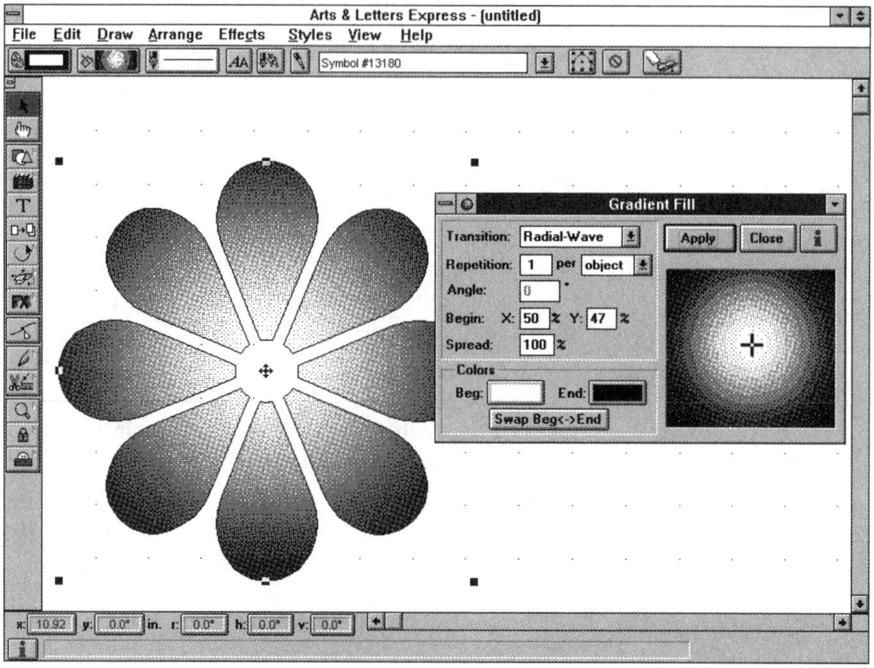

Figure 7.33
Color Gradient
The Gradient option allows you to design your own textured fill colors using a begin and end color. Features in the Gradient Fill subdialog allow you to position, angle, and set other characteristics for the resulting pattern.

Gradient Transition

Once **Beginning** and **End** colors have been selected, you have a number of options to configure the pattern, angle, repetition, and skew values for the gradient pattern. The **Transition** selection allows you to select a type of pattern for the gradient, including standard linear or radial starburst patterns.

The four options under transition are described below.

- **Linear:** Creates a standard linear gradient pattern.
- **Radial:** Creates a circular starburst gradient pattern.
- **Linear-Wave:** Creates a linear pattern with wave, or ripple, effects.
- **Radial-Wave:** Creates a starburst gradient pattern with wave effects.

Gradient Angle

Once the **Transition**, or pattern, values have been selected, you can manipulate the gradient effect by tilting it and by controlling the number of times it repeats in a defined area. You also can set the point where the first color begins to blend to the last. These features give you an extraordinary range for a wide variety of textured effects to use with backgrounds, symbols and freeform objects, and for text.

You can manipulate the angle of the pattern by entering a value in the space provided, which will tilt the gradient pattern by the specified number of degrees. An easier way to do this is to manipulate the **Control**

Bar in the **Gradient Fill** mimic display in the dialog box. The **Control Bar** appears in a number of different forms, depending on the type of **Transition** effect selected; but it primarily appears as a pair of crossed black lines, which serve as guides for your mouse. You may move the **Control Bar** anywhere in the mimic area you wish to move the start point where the first color begins to blend (**Begin X, Y**). You also may tilt or rotate it to change the angle of the gradient.

Gradient Repetition

Repetition controls allow you to condense the blend. The default value is for one complete blend to appear across a selected object or text string. You may increase that value so that the blend repeats two or more times within the selected object, which has the effect of condensing and repeating it. Repetition features may be set within a selected **Object** or defined within a single **Inch**. Using this feature, you also can use the gradient feature to set up a repeating fill pattern for backgrounds or objects.

Two of the most powerful uses for this feature are for backgrounds and text. For charts, use this feature to set the fill values for the background, backdrop, or both (to show a blended color value). For text, this feature lets you easily bring highly sophisticated blends into titles and headlines without having to create a complete color blend.

Gradient Spread

This new option in the Gradient feature allows you to control what percentage of an object will be filled with the gradient. The default value 100%. By reducing the spread percentage, you can focus the gradient to function as a focused highlight in a larger solid colored area (Figure 7.34).

Steps: Applying a Graduated Fill

1. Select the object in the working area.
2. Access **Styles | Fill | Gradient**.
3. Select **Gradient** and select **Define**.
4. Click on **First** color bar. The **Color** flyout appears. Select the desired color. You may access **Custom** from the button provided.
5. Click on the **Last** color bar, the **Color** flyout. Select the desired color.
6. Pull down the **Transition** submenu and select the desired gradient pattern.
7. Enter the desired number of repetitions per **Inch** or per **Object** in the space provided.
8. Drag and/or tilt the **Control Bar** in the mimic area to set the angle and the point at which the **First** color begins to blend. (These values may be entered numerically in the spaces provided.)

Designing with Line Attributes

A symbol is shaped by the line that defines it. The thickness, color, pattern, and style of the line can give the same symbol many different faces and moods. A thin line can give the symbol an elegant, delicate character, while a thick line can give the same image strength and power.

Line Menu

The array of features on the Color menu allow you to perform key style functions (Figure 7.35). The following is a brief review of all the color options on the menu as they appear.

Custom	Displays the **Custom Lines** dialog box to create and name unique line patterns.
Lines Palette	Displays the Lines Palette.
None	Removes the line display from the object; no color line enhancement will be accepted.
Solid	Default line displayed, changes line to a solid, unbroken display that will accept color enhancement.

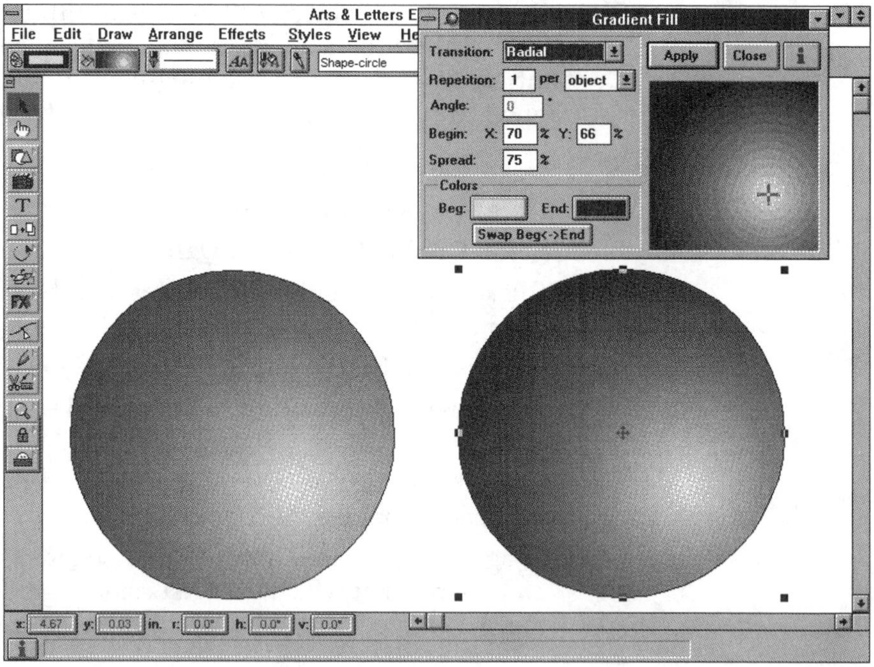

Figure 7.34
Gradient Spread
The gradient spread on the object at left is 100%. The object at right has the gradient spread set to 75%. Note that the gradient on the right creates a highlight in a richer, more solid looking object.

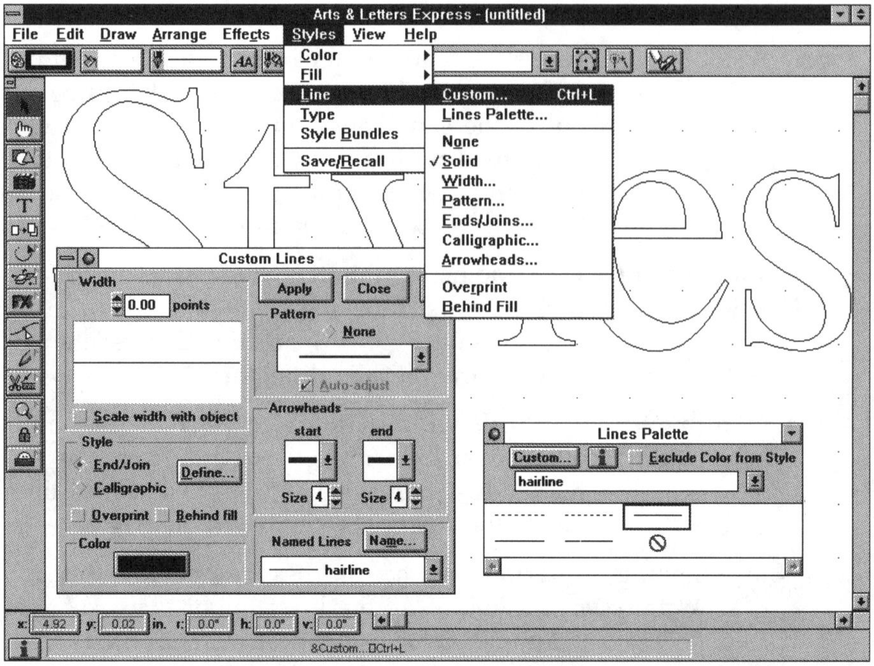

Figure 7.35
Line Attributes and Features
The Line attributes menu lets you select from an array of line enhancements, including width, pattern, special effects, and special line endings, joins, and enhancements.

Width Allows you to set the Line Width for the currently selected freeform line, text, symbol, or image. Width selections applied to groups will be applied to every individual component and group within the selected group.

Pattern Allows you to select a number of custom, nonsolid line patterns, including various configurations of dots and dashes.

Ends/Joins

Allows you to select from a group of line end and join options.

Calligraphic Allows you to design a line configuration using the calligraphic pen settings. You may create a variety of angle and depth settings that may be saved as part of a Named Line style.

Arrowheads Allows you to select from a list of available arrowheads that can be applied to freeform line segments and open-ended line elements.

Line Width

Few style features have a more dramatic impact on the look of an art form than the thickness of the line defining it (Figure 7.36). Altering this one value can change any symbol or text element in dramatic ways. Combined with other editing and special effects features in Express, you can come up with a variety of highly sophisticated variations on a theme using this one feature.

Line Weight Considerations

When adjusting line thickness, other factors may come into consideration, such as color and relative size. For example, if you increase the thickness of a red or black line and set the color to a light yellow, the effect is dramatically different.

Scale Width with Object

The **Scale width with object** selection in the **Line Attributes** dialog box allows you to increase the line thickness as the size of the text or symbol increases. In this way, the thickness of line is maintained *in proportion* to the size of the symbol in the page.

Line Drawing Weight

Altering the line thickness can change the entire character and weight of a symbol. As the line weight increases, you can also alter the line color and create dramatically different effects. The thickness of a line increases density, but a lighter color mix may soften that density and make the symbol form look entirely different from its basic configuration.

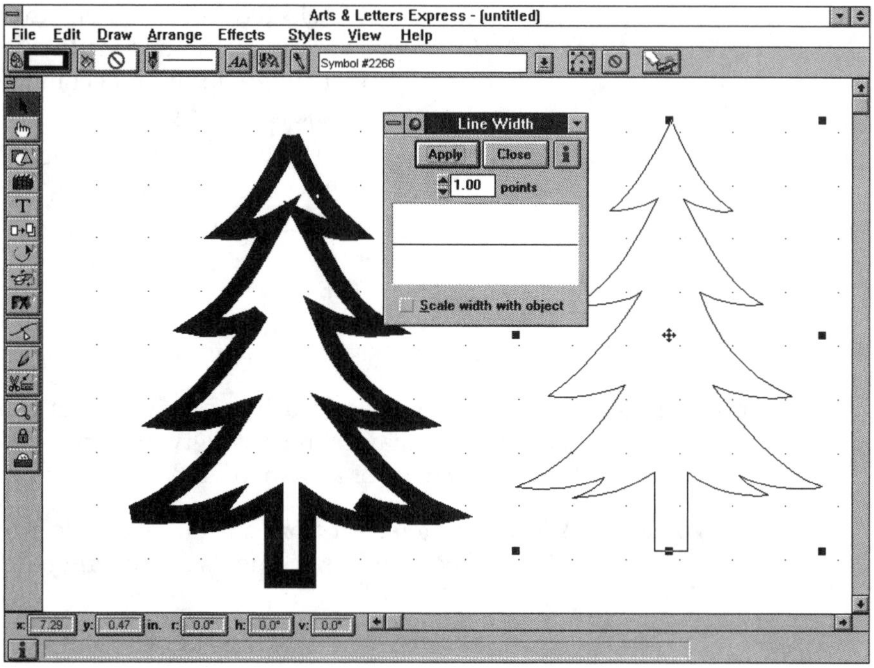

Figure 7.36
Line Width
One of the single most dramatic enhancements you can make to any symbol wireframe, the line width can add drama to a tepid, simple sketch.

Multiple Element Effects

Line width also allows you to create multielement effects with different line widths. For example, using a simple box-within-a-box effect, the outer box can have a thick line weight and progressive inner boxes can have scaled down weights, thus creating a dramatic, scaled tunnel or perspective effect using simple geometrics.

Creating Abstract Designs

By increasing the line weight and experimenting with shadings of line color, you can make simple edits such as using Slant and Rotate so that a pictorial symbol becomes progressively more stylized and abstract.

Steps: Designing with Line Width

Use this operation to set the line width for the currently selected line.

1. Select the symbol in the screen.
2. Access **Styles | Line | Width**.
3. Click on the up/down arrow scrolling buttons or enter the desired line width in points in the box provided.
4. Select the Scale Width with Object option as desired.

Line Patterns

Line patterns give you control over the quality of the line itself. Solid lines are the default in which symbols are shown. By changing the line pattern to a dashed line, a dotted line, or a combination of the two, you fragment the solid-line edge and create a rougher, less smooth edge. (See Figure 7.37.)

Arts & Letters automatically fits different line patterns into curves and straight lines. For example, a dotted or dashed line curves naturally with the shape.

Variations in Texture

Line patterns are another way of adding texture and character to the lines defining symbols and text. A solid line pattern clarifies the edges of an art form; dotted or dashed lines create a softer and more vague effect. When used in combination with internal fill patterns, line textures can enhance a very simple art form.

Variations with Calligraphic Effects

When experimenting with line patterns, try combining a selected pattern with different thicknesses or different calligraphic pens. This kind of experimentation will demonstrate to you how powerfully line attributes can affect the look and character of a symbol drawing.

Steps: Designing with Line Patterns

1. Select a symbol on screen.
2. Access **Styles | Line | Pattern**.
3. Select the desired line pattern.

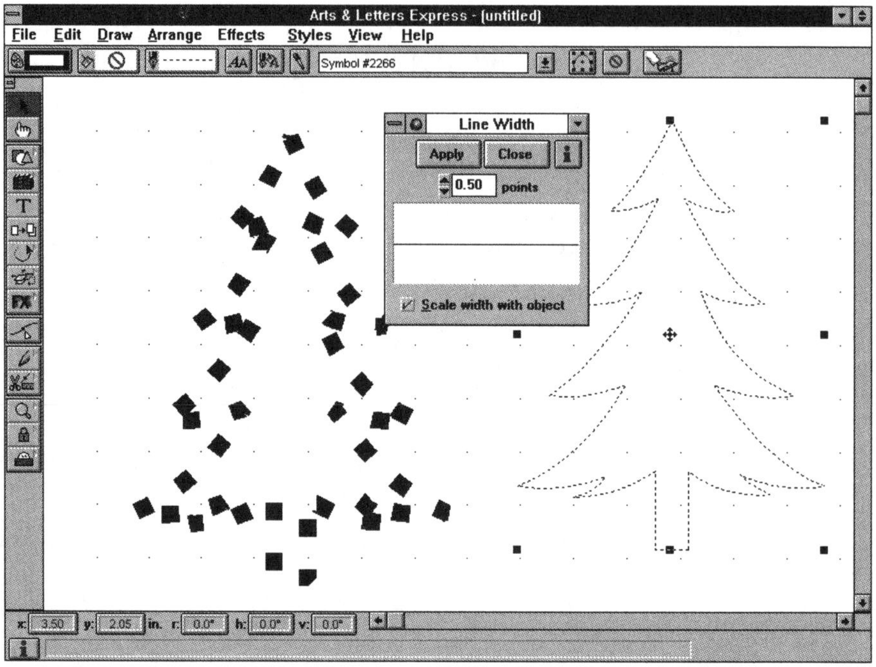

Figure 7.37
Line Patterns
A line pattern applied to the tree on the right creates a cutout image for a child's coloring book. The same pattern on an extra thick line (at left) fragments the tree into an abstract. Between these two extremes, there are many pleasing effects you can create with line patterns.

4. Enter the desired width, or use the up/down arrow scrolling buttons to set width.

Line End / Join Styles

By changing line ends and joins in a symbol or text character, every join in that character takes on the new characteristics. When combined with a solid line thickness, say three points or more, these effects can make even a standard symbol look as though it was custom designed. You can configure line ends with an end cap, a rounded end, or a squared-off end. Joins can also be configured as mitered joins, rounded joins, and bevel joins. Rounded and bevel joins in particular can give a standard symbol the appearance of being hand drawn. (See Figure 7.38.)

Line Width Considerations

Frankly, unless the line width in the symbol, text, or freeform object is thicker than a standard one point or hairline width, you won't notice these settings much. So, ends and joins generally will be more effective design tools when you are creating thicker lines or larger format artwork. You're really not likely to notice the shape of the end caps unless the line thickness is five points or more. Similarly, the joins won't really be that noticeable until you get well beyond the simple framing line.

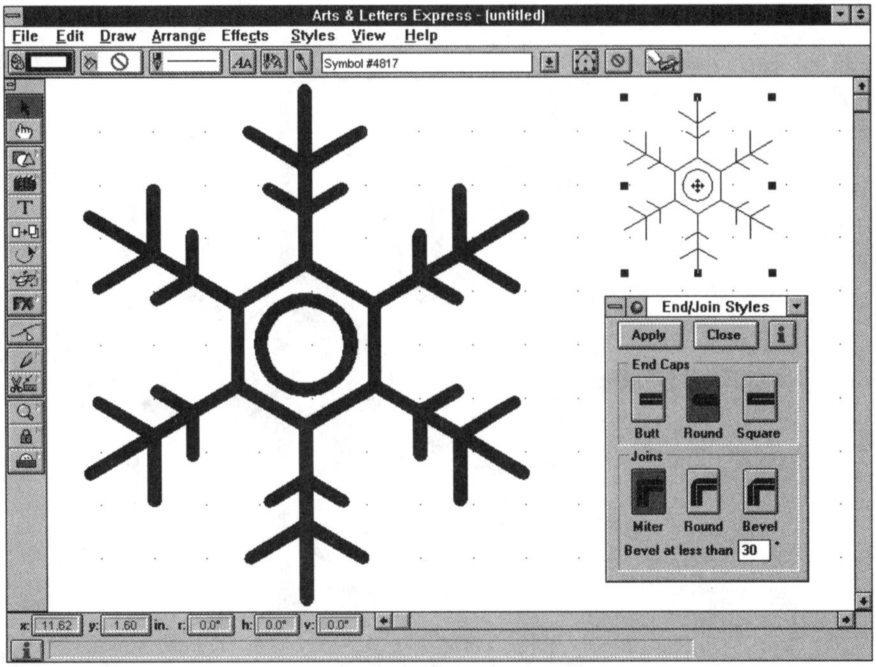

Figure 7.38
Line End / Join Styles
The simple snowflake at the upper right becomes a blizzard when the line weight is expanded (left) and the line end caps are rounded. These effects are generally more noticeable on thicker line elements.

Miter: Bevel at Less Than Option

This feature is defined for the Miter Join option only. It allows you to control the angle at which the Miter bevels out. At extremely tight angles (less than 30 degrees) the Miter effect can become very distorted looking with long narrow angles. Because this effect may be desirable for your composition, Express lets you set the threshold for beveling tight angles to a very low value. You can use this feature to suppress exaggerated Miter angle effects by setting the minimum bevel angle to a higher value.

Steps: Setting End/Join Line Styles

Use this operation to select a line end or join style.

1. Select the symbol on screen.
2. Access **Styles | Line | Ends / Joins**.
3. Select the desired end/join style and the desired join style and select **OK**.

Calligraphic Pen Styles

The calligraphic pen effects offer you the ability to mimic the effect created by a calligrapher's pen on paper (Figure 7.39). Traditionally, the calligrapher holds the point of the pen steady as the picture is drawn, and does not turn the tip of the pen as one normally does when writing by hand. With the pen tip held at a steady angle, the pen stroke is a different thickness when it is pulled vertically on the paper than it does

Figure 7.39 Calligraphic Pen Styles
Twists and turns on the line form approximate the action of a stylus. The snowflake with uniform line weight in the previous screen picture now looks almost three-dimensional as the lines are turned and angled by the calligraphic pen.

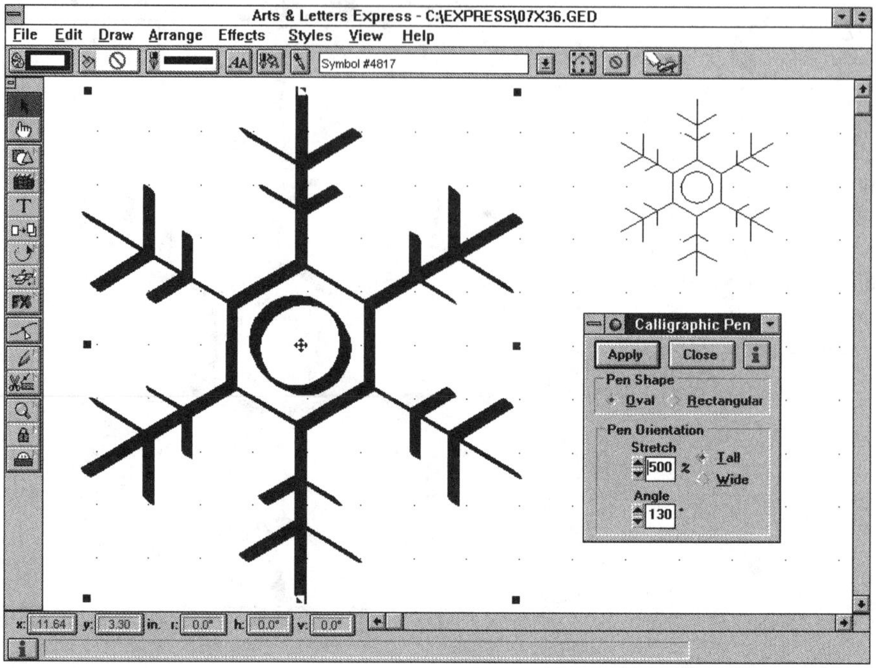

when it is pulled horizontally. This accounts for the flowing, ribbonlike quality of calligraphy. When applied to a line that defines a basic symbol, it can change the look and feel of the symbol entirely.

Variations in Line Width

As you vary line thickness in concert with changes in the calligraphic pen angle and point, the variety of effects becomes even more varied. The thicker the line width, the more dramatic will be the effects of the calligraphic twisting and shaping. To get the maximum effect while designing, set a plain geometric form or a simple curved or straight line form and practice with the controls to see how the effect changes. When you arrive at an effect you want, go to the Custom Lines dialog box and save the named configuration. Nothing can be more frustrating than trying to re-create a calligraphic line effect with all of the scaling options and choices available. Ergo, capture and save it now!

Variations in Color and Shading

When standard colors, specially mixed colors, or grayshades are applied to the line, you can create an infinite degree of textures and character. Given the richness of this feature, it is a good idea to take some time to experiment with specific effects so that you can translate the dialog box selections into specific examples that help you visualize how you would like to use this feature.

Steps: Setting Calligraphic Pen Styles

Use this operation to create calligraphic pen effects for a selected element.

1. Select the symbol on screen.
2. Access **Styles | Line | Calligraphic**.
3. Select the desired pen shape. **Oval** creates softer, more rounded effects, and **Rectangular** produces a sharper, more edged look.
4. Set the width of the pen using **Stretch** entry box.
5. Set the angle of the pen using **Angle** entry box.
6. Select **OK** to leave the subdialog box.
7. Set the **Width** of the line as desired.
8. Select **OK** to complete operation. Note that the line character in the drawing reflects your settings.

Arrowheads

Express also includes a set of arrowheads for use with open freeform shapes and any other shape as well. Arrowheads can be placed on a continuous line or used as the endpoints to straight or curved line segments. This allows you to create a variety of effects, particularly in diagrams and business artwork, where arrows can be used as flowchart symbols or as line indicator arrows (Figure 7.40).

Begin and Endpoints Two selectors are provided for arrowheads, which allow you to select one arrowhead configuration—for example, a blunt end for one end of the line, and one of the arrow options for another.

Symbol Arrow System Arts & Letters Express includes a family of over a hundred custom arrow configurations. If you are trying to create a highly stylized effect with arrowheads, review the graphic arrow pages in the *Clip Art Handbook* before attempting to design a custom effect using these arrowheads.

Ends / Joins Arrowheads are another option similar to the Ends/Joins feature. You also may combine the two—for example, using a rounded line end at one end of a line, and an arrowhead at the other. You may only select a standard line ending from the Line Arrowheads selector. If you wish one of the custom end configurations, you must access Ends/Joins and select the desired one.

Set Start / End Point To place the arrowhead within a continuous line form, such as a circle, you must convert that form to freeform and select it in standard mode. The Set Start/Endpoint feature will then become available. When

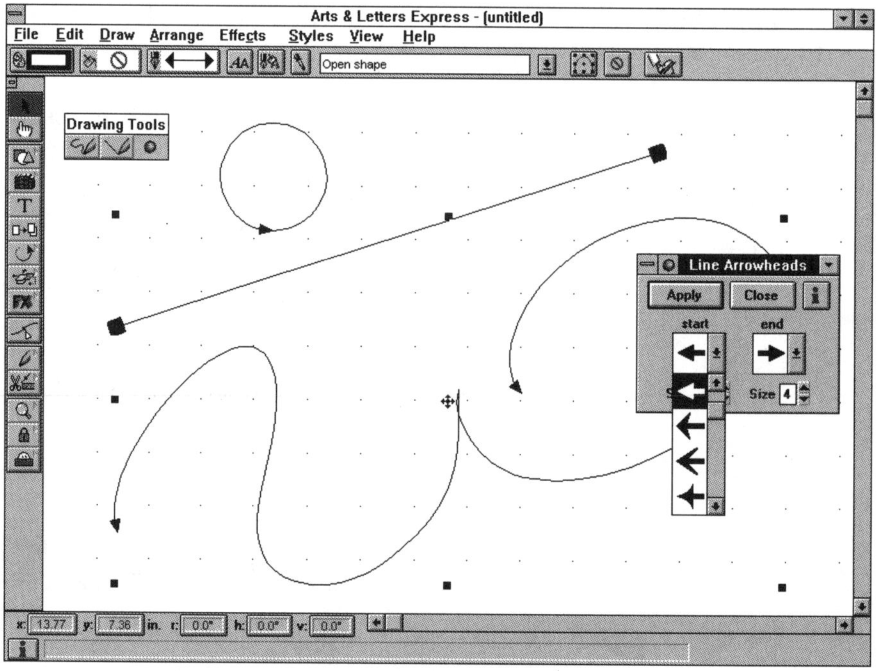

Figure 7.40 Arrowheads Arrowheads may be placed at the end of line segments or within closed freeform shapes. The symbol must be converted to freeform if you wish to use the Set Start/Endpoint feature to set the position of the arrow exactly where you want it.

selected, it changes the cursor to a freeform selection arrow and you may click at the place on the continuous line where you wish Express to place the arrowhead.

Steps: Place Arrowhead on an Open Line

Use this operation to assign an arrowhead to an open line segment.

1. Select the desired line segment.
2. Access **Styles | Line | Arrowhead**.
3. Select the desired Start and End arrow configurations. Note that the default is a standard line end.

Designing with Type

The Type style features control the display of standard text in the Express screen. When text is entered in the Enter/Edit Text dialog box and placed on the screen, it remains editable at any time. You select the text block and may change the content at any time. You may also apply attributes from the Type Attributes dialog box (Figure 7.41).

In standard text, Express is always able to recognize the object as text and apply typefaces, sizes, and typographic layout attributes like

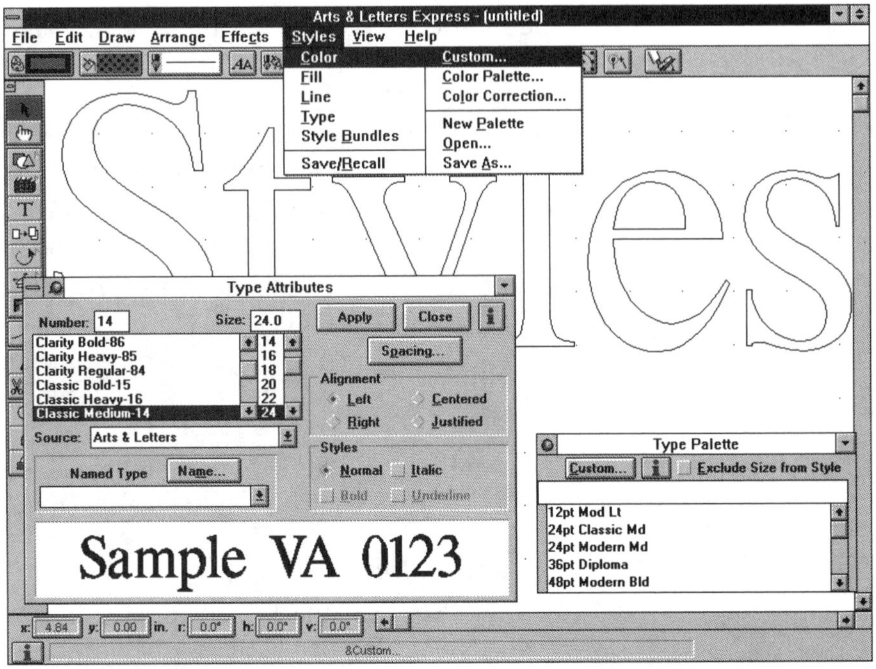

Figure 7.41
Type Features
The Type cascade allows you to access individually all the typographic and typeface controls in the Custom dialog box. Type features can also be combined with other Style features for dramatic text effects.

spacing and alignment. Once type has been converted to freeform, the connection is permanently broken and you may no longer use any of the Type Attribute features on the text.

Full coverage of the type manipulation and control features of this dialog box is presented in Chapter 4. But within the family of styles, Type Attributes may be used in combination with the other styles that regulate the color, fill, and line attributes of the displayed type. In addition, the Style Bundles option is one of the best and most effective ways to save complex type special effects.

Coverage in this section focuses on the use of Type attributes in combination with other selections and features on the Styles menu. Additional effects will be found in Chapter 8, including using type as a cutout or clipping path, warp and extrude effects, and drop shadows.

Type Menu

The array of features on the Type menu allow you to perform key style functions. The following is a brief review of all the color options on the menu as they appear.

Custom Displays the **Type Attributes** dialog box to create and name unique type styles.

Type Palette Displays the currently active named type styles on the screen. This is the same screen as the flyout from the Color icon on the Style Bar.

Face Allows you to select the desired typeface for the currently selected string.

Size Allows you to select the desired type size for the currently selected string.

Spacing Allows you to set the desired spacing for the currently selected word, phrase, or paragraph.

Type Styles Allows you to select the available type styles: Normal, Bold, Italic, and more for the currently selected typeface.

Alignment Allows you to set the alignment for any text element of two lines or more.

Type and Color

Once you have set the typographic values and typeface for text in Express, you must also set the Line and Fill color for the type string (Figure 7.42). You can vary these colors to create a variety of sophisticated effects. In many standard text presentations, solid black is the default color of choice. As always, you should be mindful of the final output of your work so that you select color accordingly. If you are outputting the final art on a black and white printer, don't use any but solid black to establish solid type. Even a solid red will print slightly different from a solid black on a standard desktop printer. There are essentially three principal color configurations you can use with type; each offers a distinct design value and look.

Uniform Line and Fill In standard black type, both the line framing the letters and the fill of the characters are set to solid black. In color applications, this would vary by the solid color selected. Uniform line and fill colors solidify the presentation of the characters on the page. Color styles do not automatically set both the framing line and the fill to the same color unless you so specify using the Fill & Line coloring set option.

The default display for Express is to show the line for type in black and the fill in the color Cyan. If you want to create a monochrome type effect in any color always use the Fill & Line option in the Color palette and verify on the screen that you have selected the desired color. If you accidentally select a shading or color mix for the line color, your characters will have a very hazy edge. Failure to check that both colors are as you want them can lead to time-consuming editing.

Figure 7.42
Type and Color
Color can make dramatic differences in how type is presented. The uniform text shows line and fill as identical colors; variable text has line and color different; outline type matches the interior to the background.

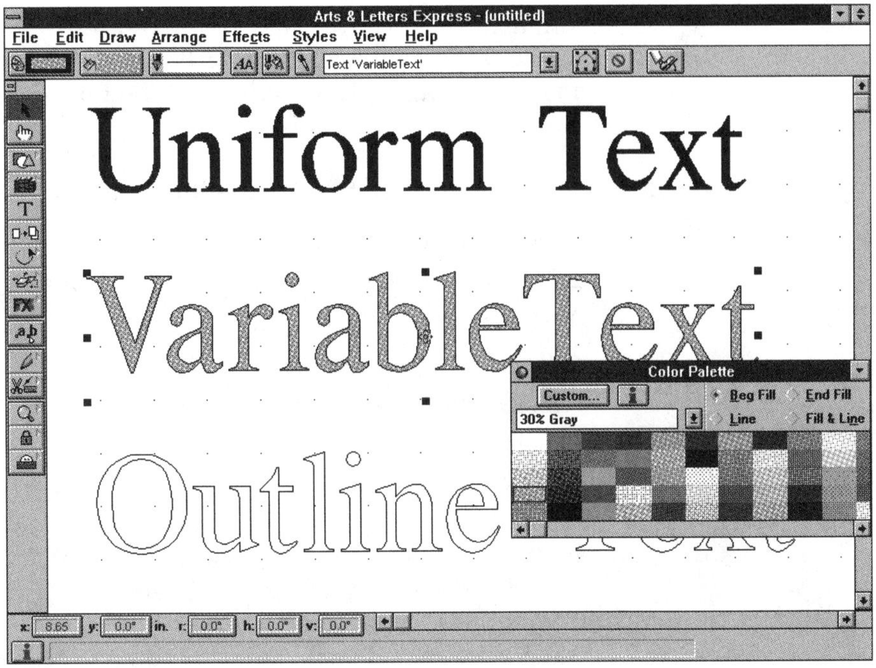

Steps: Set Uniform Color Type

Use this operation to set text with identical line and fill colors.

1. Select the desired text.
2. Select the Color icon to display the Color palette.
3. Select the Fill & Line option.
4. Select the desired color.

Variable Line and Fill

For certain effects, you may wish to vary the line and fill characteristics of the type. This is particularly true for display or designer effects which use large type sizes. The smaller the type, the less desirable it is to vary the line and fill settings. What you might end up with on the printed page is mud, no matter how nice it looks on the screen.

Variable line and fill effects are often effective when working with colored or textured backgrounds. You can set a light line color, like white, to frame the outline of the text against a dark background, and use a contrasting fill color to make the interior of the type stand out from the background.

Be sure of the effect you wish to create. Set the colors carefully. If you want to save a great deal of time, save the typographic attributes of the heading as a Named Style. Then you can use the Style Bundles option to match that typographic style with a fill or line color and save the whole thing as a named Style Bundle. Applying that style bundle to any type string will reproduce all the typographic effects, correct size, line color, and fill color in a second!

Steps: Set Variable Color Type

Use this operation to set text with variable line and fill colors.

1. Select the desired text.
2. Select the Color icon to display the color palette.
3. Select the Beg Fill option.
4. Select the desired color.
5. Select the Line option.
6. Select a color.

Outline Type

When the fill color of the type matches the background color, you have an effect called Outline Type. In this format, the external shape defines the characters. Assuming you have a white background and a black framing line, your color selections are simple. If you are using more elaborate textured backgrounds and you want a defined Outline effect, it is best to simply eliminate color settings entirely using the Fill | None option. When Fill or Line values are set to None, no color may be assigned to them. For fill values None is a much more significant setting, simply because it makes the text transparent. The only aspect of the type that has body is the framing line. Once you have set the color for the line, any background will show through. This is particularly powerful if you are setting an outline type configuration over a gradient or image in the background.

Steps: Set Outline Type

Use this operation to create outline text.

1. Select the desired text.
2. Select the Color icon to display the color palette.
3. Select the Beg Fill option.
4. Select the color to exactly match the background.
5. Select the Line option.
6. Select the color to contrast with the background.

Type and Fill Patterns

Fill patterns and colors combine to give you a multilevel enhancement capability. Since fill patterns are fundamentally texture controls, you can alter the look and presentation of type characters by varying the fill characteristics. Fill styles control only the texture pattern; you must set the fill color to express the pattern as you wish it to appear (Figure 7.43).

Solid Type

Default type is generally presented as solid characters. This is the basic fill setting for standard type. But the color or shading selected will vary the density of a solid type element. Using solid light gray or color mixes allows you to create a solid element that has a lighter texture and density. As with all style operations, experimentation will be your best guide.

Steps: Set Solid Type

Use this operation to set a solid fill pattern to a selected string of text.

1. Select the desired text.
2. Access **Styles | Fill | Solid**.

Transparent Type

Setting Fill values to None removes the interior fill characteristics of type so that it cannot accept a color. This is used to create simple outline or transparency effects. For example, a word can be used as a foreground screen through which an illustrated background can be seen.

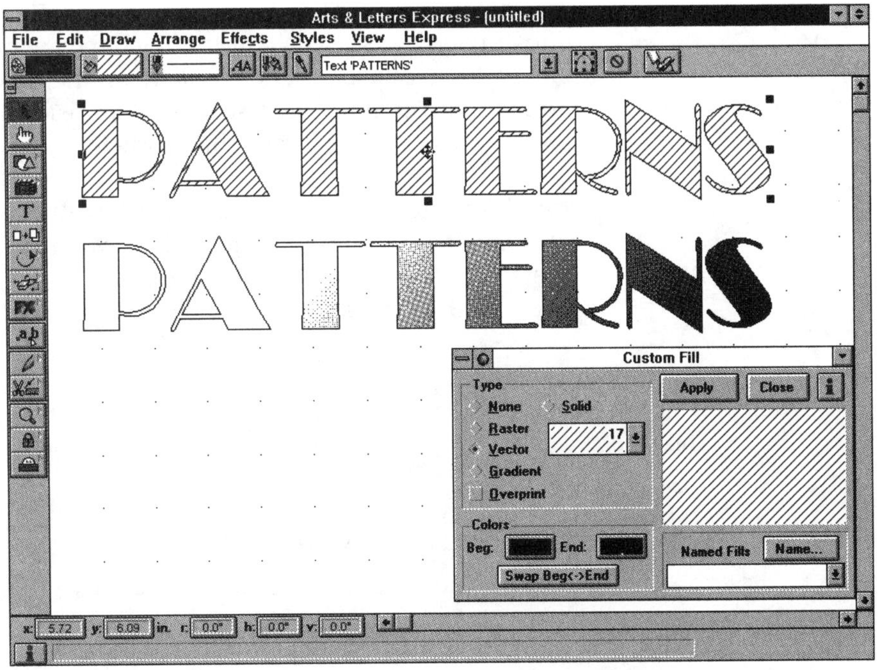

Figure 7.43
Type and Fill Patterns
The Vector pattern at the top and the grayscale gradient at the bottom both create angled dynamics within the word, but each has a special character that heightens the look of the text.

Steps: Set Transparent Type

Use this operation to make a string of text transparent.

1. Select desired text.
2. Access **Styles | Fill | None**.

Textured Type

Raster and Vector fill patterns provide a wide range of internal textures for type characters. Raster patterns are based on dots and tend to offer wider variations of density and subtle textures; Vector patterns are based in line forms and offer crisp patterns and clear effects that can be used to enhance display type. Given the detail and density of both these options, you are unlikely to use them with type unless type is scaled large, like a poster or headline element. You should not use internal textures like this for small type or text labels. Even if the effect prints on your output device, the effect is likely to be very muddled.

When using Raster or Vector fill patterns with type, be sensitive to the pattern match between the character shaping in the typeface and the specific pattern you are looking at. Vector patterns tend to be highly linear and angular. As such, they tend not to mix well with highly curvilinear script typefaces, or Italic forms. Vector fills work well with boxy, crisply linear type faces like Modern. Raster patterns offer more options for working with curved forms, but be aware that a heavy, dense fill pattern in a light, elegant face is likely to produce a muddled mismatch.

Textures are also sensitive to the character line width and thickness. Some typefaces use a slender character line, as do Light styles of standard faces. If the line is too slender, there isn't much interior to fill, and any texture you put inside the character is likely to create a confused look.

In the main, the typefaces that work well with internal Raster or Vector texturing are dramatic display faces with solid character elements, or standard typefaces in heavier styles, such as Bold or Heavy. This gives you the space for the texture effect to add a sense of style to your work.

Steps: Set Type Texture

Use this operation to set a Raster or Vector texture in a string of type.

1. Select the desired text.
2. Access **Styles | Fill**.
3. Select Raster or Vector.
4. Select the desired pattern.

Gradient Type

Gradients are the ultimate form of texturing. Unlike the preset Raster and Vector patterns provided, the gradient allows you to create a color evolution and also gives you features to frame that into a custom pattern. There are so many gradient options that this section must begin with an absolute rule: Never create a custom gradient without saving it into a Named Style in the Custom Fill dialog box or the Palette (Figure 7.44). You can capture a gradient and name it by selecting an object that carries the gradient, but that is simply catching up after the fact. Save them as you create them. You'll be glad you did.

Many of the same design considerations apply when using gradients with type. Gradient effects are dramatic and detailed. If you are using a delicate typeface with thin line elements, the gradient and its subtle variations may not establish well and the result will simply look confused. At the same time, angled linear gradients can electrify a word and move the eye pleasingly through a composition. For example, placing a radial (circular) gradient at the center of a headline can make a word pulse with life and drama.

Steps: Apply a Gradient to Type

Use this operation to apply a gradient to a string of type.

1. Select the desired text.
2. Access **Styles | Fill | Gradient**.

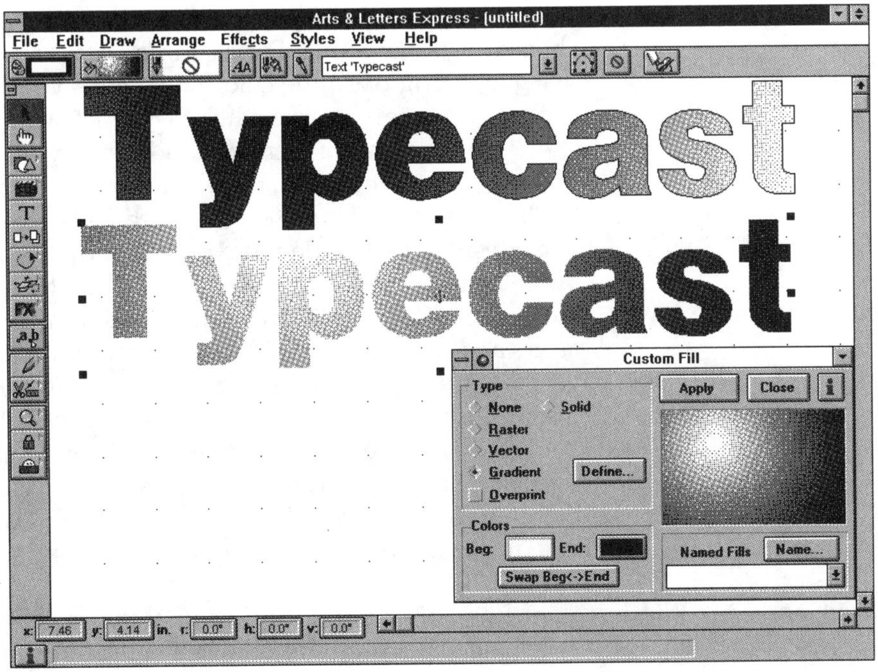

Figure 7.44
Type Gradient
The Gradient is the same in both words. The bottom one was reversed using the Swap feature in the Gradient subdialog box. Note also that the framing line is in place for the top text and removed for the bottom. Can you tell the difference?

3. Select Beg Color.
4. Select End Color.
5. Edit the Angle, Repetition, and Begin values as desired.
6. Select Apply.
7. Access **Styles | Fill | Custom**.
8. Select Name.
9. Enter desired name for the gradient.
10. Select **OK** to exit the subdialog box.
11. Select Close.

Texture and Line Variations

When textures are used, whether Raster, Vector, or Gradient, you may vary the effect further by retaining or removing the framing line around the text. This is a fundamental design issue: The line expresses the outline of the type character. If you remove it, you can have a very evocative, suggestive display of type with a subtle internal texture, or a robust and dramatic pattern that clearly defines the shape of the character without the framing line. Experimentation will help you get a sense of your options and the kind of effects you can create.

Type and Line Styles

Since all type in Express has a line component, you can alter the type characteristics of a line. For example, increasing the width of the line to match a strong or subtle color mix allows you to create diverse presentations with a few simple edits (Figure 7.45).

As a rule, you should create style effects with textures or lines but not both. If you have an elaborate interior fill, you may find that altering the line pattern will create a confused, even ugly, effect. For this reason, line effects can be made more powerful by using solid interior colors or outline effects. Some line effects really don't work very well unless they are outline effects. It looks a little weird to have a solid fill to your characters and then have a dotted line around the edge.

Line editing features give you many individual options to exercise, from width, to pattern, to calligraphic pen settings. The gradient rule applies here: Save any line effect you create immediately into a Named Style so you can apply it to other text or art elements on demand. It is no fun to re-create these things from scratch. Arts & Letters is designed as a database—not only for your art, but for your styles as well. Use it.

Type and Line Width

Adjusting line width is a function of the size of your type on the screen. Type characters are very closely shaped, and expanding the line width

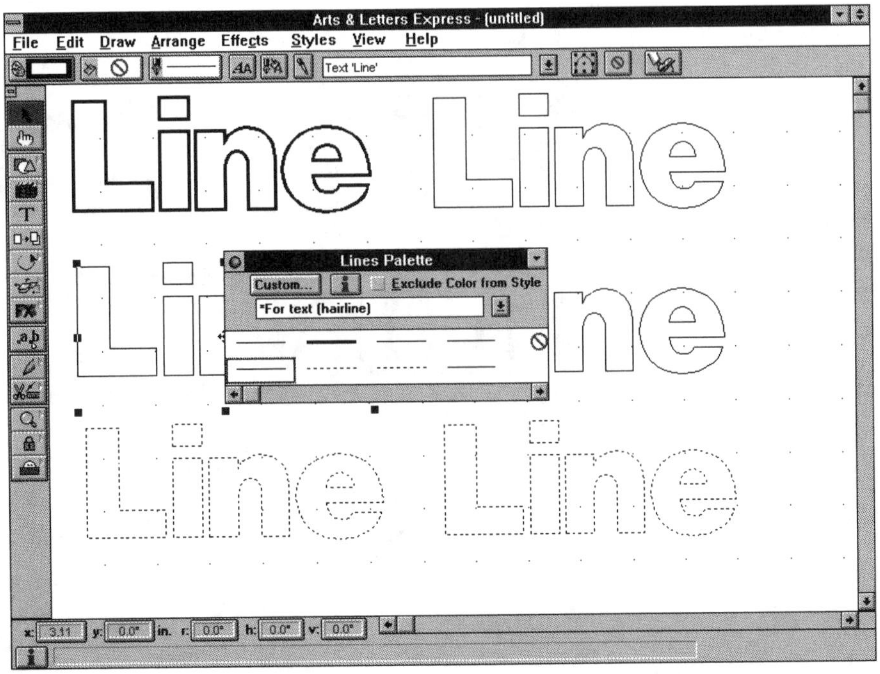

Figure 7.45
Type and Line Styles
The look of type changes as the line is strengthened or broken with dashes and dots. Line configurations may be selected and applied directly from the Lines Palette.

has an exponential effect with text. Both sides of the character get thicker with each incremental increase in the width, so you have to be careful and select just the amount of thickness to get the display effect you desire.

It is a good idea for type effects involving width to select the Scale width with object option. This will make the line thickness a function of the object size. As you edit the object size, the line will increase or decrease accordingly, but the relationship you have defined between them will remain intact.

Steps: Adjust Text Line Width

Use this operation to set the width of the framing line around text characters (Figure 7.46).

1. Select the desired text.
2. Access **Styles | Line | Width**.
3. Set the desired thickness.
4. Select Scale width with object.
5. Access **Styles | Fill | Custom**.
6. Select Name.
7. Enter the desired name for the gradient.

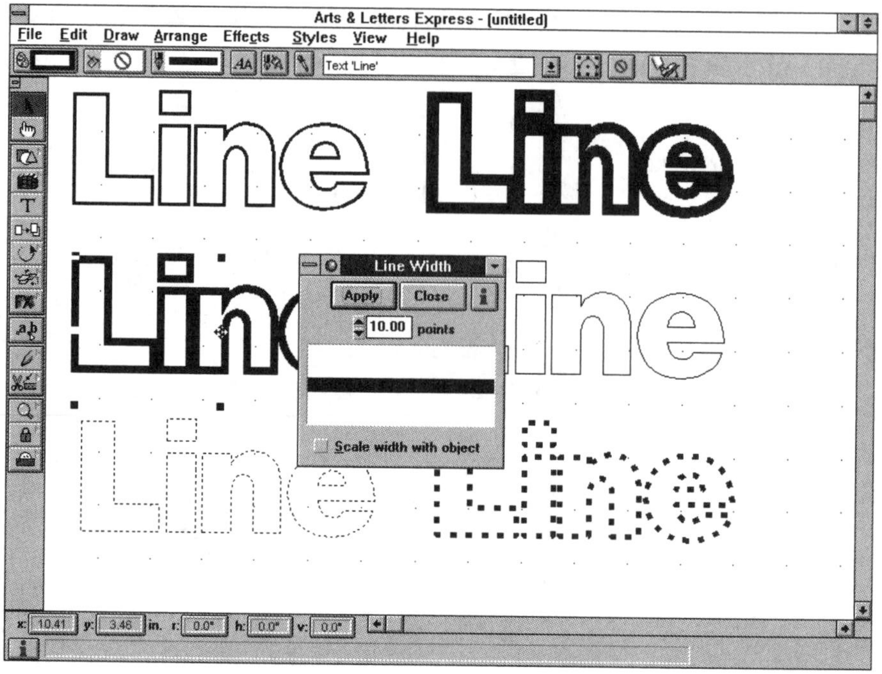

Figure 7.46
Type and Line Width
As the line gets thicker with type, the letters close in on themselves. Some of these effects can be interesting, others like the dotted mess at bottom right, just ugly.

8. Select **OK** to exit the subdialog box.
9. Select Close.

Type and Line Pattern

Fill textures are broad; line textures are thin, elegant strokes. The default pattern for most text—and all standard-size paragraph text—should be solid. As text gets larger, such as for a display or heading application, you can use some of the broken line patterns. These effects have the potential to look gimmicky, so be careful with them. You also may wish to match a line pattern on text with a dotted line around symbols or other art objects to create a uniformly textured composition.

Steps: Adjust Text Line Pattern

Use this operation to set the width of the framing line around text characters.

1. Select the desired text.
2. Access **Styles | Line | Pattern**.
3. Set the desired Pattern.
4. Select Scale width with object.

Type and Calligraphic Effects

Calligraphic and type effects were made for each other. The calligraphic pen allows you to present text with a fluid line and add a whole design layer to typefaces by simply manipulating the line. The Calligraphic pen allows you to twist the line into angles and curves.

As great as these effects are, they don't really show up unless the type is large enough and the framing line is thick enough for the eye to detect the calligraphic variations. One highly effective way to experiment with type and calligraphic effects is in outline form. Make the type a large size on the screen, with a white interior against a white background, and apply calligraphic effects. There are so many variations possible between the selected Pen Shape and Stretch/Angle Orientation that experimenting is the only real way to see the effects and find the one you want.

Calligraphic pen effects can and must be saved immediately as Named Styles. In terms of complexity, they are the Line Style equivalent of Fill Gradients; and trying to re-create one is enough of a hassle that you should always capture it as a Named Style as soon as you create it. Note that as soon as the calligraphic effect is captured in a Named Style, it shows up miraculously in the Lines Palette off the Status Bar and you can take the same style you just created and apply it to symbols and freeform drawings with a click.

Steps: Set Calligraphic Pen Style for Text

Use this operation to create a calligraphic line effect for the text framing line (Figure 7.47).

1. Select the desired text.
2. Access **Styles | Line | Calligraphic**.
3. Set the desired Pen Shape.
4. Adjust Orientation as desired.
5. Access **Styles | Lines | Custom**.
6. Select Name.
7. Enter the desired name for the calligraphic effect.
8. Select **OK** to exit the subdialog box.
9. Select Close.

Type and End / Join and Arrowhead Effects

For display type and headlines, the display of particular characters can be shaped using Join options. Miter, Round, or Bevel joins can change the look and character of type characters on the screen.

Arrowheads, as noted previously, can be placed internally in closed objects. There might be a time when the idea of having an arrowhead fly around the perimeter of the letter E would be interesting, but that time is likely to be extraordinary. Remember, to place arrowheads where you want them in a closed shape, such as a text character, you have to break the text to freeform to set the position point. Once text is in freeform it says "bye-bye" to the Styles menu, so proceed at your own risk. (See Figure 7.48.)

Figure 7.47
Type and Calligraphic Effects
The subtle calligraphic effect on the left becomes exaggerated but more three-dimensional looking as the line width is increased. Calligraphic effects require a thicker line to be noticeable.

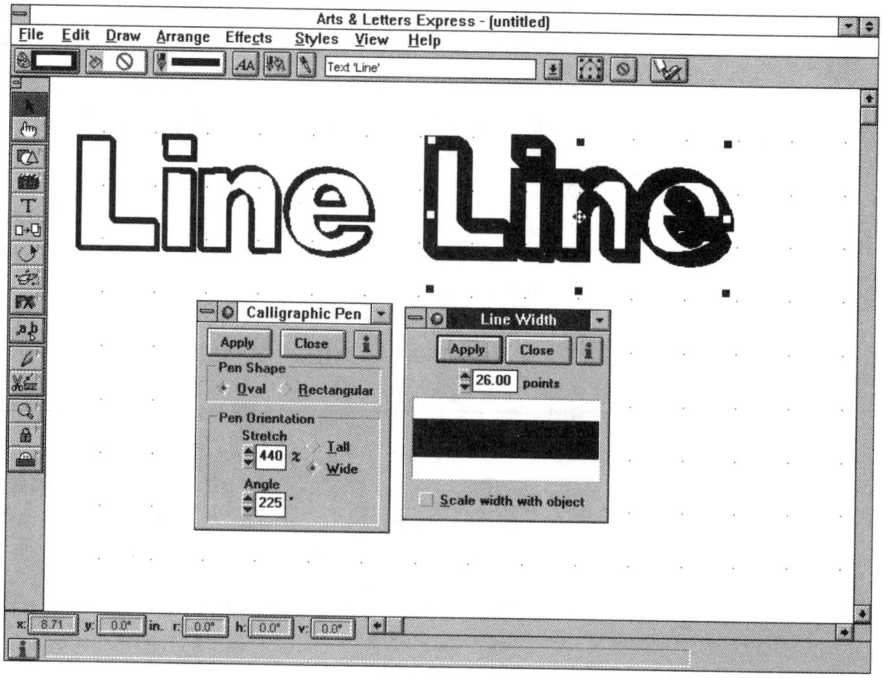

Figure 7.48
Type and Joins
The bevel effect on the text characters generally shows up as a result of the size of the word and the thickness of the line. You can use these effects to create stylized presentations of standard typefaces.

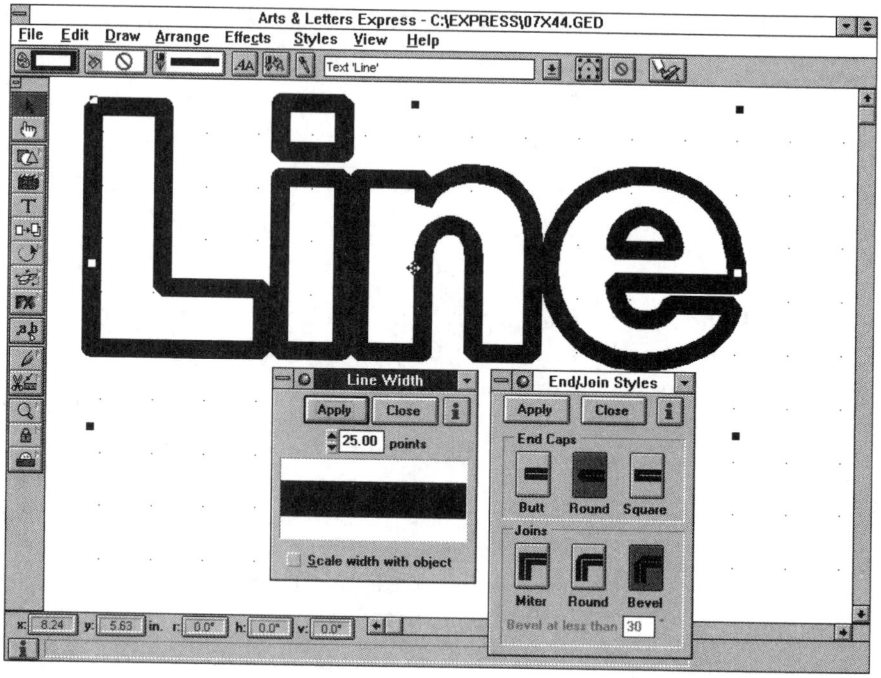

Steps: Set Ends / Joins or Arrowheads

Use this operation to set custom joins and line graphics for the text framing line.

1. Select the desired text.
2. Access **Styles | Lines**.
3. Select **Ends / Joins** or **Arrowheads**.
4. Select the desired option.

Designing with Style Bundles

Express creates and saves Named Styles just like Color Palettes. Palette files contain lists of premixed colors. By loading individual palette files, you can take advantage of wide range of named colors, stored in specific sets. The Style Bundles feature is the master control for all the other Style Naming functions on the Styles menu (Figure 7.49). All of the Named Styles you create in the Line, Fill, and Type dialog boxes are saved in special Style file collections which can be opened and closed just like palettes. In this way, you can access certain style groups, depending on the nature of the task at hand. You may also choose to create a single master Style file with all of the styles you use frequently inside it.

The Style Bundles features also allow you to interactively combine selected Named Styles from all the styles features—Color, Fill, Line, and Type—into single master styles. When these master styles are applied to a text string or art object, all the settings of all the named styles inside that bundle are applied instantly. This is a powerful automation feature with many applications. One of the most obvious and practical is storing all the style attributes to create headline text effects—typography, interior color, line color, fill patterns, line effects—all in a single, selectable style.

Style features are a parallel function of the Arts & Letters graphic database. Just as you can select symbol wireframes and images right from the database, you have the option to use and create a custom enhancement database through styles. With banks of predefined enhancement effects, you have the ability to create logos and designs automatically, depending on your needs and applications.

Style Bundles Menu

The array of features on the **Color** menu allow you to perform key style functions. The following is a brief review of all the color options on the menu as they appear.

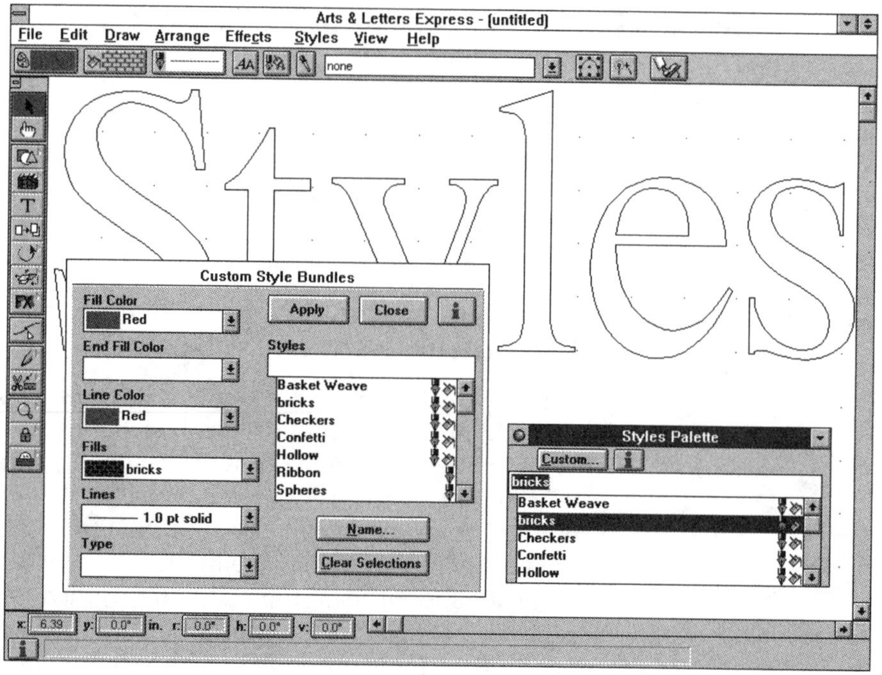

Figure 7.49
Style Bundles Features
Style Bundles features allow you to assemble Named Styles from all the other Styles dialog boxes and create grouped Master Styles.

Custom Displays the **Custom Style Bundles** dialog box to assemble style bundles.

Bundles Palette Displays the currently active collection of style bundles on the screen.

New Styles Clears the current style palette and allows you to create a new collection of named style bundles.

Open / Save As File features used to create style collections use the .STY extension. You may create style bundle collections and open them as needed. Named styles for Line, Fill, Type, and Style bundles are saved in the .STY file; Named Colors are saved in the separate PAL (Palette) file.

Assembling Style Bundles

The Custom Style Bundles dialog box is like an electronic menu. Select one from each of the drop-down style lists and create a feast. The principle is simplicity itself. As you create Named Styles for Fill, Line, and Type configurations you are using, those selections show up in the selectors in this dialog box. You may now create composite style bundles of one or more of these options. You may make a style bundle that has only a single color attribute in it, and you may create a style bundle that contains all six options:

- Fill Color
- End Fill Color
- Line Color
- Named Fill Styles
- Named Line Styles
- Named Type Styles

Once you have selected all the elements you want to combine in a single style, you select the Name option in the Custom Style Bundles dialog box and create a name for the whole bunch. Each of the components in the named style group is marked with a descriptive icon that is displayed in the Custom Style Bundles dialog box and the Style Bundles Palette display, so you can see at a glance how many components a given Style Bundle has.

Steps: Create a Style Bundle

Use this operation to assemble a style bundle. Note that the only options that will be shown in the Custom Style Bundles dialog box are Named Styles from each of the Custom screens on the Styles menu (Figure 7.50). You may not directly access individual style features to create style bundles.

1. Access **Styles | Style Bundles | Custom**.
2. Select and display all the desired Named Styles you wish to combine using the drop-down list display.
3. Select Name.
4. Enter the text of the Style Bundle name.
5. Select Name to dismiss the Name Style subdialog.
6. Repeat the operation as many times as desired to create additional Style Bundles.
7. Select Apply or Close to exit the dialog box.

Saving Style Bundles

Styles are saved in a separate STY file. This file is transportable and flexible just like the YAL format files, which are used to contain standard and custom artwork collections, and the PAL files used to store color palettes. The principle is essentially the same here. You have the option to create a variety of style files for different purposes or a single style file containing all of them.

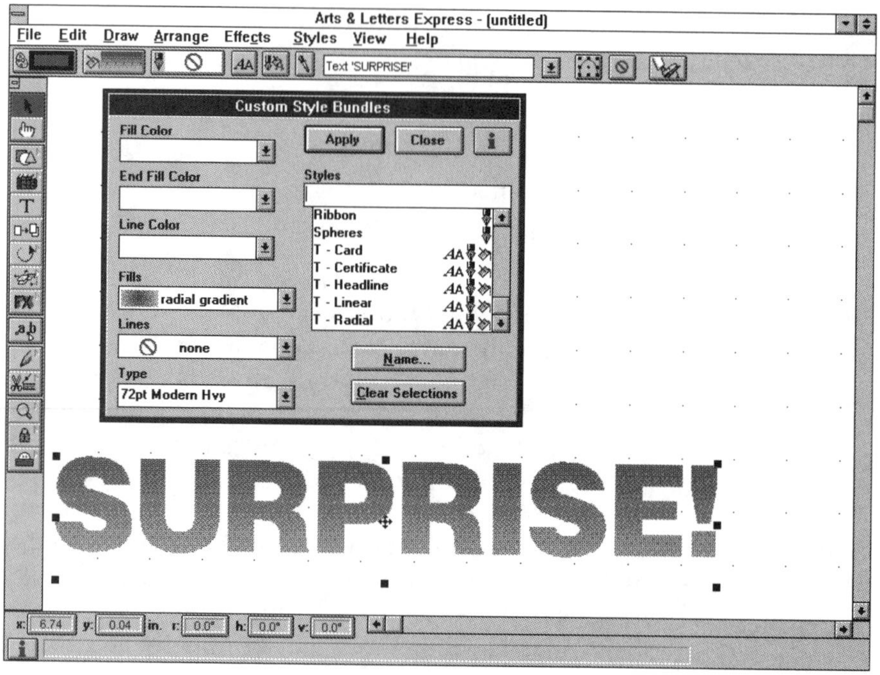

Figure 7.50
Style Bundles
A word instantly formatted by the style bundle includes a typeface and size style and a bundled gradient style. Style bundles let you create master effects that can be used on both text and graphics to create uniform design elements across a range of compositions.

Steps: Create a New Style Group

Use this operation to create a whole new style group from scratch.

1. Select **Styles | Style Bundles | New Styles**.
2. Select Yes to clear the Palette.
3. Create and Name new styles in each of the Fill, Line, and Type Custom Screens.
4. Access the Custom Style Bundles dialog box to assemble them into Style Bundles.
5. Access **Styles | Style Bundles | Save As**.
6. Enter the filename for style file.
7. Select OK.

Composition Power

The features and operations discussed in this chapter have been designed to show you just how much you can accomplish in Arts & Letters without drawing a single line. The symbol-based composition system gives you the power to create highly original artworks that don't look "canned," or as if they were cut out of a clip-art book. This is due to the extraordinary flexibility of the Arts & Letters symbol system, and the concept it embodies, which is that the base art forms are of greater use to you if they are more basic, less finished, and, hence, easier to edit.

The operations in this chapter are the basis for the advanced operations and techniques presented in the next three chapters. You can perform any of the operations shown above for freeform graphic objects or custom symbols, as long as you are working in standard editing mode. If you are a beginner with Arts & Letters, you can compose effective compositions using the techniques presented here quite easily. But you can use the features available to gain even more control and power over your system for artwork through Custom Symbols and freeform drawing, which are discussed in the chapters that follow.

CHAPTER 8

Design Effects

Customize by Components

The graphic database in Arts & Letters gives you 10,000 images to play with. Using the sophisticated, automated, and easy-to-use effects built into Express, you can multiply that number to millions. Each symbol component and image in Express can be expressed in thousands of unique variations. You can flatten or stretch the image; rotate it, slant it, and size it; and multiply it using Blends. You can explode it using Ungroup or Convert to Freeform, or explode it into a crisp 3-D image using Extrude. Warp lets you twist it like Silly Putty. The variations are infinite, and far exceed static, packaged clip art that the leading graphic software systems give you.

This chapter covers advanced design effects you can create using Express's manipulation features, which are located, primarily, on the Arrange and Effects menus. Although coverage of the Bind Text to Shape effect is located in Chapter 4, most of the effects included here can be performed without the use of the Freeform mode. If you have the artistic skill to manipulate the wireframe symbols that form the foundation of the graphic database, all the effects here can be enhanced and expanded using the Freeform mode. The fundamental principle to keep in mind is that Arts & Letters gives you systematic components to work with, and not static, canned compositions. So, even if you're not a professional artist, you can design individual components and combine them into a professional-looking drawing in minutes.

Key Concepts

Design information and operations presented in this chapter are based on a number of key concepts. Understanding these concepts will help you gain a greater practical understanding of the information presented here.

Selected Object All effects begin when you select one or more objects in the working area. Effects are not operated from Freeform mode, although several require that certain objects be converted to freeform to work properly. In some cases you may select a single object; in others, such as a shape-to-shape blend, you will be required to select two objects at the same time before the effect will work. If you are having problems activating and operating effects features, begin by checking that you have correctly selected the objects you need to complete the blend.

Beginning and End Objects A number of effects, such as Blend and Extrude, require a beginning and ending object. For example, the Blend feature requires you to individually edit and place beginning and ending objects; the Extrude feature uses an automated display in which you shape the beginning and ending objects in a single operation. This means that you select an object on the screen (the beginning object) and then create the effect by manipulating and positioning an ending object. The effect creates a controlled electronic evolution between the two objects to generate the effect.

Required Freeform Conversion Some effects, such as Merge Cutouts and Object Blends, require that one or more of the selected objects are converted to freeform before the effect will work. In these cases, Express needs to directly access the graphic information—a symbol representation is not sufficient. For example, in Binding text to a shape, you must be able to place the start point of the text string directly onto the line or form you are using for the shape. The only way to do this is in freeform. (See Figure 8.1.)

Merge Merge features operate like an overlay: They match and integrate two objects so that you can use one object as a cutout frame for another (Clipping Path); or, you can fill the interior of another object or group (such as text characters) with another (such as a brighly colored art background).

Blend Blend features multiply objects between a start and end point. You can execute a blend directly on a single object and multiply it up to 99 times to create a fluid (not solid) evolution between the start and end points. You may also use Blend to evolve one shape (for example, a spade) into another (such as a heart). You specify the number of objects used to create this evolution.

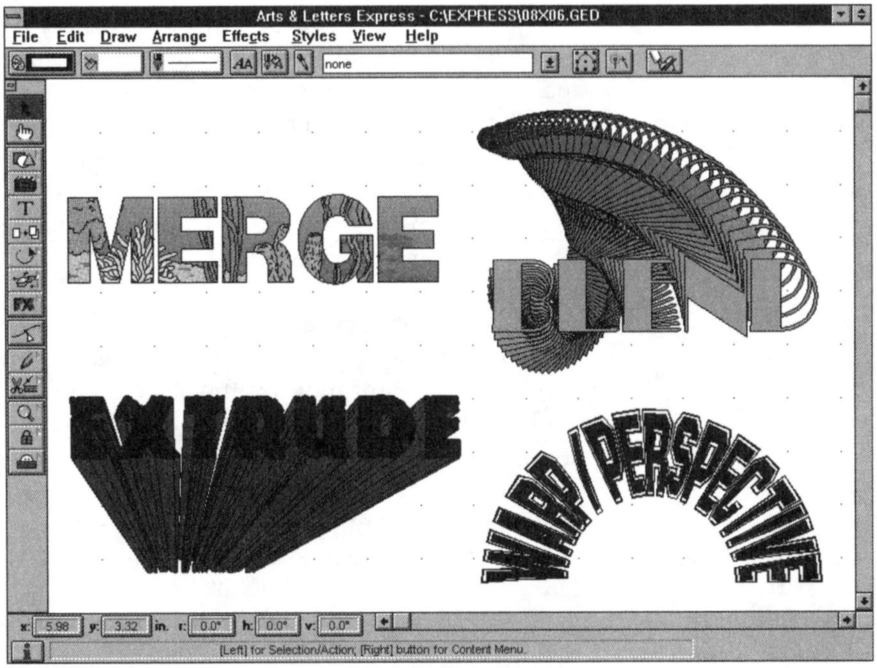

Figure 8.1
Effects
Arts & Letters gives you a variety of automated effects that let you create professional graphic effects in a few minutes, even seconds. All four of the text effects shown here were created in under five minutes.

Extrude Extrude features create 3-D point-to-point extension objects between an element start and end point. This is done using a vanishing point or trackball mimic, but the principle is essentially the same as a blend. You drag the entire shape into the configuration you want, and then the extrusion initiates at the begin point, and graphics wrap around and explode the selected object to the desired end point.

Warp Warp features operate like an electronic overlay. You select the object, then select and configure a shaping overlay to twist it into a desired appearance. You may edit and revise the overlay interactively and see the changes on screen using Apply. You may also remove the overlay at any time. Warp does not transform the graphic information itself, or destroy the symbol display; it merely acts as an overlay to shape it as you wish.

Align Align features can be used to support key effects. You can use Align within a Blend operation to make sure all the beginning and end points are on the same vertical or horizontal line. You may also use align to reassemble multielement images after they have been broken apart.

Transform Transform is home to the size, position, rotate, and slant features. You may control these features numerically rather than using mouse movements—which can be tricky for detailed editing. Transform may also be used to save and recall precise settings. For example, the most recent Transform action, such as setting an object size, can be duplicated over and over using the Transform again option. Transform also operates on two distinct levels: You can use it to set absolute dimensions and angles (such as symbol size: 2" x 4"; rotation angle: 60 degrees) or to make relative changes (such as increasing selected symbol to 150% of its current size or rotating the selected symbol 30 degrees clockwise or counterclockwise from its present angle of rotation).

Save/Recall Effects Once created, effects can be exactly duplicated, in some cases using the Save and Recall options, or Replace. Warp allows you to Save the current Warp configuration on the selected object, select another, and Recall it, and adapt the Warp shape to that object. Blend and Merge effects don't have this option, but you can duplicate the Blend, select Blend Replace, and then use Symbol Replace to change the beginning and end objects that make up the blend. Your settings for the original will be duplicated with the new art or text elements.

Tools

Design concepts and operations in this chapter make use of a number of key tools in Arts & Letters. They are summarized below.

Draw Menu The **Draw** menu is where you load standard and custom symbol forms, text, and charts into the screen. You may access symbol and text dialog boxes from the Toolbox as well. In addition, this menu contains the features that allow you to convert symbols into freeform graphics.

Edit Menu The **Edit** menu contains features that allow you to easily select groups of symbols and graphic objects as well as cut, copy, and paste symbols.

Arrange Menu The **Arrange** menu (Figure 8.2) contains composition features that allow you to automate positioning and composition, including the Group, Align, Transform, and Blend features, and a number of quick positioning features.

Effects Menu The **Effects** menu (Figure 8.3) contains automated special effects including Merge, Bind to Shape, Blend, Warp, and Extrude. Each of these effects has different operation and selection requirements, so be careful that you have properly presented the artwork in standard or freeform mode and also have selected objects correctly before activating these features. (See Figure 8.4.)

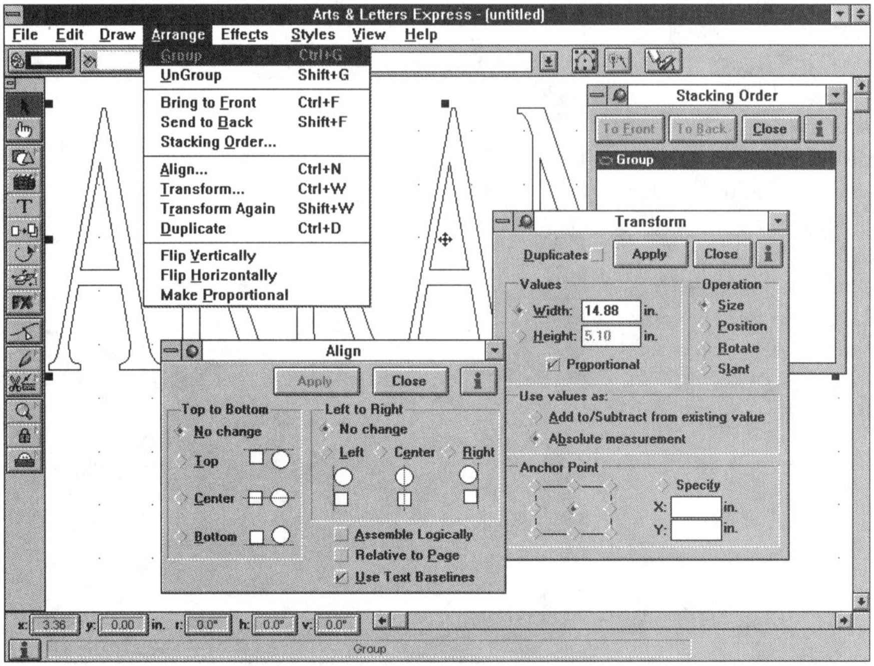

Figure 8.2
Arrange Menu
Dramatic effects can be created for symbols, images, and text using the features and screens on this menu. These features allow you to create multiple and varied effects on artwork and text.

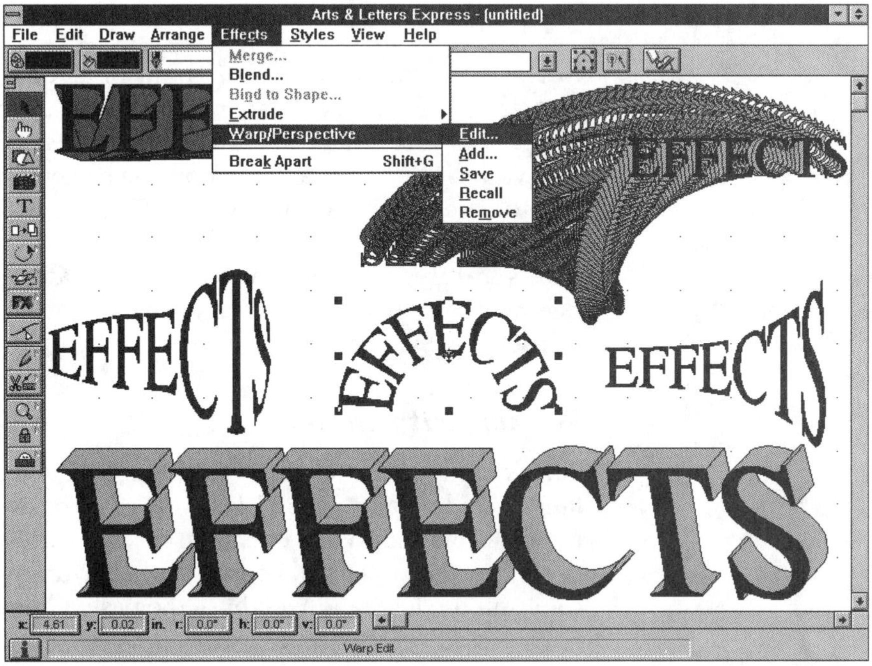

Figure 8.3
Effects Menu
Effects are automated features that instantly multiply and/or combine graphic elements that would take hours to create in freeform or standard mode. The effects shown were created with Extrude (top left and bottom), Blend (top right), and Warp (middle).

Figure 8.4
Design Layers
Each symbol and image is a template in Express. Here the simple wireframe at the top left is transformed by adding a color blend from the Styles menu. It becomes a three-dimensional color graphic with the application of the Blend effect.

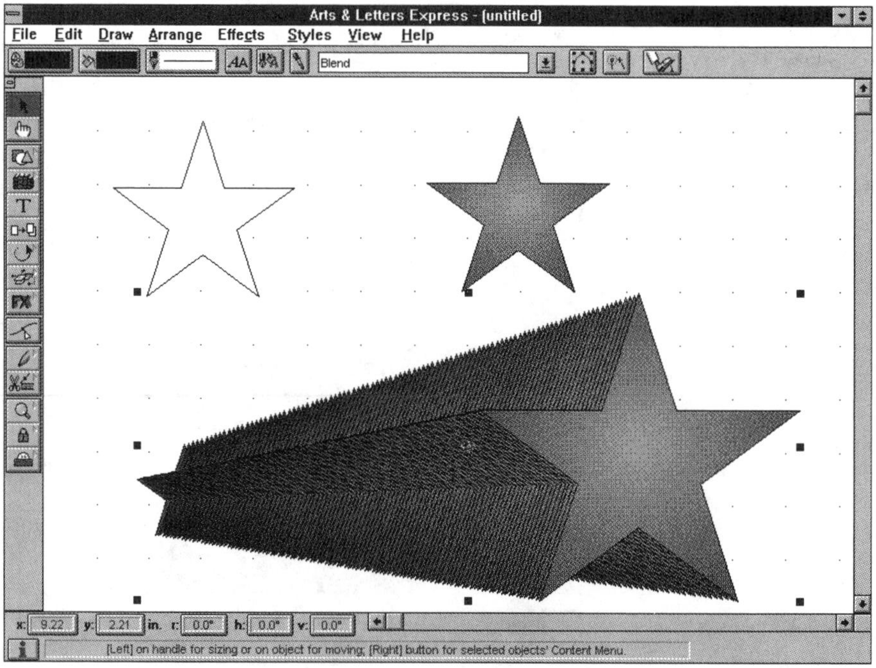

Design Layers

Express art features can be thought of as being in three tiers. On the first tier is the graphic database of text and art forms, as well as the simple presentation effects (sizing, rotation, slant, positioning, alignment) that you can use to place them in the screen. The next tier is the database of styles (covered in Chapter 7) for color, fill, line, and type that you can combine to display the image. The third tier includes the effects features, which allow you to integrate the preceding two design tiers with automated features that you control with a mouse or dialog box setting. Remember, no freehand drawing required.

Working with Effects

Since effects offer a virtually limitless array of possibilities, it is important to understand several key tips and tricks to using these features. By experimenting with effects using the variety of shapes and images in the graphic database, you will see how dramatically these effects can tranform the look and weight of the base wireframe or image.

Multiple Enhancements

The trick to mastering effects is to understand they are based on *combining the effects of other features*. You may use object rotation, slanting, and sizing effects within a blend. You may use object alignment to set up the art forms before (or within) the effect operation. Your creative options are effectively limitless, which makes for an interesting challenge. It is almost impossible to describe or demonstrate all the sophisticated effects you can create, given the breadth of art forms in the graphic database and the multiple layer of effects than can be applied to them.

Experiment with Theme and Variation

Operations in this and other chapters of this book are designed to provide you with key design concepts and relationships that you can experiment with (Figure 8.5). Once you understand the mechanics of creating a swirl or thrust blend, or generating an object shadow, you can create infinite variations of your own. It is important to try these effects on screen as you read about them. Possibilities will suggest themselves, particularly as you browse through the collections of images provided in the Clip-Art Manager.

Get Ideas from the Masters

Styles and Effects are highly subjective enhancements with infinite variations. The best way to master the integrated effects of these feature groups in Express is to begin your own styles and effects clipping file.

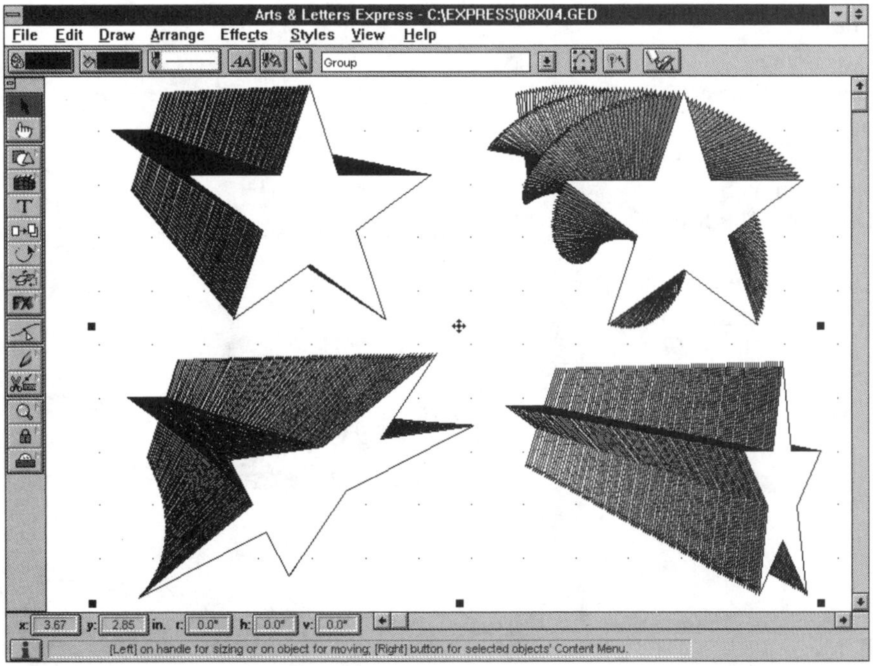

Figure 8.5
Theme and Variations
The four effects shown were developed from the exact same blend configuration. Variations from the original (upper left) were created by rotating the beginning object (upper right), slanting the end object (lower left), and flattening the width of the end object (lower right).

Tear out and save advertisement and article layouts from magazines (such as *Time, Vogue, Rolling Stone*), your local newspaper, or any form of printed communications that interest you. Look at the various components of the layout. Notice how titles are laid out, and what enhancements are used. Notice any box framing effects or highlights. Look for examples of three-dimensional design effects, drop shadow, object shadows, extrusions or distortions on art and text. If you do this consistently, in addition to the examples shown in this book, you can create a library of professional-looking effects of your own .

Design Techniques with Duplicate

The Duplicate feature on the Arrange menu (Figure 8.6), also available from the Toolbox, is the fundamental tool for creating graphic effects. Duplicate is a simple drag-and-drop object-copying tool. Just select the desired object, click the left button once, and drag a copy anywhere you want in the working area. Duplicate will stay active, and every time you click the mouse, another copy of the selected object will be placed. The Duplicate function can be disabled by simply clicking the right mouse button once.

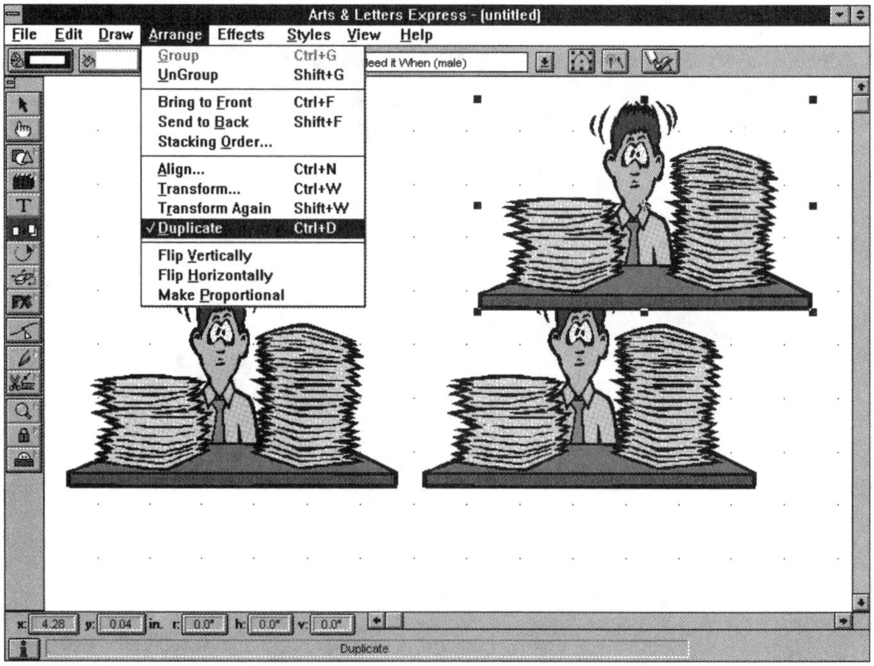

Figure 8.6
Duplicate
Drag and Drop any object in the working area instantly in a single operation with Duplicate. This feature is much more efficient than Copy/Paste while working within Express.

Duplicate Functions

Duplicate is a unique feature that forms the basis of many effects and design editing operations. Since it allows you to copy objects in a single drag-and-drop operation, it gives you a fluid means to set up and create drop shadows and multiimage effects. Since many effects operations are experimental by nature, duplicate gives you security by allowing you to duplicate your work and experiment using copies. Finally, Duplicate offers you a variety of automation capabilities that help you speed up your work across the board in Arts & Letters.

Duplicate vs. Copy Duplicate is how you make copies of objects within a given art file. When copying objects between different Arts & Letters files or to external programs, you must use the standard Copy/Paste features on the Edit menu. These features make use of the Windows clipboard and are designed to move information between different programs and files in Windows.

Layout with Duplicate When making flowcharts, illustrations, or presentation materials, you may wish to use the same symbol or image multiple times. Duplicate allows you to quickly drag as many copies as you need into the screen by just dragging your mouse for each copy of the desired object. Once you have scrambled the number of copies into the working area, you can drag them into place with the mouse, and line them up using Align.

Security Duplicates and Multiple Pages Each Graphic Environment Document (GED) file contains a variable number of pages depending on the Document Precision selected (see Chapter 2). The default precision is 1440 logical units per inch, which creates six 8½ x 11 inch portrait or landscape pages in a single GED file. For many of your compositions, you will use only a single page. But when that composition includes sophisticated graphic effects, you can use the additional pages in the GED file as security storage areas. When you create complex effects, it is a good idea to Duplicate the source art and text and store it on one of the back pages in the GED file. (See Figure 8.7.) This will simply save you the time required to search and reload them if you wish to try additional variations on the effect. More importantly, when you have created a warp, blend, or other effect, you may wish to create variations of it. In this case, use Duplicate to copy your effect to other pages. There you can break it apart and make large or small scale edits to the configuration and see the results displayed instantly. You are then free to delete your security duplicates or save the GED file containing them as a backup for reference at a later time.

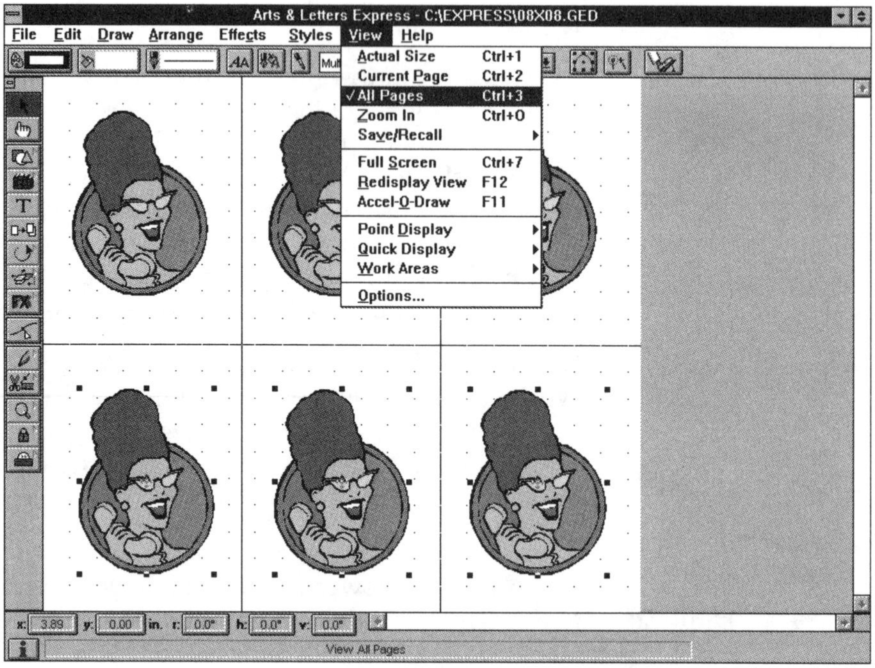

Figure 8.7
Security Duplicates and Multiple Pages
The lady with the beehive hairdo was duplicated in seconds to six pages in the current GED file. Using security duplicates, you can test out a variety of effects, save each variation as you create it, then compare and select the one you want to use.

Auto-Sizing with Duplicate and Replace

Certain projects require that you have a number of art components of the same size. Icon diagrams and flowcharts are classic examples. Express will load symbols in a consistent default size when they are placed in the working area by clicking the left mouse button. You have the option of "drawing" them in the working area to a desired size, but this kind of manual operation is notoriously imprecise. You may find yourself having to go back to make minute adjustments to size each one.

Creating Drop Shadows and 3-D Effects

Applying depth and character to symbols isn't just a function of applying attributes. You can instantly give depth and a professional quality to a simple symbol drawing by stacking one or more duplicate copies on top of one another and changing the color of the copies to create shadow and 3-D effects. (Figure 8.8.)

Adding Depth

One of the most common graphic tricks to give depth and dimension to a drawing is the drop shadow. Drop shadows can be used equally successfully with symbols and text, and drop shadow elements can be integrated into business charts to give them a strong and interesting visual

Figure 8.8
Drop Shadow Effects
Drop shadows are instant effects you create with Duplicate and the Color Palette. Drag a screen copy of the selected object, color it black (or whatever color you want), and place the shadow using Send to Back on the Arrange menu.

character. A drop shadow can be created using two copies of the same symbol, one shown as a line drawing, the other shown in solid black or shadings of gray or colors and slightly offset.

Drop Shadow Variations

Many different effects are possible with drop shadows. By adjusting the position of the drop shadow graphic to a greater offset, more exaggerated effects can be created. Visually arresting images can be created when you size the respective elements of the drop shadow differently. An image may cast a large shadow or a small one. You can even play with distortion of the drop shadow graphic, using rotation or slants to suggest the shadow reflected on an uneven surface or on a plane not parallel to the image.

When you factor in the raster and vector patterns available as shadow patterns in the Fill dialog box, you can have a field day showing textured shadows or parallel shadows.

Multiple Image Shadow Effects

A simple drop shadow consists of only two graphics. You can create even more complex effects using multiple shadows. The image can be echoed in two or more graphics with different fills, textures, or colors. This allows you to create effects, such as an image with a "ghost shadow" and a full shadow.

Figure 8.9
Soft Shadow
You can create a realistic background shadow in minutes with Duplicate. In the example shown, the duplicate was recolored by selecting a gray shade from the Color Palette flyout and Line styles were set to None.

Solid and Soft Shadows

Black shadow objects have a crisp look to them, both solid and substantial. When using any shadow graphic that is not solid black, you may set the line attributes to None, so that the line drawing element in the symbol is suppressed and the fill shape of the symbol acts as a shadow. This will create a softer shadow image, the degree of intensity a function of the density of the grayscale or color shade you select. (See Figure 8.9.)

Steps: Creating a Solid or Soft Drop Shadow

Use this operation to create a solid black drop shadow for a selected element. (Note the changes in Step 7 for soft and solid shadows.)

1. Select the object on screen.
2. Select the **Duplicate** icon in the Toolbox.
3. Depress the left mouse button and drag the duplicate to slightly offset it from the original. Release the left mouse button.
4. Click on the right mouse button to disable **Duplicate**.
5. Select the element copy on screen.
6. Select the Color Palette from the Style Bar.
7. For solid shadows, select **Black**. For soft shadows, select desired grayscale or color mix to serve as the shadow color.

8. Use **Arrange | Send to Back** to position the solid black copy.
9. Use the mouse to position the drawing in the desired relationship to the shadow copy. Take time to experiment!

Slanted Drop Shadow Effect

Drop shadows expand the depth of art forms or text by implying a three-dimensional space. The Slant feature lets you experiment with this virtual art space by slightly tilting either the primary graphic or its matching shadow. The tilt will imply a different angle for light entering the composition space and can be used to create arresting visuals that command and engage the eye. (See Figure 8.10.)

Steps: Creating a Slant Shadow

Use this operation to create a slant shadow for a selected element.

1. Select object on screen.
2. Select the **Duplicate** icon in the Toolbox.
3. Depress the left mouse button and drag the duplicate to slightly offset it from the original.
4. Click on the right mouse button to disable **Duplicate**.
5. Select the element copy on screen.
6. Select the Color Palette from the Style Bar.

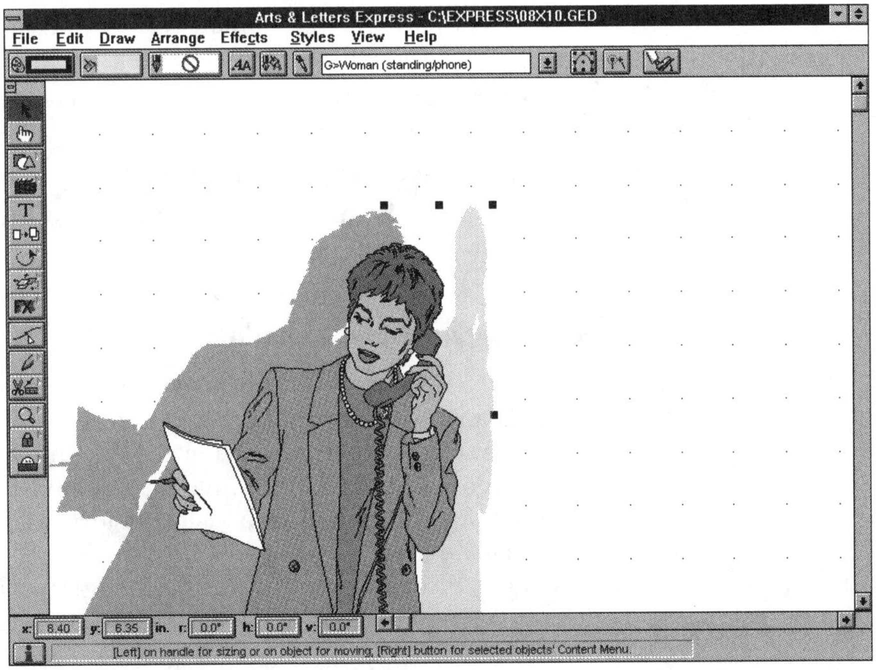

Figure 8.10 Slant and Multiple Shadow Effects Varying the slant and flattening the shadow graphic creates the suggestion that this woman is standing in the corner of the room. Varying the shading of the shadow object creates dramatically different presentation effects.

7. Select desired grayscale or color mix to serve as the shadow color.
8. Use **Arrange | Send to Back** to position the solid black copy.
9. Access Transform Objects flyout in the Toolbar; select the **Slant** icon (second from left).
10. Select either the primary graphic or drop shadow and experiment with different angles.
11. When using gray or color shades, either set Line Style to None, or set Line Color to match the background (default = White). A box line around a soft shadow looks strange and detracts from its overall impact.

Creating Slant Shadow Multiples

Slant shadows can create a dynamic image of three-dimensional space within a composition. If you are using this effect throughout a single composition or series of compositions, you should verify that the slant angle of the shadow or foreground object is consistent. You can do this easily with the Transform feature group. (See Figure 8.10.)

Steps: Consistent Slant Shadow Multiples

Use this operation to maintain consistent slant shadow angles for a series of selected elements.

1. Select the slanted object (foreground or drop shadow).
2. Select **Arrange | Transform**.
3. Select **Slant**. The horizontal and vertical slant angles for the selected object will be displayed onscreen.
4. Select **Apply**. These angles have now been saved into Transform's Save/Recall system.
5. Select another object that you wish to match the slant angle.
6. Press **Shift-W**, or access **Arrange | Transform Again**.
7. Verify that the angles match.

Creating an Object Shadow

One of the most difficult things to create if you are not an accomplished artist is a realistic object shadow (Figure 8.11). Where a drop shadow is a simple offset process involving two pictures or strings of text, an object shadow is a projection involving the base drawing and a second shadow drawing shown in a distorted form and placed at a realistic angle to create the illusion of an object shadow.

For a novice artist, one of the most magical experiences in Arts & Letters is the ease with which a realistic object shadow can be created.

Figure 8.11
Object Shadow
The series of actions to create a realistic object shadow is surprisingly simple. After creating the duplicate of the shadow graphic (upper left), rotate it on its side (middle left), slant it to the plane, and flatten the width with the side sizing handle (bottom left).

Object Shadow Process

This process is simple and can be done entirely with the mouse using the Duplicate, Rotate, and Slant tools. By duplicating the original drawing and coloring it black, the shadow graphic is created. The Slant tool can be used to distort and flatten the shadow graphic to approximate a shadow projection at a variety of angles. The Rotate tool can then be used to turn the finished object shadow to a desired angle. When moved into place, the finished shadow creates the complete progression between the two in size and shape.

Object Shadow Effects

Object shadows allow you to place shadows anywhere around an art form or text in seconds using only the mouse and a few fluid screen features. You can create front shadows of text, side shadows of trees, and so on. You can use a variety of sizing and positioning effects to shape an image into three-dimensional space. Once you have slanted and rotated the shadow into place, you may distort the shadow effect by stretching its width or flattening its height. You may elect to make the shadow much larger or smaller than the primary object to achieve stylized looks and effects. Check the comic pages in your local newspaper or illustrated books and magazines to get ideas. Creating shadows is one of the most important techniques in a professional artist's repetoire for creating depth and space.

Steps: Creating an Object Shadow

Use this operation to create a simple front or side shadow of an object.

1. Place the primary object into the working area.
2. Select the **Duplicate** icon in the Toolbar.
3. Drag a copy of the primary object next to it.
4. Select the **Rotate** icon from the Transform Objects flyout (first icon).
5. Turn the copy of the primary object to the desired shadow angle; a quarter turn to lay it on its side, upside down, or any desired angle.
6. Select the **Slant** icon from the Transform Objects flyout (second from left).
7. Slant the copy of the primary object to flatten and angle it as desired. The angle should represent the flat plane on which the shadow appears. For a standing figure in a room, the shadow angle should match that of the floor or wall where it appears.
8. Move the slant object into position at the base point of the primary object. The bottom of the shadow object should touch or be near to the bottom of the primary object.
9. Select the shadow object. Access **Arrange | Send to Back**.

Steps: Varying Shadow Appearance

Use this operation to experiment with the presentation of the shadow object.

1. Select the shadow object in final position with the primary object.
2. Expand/reduce the size of the object by dragging on the corner sizing handles.
3. Stretch/flatten the dimensions of the object by dragging on the middle sizing handles.
4. Make any final repositioning moves to align the bottom of the shadow object with the bottom of the primary object.

Automatic Front Shadow Effects

You can make text three dimensional by casting a shadow directly in front of an object, adjusting its size, and stretching or flattening it for added impact. (See Figure 8.12.) Also, you can slant the shadow to create a more dynamic effect. You may slant symbols and images in their standard form; however, text must be broken into freeform for the slant features to work correctly. After making the shadow copy of the original text, select it, press F8, and verify that the Viewer box in the Style Bar reads "Group." When text or symbols are broken into freeform, Express automatically holds them in a group configuration. You may ungroup the selection or use a section within groups to select individual closed and open shapes, if you wish.

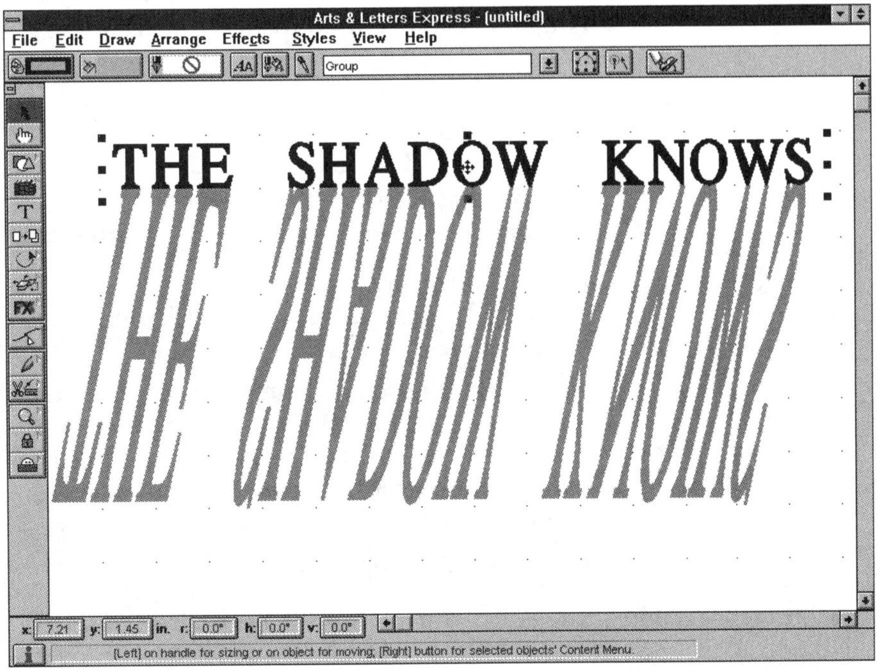

Figure 8.12
Front Shadow Effects
This effect was created in a couple of minutes by duplicating the base text at the top, flipping it vertically, distorting the shadow's vertical dimension using the middle sizing handle, converting it to freeform (F8), and slightly slanting the shadow.

Steps: Front Shadows with Flip Vertical

Use this operation to create a front shadow for text or artwork with Flip Horizontal.

1. Place primary text or art into the working area.
2. Select the **Duplicate** icon on the Toolbar.
3. Drag a copy of the object immediately below the original.
4. Select **Arrange | Flip | Vertical**.
5. Select the Color Palette from the Style Bar.
6. Select the desired contrasting shadow color: solid black for colored or line objects; grayscales or color shades for different effects.
7. Use sizing handles to flatten or lengthen the shadow.

Composing with Alignment

Alignment places objects vertically, horizontally, or assembles them in some logical order. Laying out a composition on the screen is easy with the mouse, but finished work requires some form of precision editing, otherwise you can spend hours micro-adjusting individual components.

Alignment can be used to create special design effects; it is also a foundation tool for creating may of the effects profiled in this chapter.

Alignment Options

Aligning objects is a key element in creating and editing effects (Figure 8.13). Express gives you three ways to align objects:

- The mouse and rulers. To turn rulers on, use the Work Areas option on the View menu. To set ruler increments, use the Options selection on the View menu.
- The position selection in the Transform dialog box to set X (horizontal) and Y (vertical) positions. If you select the X or Y displays from the Hint line at the bottom of the screen for the anchor object, you may then select Apply to save that position. It can then be applied to other objects by selecting them and pressing Shift-W.
- The Align dialog box.

Alignment Dialog Box

The Align feature is not a numeric precision option. It operates on two or more selected graphics and automatically positions them based upon selections you make. The Align dialog box contains a group of options

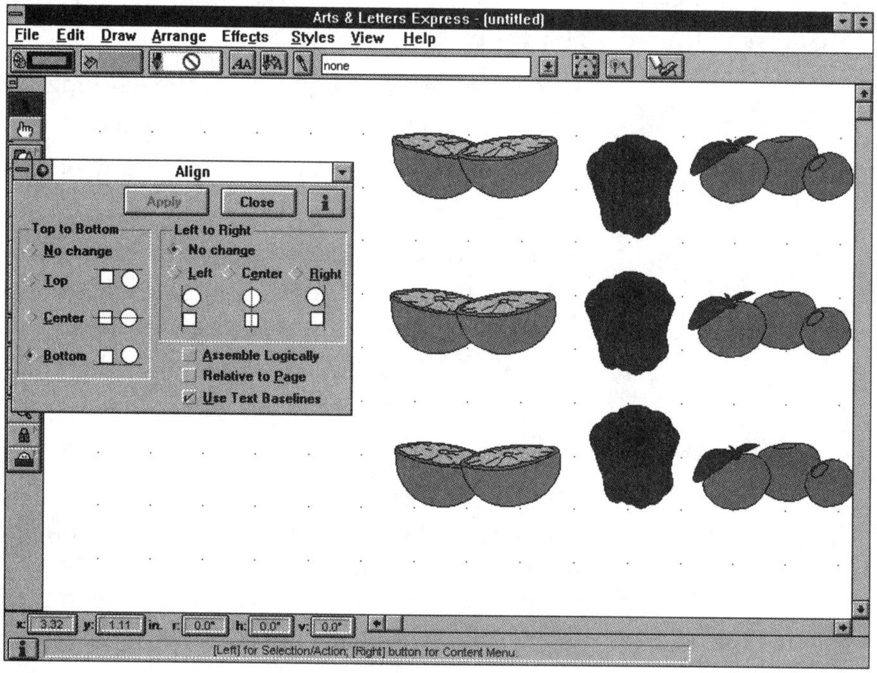

Figure 8.13 Alignment Options The top row is aligned to the Top, the center to the Center, and the bottom to the Bottom. The same principle works for the Left to Right Alignment selector as shown. All objects to be aligned must be selected at the same time.

that offer many specialized alignment configurations. The Alignment dialog box allows you to interactively align based on:

- Top to Bottom alignment
- Left to Right alignment
- Top/Bottom and Left/Right alignment

Each of these three options may be activated in two distinct ways:

- Relative to selected objects
- Relative to page

In addition, the Alignment dialog box provides you with two separate alignment options:

- Assemble Logically—assembles symbols in a master drawing or free-form objects into a complete drawing in seconds.
- Use Text Baselines—aligns text based on the baseline when text is in standard format. This is important because in upper- and lowercase text, letter elements rise and descend from the baseline; it is not the bottom of the text element. Using standard bottom alignment with text could seriously scramble letter characters.

Alignment to Page

You may use any of the Top/Bottom or Left/Right alignment options in relation to the current page in the screen. This allows you to place objects at the exact center of the page or align them to the left or right. This is useful in placing text headlines or centering art elements within a single composition or a group of pages, such as a set of presentation overheads. (See Figure 8.14.)

Steps: Alignment in the Page

Use this operation to align objects in the current page.

1. Select any symbol in the screen. You may select more than one symbol at a time using **Shift-Select** or **Block Select**.
2. Access **Arrange | Align**.
3. Select **Relative to Page**.
4. Select the desired alignment position from the groups provided: Top to Bottom, Left to Right.
6. Select **OK**. The symbols are aligned as directed.

Multilevel Alignment

You may position individual objects in the page precisely and quickly using multilevel alignment operations. This means that you select an

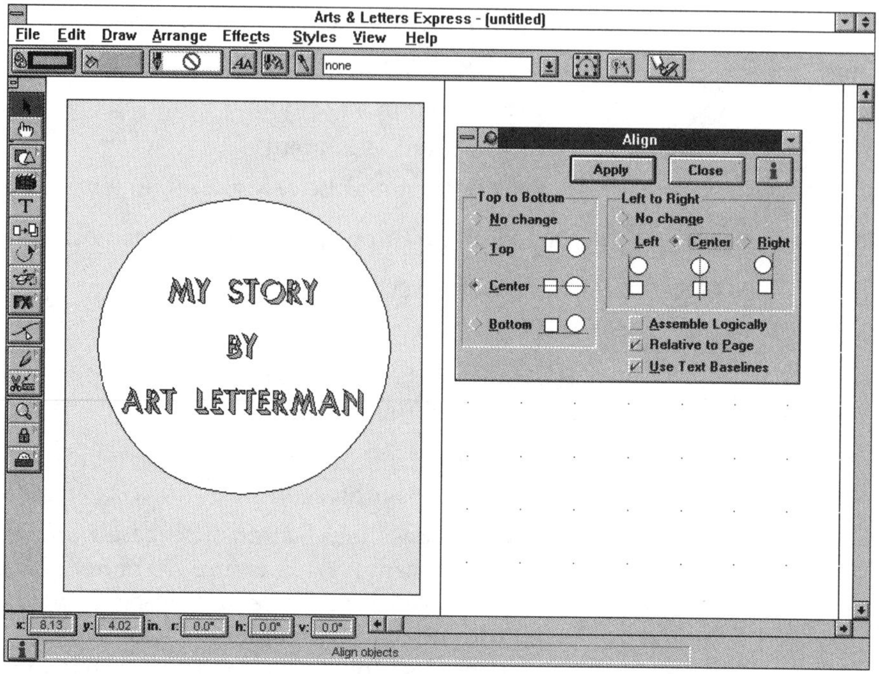

Figure 8.14
Page Alignment
The shaded box, the white circle, and the text block were all selected and centered on the cover page using Relative to Page alignment. This feature is particularly useful in final preparation before printing.

option from the Vertical alignment group (Top to Bottom) and one from the horizontal group (Left to Right). Selecting an object and Aligning Center-to-Center will instantly move that object to the exact center of the current page.

Steps: Multilevel Alignment in the Page

Use this operation to place a single selected object to a desired position in the page.

1. Select the desired object.
2. Access **Arrange | Align** or select the Object Alignment icon in the toolbar.
3. Select the desired alignment for Top to Bottom.
4. Select the desired alignment for Left to Right.
5. Select **Apply**.

Automatic Object Alignment

Begin with two or more objects selected on the screen. When the **Object** reference in the **Align** dialog box is selected, you may snap this group of objects into a variety of different alignments, including placing them in a straight row.

Alignment to Object

The most common use of the Align features is to use them relative to a group of selected objects. If you want to horizontally align a group of flowchart boxes, select all of them and select Align to Bottom, or Center, or Top. Express will then automatically move all the objects to the closest position. For example, if you align all the selected objects to Top, Express will align them with the top edge of the uppermost graphic you have selected. If you align them to Bottom, Express will move them to the bottom edge of the lowest graphic in the group. If you align Center, the objects align to the center of the center graphic in the selection.

Single-Level Alignment

You may align a selected group based on one level of alignment: Top to Bottom or Left to Right. (See Figure 8.15.) There is a kind of cross dynamic working here. Generally if you have a group of objects laid out horizontally, you will use the vertical (Top to Bottom) alignment selection to bring them to a common vertical position in the working area. A group of vertically arranged objects will use the horizontal (Left to Right) group to move them to a standard horizontal position.

When alignment is based on one level, you should make sure that the other level has the No Change option selected. The Align dialog box remembers your most recent operation, and therefore if you have just made a vertical alignment operation and now want to do a horizontal alignment, the vertical option you just used will be default-selected in the dialog box.

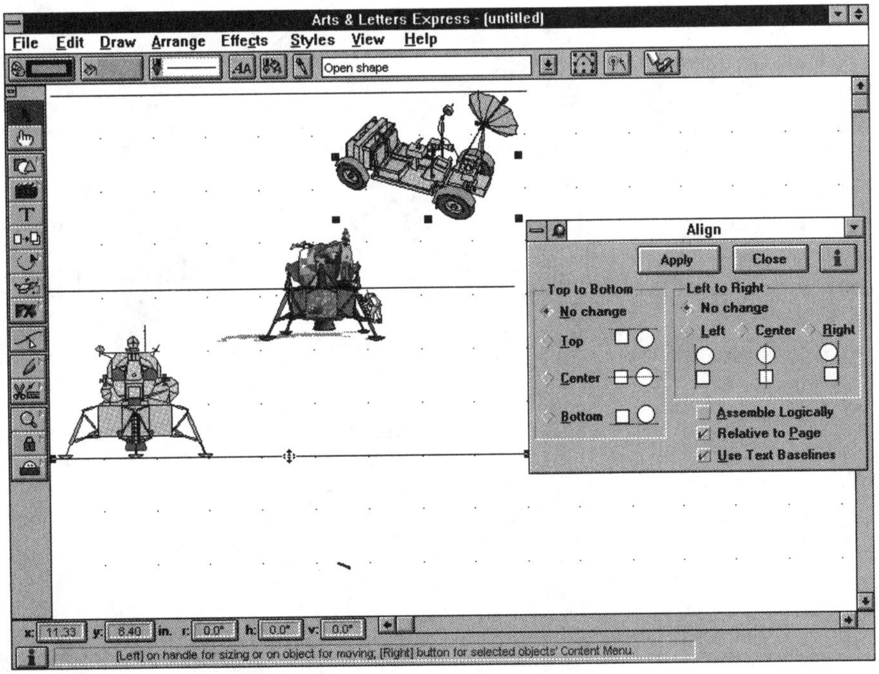

Figure 8.15
Alignment to Object
If this group were aligned to the Top, the top edge of each element would rise to the line at the top of the screen. Center aligns to the Center position in the Center object. Bottom aligns to the bottom of the bottom object.

Multilevel Alignment

You may use both levels at the same time to align a group of objects, but the impact of multiple alignment operations with multiple elements is to stack them on top of each other in the same place. If you have three elements selected and tell them to align to Top-Right, all of the elements will move to the exact same place on the screen.

Steps: Object Alignment

1. Select a group of objects in the screen.
2. Access **Arrange | Align**.
3. Select the desired alignment for the group from either the Top to Bottom or Left to Right groups.
4. Verify that the group you did not use has the No Change option selected.
5. Select **Apply**.

Object Assembly with Logical Alignment

Logical alignment is an assembly feature used to assemble master symbol images and freeform compositions (Figure 8.16). It is one of the truly unique features developed by Arts & Letters, and like the Replace option, it is a direct outgrowth of the unique graphic database design in the program.

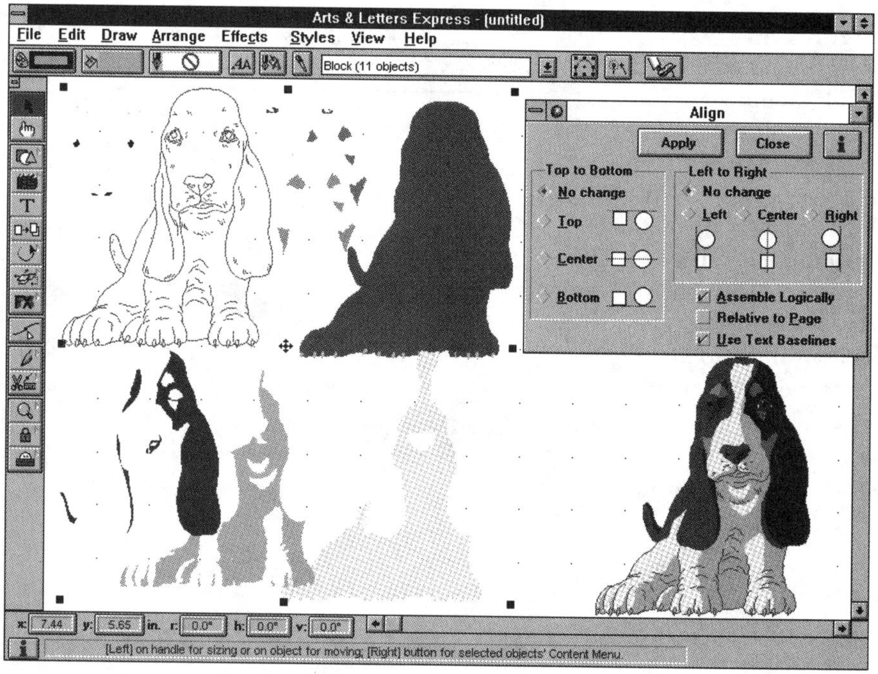

Figure 8.16
Logical Alignment
The dog at bottom right is composed of all the symbol components at left. You may break up the dog and assign colors to the various components, then select all of them and reassemble the finished drawing using Assemble Logically.

Logical Alignment and Master Symbol Drawings

The graphic database in Express was designed as a series of symbol art forms. To create more complex images, additional numbered symbol accents were developed. These accents were positioned as precise overlays to the master drawing. So the master drawing showing a human face could have additional accent graphics that contained only the eyes, on another only the hair, on another only the shirt or coat, and on another only the tie. In older versions of the program, you had to load these symbols, one by one, set color for them, and then assemble them into a finished image.

How Logical Alignment Works

When all components in an image are selected, Assemble Logically instantly assembles them into a finished object through a unique construction that sets up each separate symbol in a box space representing the total area of the drawing (see Figure 8.16). When Assemble Logically is activated, it stacks each of the boxes on top of each other and the complete drawing is instantly assembled.

Logical Alignment and Editing Options

Logical Alignment has been present in previous versions of Arts & Letters. It was used primarily to assemble master symbol drawings. But since virtually all of the master symbol drawings come pre-assembled and colored in the Clip-Art Manager, you don't need to individually load all the symbols to create master drawings anymore. In addition, the new Express "select within group" feature allows you to select any one of the symbols in a Clip-Art Manager image and select color and enhancements without breaking up the group. Finally, the new Color Correction feature allows you to apply multiple levels of color to a grouped image systematically, so again, you don't need to break up the group and reassemble it.

Image Editing

The bottom line is that Express gives you many choices on how to edit the clip art contained in the Clip-Art Manager. Many of the images are complex and contain many small symbol components. In this case, you may want to break apart the image and pull it apart to see the various components and apply styles and color edits to them individually. In these situations, you can use Assemble Logically to reassemble the composition.

Warning

Logical alignment works when the selected components are either all standard symbols *or* all freeform objects, but not both. If you convert some of the symbols in a broken out image to freeform, the image will not reassemble correctly. When using this feature, make sure you are dealing with all symbol or all freeform at the start! Use the Object Browser or Viewer to check.

Steps: Logical Alignment Use this operation to assemble two or more symbols that make up an image.

1. Select two or more symbols which are part of a master drawing.
2. Access **Arrange | Align**.
3. Select **Reference/Object**.
4. Select **Logical** and select **OK**. The composite is instantly assembled.
5. Access **Arrange | Group** to group the composite.

Steps: Editing Clip-Art Manager Images Use this operation to break apart and enhance individual elements within a symbol-based Clip-Art Manager image.

1. Access the Clip-Art Manager from the Toolbox or the Draw menu.
2. Select the desired image and place it in the working area.
3. Select **Arrange | Ungroup**. (Note: Certain images may have symbol groups within the master group so you may have to perform a series of ungroup operations to reach the base symbols.)
4. Select the desired symbols and apply color and styles as desired.
5. Access **Edit | Select All** or use Block Select cursor to select all symbols in the image.
6. Access **Arrange | Align**.
7. Select **Assemble Logically**. (Note: Both Top/Bottom and Left/Right automatically set to No Change when Assemble Logically is selected.)
8. Select **Apply**.
9. Select **Arrange | Group** to regroup the image.

Creating Your Own Auto-Assembly Artworks

Logical Alignment works with freeform objects as well as symbols. This allows you to create your own auto-assembling artworks in Freeform mode. You may include any symbols converted to freeform, any drawing shapes converted to freeform, and any freehand drawings made with the line and curve features. For the auto-assembly feature to work, you may not include any symbol art forms; all elements must be freeform art or converted to freeform, including text.

Group Activation The auto-assemble activating feature is the Group command. When you assemble your drawing and group it, Express remembers the virtual position of each object in the group. From that point on you may break apart the group, edit it with Styles and enhancements, and reassemble the entire drawing exactly as you drew it, using the Assemble Logically option in the Align dialog box.

Steps: Create Your Own Auto-Assembly Artworks

Use this operation to assemble, ungroup, and reassemble an original composition in Freeform mode.

1. Verify that all artwork in the composition—converted to freeform symbols, text, and freehand drawings—is freeform art.
2. Select **Edit | Select All** or use Block Select icon to select all components in the composition.
3. Select **Arrange | Group**.

Steps: Edit Your Auto-Assembly Artwork

Use this operation to break apart and edit your custom artwork.

1. Select group object containing artwork.
2. Select **Arrange | Ungroup**.
3. Edit individual components in the group as you wish. You may move them around on the screen to facilitate editing.

Steps: Reassemble Custom Artwork

Use this operation to reassemble custom freeform artwork using Logical Alignment.

1. Select **Edit | Select All** or use Block Select icon to select all components in the composition.
2. Access **Arrange | Align**.
3. Select **Assemble Logically**.
4. Select **Apply**.
5. Select **Arrange | Group**.

Text Baseline Alignment

Alignment gives you a general Use Text Baselines in Alignment (Figure 8.17) option to use in text only operations so that separate groups of text can be aligned to the Top, Center, and Bottom positions (unless text is rotated sideways, you are unlikely to use the horizontal features for text), and the alignment will be based on the position of the text baseline.

Alignment with Objects

If the alignment operation involves both text and graphic objects, then text is treated like any other graphic object. When Bottom alignment is selected, the bottom of the text string will align to the bottom position. If the text is all caps, the actual baseline sits at the bottom position; if it is upper- and lowercase, the bottom of the descenders on characters like p, g, and j will sit on the bottom position. When the Top option is

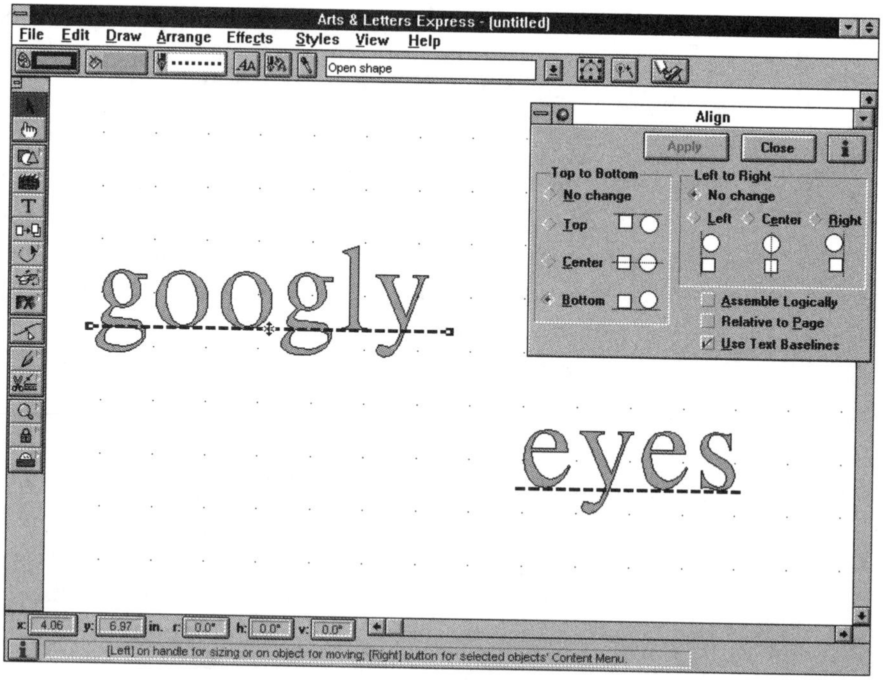

Figure 8.17
Align to Baseline
The baseline is the home base for text with parts of letters above and below it. Alignment to Baseline is an option that operates with any of the alignment options. Text converted to freeform will not recognize a baseline and be aligned like a common graphic.

selected, the top of capital letters, or lowercase ascenders in letters like l, f, and d will align with the top position. When the Center option is used, the text expression from the top of the ascenders to the bottom of the descenders will center over the center alignment position. Given that different fonts have different metrics that determine the height of character components, the look of aligned text is somewhat dependent on the font you use.

Steps: Align Multiple Text Objects

Use this operation to align multiple text objects to the same baseline.

1. Select all desired text objects in the working area.
2. Access **Arrange | Align**.
3. Select **Use Text Baselines**.
4. Select **Bottom**.
5. Verify that all text is aligned to the baseline.

Creating Effects with Transform

In Standard editing mode, Arts & Letters gives you a set of manipulation tools to slant, rotate, and duplicate symbols. You may, of course, access each of these features directly from the Toolbox and implement them directly on the screen with the mouse. This has a speed advantage but at a loss of precision. The Transform dialog box (Figure 8.18) is the home base of these fundamental manipulation features, where you control them through numeric settings.

Transform Options

Size, Position, Rotate, and Slant are all controlled by numeric values directly from the Transform dialog box on the Arrange menu. Transform is one of the most powerful dialog boxes in Arts & Letters because it allows you to make edits to symbols based on precise measurements according to either relative or absolute values.

Transform Numeric Bar

At the bottom of the screen is the Hint Line, showing information on the selected icon, features, or current operation. Directly above it appears the Transform Numeric Bar. This line is a direct portal to key numeric settings for objects in the screen. Selections on the Numeric Line represent key options in the Transform dialog box.

- x = width of currently selected object
- y = height of currently selected object
- r = angle of rotation of currently selected object

Figure 8.18
Transform Options
The Transform dialog box is a technical control center for the size, position coordinates, rotation, and slant angles. Clicking on the numeric boxes shown at bottom left will auto-display Transform with the selected numeric value displayed.

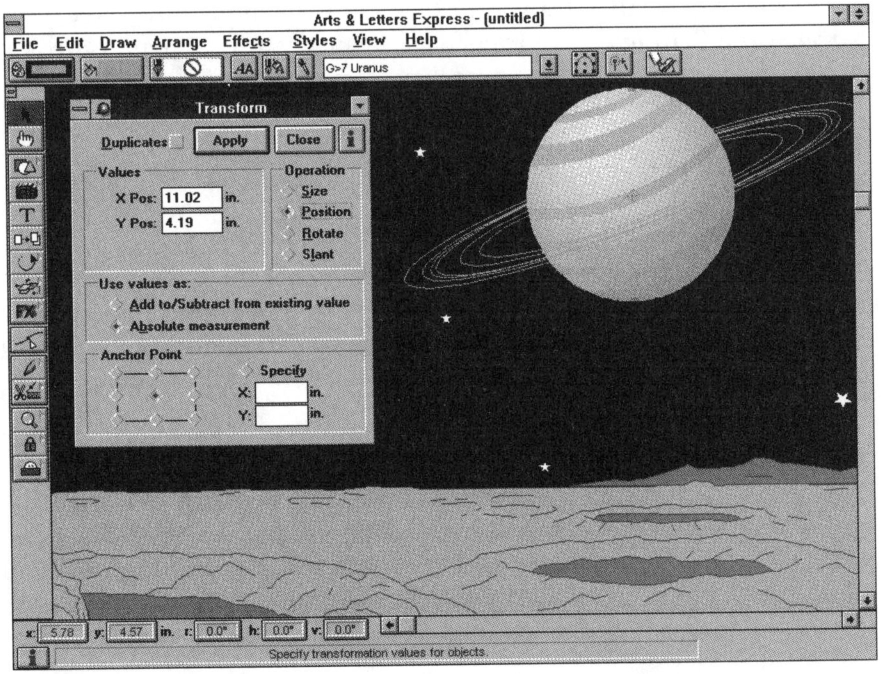

- h = horizontal slant angle of currently selected object
- v = vertical slant angle of currently selected object

By clicking on the the desired measurement display, the Transform dialog box appears with that option already selected and ready for editing.

Absolute and Relative Transform

The Transform dialog box is really two displays in one. The default display shows absolute measurements of dimensions and angles. So if you select a graphic, the absolute size will be its exact dimensions in inches. A rotated or slanted object will show the exact angle of rotation or slant. The second option, somewhat confusingly titled *Addto/Subtract from existing value* represents the Variable Transform option. You may increase the size of an object here using percentages, such as increasing the size of an object by 100%. With the Position, Rotate, and Slant options, you may add to the existing values of the object. So if an object is rotated at 30 degrees, and you enter 40 degrees in the Variable rotation option, the angle of rotation is increased by 40 degrees to an angle of 70 degrees rotation.

Relative or Variable Transformation takes a little getting used to. The more you work with Express, the more you can see the effective value of this option and the fluid options it gives you to adjust the position, size, rotation, and slant of objects from where they currently are set. Absolute measurements are easy to understand and use any time.

Save/Recall Transform Settings

Transform has its own unique Save/Recall feature operated through the Transform Again feature. When you complete a transform operation and select Apply in the dialog box, they become the most recent transform values and are saved in Transform's memory. You can then select any object in the screen and activate Transform Again, and the same transformation operation will be performed on the selected objects. To see the power of this, imagine you have done a transform to increase the size of an object from one inch to five inches in height. You may select any other object in the screen and apply Transform again, and it will instantly be transformed to five inches in height. You can repeat this process until you make another transform setting, and Transform Again will operate with that setting.

Save/Recall with Duplicates

Transform allows you to select an object, set its vital details numerically and activate a duplicate option. When Make Duplicates is selected, Transform will make up to 99 duplicates of the edited art form when the Apply selection is selected. In addition, each time that Transform Again is activated, another single duplicate will be created. This allows you to load a transform operation and simply press the Shift+W shortcut for Transform Again to make many duplicates of it.

Size Transform

Size transformation allows you to set the exact dimensions of any object. In Absolute measurement mode, you set the exact dimensions of the object using the default unit of measure displayed in the dialog box. Units of measure may be changed using the Options selection on the View menu. In Variable mode, size may be altered by percentage, greater or less than the size of the current object.

Proportional Size

Size transform includes a Proportional checkbox settings (Figure 8.19). When proportional is checked, you may change either dimension and the other dimension will automatically adjust to keep the object in proportion. This is the equivalent of increasing and decreasing the size with the corner sizing handles. When Proportional is turned off, you may independently specify the height and width and distort the object shape. This is analogous to sizing with the middle handles.

Steps: Set Absolute Size in Proportion

Use this operation to set the size of an object using either height or width and maintain the object proportion (aspect ratio).

1. Select the desired object.
2. Access **Arrange | Transform**.

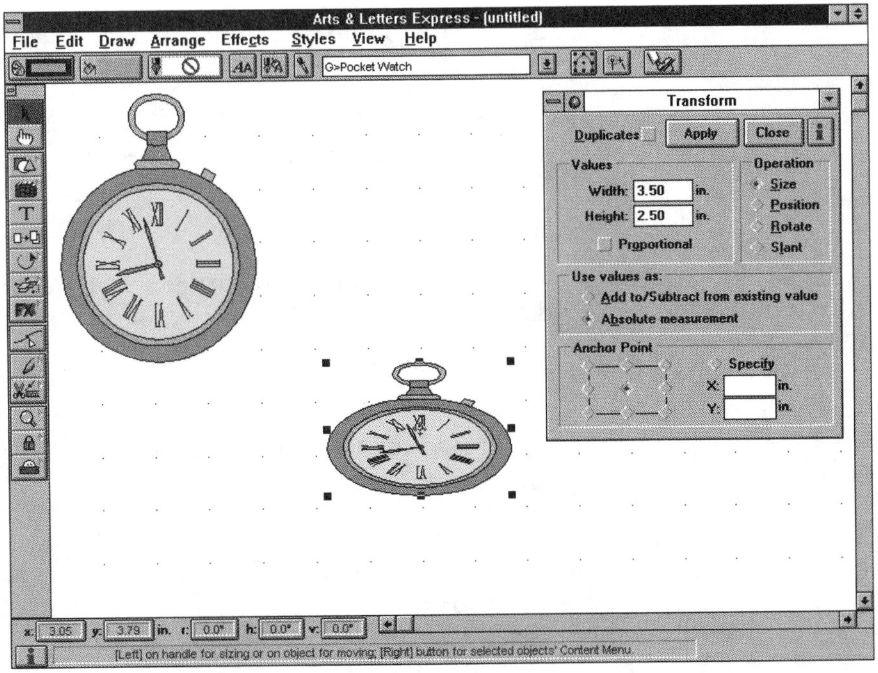

Figure 8.19 Proportional and Distorted Size
The watch to the left is sized with the Proportional option enabled. The squashed watch, center, was sized (see dialog box settings) with Proportional sizing turned off.

3. Select **Absolute**.
4. Select the size.
5. Verify that Proportional is selected.
6. Enter new size in either the Width or Height entry boxes.
7. Select **Apply**.

Steps: Set Absolute Size in Distortion

Use this operation to set the size of an object using either height, width, or both to distort object proportion (aspect ratio).

1. Select the desired object.
2. Access **Arrange | Transform**.
3. Select Absolute.
4. Select Size.
5. Verify that Proportional is not selected.
6. Enter new size in either the Width or Height entry boxes, or both.
7. Select Apply.

Steps: Set Variable Size in Proportion

Use this operation to vary the size of a selected object in proportion by percent (Figure 8.20).

1. Select the desired object.
2. Access **Arrange | Transform**.
3. Select **Add to/Subtract** from existing value.
4. Select Size.
5. Verify that Proportional is selected.
6. Enter percentage transformation in either the Width or Height entry boxes.
7. Select **Apply**.

Steps: Set Variable Size with Distortion

Use this same operation to vary the size of a selected object by percent and also to allow distortion of the aspect ratio.

1. Select the desired object.
2. Access **Arrange | Transform**.
3. Select **Add to/Subtract** from existing value.
4. Select Size.
5. Verify that Proportional is not selected.
6. Enter the percentage of transformation in either the Width or Height entry boxes.
7. Select Apply.

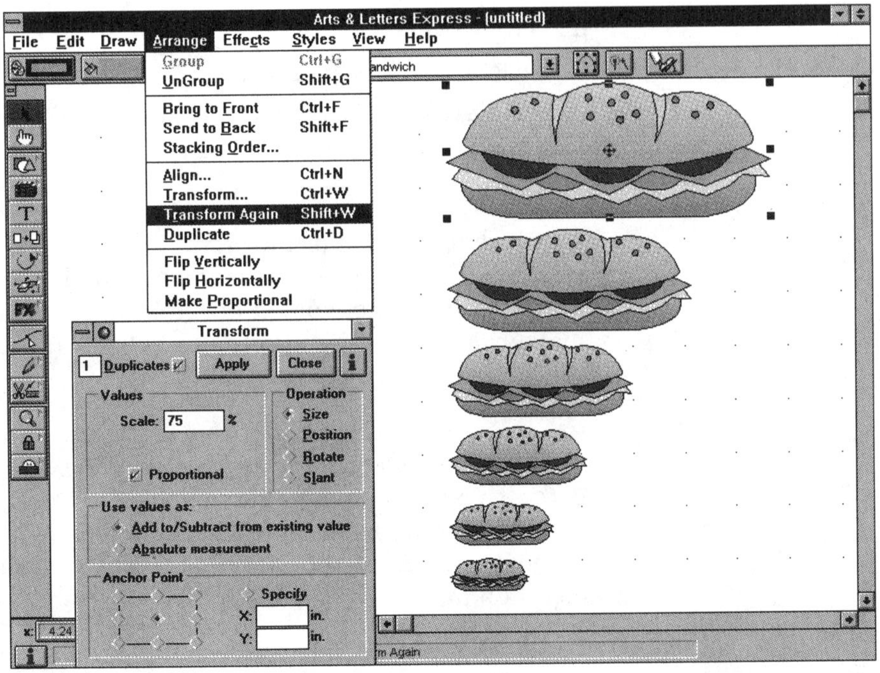

Figure 8.20
Variable Size in Proportion
Using Variable sizing you can increase or decrease the size of an object by percent. In the example shown, each time the percentage reduction is executed it takes a progressive bite out of your lunch.

Steps: Auto Duplicate Object

Use this operation to set custom size and create a stack of duplicates of the transformed object. Note that any multiples of duplicates created using the Duplicates option in the Transform dialog box stack directly on top of one another and must be dragged from the stack in position. This same operation can be created using the Variable option.

1. Access **Arrange | Transform**.
2. Select **Add to/Subtract** from existing value.
3. Select Size.
4. Verify that **Proportional** is selected.
5. Select **Duplicates** and enter the desired number of duplicates to be created and stacked.
6. Enter the percentage of transformation in either the Width or Height entry boxes.
7. Select **Apply**.

Steps: Apply Absolute/Variable Size

Use this operation to apply the current Absolute or Variable size values to any selected object in the working area.

1. Set desired Absolute/Variable size values in the Transform dialog box (see above).

2. Select **Apply**.
3. Select the object to be sized.
4. Select **Arrange | Transform Again** (Shift-W).

Position Transform

The anchor position of the working area is the upper-left corner of the screen. At this point both x (horizontal) and y (vertical) equal 0. Positioning coordinates are worked out from this position. Horizontal positions measure across and right; vertical positions measure down from the top.

Absolute vs. Variable

In Absolute mode, an exact position in the working area is specified. In Variable mode, offset positions are specified in relation to the position of the current object. You may set only the horizontal or the vertical or both. If you apply the Transformation to the same object repeatedly, it will jump each time by the offset increments. If Duplicates are enabled, they will be added and placed at the offset amounts from the selected object on the screen.

Anchor Point

The Anchor point display at the bottom of the Transform dialog box (Figure 8.21) sets where position coordinates for the object are calculated. The

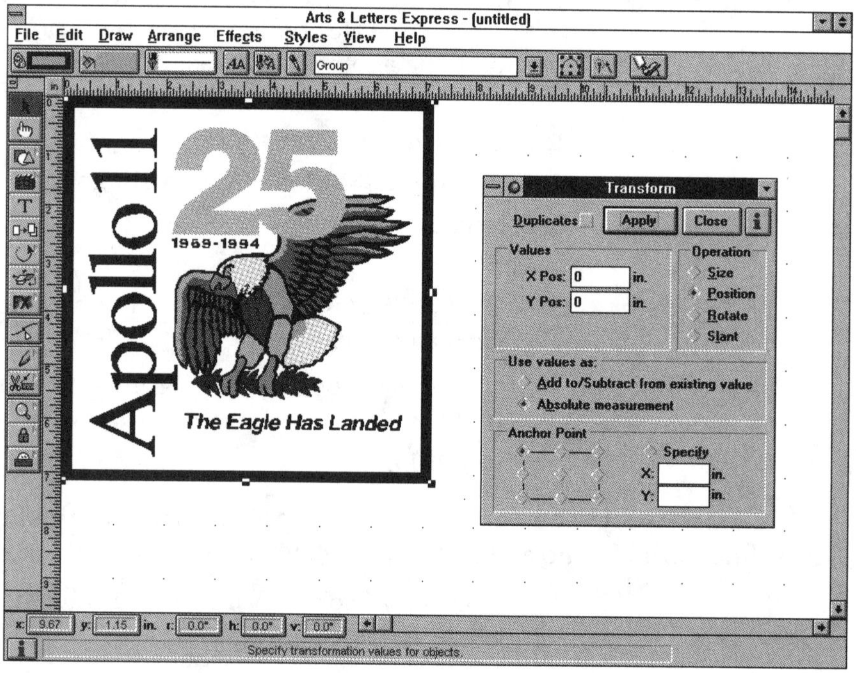

Figure 8.21 Anchor Point
The Anchor Point display at the bottom of the dialog box determines how measurements of objects are made. Set at the upper-left corner of the object, it forces the object to position exactly at the Ruler intersection point, 0,0.

default is the center of the object. You may select any of the points at the corner of the object or specify specific coordinates in inches for the anchor point. When setting numeric positioning, check the Anchor Point before executing the operation. You should be using the same anchor point for all alignment operations to assure consistency.

Position Alignment

Position features can be used to set the alignment numerically—something the Align dialog box does not allow you to do. If you wish to set numeric alignment, the position of the anchor becomes critical. To exactly align the left side of a group of graphics to a numeric position, you should make sure that you have selected one of the left side anchor points. If you wish to align the center of a group of graphics to a numeric position, set the anchor point at the center. If you wish to align numerically the right side of a group of graphics, set the anchor point.

For most object positioning and alignment operations, it is best to set the anchor point to the upper-left corner. This matches the zero point on the rulers at the upper-left corner of the screen. So if your positioning coordinates are set at 0,0 (horizontal = 0 inches, vertical = 0 inches), the graphic will position snugly at the intersection of the X and Y axis.

Steps: Set Absolute Position

Use this operation to set the position of an object.

1. Select the desired object.
2. Access **Arrange | Transform**.
3. Select Absolute.
4. Select Position.
5. Verify that Anchor Point is set to the desired point of reference.
6. Enter new values in X (horizontal) or Y (Vertical) position.
7. Select **Apply**.

Steps: Set Variable Position

Use this operation to set the specific measurements of an offset from the current position of a selected object.

1. Select the desired object in the working area.
2. Access **Arrange | Transform**.
3. Select **Add to/Subtract** from existing value.
4. Select Position.
5. Verify that Anchor Point is set to the desired position as the positioning point of reference.
6. Enter new values in X (horizontal) or Y (Vertical) position.
7. Select **Apply**.

Steps: Create an Offset Series Effect

Use this operation to automatically create a set of duplicates each time the Transform Again option is selected. (See Figure 8.22.)

1. Select the desired object in the working area.
2. Access **Arrange | Transform**.
3. Select **Add to/Subtract from** existing value.
4. Select **Position**.
5. Select Duplicates, Quantity=1.
6. Verify that Anchor Point is set to the desired point of reference.
7. Enter the desired offset values in X (horizontal) or Y (vertical) position.
8. Select **Apply**.
9. Select Transform Again (Shift-W) as many times as necesary to create the desired number of copies.

Steps: Apply Absolute/Variable Position

Use this operation to apply the current Absolute or Variable position values to any selected object in the working area.

1. Select the object to be positioned.
2. Set desired Absolute/Variable position values in the Transform dialog box (see above).

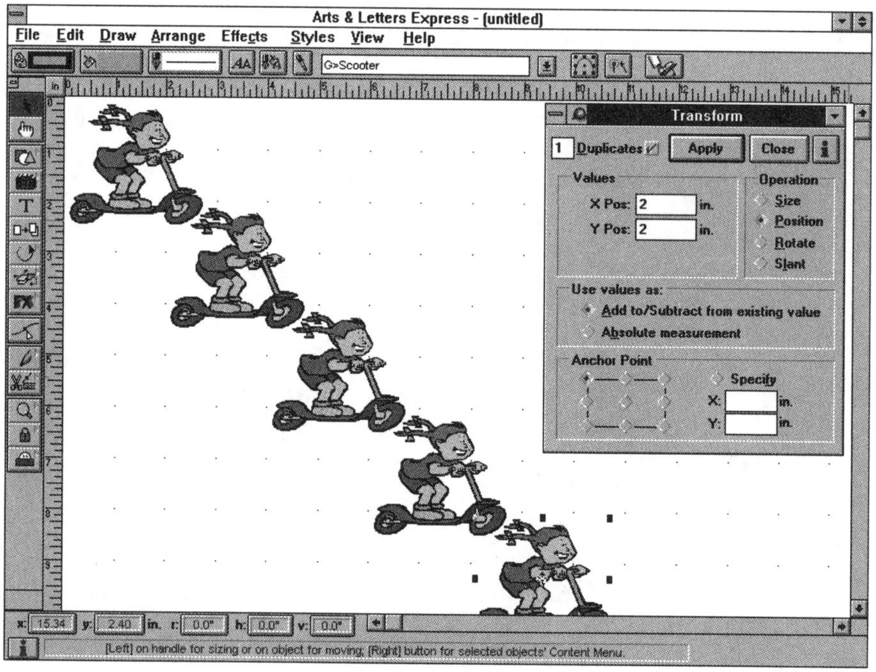

Figure 8.22
Offset Series Effect
The offset is set at two inches across and two inches down, with duplicates enabled. Each time Transform Again is selected a new duplicate is made with these offset values.

3. Select **Apply**.
4. Select **Arrange | Transform Again** (Shift-W).

Rotate Transform

An object may be rotated from its center or from an infinite number of anchor points placed in the object. Rotation transform features allow you to set the exact angle of rotation of an object. This is particularly useful to set standard 45 degree and 90 degree increments. A 90 degree rotation represents one quarter turn, clockwise. A 270 degree rotation represents one quarter turn counterclockwise. These settings allow you to turn objects on their sides and are highly useful to position and turn display graphics, such as arrows, and flowcharting elements to the exact direction and angle you wish.

Absolute vs. Variable

Absolute rotation settings determine the angle of rotation. (See Figure 8.23.) When Transform Again is activated, it duplicates this exact angle on any selected object; the duplicates will always rotate to the same angle. Variable rotation settings are added to the angle of rotation of the selected object on the screen. So, if you have a Variable setting at 60 degrees applied to an object already rotated at an angle of 30 degrees, the

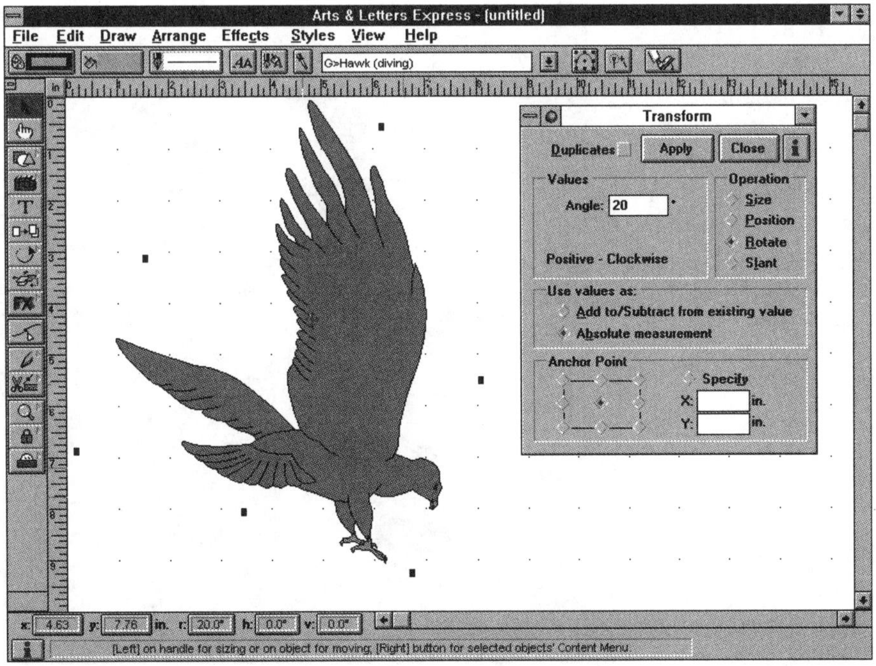

Figure 8.23
Absolute Rotation
The bird is set to an absolute angle of 20 degrees. This same rotation setting can now be applied to any other object in the screen using Transform again. This is a highly efficient way to control the angles of a series of different objects.

two values add and the object is rotated at 90 degrees. When Transform again is activated, it adds the Variable value to the angle of rotation of the selected object (Figure 8.24).

Anchor Point

The most common anchor point for rotation is the centerpoint. You may select any of the points around the edge of the graphic as its anchor point. These points are useful if you wish to spin an object based from its corner and create a progressive effect based on that rotation. You also have the option to drag the anchor point in the working area with the mouse, but if you don't want to take chances on an uneven rotation, simply select the center or other desired anchor point in the Transform dialog box before beginning numeric or screen rotation operation.

Steps: Set Absolute Rotation

Use this operation to set an absolute rotation for an object.

1. Select the desired object.
2. Access **Arrange | Transform**.
3. Select Rotate.
4. Select Absolute.
5. Verify that the Anchor Point is set to Center or other desired position.

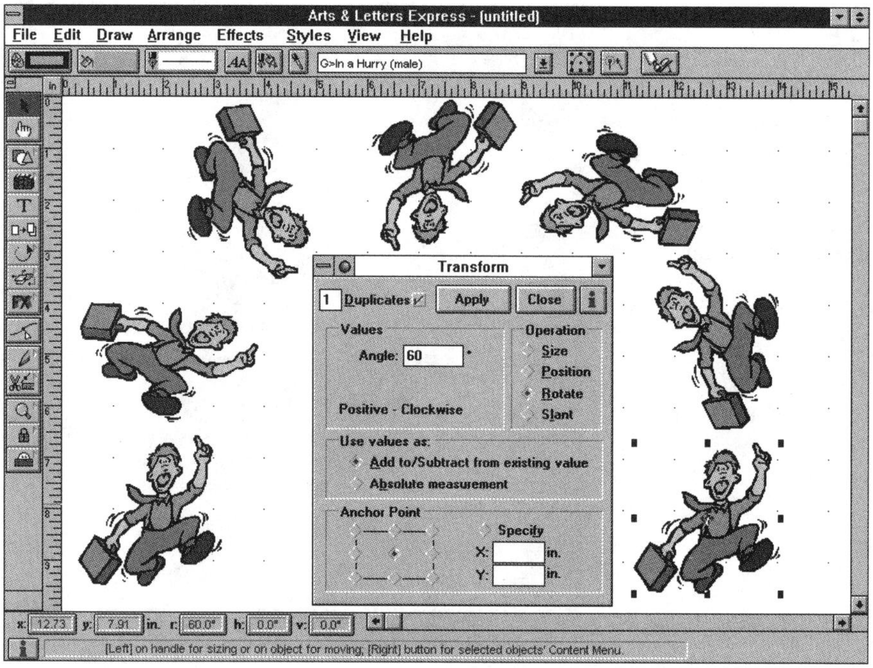

Figure 8.24
Variable Rotation
In the example shown, variable rotation is set to 60 degrees, with Duplicates enabled. Each time you select Transform Again, a new copy is made at an angle 60 degrees greater than the preceding image.

6. Enter the desired angle. (Note: Positive values move clockwise, negative values turn the object counterclockwise.)
7. Select **Apply**.

Steps: Set Variable Rotation

Use this operation to set a variable rotation for an object. The rotation angle specified here will add to the rotation angle of the specified object.

1. Select the desired object.
2. Access **Arrange | Transform**.
3. Select Rotate.
4. Select **Add to/Subtract** from existing value.
5. Verify that the Anchor Point is set to Center or other desired position.
6. Enter desired angle. (Note: Positive values move clockwise, negative values turn the object counterclockwise.)
7. Select **Apply**.

Steps: Apply Absolute/Variable Rotation

Use this operation to apply the current Absolute or Variable rotation values to any selected object in the working area.

1. Set the desired Absolute/Variable Rotation values in the Transform dialog box (see above).
2. Select **Apply**.
3. Select object to be rotated.
4. Select **Arrange | Transform Again** (Shift-W).

Slant Transform

Slant is created by manipulating angles on the sides of a graphic around a centerpoint, like rotation. It is difficult to see how slant works using the mouse, because things happen so rapidly and fluidly, so it just looks like the object is flipping and shaping wildly. Do it in Transform and you can see exactly what is happening. Set Horizontal slant for a square at 30 degrees and both left and right sides of the square will tilt 30 degrees, forming a parallelogram. Set the vertical slant for 40 degrees and the top and bottom sides of the square will tilt 40 degrees.

Slanting Constraints

There are constraints in slanting. For example, the vertical and horizontal angles can't change so as to flatten the object into a straight line. A slant of 90 degrees would do that, so you are constrained to enter values of + or – 80 degrees.

Applications

Numeric slanting operations have a number of specific and practical applications. You can use them to transform simple graphics like a square or rectangle into controlled geometric shapes at specific angles. In operations like object shadows, you can use this feature to capture object slant angles and use Transform Again to apply them to multiple objects to mirror the same shadow effect.

Slanting and Text

Note that with Transform, as with the mouse, text must be broken into freeform objects and edited as a group for slant operations to work. Slant operations will not be shown on the screen or print correctly unless you break up the text and edit it in freeform mode.

Steps: Set Absolute Slant

Use this operation to set an absolute slant for an object (Figure 8.25).

1. Select the desired object.
2. Access **Arrange | Transform**.
3. Select **Slant**.
4. Select Absolute.
5. Verify that the Anchor Point is set to Center or another desired position.

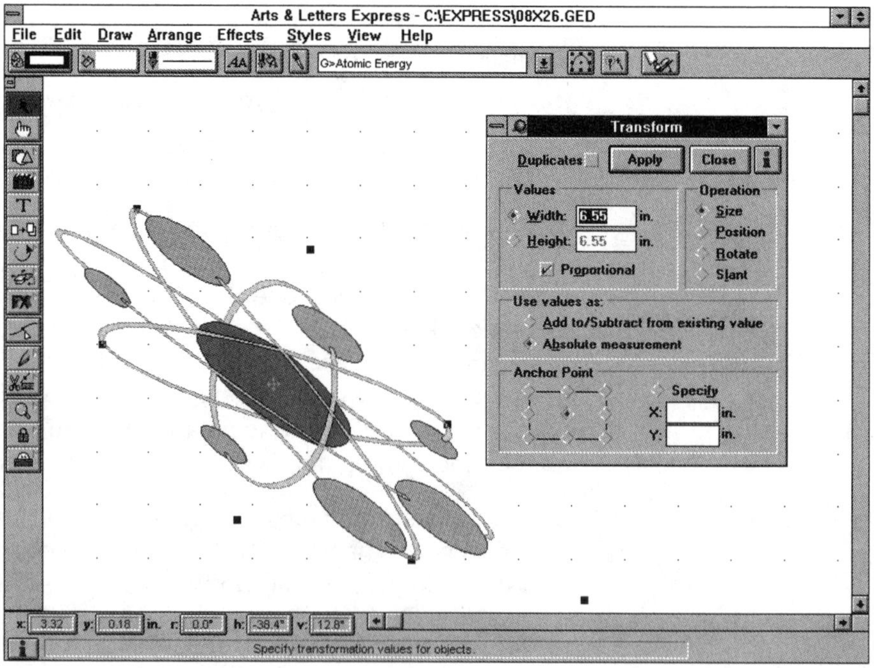

Figure 8.25 Absolute Slant
Slant is set using two angles—Horizontal and Vertical. As angles are set, the object slants to different planes. Slant is used to create 3-D and a variety of distortion effects.

6. Enter the desired horizontal and vertical angles. (Note: Positive values move clockwise, negative values turn the object counterclockwise.)
7. Select **Apply**.

Steps: Set Variable Slant

Use this operation to set a variable slant angle for an object. The slant values set here will add to the slant value set for the selected object.

1. Select the desired object.
2. Access **Arrange | Transform**.
3. Select **Slant**.
4. Select **Add to/Subtract** from existing value.
5. Verify that the Anchor Point is set to Center or other desired position.
6. Enter the desired angle. (Note: Positive values move clockwise, negative values turn the object counterclockwise.)
7. Select **Apply**.

Steps: Apply Absolute/Variable Slant

Use this operation to apply the current Absolute or Variable slant values to any selected object in the working area.

1. Select the object to be slanted.
2. Set the desired Absolute/Variable slant values in the Transform dialog box (see above).
3. Select **Apply**.
4. Select **Arrange | Transform Again** (Shift-W).

Automated Offset Duplication

Duplicates work magically in combination with the Variable (Add to/Subtract from...) mode in the Transform dialog box. Since Variable transformations are progressive, each time a duplicate is made, it changes based on the settings of the previous copy.

Size Example

If you set the Variable Size option to 25% with duplicates active, the first duplicate will be 25% the size of the original, the second will be 25% less than that and so forth.

Position Example

If you set the position setting to ¼ inch horizontally and ⅛ inch vertically, each time you activate Transform Again, a new copy is made ¼ inch to the right and ⅛ inch higher than the one that preceded it.

Rotation Example

For example, if you set the Variable Rotation angle for an element to 30 degrees, the first duplicate will have an angle of rotation of 60 degrees, the next will have an angle of rotation of 90 degrees, and so forth. The same general principle works for slant angles.

Steps: Create Spinning Stack

Use this operation to set a variable angle rotation for an object with duplicates enabled. This will create a progressive "spinning stack" of graphics (Figure 8.26). Each time that Transform Again is enabled, a new graphic will be created and incrementally rotated based on the angle of the previous graphic. This can be used to create "wheel" or "whirl" effects.

1. Select desired object.
2. Access **Arrange | Transform**.
3. Select **Rotate**.
4. Select **Add to/Subtract from** existing value.
5. Select **Duplicates**, Quantity=1.
6. Verify that the Anchor Point is set to Center or other desired position.

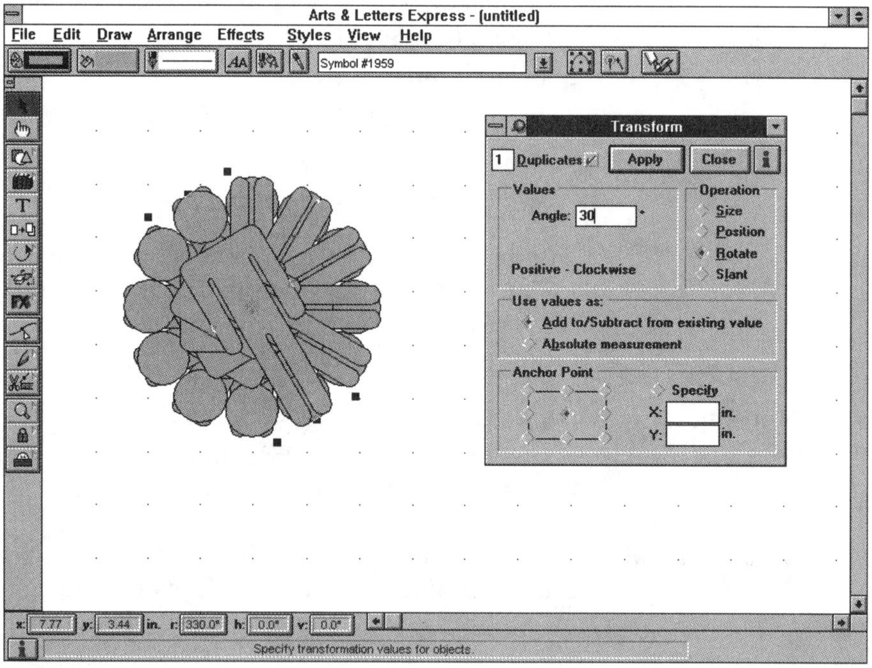

Figure 8.26
Spinning Stack
With Variable rotation set to 30 degrees in the Transform dialog box, and Duplicates enabled, each time that Transform Again on the Arrange menu is selected a new duplicate is made at 30 degrees from the preceding graphic. This is similar to, but more numerically precise than, a rotation or spin blend.

7. Enter the desired Angle. (Note: Positive values move clockwise, negative values turn the object counterclockwise.)
8. Select **Apply**.
9. Select **Arrange | Transform Again** (Shift-W).
10. Repeat the operation to continue the spinning stack.

Object Series

For technical drawings or any application requiring exacting measurement for different aspect views of an object such as a jet fighter or a map, you may wish to specify an exact angle of tilt or slant. You can use the Transform dialog box in a series of operations to set the size and then create a series of duplicates that tilt at incremental angles (Figure 8.27). Each of these duplicates and its exact angle of rotation can be saved in a Clip-Art Manager collection. This is particularly useful for arrows and flowchart or diagram components.

Steps: Create Incremental Series Variation in Slant or Rotation

Use this operation to create a series of graphics that turn at incremental rotations. For example, at an incremental rotation setting of 30 degrees, you can create 12 progressive duplicates that go full circle.

1. Select the desired element in the working area.

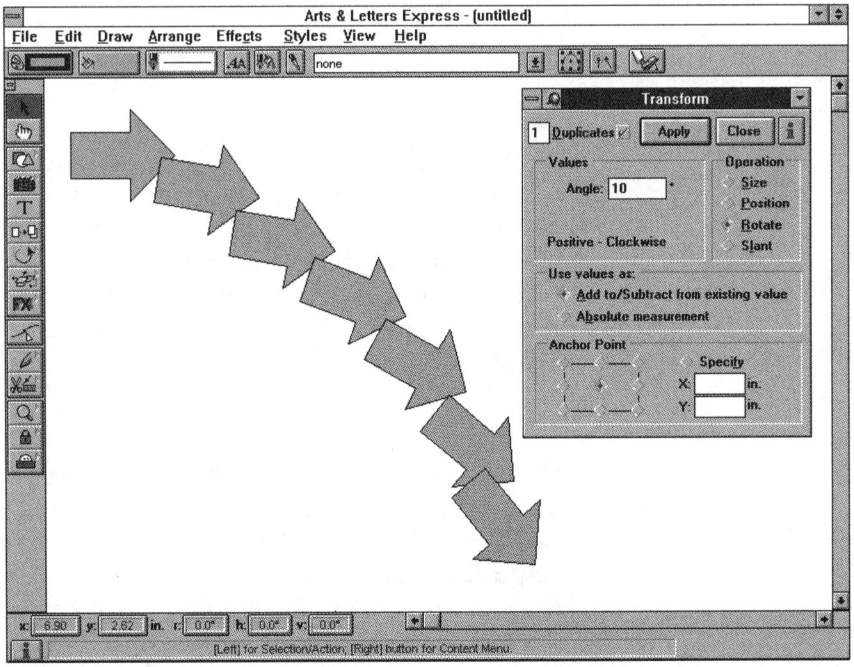

Figure 8.27
Object Series
Use Transform and Transform Again to create a series of precisely angled elements. Here a series of arrows shown in 10 degree increments allows you to save the set into a custom collection.

2. Select group and access **Manipulate | Transform**.
3. Select **Add to/Subtract** from Existing Value.
4. Select Duplicates, Quantity=1.
5. Enter the degree of desired slant or rotation increment.
6. Select **Apply**.
7. Select **Arrange | Transform Again** (Shift-W) as many times as necessary to create the desired series of duplicates.

Steps: Create Series Collection

Use this operation to place each graphic in the series into a single series collection for use from the Clip-Art Manager.

1. Access **Draw | Clip-Art Manager**. Press pushpin.
2. Access **Collections | New**.
3. Enter Filename, Collection Name, and Additional Information. Select **OK**.
4. Verify that New Collection is selected in the Clip-Art Manager Collection List.
5. Select the first graphic in the series.
6. Select **Save to Collection**.
7. Enter Name. Include the angle of slant or rotation. Select **OK**.
8. Repeat the operation for each graphic in the series.

Flip Effects

The Flip option on the Arrange Menu allows you to perform instant horizontal and vertical flips of selected object(s) in the working area. Flip operations may also be implemented directly with the mouse. If you drag any selected element from one corner or side, the minute your mouse cursor crosses the line or point on the opposite side of the element, it will flip automatically. Depending on whether you are dragging up or across will determine what kind of screen flip you get.

Mirror Effects with Flip

One very interesting visual effect that can be created using Arts & Letters is to mirror a symbol by creating its visual match in a flipped duplicate. (See Figure 8.28.) This is a simple operation, but it illustrates the composition power you have at your fingertips when you have a library of ready-made symbols used in combination with simple **Duplicate, Flip Horizontal**, and **Flip Vertical** features.

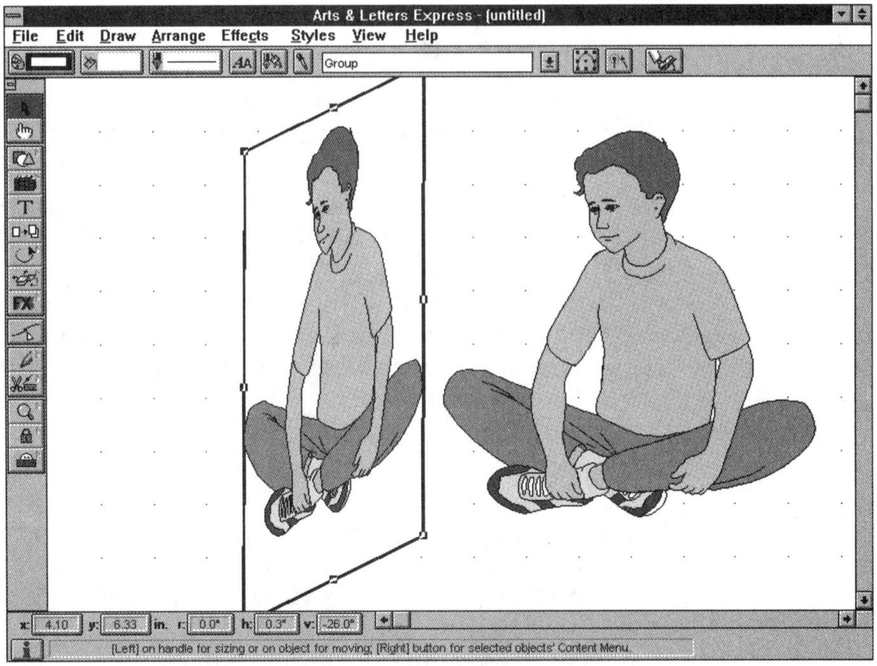

Figure 8.28
Mirror Effects
The figure of the boy was duplicated, and then slanted. To heighten the mirror effect, the width was flattened using the middle sizing handle. The effect took under two minutes to create.

If you begin with a basic symbol on the screen, you can instantly create a mirror image by making a copy and flipping it horizontally.

You may also create a vertical mirror effect using the flip vertical option. The basic mirror effect can be enhanced through drop shadows to one or more of the graphics, or by distorting one of the copies through use of the **Slant** or **Rotate** tools.

By adding attributes, such as line weight, color, and other effects, you can create a highly effective mirror effect in a few mouse movements.

Steps: Creating Mirror Effects

Use this operation to create a mirror effect of a selected string of text or graphic.

1. Select the symbol on screen.
2. Select **Duplicate** icon in the Toolbox.
3. Click on the symbol, press and hold the mouse button, and drag duplicate to the side of original.
4. Click on the right mouse button or select the **Arrow** icon to disable **Duplicate**.
5. Select Copy and access **Arrange | Flip Vertically** or **Arrange | Flip Horizontally** to create a mirror image of the original.
6. Use the mouse to move the original and its mirror into desired position.

Merge Effects

The Merge feature group contains two distinct features that perform different types of shape cutting operations. The Cutout option works only with closed freeform shapes, and allows you to use one closed freefrom shape to cut a hole in another. Objects placed behind the hole will show through the hole but not through the surrounding shape. The Clipping Path option is more flexible and works with standard images, symbols, and text. It allows you to place a shape over another graphic or background and fill the shape with the background. This allows you to create custom fill effects for objects or text and to use simple shapes to electronically clip and cut segments out of larger compositions.

Technical Issues and Options

Like Warp and Extrude effects, Merge features are created as special group graphics. When a Merge effect has been created, it will be specially identified as a Hole Group (Cutout) or Mask Group (Clipping Mask). The group contains both the background file and the clipping object, be it the hole shape or the mask.

Object Size Since Merge objects are composite graphics, you should be mindful of the size of the objects you are creating and the frequency with which they are used in an individual file. If you are creating Merge effects using highly complex (therefore large) freeform graphic or image groups, you may strain your system resources in performing the processing and displaying all elements of the group on the screen. These effects are some of the highest level features in the product and demand a significant amount of processing. If you are on a shoestring system, big merge groups could leave you untied.

Printing Issues Merge groups can be printed from within Arts & Letters, but when you need to export them to external file formats, certain problems will arise. Vector formats like CGM will present an accurate representation of most effects created by Arts & Letters, but don't have the programming structure to handle the Hole Group or Mask Group configuration. What you will get in export to these formats is the entire graphics that make up the whole group, not the effect itself.

Bitmap export file formats, like TIFF, offer you the ability to translate the effect and turn it into a bit-mapped dot pattern. This may not be acceptable from a clarity or quality standpoint, because you will lose the seamless bezier curves that the vector engine in Express generates.

The ultimate solution to file export where Merge effects are concerned is our old friend Postscript. Express, like most other top-of-the-line graphics packages, is optimized around the PostScript language. It has the ability to translate the final effect into an export file and print it cleanly, crisply, and clearly.

Copy/Paste and Merge The same problems that arise in exporting a Merge effect to a CGM file will arise when pasting the effect from Arts & Letters to the Clipboard.

Hole Cutting

Cutouts are especially useful with text because they can be used to create "show-through" effects, in which case a pattern or a drawing hidden behind a solid graphic overlay will only show through in the text letters.

This effect is best used when a textured pattern or drawing is hidden behind part of a drawing or a neutral background. The cookie cutter elements are then positioned over the background, and, when the cutting is finished, it creates a hole in the background. All elements in the operation must be *closed freeform shapes* for the merge feature to work.

Steps: Hole Cutting Use this operation to cut a hole in a graphic form (Figure 8.29). Note all selected graphics must be closed freeform shapes, not groups, not symbols, and not images. Otherwise the operation will not work correctly!

1. Create a background graphic or textured panel.
2. Create a neutral background or drawing to overprint the background graphic.
3. Create a cookie cutter element. It must be a closed freeform shape.
4. Use **Block Select** or **Select All** to select all elements.
5. Access **Effects | Merge**.
6. Select **Cutout**.
7. Select **Add**.
8. The cutout effect is created and labeled as a Hole Group in the Status Bar. As with any other object grouping, to change a hole group, it is necessary to use **Effects | Break Apart**.

Cropping with a Clipping Mask

You can also crop or "cut out" a desired section of a freeform object, symbol, or text. The procedure is simple. Just place the composition you wish to crop or clip from in the screen and create a clipping mask (Figure 8.30). This can be a basic symbol, such as a circle or rectangle, a

Figure 8.29
Hole Cutting
The background is a rectangle containing a color blend; the cutout object is an 8-point star. The woman's face shows through the cutout hole. The hole effect may be broken apart at any time for editing.

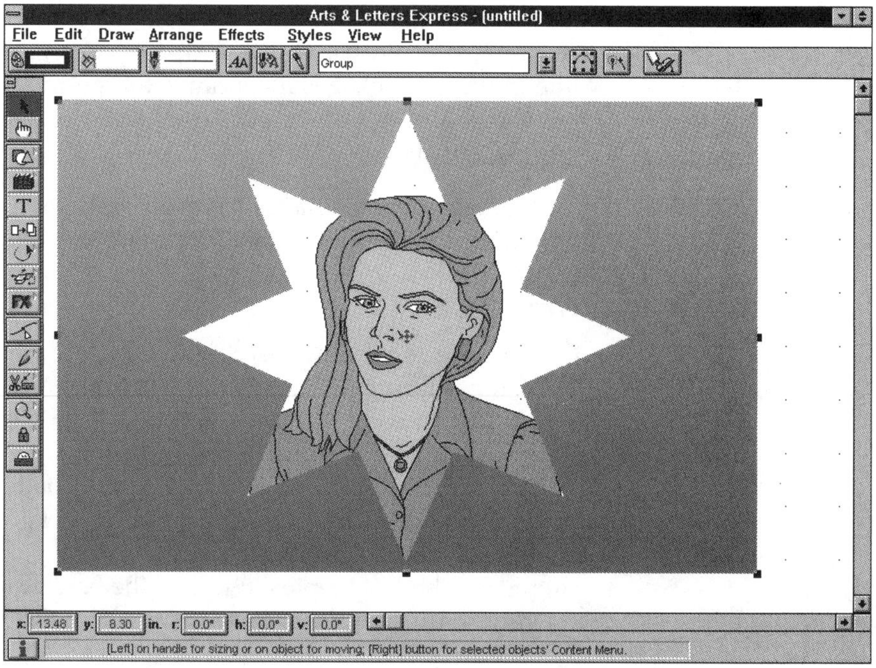

Figure 8.30
Cropping with a Clipping Mask
The background picture of the volcano was clipped using an inverted triangle as shown. This is a simple overlay and selection procedure that does not require that either background or clipping object be in freeform mode.

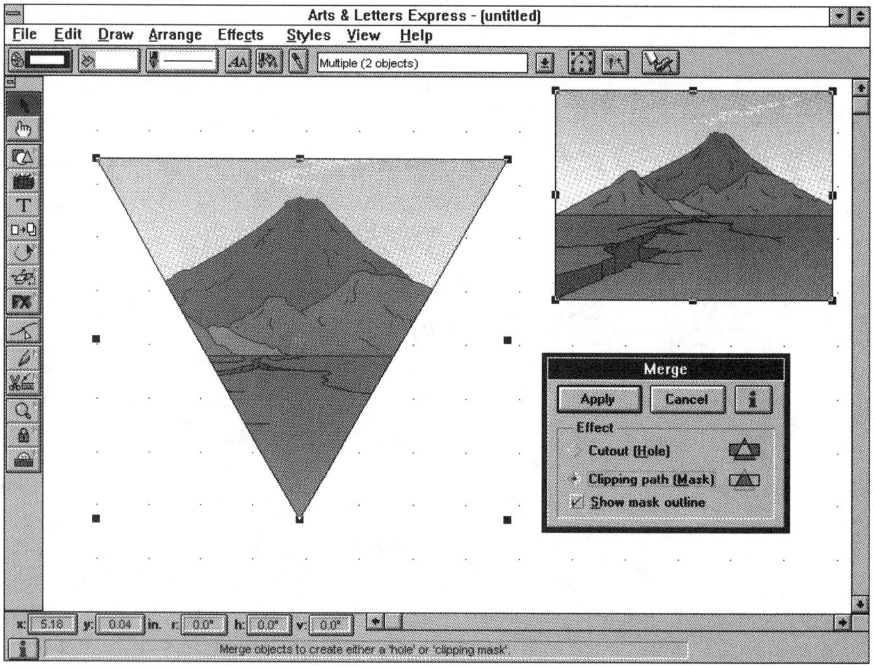

closed freeform shape, or a string of text. Position the clipping object over the background and access the **Clipping Path** feature, located in the **Merge** dialog box from the **Arrange** menu. The area of the base drawing overprinted by the mask will be cut out and fitted into the mask.

Cropping with a Clipping Path

Use this operation to crop a selection using the Clipping Path Merge operation:

1. Place the base drawing that you wish to crop or clip on the screen.
2. Create a clipping path by selecting a symbol form, drawing a closed freeform object, or positioning a text string.
3. Position the clipping path directly over the area of the base drawing you wish to clip.
4. Select both the base drawing and the clipping path.
5. Access **Arrange | Merge**.
6. Select **Clipping Path**.
7. If you wish the clipped object to have a line around it, select **Show Outline**. If you don't want a line, leave it blank.
8. To break up the Mask Group, select **Arrange | Break Apart**.

Cropping Images with Select Area

In previous versions of Arts & Letters, the clipping mask was the only effective way to crop images and print them. In Express, the Select Area command on the Edit menu allows you to crop images for copying, exporting, and printing (Figure 8.31). Select Area is not formally a design effect, but it can be used for that purpose.

Raw Edges and Output Options

When creating complex compositions made up of many art elements, it can be time-consuming to fit all of the elements into a neat rectangular, page size layout. Elements may overlap and extend out from the composition, and the whole layout may have a number of jagged edges. For final presentation, you need to be able to show the composition with crisp, clean edges. You have the option to use a square or rectangle or any other simple shape as a frame for the final version and use the Clipping Path option. But for output purposes it makes more sense to use the Select Area option.

Select Area Operations

Select Area is a command that must be activated and deactivated as it is used. When you activate Select Area, the system prompts you to draw a square or rectangular bounding box on the screen around the graphics

Figure 8.31 Cropping with Select Area
The rectangular box around the city is the selected area that you can print, export, or copy to the Clipboard. This allows you to cut precisely what you want from the screen and avoid loose ends or overlapping objects.

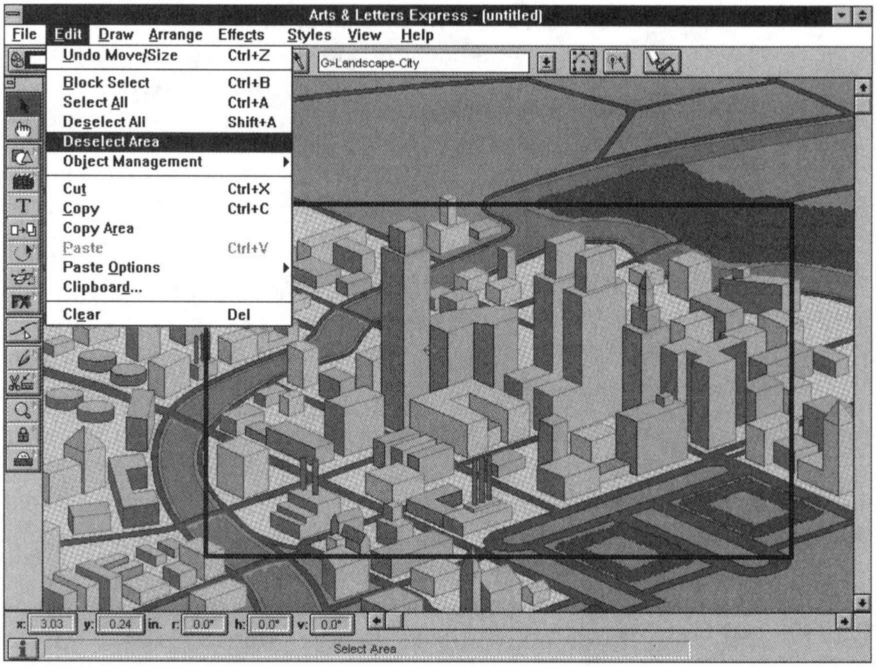

you wish to output. The area is shown on the screen by a heavy black line. This line may be adjusted and resized interactively from any point. Just like a program Window, when the cursor is placed over any part of the line, the line or double-arrow corner adjustment appears and you may drag the sides of the box to the exact configuration desired.

The Select Area bounding box remains active in the working area until you choose Deselect Area from the Edit menu to remove it. You may use the Select Area option when using the File: Export option, or the File: Print option. To use this option with Copy/Paste features, select the Copy Area feature available on the Edit menu.

Steps: Cropping with Select Area

Use this operation in Express to crop a portion of a composition on screen for output via print, file export, or the Windows Clipboard.

1. Select **Edit | Select Area**.
2. Drag the mouse to place the bounding box over the area of the artwork you wish to export, print, or copy.
3. Place the cursor over the bounding box line to activate the resizing cursor and make any adjustments to the position or size of the bounding box.

4. Activate the desired feature (Export or Print) and select the output Area option or select **Edit | Copy Area**.

Visual Callouts and Framing Effects

Merge functions as an electronic cookie cutter. Place a shape over a background and the shape clips out only the portion of the background graphic it covers. This can be used artistically, but can also have a great deal of practical value. When used with maps and backgrounds, even charts, it allows you to clip and blow up a special area of a graphic for emphasis (Figure 8.32). If you create two copies of the background graphic, you can use one to create the Clipping Path cutout and then resize the cutout and match it to its original. In the illustration shown, a cutout has been matched with its source graphic with a circle blend used to enhance the three-dimensional expansion of the cutout. This 3-D effect could also be created using Extrude.

Express comes with a large collection of scenic systems: the Dinosaur collection, Aircraft, Space, and a variety of business art and charting designs. Clipping Path Merge operations allow you to make art objects in any shape using any part of these art forms or any complex composition you make. The ease with which you can do this makes it an attractive way to enhance even traditional flowcharts and graphics. Place a box, circle, or triangle over the graph or flowchart and pull out points

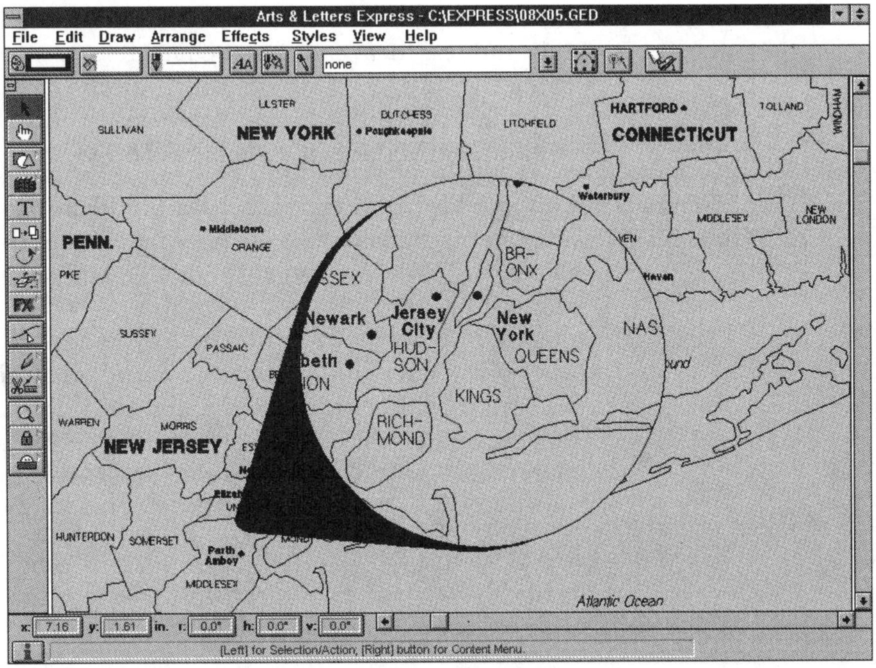

Figure 8.32
Visual Callouts
The circle cutout was created using Merge | Clipping Path. The map is contained in the Merge group object. To edit the clipping selection just break apart the object, or select it within the group, move the circle slightly, and re-Merge the two.

Steps: Creating Callouts with Clipping Path

of emphasis using a cutout. You can then use these individual selections to highlight slides in a presentation.

Use this operation to create a callout with the Merge | Clipping Path feature.

1. Create or select an artwork to be the basis of the callout.
2. Create or select a masking graphic to act as the clipping path.
3. Use **Shift-Select** or **Block Select** to select both graphics.
4. Access **Effects | Merge**.
5. Select **Clipping Path**.
6. Optional: If you want the line around the masking graphic to show, select the Show Mask Outline option.
6. Select **Add**.
7. The clipping path is created and labeled a Mask Group in the Status Bar.

Create Custom Text and Object Fills

The Clipping Path is a dramatic feature that lets you create your own custom graphic fill patterns for objects and text. You can take any of the images from the clip-art library and use them as a background for art objects or text. You can create custom blends or specialized color layouts and use them to fill text characters or as fill patterns for graphics. Using the Clipping Path option, you can stack any outline form on top of a color background, and the background clips to the shape of the outline form and fills it. (See Figure 8.33.)

Blends as Text/Object Fills

Clipping Path allows you to use the Blend feature to generate special fill patterns, either based on color patterns or using objects and pictorial elements. This gives you a formidable array of capabilities to create customized backgrounds and text. You can build color patterns based on shapes, and ranges of color. The following section covers design effects with blends and will provide a number of ideas for Clipping Mask backgrounds. As with all Clipping Mask operations, you simply position the text or object you wish to fill over the place on the background that has the texture or design elements you wish to include.

Images as Object Fills

You may use graphic images from the Clip-Art Manager as object or text fills with the Clipping Mask feature. Simply place or compose the images you want on the screen and place the Clipping Mask graphic over the composition and Merge.

Figure 8.33
Text and Object Fills
The text at the upper-left was created by selecting the graphic and text in the lower right and activating the Clipping Path. Instead of a textured fill or gradient, this text is filled with the image of a city. The entire effect was created in under two minutes.

Drop Shadow with Text/Object Fills

One way to expand the depth and presence of a text or object effect created with Clipping Path is to add a drop shadow behind or in front of the element. To make this operation easy, duplicate your Clipping Mask text or object before you create the Clipping Mask and store it in some other place inside the same GED file. Once the Mask Group has been created, you will have the matching sized object ready to put in place.

Steps: Create Custom Text/Object Fills

Use this operation to create your own custom art or texture fills for objects or text.

1. Create the fill background using any of the features of Express, including the Clip-Art Manager, Symbol selector, Charting feature, or special graphic configurations, including Blend.
2. Create the mask object, either a text or graphic component.
3. Select the background graphic and the mask object at the same time. Do not Group them.
4. Access **Effects | Merge**.
5. Select Clipping Path.
6. Set the Show mask outline option as desired.
7. Select **OK**.

Blends

Blend is an object multiplier that allows you to create a variety of highly sophisticated effects. On one level, Blend is an automated version of the Duplicate feature. When you create a blend, you specify the beginning object, the ending object, and the number of copies to be generated to create the evolution between them.

Design Options

Blend effects are not group graphics like Merge objects are. When you generate a Blend, the system will label and identify it as a Blend group, but the effect is fully generated on screen by multiplying and positioning graphics. You can break apart the blend group and access any of the individual copies that make it up. Because blends are naturally generated on screen, in most situations you will have none of the printing or Copy/Paste issues that arise with composite effects like Hole and Mask groups.

Colors and Textures

Blends can be used to evolve colors from one shade to another. This is similar to the Gradient feature offered under the Styles: Fills feature group. Blends allow you to use any symbol wireframe as the frame for the color. You can assign a color to a stylized shape and evolve it to another shade and another stylized shape. Unlike the simple linear and radial gradient configurations offered, the shapes and color pattern designs available through Blend are limitless.

Object Shape, Size, and Position

Blends may also be used to evolve an object in shape, size, and position. You may show a small version of an art form growing progressively to a new size and position. These effects are similar to some of the effects that can be created using the Extrude and Warp options. Blend (Figure 8.34) allows you to fluidly select from any of the graphic database components, either symbols, images, or text, and evolve them from one shape to another. You may use this capability to create three-dimensional effects from a single graphic, to auto-duplicate a selected graphic, or to use multiple blends to automatically create layout fields, grids, and backgrounds.

Shape Evolution

Blend may also be used with simple freeform shapes to dynamically evolve between shapes. A simple example of this is turning a heart into a spade. When these symbol drawings are loaded and converted to freeform, they are both selected and Blend creates a continuum of copies that evolves from one of the selected shapes to another. This is useful to create progressive evolution effects that can be combined with changes in object color and texture as well.

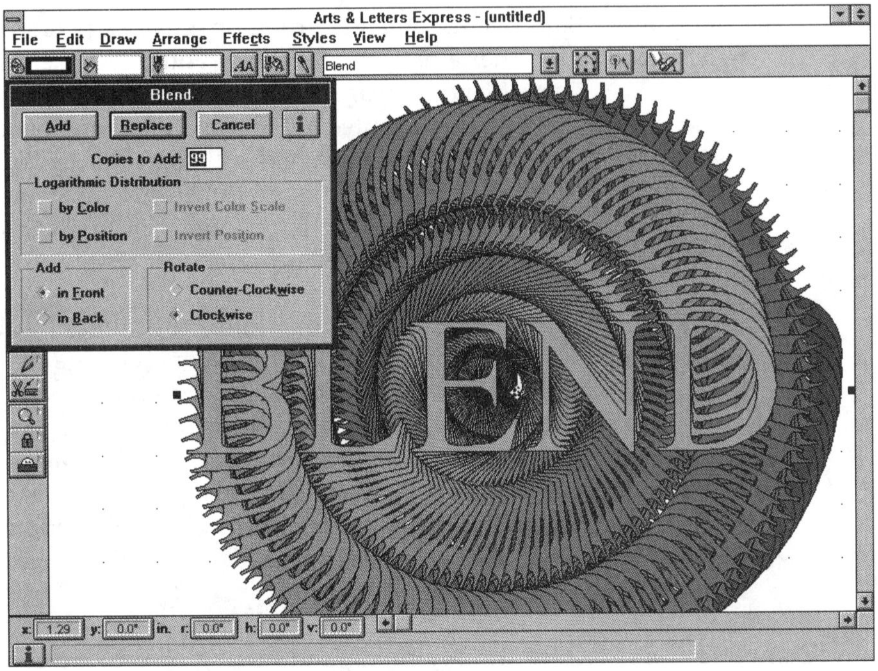

Figure 8.34
Blend
The workhorse of all the effects features, Blend is simple and easy to use and creates high-impact graphics in seconds. The stylized Blend at right was created by manipulating the Begin and End objects of the word with the mouse.

Shape evolution does not work with complex wireframes. There's simply too much going on inside complex symbols, such as those representing a human face; when shape evolution is attempted, you get mush. This option works the best using simple outline shapes.

Blend Group and Stack

A Blend is auto-generated as a graphic group, but the effect does not depend on the group, as Merge or Warp do. Express generates all levels of Blend and Extrude on the screen. This gives you the unique option of using the entire Blend group as created, or breaking it apart and moving individual elements in the Blend stack as you wish. Think of the Blend stack as a pack of up to 99 playing cards. The cards are spread out on the screen in an array in the base blend. When broken apart, you may select any of the playing cards and move it slightly, or pull it out entirely.

Blend Options and Controls

The Blend feature group allows you to execute a procedure to create and edit a variety of blend effects. The options and controls within the feature set can dramatically impact the look and form of the blends you create. The basic options are profiled here; advanced logarithmic distributions are covered later in this section.

Begining and Ending Objects Both beginning and ending objects of a position blend must be created from the same element. When you select the element on screen and activate Blend, you are prompted in the dialog box to enter the number of copies to be generated in the blend effect and offered several configuration options. When you leave the dialog box, the Blend design really begins. Blend changes the cursor to the Duplicate format and auto-generates an Ending object, which is offset stacked on top of the Beginning object you originally selected.

Editing Blend Objects You can make custom edits to the symbol at both ends of the blend process using Rotate and Slant, and change the aspect ratio so that one distorted version of a symbol blends to another distorted version. Many of the editing features in Express are available, including Align and Transform, the entire Style menu, and all of the basic Edit and positioning features. You are not required to make edits in any particular order. You simply select the beginning or ending object as needed and make the desired changes to color, size, position, alignment, and so forth.

Complete Blend Once the beginning and ending objects are in place and configured as you want them, you may activate Complete Blend by clicking the right mouse button. The dialog box will not redisplay, the system will simply auto-calculate the copying process and the series of copies you specified will be generated on screen into a Blend group object.

Editing Blends with Replace Blends can be complex and detailed. The Blend feature does not include a mimic or preview feature as the Warp and Extrude screens do. So, to a certain extent, each blend you make involves guesswork, and trial and error. You can interactively edit your blends without re-creating them from scratch using the Blend Replace option. With the completed blend selected, re-access the Blend dialog box and respecify any of the settings pertaining to the number of copies, position, or front/back origination. Then select Replace. You will be given the beginning and ending objects as they appeared before you initiated the Complete Blend command. You may now start your editing cycle all over again and make changes, and Complete Blend again.

Blend Add Options The normal blend generation is to stack copies in front of the beginning object moving toward the ending object. So the beginning object represents the back of the blend, and the ending option represents the front. You can reverse this flow so that copies are added in back of the beginning object. This is an interesting option to experiment with on the same blend configuration. The stacking direction of objects within a blend can affect the areas of graphics shown in the effect. This is particularly important if you are stacking representational artworks like people, animals, buildings, and so forth.

Blend Rotate Options Rotation controls are active only when either the beginning or ending point of the blend has been rotated. Again, this is an experimental issue. You may even want to Duplicate the entire blend and see what happens to it when you Replace it and change the angle of rotation. When using abstract designs or objects, in particular, you will find that the effect dramatically changes when the rotation direction changes.

Blends by Position

Blends by position allow you to create a physical flow of an element from a starting shape to an ending shape and show all the stages of evolution in between. The process to create a blend by position simply involves specifying a starting symbol in the shape, size, and configuration, specifying the number of copies, or "stages of evolution" you wish to see, and specifying the ending shape, size, and position of the graphic. (Figure 8.35.)

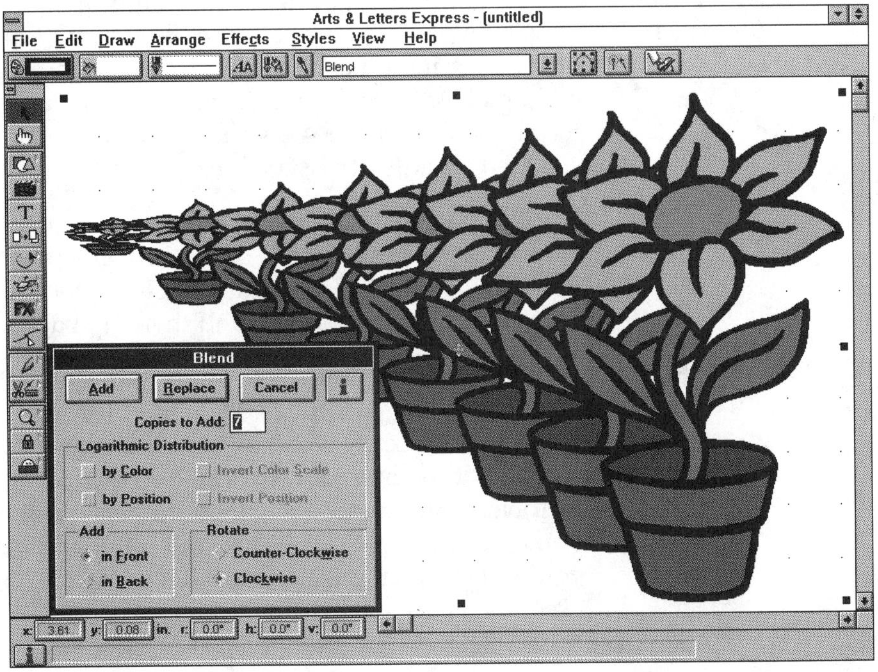

Figure 8.35
Blends by Position
Multiplied by seven and flattened at the start, this flower grows through the evolution of a position blend. Blends allow you to show objects actively changing shape and position on the screen. They are fully editable at any time using the Blend Replace option.

Size By varying the size of the graphic or text between the beginning and ending object, you can create an exploding blend that fluidly transforms in size from large to small or small to large. This effect can be created using Extrude but you can achieve some interesting and textured variations on it with the Blend feature. Position blends can be configured using a number of parameters either singly or in combination.

Shape Use Transform or the middle sizing handles to flatten or stretch the dimensions of the text or object and Blend will fill in the rest. This can be combined with Size variations to show the evolution of a single shape.

Rotation Simple size and shape blends explode like clean vectors. Changing the rotation angle of the beginning or ending object allows you to twist the blend like bread dough. Objects spin out and twist dramatically, creating an expanded and intense effect. Don't forget to experiment with the rotation direction option in the Blend dialog box.

Slant Like Rotation, Slant adds a twist to dramatically enhance the three-dimensional character of the final blend effect. If you slant the beginning or ending object, the copies move dynamically and turn corners to twist from the flat plane of the screen and suggest a full three-dimensional object.

Stacks and Progressives Positioning the beginning and ending objects creates additional variations. By placing the end object directly on top of the beginning object, or stacking it, you expand the depth of the object itself. By moving the ending object across the screen, you create a broad and expansive look to the blend and see the various shapes spread out like playing cards smeared broadly across a table.

Flips Some of the most interesting basic blends can be created by flipping the end or beginning object. If both horizontal and vertical dimensions are flipped, the blend can literally reach the vanishing point, narrowing to a single point on the screen and then flip back to full size.

Styles Position blends are affected by the color and styles you select, in particular, the Line Attributes. In dense blends of 25 copies or more, lines around the selected blend object can become so tightly clustered in the copies that the interior color can be obscured. For dense blends, setting the object framing line thickness to hairline or none can help the color of the objects come out. When the fill of an object is set to solid colors, you'll get a very crisp blend effect. When shades and grayscales are used, the effect softens.

Steps: Symbol Blends by Position

Use this operation to set up a symbol blend by position.

1. Place the symbol, image, text, or freeform object to be blended.
2. Access **Effects | Blend**.
3. Enter the desired number of copies or "stages of evolution" between start and end form of the blend.
4. Select any of the desired Blend options in the dialog box to configure the blend.
5. Select **Add**.
6. A duplicate of the symbol appears on screen. Drag it to desired position.
7. Use any manipulate tools including Rotate, Slant, and reshaping operations with the mouse to configure the beginning and ending objects as you wish them to appear.
8. Select **Effects | Complete Blend**.

Steps: Edit Position Blend with Replace

Use this operation to fine-tune corrections to the Blend configuration.

1. Select the Blend group by itself in the working area.
2. Access **Effects | Blend**.
3. Make any desired changes to blend options including number of copies.
4. Select **Replace**.
5. Make edits to the Beginning and Ending objects as desired using any of the available Express features.
6. Click the right mouse button to activate Complete Blend option.

Steps: Create Blend Theme and Variations

Use this operation to duplicate the original blend and make adjustments to copies. This operation allows you to save each variation on the blend within a GED file and select the one you like based on experimentation and observation.

1. Select **View | All Pages**.
2. Select the Blend group by itself in the working area.
3. Select the **Duplicate** icon in the Toolbar.
4. Drag one or more duplicates of the original Blend and position them in the available pages of the current GED file.
5. Select one of the copies and enter variation edits using Replace as described above.

Blends by Color

Using blending by color, you can give an individual symbol a highly sophisticated texture of gradations in color or grayscales (Figure 8.36). The principle here is to set a starting point in the desired color, select Blend, and define the number of "copies" or gradations you wish to see on screen. The Blend command automatically places a duplicate of the original symbol, which you may use to specify the ending color of the blend.

Color Distribution and Stacks

Unlike Blends by Position, which distributes an array of copies *across* the screen, color blending lets you see the color distributed within the same symbol. This involves stacking a smaller ending object on top of a larger beginning object. Stacking color objects allows you to create a blend of a single graphic shape in which the color variations shift and change.

Bounding Line vs. Object Line

Since color blends are intended to create a variety of color effects within a single object, the framing line around each object is a critical factor. If the line is a different color (such as black) from the interior, the multiple copies generated by the blend will show the black lines around each copy and the blend will look like a stack of layered objects. This can be a highly desirable effect, particularly when used with freeform or ripple objects.

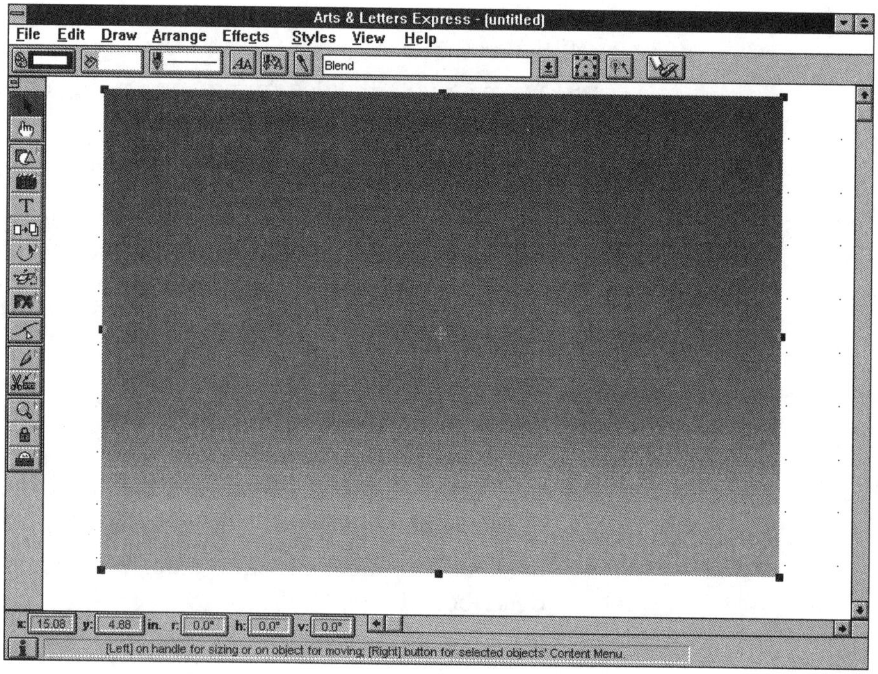

Figure 8.36
Blends by Color
This gradient background was created by blending a red rectangle at the top with a same-size yellow one at the bottom. Line attributes on both were set to None and number of Blend copies set to the maximum: 99.

For subtly textured variations in color, the object line can be a limitation; the multiple copies of the object line get in the way of the color transformation. You have two options: either remove the line entirely by setting the object line attributes to None, or change the color of the object line to exactly match the interior. Either way, the color evolution will be seamless and fluid.

Once the effect is complete, you may want a single bounding line around the entire object. You can place a line around the base graphic by selecting that one graphic within the Blend group. It will be the top graphic in the list displayed in the Object Viewer on the Style Bar.

Ending Object Position By varying the position of the ending object within the base graphic, you can change the flow of color evolution dramatically. Positioning the ending object in the center of the background graphic will create symmetrical color evolutions. Moving it to an offset position or an extreme edge position will skew the color distribution accordingly.

Ending Object Distortion When adding blended color highlights to an object, the ending object represents the color highlight. You can, of course, blend to a matched copy of the beginning object to create the color distribution. To create more stunning effects and textures, you can distort the ending object by stretching, flattening and/or slanting it. Changing the character of the ending object will bring about twists and shifts in the pattern of the color evolution, even giving it a dramatic patterned character similar to a gradient.

Compound Blends You may create a series of individual object blends and then group them over a blended background to create intricate color mixes and highly textured backgrounds. When doing effects like this, you should turn off the object line in most cases, unless you are looking for an exaggerated, highly terraced graphic effect.

Steps: Creating a Color Blend Use this operation to create a color blended graphic object. This technique works best with simple graphic shapes, forms, and outline drawings. Complex drawings with many elements can create interesting effects if the object is selected and all external and internal framing lines are set to None.

1. Place the symbol to be blended in screen.
2. Set color, using basic color options, or one of the available color palettes, or your own color mix.
3. Set size, shape, and any other changes you wish to create the beginning object for the color blend.

4. Access **Effects | Blend**.
5. Enter the desired number of copies, or color gradations.
6. Make all option selections you wish inside the dialog box.
7. Select **Add**. A copy of the original symbol appears to create the ending point of the blend.
8. Access **Styles | Color | Color Palette** and select the ending color of the blend.
9. Use handles to size the ending object and position it within the original graphic. Remember, the color blend involves a progressive change of colors, size, and position to create a color gradient.
10. Select **Complete Blend**. The Blend is drawn on screen.

Steps: Edit Color Blend with Replace

Use this operation to fine-tune the Blend configuration.

1. Select the Blend group by itself in the working area.
2. Access **Effects | Blend**.
3. Make any desired changes to blend options including number of copies.
4. Select **Replace**.
5. Make edits to the beginning and ending objects as desired using any of the available Express features.
6. Click the right mouse button to activate Complete Blend option.

Steps: Create Color Blend Theme and Variations

Use this operation to duplicate the original blend and make adjustments to copies. This operation allows you to save each variation on the blend within a GED file and select the one you like based on experimentation and observation.

1. Select **View | All Pages**.
2. Select the Blend group by itself in the working area.
3. Select the **Duplicate** icon in the Toolbar.
4. Drag one or more duplicates of the original Blend and position them in the available pages of the current GED file.
5. Select one of the copies and enter edits using Replace as described above.

Understanding Logarithmic Distributions

Logarithmic distributions give you the means to skew, or weight, the distribution of objects or the flow of color toward the beginning or ending object. This allows you to create distribution emphasis at certain points in a Position or Color Blend.

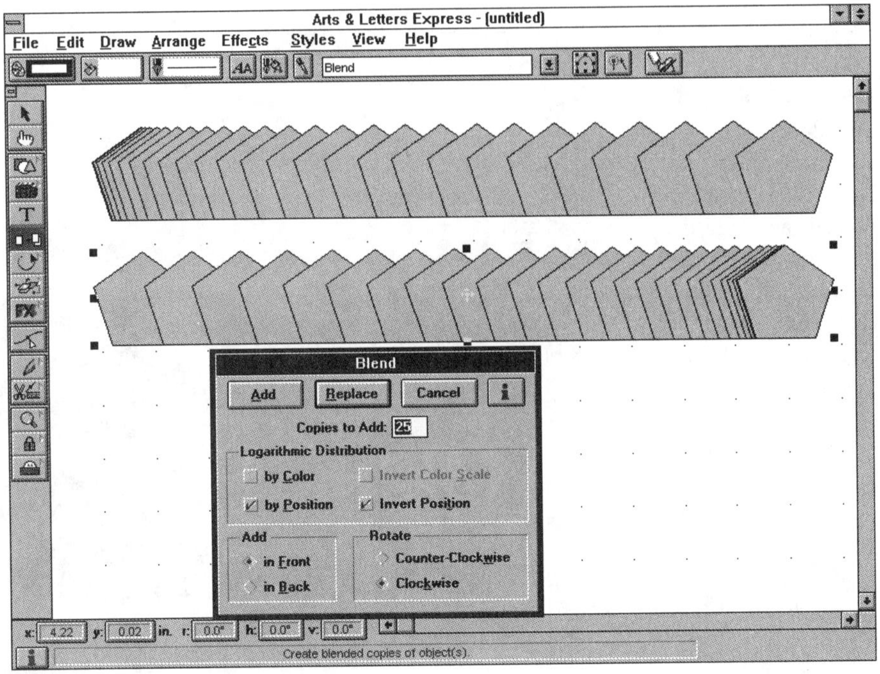

Figure 8.37 Logarithmic Distributions by Position
The Blend at top shows a standard Logarithmic Distribution by Position, with the stack of graphics skewed left. The bottom has Invert Position selected and the exact settings used to create the effect.

Logarithmic Controls

The **Blend** dialog box (Figure 8.37) includes the option for logarithmic distributions by color and position. The dialog box is slightly confusing in that you may think you must select **by Color** or **by Position** to implement either of these blending options. You can implement a color or position blend simply by configuring the start object color and position, the end object color and position, and specifying the number of gradations between them. Logarithmic Distributions are another matter entirely.

Logarithmic Distribution by Position and by Color (Figure 8.38) are skewed, exaggerated forms of blending in which the color and position distribution of the copies is not evenly distributed.

Experiment with Multiple Effects

The best way to understand these features is to experiment with them and look at the results on screen. You do not have to activate logarithmic options for any blend. If you wish to use them select either the Logarithmic Distribution options **by Color** or **by Position** or both at the same time. If you wish to invert the scale, that is, have the logarithmic pattern work in reverse, select the appropriate box. All other operations in the blend are exactly the same.

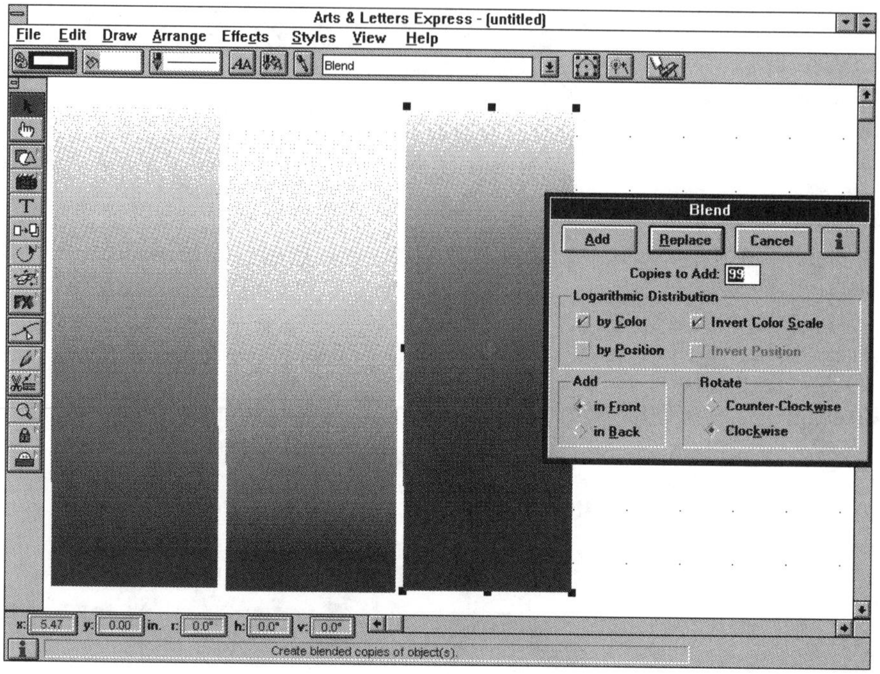

Figure 8.38 Logarithmic Distribution by Color The blend at the far left shows a standard color blend distribution; the middle, a standard logarithmic color distribution; and the right blend, a logarithmic color with position inverted.

Steps: Using Logarithmic Distributions

Use this operation to activate logarithmic distributions for any blend.

1. Select the object to be blended in the working area.
2. Access **Arrange | Blend**.
3. Select either one or both of the logarithmic distribution options in the desired configuration.
4. Select **Add**.

Blending between Shapes

Blending is one of the most powerful design features in Arts & Letters; it can be used to create an array of dazzling effects from simple forms in minutes. In Chapter 6 of this book, the blend features are covered as they relate to color blends and blends by position for symbols. Blends have an additional dimension when used with freeform objects, or symbols converted to freeform. They may literally be used to blend one shape into another, not just one version of a symbol to another. So you can start with a couple of shapes on the screen. (See Figure 8.39.)

Specify Evolution Stages

By selecting both shapes and accessing **Blend**, you can specify the number of stages of evolution between the two shapes that you wish to see.

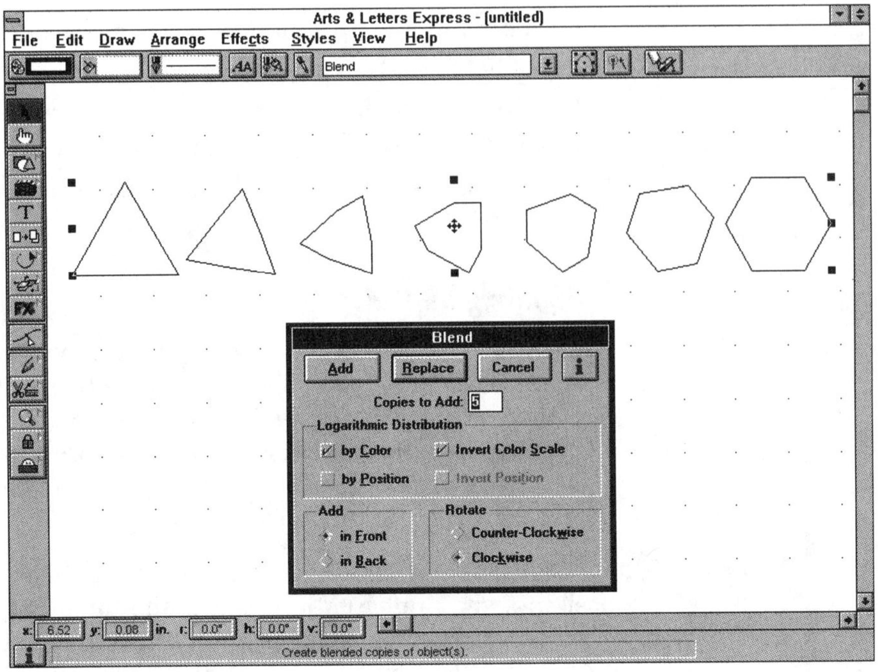

Figure 8.39 Blend between Shapes
The freeform triangle and hexagon shown evolve through five blended copies into one another. This operation must be done with both objects in freeform.

If you space the shapes to allow for the copies to be displayed independently, you will see one shape turn into another.

Avoid Logarithmic Selections

Note that logarithmic distributions should not be used for these operations, unless you want to create a special effect. Logarithmic distributions will distort the spacing so that some of the evolutions in the shape will overprint each other.

Once created, you may **Break Apart** the blend from the **Effects** menu and edit the elements in the blend, either in standard editing mode, or in freeform editing.

Steps: Blending between Shapes

Use this operation to evolve one freeform shape to another. This operation should be used with simple shapes or outline drawings. (More complex artwork will very likely get scrambled.)

1. Select two freeform objects on the screen.
2. Align the objects as desired.
3. Access **Effects | Blend**.
4. Specify the number of copies or stages of evolution between the two shapes. Select **OK**.

5. Check the color, position, and size of the two shapes before completing the blend.
6. Select **Effects | Complete Blend**.
7. The shape-to-shape blend appears on the screen.
8. Optional: Select any of the elements within the Blend group and edit as desired.

Blending and Text

Blend allows you to create three-dimensional text effects, but Extrude creates cleaner 3-D text. One advantage Blend offers is that Extrude operations work only on freeform objects, so you must convert the text to freeform to Extrude it. That means you lose the ability to edit using the Text Attributes and styles features, and can't change the content of the text or use Point Edit adjustments.

Dynamic Text Effects

Because Blend allows you the full array of Arts & Letters features—sizing, shaping, rotation, slant, alignment, styles—you can create a broader array of text effects with Blend than you can with Extrude. You can show text evolving through a series of colors and shapes, distort the shape, create spin blend effects with text, and more. You may also combine text in logo arrangements or groups with art objects and blend them as a whole.

Automatic Duplication: Blending a Grid

Blend can be used to create a custom grid design for background purposes or for precise business applications. At its base, Blend is an automatic copying system, and you can use this to create precise consistent grid effects. Choose the basic element of the grid—it can be a square, a circle, a triangle, or any of thousands of ready-made symbols. Once the base object has been selected, size it so that you can create a horizontal or vertical blend using the number of grid positions you desire. If you want a grid that is seven objects across, make sure that the object is sized to permit that. (See Figure 8.40.)

Create Grid Component

To create the first horizontal or vertical component of the grid, activate the blend feature and specify the number of copies desired. When positioning the beginning/ending objects, you may wish to use the screen ruler to set the positions. Before initiating the Complete Blend, select both objects and use Align to place them in line horizontally or vertically. Activate Complete Blend, and the component is complete.

Figure 8.40
Blending a Grid
Use Blend to auto-copy a string of graphics to the base of the grid. Then blend the string into itself to create a grid effect. You can use any image or graphics to create a technical grid design or background.

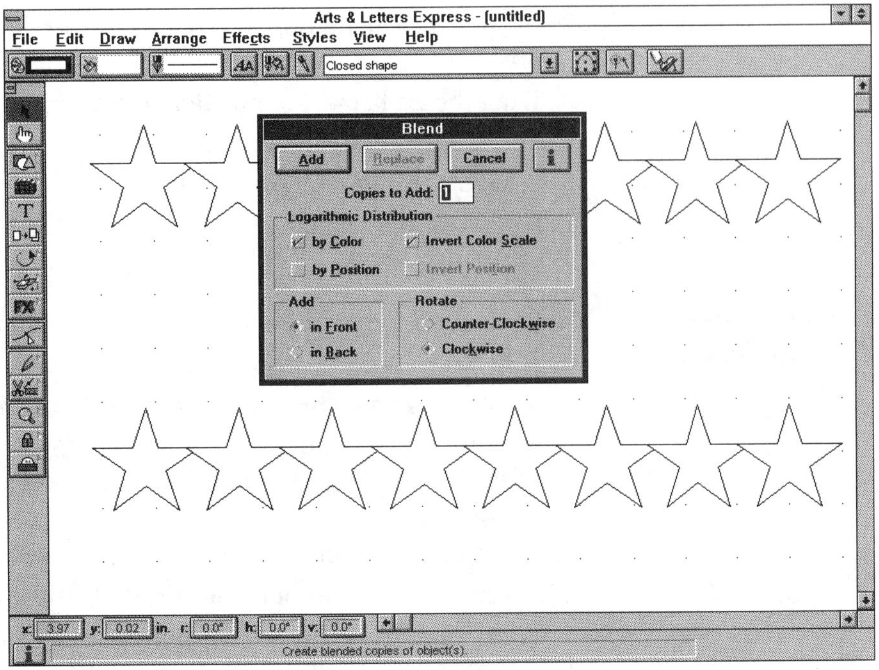

Expand Grid To expand the component into a full grid, you will now repeat the process with the blend you just created. Activate Blend with the component selected. If you have a horizontal component, drag the ending object down vertically to form the grid; if your component is vertical, drag the ending object across the screen. Once again, be sure to Align both components before selecting Complete Blend. Don't try to eyeball it! Even small errors will be evident in the final product.

Steps: Blend a Grid Component Use this operation to create a simple horizontal distributed strip of an object to make one line in a grid. You can use any symbol, text character, or image to create the grid.

1. Select grid symbol, text, or image.
2. Size the object based on the number of copies desired in the grid line. Size it small enough so that the multiple copies will not overlap.
3. Access **Effects | Blend**.
4. Specify the number of copies desired.
5. Verify that Logarithmic Distribution by Position is not active.
6. Select **Add**.

7. Position the begin object at the upper-left corner of the working area.
8. Drag the end object to position across from the beginning object.
9. Select both begin and end objects.
10. Access **Arrange | Align**.
11. Select Bottom.
12. Click the right mouse button to Complete Blend.

Steps: Cross-Blend the Grid Component

Use this operation to blend the grid component as a whole to create the full grid.

1. Select the grid component in the working area.
2. Size the grid component based on how many vertical lines you wish in the grid. It should be sized small enough to prevent overlapping.
3. Access **Effects | Blend**.
4. Specify the number of copies desired.
5. Verify that Logarithmic Distribution by Position is not active.
6. Select **Add**.
7. Position the begin object at the upper-left corner of the working area.
8. Drag the end object to position down from the beginning object.
9. Select both begin and end objects.
10. Access **Arrange | Align**.
11. Select Left.
12. Click the right mouse button to Complete Blend.

Object Distribution with Blend

Alignment is a function to make sure that objects line up; Distribution controls the spacing between multiple objects. Blended objects without logarithmic distributions activated are always evenly distributed. You can use this capability as a design tool.

Create a Distributed Replace Grid

If you have a series of different objects that are about the same size, such as flowchart boxes and graphics, you can use a Replace Blend to set up even distribution between them. Using the same technique described above to create a Grid Component, you blend one base object, sized to represent the desired size of each element in the array. Now

UnGroup the blend, and select each of the base object components and Replace it with the desired graphic. This effect will work seamlessly with numbered symbol art forms, because Replace will reproduce the sizing, positioning, and style enhancements to a selected object. At the same time, Replace will force the new object into the aspect ratio of the old one.

Replace Matrix

Clip-Art Manager Replace does not exactly reproduce the size and dimensions of the base object when a new object is put in its place. So in this case, you can use the blend array as a matrix or positioning guide. But do not break up the Blend group. Place the images over each of the base objects and use them as a guide to position the images. When complete, simply delete the Blend group. You may also wish to use the Transform Again command to distribute the images. Select an object of the desired size you wish to apply to all and access Transform. Make no changes; simply select Apply. Now that size is loaded into Transform's Save memory, you can apply it by selecting any object and activating Transform Again.

Steps: Create Object Distribution with Blend

Use this operation to create a simple horizontal strip of an object to serve as framework to distribute a group of different objects.

1. Select the grid symbol, text, or image.
2. Size the object based on the desired size of each object in the distribution and the desired space between them.
3. Access **Effects | Blend**.
4. Specify the number of copies desired.
5. Verify that Logarithmic Distribution by Position is not active.
6. Select **Add**.
7. Position the begin object at the upper-left corner of the working area.
8. Drag the end object to position across from the beginning object.
9. Select both begin and end objects.
10. Access **Arrange | Align**.
11. Select **Bottom**.
12. Click the right mouse button to Complete Blend.
13. Access **Arrange | Ungroup**.
14. Select the first graphic in the array. Access **Draw | Symbol**. Enter the symbol number of the desired artform. Select Replace. Complete this process with each additional symbol.

Three-Dimensional Objects and Backgrounds

Let's say you want to take a simple circle and use blending to add shading to suggest a spherical shape (Figure 8.41). To make it simple, let's say the circle blends from black to white. So you start out with a black circle.

Stacking Color Objects

Once you activate the Blend command, select Blend by Color, and specify the number of copies, or gradations of gray, that you wish to see between black and white. You may enter up to 99 gradations. When you select **Add** in the **Blend** dialog box, a duplicate copy of the circle automatically appears, slightly offset. You use this circle to specify the color, size, and position of the ending graphic. Obviously, then, you change the copy's interior color to white, and set line thickness to None. However, you must also change its size and position to a small white circle placed within the larger black circle.

Blend Operations

Now you are ready to complete the Blend operation. Return to the **Arrange** menu, and Arts & Letters will create a progression of copies, each in a different color and shape, moving from the original black circle to the small white one. The result is a circle transformed into a seemingly spherical object.

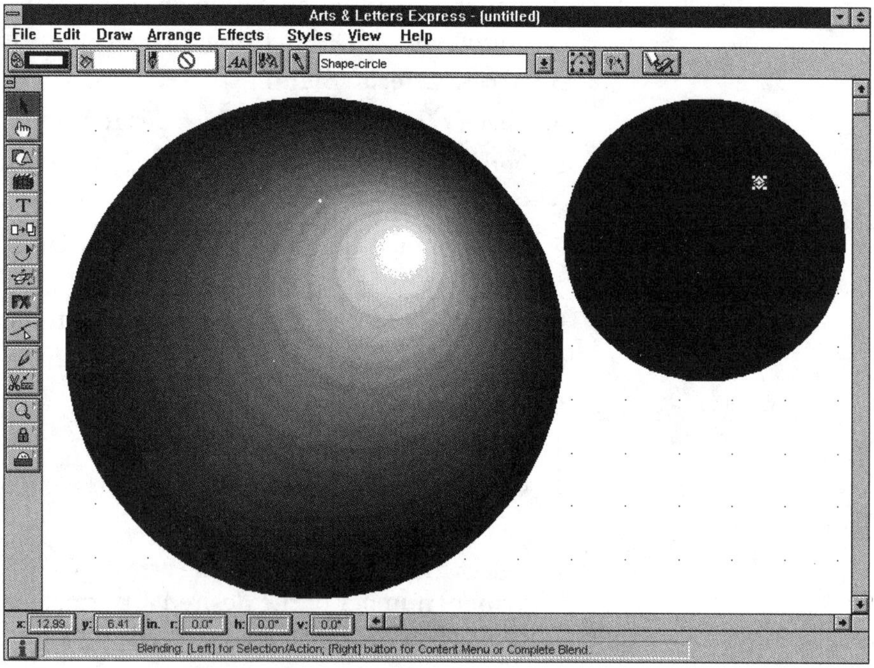

Figure 8.41 Creating Three-Dimensional Objects
Blend evolves the two objects together, the finished effect on the left, and the blend starting point on the right, showing the large black circle and tiny white highlight. Note that line styles for both circles were set to None.

Color Blending may be used to create 3-D effects such as this, or to create shaded backgrounds. But remember, the start point and end point should be of a different size and color, and Arts & Letters will fill in all the steps, in tight, closely packed copies to give the impression of a color or grayscale progression.

Steps: Create Three-Dimensional Objects with Blend

Use this operation to create a three-dimensional circle with blend. This technique can be used with any desired wireframe symbol or closed freeform shape.

1. Access **Draw | Shapes**.
2. Place a circle in working area.
3. Select the circle and press F8 or select **Draw | Cvt to Freeform**.
4. Access **Effects | Blend**.
5. Set number of copies up to 99.
6. Size the beginning object circle to a large size and set the color as Black.
7. Set ending object circle to tiny size and set color as White.
8. Position the white circle over the black circle where the highlight is to appear.
9. Select both the begin and end objects and set Line Styles to None.
10. Click the right mouse button to Complete Blend.

Freeform Ripple Objects

The same principle used to create a three-dimensional circle can be expanded and used with freeform objects. If the base circle is converted to freeform, you can blend it to a hand drawn freeform object. This allows you to create custom highlights.

Texture Effects within Backgrounds

Selecting both freeform objects at the same time will allow you to blend one into the other. This effect creates dramatic textures, particularly if you create a large rippling object and blend it to another. The blend resulting from this effect can be placed within a larger background as highlights, on the surface of water, or as a pure abstract design. (See Figure 8.42.)

Steps: Create Freeform Ripple Effects

Use this operation to create a three-dimensional circle with a ripple highlight in the blend. This technique can be used with any desired wireframe symbol or closed freeform shape.

Figure 8.42 Freeform Ripple Objects
The same freeform scribble was rotated and blended together to create this effect: the finished effect on the left, the blend starting point on the right.

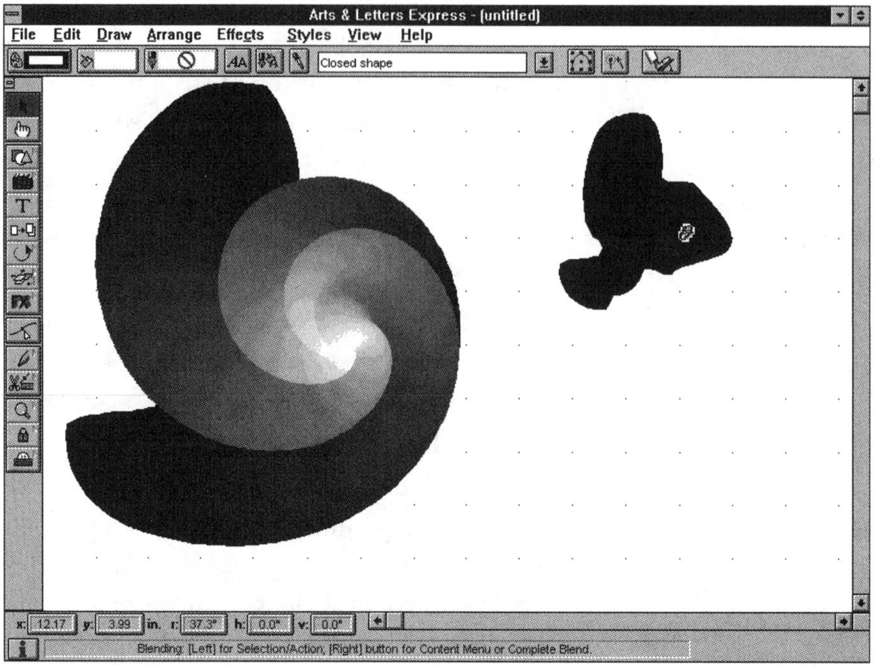

1. Select **Draw | Curve**.
2. Draw a freeform highlight and connect the start of the line with the end.
3. Click the right mouse button to return to standard mode. Verify that the freeform highlight is selected.
4. Verify that the Object Viewer displays "Closed Shape." (If it displays "Open Shape," go back to Freeform mode and create the highlight again.)
5. Access **Draw | Shapes**.
6. Place a circle in the working area.
7. Select the circle and press F8 or select **Draw | Cvt to Freeform**.
8. Select both begin (Circle) and end (Freeform) objects and set Line Styles to None.
9. Access **Effects | Blend**.
10. Set the number of copies to 99.
11. Size the beginning object circle to a large size and set the color as Black.

12. Set the ending object (freeform highlight) to tiny size and set color as White.
13. Position the white circle over the black circle in the position where highlight is to appear.
14. Click the right mouse button to Complete Blend.

Creating a Spin Blend

One highly creative way to create backgrounds or elaborate abstract art effects is a Spin Blend (Figure 8.43). You simply stack the ending object directly on top of the beginning object and Rotate it. You set the color or shade of each object depending on the effect you desire. You may want to offset the two objects slightly, to create a slightly off-center spin.

Icons and Abstracts

Some of the best elements to use for spin blends are the simple icons, pictorials, and abstract elements that are indexed by number in the *Clip Art Handbook*. These simple line drawings can be colored and then spun to create a dazzling background. Depending on how you color them and present their framing line attributes, these little icons can be used to create incredible backgrounds or custom fill patterns for use with Merge Clipping Path.

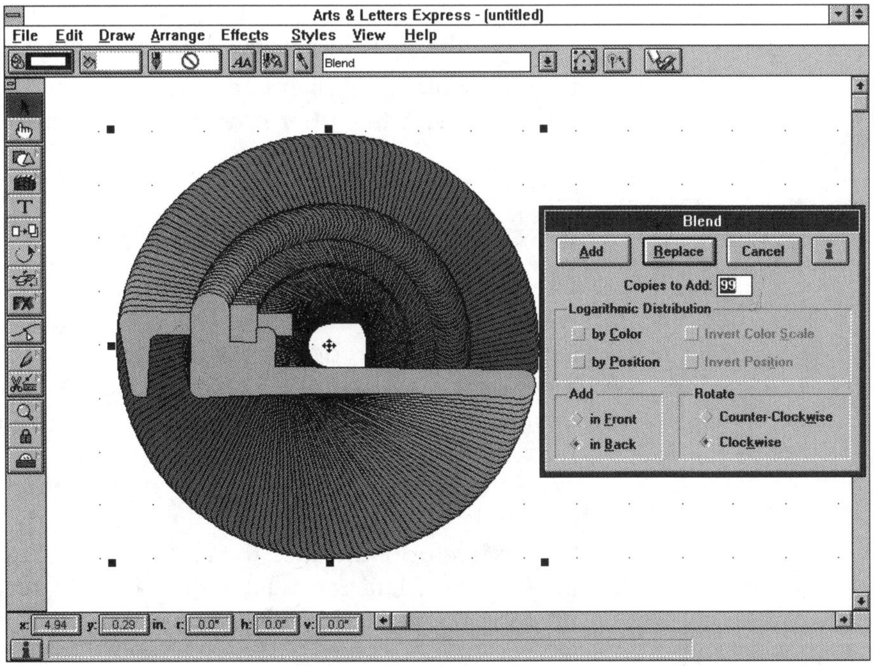

Figure 8.43
Spin Blend
A simple wrench graphic was used to create this effect—dramatizing how virtually any art object can take on a new look, here using a simple spin blend.

Editing Spin Blends Creating any custom blend is a trial and error process. You can use the Blend Replace command to go back and reposition elements in the composition. Remember to experiment with the direction of Rotation in the Blend dialog box. You may also wish to exaggerate the sizing of the beginning object so that it is somewhat larger than the ending object. Also, be mindful of the line weight for the Blend objects. If you have a large number of copies specified in the blend, you may find that the black lines around the edge are overpowering. Reduce the line thickness to a hairline, color it in a light grayshade, or remove it altogether.

Steps: Create a Spin Blend Use this operation to create a blend effect by spinning one object on top of another.

1. Select the object to blend.
2. Access **Effects | Blend**.
3. Set Number of Copies to a high number (25 or greater).
4. Verify that Logarithmic Distribution by Position is not active.
5. Select **Add**.
6. Drag the ending object on top of the beginning object.
7. Select the ending object and the Rotate tool from the Toolbox.
8. Spin the ending object. (You may also spin the beginning object if you wish.)
9. Click the right mouse button to Complete Blend.
10. Optional: Select Blend and access **Effects | Blend** and select Replace if you wish to edit or fine tune the effect.

Extrude

The newest member of the Express effect family, Extrude (Figure 8.44) is a feature that creates three-dimensional text and objects. Where Blend is a muliplier, Extrude is a connector. Rather than stack copies between a beginning and ending point, Extrude simply draws lines between them and creates graphics to bridge the difference.

Extrude works only with objects and text that have been converted to freeform. This means that when you convert text to freeform you lose all standard text editing capabilities. Similarly, you must convert symbols to freeform and lose the ability to Replace them. All images from the Clip-Art Manager must also be broken down into their constituent freeform objects and symbols before the extrusion operation begins.

Figure 8.44
Extrude Options
The Extrude is a simple feature to operate in the dialog box. Most of the hot design options with Extrude involve breaking up and manipulating the Extrude object after it has been created.

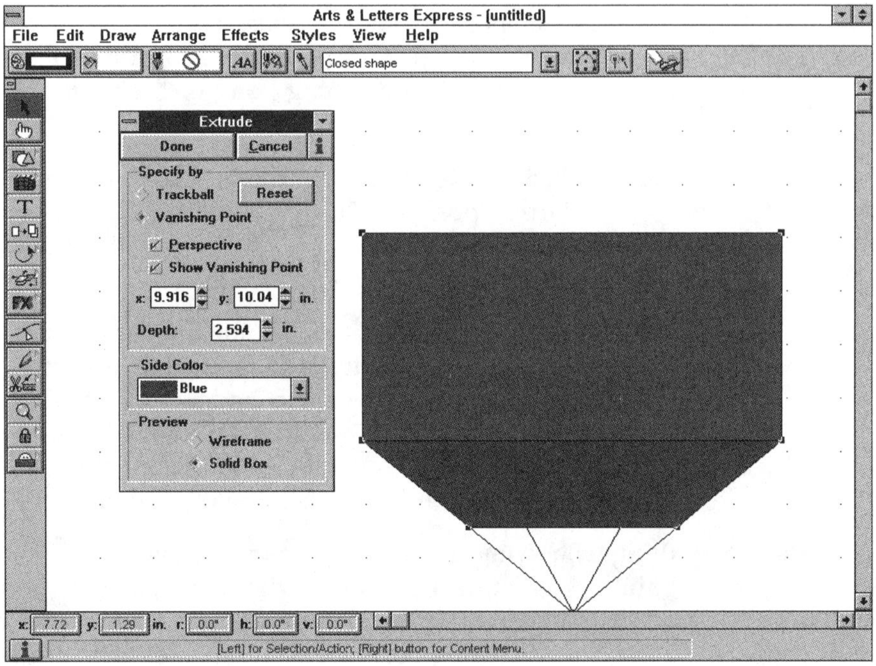

Extrude Options

Extrude allows you to shape a three-dimensional object using a movable mimic. This screen representation shows you a simplified preview of the finished effect. Extrude works directly on a selected group or object and expands it into three dimensions, so you have to use your imagination. The angle of the extrusion and the placement can dramatically impact the overall look of the effect. When first using this feature, it is wise to create multiple duplicates of your extrude effects and experiment with variations so you can see the differences on screen. When you select the one you like, delete the others, or save the ones you like in a custom Clip-Art Manager Collection.

Trackball The Trackball is one of the forms of the Extrude screen mode. It appears as a solid box that moves in space.The box represents the shape of the three-dimensional effect created from your selected graphic, expanded into space. Experiment frequently with different effects, but remember, once the Extrude object has been created, you can edit its position, size, angle of rotation, and slant using standard Express features.

Vanishing Point The Vanishing Point is the other format of the screen mimic. Where the trackball spins freely in space, the Vanishing Point mimic is anchored to a perspective point in space. This allows you to shape extrusions that taper into a distant perspective. To turn or rotate the image here, you may drag the vanishing point or the front or back faces of the extrude box.

Reset Clicking Reset returns the Trackball or Vanishing Point mimic to its starting position. This can be useful when you have lost track of how the effect will look or wish to bring the vanishing point back into the working area.

Perspective Perspective extrusions include a taper to a vanishing point. That is, the three-dimensionality is exaggerated. This effect is one of the staples of Hollywood movie posters and advertising. The alternative is a solid extrusion that goes straight back, maintaining the size of the object all the way through. You may have perspective enabled or disabled when working with the Vanishing Point mimic.

Show Vanishing Point Showing the vanishing point allows you to manipulate it. This can be frustrating, however, in that the vanishing point will frequently extend outside of the working area. You may use the scroll bars while the Extrude dialog box is active to display the vanishing point. You may also change the vanishing point x or y values in the dialog box. It is the anchor of the effect in this view, and you can manipulate the angle and depth of perspective by extending the vanishing point, shortening it, and turning it as you desire.

Numeric Settings and Depth You can control the size of the base object and the depth of the extrude effect by manipulating the sizing handles. These boxes change and display current statistics following each edit (they do not change while you are dragging the mouse to operate the Extrude handles).

Side Color Whatever the color of the base object, this feature controls only the color of the extrusion graphics created for the three-dimensional effect. Select the side color from the drop-down display and all the graphics that make up the extrusion will carry this color.

For more exotic presentations, you have the option to break up the Extrude object after it is complete using the UnGroup command on the Arrange menu or the Break Apart option on the Effects menu (they are the same command). You can then select individual graphics that make up the extrusion effect and then color or texture them individually, if you like. You may also use Select within a group to do this.

The side color is shown in the Trackball and Vanishing Point mimic, with a different color used for the front of the extrude box for ease of identification.

Preview You may chose between a simple wireframe display or a solid box. While the mouse is active on the Extrude handles, a wireframe is shown anyway, so it makes sense to select the Solid Box option. In this configuration, the sides of the extrusion are shown in the selected Side Color, which helps you quickly identify the front of the ultimate effect and check its size and position. But with all the turning and twisting that goes on in this effect, it's easy to forget which side is which.

Creating and Editing an Extrusion

Extrusions are relatively simple to create once the basic operational features are understood. There are fewer options and variables here than in Merge, Blend, or Warp. You select the object you desire to extrude and make sure all elements of that object are in freeform. These freeform objects may be in a group format, but they all must be freeform, or the feature will not work. (See Figure 8.45.)

Steps: Create an Extrusion Use this operation to create an extrusion of text or art objects.

1. Place the object or group to be extruded in the working area.
2. Verify that the object or all the components of the group are in freeform.

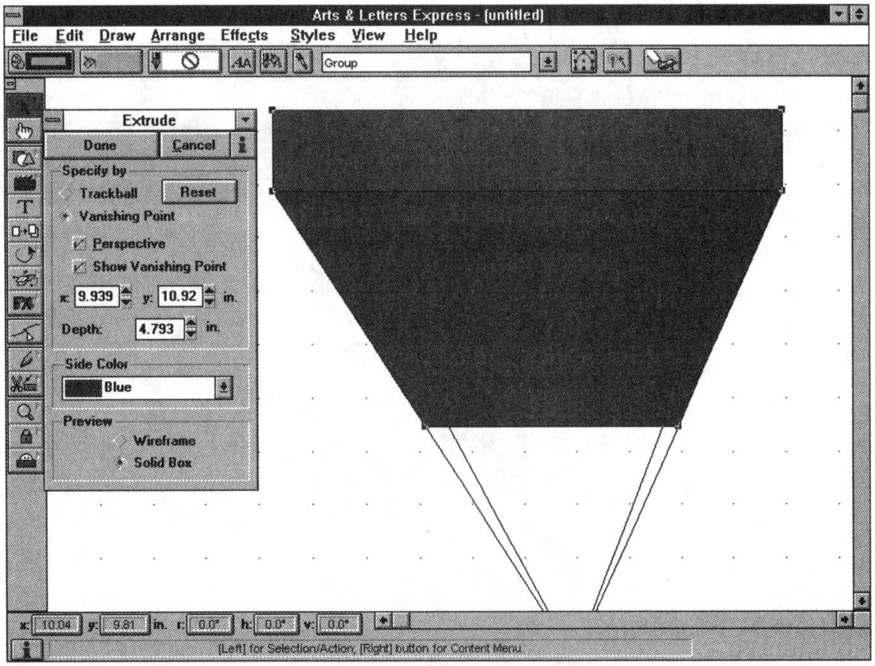

Figure 8.45 Creating an Extrusion A string of text is seen in the Extrude Vanishing Point display mode, with the base object at the top and the Extrude sides shown in the selected side color. Note that this extrude will taper to the Vanishing Point.

3. Access **Effects | Extrude**.
4. Select **Add/Edit**.
5. Select the desired mode: Trackball or Vanishing Point. (You may move between these displays at any time during creation.)
6. Drag handles on the 3-D box to shape the extrusion as desired.
7. Select Done to display the finished effect in the working area.

Editing Extrusions

You may select and edit any extrude object at any time, unless it is within a larger graphic group. Unlike some of the other effects, you cannot Save and Recall effects created here. When editing Extrusions, it is a good idea to keep a security duplicate of the original somewhere in the current GED file. This way, you won't lose the original in the editing process, and, given the trial and error nature of this feature, you can compare the edited version on screen with any variations before selecting the final one you want. To do this, select the Extrude Object on the screen, activate Duplicate, then drag a number of duplicates and store them on other pages in the current GED for later reference. (See Figure 8.46.)

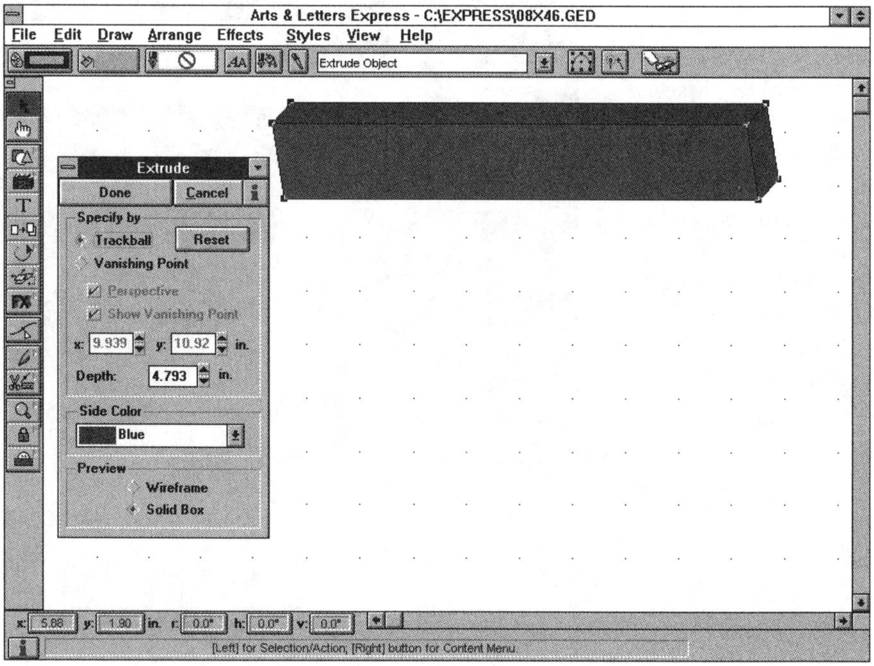

Figure 8.46
Editing Extrusions
The same text in Trackball display: Note that there is no taper and that the extruded object will be previewed as a solid box with the front dimensions extending directly to the back.

Steps: Edit Extrude Object

Use this operation to make changes to a current Extrude Object.

1. Select the EXTRUDE OBJect in the working area. The Object Viewer in the Style Bar will display either "Extrude Object" or "E."
2. Access **Effects | Extrude**.
3. Select **Add/Edit**.
4. Make the desired changes.
5. Select Done.

Removing Extrusions

Extrude works with freeform objects but it doesn't permanently change their graphic configuration. It creates a matching overlay that can be removed at any time. So if you want to use some other effect on an object you have created, you simply remove the extrusion overlay.

Steps: Remove Extrude Object

Use this operation to remove a current extrude object.

1. Select the Extrude Object in the working area. The Object Viewer in the Style Bar will display either "Extrude Object" or "E."
2. Access **Effects | Extrude**.
3. Select **Remove**.

Ungrouping Extrusions

Extrude creates a series of graphic components that make up the three-dimensional effect. You may ungroup the Extrude Object using Un-Group on the Arrange menu or Break Apart on the Effects menu. Express will break the Extrude Object into the base element and another group called Extrusions. You may break this group apart or use Select Within Group to select individual graphics that make up the extrusion and apply styles, delete individual graphics, and resize or distort them.

Steps: Ungroup Extrude Object

Use this operation to break apart the Extrude Object and edit individual graphics making up the 3-D effect.

1. Select the Extrude Object in the working area. The Object Viewer in the Style Bar will display either "Extrude Object" or "E."
2. Access **Effects | Break Apart**.
3. Select Extrusions Group.
4. Access **Effects | Break Apart**.
5. Select graphics as desired.

Hollywood Text

Extrude and text go hand in hand for dramatic headlines and text elements. Think of the word "colossal." It's an ideal word for the Extrude feature. (See Figure 8.47.)

Text Groups

When text is converted to freeform, Express keeps it in a group. Extrude can access the text freefrom objects inside it and you eliminate the risk of scrambling some of the overlay components that make up individual letters.

Steps: Create Hollywood Text

Use this operation to create three-dimensional text effects.

1. Select the text to extrude in the working area.
2. Press **F8** or select **Draw | Cvt to Freeform**.
3. Select the text and verify that "Group" displays in the Object Viewer in the Status bar.
4. Access **Effects | Extrude | Add/Edit**.
5. Drag the Extrude mimic to set the effect as desired.
6. Select the desired side color.
7. Select Done.

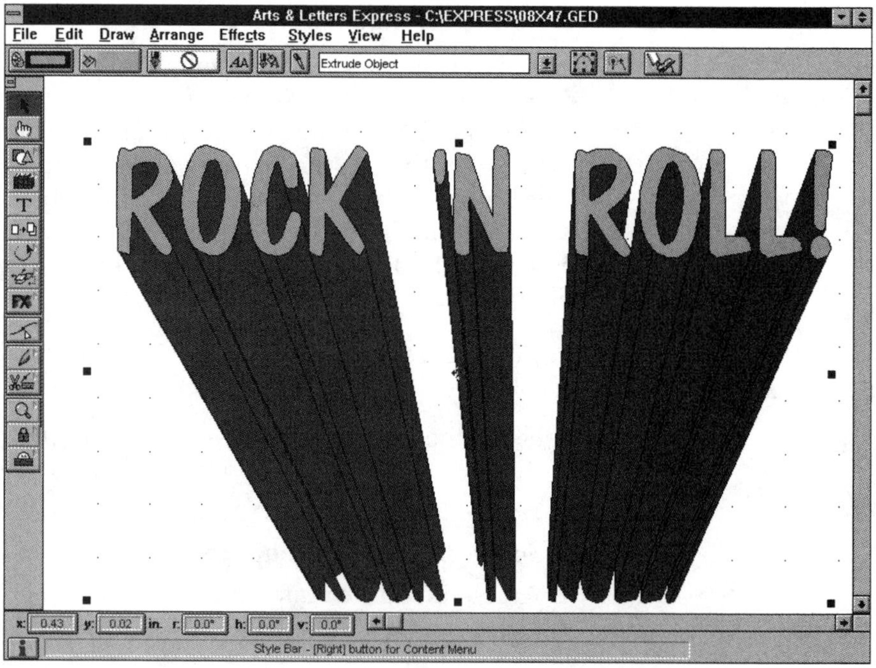

Figure 8.47
Hollywood Text
The final effect chosen for the extruded word is a Hollywood favorite, and an advertising staple.

Design 3-D Geometrics, Abstracts, and Icons

Since Extrude works with freeform objects, some of the hottest art forms to use with this feature are the simplest. Abstracts, arrows, simple people icons all have the virtue of simplicity and lend themselves to dramatic extrusion. You can make them into solid three-dimensional objects with narrow depth for use as backgrounds or as design components.

Simple extrudes of icons represent an alternative to drop-shadows. You can take drawings of objects and make them solid, colorful, and interesting using fill patterns and a matching or contrasting side color. And remember that you can break out the Extrusions as selectable graphics and edit them as desired.

Steps: Create 3-D Geometrics, Abstracts, and Icons

Use this operation to make 3-D backgrounds and design elements out of simple geometric drawings available through the Symbol dialog box or from collections in the Clip-Art Manager (Figure 8.48).

1. Place the desired icon symbol in the working area.
2. Press **F8** or select **Draw | Cvt to Freeform**.
3. Access **Effects | Extrude | Add/Edit**.

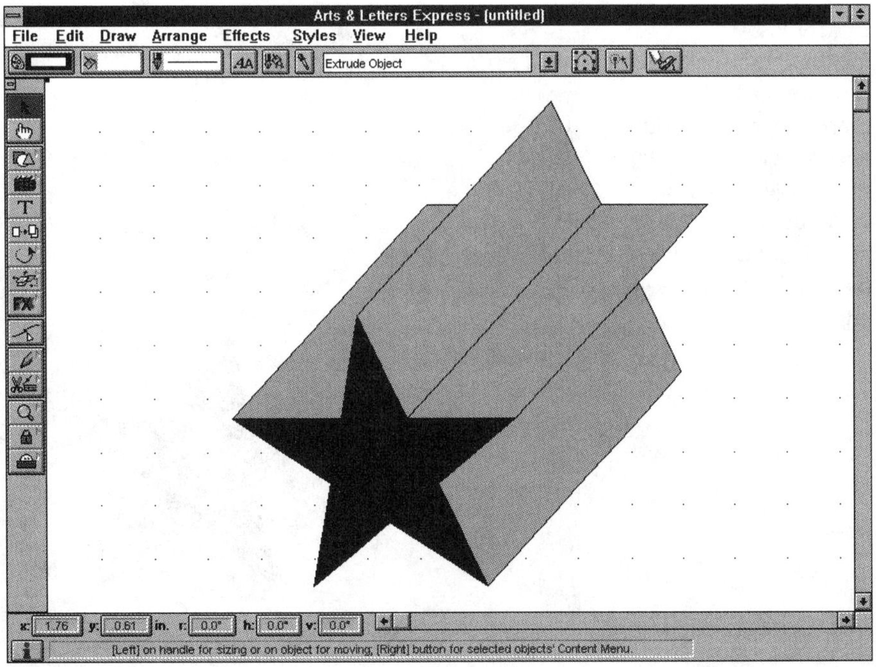

Figure 8.48
3-D Geometrics
You can rotate and extend a simple form into three-dimensional space. Symbol art forms, including people icons, are ideal for extrusions. Use this effect in place of simple drop shadows.

4. Drag the Extrude mimic to set the effect as desired.
5. Select the desired side color.
6. Select **Done**.

Create Hollow Box Extrudes

Breaking up the Extrude Object allows you to separate the base object from the extrusions generated around it. You may also select extrude components using Select within Group. You can use this to create hollow box extrusions of any text or art object. Simply remove the base object. You can now see inside of the extrusion. (See Figure 8.49.)

Crazy Design Tricks

This is fun to do for simple geometrics: You create a three-dimensional hollow box that can function as a background for text and graphics. You may also break up the Extrusions group and select and color individual components within the hollow box to emphasize its three dimensionality. Once you have access to the extrusion graphics themselves, you can do anything you want, including resizing them, applying color, line, fill styles, and even fancy gradients. You can easily take these graphics and use them as a template to cut a hole or as a clipping path using Merge operations.

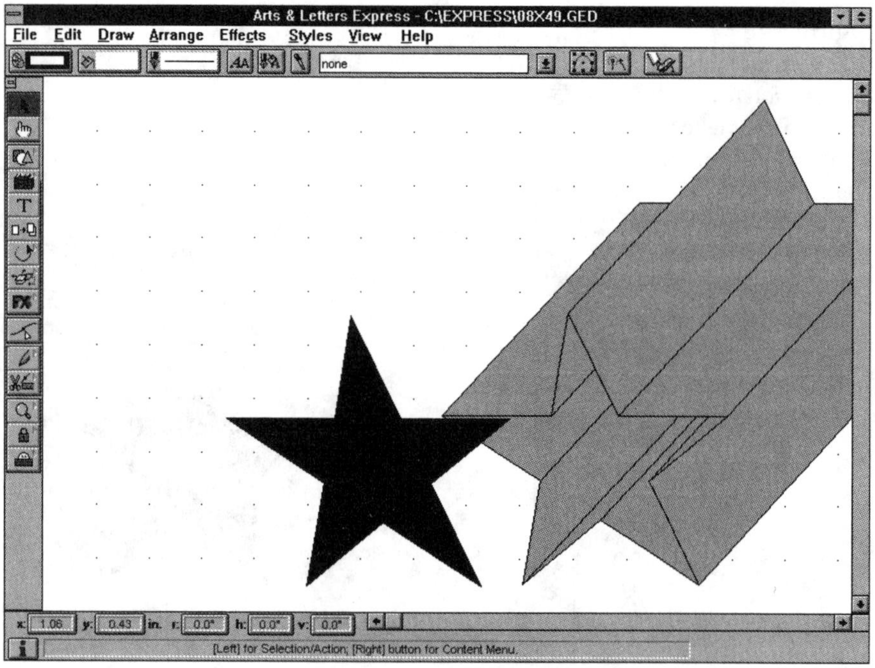

Figure 8.49
Hollow Box Extrudes
Remove the base graphic from the front and you can see inside of the extrusion. If you break up the Extrusions graphic group, you can create additional design effects.

Steps: Create Hollow Box Extrudes

Use this operation to create hollow 3-D effects where the interior is visible.

1. Place the desired art form or text in the working area.
2. Press **F8** or select **Draw | Cvt to Freeform**.
3. Access **Effects | Extrude | Add/Edit**.
4. Drag the Extrude mimic to set the effect as desired.
5. Select the desired side color.
6. Select **Done**.
7. Select the Extrude Object.
8. Select **Effects | Break Apart**. Two objects will result: an Extrusions group and a Closed Shape.
9. Use the Object Viewer to select the closed shape.
10. Move the closed shape, base object away from the extrusions group or delete the closed shape with **Edit | Cut** or the Delete key.

Breakout, and Explode Extrusions

Once the Extrusions group has been broken out, you can create a breakout configuration by pulling it apart or deleting selective extrusion strips to create a variety of interesting visuals (Figure 8.50). Since extrusions give the appearance of three-dimensionality, this allows you to create graphically credible object explosions.

Breakout effects can also be used in a kind of cinematic series. Show the exploded graphic of a simple object—a house, for instance—and show a companion graphic with the house completely assembled and three-dimensionally in place. Advertising design is full of effects like this. Using Extrude lets you have fun with them.

Steps: Create Breakout and Explosion Extrusions

Use this operation to create hollow 3-D effects where the interior is visible.

1. Place the desired art form or text in the working area.
2. Press **F8** or select **Draw | Cvt to Freeform**.
3. Access **Effects | Extrude | Add/Edit**.
4. Drag the Extrude mimic to set the effect as desired.
5. Select the desired side color.
6. Select **Done**.
7. Select **Effects | Break Apart**. Two objects will result: an Extrusions group and a Closed Shape.

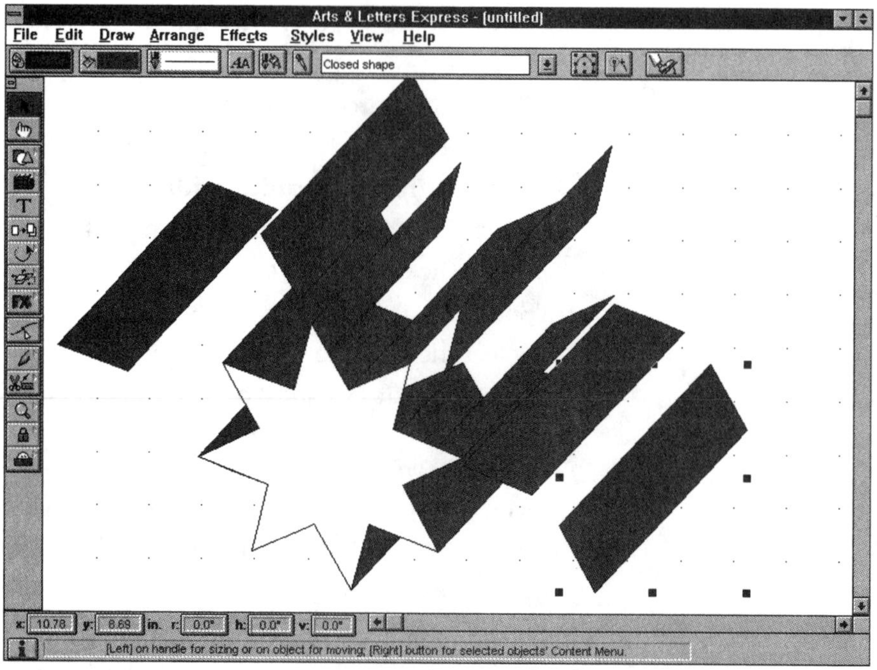

Figure 8.50 Breakout and Explode Extrusions Breaking apart the Extrusions Group inside the Extrude Object lets you pull the effect apart and make it look like a bomb went off. Add one of the explosion graphics from the graphic database, and you're all set.

8. Use the Object Viewer to select the Extrusions group.
9. Select **Effects | Break Apart**.
10. Select individual extrusion strips and move them as desired.

Design Spectrum and Zebra Extrusions

Working with the Extrusions group within the Extrude Object, you can create an interesting effect by varying the color of the different bands that make up the extrusion (Figure 8.51). Using black and white, you can create a Zebra effect or, using colors, you can alternate the shades and/or color range in the extrusion.

The shape of the bands will depend on the angle and the presentation of the extrusion itself. You may wish to create a series of security duplicates in the same GED file and try tilting the object using the Extrude Trackball mode in a variety of ways to see how the different bands take shape.

Steps: Spectrum and Zebra Extrusions

Use this operation to create hollow 3-D effects where the interior is visible.

1. Place the desired art form or text in the working area.
2. Press **F8** or select **Draw | Cvt to Freeform**.

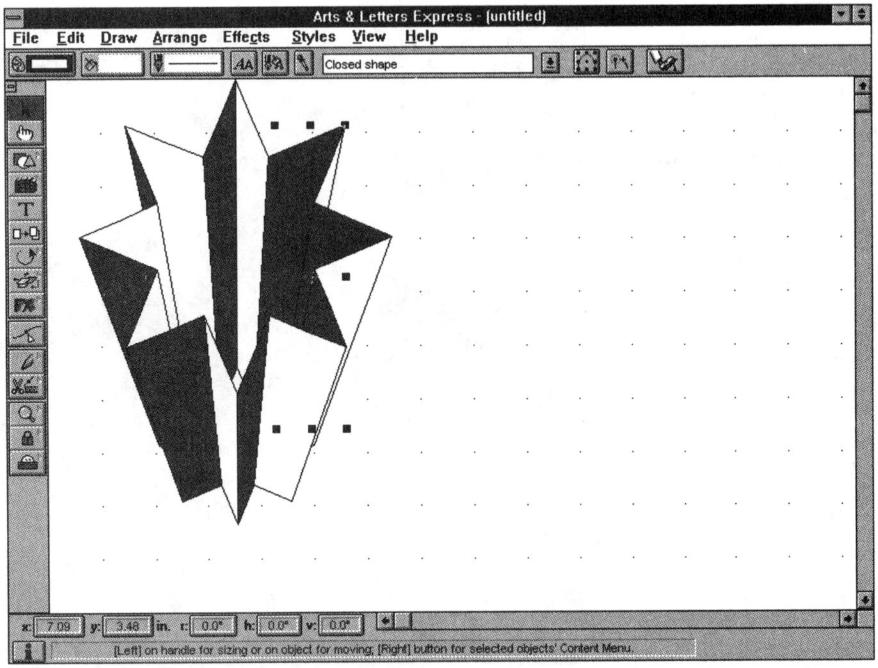

Figure 8.51
Spectrum and Zebra Extrusions
When the Extrude group is broken apart, you can selectively color the extrusion strips to create interesting graphic variations on a solid side color.

3. Access **Effects | Extrude | Add/Edit.**
4. Drag the Extrude mimic to set the effect as desired.
5. Select the desired side color White.
6. Select **Done.**
7. Select **Effects | Break Apart.** Two objects will result: an Extrusions group and a Closed Shape.
8. Use the Object Viewer to select the Extrusions group.
9. Select **Effects | Break Apart.**
10. Select individual extrusion strips and apply color styles as desired.

Warp/Perspective

Warp allows you to distort and twist objects along a straight line or a curved form (Figure 8.52). You can instantly reshape text and art forms to fit irregular forms. The closest equivalent to warping an object is to slant it. A slant can tilt an object around an axis, thus creating distortion effects. However, slant is essentially changing only the angle of perspective for the object, not fundamentally redrawing it.

Figure 8.52
Warp/Perspective
Unlike Extrude, Warp deals with any standard symbol, text, or image. The Shapes shown allow you to create a number of controlled distortion effects on any artwork in the graphic database.

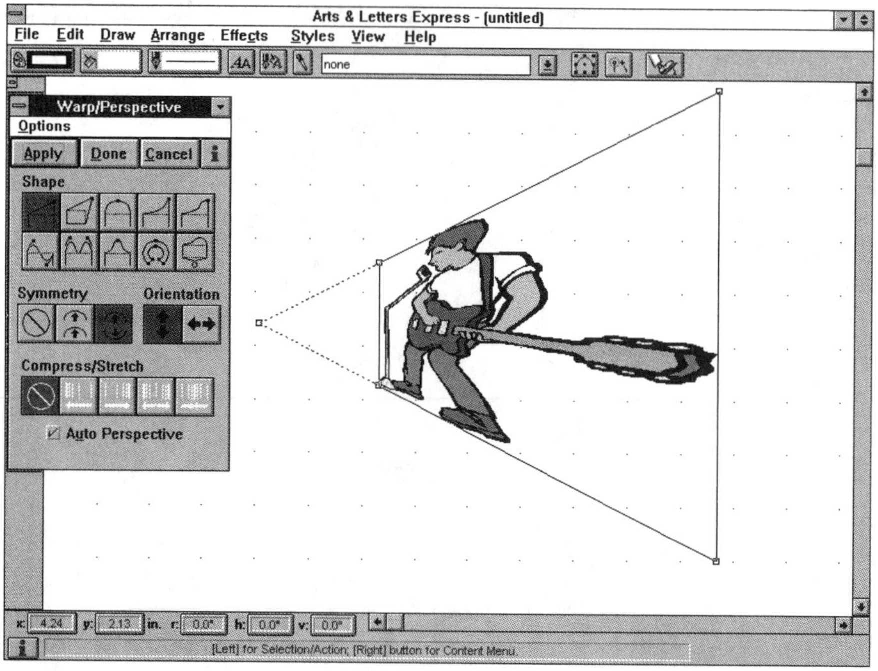

Warp Overlay

Warping operations create a shaped overlay and pour the objects into it. Warp does not change the actual graphic information of the object. Unlike Extrude, Warp operates with standard text, symbols, images, and freeform objects. Using this feature, you can twist a string of text, exaggerate several letters in the center of a word so it is shaped like a mountain, for example. You can create elaborate three-dimensional effects, in which a word seems to explode from the distance into the foreground.

Warp Editing and Applications

Warped objects and text are created by a two-level process in which the base object is retained and a warp overlay is displayed on the screen. This construction allows you to remove the warp if you're not happy with the result. Note that once the warp values are applied, the resulting object is a Warp object.

Compound Warps

Using compound warps you can stretch any text string or graphic object any way you wish in a matter of seconds without detailed or time-consuming freeform editing.

In practice, you will find that the warp features in Arts & Letters function as an automated form of freeform editing, permitting you to instantly reshape any object by simply dragging your mouse. This capability allows you to experiment and realize your ideas instantly.

Using Warp

There are a number of options in the **Warp/Perspective** dialog box on the **Effects** menu which allow you to control sophisticated warping effects.

Shape The drawings on the selection buttons approximate the shape of the warp and, when selected, place an outline on the screen that demonstrates the shape of the selected warp. The outline has handles and control points in place (just like those used for freeform drawings) which allow you to easily manipulate the outline. Names for all shapes may be directly selected from the **Shape** menu as well.

Symmetry You may control the symmetry as the object is warped in any of the selected shapes. If symmetry is turned off, each adjustment you make to the outline points will affect that area of the warp outline only. The second symmetry selection allows you to warp in parallel, so that if you pull on an outline point, the corresponding point at the opposite side of the outline will move in the same direction, maintaining parallel position. Finally, if you select the final button, each adjustment you make will be mirrored on the opposite side of the drawing. That is, if you pull up on a point at the top of the drawing, the opposite point at the bottom will move down exactly the same distance.

Orientation You may set up warping to take place horizontally or vertically. If you set up a vertical warp, the point handles will appear along the top and bottom edges of the warp outline. When horizontal warping is selected, point handles appear on the left and right sides of the outline.

Compress/Stretch This option lets you distort the warp values further through compressing or stretching the warp. In effect, these selections skew the perspective of the graphic object. The first button on the left turns off the feature, and the patterns on the remaining four buttons present a visual approximation of the type of compression and stretch values that can be created. The first option will skew perpective to the left, the second skews it to the right, the third skews it to the outside edges, the final selection skews it to the center. When any of these four options are selected, you have the additional option to select a position along a **Min..Max** scaling bar. By combining the **Stretch/Compress** feature with this intensity scale, you can apply a virtually infinite number of perspective variations and create many dramatic effects.

Auto Perspective This is a special control option available with two of the shape options only. When using either of the two linear shape options, 1 pt Perspective or 2 pt Perspective, this feature automatically enables "true perspective," which presents objects or text in a mathematically precise perspective relationship, based on the positions of the vanishing point and the text. Turning this option off allows you to distort perspective as you wish. Note that when this feature is enabled, the Compress/Stretch selector "grays out" because all perspective values are being automatically calculated by the software.

The main warp features just described form the basis of the warping features. In addition, there are a variety of constraints, or editing controls for warps which are available from the **Options** menu in the **Warp/Perspective** dialog box.

Allow Horizontal/Vertical Moves When you warp an object, you may wish to stretch it in one direction only. This feature is a toggle which changes the vertical/horizontal orientation. When you select **Horizontal** orientation, the **Allow Vertical Moves** option will be available; when you have **Vertical** orientation selected, the **Allow Horizontal Moves** option will be available. An object may stretch horizontally when vertical warp is applied or vice-versa. You can also freeze one dimension and apply the other.

Maintain Lines When applying one of the curvilinear warp options, straight lines in the object will be warped to follow the curved shape. Enabling this option allows you to maintain straight lines in the object even as it follows a curved path. This feature can be used to create interesting text effects because it allows you to warp text along a curved path, and still keep the tops of the letters straight and angular, rather than forcing them to follow the curve. Take time to experiment and see the results created with this option.

Show Perspective Lines The **1 pt Perspective** and **2 pt Perspective** Shape options shape an object in perspective lines that intersect a common vanishing point. When you use either of these options, enabling this feature will display the perspective lines leading to the vanishing point as dotted lines on the screen. You can then edit the warp by dragging the vanishing point with the mouse.

Auto Apply The Warp/Perspective dialog box contains the **Apply** option which allows you to complete the specified warping operation without removing the dialog box from the screen. When **Auto Apply** is enabled, warping operations are displayed *automatically* as you shape the object on the screen. Each time you release the mouse button, the warp operation will be completed and displayed so you may make any necessary corrections immediately, and without having to select the **Apply** option each time.

In addition to features in the dialog box itself, there are a number of different selections that may be made from the Warp submenu off the Effects menu.

Specify This displays the Warp dialog box so that you can specify the desired warp pattern, mirroring, orientation, and compress/stretch values.

- **Save/Recall** Just like all Save/Recall features in Arts & Letters, this allows you to save a particular warp configuration and recall it to apply the same warp to a different text string or object. If you have a series of objects that you wish to share the same warp values, this is an enormous time saver. The recalled Warp will be stretched to fit the size and aspect ratio of the selected object.
- **Remove** If you wish to cancel a specified warp, select the warped object and use this command to return the object or text to its original appearance.

The following step-through demonstrates the correct procedure for completing a simple warping operation. Keep in mind that many of the effects in Warp can be created manually in Arts & Letters by editing individual characters, but many are not possible without highly sophisticated freeform editing. This feature automates the process of stretching and twisting text and objects, which puts a great deal of sophisticated design power in your hands.

Steps: Warping Text Use this operation to apply a warp shape to a selected string of text (Figure 8.53).

1. Select the **Text** icon.
2. Enter the desired text string in the **Insert/Edit Text** dialog box. Select **Add**.
3. Click the mouse on screen to place text. Use the sizing handles to adjust text to the desired size.
4. Access **Draw | Cvt to Freeform** or press **F8** to convert text to freeform objects.
5. Access **Arrange | Group** to group the text.
6. Access **Effects | Warp/Perspective**, and select **Add** in the submenu. The **Warp** dialog box is displayed.
7. Select the desired **Shape**, **Mirror**, and **Orientation**.
8. Use the point handles on the shape outline to adjust the warp as desired. Note that you may change shapes, mirror values, and orientation at any time as needed.

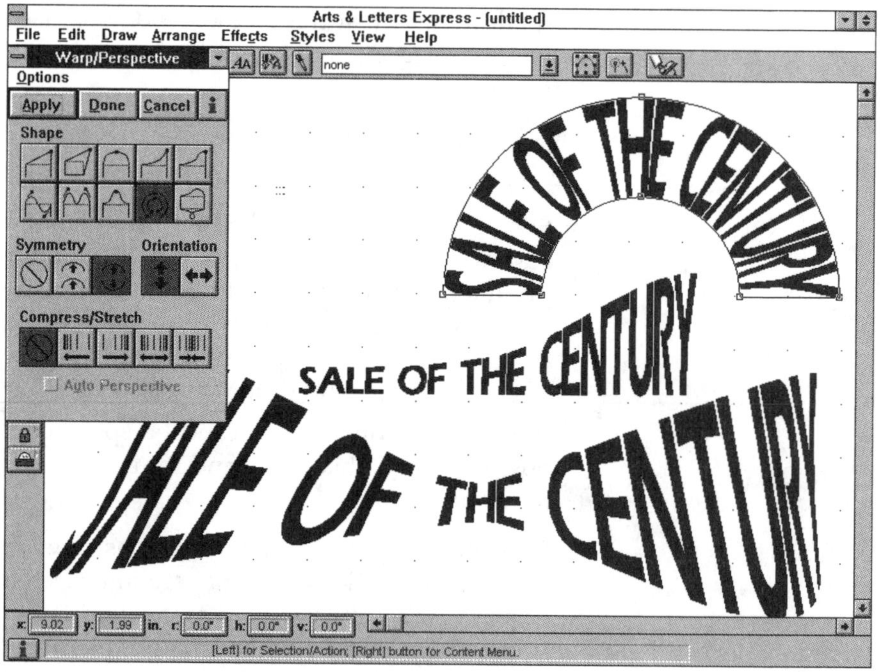

Figure 8.53 Creating/Editing Warps The same hustle, duplicated three times, shows up in three different warp faces. You simply tug on the control points of the framing graphic shown at upper right to adjust the presentation of each of the available Warp Shapes.

9. Select the desired **Compress/Stretch** values and the degree of compression or stretching using the **Min...Max** scale.
10. To see the result and leave the **Warp/Perspective** dialog box displayed, select **Apply**. To implement the operation and remove the **Warp** dialog box, select **OK**.

Steps: Using Warp Save/Recall

Use this operation to apply the warp shape and settings from a currently selected warp object to any other object in the working area.

1. Select a warped object on screen.
2. Access **Effects | Warp/Perspective** and select **Save** on the submenu. The Warp values are now saved.
3. Select another, non-warped object. Access **Effects | Warp/Perspective** and select **Recall** on the submenu. The warp values from the first object have now been applied to the second.

Steps: Removing a Warp

Use this operation to remove the warp shape and settings from any warp object.

1. Select a warped object or text string.
2. Access **Effects | Warp/Perspective** and select **Remove**.
3. The text or object returns to its original appearance.

Steps: Editing a Warped Object in Freeform

1. Select the warped object.
2. Access **Draw | Cvt to Freeform**, or press **F8**.
3. Click on the **Edit Freeform** icon to enter freeform editing mode. The warped object may now be directly edited.

Automated Freeform Drawing with Warp

One of the main benefits of warping features is that it functions as a *guided form of freeform editing*. When you specify a warp pattern, an outline immediately appears on the screen. You can instantly select another warp pattern and see the outline result on screen. You are free to manipulate the outline on the screen using the point handles to achieve exactly the effect you wish. You also have the option to mirror your edits at the opposite side of the form or parallel to them, to set the warping to take place vertically or horizontally, and to set a number of sophisticated object stretching and compressing values. The number of effects you can create with a few simple keystrokes are virtually without end.

Warp Directions and Angles

Before getting into specific techniques, a couple of words about horizontal and vertical warp values. Warping operates horizontally or vertically. That is, you have the option to warp a string of text horizontally so that it ripples inside a horizontal "banner."

Warp Handles and Operations

When a vertical warp is selected, point handles appear along the top and bottom edges of the shape; when horizontal warping is selected, they appear on the left and right sides. However, when in a vertical warp, you can use the point handles on the far corners of the top and bottom to actually "pull" the object horizontally. So, technically, you can perform both horizontal and vertical moves within a "vertical" warp operation. You can suppress horizontal moves in a vertical warp, however, by enabling **Allow Horizontal Moves** in the **Options** menu so that the white selection box is empty.

Warp Banner Effects

The most visual and practical application that can be created with warping is the "waving banner" effect. Using this effect, you can shape a word to fit into a pointed, triangular banner shape. Once in the shape, you can pull on elements in the word to add ripples so that the word wraps to fit inside the banner and appears to exist in three-dimensional space (Figure 8.54).

Figure 8.54
Banner Effects
Using the freehand warp shape—bottom right in the Warp Shape selector group—a word can be twisted to look like a floating banner. Add a dropshadow for depth and use it as a title!

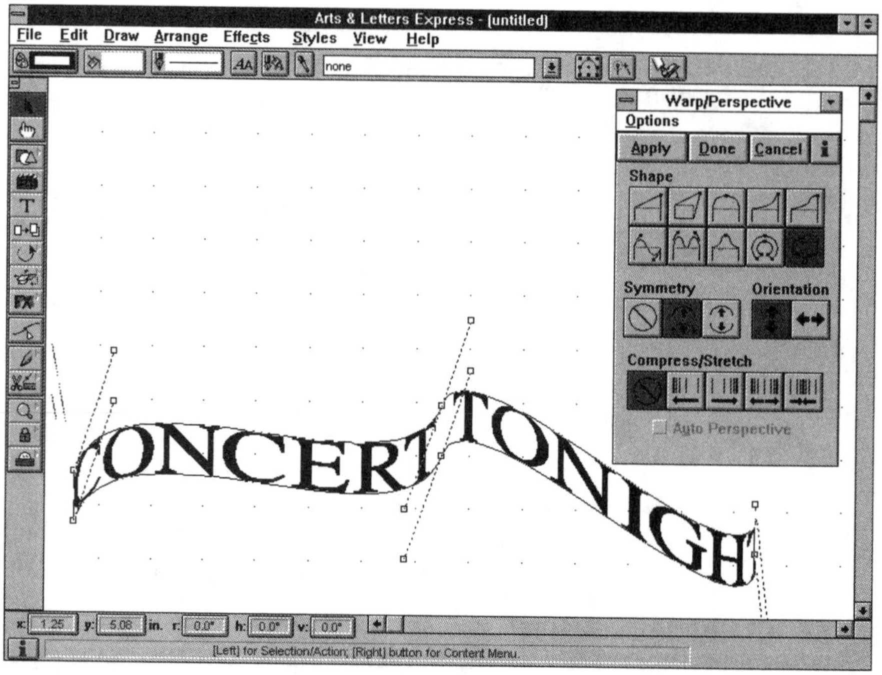

Steps: Creating a Text Banner Effect with Warp

Use this operation to shape text into a waving banner. This same technique may be used with any symbol or image in place of text.

1. Select the **Text** icon.
2. Enter text in **Insert/Edit Text** dialog box. Add text.
3. Access **Effects | Warp/Perspective | Specify**.
4. Select the final **Shape** icon (lower row, far right).
5. Select **Vertical** orientation.
6. Select the **Parallel Symmetry** icon (middle).
7. Use point handles to tighten one end of a word to a point.
8. Use point handles to expand the opposite end to form a wide end of the banner.
9. Pull on the middle handles to create ripple elements within the banner.
10. Select **Apply** to display the effect.
11. Continue adjusting handles and selecting **Apply** until you achieve the exact effect desired, then click on **Done**.

Warp and Text Wraparound Effects

Wraparound is an effect in which an object or text appears to twist partially or entirely around an invisible cylindrical shape. This effect is particularly effective with text because you can turn the text back on itself and see the text backward from behind as it loops around into the foreground.

This effect is a powerful way to suggest three-dimensionality and can be combined with the banner effect so that you have a banner wrapping around a pole, or realistically waving in the wind and accomplish this tricky effect without drawing a single line (Figure 8.55).

Warp Freehand Shape

To create wraparounds, you should use the **Freeform** shape button, which gives you a set of flexible point handles on both the top and bottom of the shape in a vertical warp. As you pull on these points horizontally, the side of the shape moves as a unit. (In a vertical warp, the horizontal edge of the shape remains rigid.) As you drag one set of points over another the text or freeform shape folds over and wraps into three-dimensional space. Text printed on this three-dimensional surface will logically follow the shape so that on the folded areas, the text reads backward.

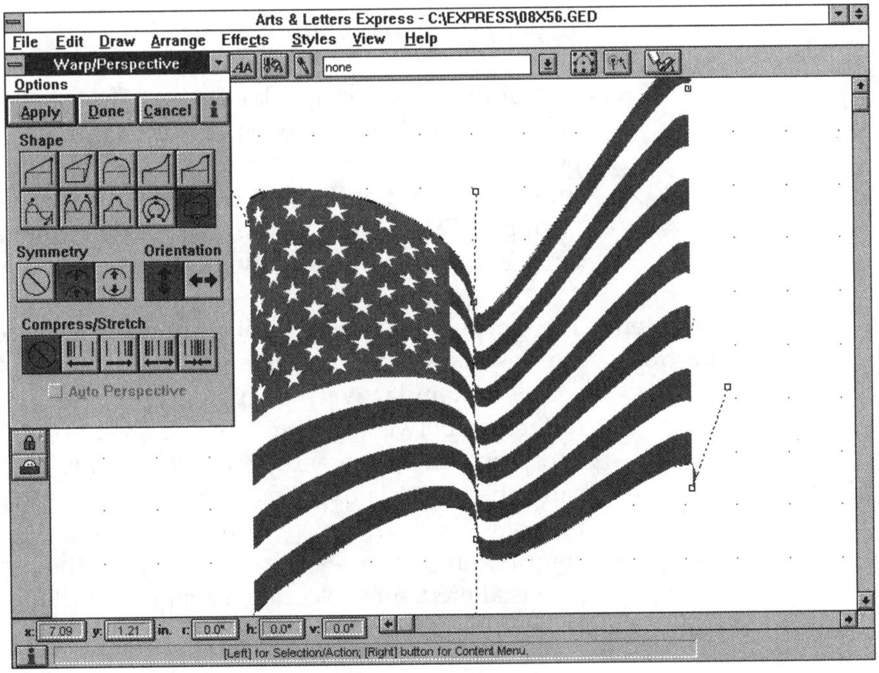

Figure 8.55
Wraparound Effects
Twisting text or objects around a corner lets you create three-dimensional space in different ways from Slant, Blend, or Extrude. It's ideal for flags. You make the breeze.

The following technique is a suggested method to accomplish this effect using text as an example only. You are encouraged to experiment on your own to see what effects you can create.

Steps: Creating a Wraparound Effect with a Warp

Use this operation to create a text wraparound. This technique will work with any symbol or image in place of text.

1. Select **Text** icon.
2. Enter text in **Insert/Edit Text** dialog box. Add text.
3. Access **Effects | Warp/Perspective | Specify**.
4. Select the **Freeform** shape icon (lower row, far right).
5. Select **Vertical** orientation.
6. Select the **Parallel Symmetry** icon (farthest to right).
7. Drag the point handles at the far right edge of the word over the next set of point handles; or: drag the point handles second from the far right corner over point handles at the far right corner.
8. In both cases, the text has "folded" into three-dimensional space.
9. Select **Apply** to display the effect.
10. Continue adjusting the handles and selecting **Apply** until you achieve the exact effect desired, then click on **Done**.

Warp Perspective Effects

One of the more spectacular design effects is to present a word or symbol in highly distorted perspective so that one end of the drawing appears tiny in the far distance, and the rest of the drawing "explodes" into the foreground. This effect is a visual equivalent of the audio "Doppler Effect" in which a train whistle that sounds faint in the distance becomes progressively louder as it approaches. (See Figure 8.56.)

Controlled Distortions

The warping features contain a number of shapes that allow you to create this distorted perpective with text or freeform drawings. Choose a simple triangular warp shape and the word fits into it. The degree of difference between the size of the start point (the small end) and the end point (the large end, in the foreground) determines how dramatically the effect is expressed. You can complement this effect with a number of additional feature adjustments, including stretching and compressing, suppressing mirroring so that only one vertical dimension is altered, and selecting a shape that allows you to place "ripple effects" in perspective.

Figure 8.56 Warp Perspective Effects
The expression reads: "Help I'm going flat!!" The middle Compress/Stretch option created this exaggerated skew effect, which is similar to Logarithmic Distributions in Blend.

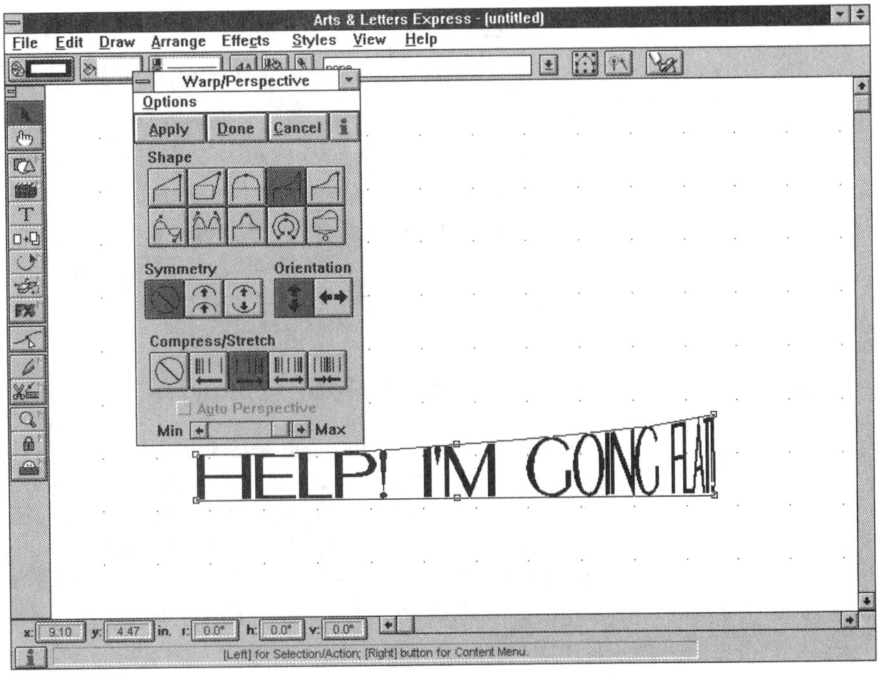

Designer Effects for Text and Art Forms

This capability is great for designer headlines and similar text effects, but it can be applied in a creative way even in simpler applications. Say you have a flowchart or a diagram and need to create callouts or titles. Perspective text and symbol warping allows you to create a flowchart or diagram that has a three-dimensional effect in which the words look like they are jumping off the page.

The following example uses text and is only one suggested way for you to achieve this design effect. There are a variety of ways to twist perspective using **Warp/Perspective** features, but it's a good idea to experiment with all the available shape selections.

Steps: Creating a Distorted Perpective Effect with Warp

Use this operation to create a distorted perspective effect with Warp text. This same technique works with any symbol or image in place of text.

1. Select the **Text** icon.
2. Enter text in the **Insert/Edit Text** dialog box. Add text.
3. Access **Effects | Warp/Perspective | Add**.
4. Select a perspective warp icon (upper row, second from right).

5. Select **Vertical** orientation.
6. Use point handles to set the vertical height of the far point of perspective.
7. Use point handles to set the vertical height of the near point of perspective.
8. Select **Apply** to display the effect.
9. Continue adjusting handles, selecting **Apply** until you achieve the effect desired. Then click on **Done**.

Warping Effects with Symmetry

Selecting the warp shape lets you pick a target shape for your warped object. Once this is done, you can control how that shape is implemented through the **Symmetry** controls (Figure 8.57). With mirroring turned off (First icon, closest to the left), every move you make on a point handle is an individual edit, reflected nowhere else in the drawing. Use this selection to redraw text and symbols in highly original forms.

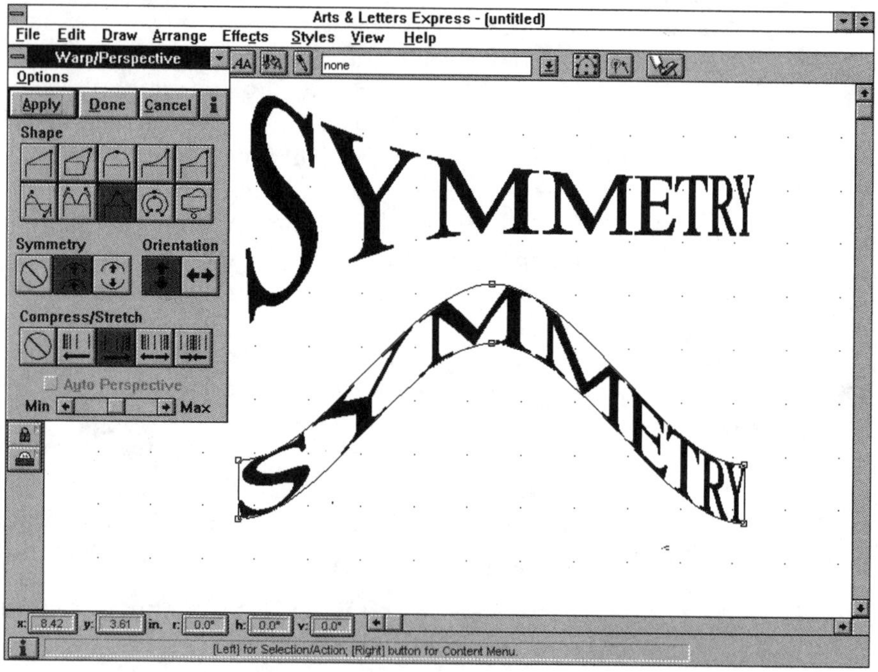

Figure 8.57
Symmetry
At bottom is Parallel symmetry, in which both sides move in tandem; at the top is mirrored symmetry, in which a tug of the mouse on one handle generates an equal and opposite reaction on the opposing handle.

Symmetry Options

If you select the Parallel symmetry option (second icon from left), each move you make on a point handle is matched *by the same distance, in the same direction* on the opposite side of the object. This allows you to create snaking patterns of text and long narrow objects. The final icon, mirrored symmetry (third from left) is the default, which makes every movement an equal and opposite movement.

Compared to using freeform editing to create a snaking strip of text, the **Warp/Perspective** feature is all the more miraculous. The following exercise is an example of how you can use parallel mirroring with text, but it also works with any symbol or image.

Steps: Parallel Mirroring with Warp

Use this operation to create parallel mirror effects with warp. This technique works with any symbol or image in the place of Text.

1. Select the **Text** icon.
2. Enter text in the **Insert/Edit Text** dialog box. Add text.
3. Access **Effects | Warp/Perspective | Add**.
4. Select the **Freeform** shape icon (lower row, far right).
5. Select **Vertical** orientation.
6. Select the **Parallel Symmetry** icon (farthest to right).
7. Drag the point handle on top of the text to pull it to a curve. The bottom edge matches the move.
8. Drag the point handle on the bottom of the text to pull it to another curve. The Top edge matches the move.
9. Select **Apply** to display the effect.
10. Continue adjusting handles and selecting **Apply** until you achieve the exact effect desired, then click on **Done**.

Warp Shape Matching

Warping can be used to fit text into an irregular shape. It can also be used to match text with a symbol icon which can serve as a "shape template." Say you want to make your name shaped so that it fits into the outline of an automobile. The easiest way is to display the automobile symbol and place your name on top of it. Then convert your name to freeform and access the **Warp/Perspective** features. The final selection (lower row, far right) is the most flexible of the warping shape selections. You can combine the finished shape with the symbol template to create a composite effect, or let the shaped text stand on its own.

Warp Templates

There are a variety of ways to apply overlays and templates using the Warp feature, because, in a very real sense, it is a kind of automatic editing mode in itself. It operates very much like the Freeform Edit mode, and when the warped object is converted to freeform (using **Cvt to Freeform** on the **Edit** menu or by pressing **F8**) it becomes fully editable in freeform. You can use the warp features to shape the text close to the desired form and finish up the work in Freeform.

The following example shows one way you can apply the concept of warping to a template. Again, take time to experiment.

Warping with Symbols

In this operation you can use a symbol as a warp template for text or other symbols.

1. Select the **Symbol** icon and select **Add** to use the symbol as a template, or use **Line** and **Curve** drawing tools to draw the template form.
2. Select the **Text** icon.
3. Enter text in **Insert/Edit Text** dialog box. Add text.
4. Access **Effects | Warp/Perspective | Specify**.
5. Select the **Freeform** shape icon (lower row, far right).
6. Select the desired orientation and mirroring.
7. Use the point handles to shape the word to a close approximation of the template form.
8. Select **Apply** to display the effect.
9. Continue adjusting handles, selecting **Apply** until you achieve the effect desired. Then click on **Done**.

Double Warps

Each warp shape stretches the text or graphic object in a specialized and defined way. Linear warps allow you to create exaggered 3-D effects, showing the object moving into the foreground from a vanishing point. Curvilinear shape options give you the ability to create 3-D effects and stretch, twist, and reshape the object as fluidly as putty. You can apply multiple warps to the same object, in effect combining a linear and a curvilinear effect, or applying multiple twists and turns to the shape. As you experiment with this feature, you will find that you can create spectacular effects by warping an object with one shape, then returning and warping with a different one. (See Figure 8.58.)

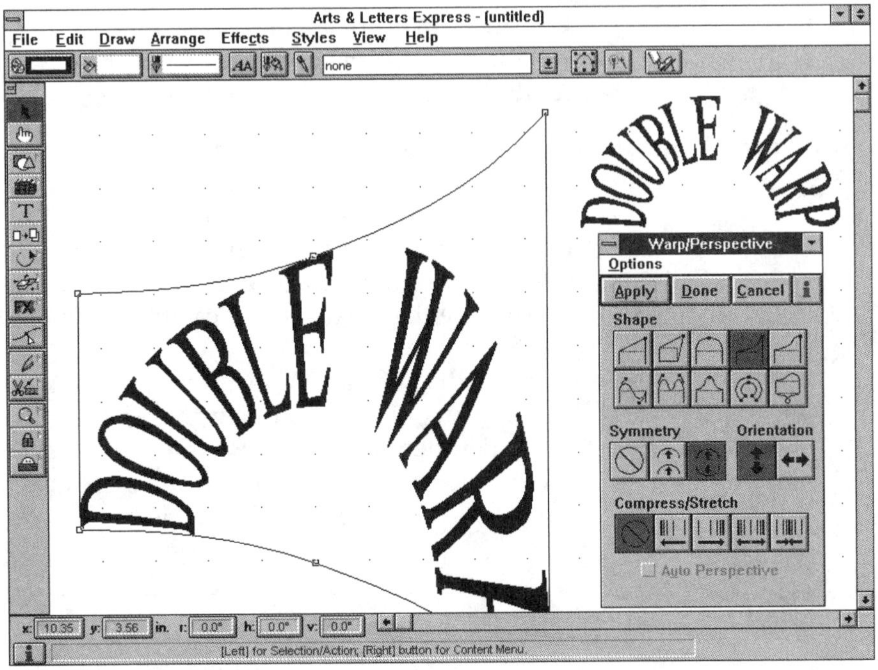

Figure 8.58
Double Warp
The object at the upper right is the first warp. Reprocessed with another shape model, it acquires a new look. When warps are converted to freeform, they can be edited right down to the base line and curve forms.

Vertical/Horizontal Warp

One use of this capability is to vertically and horizontally warp dimensions in the same object. Perform a vertical warp in one operation, and then perform a horizontal warp operation on the result.

The design possibilities with double warps are virtually endless. The following sequence lists the technical steps for making a double warp. As you become aware of the warp effects created by the various shapes, take time to mix and match them.

Steps: Creating a Double Warp

Use this operation to create a double warp for text or art forms.

1. Enter the desired symbol or text string into the screen.
2. Access **Effects | Warp/Perspective | Add** and perform the desired warp operation. Select **OK.**
3. Select the warped object onscreen. Access **Effects | Warp/Perspective | Add** and perform the second warp operation.
4. Repeat this process as many times as desired until the complete effect is achieved.

Manipulating and Enhancing Warped Objects

Once a warped object has been created, it can be manipulated and edited using the family of features available in the Arts & Letters Screen.

You can use **Duplicate** and color them as drop-shadow forms, **Rotate** and **Slant** to tilt or slant the warped object, and commands on the **Attribute** menu to change the line, fill, color, and so forth.

Warp and Gradient Fills

One of the most powerful options to keep in mind is how warps accept gradient backgrounds. A gradient is an automatic blend (new with Version 3.1), which is accessible through the **Fill** dialog box on the **Attributes** menu. Linear gradients can be used to accentuate the three-dimensional look of a "banner" warp, just as radial gradients can be used to enhance the spherical, three-dimensional character of round objects.

Warping is such a rich feature that it is impossible to cover all of its permutations in a few paragraphs. The key to understanding warping is to experiment on screen. Seeing is understanding, and the more you take time to see and experiment, the more effectively you will be able to design and compose with this feature.

Effective Communication

The look and presentation of artwork affects its ability to communicate. Effects allow you to transform the basic alphabet of images, wireframes, and text in Express and make these standard forms your own. These features are not only powerful graphic tools, they are fun to experiment with. They allow you to achieve graphic effects previously reserved for professionals.

The only limit in your use of Express is your imagination. Ideas are all around you; in magazines and newspapers, on television, and on streets signs, billboards, and advertisements. Take a moment and experiment with these effects and see how they can help you realize your vision.

CHAPTER 9

Idea Gallery

Creative Applications

Creating applications in Arts & Letters is a cumulative process. You compose components from the graphic database in desired relationships, enhance them with styles, and add one or more graphic effects. Arts & Letters Express can be used as a standalone graphics environment to generate documents, or you can use it as foundation art for all Windows programs.

This chapter covers special features, techniques, and ideas you can use within Arts & Letters, including key libraries in the Clip-Art Manager and template systems contained in the Activity Manager. Full coverage for using Arts & Letters as foundation art for Windows programs is included in Chapter 10.

Fast Track Orientation

Information presented in this chapter is based on a number of key concepts and sofware features. These concepts are defined to help bring you quickly up to speed.

Key Concepts

Series Composition Express allows you to build final graphic documents in a series of operations by combining a standard set of graphic components. Titles, standard backgrounds, images, and other components can all be saved in a custom Clip-Art Manager Collection and literally "plugged in" wherever needed. This approach allows you to use the same graphic components in a wide range of documents, including color slides, overheads, posters, presentations, brochures, and signs.

Activities/Templates Express includes a series of template and automated effect files that you can use to create custom effects. You can use custom warp and Bind to Text effects by simply loading and selecting them. In addition, there are a variety of complete compositions, including certificates, posters, and bullets that you can load, adapt, and customize for text and graphics using the Replace option.

Models The hard part in graphic composition is developing a concept. If you are an experienced artist this is less of a challenge. If you are not an experienced artist, one quick way around this problem is to maintain a graphic file of clippings to serve as models or examples.

Electronic Style Standards The simple selection of color and basic typeface, line, or fill styles can be significantly complicated. Applying style standards within a composition becomes a paramount issue when you are developing presentations, brochures, logos, stationery, and so on. It is essential that you get into the habit of naming and saving styles as you create them, and applying these named styles to text, art forms, and all aspects of your compositions. This will not only save you time in application, it will help you create standards that can be used by you or anyone involved in a project.

Tools

Clip-Art Manager The Clip-Art Manager is the central access for the Express graphic database. You can access all of the images and symbols directly from the collections contained here. Certain libraries provide you with images to use as the basis of your work and contain practical business images that can be used for a variety of applications.

Activity Manager The Activity Manager (Figure 9.1) is a twin dialog box to the Clip-Art Manager; it operates in exactly the same way to place selections from within a collection. It does not contain the Replace command, nor does

Figure 9.1
Activity Manager
Before creating your own textured backgrounds, check out the ready-made components here. Any of the backgrounds shown can be placed in the working area and configured with different colors and shapes, and sized on demand.

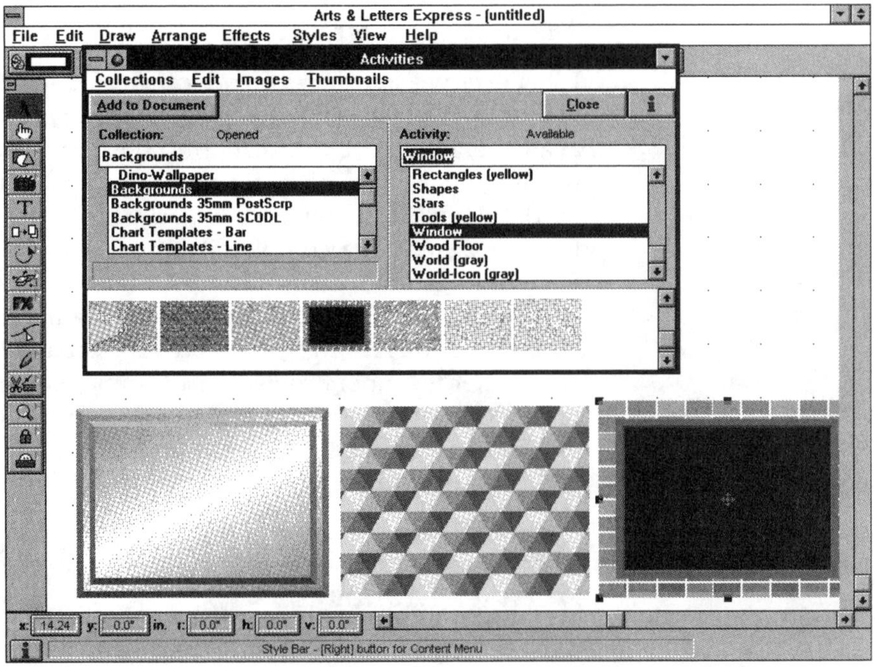

it contain any of the features to save and name individual images. Aside from these variations, the Activity Manager can function as a second Clip-Art Manager, used to store clip-art collections and, less frequently, to store templates and other performance enhancers included with Express.

Import The Import command on the File menu is an invaluable means of importing art from other graphics packages, including Micrografx, Corel, Adobe Illustrator, and also for accessing common file formats such as CGM, TIFF, and Windows Metafile. Using Import, you also can bring in works or art components created elsewhere and edit them in the Arts & Letters screen.

Visual Communication

To understand any software program, you have to know how to use its features and functions. You must be able to combine features to create finished work or applications. With Arts & Letters you can create just about any visual element you want for any purpose. But the question is, *how* to make the best use of the program to create the images, business graphics, and technical illustrations that you want.

The Best Tools for the Job

Whenever we sit down to work on any job, the first question should be: "What is the most effective way to perform it?" Given all the choices available, it is a tricky question to answer. Today, we have an array of sophisticated publishing, information management, presentation, and graphics tools available on the market. Many, if not most, of these products are based on a compatibility that allows you to create files internally and export them through commonly used file formats. The general philosophy is that one piece of software can be read and used by another. Increasingly, the software capabilities on the PC have become interdependent tools. For example, you can create a spreadsheet on Excel, import a range into Arts & Letters to create a chart, and export the chart in a file format to be read by Ventura Publisher to be included in a report.

Activity Manager

The Activity Manager could as easily be called the Template Manager. It contains a group of special files that help automate composition, create special effects, and even generate certain custom documents automatically.

Using Activities

It is easy to forget that the Activity Manager even is available. It is displayed at the bottom of a list of key drawing options on the Draw menu. It is a good idea to review all of the Activity Manager as soon as you install Express 5.0 so you can discover the magical files tucked away here. (See Figure 9.2.) There are templates for special warp effects, text binding curves, chart templates that allow you to enter your own data, ready-made templates for forms and greeting cards, and a complete set of components for musical notation that allows you to publish musical scores. Make a note of the Activities effects you are interested in and keep a written note close to your screen so you remember these power tools when the situation warrants it.

Activity Instructions

In all template activity collections, one of the selectable items is a text block of instructions. In some cases, text instructions are contained directly with the template. In these cases, you simply select the instruction block and place it in the working area, size it to read it, and delete the instruction text once you have read it. Like any collection element,

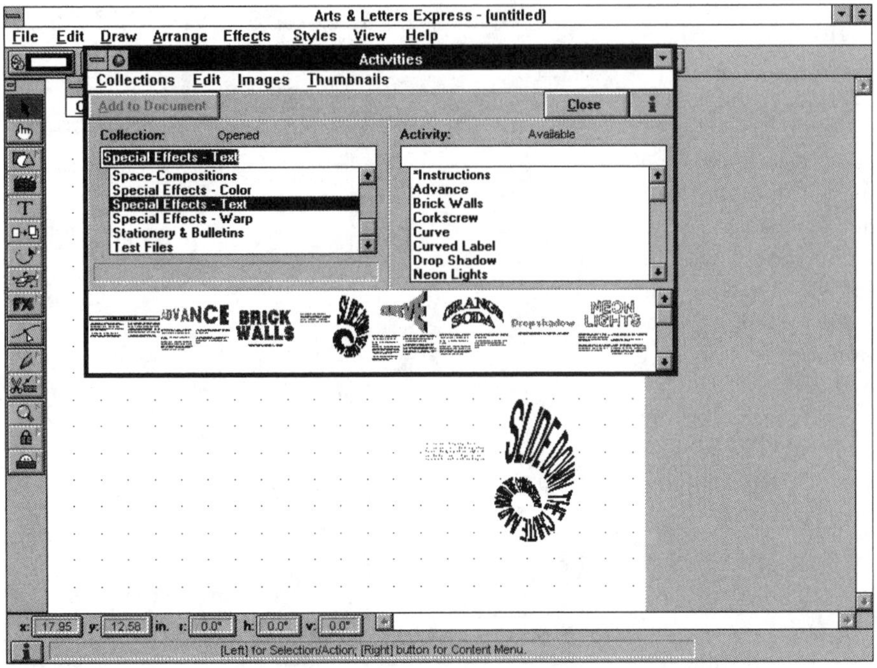

Figure 9.2
Text Effects
You can create highly sophisticated text effects using these activity selections. Each comes with directions built into the effect. Break apart the activity group, read the directions, and keep them onscreen until you have created the desired result, then delete them.

you cannot delete the original unless you delete the entire YAL file, so you can regard these instruction blocks as disposable elements to be displayed as you need to use them.

Activity Files

Activities are stored in standard YAL file format—the same format used for the Clip-Art Manager (Figure 9.3). You can store any of the Clip-Art Manager files you don't use frequently in the Activity Manager and thereby focus the Clip-Art Manager on those parts of the graphic database you use more consistently. The easiest way to do this is to use the default directories designed to contain the Clip-Art Manager and Activity YAL files.

Under the master \A&L directory is the \CUSTOM subdirectory that contains all Clip-Art Manager files. All Clip-Art Manager files stored in this directory will automatically be opened when you boot Express. Also under the \A&L directory is the \ACTIVITY subdirectory that contains all the Activity YAL files. If you wish to move Clip-Art Manager collections over, first make sure you know the exact YAL filename of the collections you wish to move. The Collection name that appears in the Collection list in the dialog box may be substantially different from the actual filename. You can check the filename by selecting the desired collection and selecting **Change Name/Info** on the Clip-Art Manager or Activity Manager from the **Collections** menu.

Figure 9.3
Activity Files
YAL Collection files are stored in different subdirectories under the master \A&L directory and are loaded automatically when the software boots. You can move seldom-used files from the Clip-Art Manager group to the Activity group, or copy them to disk for backup and delete them from your hard disk.

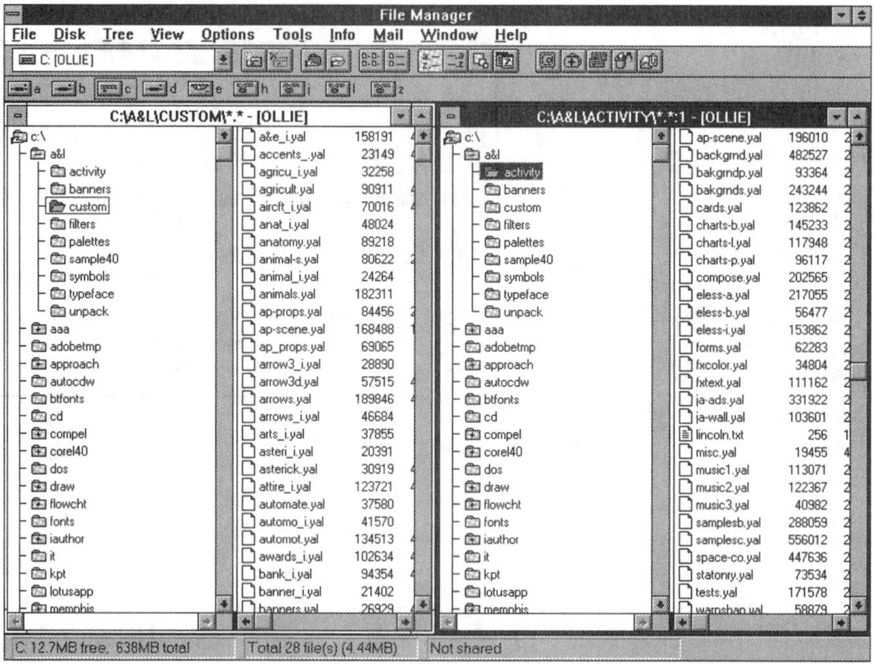

Once you have identified the correct filenames, use the Windows File Manager to select all the files in the Clip-Art Manager to be moved to the Activity Manager and drag them to the \ACTIVITY subdirectory icon.

Clip-Art Manager Production Techniques

The Clip-Art Manager is both a means to place prepared artwork from the graphic database and an alternative Save option for your creations. There are a variety of ways to use the Clip-Art Manager. You can access the standard graphic database components or use the collection system to capture elements that can automate your work.

An Open System of Capture Collections

The urgency of getting work done often prevent us from developing a workable system. Everybody thinks it would be great to have a system, but nobody's got the time to do it and one usually ends up constantly performing repetitive tasks in a lurching race to beat a deadline.

Create Ready-Made Capture Collections

To effectively apply this concept, it is a good idea to define each collection for a specific set of drawing elements. (See Figure 9.4.) As you perform your everyday work, take time to capture useful elements into

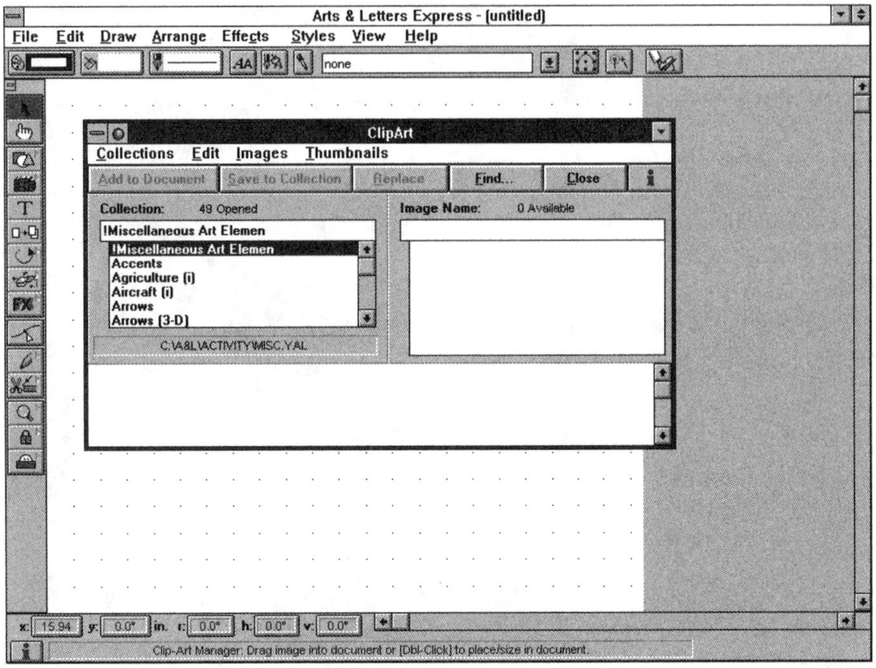

Figure 9.4
Capture Collections
In the example shown, a miscellaneous clip-art collection is ready to accept anything you want to save at any time. This saves you from waiting to categorize. The point is to save art objects as you create them. You can always place and save them to another collection anytime you want.

these collections *as you create them*. Don't try to create a complete drawing library at one time. Just set up your system so you can save images and elements as you need them. You'll be surprised how fast you can assemble a highly useful library of ready-made drawing elements and how much time it can save you when the heat is on.

Art Forms as Drawing Templates

Symbols and images make ideal templates for sketching and drawing. Let's say that you want to make a freehand drawing, but you'd like to have a general frame to work from. You can use the prepared symbols in Arts & Letters and group them into a single composition.

Display Art Forms as Drawing Guides

Once the symbol composition exists, you can use it as a visual template for freehand sketching (Figure 9.5). To speed up your drawing, you can use the **Quick Display | Show Outlines Only** selection on the **View** menu to remove all special attribute effects from the grouped symbol sketching template.

At any time, you may select the grouped template of symbols and delete it from the screen, so that you can work directly on your sketch.

Figure 9.5
Art Forms as Drawing Guides
Place any art form in the screen and draw freeform using the elements as a guide. You can make many variations using the art forms as templates for your freeform drawings.

Integrate Freehand and Art Form Elements

You may wish to redraw only a part of an image. For example, in a drawing of a person's face, you may wish to only change the look of the eyes, the mouth, or the nose. You can break apart the image and redraw these sections in freeform, or you may draw new components in freeform, or you may combine pieces from other Express images. The Portrait Gallery contains a variety of ready-made faces and expressions for men and women. Just load one or more of these faces and swap different facial components to create your own unique facial expression by simply dragging and dropping components.

Assembling a System of Icons

Icons are simple, stylized elements that symbolize everything from people, professions, and objects to ideas and concepts. Arts & Letters has an excellent and comprehensive library of icons that are perfect for creating overhead transparencies, business reports, technical manuals, and many other applications (Figure 9.6).

Building on Base Drawings

In their basic symbol form icons are simple drawings, but they can very quickly be converted into professional-looking images with drop shadow effects, frames, and textured backgrounds.

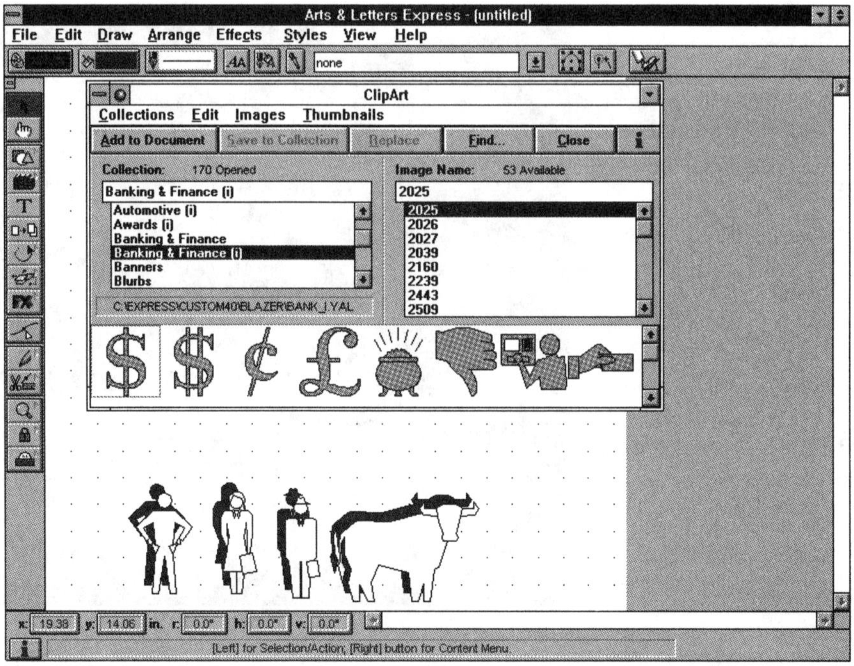

Figure 9.6
System of Icons
You can take a series of icon forms as shown and add group enhancements, then save the enhanced icons back into Clip-Art Manager Collections. This allows you to create systematic, custom variations on simple art forms for use in larger publishing projects, or to create your own ready-made databank of effects for a series of documents and presentations.

Adding Dimension To add dimension to the icon, you can add a drop shadow by simply duplicating the original icon, shading it, and offsetting the position of the copy. Now, to the drop shadow icon, add a framing line with one of the standard flowchart boxes, or a rounded rectangle, or use one of the 3-D geometric icons.

Presentation Graphics Applications

Arts & Letters is an excellent tool for developing presentation graphics applications, such as charts, illustrations, overhead transparencies, and color slide presentations.

This section focuses on design and production techniques for presentation graphics. Concepts will be illustrated with a sample graphics created using Arts & Graphics files and original artwork. Case studies provide real-world examples of the concepts presented.

Overheads

Overheads can contain anything from text to complex graphics and pictures (Figure 9.7). Overheads are commonly used for customer presentations, and typically, are produced in numbered sequence for a presentation.

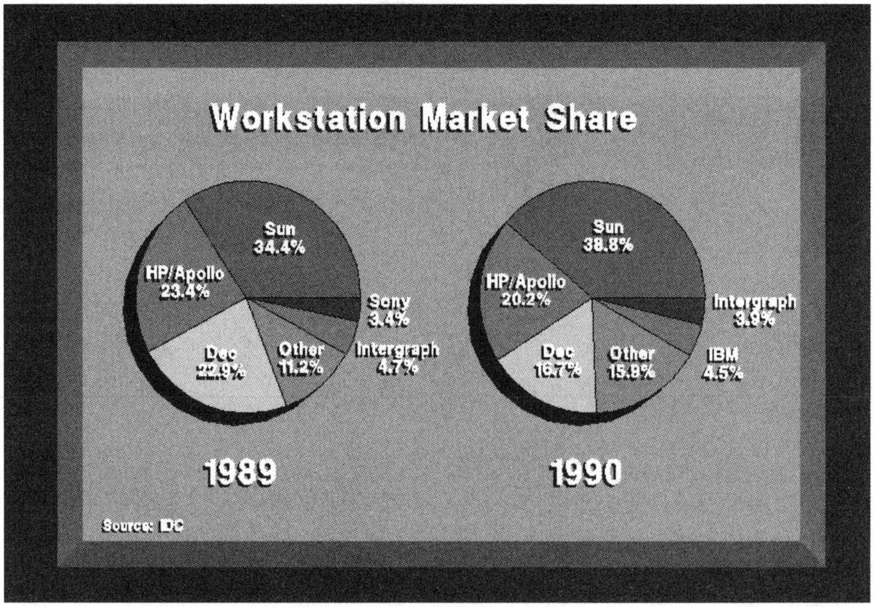

Figure 9.7
Overheads
You can create a set of overheads using multiple pages within a single GED file. Use ready-made backgrounds and/or the overhead templates provided, or create your own designs and save them in a custom Collection. You can place your design anywhere and change the text and bullet content using Text Replace.

People who regularly give presentations often store and use the same slides over and over again, making selective revisions within the set as necessary. Overheads may be printed and stapled into handouts so that the audience can follow along and make notes on the actual overhead itself.

Arts & Letters is an excellent tool for creating overheads, given its superior text-handling capabilities, its built-in charting, and its ability to develop sophisticated diagrams from standard flowchart symbols included with the software.

Tips: Overheads

- Create a standard design style for overheads and include page size, margins, text style, heading characteristics, and so forth.
- Use a standard overhead as a template. If all text elements are in the correct place and the text has not been converted to freeform, you can select any text element in the template, replace the text using the **Text** icon, and the new text will instantly take on everything that was in the template, including position, size, typeface, etc.
- You can use Arts & Letters to create a variety of interesting bullet characters for text-only overheads.
- Use charting features in combination with text to create a system of overheads with uniform titles that can display charts.

Color Slides

Color slides are one of the most common forms of presentation. Color text, charts, and graphics can all be generated and output directly through Arts & Letters (Figure 9.7). In addition, Arts & Letters files can be exported in popular vector and bitmapped file formats for use in a variety of presentation programs and slide-show generating packages (Figure 9.8).

The major problem with using color in presentations is that it requires a careful and consistent design and application of style standards. Eye-balling color mix and typefaces is simply not good enough: even small bits of guesswork will become glaringly evident when the slides are printed and shown. Also, without careful color selection, a presentation can be overpowering or jarring. A good rule of thumb when using color in presentation applications, particularly slides, is to select colors according to mood. Use bright, hot, colors for emphasis, and to attract the audience's attention to what you think is important in the slide, and use softer, mellower colors for backgrounds and framing aspects.

Tips: Color Slides

- For backgrounds use color blends for your slides that show a soft evolution between colors. Not only does this suggest three-dimensionality, but it gives your slides a professional look that solid color blocks do not.

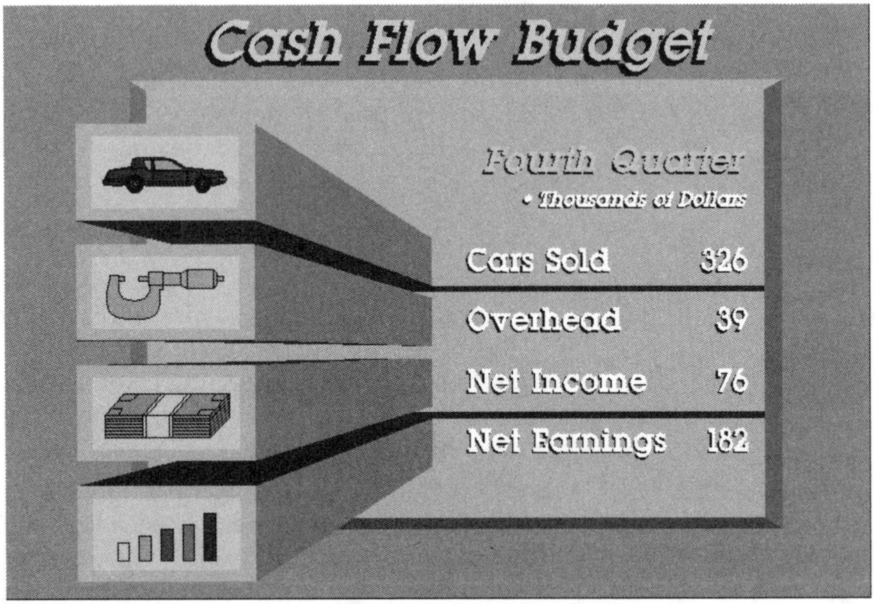

Figure 9.8
Color Slides
The Activity Manager contains a number of color slide templates and layouts to use as the beginning of your design. Save style standards for color mixes you use in text titles, and use a style bundle to save your slides' typographic attributes, color, line, and fill characteristics. This will let you create text elements in a single mouse click.

- Use color blends in graphic art forms, text, and charting elements to give a rounded, solid look to these elements. This is particularly effective when you are simply assembling standard symbols into a chart. A color blend can make the standard symbol look finished, original, and professional in seconds.
- Experiment with picture charts so that your message can be carried as visually as possible. Use pictorial elements as backgrounds and framing elements for charts. Your audience may not remember all the text labels in the chart, but they will remember the visual image.
- Create a custom symbol library that contains your basic slide element set of symbols. This allows you to consistently use the same art and text elements without searching through the *Clip Art Handbook* to find the correct symbol numbers.
- As you develop color slides, particularly if you are using custom color mixes and blends, use named attribute styles to save your color mixes so that they are easily accessible. This not only saves time, it makes it easy for you to create consistent blends from one custom color mix to another.

Report Graphics

In many cases, charts, diagrams, and other visual presentation materials can enhance printed or desktop published reports (Figure 9.9).

When creating your overheads or slides, keep in mind the concept of the "exploded" graphic. Ideally, you should be able to create a graphic for an overhead or slide and use the various elements—the text title, charts, and graphic elements—in a desktop publishing program. It's best to neatly group individual elements within the overhead or slide so they can be selected and exported instantly.

Tips: Report Graphics

- Exporting a color file to an external application where it may be printed in black and white can cause problems with texture. Translating color to gray values may instantly remove some of the emphasis in the design simply because a soft red and a soft blue often read as the same gray. Before exporting color layouts, take a look at the color pattern and decide if you need to make adjustments in contrast in order to present the image in black and white.
- Support for pattern fills is dependent on your printer. It is often better to stick with shades of black and white rather than colors if you are printing to a black and white printer. If you need to use patterns, it is a good idea to run a test sheet to see how they will print.

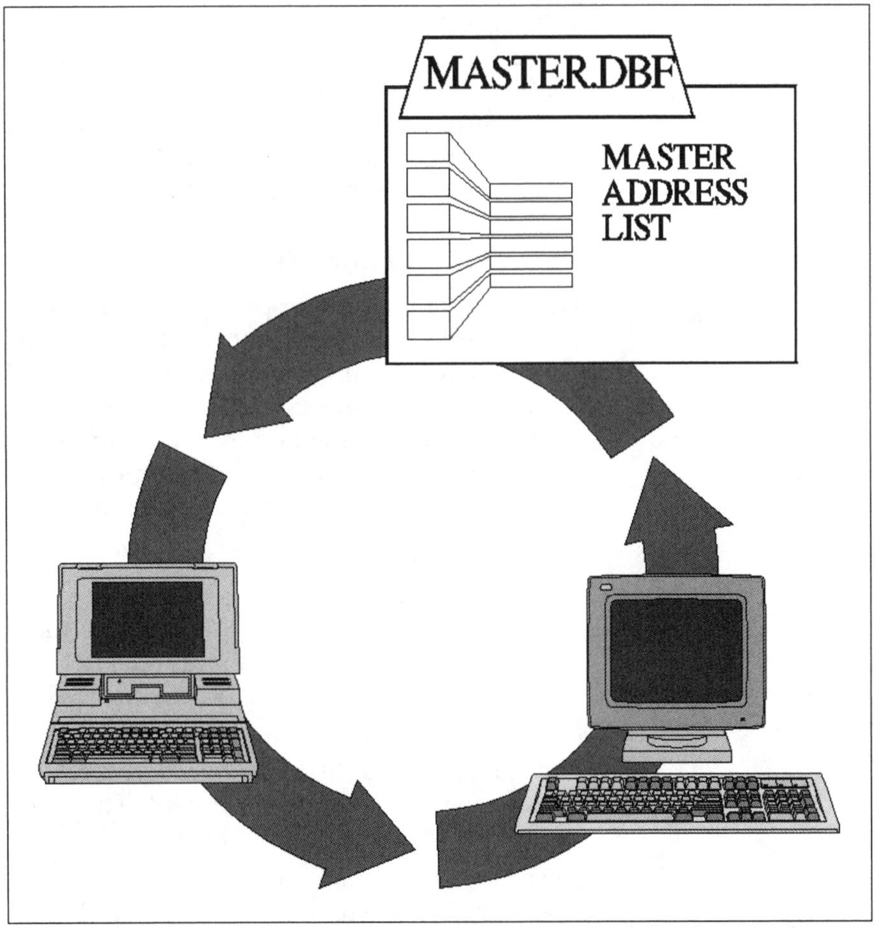

Figure 9.9
Report Graphics
In reports, try to maintain style standards in all graphic elements, including titles, diagrams, and charts. Electronic style standards are invaluable. To apply standards, click on the desired style from the palette. Create a single master chart design, save it in a custom collection, and enter the various data blocks into the template for each time you need a chart.

- Computer Graphics Metafile (CGM) is an excellent format for exporting files to Ventura Publisher and PageMaker. Conversion is fast and direct. Encapsulated PostScript (EPS) is also good, but involves a two-file conversion process: the EPS file itself must be written along with a "header" representation in TIFF format, which allows the file to be seen on screen. This takes more time in conversion, and the screen result in your desktop publishing program is not as clear. Another factor to note is that some applications, notably Ventura Publisher, can have trouble reading the file header in TIFF or WMF format, so you may have to export EPS files to such applications without a header, meaning you will see only an "X" on the screen in place of the picture in the destination application.

- Encapsulated PostScript is the file format of choice if you are printing to a PostScript printing device. EPS with a WMF (Windows Metafile) header is as clear, if not clearer, than CGM format. WMF supports all patterns and colors available in Arts & Letters, while CGM supports all colors, but only vector patterns. Raster patterns will not be interpreted properly.

Presentation Booklets

When you are designing presentation graphics that will exist both as a set of overhead or color slides and as a printed booklet, you must keep in mind what the finished application will look like in both forms. For black and white slides, this is relatively easy, since what works as an overhead slide will generally work well on paper. The translation of color slides to black and white printouts is more problematic, largely because color tones used for emphasis are washed out or look identical in black and white.

Tips: Presentation Booklets

- Run a simple test on a couple of initial slides to see how they look on paper versus on the slide. Make sure that you haven't overloaded the slides with too many graphic effects. What looks dramatic on screen may look cluttered on paper.
- Set up your slides using multiple pages in the same Arts & Letters document file. This means that you will have perhaps six or eight slides within a single document. This allows for faster printing of slides from a master set of art files.
- The number of pages in your Arts & Letters document is dependent on the document precision setting. The lower the document precision, the more pages are available. For a set of slides, the document precision (entered through the **Page Setup** dialog box on the **File** menu) could be set as low as 720 logical units, thus creating a document with 36 separate pages.

General Business Applications

In an office, there are limitless opportunities for using graphics. Everything from posters, memoranda, diagrams, signs, labels can all be enhanced by professional looking text and graphics.

With Arts & Letters you can create designer signs, labels for reports, computer diskettes, archives—anything you want. The only limit to what you can do is your own imagination and creativity. And with the symbol system in Arts & Letters, you can make these applications so that the reader can instantly visualize the material through an icon or graphic rather than having to read text. Using pictorials and icons for stored reports and shelf materials is also a powerful way to label your documents.

General business graphics include flowcharts, diagrams, and icon systems. These things could be considered presentation graphics, but they also can be used as posters, for memoranda, in press releases, or in published materials. If you take the time to create a ready-made system of icons, flowchart elements, and diagram elements, save them in a clip art collection, and distribute them within the organization, everyone will be working with the same visual elements, allowing you to bring a visual consistency to a variety of business communications.

Creating a System of Business Icons

Icons are visual keys that allow you to summarize a complex idea in a simple graphic (Figure 9.10). Their power lies in instant recognition. The effect and utility of icons is similar to logos. When we see a logo of a company or product, we react instantly to it. The visual character of an icon should also draw us in and interest us. Arts & Letters includes a system of ready-made icons and pictorials that you can enhance and use in labels, signs, flowcharts, books, reference materials, marketing, brochures, newsletters, and more.

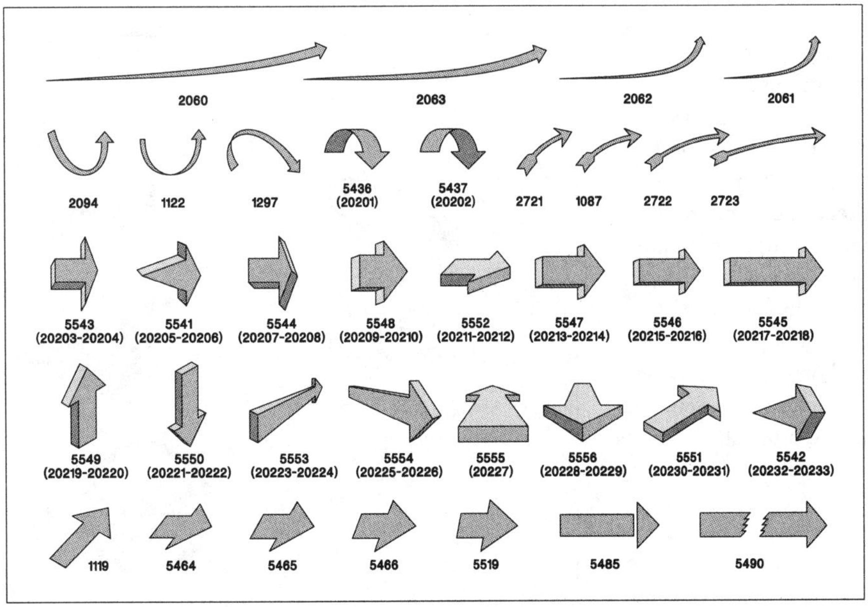

Figure 9.10
General Business Uses
The graphic database has many ready-made elements such as these arrows you can use to dress up your office communications—everything from icons representing computers and business equipment to graphics and components that you can use to create maps of your office layout.

Tips: Creating Icon Systems

- Create a standard framing background and then load a series of ready-made Arts & Letters icon symbols into the background. In this way you can customize a whole set of icons in under half an hour.
- Simple symbol icon forms can instantly be enhanced so that they have 3-D qualities and color. A few simple changes will make the plain symbol look professional and visually interesting.
- Combine multiple icons to create more complex "visual sentences." You can show a simple "stick-figure" as an icon, or add a pictorial background to the icon to enhance its visual character or communicate a technical concept.
- By scanning and tracing your company logo or other business graphic, you can save them in a clip art collection along with the rest of your icons.

Developing a Set of Flowchart Symbols

Flowcharts demonstrate relationships. Where a written description of a complex process might take a long time to visualize, a flowchart can graphically communicate the same information so that the reader cannot only see the elements in the process, but how they relate to one another (Figure 9.11).

Box Graphics and More

Flowcharts work best when designed around a core set of graphics. The graphics should provide a visual key to content. This is particularly

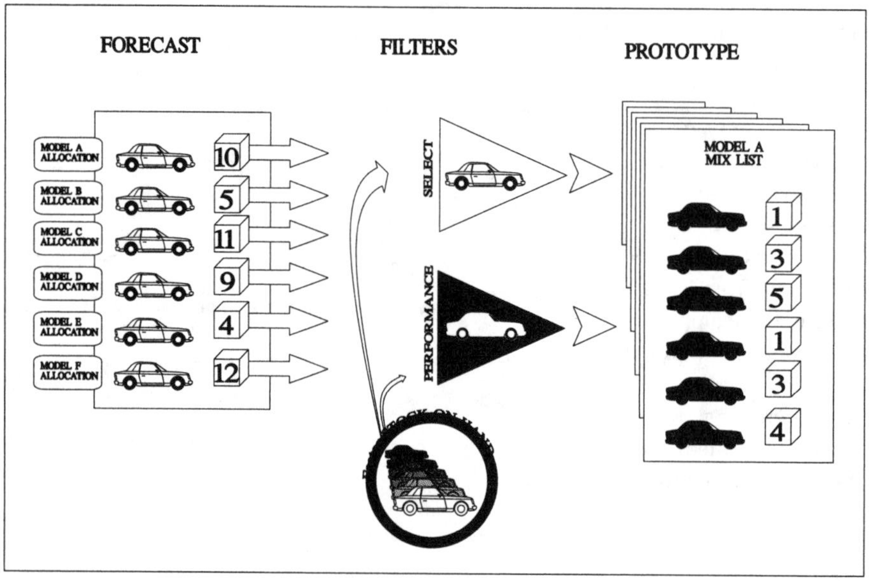

Figure 9.11 Flowcharts
Using simple art icons to enhance flowchart graphics helps you break the standard box used in many diagrams and flowcharts. Using an art image to represent people, tools, and objects has greater impact, recognition, and visual interest.

important in technical flowcharts, but the concept can be applied broadly to include any other type of simple business flowchart.

Flowcharts as Art Images

Where flowcharts created in traditional graphics packages are often made with simple geometrics, such as boxes, circles, triangles, and polygons, Arts & Letters gives you the option to create pictorial, icon-based flowcharts. Using pictorial icons that represent the element can create visual impact. Your reader can react to the visual elements without having to read the text labels.

If you define your basic graphics and save them in a clip art collection, that collection can be copied into other Arts & Letters applications.

Tips: Creating Diagram and Flowchart Systems

- To add depth and interest to your flowcharts, add 3-D effects, such as drop-shadows, and save the completed element into your custom symbol library.
- Because flowcharts may require lines and arrows moving in many directions, it is a good idea to apply the concept of variations on a theme and save connector arrows and other elements in a variety of different angle positions. This will save you the time when assembling the flowchart.
- If you use your flowcharts in published applications, it is a good idea to select the flowchart text font in Arts & Letters that most closely matches that used in your publishing program. You may then export the flowchart with text in place via an EPS file and the text will appear with the same level of clarity as your published text.
- When entering flowchart text, use the type size entry line in the **Type Attributes** dialog box to specify the exact type size required. This is much easier than attempting to eyeball elements and size them from the screen.
- If you regularly create flowcharts of a similar type, it is a good idea to retain all your finished work in a GED file. Your old flowcharts may serve as ready-made templates for new ones in which only a few elements have to be moved and adjusted.
- If text in your flowchart remains in Word Text form and is not converted to freeform graphics, you can instantly replace text in existing flowcharts by selecting any text element, going to the **Type** icon, entering the new text, and selecting Replace. The new text will instantly appear with the correct typeface and with all attributes assigned to the existing text.

Signs

A sign may be a handwritten notice, an office memo about the company picnic, or a taped note describing the peculiarities of the office copier. Whatever your need for signs, you can use Arts & Letters to instantly create highly visual and effective announcements, notices, warnings, mini-posters, and other display applications (Figure 9.12).

Figure 9.12
Signs
Aside from the collections of standard signs in Express (the universal No Smoking sign is very popular now), you can create your own posters and integrate these symbols with backgrounds, text, your own logo, and any other sign elements you like.

Although you may create signs in text only, the basic symbol set contains a full complement of familiar signs, and any of the icons, pictorials, images, or cartoons can be used to create signs.

Tips: Signs

- Cartoon symbols are an interesting and amusing way to get people's attention, particularly if you are developing a sign for in-house use. If you really want to play with this, remember that the basic symbol set contains not only the cartoon figures, but dialog balloons as well.
- If you regularly post signs, it is a good idea to set a standard design so that your sign will stand out wherever it is posted.
- For signs used in trade shows and any event involving customers or outsiders, it is a good idea to scan in your company logo so that it is available in Arts & Letters as a clip art image. You'll find that you can create quite an impact by generating signs that carry your company identity.

Labels

Think of how many office items require labels: diskettes, diskette boxes, reports, bound magazines, file drawers, storage bins, and many more. You can make simple labels by scribbling on a Press-N-Stick sheet, but if you want to create visually interesting labels, Arts & Letters can help you do it (Figure 9.13).

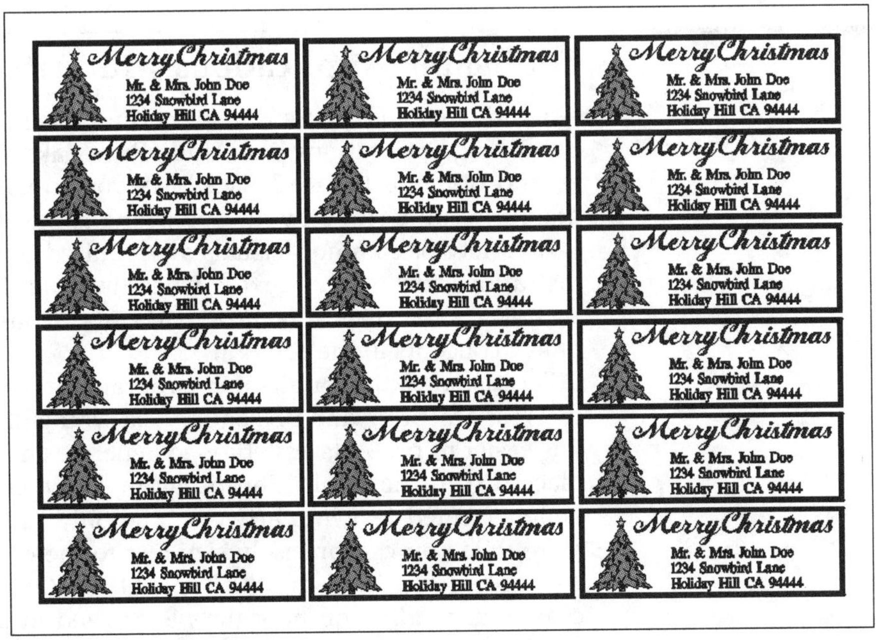

Figure 9.13
Labels
You can buy labels by the sheet and feed them through a laser printer. With Express, you can dress up your diskette labels or any other label you use routinely with descriptive or logo graphics and stylized text.

Keep in mind that labels done in Arts & Letters don't have to be text. You can use icons, symbols, pictorials, or any of the ready-made graphics to instantly add life to labels. Using drop-shadows, blends, and all the other available enhancements, you add depth and attention-getting power.

At meetings and trade shows, attendees are frequently given stick-on labels to identify themselves. You can dress up these labels with decorative text, your company logo, or any visual element you want.

Tips: Labels

- Set up your labels to correspond with the arrangement of labels on the sheet you run through your printer. If necessary, use screen rulers to arrange items on the page. You can size individual graphic objects and graphic groups to precise measurement using the **Transform** dialog box.
- Create a basic label in the correct size and shape and use the **Duplicate** tool to copy it to all positions in the page. To save time on the screen, activate **Show Outlines Only** in the **View** menu so that all attributes on labels will not be drawn individually.
- Save a finished label sheet in a GED file in your system. When you next sit down to create labels, you will already have the correct relationship of graphics for printing and you can use the old label sheet as a template for others you make.

Publishing Applications with Arts & Letters

Artwork created in Arts & Letters can be exported for use in desktop publishing applications like Aldus PageMaker, Xerox Ventura Publisher, and other software. This allows you to use Arts & Letters as the graphic resource for all your publishing applications.

A variety of common visuals are required in publishing including illustrations, decorative text for headings, and presentation graphics such as charts, diagrams, flowcharts, and icons to mark section heads or key concepts in the content.

Because desktop publishing programs have highly developed systems for accepting and presenting text, you will have to decide whether it is easier to use Arts & Letters to generate charts and art forms and to place text in the publishing program, or whether to integrate Arts & Letters-created text into artwork. The only caution to keep in mind is that while you can precisely size text to the desired point size in your Arts & Letters files using the **Type Attributes** menu, the text size may change depending on how the file is sized in the publishing program page. In other words, you may have a full-page text chart with a title in 18-point Modern Bold created in Arts & Letters, but if that file is exported and placed in a half-page-sized frame in the publishing program, the text will no longer appear in 18 points. The overall issue here is document consistency: If some of your charts in the published program are shown as full pages and others as half pages you may have a considerable play of font sizes and an uneven look across the document.

Desktop publishers often make use of packaged clip-art to spice up the page. You can use Arts & Letters as a "custom clip-art generator" by assembling standard or custom symbols into your own custom library of ready-made clip-art, which can be instantly brought into your publishing program. By exporting a series of icons, drawings, symbols, and other art forms, customized in Arts & Letters to CGM or another preferred format, you can create a library of foundation art that is instantly available for use in any of your published pages.

Newsletters

Newsletters are the most common desktop publishing applications, both on Ventura and PageMaker. Be it an in-house organ or a customer bulletin, your newsletter is more effective if it uses visual elements strategically to interest the reader and involve them in the content.

Arts & Letters includes many different pictorials that can be combined with backgrounds to illustrate stories, articles, sidebars, and other content elements. Use Arts & Letters to create a decorative text logo for the cover (Figure 9.14), as well as decorative text headings for articles. By combining decorative text with symbol elements or icons and sizing them exactly to fit a specified area, you can create ready-made headings. You can use the same principle to design boilerplate headings for each issue, and simply replace the text in the ready-made heading for each article in the publication.

Tips: Newsletters

- Be careful to match the font used for your decorative text effects created in Arts & Letters with the font used for text and other elements in the publishing program. You may match Arts & Letters to their commercial counterparts using the typeface section in the *Symbol Handbook*.
- For feature articles, you may need to create images in which the same graphic appears in different aspects, with different backgrounds, or "growing" from a simple drawing to a more complex illustration, as the article proceeds. Arts & Letters symbols allow you to take a standard graphic and make a number of evolutionary changes without drawing a line.

Figure 9.14
Newsletters
You can use Express artwork and text right out of the box to dress up your newsletters. You can also add a few jazzy effects and framing elements to create a magazine- quality look to a simple newsletter you run through your laser printer.

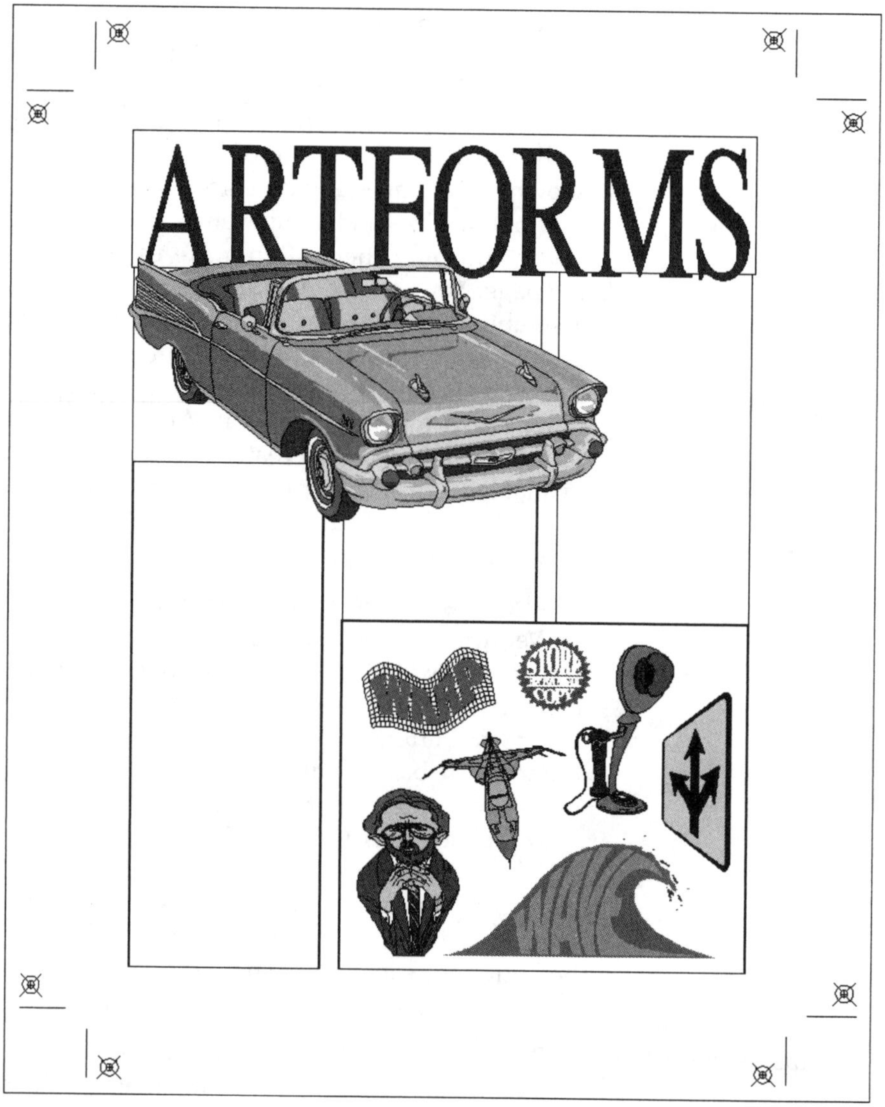

- Blending is an effective technique making text appear textured and three-dimensional. Experiment with blending letters in gray shades and colors to give them a rounded, textured look.
- Merging can be used to create "see-through" decorative text headlines and logo effects that work well on the cover of a newsletter or as header graphics.
- Icons or simple pictorials can be used in place of subheadings to carry a reader through a story by illustrating the written content.

- Text features can be used to create interesting "drop-caps" for the first character in a paragraph or story. For more impact, you can make the initial capital a "picture letter." Place the stylized drop-cap over a pictorial graphic that represents the content of the article.

Books

Arts & Letters can be used to support your book publishing software to provide the images, illustrations, graphics, charts, design elements, and any other graphics that you require for books. In fact, the book applications made possible by Arts & Letters are illustrated by this book itself. Traditional books contain illustrations, graphics, and diagrams that are often created by professional graphic artists. Adding art to a book can significantly increase its budget if the author is not able to create and deliver the finished artwork.

Arts & Letters is so flexible a tool, however, that you cannot only create standard book illustrations, you can actually create inset artworks, similar to the ones used in the preceding chapters, to illustrate a concept right in the flow of the text. Also, rather than describing a concept and referring the reader to an illustration, possibly located on another page, you can create symbol-based drawings or sketches that present a point and place one right at the point where it is described. This allows you to write a book differently, drawing as well on your power to illustrate what you're talking about right on the page.

Tips: Books

- When creating artwork for a book, make the illustrations look like they came from a single source, not from a random collection of clip-art packages. You may wish to consult a graphic design expert to help you get an overview of the "look" of art that will complement the book.
- For books with technical content or complex material, you can develop a system to highlight different content points. This allows the reader to scan pages using visual cues.
- Icons also can be used as section heads, main headings, and subheadings to create an entire visual reference system supporting the content.
- Even if you don't want to create the final art for your book, you can use Arts & Letters to sketch-out the type of finished illustration that will best support the content. These quick electronic sketches can then be used as reference by a professional for the final drawings and illustrations.

Case Study: Book Illustrations

The power of Arts & Letters to develop complex art projects under very tight deadlines is dramatically illustrated by an actual case study involving a recently published book on chess strategy. *Play Winning Chess* is a book by Microsoft Press. The content covers detailed chess moves and gambits, which are illustrated by exact representations of the chessboard pieces (Figure 9.15).

The book required 139 chessboard illustrations and a chessboard. (A chessboard is a black and white grid of 64 squares, eight by eight. There

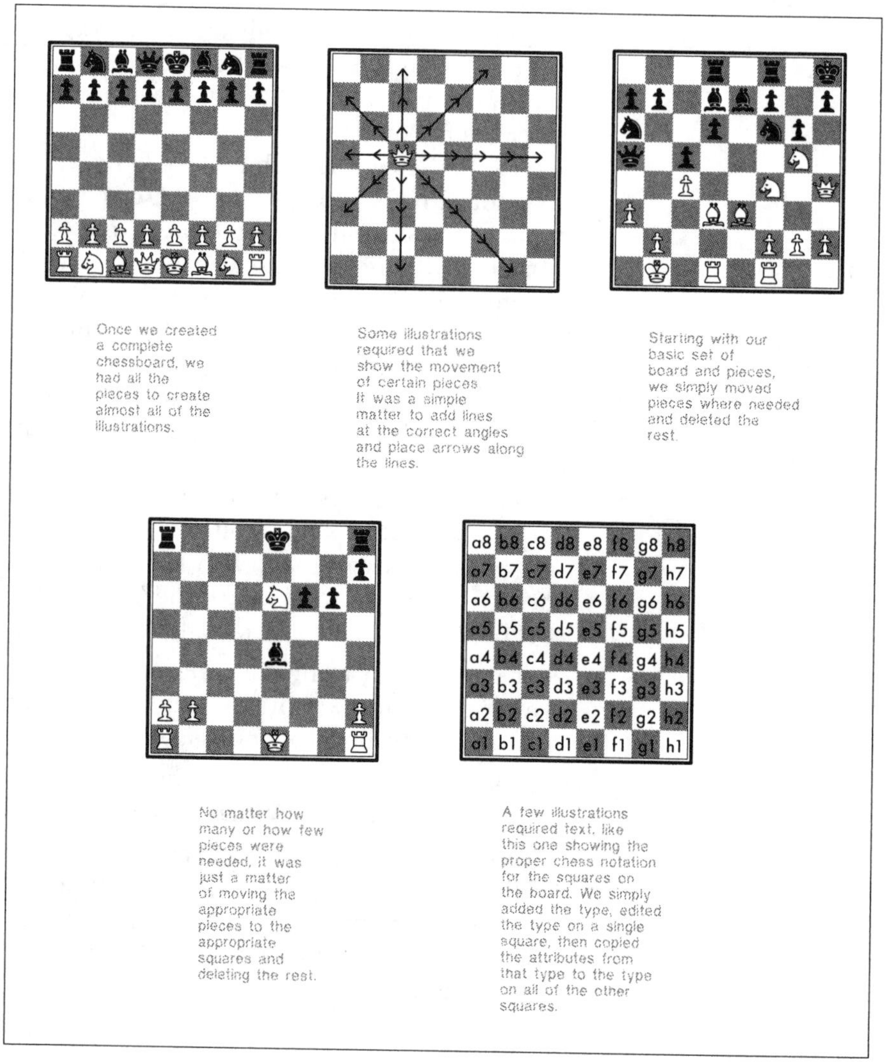
Once we created a complete chessboard, we had all the pieces to create almost all of the illustrations.
Some illustrations required that we show the movement of certain pieces. It was a simple matter to add lines at the correct angles and place arrows along the lines.
Starting with our basic set of board and pieces, we simply moved pieces where needed and deleted the rest.
No matter how many or how few pieces were needed, it was just a matter of moving the appropriate pieces to the appropriate squares and deleting the rest.
A few illustrations required text, like this one showing the proper chess notation for the squares on the board. We simply added the type, edited the type on a single square, then copied the attributes from that type to the type on all of the other squares.

Figure 9.15
Creating a Chessboard
This chessboard was created from a series of grid activities. The chess pieces were already in the Express graphic database, so the game images could be created by dragging and deleting elements directly on the screen.

are six different types of chess pieces, and 16 pieces per side—1 King, 1 Queen, 2 Bishops, 2 Knights, 2 Castles, 8 Pawns.

By any measure, the prospect of creating 139 chessboard illustrations, given this level of complexity, is a daunting and potentially time-consuming project. Against a tight deadline, Microsoft Books contacted Genesis Publications, a book production house, for advice and guidance. The people at Genesis estimated the task would require a minimum of 70 hours of work in CorelDraw. Genesis contacted Arts & Letters and asked for their estimate of time. Arts & Letters said the task could be completed in approximately *8 hours*.

Composition Power

To create the chessboards in so short a time, Arts & Letters staff used a systematic approach to creating the art. The board began with the symbol for a square which was auto-duplicated using the Transform features to create a chessboard grid. The entire board was sized to the publisher's specifications and saved as a graphic group to keep all elements in the correct relationship. Instead of using the ready-made clip-art symbols for individual chess pieces, which are included in Arts & Letters, line drawings of chess pieces from the publisher were scanned, and auto-traced in Arts & Letters.

A complete set of chess pieces in white and black was created and sized to the chessboard spec using precise numeric sizing controls. The entire chessboard and pieces were assembled and then saved as a group.

Fast Editing and Assembly

To create individual chessboards, the complete chessboard group was copied as a complete entity. From that point on the task was simply to delete unnecessary pieces and move the remaining pieces into the correct position on the chessboard grid. Using Arts & Letters, a complete draft set of 139 illustrations was completed, start-to-finish, in eight hours. Later revisions from the publisher were created and turned around virtually on demand.

This case study illustrates how the composition power in Arts & Letters can make a complex job easy. At all times, artists were working on the screen with the real chessboard, not a clumsy "wire-frame" representation. By composing with graphic objects, a job that could take a draw program at least 70 hours was completed in a fraction of the time.

Graphic Arts Applications

Arts & Letters supports a full range of graphic arts and design applications including professional-quality color images, calendar art, posters, brochures, advertisements, product packaging, point-of-purchase sales materials, and more (Figure 9.16).

Art Strategies

There are a variety of ways that a seasoned artist can make use of Arts & Letters. You can sketch out roughs by hand or use symbols as the basis for your work. The advantages of symbol composition is that it is extremely fast and requires no drawing. So you can quickly assemble your idea on screen, place foreground and background elements, add color, shading, and attributes and come up with a reasonably well-worked preliminary composition in 15 minutes or less.

Editing Compositions

Once the composition has been sketched out, you can dispense with it and sketch freehand, or convert the entire composition into freeform graphic objects that can be manipulated, sized, enhanced, and worked

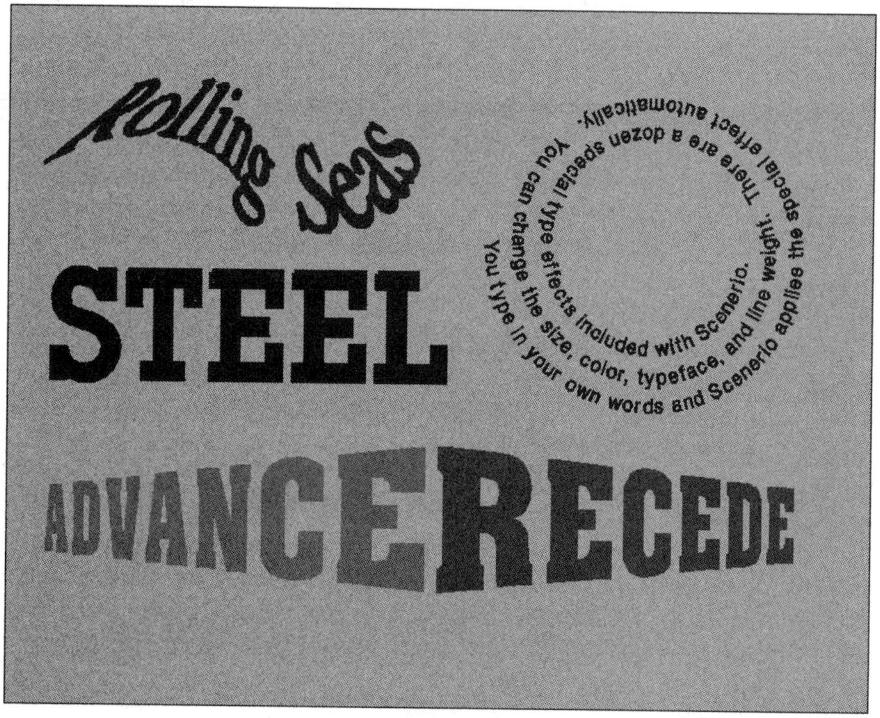

Figure 9.16
Graphic Arts
There is no limit to the type and range of graphic arts effects you can create with Express features. Stacking shapes and using different fills and object effects lets you create components that can be assembled into a variety of professional-quality illustrations.

into the final form. Even if you don't want to sketch initially on Arts & Letters, you can draw freehand on paper and scan the result so that it can be traced and edited in freeform on the screen.

Bitmaps and TIFF Insertions

Experienced artists should also note that the Arts & Letters GED file format can accept and access scanned color backgrounds in TIFF format, or backgrounds converted from high-end PC graphics formats, including Targa, GIF, and PCX 3.0, to serve as textured color backgrounds. Once the color background is in place, you may create a series of graphic objects to overlay the background, including custom text, charts, and symbols. Keep in mind that all Arts & Letters graphic objects may be easily enhanced with subtle variations in color using the premixed color palettes or your own custom color mixes. Using the **Blend** feature or a gradient fill, you may quickly customize your freeform sketches, symbols, text, or charts, with color gradients that suggest a three-dimensionality and help to fit the artworks into the color background you have selected.

Creating Custom Graphic Collections

The final components to consider are the Collection files. No other PC graphics package gives you the ability to create computer libraries of your own ready-made art elements. You can set up a system so that you can save sketched objects as you create them and recall those sketches at any time.

Brochures and Advertisements

Brochures and advertisements have one function: to get the reader interested in whatever you're selling. These applications are, by definition, designed to get attention (Figure 9.17).

Use Arts & Letters to create full-page images using all of the design, freeform drawing, and color capabilities available

You can also develop stylized logos, decorative text for headlines, subheadings, and picture captions. Icons, pictorials, and other art forms can be used to highlight paragraph text and visually carry the reader through the brochure or ad.

Ads and brochures can be created entirely within Arts & Letters itself, or in a dedicated desktop publishing program. Within Arts & Letters, you can set up a double-page advertisement or a short brochure in a single document and save the entire thing in a GED file. If you want to export art to your desktop publishing program, you can do so in a variety of formats.

Tips: Brochures and Advertisements

- If you are using a desktop publishing program to assemble the brochure, be sure to match fonts and font sizes. You should know the

Figure 9.17
Brochures
Brochures may involve using common elements from presentations as well as your company logo. Make sure you use custom styles systematically, so that you can control style standards. Then, every time you need an image for a brochure or supporting document, it is consistent with others.

size of the area that will contain the artwork in the published page so you can configure the art to match that size in Arts & Letters.

- Brochures and advertisements often require decorative text. In Arts & Letters, you can work with text as a graphic form and mix it in with symbol drawings to create illustrative text effects.
- Charts and graphs can be presented in pictorial ways. Stacked symbol charts allow you to convey data pictorially without complex text labeling or titling. This feature is very useful and visually dynamic as part of an ad layout.

Illustrations

Illustrations can be anything from black and white drawings to full color artworks. The most important capability Arts & Letters offers to illustrators is the natural way in which your sketches are translated into graphic objects and the extraordinary number of editing controls and selections available (Figure 9.18).

Figure 9.18
Illustrations
You can create illustrations by combining figures with ready-made Arts & Letters images and backgrounds or create your own art backgrounds directly using the components in the graphic database. Experiment with different components to sketch out an image using the graphic database before deciding to draw everything from scratch.

Drawing Preferences Drawing preferences allow you to control within a specific pixel range how close the line on the computer screen matches the line you draw by hand. You can opt for a precise translation or allow Arts & Letters to translate your sketched lines into smooth, seamless Bezier curves. You may then quickly reshape the line by moving handles on the screen and see the results immediately.

Color Handling A final consideration is color handling. Arts & Letters remains one of the most powerful products on the PC for doing color work. You can import bitmapped color files to use as backgrounds and design elements in your compositions, and you have at your disposal the best capabilities available for output to a variety of color devices, including high-end imagesetters.

Tips: Illustrations

- One way you can work quickly is to compose with standard or custom symbols and edit them in freeform. Symbols can reduce the amount of work and time you spend drawing and provide a foundation for your finished work.
- Simple manipulation controls such as Rotate, Duplicate, Slant, and resizing with object handles let you view an element in your composition from a variety of aspects.
- Color and object blends are a limitless source of automated effects for layout, design, and object textures. You can create your own textured color backgrounds in Arts & Letters using a combination of shapes, slants, rotated angles, and more.
- Logarithmic Distribution in blending allows you to create dramatic variations on blends in shape and color for interesting effects with text and artwork.

Case Study: Package Design

Arts & Letters was used to design all of the packaging for a new computer product developed by the Schenechtady, New York advertising agency, Egeland, Wood & Zuber. The product was called "ZEW Software for Advertising Agencies" (pronounced "zoo") (Figure 9.19a). In developing the design, the agency took a number of key factors into account, including the overall look of the design and how well it expressed and enhanced the product, the client's budget, and the impact of the design. Would it stand out when placed side by side with other packages on store shelves?

Concept Development The name "ZEW" ("zoo") suggested an animal theme and the decision was made to design the packaging in distinctive zebra stripes. This had the advantage of being striking and, at the same time, require no more than two colors, thus conserving the client's budget.

Figure 9.19 (a and b)
Package Design
This Zebra box design was easy to create in Arts & Letters. The base design was then configured into the various positions necessary to print the box wrapping and related marketing materials.

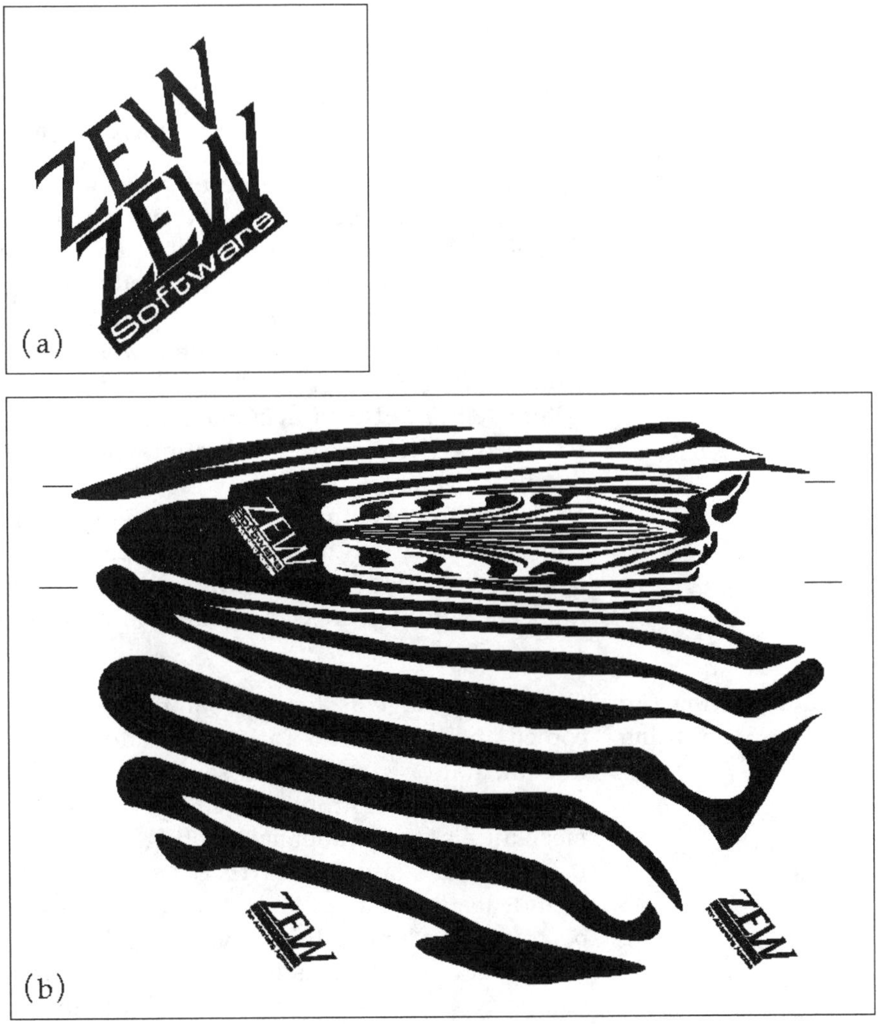

Creating Package Design

To form the basis of the design, a photograph of a zebra's face and neck were scanned and saved as a bitmapped file in .TIF (Tagged Image Format). The bitmapped file was scanned at 300 by 300 dots per inch, which is an acceptable desktop scanning standard, but not acceptable as professional quality. To clarify and manipulate the image, the .TIF files had to be converted into vector graphics so that all line edges and curves could be smoothed to create a more professional form.

The TIFF image of the zebra was imported into Arts & Letters Graphics Editor and converted into vector graphic objects (Figure 9.19b), and saved as an Arts & Letters GED file. This conversion was accomplished using the AutoTrace tool, which traced the bitmapped zebra stripes from the TIFF original and made each into a separate vector object. Once converted to vector form, each stripe could be moved, sized, smoothed, and stretched to form the desired pattern of zebra stripes that would appear on the front, spine, and back of the package.

Logo Text Development

Once the background pattern of zebra stripes had been designed and edited in Arts & Letters, a logo type had to be developed. To do this, the Arts & Letters typeface Quadrille (which resembles Fritz Quadrata) was used. The logo was typed directly into the Arts & Letters screen and letters for the focal point of the logo "ZEW" were sized and grouped. Additional text elements were added, including having the word "Software" set in reverse on a black strip beneath the large-scale letters "ZEW." It was decided that the "W" in "ZEW" needed to be reshaped so that it would look right when the entire logotype was tilted on an angle. The letter form was edited in Arts & Letters in Freeform Mode and the resulting logo was then grouped and saved and matched with the background. The complete package design was printed with crop marks added in. Beginning with source art scanned at 300 dpi, the final package design was printed on a Linotronic 200 imagesetter at 1693 dpi resolution.

Final Editing and Printing

Once the package design was completed, the files used to create it were copied and edited into a variety of additional art pieces, including the documentation cover and diskette labels. All additional artwork was printed on the Linotronic 200 and pasted on boards to create traditional mechanicals for commercial printing.

The benefits offered by Arts & Letters for this graphic design project include its flexibility in importing and tracing bitmapped art, which can be translated into editable vector objects with all the rough edges smoothed out as well as its high degree of flexibility in presenting and editing typefaces. On a production level, the software made it possible for designers to experiment with different ideas much faster than traditional processes permit.

Technical Applications

Technical operations and concepts are often best represented visually. Industries such as aerospace, engineering, computer; scientific applications, such as zoology, medicine, and chemistry; and other technical fields, require pictures. This can save literally thousands of words.

Technical art often requires more precision than most commercial art. Measurements must be accurate and scaled correctly, and details must be precisely pictured. The drawing is developed to help the reader see and interpret precise technical details.

Arts & Letters freeform drawing mode has been designed with technical illustrators in mind (Figure 9.20). The highly developed system of drawing constraints supports a high level of precision both in drawing and editing technical illustrations. Points can be moved to specific coordinates instantly, and lines may be defined to an exact length and angle without a lot of manual micropositioning or "guesstimates" from screen rulers. Drawing features may be customized to support the highest level of precision on the screen; and the output features support extremely high resolution printing for technical drawings, if required.

Figure 9.20 Technical Illustrations
Arts & Letters has detailed editing capabilities on the Construct flyout in the Draw menu that permit micropositioning of points and line elements. This is ideal for technical illustrations and schematics.

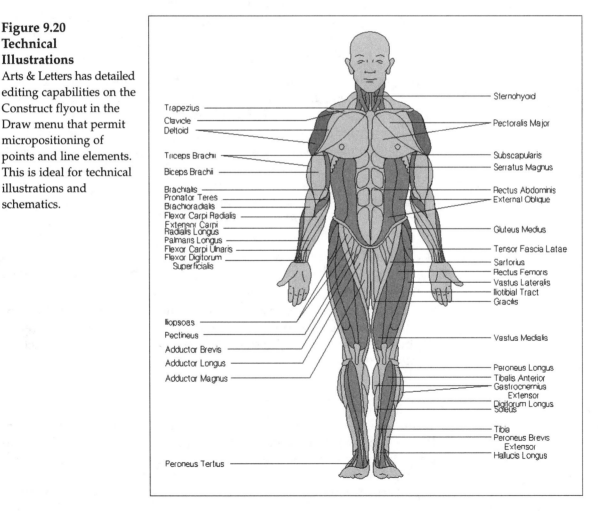

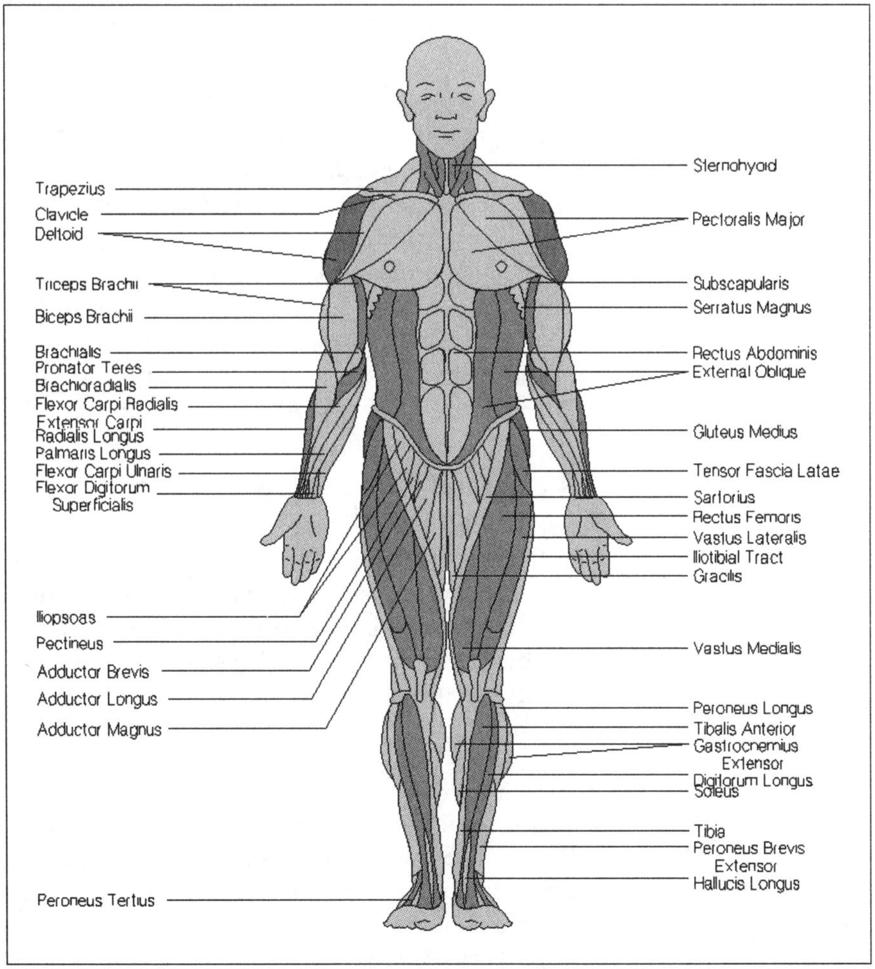

Clip art collections are a convenient way for technical illustrators, particularly those involved in developing schematics or diagrams, to save precise schematic elements and place them on the screen, fully drawn, in seconds. In addition, image collections may be copied and distributed to other users of Arts & Letters who can use exactly the same schematics and ensure consistency among an entire group.

Technical Illustrations

Arts & Letters offers direct support for many technical illustrations in a group of optional symbol libraries. Many of these libraries have been designed to meet the needs of specific technical industries, such as aerospace, and for computers. Others cover such things as medical illustration, zoology, and chemistry (Figure 9.20). Optional symbol libraries are available from Computer Support Corporation, the developers of Arts & Letters, at additional cost.

Tips: Technical Illustrations

- Alignment features are an effective way to combine and place individual elements in relationship to one another. Logical alignment, in particular, allows for instant assembly of a number of standard symbols into complete compositions.
- Use the screen rulers in combination with an active snap-to grid if you need to make precise, measured lines during freeform drawing. The rulers contain tracking lines that mark the cursor position and its exact place on the horizontal and vertical axis on the screen. Properly configured, the snap-to grid will force lines to snap exactly to major measurements on the rulers.
- Save and Recall features control precise relationships between angles, line lengths, perpendicular lines, and the location of specific horizontal and vertical point values.
- Technical drawings on paper can be scanned into Arts & Letters for editing. A scanned file of a drawing on paper may be traced into vector objects in Arts & Letters itself or in an external package such as Adobe Streamline.

Technical Schematics

Technical schematics are a specialized kind of diagram in which relationships between elements in a technical process or product are demonstrated using specialized symbol sets. Arts & Letters offers direct support for certain technical schematic applications including electrical engineering, chemical process flow, and more. Optional libraries contain a custom symbol set for these applications and are directly available from Computer Support Corporation.

Tips: Technical Schematics

- Image collections are an effective way to store individual schematic symbols for easy access on the screen. You can use collections for specialized products or groups of symbols, which can be copied and distributed as standard drawing elements for all individuals involved in schematic drawing.
- The snap-to grid is an effective way to create a live workspace that forces schematic symbols to align to precise points within a grid. This can save you a great deal of time positioning symbols.

The Power of the Imagination

If you had to create a masterpiece from nothing, you'd probably scratch your head for a while, simply because you'd be trying to figure out where to start. Arts & Letters gives you a lot to start with. Shopping through the Clip-Art Manager can give you many ideas for your business and professional communications. Each element you select can then be enhanced with styles and effects and composed with the many ready-made elements and art components.

Express provides a flexible system of graphics for you to work with. When you're solving a graphic design problem, take time to explore the graphic resources, not just the graphic database in the Clip-Art Manager, but the full range of activities and supporting tools available. The more you know about what is available, the more intelligently you can assemble them to get the results you want.

PART THREE

Advanced Operations and Techniques

C H A P T E R 1 0

Express & Windows

Foundation Art

The graphic database in Express can be used as a complete, Windows-wide system for artwork and text. Using the new Clip-Art Server function within the Clip-Art Manager, you can bring a window full of collections and thumbnails over any other Windows program screen and either copy the selected art or place it using OLE. The advantages of the Express system of images, styles, and effects is that, in effect, Arts & Letters becomes a complete graphic menu for each of your Windows programs.

This chapter covers design techniques, operations, and creative suggestions for how to use Arts & Letters with a variety of Windows programs. The central assumption here is that, unlike simple drawing software, Arts & Letters is ideally positioned as a core image database and engine that can be easily used with many major applications.

Fast Track Orientation

Key Concepts

Foundation Art Because Arts & Letters images are designed to work as components, the Express graphic database gives you a richer variety of options and capabilities than random clip-art collections. Commercial clip-art libraries aren't as systematic as this. At best, they are a grab bag of what a given art vendor has available. You can easily select a broad range of images and style them for documents, presentations, charts, listings, and other output created in other Windows programs.

OLE Client An OLE Client program is one that accepts embedded or linked OLE objects. Most word processors, spreadsheets, databases, and publishing software include OLE Client technology. OLE Client operations are generally activated using the Paste or Paste Special command on the Edit menu. Arts & Letters images may be placed as OLE objects in any Windows package that is an OLE Client.

OLE Server An OLE Server program is one that generates OLE objects. Express is an OLE Server, under Version 1.0 of OLE technology. Many programs are both OLE Client and Server. (You should verify from the program documentation what the configuration is.) Express is only an OLE Server and cannot function as a client. That is, you cannot place OLE objects created in other Windows programs inside Express.

Paste as Bitmap The Cut, Copy, and Paste features in Windows programs form the activating toolkit for OLE objects. You retain the option of not using OLE and pasting Express artwork as a bitmap in external Windows programs. In this configuration, Windows will place any selection you copy from Arts & Letters into another Windows program as a bitmapped artwork. You will lose the vector components in the art and it will not be as easy to edit.

Tools

Clip Art Server When the Always On Top option in the Clip-Art Manager System menu (the menu button at the far upper-left corner) is selected, the Clip-Art Manager floats on top of the screen (Figure 10.1). It will also flow on top of other Windows programs, allowing you to select a thumbnail, copy it, and then either paste it as a bitmap to another Windows program, or use Paste Special for an OLE object.

Cut, Copy, and Paste Cut, Copy, and Paste are virtually universal features in Windows. They are the port of access to the central Windows Clipboard. When you Copy or Cut any selected graphic or text in any program, it is sent to the Windows Clipboard where you can then Paste it as many times or to as many places as you like before the next Cut/Copy operation displaces it. In Windows for Workgroups, you get the more robust Clipbook, which allows you to retain Cut/Copy blocks and share them for Paste operations over the network.

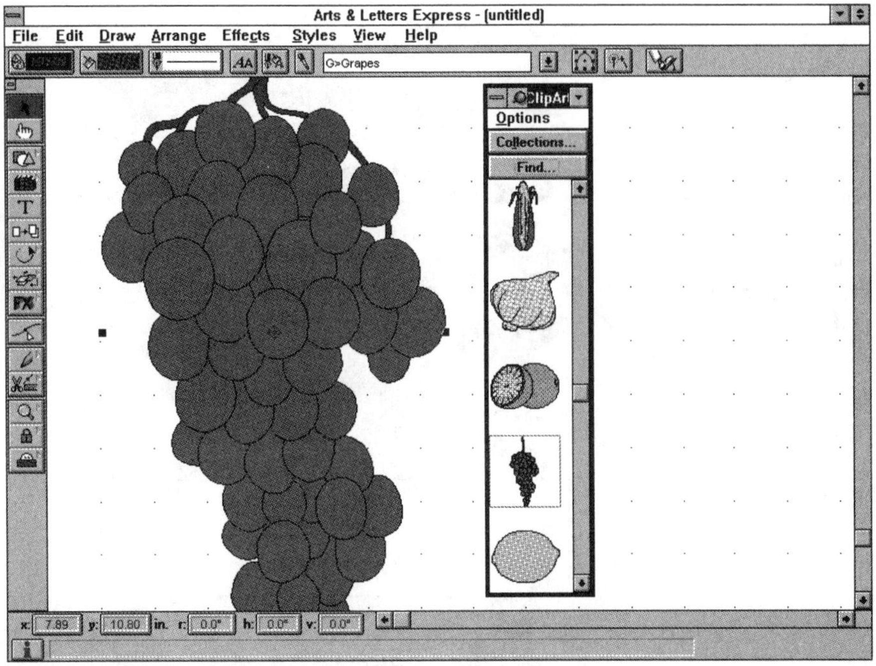

Figure 10.1
Clip-Art Server
When the Clip-Art Manager is set to Always On Top (a feature available on the System menu at the upper-left corner of the dialog box) and the thumbnail display is set to Only, you get this floating column of selectable images that can be placed into any Windows program.

Bitmap Tracing Bitmap tracing is a feature that allows you to convert a bitmapped image, such as a scanned picture in TIFF format, into a vector graphic format made up of graphic objects. Arts & Letters includes its own on-board bitmap tracing capability that allows you to directly import TIFF files into the screen and read the line and forms within them into graphic objects, which are manipulable using the full capabilities of Arts & Letters itself.

Import/Export The Import/Export system in Arts & Letters and other Windows programs still provides you with a highly accurate and effective means of sharing information between programs. You may export Express artwork to a standard file format and then load it through import filters into another file. This is particularly effective when PostScript export and import is used: You can export even complex compositions to a PostScript file and import them into other programs, and realize very high quality output printing of both art forms and text.

Linking to Other Programs

To take full advantage of Arts & Letters, think of it as your central resource for art in support of all the other applications you are currently

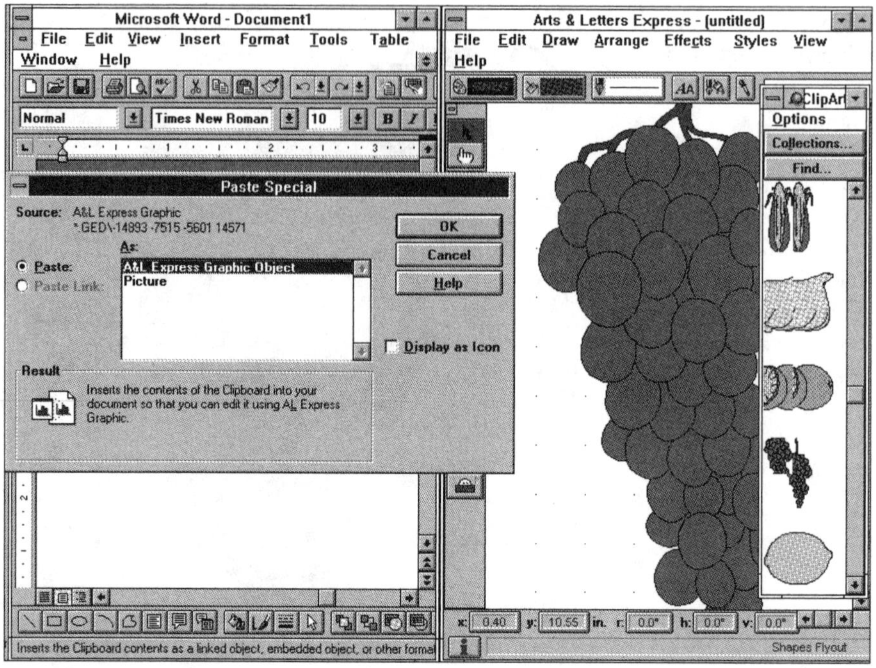

Figure 10.2 Linking to Other Programs
The grapes in Express are ready to become an object in Microsoft Word. When placed in Word as an object, you can summon Express to edit the image by simply clicking on the grapes in the Word page.

producing with other software programs (Figure 10.2). If you are currently publishing with Ventura and PageMaker, Arts & Letters allows you to create anything you need for your Ventura and PageMaker documents and export them in a compatible format to be ready for use in minutes. If you are interested in producing art for presentation graphics, use Arts & Letters to develop the art and use a program such as Show Partner or Microsoft Powerpoint to automate it into a complete slideshow.

Graphic Database vs. Clip Art

The value of Arts & Letters to Windows is that the database of art forms is ready to use in a moment's notice. Much has been made in this book about the difference between Arts & Letters art forms and traditional clip art, and for good reason. Clip art is, by definition, not highly editable. Arts & Letters symbols are ready-made frameworks for you to create your own variations. This principle is very powerful when placed in the context of daily business deadlines, constant changes, last-minute edits, and so forth. In many if not most cases, when you are developing applications in your art package, you don't have the luxury or time to start with a blank screen. Most conventional drawing programs don't really have a way to help you out of that dilemma. Arts & Letters does.

Word Processing Packages

Word processing packages under Windows have evolved from sober business typing tools into a Big Top full of clowns, jugglers, and sideshows. Despite the many add-ons and (pardon the expression) outright gimmicks, Windows word processors have come into their own as full-featured business tools. The core of any Windows word processor is the graphical interface and the integrated typography and formatting system.

In the new Windows OLE and integrated technologies, word processors are the host application for a company's output documents. They are relatively simple to use, page driven, and now include the almost obligatory table grid feature, which allows them to double as simple spreadsheets. The leading word processors also have borrowed a couple of key publishing features, such as editable frames for picture art and systems for text styles to give you greater control over typography

Word for Windows, Version 6.0

Microsoft's word processor comes dressed up with a full complement of features and a crisp screen design. This package bristles with add-ons. Its only real rival is WordPerfect for Windows. Word even includes a built-in, vector-based Draw package and a variety of available clip-art files. However, there is nothing here that can rival the collection of art included with Express. And, you can use Express to provide you with an immense library of ready-made images that will work in Word.

Word is also fitted out with the latest in OLE technology, Version 2.0. The short statement is that your Express objects will work fine here. (Even though Express is Version 1.0 OLE, there are no compatibility problems or issues.)

WordPerfect for Windows, Version 6.0

WordPerfect built its reputation on service. It has dominated the marketplace for word processing for years with a product that is complicated yet user friendly. WordPerfect for Windows puts many options on its menus and makes extensive use of cascades so you can find and execute even esoteric features directly from the screen. The screen design of the product is superb. No other vendor has really matched the quality of WordPerfect's interface button bars, all of which are customizable and allow you to assign features, your macros, and more directly to the button bar for easy access. Even the Open dialog box—an afterthought in most packages—is a fully articulated file management system that lets you perform sophisticated File Manager functions right from the point where you load files.

WordPerfect for Windows includes a bank of ready-made artworks. Most of them are simple ornaments or practical labels and enhancements. Coupled with the 10,000 images in the Express graphic database, you can create some sophisticated publishing effects within your WordPerfect documents (Figure 10.3).

Steps: Paste Express Art as a Bitmap to Word or WordPerfect

Use this operation to paste a selected Arts & Letters page, selected objects, or selected area as a bitmap into a Word or WordPerfect document.

1. Select Express art to be copied.
2. Access **Edit | Copy**.
3. Display Word or WordPerfect.
4. Click in text or in page where you wish to paste the art.
5. Select **Edit | Paste**.

To paste a selected Arts & Letters page, selected objects, or selected area as an object into a WordPerfect document, in Step 5, select **Edit | Paste Special**, and select A&L Express graphic object.

Figure 10.3 WordPerfect for Windows
The Arts & Letters object displays in the WordPerfect screen where you can design, layout, and publish just about any document you want. WordPerfect includes its own graphic features and subsystems; Express provides the database of graphics.

Spreadsheets and Databases

Despite their different business functions, spreadsheets and databases work in much the same way. They store data in discrete chunks and allow you maximum control of data to derive specific results. Relational, or grid-based, databases are coming into currency under Windows, and these are presented much like a spreadsheet, with the data in rows and columns. Links can be built between addresses in the respective grids allowing for higly integrated access and connection to data.

Data and Graphics

Spreadsheets and databases are more data-focused than word-processors; because of their grid layout, they are not used for applications that are art-intensive. However, they do make substantial use of artwork in a number of specialized areas.

Charts and Reports Given the competition under Windows these days, database and spreadsheet packages are becoming more self-contained with their own art and composition features. You can go into a spreadsheet like Excel and have a lot of the page composition features, as well as graphics, to make reports and charts. Similarly, Windows databases include not only the traditional data reporting structures, but complete page design functions so you can typeset the database report within the one program. Arts & Letters provides many simple but invaluable page composition frames, icons, and diagramming visuals that are available on demand through the Clip-Art Server.

Cell-Embedded Artwork OLE technology allows you to store artwork within a database cell. This capability permits a data record to contain a field to hold OLE video, audio, graphic, or other objects. So, in a real estate database, one cell could contain a play-on-demand video clip of the house in the data record. For a variety of other applications, such as a parts catalog, the database record can contain OLE objects with graphic representations of each part. The extensive collection of icons and customizable art forms in Express can be used to create an art database, as well as flowcharts and diagram components. Using a graphic scanner, you can also capture visual information, edit it in Express, and load into a cell storage in an external database.

Microsoft Excel

Excel has access to the Microsoft Draw system used in Word (the most space-saving way to install these two together is through the Microsoft Office system), but, as noted, this system is simple business art. When combined with the full graphic database in Arts & Letters, you have a set of composable art forms that can add picture power and enhancement to Excel charts. You have the option to add Express images directly to charts generated in Excel, or convert Excel data to be processed in the Express Chart engine, and place the resulting chart as an object in the source Excel spreadsheet.

Lotus Approach for Windows

Lotus Approach for Windows is a full-featured and practical database that almost anyone can use without training or armies of consultants. In a flash of wisdom, the Approach developers did not develop a unique data storage format for the product. Rather, they used filters for all the prevailing industry standards, including dBASE, Paradox, FoxPro, Oracle, and more, to store data, and created a graphic overlay file, called a VEW file, to display whatever data you have created in whatever format.

Approach Graphics

Approach lets you paste pictures into database VEW files as design objects or paste pictures into specially configured Picture Plus fields. The Picture Plus field is a designation assigned to the field characteristics, like Text, Numeric, and so forth. So, you can store data in fields or to ornament reports you generate with Approach data.

Folio Views, Version 3

Folio Views is something of an anomaly: a database that works like a word processor, or a word processor that thinks like a database. This is a new-generation type of software that treats paragraph text with all the structure and local control that is associated with databases. You can import text from other applications and it will automatically be indexed and fitted out with an on-demand electronic table of contents. As you select lines in the table of contents, text is instantly displayed. Using many hot access features, you can access as much as a complete book inside a Folio Views information base.

Folio Views accepts graphics just like a Folio Views processor or publishing package. The form of the data is paragraphs just like any book. You can load individual Express artworks, or complete compositions as you need (Figure 10.4).

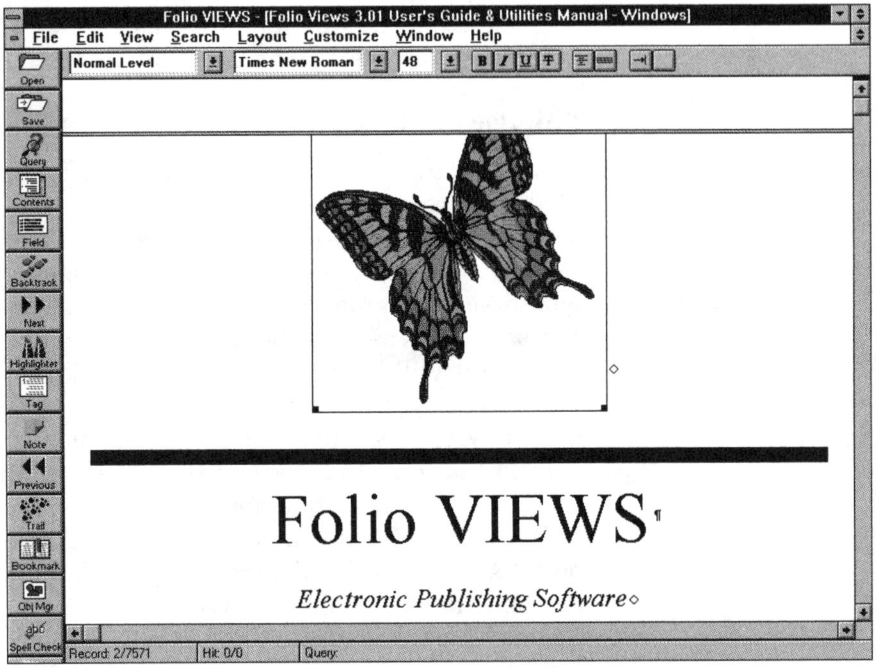

Figure 10.4
Folio Views
This interactive word processor thinks like a database. You can paste artworks here just like you would in any word processor or publishing document. You can also build dynamic links to all your pictures and display them on demand electronically.

Steps: Paste Express Art as a Bitmap or as an Object to Excel, Lotus, or Folio Views

Use this operation to paste a selected Arts & Letters page, selected objects, or selected area as a bitmap into an Excel, Lotus, or Folio Views document.

1. Select Express art to be copied.
2. Access **Edit | Copy**.
3. Display Folio Views.
4. Click in text or in page where you wish to paste the art.
5. Select **Edit | Paste**.

To paste a selected Arts & Letters page, selected objects, or selected area as an object into a Folio Views document, in Step 5, select **Edit | Paste Special**, and select A&L Express graphic object.

Graphics Packages

Arts & Letters is an ideal companion to other Windows graphics package, because none of them can equal the quality and integrated design of Arts & Letters graphic database. Off-the-shelf clip-art collections are the common coin of the graphics marketplace. But off-the-shelf clip art is not customizable, and accordingly not very useful.

CorelDraw! Version 4

Corel has always been great at handling type. Dating back to the late 1980s when it was a DOS utility called Corel Headline, its main business was creating display type. Today it is a Windows staple, and has become a multi-product system that includes a separate paint package, type design program, presentation package, and other units. Corel, of course, also owns Ventura Publisher (the software used to produce this book) and will be advancing new versions of that product as well. Corel has artwork by the numbers, but nothing to approach an integrated system of clip art. It includes some of the better off-the-shelf clip-art libraries, but none of these are designed with the integrated composition and combination capability of Arts & Letters.

Corel's drawing features are similar to Arts & Letters so you can export A&L art into CorelDraw, or export CorelDraw images and text into Arts & Letters. CorelDraw's typeface controls and design tools are excellent. Working together, the two packages let you create extraordinary results.

Visio, Version 2

Express began life in the '80s based on a package designed to draw schematics. Like flowcharts, engineering diagrams are a type of art in which individual components are connected, and edited, in related structures. The connections between each art component creates a set of relationships that communicate an idea. Express evolved into a full art and illustration package, but without developing elaborate flowchart systems and subsystems.

Windows Charting

Visio is a new Windows package designed as a charting and mapping package. Visio comes with a set of predefined art components grouped by tasks into Stencils. There is a stencil for flowcharting, organization charts, office space allocation, engineering applications, and more. Visio, however, does not include general art and composition functions. It is designed specifically to focus on certain types of business-related art. Arts & Letters is an ideal companion to Visio, because both packages are based on a system of composable objects. You can create new Stencil groups in Visio and use Arts & Letters' 10,000 images with Visio to create more. In addition, Express artwork can be used to generate backgrounds or to highlight Visio designs.

Adobe Photoshop

There are a variety of dedicated scanning packages available, and most scanner hardware vendors include some kind of package with a scanning device. Generally, standalone graphic scanning packages are not as good as full-featured image- and photo-editing software. The package setting all the standards is Adobe Photoshop.

Image Editing and Filters

Photoshop not only includes complete scanning drivers and supporting software, it is arguably the best editing system in the business for scanned bitmapped images (Figure 10.5). Photoshop was designed to provide a professional image editing and effects system. The result is a full-featured package that includes standard bitmap and color editing functions. Photoshop also pioneered the use of specialty effects filters that function like an electronic airbrush. A variety of products have adopted Adobe's filter technology, making it possible for you to purchase custom and add-in filters that manipulate bitmaps in a variety of sophisticated ways to create textures, patterns, and twists on bitmapped images and photographs.

Graphic Components

Photoshop actually can blur the point where a photograph ends and graphic arts begin. Its powerful texturing and image-editing tools allow you to use a photograph as a basis for an artwork. Accordingly, Express

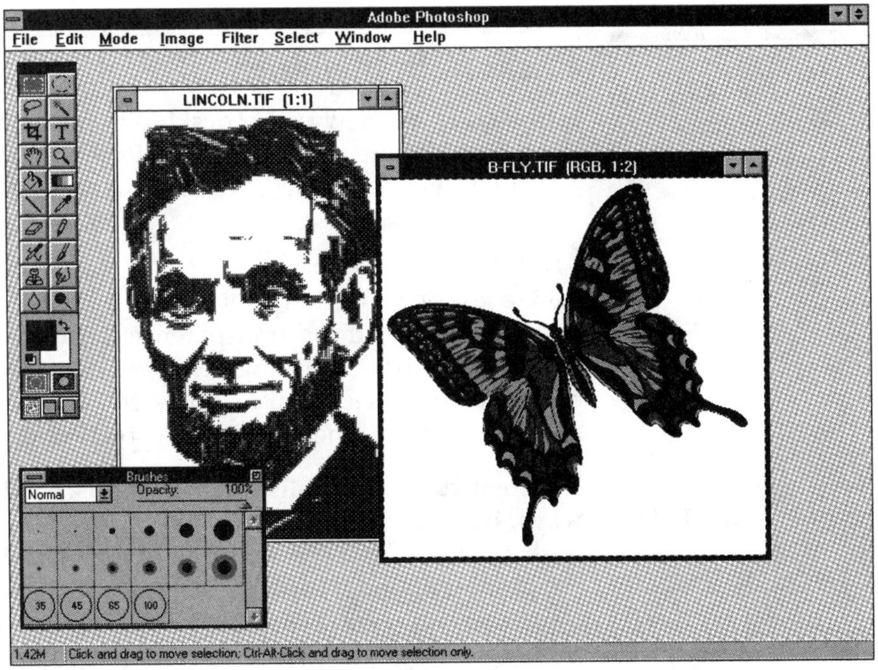

Figure 10.5 Photoshop
The leading photo and image editing package lets you scan, edit, and enhance images with a variety of visual filters. Express provides thousands of composable components that can be used very effectively in developing compositions in Photoshop.

and the graphic database have many elements that can be used productively with Photoshop. Express has thousands of simple line drawings and geometrics that can be used as shape frames for photographic elements, and it has ready-made art images that can be combined into complete compositions in Photoshop. Elaborate picture framing elements, cartoons, and composable backgrounds all can be used in combination with photographic components to create powerful images that use the full set of Photoshop's composition tools.

Steps: Paste Express Art as a Bitmap or as an Object to CorelDraw, Visio, or Photoshop

Use this operation to paste a selected Arts & Letters page, selected objects, or selected area as a bitmap into a CorelDraw, Visio, or Photoshop document.

1. Select Express art to be copied.
2. Access **Edit | Copy**.
3. Display CorelDraw, Visio, or Photoshop.
4. Click in text or in page where you wish to paste the art.
5. Select **Edit | Paste**.

To paste a selected Arts & Letters page, selected objects, or selected area as an object into a Photoshop document, in Step 5, select **Edit | Paste Special**, and select A&L Express graphic object.

Desktop Publishing

In the space of a few years, desktop publishing programs like Ventura Publisher, IBM Interleaf, and Aldus PageMaker have brought extraordinary publishing capabilities to individuals as well as companies.

Publishing Packages

Where text developed in Arts & Letters is generally for display applications, such as overhead transparencies, slides, signs, and similar applications, desktop publishing packages allow you to publish and print complete books, technical manuals, brochures, magazines, newsletters, and virtually any other application you desire.

Graphic Arts Integration Filters

Different desktop publishing programs handle art files in different ways, but all of them have a means to accept files from outside art packages like Arts & Letters. Two of the most common line-art, or vector graphic, import formats are Encapsulated PostScript (EPS) and Computer Graphics Metafile (CGM). Desktop publishing applications running under Microsoft Windows including Aldus PageMaker and

Ventura Publisher (Windows version), may accept files loaded through file filters or directly via the Windows Clipboard.

Corel Ventura Publisher

Ventura Publisher is the most powerful publishing package for the PC. Its features and capabilities are superb for the design and production of books and technical documents, for published database listings, as well as for a plethora of general business documents like reports, proposals, memoranda, and more.

Ventura Graphic File Support

Ventura is built around an open architecture that can accept files from external graphics packages in a variety of output formats. Through the Load Text/Picture option on the File menu, Ventura contains a selection of import filters supporting Arts & Letters vector-graphic export formats including Computer Graphics Metafile (CGM) and Encapsulated PostScript (EPS) formats. You may generate drawings or illustrations in Ventura and export either the page or selected objects on the screen to either of these formats, which Ventura will read and display on the screen. Arts & Letters allows you to include a file header in TIFF or WMF format when you export an EPS file. Ventura, however, has trouble reading these file headers, so it is best to export EPS files from Arts & Letters to Ventura with neither header option selected. Ventura also accepts importation of TIFF files and several other bit-mapped formats. You may export Arts & Letters files to a TIFF format for black and white and color applications.

Steps: Paste Express Art as a Bitmap or as an Object to Ventura

Use this operation to paste a selected Arts & Letters page, selected objects, or selected area into a Ventura document.

1. Select Express art to be copied.
2. Access **Edit | Copy**.
3. Display Ventura.
4. Click in text or in page where you wish to paste the art.
5. Select **Edit | Paste Object** for an object, or select **Edit | Paste Special** and select Bitmap.
6. Enter the filename for the pasted object when prompted.
7. Select **OK**. Verify that the art is displayed.

Aldus PageMaker for Windows

Aldus PageMaker is the most venerable of the popular-priced desktop publishing programs. In its original Macintosh format, it helped to spark the desktop publishing revolution by offering a set of easy-to-use page layout capabilities that enabled users to easily integrate text and graphics. PageMaker has traditionally been used more for design applications which require more control over the positioning of text and graphics. It is generally used for brochures, advertisements, and flyers, although the truly determined can use it to produce longer applications, like books. With the expected addition of new, more powerful publishing features under Version 5.0, PageMaker can more easily accommodate larger and longer applications.

PageMaker accepts files from external packages through a set of file filters loaded at the time of installation. File formats, including WMF, CGM, TIFF, and EPS can be loaded into the page using the **Place** command on the **File** menu.

Steps: Paste Express Art as a Bitmap to PageMaker

Use this operation to paste a selected Arts & Letters page, selected objects, or selected area as a bitmap into a PageMaker document.

1. Select Express art to be copied.
2. Access **Edit | Copy**.
3. Display PageMaker.
4. Select **Edit | Paste**.
5. Select **OK**. Verify that the art is displayed.

Steps: Paste Express Art as an Object to PageMaker

Use this operation to paste a selected Arts & Letters page, selected objects, or selected area as an object into a PageMaker document.

1. Select Express art to be copied.
2. Access **Edit | Copy**.
3. Display PageMaker.
4. Click in text or in page where you wish to paste the art.
5. Select **Edit | Paste Special**, select A&L Express graphic.
6. Select **Paste**. Verify that the art is displayed.

QuarkXPress for Windows

For the past few years, the chief rival to PageMaker in the Macintosh corral has been QuarkXPress. This elegantly designed desktop publishing solution works very much like a graphics package. It is widely noted for the clarity of its page layout features and the flexibility of the design it supports. Quark allows you to draw non-rectangular illustration frames—circles, freeform graphics, trapezoids—and flow text around them. You may also save graphic components you create in

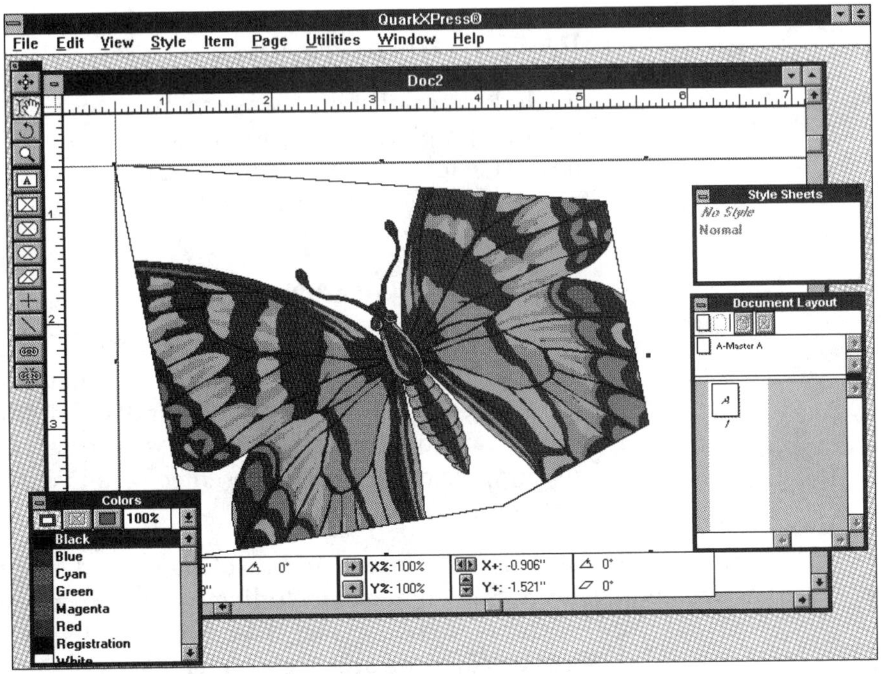

Figure 10.6
QuarkXpress
This package lets you manipulate and shape objects into the page much more fluidly than most other packages. It also includes a feature that lets you save components as you create them (like the Express Clip-Art Manager).

Quark in a special library system very similar to the Arts & Letters Clip-Art Manager (Figure 10.6).

Superior type handling is supported by a well-articulated graphics and object-management system that lets you freely position elements in the page. Art objects may be turned and positioned through continuous angles of rotation—not the static, 90 degree increments that are common in simpler packages.

Steps: Paste Express Art as a Bitmap to QuarkXPress

Use this operation to paste a selected Arts & Letters page, selected objects, or selected area as a Bitmap into a Quark document.

1. Select Express art to be copied.
2. Access **Edit | Copy**.
3. Display Quark.
4. Draw frame to hold graphic and select it.
5. Select **Edit | Paste**.
6. Select **OK**. Verify art is displayed.

To paste a selected Arts & Letters page, selected objects, or selected area as an object into a Quark document, in Step 5, select **Edit | Paste Special**, and select A&L Express graphic; in Step 6, select **Paste**. Verify art is displayed.

Presentation Graphics

If "desktop publishing" was the buzzword of the Eighties, then "presentation graphics" is the term humming at the beginning of the Nineties. The term "presentation graphics," like "desktop publishing" before it, conceals much more than it communicates.

Presentation Packages

There are many different facets to presentation media, such as overhead transparencies, foils, color slides and animated slide-shows that present still images in a timed sequence, and so on. But presentation graphics may mean something else too. Essentially, presentation graphics are any graphic applications presented to a live audience or via electronic media.

Presentation Components

Graphics, charts, art, and text lists created for presentations are used in business documents, including reports, memoranda, and press releases, by corporations for a speaker to distribute printed copies of overheads or slides to those attending a meeting.

Microsoft Powerpoint

Microsoft Powerpoint is one of a new generation of desktop presentation products that, purportedly, allows you to generate an entire presentation without using any other software. It includes a spelling checker, text handler, built-in graphing capability, and a library of—count 'em—400 clip-art images. Users of Arts & Letters may find some of the slide-making capabilities of interest, but essentially, on every level of composition, you have more power to create artistically interesting slides within Arts & Letters. What is of interest here is the slide-show capability, which can be used to sequence and control the presentation of Arts & Letters files and develop highly professional color graphic presentations.

Steps: Paste Express Art as a Bitmap to Powerpoint

Use this operation to paste a selected Arts & Letters page, selected objects, or selected area into a Powerpoint document.

1. Select Express art to be copied.
2. Access **Edit | Copy**.
3. Display Powerpoint.
4. Click area in open file where art is to be pasted.

5. Select **Edit | Paste**.
6. Select **OK**. Verify art is displayed.

Steps: Paste Express Art as an Object to Powerpoint

Use this operation to paste a selected Arts & Letters page, selected objects, or selected area into a Powerpoint document.

1. Select Express art to be copied.
2. Access **Edit | Copy**.
3. Display Powerpoint.
4. Click in text or in page where you wish to paste the art.
5. Select **Edit | Paste Special**, select A&L Express Graphic.
6. Select **Paste**. Verify art is displayed.

Aldus Persuasion

Persuasion is part of the integrated family of Aldus Publishing products designed specifically for presentations. Persuasion makes use of a unique outline-based approach that allows you to convert a text outline into a set of presentation slides. Persuasion works very much like its cousin, PageMaker, does, and provides many of the same editing features and assumption in designing presentation pages. You have the option here to create entire slide layouts in Arts & Letters and use Persuasion as the showing device, or you can send components here to be combined with text and other elements created in Persuasion itself.

Steps: Paste Express Art as a Bitmap to Persuasion

Use this operation to paste a selected Arts & Letters page, selected objects, or selected area into a PageMaker document.

1. Select Express art to be copied.
2. Access **Edit | Copy**.
3. Display Persuasion.
4. Display file to receive artwork.
5. Verify View is set to Slide.
6. Select **Edit | Paste**.
7. Select **OK**. Verify art is displayed.

Slide-Show Output to Videotape

Up to this point, the slide-show options for presentation graphics discussed have been *computer-driven*. That is, the presentation must take place within your computer system, running under a specific piece of software, or running from a run-time command program on a diskette. While these are wonderful capabilities, the number of computer systems adequately equipped with the right hardware, color display, and other components necessary to run your slide show pales in comparison to the number of video cassette recorders (VCRs) in this country. The VCR is the most popular recordable color presentation technology today. Wouldn't it be great if you could make a really excellent slide presentation, sequence it into a slide show, and port that to videotape—without spending a fortune?

Presenter Plus Sound

Presenter Plus Sound is a unique, highly portable device that allows you to convert the VGA output on your computer screen to the screen configuration of a standard television set. You basically use this device as an electronic bridge from your computer's parallel port to the input jacks on the TV set or VCR. This allows you to create entire running presentations with a Powerpoint or Persuasion and play them right onto a videocasette. The obvious advantage of technology like this is that it not only bypasses the costs of transferring your computer disk, it also saves you time.

Multimedia Programs

Multimedia is the next evolution in computer technology. Until the advent of popular desktop publishing packages like Ventura and PageMaker, you developed your work, saved it in a file format defined by the software, and then (in most cases) printed it. Desktop publishing packages were the first integrated software packages designed to combine the output of other programs, including importing files for graphics, data, lists, and text, and using a large set of file filters. The user could then assemble complete documents using files created in all the familiar packages a customer was using.

Media Integration

Where the publishing package assembled all the components into document pages, multimedia packages tend to build an interactive structure or map. You can then display text, graphics, animation, video, text, and combinations of these components in a seamless, integrated show, or presentation.

Graphic Components for Multimedia Express is a natural graphic feeder for multimedia. Many programs have a lot of static and disposable clip-art images, while Express offers a set of building blocks, including frames, abstracts, figures, backgrounds, and more. This component-based approach is ideal for multimedia. Select the components you want and combine them to fit your particular design and production requirements.

Animation Blocks Express artwork also is ideal for animation functions. Computer animation basically involves moving objects in space: Show a static airplane or string of text moving across the screen space; show a single object growing in size and filling the screen, or shrinking to a tiny dot. Actual object animation is possibile as well, particularly using the Flex-Art dinosaurs and space images included with Express. Using animation packages, you can select elements within a figure drawing—legs, arms, jaws—and make them move naturally by manipulating these elements and creating movement sequences in the software.

Multimedia Toolbook

Multimedia is something like a wild west technical frontier. Many of the applications that have been developed arise from custom programming by deep tech-heads. Toolbook is designed to make an end run around this problem by providing a multimedia publishing and development platform to assemble full multimedia presentations, reference applications (such as encyclopedias), and for customized multimedia front ends for existing programs.

Dynamic Link Libraries Toolbook allows you to do all this by providing a framework of pages to create a multimedia "document" as well as the ability to access and control Windows Dynamic Link Libraries (DLL) files. Windows is notable for the way it has changed programming. Most programs, including Express, are written in components. The main program file is called an executable (EXE) file, and special feature groups, for example, the type features, are stored in "plug in" DLL modules. Toolbook gives you the ability to activate and use multimedia DLL files as part of your program. You can literally assemble active program components that perform certain tasks and build them in to create a multimedia document that you can operate just like a regular computer program.

Express and Toolbook Express artwork can be imported or pasted in a Toolbook document. You can use Express as a system of graphics to support multimedia applications generated in Toolbook. (See Steps head after Icon Author; below.)

Asymmetrix Compel

Compel is produced by Asymmetrix, the people who gave you Toolbook. It is designed specifically as a presentation package, just like Powerpoint and Persuasion. The key difference is that Compel is designed to accept multimedia components including animations, voice and sound clips, video components, and more. The architecture of the program is exactly like the slideshow formats used by the leading presentation packages.

Compel integrates many of the new presentation technologies under one roof and makes it possible to take even a large presentation on the road. The program allows you to break up large media files into chunks that can be copied to disk and moved to a laptop for portable presentation. Express serves this software exactly as it does any presentation or publishing system—as a databank of components that can be combined easily into larger and more sophisticated compositions.

Icon Author: HSC Interactive

Before multimedia there was CBT (Computer Based Training). CBT programs were the development engines that made it possible to create user-operable computer documents. Primarily, CBT programs were used to develop user-driven kiosk displays and educational programs. The user is presented with a topic and an array of options and then taken step by step through a lesson plan (Figure 10.7).

Flowchart Design Icon Author does not create multimedia presentations as slides, as does Compel. It lets you build a flowchart of individual components and control how these components interact and map to each other. Building the flowchart lets you control relationships between media and combine a variety of data elements including text, graphics, animation, sound, video, database elements, spreadsheet data, and more. Icon Author is available in a powerful presentation version called HSC Interactive, which contains the hottest presentation features, but *not* some of the more complex, high-end programming features.

Editing Systems The main Icon Author development screen lets you assemble the flowchart. The software comes with a set of editing components that let you draw screen designs, set text components, place buttons, and create animations. You can assemble animations from simple shape movements in space to more complex effects and then integrate them into the whole show. You may bring Express graphics directly into the Icon

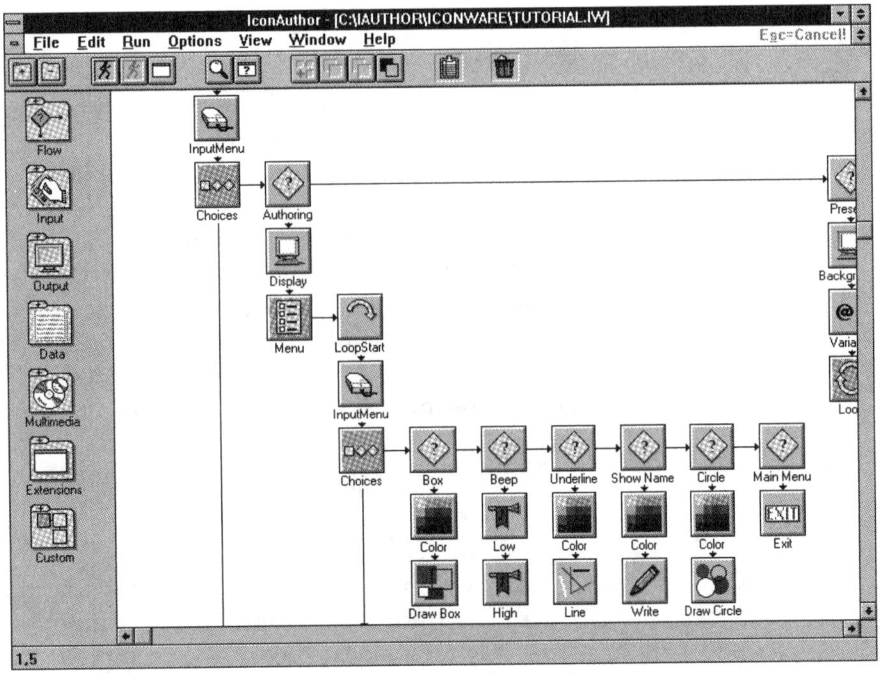

Figure 10.7
Icon Author
The flowchart is the matrix for the multimedia show. You can use Express artwork in the Graphics Editor and even use Express components in the special Animation editor program.

Author Graphics Editor for use in creating screen and text designs using Cut/Copy/Paste features.

Steps: Paste Express Art as a Bitmap to Icon Author

Use this operation to paste a selected Arts & Letters page, selected objects, or selected area into the Icon Author Graphics Editor.

1. Select Express art to be copied.
2. Access **Edit | Copy**.
3. Display Icon Author.
4. Click area in open file where art is to be pasted.
5. Select **Edit | Paste**.
6. Select **OK**. Verify that the art is displayed.

To paste a selected Arts & Letters page, selected objects, or selected area as an object into a Compel document, in Step 5, select **Edit | Paste Special**, and select A&L Express Graphic; in Step 6, select Paste. Verify that the art is displayed.

Working with Scanned Files

A scanner is an electronic page reader. It translates whatever it sees into a pattern of dots that are stored into a bitmapped computer file. Scanners have been around the desktop publishing and computer graphics marketplace for a long time, and are a commonplace item.

In the past few years, scanners for the PC have begun to evolve in complexity and quality to the point that you can now scan line art files, highly textured black-and-white artwork, and color images. Arts & Letters can make use of all of these capabilities; therefore, a scanner will enable you to make much more effective use of the program. Essentially, a scanner allows you to import just about any art that exists in hard copy (keep the U.S. copyright laws in mind, though). And, with that kind of power, Arts & Letters can do anything you want.

Book Clip-Art

One of the richest sources for clip art is not in a computer field, but in books. The traditional graphic arts business has used book clip-art for years. It is presented in books with complete ready-made drawings, usually developed as finished art designed for insertion with no editing.

Scanning Art You can scan book clip-art into individual computer files using a scanner and then auto-trace them in Arts & Letters for editing on the screen. Keep in mind that once in Arts & Letters format, you can combine any image you find in a book of clip art with all the symbols that exist with Arts & Letters itself. This enables you to combine book and Arts & Letters art forms and save them in a symbol library.

Scanning Drawings If you are uncomfortable with sketching on the computer screen, or you wish to achieve effects of shading and nuance not possible using the computer, you can draw on paper and scan it.

Scanned sketches can be auto-traced into Arts & Letters form so that you can bring all features into play to finish the drawing or integrate it into an already existing composition.

Bitmap Tracing Operations

The Arts & Letters auto-trace operations offer simplicity and power. The basic concept is to import a bitmapped file in one of the supported formats, such as TIFF. The file will appear in the screen in its complete form; however, it will not be editable in Arts & Letters until the lines and shapes in it have been traced and can be recognized by Arts & Letters as graphic objects.

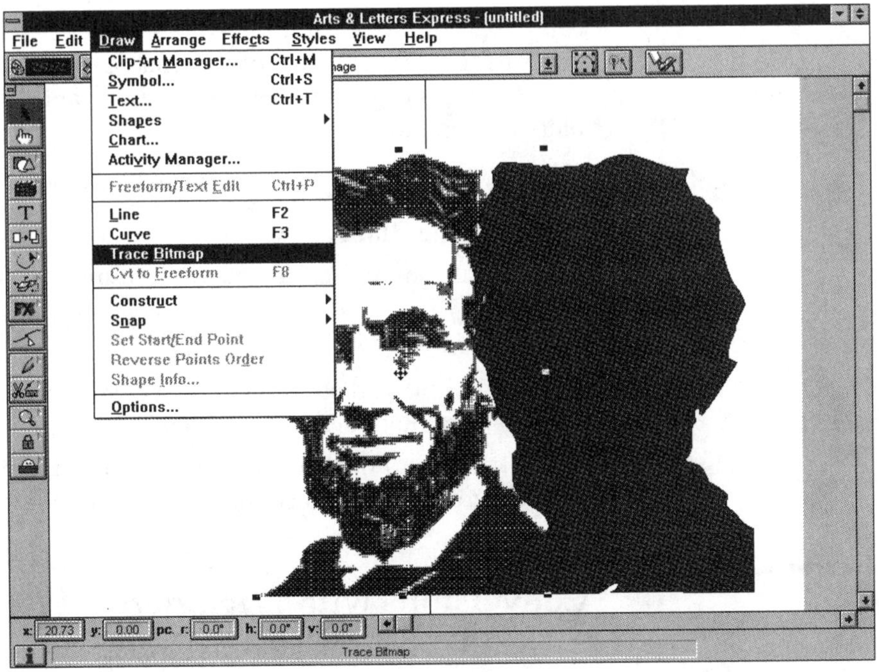

Figure 10.8
Auto-Tracing
Touch the tracing cursor to the line in the bitmap file and it automatically generates a freeform line following the shape. Auto-tracing lets you bring forms from bitmaps into Express-editable format.

Auto-Tracing

To trace a bitmapped image in Arts & Letters, it must be a monochrome or black and white image (Figure 10.8). Uncompressed files will trace more quickly than compressed images. A math coprocessor version of Arts & Letters is available and will dramatically increase tracing performance and also speed up other aspects of the program. Tracing with the coprocessor version is approximately four times faster than without it. With the bitmap tracing features, you have a great deal of control over the quality of the traced image. Keep in mind that tracing is, in effect, automated freeform drawing. You can set up your drawing preferences in the **Preferences** dialog box of the **Draw** menu for faster tracing, more precise tracing, and so forth, just as you would set parameters for freeform drawing.

Select and Auto-Trace Line Forms

To auto-trace the bitmapped image, enable the auto-trace cursor using the **Trace Bitmap** option on the **Draw** menu. Once selected, you may click the auto-trace tool on any line within the drawing and Arts & Letters will automatically generate a freeform line matching the original. You must continue to select line forms within the drawing until the complete drawing has been traced.

Once the traced freeform objects are on the screen, they may be moved and edited. The original TIFF file is no longer necessary. Auto-tracing is a complex technical operation, so it tends to be memory intensive. If you don't have sufficient memory available, you may get an overload message saying that you ran out of memory and Arts & Letters can't complete the operation.

Steps: Bitmap Tracing

Use this operation to trace line forms in a bitmapped image in Express.

1. Access **File | Import**.
2. Select format of the file you wish to import, such as TIFF.
3. Access the correct drive and directory containing the file. Select the file.
4. After the file is displayed in the screen, access **Draw | Trace Bitmap** to display the Trace Bitmap Tool.
5. Click the Auto-trace tool on a line edge in the drawing. Arts & Letters will automatically trace the form and display it on the screen.

Conversions with Decipher

Arts & Letters includes its own special conversion utility, which has been designed to increase the number of direct conversions into Arts & Letters.

File Conversion Operations

You may import and export color bitmapped files, including high-resolution Targa, GIF, and PCX images, into TIFF format files that can be accepted by Arts & Letters and used as backgrounds for graphic objects drawn on your screen. Finally, you may capture screens directly with Decipher, either the whole screen or a specific part of it. You may also use Decipher to capture any Windows application screen that you wish. Decipher is really two programs: one handles import/export of various raster (bit map) file formats, and a new component that expands Express' capability to Import vector (object) formats, including Windows Metafile, CGM, CorelDraw, Postscript (EPS), AutoCad, Micrografx and WordPerfect, directly into Express GED file format (Figure 10.9). Each of these modules may be run independently of Express, and each has its own icon in the Express program group.

PostScript Conversions

One of the most difficult transitions to make in PC computer graphics is to move a bitmapped file directly into a vector-editable format, such as an Arts & Letters GED file format. The most common way to bring bitmapped files over is auto-tracing. Arts & Letters includes a built-in auto-tracing capability that can be used effectively with line art files and some more densely drawn bitmapped images.

Importing to GED Format

The Decipher EPS conversion is useful for bringing in EPS files generated in other applications, such as CorelDraw, for editing in Arts & Letters. You can even use it to bring in EPS files created on the Macintosh. Since EPS is a vector format, Decipher can reliably interpret these files into a fully editable GED file.

EPS Conversion vs. Tracing

While this two-step conversion process may seem cumbersome and time-consuming, consider the alternative. Unless you are willing to use the auto-tracing features within Arts & Letters to manually select line forms for tracing—which in a complex file could take a long time—this conversion is virtually impossible to make. Bitmapped and vector file formats share absolutely no common computer algorithm that would make it possible to electronically translate them in a simple electronic operation.

The way to bring files over from bitmapped format to the more complex vector format is to read the surface file values, and interpret them into the coordinate values required by the vector graphic file. The following instructions cover steps necessary to load Decipher from within Arts & Letters. The Decipher Vector module is a dedicated Windows application. You may not run EPS conversion operations from the DOS command line as in previous versions. Decipher Vector does provide features that allow you to automate conversion of large batches of vector files into GED format.

Steps: Converting EPS to GED with Decipher

Use this operation to convert an EPS file to a GED File.

1. Access the **Decipher/PS** icon in the Program Manager.
2. Select the Open File icon, and select the EPS file to convert.
3. Select **Adobe PostScript.**
4. Specify the drive and directory where the Postscript file is located and select the file.
5. The screen will go to a character screen as the file is processed.

Bitmap Color Conversions

You may create color files using your scanner in high-resolution color formats such as Targa, GIF, and PCX 3.0. You may import these files for use as backgrounds and graphic elements for Arts & Letters artwork using Decipher's Bitmap conversion utility features. The operation is quite simple: Access the Bitmap selection on the Decipher screen, open the file you wish to convert, and begin the operation. Decipher does all the rest.

Steps: Bitmap Color Conversions with Decipher

Use this operation to import high-resolution color files into Express.

1. Access **System | Decipher**.
2. Select **Bitmap**.
3. Select **File | Open**.
4. Select the bitmap file desired and click on **OK**.
5. Select **File | Save As**.
6. Choose the format desired and click on **OK**. The original file is translated to the chosen format.

Screen Capture

As you work in Arts & Letters and other Windows applications, you may wish to take color snapshots of the screen interface and its contents. The Decipher utility offers you the ability to directly shoot the entire Windows screen containing Arts & Letters or any other Windows application, or part of a screen, and save it into a computer file.

Capture Operations

All screen capture utilities are essentially the same in that they run in a small area of memory beneath the main application like a camera loaded with film. When activated, they write exactly what they see on the screen in a bitmapped format into a computer file, which can then be edited, manipulated, and used in a variety of applications.

Capture Control and Editing

What makes the Arts & Letters Decipher utility exceptional is that it allows you to either shoot the entire screen or pre-edit and shoot exactly the part of the screen you wish to capture. In some ways this capability is a mimic of the Windows Clipboard, which can do some of the same things. But the Windows Clipboard is designed for cut and paste operations and can be time-consuming to use if you have a great number of files to create. Decipher's screen-capture utility immediately writes what it sees to a variety of formats including TIF, GIF, and PCX in a directory you specify. Once there, you may edit it like any other TIFF file.

External Tracing Software

One key factor to consider in bitmap tracing is file complexity. Bitmapped files may be simple line art drawings, similar to Arts & Letters symbols in their unenhanced form. However, some bitmapped images may be highly textured, with gray highlights and shading. It is at this point that bitmap tracing becomes problematical, not only in Arts & Letters, but in virtually every graphics program that offers it. Heavily shaded and textured drawings are difficult to translate into vector-based graphic objects without having a lot of tracing power at your disposal. For this type of file, you may have to look elsewhere.

Adobe Streamline

One of the most powerful external bitmap tracing utilities is Adobe Streamline. Streamline allows you many automatic options for tracing the outline, centerline, or both aspects of a bitmapped file, and it performs the operation automatically. You can use Streamline to bring a TIFF format bitmapped file directly into standard Encapsulated PostScript (EPS) format, then use Decipher to translate the EPS file into an Arts & Letters GED file, which is fully editable as a collection of graphic objects as soon as you load it into the screen.

Steps: Converting Bitmapped Files with Streamline

Use this operation to trace a bitmapped file to an EPS format using Adobe Streamline.

1. Create a bitmapped file in Streamline supported TIFF, PCX, or PNT formats.
2. Open Streamline through Windows Application Manager.
3. Access **File | File Setup**.
4. Select **Art Format:** Adobe Illustrator (EPS).
5. Select the type of bitmapped file you wish to convert. Select **OK.**
6. Access **File | Conversion Options** and select the desired conversion options.
7. Access **File | Convert**.
8. Select the type of bitmapped file you wish to convert. Display the drive and subdirectory containing the file. Select the desired file.
9. Accept the default filename for the EPS file or enter a new one. Select **Convert Image(s).**
10. The file will be converted into an EPS format file.
11. Use Decipher's EPS conversion process to change the file to an Arts & Letters-supported GED file.

Scanned Color Backgrounds and Bitmapped Files

The Arts & Letters GED file format can accept and reference color TIFF files used as backgrounds for graphic objects created on the screen. If you have a color scanner available, such as a Microtek 300Z, you can scan your own color backgrounds, which you can use directly in Arts & Letters.

TIFF Files as Color Backgrounds

The Arts & Letters GED file format recognizes and imports TIFF images for you to use in your files. Once drawn on the screen, the TIFF image is recognized as an image, and can be integrated into a variety of screen operations, including hole cutting and clipping masks. You can manipulate the image in the Arts & Letters screen with editing features such as Duplicate, Slant, and Rotate, and size the image proportionally or change its aspect ratio. The bitmapped file is saved by the GED in the Arts & Letters document so that it functions as another drawing element in your whole composition.

Color Scanning File Size

Color file scanning is a highly sensitive operation that requires some knowledge of various file formats, how they process color, and the optimal way to balance resolution and file size. Even grayscale images without any color can reach a huge size (1 to 2 MB). So, when you add color, you can end up with files so huge that they are slow and difficult to process. For more information about color, turn to Chapter 11.

A World of Options

Arts & Letters gives you many options for using it with other programs. The options described in this chapter are just a few. Keep in mind that any application that accepts files in formats supported by Arts & Letters **Export** option or **Decipher** can accept these files into other work you are doing. When you add the power to compose art, text, and charts to the ability to export work electronically to other powerful applications, you have a communication tool with a virtually endless number of uses.

CHAPTER 11

Printing Operations and Color

Printing and Color

Printing remains one of the diciest of all computer operations for any software package. It involves sending your work to one or more external devices, all the while making sure that the data is presented correctly, and in a way the device can understand. Even though fonts and font management have become much simpler, typefaces from a variety of vendors must be matched with your document and also with the printer.

This chapter covers features and operations for printing Arts & Letters drawings, either directly from the software, or exporting files for printing through desktop publishing or other software. The focus here is to make you aware of the range of choices available to create printed output and how to control the quality of it. Where appropriate, step-by-step instructions will be provided to help you. A listing of technical tips and techniques on printing and color separation operations is included at the end of this chapter.

Key Concepts

File Import Color files may be imported into Arts & Letters directly through the Import/Export filters, or may be processed through the Decipher utility for use as color backgrounds.

File Export Instead of printing your files directly from Arts & Letters, you have the option of exporting the file to a commonly accepted file format for use in third-party desktop publishing, presentation graphics, or other software.

Print and Output Operations

Arts & Letters has a highly developed system to allow you to print your files or to export them to other software, such as desktop publishing programs. You have the option of printing your files on a local desktop laser printer, printing to a printer-output file, or exporting pages to specified output formats or for use in other programs.

Controlling Document Size and Attributes

Arts & Letters printing features are straightforward and easy to use, but printing correctly involves understanding and applying several operations not directly connected to the Print features themselves.

GED File Format Arts & Letters stores files in what is called a Graphic Environment Document (GED). To print accurately, the page size defined in the **Page Setup** option on the **File** menu must match the paper size available in the printer. Attempting to print a legal-size page defined in the computer on standard letter-size paper will result in problems, and you won't be able to print correctly.

Document Precision Arts & Letters controls document precision through a logical system of units per inch. These logical units define the invisible grid within Arts & Letters, which determines the precision with which files are sent to the printer. As precision increases, the available size of the printed area decreases; so you must choose what is the most desirable match of precision to page size.

Generally speaking, 1440 logical units per inch is considered the standard setting for most applications, particularly those printed on a desktop laser printer with a standard resolution quality of 300 x 300 dpi (dots per inch). Documents printed on higher-end machines, such as a Linotronic Imagesetter, may require higher document precision for them to appear at the best possible output quality. When in doubt, experiment. Run several printouts of the same file at various levels of precision and examine the results.

When setting up a document for printing, keep in mind that the page setup must match the printer setup. The operation below details the correct steps for defining the page using the **Page Setup** dialog box. You also have the option to set up the print job in the **Print** dialog box and click on the **Printer Page** option which will automatically match your page setup to the print job.

Steps: Setting Up a Document for Printing

Use this operation to set up a document for printing.

1. Access **File | Page Setup**.
2. Set page orientation: portrait (tall) or landscape (wide).
3. Select paper size.
4. Define page margins in the spaces provided.
5. Select **Document Precision**.
6. Select the level of document precision required; 1440 logical units per inch is the recommended level, except for high-resolution applications.
7. Select **OK** to leave the subdialog box. Select **OK** again to return to the screen.

Printing to a Local Printer

To print to a printer connected to your computer, you must make sure that the correct printer is selected in the **Printer Setup** dialog box before accessing the **Print** dialog box itself. Arts & Letters must know what printer is enabled and which port it is connected to before printing can commence. This is especially important if you have more than one printer connected to your system, such as a black-and-white PostScript laser printer and a color output device.

Once the correct printer has been selected, the **Print** dialog box on the **File** menu gives you the option to select the number of copies and to print the current page in the document, all pages of the document, or only objects currently selected on the screen. Keep in mind that if there is a mismatch between the page size defined in the **Page Setup** dialog box and the size of paper in the printer, you may experience problems.

Steps: Printing to a Local Printer

Use this operation to print to a local printer.

1. Access **File | Printer Setup**.
2. Select the local printer desired for output.

3. Select **Setup** in the dialog box.
4. Verify all printer settings are as desired. Make any changes necessary.
5. Access **File | Print**.
6. Specify the number of copies desired.
7. Select the range of printing desired: the current page, all pages (in the document), or currently selected objects.

Printing to a Filename

The **Print** dialog box gives you the additional option of printing a document, page, or selected objects directly to a computer file. The resulting file is called a printer output file (Figure 11.1). This option is most commonly used with PostScript applications when printed on a high-end Linotronic or other PostScript imagesetter. The printer output file contains all the necessary information for the imagesetter to print the complete image without having Arts & Letters installed and available.

Steps: Printing to a Filename

Use this operation to print to a filename.

1. Verify the printer has been set up for use.
2. Access **File | Print**.

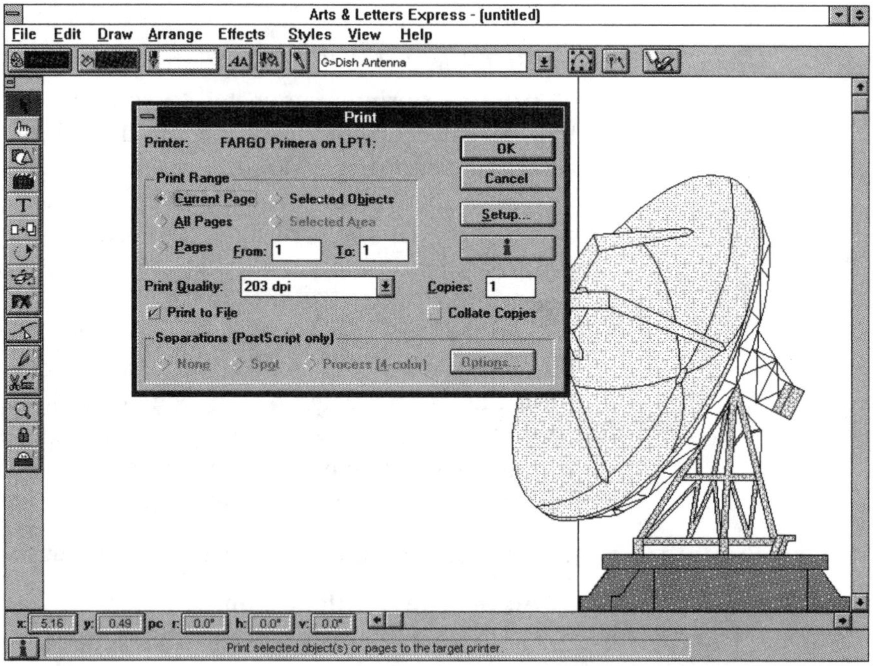

Figure 11.1 Printing to a Filename
You specify the filename and Express prints the page to a file that can be later printed on a PostScript device. Files printed this way are positioned correctly on a page just as they would be if printed on a printing device. This is the principal difference between this technique and creating a standard EPS export file.

3. Verify that number of copies is set to 1.
4. Select the desired print range.
5. Select **Print To File**.
6. Select **Print**.
7. Select drive and/or subdirectory where the file is to be written.
8. Enter name of printer output file.

Exporting Files

Another output option is simply to save the Arts & Letters image you have created into a computer file that can be used in some other software package such as desktop publishing or presentation graphics software. This option is your port of entry into Ventura, PageMaker, and Interleaf, as well as other applications in the PC. This is also where you may export files in SCODL format for use in printing color slides.

Export Options When exporting files, note that you do *not* have the option to export the entire document, only a single page at a time, or a group of selected objects or a selected area. So, to export all elements in a document, you may have to export a file for each page in the document.

Export Filters The export file filters available do not include all possible file formats you may wish to use. No computer graphics program can cover all formats available in the PC, there are simply too many to choose from. Arts & Letters Decipher can translate files into a variety of formats not directly supported in the **Export** dialog box, including ZSoft PCX and CompuServe GIF. Using an external computer graphics conversion package like the Graphics Link Plus you may be able to translate files to even more formats. Files exported from Arts & Letters in TIFF can be instantly and accurately translated individually or in batched groups from the originating TIFF format into ZSoft PCX format, GEM IMG format (for direct loading into Ventura without file conversion), Halo CUT format, WordPerfect WPG format, and other common standards including CompuServe's GIF, Show Partner's GX1, and more. Using such a utility expands the reach of your Arts & Letters output and lets you use your creations in Arts & Letters in a variety of other applications not directly supported under the Export features.

Steps: Exporting Files Use this operation to export Express artwork to other formats. Note you may Export an entire page, a selected group of objects, or a selected area.

1. If you wish to export selected objects only, select them prior to opening the **Export** dialog box.
2. Access **File | Export**.
3. Enter up to an eight-digit filename for export.
4. Select the export conversion filter.
5. Select **Setup** and enter the desired export values for the selected export conversion filter.
6. Select export range—the current page or currently selected objects.

Color Printing

If you've been working with color graphics and desktop publishing on the PC, the terms and concepts of black-and-white laser printing are probably fairly familiar. But color printing, for many PC users, is a new world, full of complex concepts, technical details, and a profusion of different options. Color printing is in a constant state of development and advancement. If you're serious about making use of the technology, you should keep in touch through the various magazines and computer newsletters on the market.

Color Printing Operations

Color is difficult because of the many control factors required to ensure quality output. On a black-and-white laser printer, all you have to worry about are black, white, and shades of gray. In color printing, you have to worry about the quality of many color shades, how well they blend in the finished composition, and many other details. Add to that the fact that color printing, either from a desktop machine or from your local service bureau, is significantly more expensive than black and white. This is a world in which mistakes can be costly and very time-consuming. It is one where you should take the time to make sure you're making the right choices.

Output Choices

There are a variety of different technologies and equipment available that can output your Arts & Letters files in color. Each has advantages and disadvantages, and the available technologies vary widely in output quality and resolution.

Dot-Matrix Printers

The original desktop color printers were dot-matrix printers, specially designed to create a pattern of color dots. Dot matrix is one of the cheaper technologies available. Its main liability is that it involves an *impact* printing process. That is, the impression on the page is created by a printhead physically "typing" a pattern of dots onto the page. In addition to being rough on the paper, the resolution these printers are capable of is limited to the size of the dots in the impact printhead.

Dot-matrix color printers are still available and they can provide a cheap, workable option for printing color drafts. You will probably find that the output resolution is grainy and that the supplies, notably the color inks used, tend to be very expensive, considering the results you are getting.

Thermal, Laser, and Ink-Jet Printers

A cleaner color impression is created by nonimpact formats, such as thermal, laser, and ink-jet printers. While each of these technologies is in a way different, they are alike in that they create the color image by moving the paper over a smooth printhead, without any impact devices to the page.

A variety of these products available on the marketplace are capable of delivering much higher quality results than the old-fashioned dot matrix variety. Certain manufacturers, such as QMS, offer a desktop color printer with true Adobe PostScript, capable of outputting files at a solid resolution of 300 x 300 dpi. The quality of the output is good, but it isn't as good as you're going to get from a commercial printer at a service bureau. A new generation of these desktop color machines is moving into the market with more features and at lower cost. For many of your color applications, a printer such as this may offer a reasonable solution.

Digital Color Printers

One of the trickiest problems with color printing has been finding a way to make copies of a color printout. Most office copiers are black and white, or they have special color cartridges available that can provide "color highlights" or "spot color." But color copying, up to now, is not generally available.

A new generation of color printers is making its way to market that may resolve this problem by combining color printing and color copying in the same machine. This is done through the use of a new technology called "digital reprographics," or "laser copying." Instead of using the traditional light-lens copying technology, these machines have incorporated a complete color page scanner in the same box with a color laser printing device. You may connect your computer directly to the color laser copier through special adapter modules, and use it like a color printer. You may also take color hard-copies and copy them using the same machine.

Digital copying and printing is an emerging technology that represents the wave of the future. In the 1990s, expect to see many more "intelligent" copier-printers emerge. Some of these machines will have additional direct-connect options, including the ability to reproduce color slides. And they will contain additional capabilities, such as a built-in fax machine and a complete user interface, with screen and keyboard, built right into the machine.

These machines offer very high quality printing, particularly when compared with dot-matrix output. But, as you might suspect, the price tag is still up there. Canon USA, which has a number of these on the market, is charging anywhere from $15,000 to $50,000 for its line of digital color copiers. Other vendors coming into the market can be expected to charge similar prices.

Plotters

Plotters have traditionally been used to output color files developed for specialized applications, such as Computer-Assisted Design (CAD). A plotter is an excellent tool for technical color applications and drawings because it uses a series of pens to literally draw the picture in color on the page, or place the line on the page using a similar drawing printhead.

But plotters place points on a page; they are not the technology of choice for applications like full-color illustrations, which have many subtle shades of colors and large object and background areas with many different colors.

Film Recorders

Film Recorders take a color image and write it directly onto film instead of paper. One of the most popular film output applications is used to create instant color slides directly from computer files. There are a number of national slide reproduction services that specialize in turning your files into slides overnight from a variety of color formats.

Commercial Presses and Imagesetters

The highest-quality color printing available is still in the commercial realm, using equipment that is far too costly to maintain in the average business office. Color printing on a commercial press requires specific preparations based on the final printing form to be used. Concepts and operations used in preparing for commercial color output are covered in the following sections of this chapter.

Color Printing Terms and Concepts

Most people who have used computer graphics or desktop publishing are familiar with the concept of *output resolution*. Output resolution is a means of measuring the level of detail, line clarity, and precision for the image placed on the page. For most desktop technologies, an accepted standard of resolution has been the magic 300 x 300 dpi, which is found in most commercially available desktop laser printers. This standard produces clear graphics, clean type characters, and a generally professional-looking black-and-white document.

Output resolution, however, is only a part of the color printing story. You also have to be concerned with *color quality*. That is, are the colors on the screen accurately reproduced on the page? Or is something you drew as bright red coming out as a washed-out pink? Additionally, there is the problem of *color mixes*. Color printing is made possible by adopting a small group of basic colors that provide the foundation for the process. These colors, when combined in varying levels of intensity, create the color mixes. Since there are thousands upon thousands of possible color mixes, getting the right mix is tricky. (See Figure 11.2.)

Color Separations

If you've created an illustration in Arts & Letters and you want to print it in color, you also have to understand the concepts of *spot color* and *process color*, and how they relate to color separations.

Color separation is a fairly simple concept. The printer can't print all the colors in the spectrum in one continuous process; it has to break

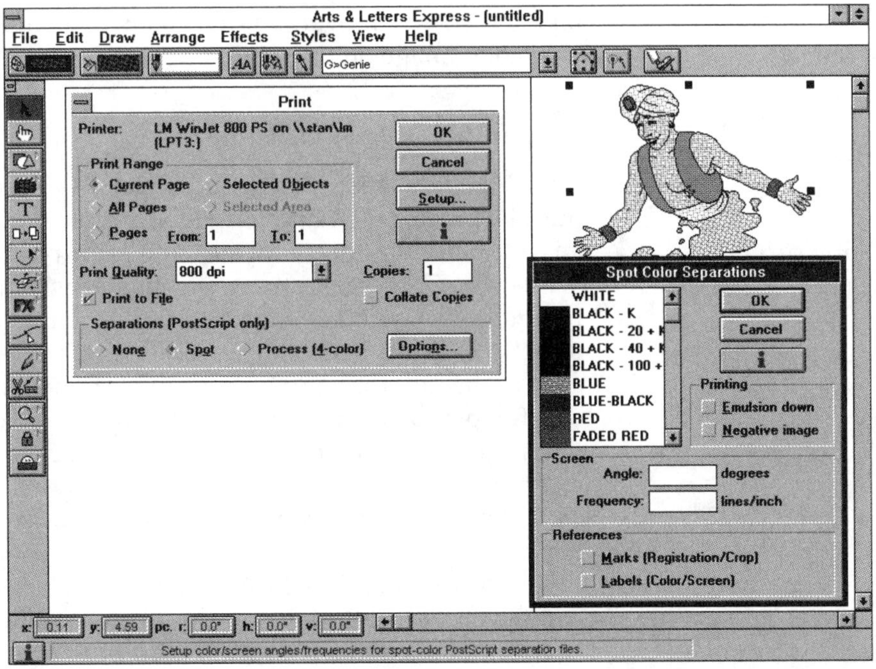

Figure 11.2
Color Printing Features
Express provides you with detailed controls for color printing. When performing color printing operations, be sure you communicate with your service bureau or printing specialist before you finalize the artwork.

down the color layout into its constituent elements and "paint" them one at a time. To do this, the various color elements in the layout must be "separated" out from the design so that they can be printed separately. When the layers are complete the complete color image is formed.

Spot Color Spot color is the simplest form of color separation. If you have created a sign that uses a blue background and bright red lettering, a spot color separation prints the red elements on one sheet and the blue ones on another. The results can then be combined by a professional printer into a complete color image.

Process Color Spot color works when you have a simple set of colors in a composition. But what happens when you have a highly involved continuous-tone composition, such as photography, that can't be easily broken down into a handful of discrete colors? This is where process-color separation comes in. Rather than breaking down the layout into separate fields of color, a process-color separation identifies and prints out four separate pieces of film based on the components of cyan (C), yellow (Y), magenta (M), and black (K) found in the image (CMYK are the primary colors used on a printing press to create full-color images.) The color separation program finds and prints all cyan values on one sheet of film, yellow values on another, magenta on another, and black on another. When overlaid, the colors combine to create a continuous-tone color image on the page.

Printing Color Separations

Arts & Letters creates color separations as PostScript output files that must be printed on a PostScript-compatible output device. Before going any further, note that your desktop laser printer is suitable as a draft printer for color separations, but to achieve true, professional quality results, you should have the separations printed at your service bureau directly or from print output files on a high-resolution imagesetter, such as the Linotronic 300. Your service bureau may have specific methods for preparing the final result, such as Negative separations, or Emulsion Down, so you should consult with your printer in advance to make sure that you have all the technical specifications fully addressed. Note that if your desktop laser printer is not PostScript, separations are not available.

The **Print** dialog box in Arts & Letters allows you to define specific parameters for spot and process color separations. But to do this, you have to understand a couple of additional terms and concepts to create the separations that you give to your printer to create the final result. Note that both of these values are controlled through the **Setup** selection in the **Print** dialog box, which appears opposite, from the available color separation options.

Frequency

When you make a spot or process color separation that incorporates continuous-tone images, you must specify a screen frequency. Frequency is related to resolution quality in your desktop laser printer, and is specified in lines per inch (lpi). Standard line frequencies in the printing industry range from a low-resolution 55 lpi, which creates a rough, coarse image, to 150 lpi, which creates a much higher resolution printout, with greater clarity of line and form in the final product. Generally, your lpi should be about half the value of your target dpi. You should check with your printer if you're unsure of which line frequency to specify when making the color separations.

Screen Angle

Screen angle affects the color quality in the printed image. The dots that make up each CYMK color are set at a unique angle so that when the four process colors are overlaid they fit together properly to create the desired final hue. Different screen angles, therefore, can have a marked effect on the quality of tones and shades within the final printout. As a general rule, the darkest color in a process separation, black, gets a setting of around 45 degrees; the lightest color, yellow, is given a setting of zero degrees; and the intermediate colors, cyan and magenta, are given values about 30 degrees above and below the setting for black, at 15 and 75 degrees. The result is that each color in the separation has a distinctive screen angle setting.

If you are in doubt about the correct screen angle setting when making your separation, *call your service bureau or printer*. The process color separation subdialog box displays default screen angles set by Arts & Letters, but these may not be preferred by your printer.

Output Options

In some ways, there's nothing worse than having too many choices. And choices are what the world of printing is about. There are so many available types of hardware, output technologies, file formats, technical considerations, and other details for getting your files printed at the quality level you want that the choices can be more than a little overwhelming.

For the best, most professional results, go to a competent commercial printer or service bureau that can advise you on the details necessary to get your files printed correctly. But the world is changing radically. Emerging technologies like digital copying and the rapid advances made in desktop color printers promise that sometime in the not-too-distant future, you may be able to have professional, full-color printing from your desktop.

Printing and Resolution Tips and Techniques

The quality of a printed Arts & Letters document depends on the quality of the printer. A 72 dpi dot matrix printer will not produce an image as clear and sharp as a 300 dpi laser printer, which in turn will not produce an image as clear and sharp as a 1270 dpi imagesetting machine. Many service bureaus and print shops now provide printing on laser printers and imagesetters.

The Logical Coordinate System

The logical coordinate system is an internal grid that Arts & Letters uses to determine the precision of a document. It is not related to the grid you set using the **Preferences** command in the **View** menu.

Precision and Resolution

The document precision determines both the maximum resolution that Arts & Letters can output, and the maximum size of the Arts & Letters document. The higher the precision, the smaller the document. For most purposes, the default setting of 1440 is appropriate; certain special cases may require different settings. As a general rule, the document precision should be at least twice the resolution of your output device.

Selecting Precision

For example, 1440 logical units per inch is adequate for most printers, including laser printers, which generally have a resolution of 300 dots per inch. Imagesetting machines and some other output devices can print at much higher resolutions and, depending on your purposes, may require a Document Precision setting of 2880. (Note that changing the Document Precision does not change the resolution of your output device, only the precision of the output that Express can send to the output device.) To obtain the highest precision possible when drawing, set the Document Precision to 2880 and use as much of the work area as possible, then scale your completed image down to the size desired.

Banner, Poster, and Oversized Paper Applications If you need to print a document on oversize paper, you may have to reduce the Document Precision to make the document the size required. An Arts & Letters document is 32,768 (32k) logical units in size. The maximum size of the document in inches is 32k divided by the selected Document Precision and then squared, as shown:

Document Precision	Maximum Document Size
2880	129.50 square inches
1440	517.56 square inches
720	2071.16 square inches
360	8284.64 square inches
180	33138.56 square inches

Check Precision at Outset Note that these are the maximum sizes for a document at a given precision setting. The actual size of the document depends on the selected page size (letter, legal, etc.) and the selected margins.

You should make certain that the Document Precision is correctly set before starting to work on a document.

Symbol and Freeform Object Measurement The logical coordinate system is also Express's internal measurement system for symbol and freeform objects. Although you can specify and work with sizes in picas, centimeters, and inches, Express internally stores the size of symbol and freeform objects in logical units. Because of this, you might think that changing the logical units per inch would change the size of objects on the screen. However, Express automatically readjusts the sizes of objects to compensate for changes in the document precision, with one exception. If you cut or copy symbol and freeform objects to the clipboard, and then paste those objects into a document with a different precision setting, the size of the objects will change. For example, objects cut from a document with a precision of 1440 will be twice their original size when pasted into a document with a precision of 720.

Creating Printable PostScript Files

You can print directly to PostScript devices from Express or you can use the following two methods to create a PostScript file: Use the **Export** command to export a document in EPS format, or use **Print to File** to create a PostScript print file.

EPS File Output Both methods create a printable PostScript file; however, the EPS file does not include any page position information and will print at the bottom left of the page. Because of this, it is preferable to use the Print to File command to create a PostScript file for printing. Use the Export command to create an EPS file for import into other programs.

Print to File When you use Print to File to create a printable PostScript file, the Windows driver inserts Control-D characters at the beginning and end of the file. Some print utilities recognize ASCII information only, and will generate an error message when you use them to print a file containing control characters. If this happens, use a text editor to remove the Control-D characters from the PostScript file, then print again.

Nonstandard Registration Marks

The automatic registration marks generated by Express for color separations are positioned in the margin area at the four corners of the page. There may be occasions, however, when you need registration marks in different positions. If you specify a page size with no margins, Express cannot automatically print registration marks since there is no margin area for them.

If you have multiple images on a single page, you may want registration marks for each image.

Steps: Create Registration Marks Manually

Use this operation to create registration marks manually:

1. Add symbol 1620 (registration mark) to your document. In the Attributes menu, use the Fill command to set the fill to None, and the Line command to set the line width to 0.5. Make sure the color is 100% of CMYK.
2. Duplicate the symbol to create the number of registration marks needed, then position them as desired.
3. If you have a single image on a page, you can use the Page Setup command to set the page size and margins to fit the image. The automatic registration marks and labels will then be positioned properly.
4. When you print, you will see that the message Printer page size does not match document page size. Click on **OK** to continue printing.

Color Separation Techniques

The automatic labels generated by Express for color separations are positioned in the margin area at the bottom of the page. There may be occasions, however, when you need labels in different positions.

If you specify a page size with no margins, Express cannot automatically print labels, since there is no margin area for them. If you have multiple images on a single page, you may want to place labels for each image.

Steps: Create Color Registration Labels Manually

Use this operation to create labels manually:

1. Add a text object to your document containing the filename, the date, and any other information you want. Color this text object 100% CMYK.
2. Add the text objects Cyan, Magenta, Yellow, and Black. Color the Cyan text object 100% cyan, the Magenta text object 100% magenta, the Yellow text object 100% yellow, and the Black text object 100% black.
3. Size and position the text on the page as desired.
4. Print the separations. The 100% CMYK text object will print on each separation, while the color names will print only on their corresponding separation.

Reference Marks: Crop and Fold Indicators

If you are printing a document that will be trimmed or folded, you may want to add reference marks to show the exact position of the trim or fold. To make the best use of reference marks, you should create them before working on your image, or create them in a blank area of your document and then move your completed image on top.

Step: Create Reference Marks

Use this operation to create reference marks:

1. Add symbol 1001 (rectangle) to your document. Use the **Transform** command to size the rectangle to the final trim area desired, then use the **Lock/Hide/Name** command to name it Trimming Rectangle.
2. Use the Duplicate tool to create a second rectangle, then use the **Lock/Hide/Name** command to name it Cropping Rectangle. Use the **Transform** command to size it an inch (or 2 picas) larger than the trimming rectangle in both width and height. Set the width of the cropping rectangle to 0.00 and the color (both interior and line) to white.
3. Select both rectangles and use the Align command to align center.
4. Select the cropping rectangle and choose the **Stacking Order/ Send to Back** command, then use the **Lock/Hide/Name** command to lock the cropping rectangle.

5. Draw a vertical line through the trimming rectangle. Size the line so that it extends at least a ½ inch beyond the top and bottom of the trimming rectangle. (To ensure that the line is exactly vertical, hold down the Shift key as you draw it.) Set the color of the line to 100% CMYK, the width of the line to 0.5 points, and make certain that the scale width with object option in the Line Attributes dialog box is not selected. Select the line and the trimming rectangle and Align left.
6. Select the line and use the **Transform** command to duplicate it at the exact positions where vertical fold or crop marks are required.
7. Draw a horizontal line through the trimming rectangle. Size the line so that it extends at least an inch beyond the left and right sides of the trimming rectangle. (To ensure that the line is exactly horizontal, hold down the Shift key as you draw it.) The line should have the same attributes as the vertical line you drew in Step 4. Select the line and the trimming rectangle and Align left.
8. Select the line and use the **Transform** command to duplicate it at the exact positions where horizontal fold or crop marks are required.
9. Select all lines that are to be fold indicators and change them to dashed lines.
10. Use the **Lock/Hide/Name** command to unlock the cropping rectangle. Use the **Stacking Order/Bring to Front** command to place the cropping rectangle at the front of all the lines. Select all of the reference marks (rectangles and lines) and Group them, then use the **Lock/Hide/Name** command to name them Reference Marks and to lock them in place.

Note: It is sometimes helpful to leave the trimming rectangle or lines exposed to use as guidelines while creating an image. If this is the case, leave the cropping rectangle in back while working on the image, then bring it to the front of the trimming rectangle and reference lines before printing.

Steps: Create Crop Indicators for Bleeds

Use this operation to create crop indicators for bleeds:

1. Use the **Page Setup** command to specify a page size larger than the print area of your image.
2. Add a rectangle to the page, and size it to the exact image area desired.
3. Hold the **Shift** key to constrain the drawing tool as you draw line segments at the corners of the rectangle.

4. Use the CMYK model in the Color dialog box to color all the lines 100% CMYK.
5. Use **Shift** + click to select the rectangle and the two horizontal lines near the top of the rectangle, and Align Top. Use this method to align the two lower horizontal lines with the bottom of the rectangle, and the two left vertical lines with the left edge of the rectangle, and the two right vertical lines with the right edge of the rectangle.
6. Select the rectangle. Choose **Transform** from the **Manipulate** menu, select **Relative** and **Size**, and enter **110**.
7. Bring the rectangle to the front, then Group the lines and the rectangle. Place your image in the area defined by the rectangle. Before printing, ungroup the lines and rectangle and delete the rectangle.

Rotated and Slanted TIFF Images

If you print to a PostScript printer, you can print rotated and slanted TIFF images. When a TIFF image is rotated in the Express screen, a grayed-out representation will appear with the TIFF filename imprinted. The following instructions are used to print the full image on a Postscript device.

Steps: Printing Rotated or Slanted TIFF Images

Use this operation to print rotated or slanted TIFF images:

1. Use the Rotate or Slant tool or the **Transform** command to rotate or slant a TIFF image. The rotated or slanted image is displayed on the screen as a box with the filename of the TIFF image inside.
2. Print the file. Because of the extra computation involved in printing a rotated or slanted TIFF image, printing time should be approximately 10% longer than printing the file with a nonrotated or slanted TIFF image.

Note: If you are printing a color TIFF image directly to a black & white printer, the computation time greatly increases. It may be preferable to use the Arts & Letters Decipher utility to convert the image from color to black and white before printing.

Line Screens, Printer Resolution, and Image Appearance

If you print to a PostScript printer, you can lighten and soften images by specifying lower line screens, and create darker, sharper images by specifying higher line screens. The appearance of the images at different line screens is determined by the resolution of your printer.

Clip-Art Image Printed at 1270 DPI

45 Line Screen

80 Line Screen

133 Line Screen

Scanned Image Printed at 1270 DPI

45 Line Screen

80 Line Screen

133 Line Screen

As you decrease the line screen, the dot size becomes larger, and can reach the point where the image becomes too grainy. Experiment to determine the best line screen for the job. (Note: If you do not specify a line screen, Express uses the printer's default setting. See your printer documentation to determine its default line screen setting.) Line screen information cannot be saved in an EPS file, since the program that does the importing (such as PageMaker, QuarkXPress, or Ventura Publisher) controls the line screen.

Output Options

Express is designed to provide you with a full range of capabilities. The system design can provide an entry-level graphics user with support to create professional results on a desktop printer. Advanced color and printing features are meant to work within professional standards. The best way to make use of these features is to talk to your service bureau, and design your files from the ground up to meet the standards required when they are output.

Appendices

APPENDIX A

Picture Wizard

Overview

All work and no play make computers dull toys. Arts & Letters Picture Wizard, first released in 1991, was the first of a line of educational and entertainment products based on the award-winning Arts & Letters system of computer clip art. Specifically designed for use by children in the home or at school, Picture Wizard contained a selected group of features from the full Arts & Letters Express combined with specially created activities, art files, and games. In practice, Picture Wizard operated as a miniature version of the full Express product. The current shipping version of Picture Wizard uses the same interface as the Version 3 series products and contains simplified icons for the major features and functions in the product.

Features and Capabilities

Picture Wizard contains the four basic functions of the full Arts & Letters software: symbols and images, text, charts, and freeform drawing. With 1,500 art forms and clip-art images and 15 typefaces, Picture Wizard has formidable range for a child's creative interests and requires significantly less installation space than the full software (a total required of about 10 megabytes).

The art system in Picture Wizard includes the Clip-Art Manager and freeform tools, allowing for line and Bezier curve drawing. The Text

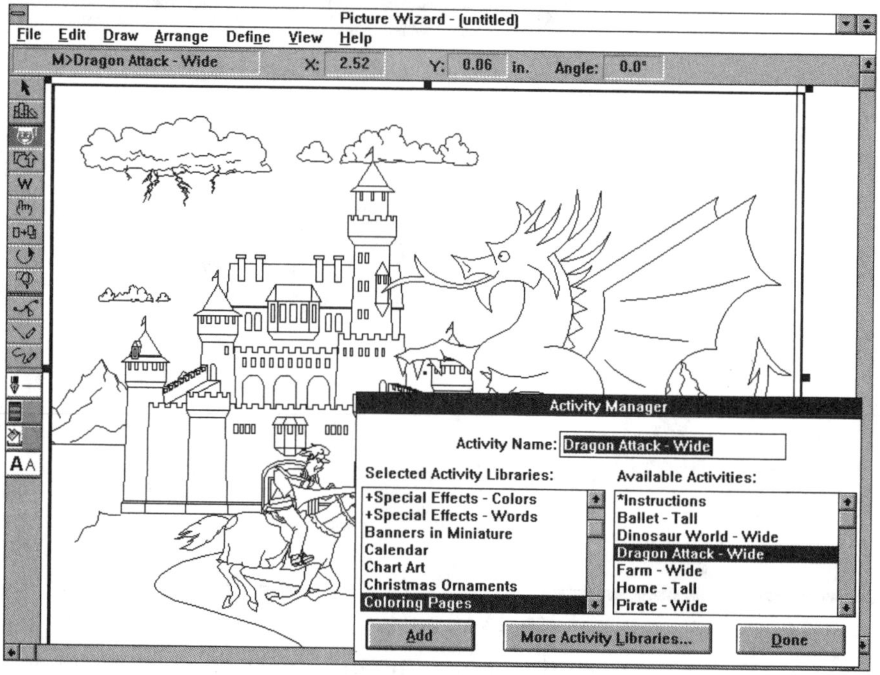

Figure A.1
Picture Wizard
Designed especially for children, Picture Wizard includes art composition, text, chart, and freeform features, along with a specially designed set of art files, activities, games, puzzles, and tutorials to help kids create their own unique compositions on the computer.

system includes full typographic controls, typeface preview, even kerning controls. Kids can also create full data-driven charts using the Chart features included.

The unique focus of Picture Wizard is in the Activity Manager. This twin screen to the Clip-Art Manager contains a group of specially created art files which are used for special projects. The basic projects serve as tutorials to teach children how to place and manipulate objects and create their own art, using the included art forms or by drawing from scratch. Additional projects allow children to make a variety of graphics by editing special files provided. Kids can create their own banners, customized words, calendars, stationery, signs, charts, holiday ornaments, coloring books, paper dolls and fashions, greeting cards, and more. Additional activities include puzzles and games in which the user unscrambles graphics to create a complete picture or negotiates a maze. Art files are also provided for children to create and print music.

Coverage of key features contained in Part I of this book is valid for Picture Wizard. Note that the interface design is based on Version 3 Arts & Letters products. Operations and design concepts for the four key functions of Arts & Letters contained in Chapters 3 through 6 also can be used as guidelines for learning and using Picture Wizard.

APPENDIX B

Arts & Letters Draw

Overview

Many users have a need for a simple graphics package that produces basic, practical art output. Arts & Letters Draw replaces the old Scenerio package as the base product of the entire line. It is sold both as a free-standing product, and is included as the Drawing component in several of the new Expo series products, such as Space Age and Jurassic Art. Draw provides basic art and text functions, without charting features and none of the higher-end effects. It is intended to serve simple business purposes for sketching and illustration. Draw comes with a minimal collection of art forms and images, but may accept additional clip-art libraries available from Computer Support Corporation, developer of Arts & Letters.

Features and Capabilities

Draw includes the same feature group as Picture Wizard, without the Charting features or the specially developed Activity files, games, puzzles, and musical notation files included in that product. But as a low-end product, it includes 350 art forms and images and 9 typefaces,

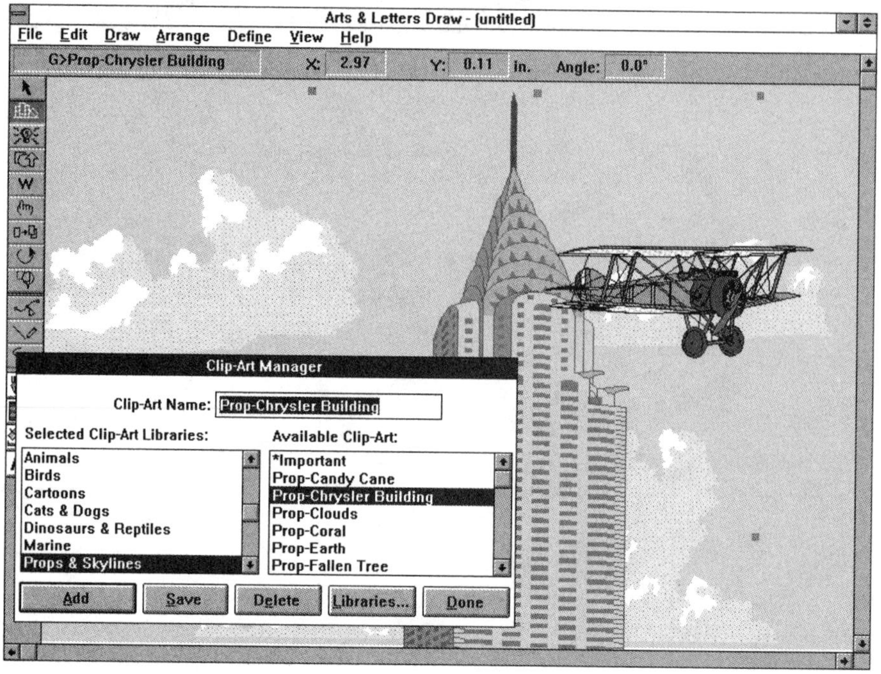

Figure B.1
Arts & Letters Draw
The basic package of the Arts & Letters line, Draw is also included in Arts & Letters multimedia products as the drawing system. It permits you to create basic business and presentation art and text using a reduced set of artforms and typefaces.

sufficient to create basic business and presentation artwork. The Type system includes typographic controls, and the art manipulation system allows you to size, rotate, duplicate, and align objects. Styles supported (on the Define menu) include Color, Line, Fill, Type, and Style Bundles. These style options are basic and do not include advanced style features such as Color Mixing, Color Filters, and Calligraphic Pen designs for Line styles, or Gradients for Fill styles.

Draw does not include any of the elaborate special effects options such as Blend, Merge, Warp, and Extrude. It also does not include any of the precision freeform editing features in the full Express product, or the ability to convert symbols to freeform objects for editing. It functions as a simple assembly and drawing package.

Coverage of feature operations for the key art and text functions in Chapters 3, 4, and 6 of this book can be used as guidelines for Arts & Letters Draw. Note that most features carry the same names as in Express, but in a few cases, they differ. For example, The Text feature in Express is called Words in Draw. Otherwise, these core features and dialog boxes operate in the same way between the two products. Like Picture Wizard, Draw is being shipped, as at this writing, with the interface for the Version 3 products, so that Version 5 elements like the Style Bar are not present.

APPENDIX C

Arts & Letters Home & Office

Overview

Arts & Letters Home & Office is the intermediate level business product in the line. With significantly greater power than Draw, Home & Office is keyed to the individual who needs to create a wide range of business artwork, text, and charts. Home & Office is offered only on CD-ROM and contains the feature array included in the previous flagship product, Arts & Letters Version 3.1. None of the new features or the interface developed for Version 5 is included. In effect, Home & Office replaces the popular Arts & Letters Apprentice package.

Features and Capabilities

Home & Office includes the entire feature set of the Arts & Letters Editor, Version 3, and uses the same interface as the older product. This includes full systems for symbols/images, text, charts, and freeform editing. It also includes full Style/Attribute features, and powerful effects, including Blend, Warp, Merge, and Wrapping Text to Shape.

Home & Office does not include the new interface design used in Version 5 products, nor specific features, such as Extrude, advanced typographic controls, the new drag-and-drop Clip-Art Manager, Color Filters, Select Within Group, or the new Import filters.

Coverage in this book for Home & Office is valid for the four key function chapters on art composition, text, charts, and freeform (Chapters 3 through 6). Style and Attribute features in Express (covered in Chapter 7 of this book) are more elaborate than those included in Home & Office, but operation of key functions, such as color mixing, placing calligraphic pens, setting a gradient, are identical or highly similar between the two products. Coverage of Effects in Chapter 8 is valid for Blend, Merge, and most Transform and Align operations, but again, these features have additional functions in Version 5 that will not be present in Home & Office. Coverage of Warp features for Version 5 reflect the new programming that allows Warp operations to be performed directly on any symbol; in Home & Office, Warp objects must be freeform for the feature to work. Exporting artwork to other Windows programs, covered in Chapter 10, is confined to file export or Clipboard operations; Home & Office does not yet support OLE Version 1.0.

APPENDIX D

Jurassic Art

Overview

The first of the special interest and educational products developed by Computer Support Corporation, Jurassic Art, is a specialty art product and learning tool that allows people of all ages to learn about the prehistoric era. Jurassic Art includes Arts & Letters Draw or Scenerio, along with a specially created family of art forms, images, and backgrounds that are installed with it. In addition, Jurassic Art contains a unique "Dinosaur Database" that provides text and graphic references and instruction on the period of the ancient dinosaurs.

Features and Capabilities

The operational considerations for Jurassic Art are the same as for Arts & Letters Draw. Basic art, text, and freeform operations are covered in Chapters 3, 4, and 6 of this book. Dinosaur clip art is installed directly into the Clip-Art Manager and may be accessed like any other of the collections included in the basic Draw product.

Dinosaur Clip Art includes a set of specially created Flex Art figures. Flex Art is a trademark of Computer Support Corporation and represents a component-based approach to create posable figures. Each figure is

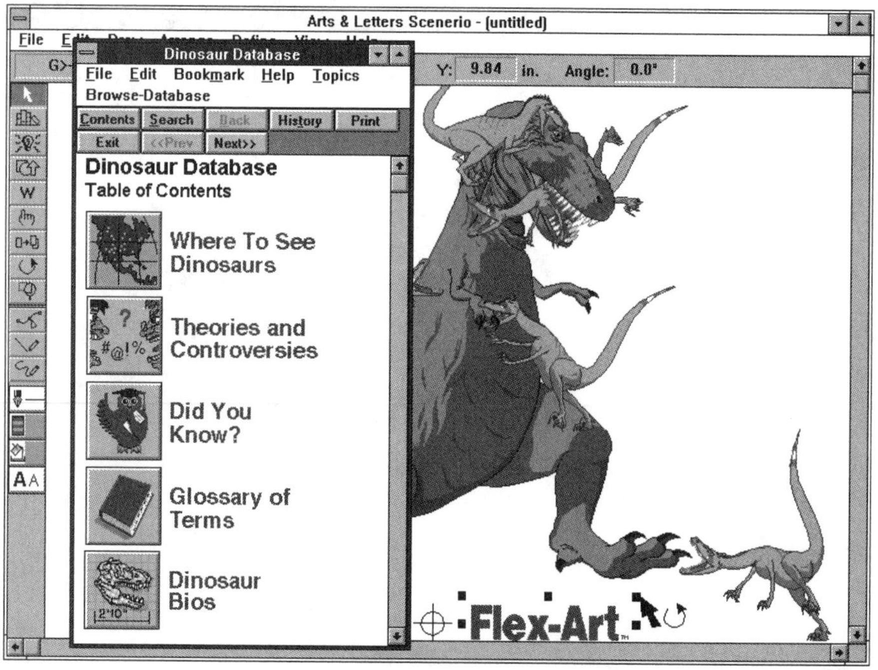

Figure D.1
Jurassic Art
The Flex Art Dinosaurs in the drawing screen may be posed as you like: just break apart the figure and move the arms, legs, and body as you wish. The Dinosaur Database is an electronic book full of interesting insights and visuals covering the history of the dinosaurs.

drawn and broken into logical components: arms, legs, jaws, body, head, and so forth. By ungrouping or breaking apart the figure, you can rotate the arms and legs at their pivot points to pose the figure in thousands of different ways. The best way to use Flex Art figures is to make several duplicates of the same figure, then break it apart and compose it as you like. You may then compose the other duplicates in different poses. Add a background and several other Flex Art figures and you can create your own prehistoric scene by manipulating the images as you like.

The Dinosaur Database may be accessed from a separate icon in the Jurassic Art program group. It is a kind of Dinosaur Help system, which includes fascinating facts, figures, illustrations, maps, and scalable comparisons of size so that you can see just how big and powerful these creatures were. The Dinosaur Database is designed graphically to make it easy to access the various features and points of information.

APPENDIX E

Arts & Letters Space Age

Overview

The first, full multimedia product from Arts & Letters, Space Age is the most complete media encyclopedia on the exploration of space on the market. In addition to the multimedia program (which comes complete with audio and video components), Space Age includes Arts & Letters Draw and a complete set of composable space clip art and backgrounds, which allow you to design and assemble your own space vehicles using a set of electronic building blocks. The depth of the research and the included encyclopedia has gained public accolades and endorsements from NASA, The National Space Society, and U.S. Space Camp.

Features and Capabilities

Space Age is available both on disk and in an expanded version on CD-ROM. The full, multimedia program installs and runs from the CD-ROM. You may install Arts & Letters Draw and then take advantage of the separate art system included, and the hundreds of space age components developed specifically for this product. The entire space collection

Figure E.1
Space Age
The main screen of the Space Age multimedia product lets you select from a range of space related topics and directly view video and multimedia components in the SpaceAGE Theater.

of clip art is included with Express so that you may have access to it directly from the Express screen as well.

The Space Age Multimedia program includes comprehensive coverage of space flight, including Human Missions, Robotic Missions, Launch Vehicles, Space Stations, Space Spinoffs, History and People, Space Centers, and space exploration in the future.

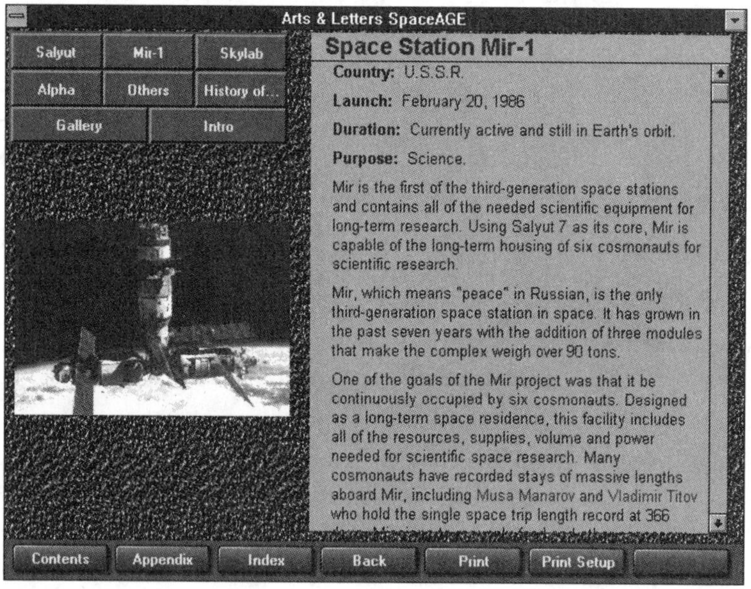

Figure E.2
Space Information
SpaceAGE is an in-depth encyclopedia with detailed coverage of both U.S., Soviet, and other space programs. Each point of content is supported with buttons allowing you to navigate to areas of related interest.

Index

D

E

Q

R

S